CHARLES TOWNSHEND

Easter 1916

The Irish Rebellion

LIBRARIES NI
WITHDRAWN FROM STOCK

PENGUIN BOOK

D0184819

PENGUIN BOOKS

Penguin [...] [...] 014, USA
Penguin Group [...] Canada M4P 2Y3

Camberw[...] [...] p Pty Ltd)

Aud[...] [...] Ltd)

Penguin Books Ltd, Registered Offices: 80 Strand, London WC2R 0RL, England

www.penguin.com

First published by Allen Lane 2005
Published in Penguin Books 2006
11

Copyright © Charles Townshend, 2005
All rights reserved

The moral right of the author has been asserted

Lines from W. B. Yeats' 'Easter 1916' reproduced by permission of A. P. Watt Ltd,
on behalf of Michael B. Yeats

Set in Linotype Sabon
Typeset by Palimpsest Book Production Limited, Polmont, Stirlingshire
Printed in England by Clays Ltd, St Ives plc

Except in the United States of America, this book is sold subject
to the condition that it shall not, by way of trade or otherwise, be lent,
re-sold, hired out, or otherwise circulated without the publisher's
prior consent in any form of binding or cover other than that in
which it is published and without a similar condition including this
condition being imposed on the subsequent purchaser

ISBN-13: 978-0-141-01216-2

www.greenpenguin.co.uk

Penguin Books is committed to a sustainable future
for our business, our readers and our planet.
The book in your hands is made from paper
certified by the Forest Stewardship Council.

LIBRARIES NI

C700892557

RONDO	02/02/2012
941.50821	£ 10.99
BUIS	

'Before the Last Battle'

God, we enter our last fight;
Thou dost see our cause is right;
Make us march now in Thy sight
    On to victory
Let us not Thy wrath deserve
In the sacred cause we serve;
Let us not from danger swerve.
    Teach us how to die.
Death for some is in reserve
    Before our flag can fly.

All the agony of years,
All the horrors, all the fears,
Martyrs' blood, survivors' tears,
    Now we offer Thee
As an endless holocaust
For the freedom we have lost.
God, restore it, tho' the cost
    Greater still must be.

Terence MacSwiney

Contents

List of Illustrations		viii
List of Abbreviations		x
Maps		xii
Preface		xvi
1	Revolutionism	1
2	The Militarization of Politics	28
3	England's Difficulty	60
4	Ireland's Opportunity	90
5	To the Brink	122
6	The Battle of Dublin I: to the Barricades	152
7	The Battle of Dublin II: the Counterstroke	183
8	The National Rising	214
9	Surrender	243
10	Punishment	269
11	Transformation	300
12	The Politics of Militarization	324
	Epilogue: The Rebellion in History	344
	Notes	360
	Biographical glossary	407
	Bibliography	414
	Index	430

List of Illustrations

Photographic acknowledgements are given in parentheses.

xx. The proclamation of the Irish republic, printed at Liberty Hall on 23 April 1916 (National Museum of Ireland).

xxi. The proclamation of martial law by the Lord Lieutenant, Lord Wimborne, 25 April 1916 (National Army Museum).

PLATES

1. 'The North began': the UVF struts its stuff, January 1914 (Hulton Getty).
2. Molly Childers and Mary Spring Rice aboard the 'Asgard' with the shipment of Mauser rifles, July 1914 (George Morrison).
3. Irish Volunteers carrying the rifles back from Howth, 25 July 1914 (National Museum of Ireland).
4. The crowd of mourners crossing O'Connell Bridge on 29 July 1914, following the funeral procession for those killed in the Bachelor's Walk shooting (Getty).
5. The Irish Citizen Army parading in front of Liberty Hall in 1915 (George Morrison).
6. Sir Roger Casement with John Devoy in New York, 1914 (National Museum of Ireland)
7. Thomas J. Clarke, President of the Supreme Council of the Irish Republican Brotherhood (National Museum of Ireland).
8. James Connolly, leader of the Irish Citizen Army, and

commander of all republican forces in Dublin in April 1916 (Hulton Getty).

9 Patrick Pearse, the Irish Volunteer Director of Organisation, President of the Provisional Government and Commander-in-Chief of the Army of the Republic in April 1916 (National Museum of Ireland).

10. Sean MacDermott, the most tireless of all republican organisers (National Museum of Ireland).

11. The warrior aesthete: Grace Gifford's sketch of her fiancé Joseph Plunkett in Volunteer uniform (Irish Military Archives).

12. Are you looking at me? Constance, Countess Markievicz, in characteristically combative pose (National Museum of Ireland).

13. Mobilisation order for the 4th Battalion of the Irish Volunteers on Easter Sunday 1916 (National Museum of Ireland).

14. The 'Starry Plough', the Citizen Army flag raised over the Imperial Hotel during Easter week 1916 (National Museum of Ireland).

15. Waiting for the counterattack: Irish republican forces inside the GPO, Easter week 1916 (Irish Military Archive).

16. 'Soldiers are we': two men of the GPO garrison show off their eclectic mix of clothing and equipment (Irish Military Archive).

17. Into captivity: Eamon de Valera marching at the head of the 3rd Battalion after the surrender (National Library of Ireland).

18. The war zone: a German image of the ruins by O'Connell bridge after the 'Aufstand' (insurrection) (AKG).

19. 'Conky' and the 'Gorgeous Wrecks': General Sir John Maxwell inspecting the Volunteer Training Corps shortly after the rebellion (RTE/Cashman).

20. Resistance commodified: postcards of de Valera and other rebel leaders sold widely after the rebellion.

21. Incarceration: Irish internees in Stafford gaol, May 1916. Michael Collins is under the cross (Irish Military Archive).

List of Abbreviations

AOH	Ancient Order of Hibernians
BL	British Library
BMH	Bureau of Military History records, IMA
Bod	Bodleian Library, Oxford
CAB	Cabinet records, PRO
CCORI	Central Committee for the Organization of Recruitment in Ireland
Cd, Cmd	Command Paper (British Parliamentary Papers)
CI	County Inspector, RIC
CIGS	Chief of the Imperial General Staff
CO	Colonial Office records, PRO
DAG	Deputy Advocate General
DATI	Department of Agriculture and Technical Instruction
DMP	Dublin Metropolitan Police
DORA	Defence of the Realm Act(s)
DRR	Defence of the Realm Regulation
GAA	Gaelic Athletic Association
GOC(-in-C)	General Officer Commanding (in Chief)
HC Deb.	House of Commons Debates (Hansard)
HLRO	House of Lords Record Office, London
HO	Home Office records, PRO
ICA	Irish Citizen Army
IMA	Irish Military Archives, Dublin
INA	Irish National Archives
INAA	Irish National Aid Association

INV	Irish National Volunteers
IPP	Irish (Nationalist) Parliamentary Party
IRA	Irish Republican Army
IRB	Irish Republican Brotherhood
ITGWU	Irish Transport and General Workers' Union
IV	Irish Volunteers
IVDF	Irish Volunteers Dependants' Fund
IWM	Imperial War Museum
JAG	Judge Advocate General
NA	National Archives, Dublin
NAM	National Army Museum
NLI	National Library of Ireland
OC	Officer Commanding
OTC	Officers' Training Corps
PRO	Public Record Office, London
PRONI	Public Record Office of Northern Ireland, Belfast
RIC	Royal Irish Constabulary
RIR	Royal Irish Regiment
SDU	South Dublin Union
TCD	Trinity College, Dublin, Library
TD	Teachta Dála [member of parliament, Dáil Eireann]
UCD(A)	University College, Dublin (Archives)
UIL	United Irish League (Parliamentary Party)
UUC	Ulster Unionist Council
UVF	Ulster Volunteer Force
WO	War Office records, PRO
WS	Witness Statement, BMH

Ireland in 1916

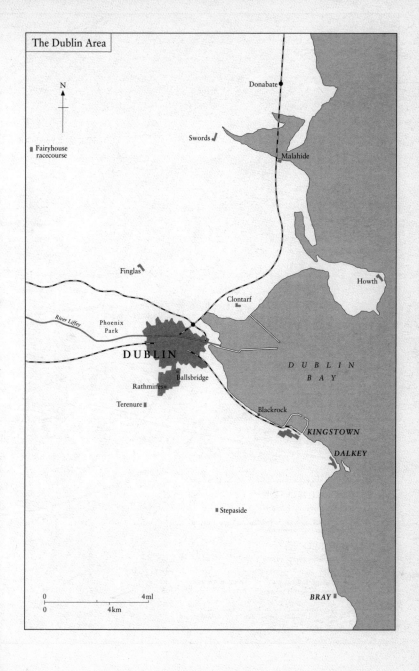

The Dublin Area

N

Fairyhouse racecourse

Donabate

Swords

Malahide

Finglas

Howth

Clontarf

River Liffey

Phoenix Park

DUBLIN

DUBLIN BAY

Rathmines

Ballsbridge

Terenure

Blackrock

KINGSTOWN

DALKEY

Stepaside

0   4 ml
0   4 km

BRAY

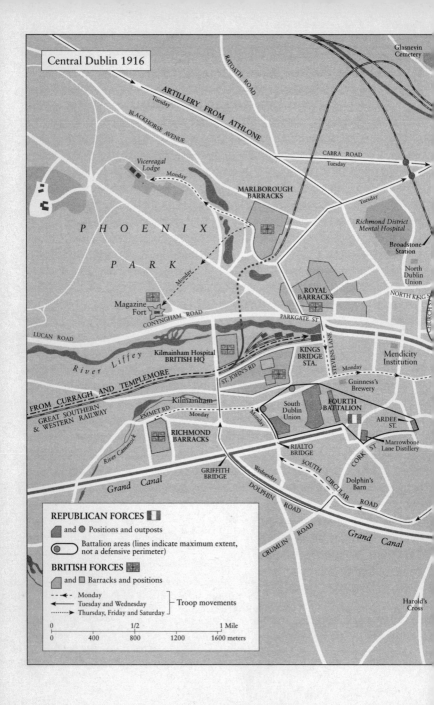

Central Dublin 1916

Glasnevin
Cemetery

RATOATH ROAD

ARTILLERY FROM ATHLONE

BLACKHORSE AVENUE

Tuesday

CABRA ROAD

Tuesday

Vicereagal
Lodge

Monday

MARLBOROUGH
BARRACKS

Tuesday

P H O E N I X

Richmond District
Mental Hospital

Broadstone
Station

North
Dublin
Union

P A R K

Monday

ROYAL
BARRACKS

NORTH KING ST

Magazine
Fort

CONYNGHAM ROAD

PARKGATE ST

CHURCH

LUCAN ROAD

River Liffey

Kilmainham Hospital
BRITISH HQ

ST. JOHN'S RD

KINGS
BRIDGE
STA.

Mendicity
Institution

Monday

Guinness's
Brewery

FROM CURRAGH AND TEMPLEMORE

GREAT SOUTHERN
& WESTERN RAILWAY

Kilmainham

Monday

EMMET RD

Monday

South
Dublin
Union

FOURTH
BATTALION

ARDEE
ST.

Marrowbone
Lane Distillery

River Cammock

RICHMOND
BARRACKS

RIALTO
BRIDGE

CORK ST

SOUTH

Dolphin's
Barn

GRIFFITH
BRIDGE

Wednesday

DOLPHIN ROAD

CIRCULAR ROAD

Grand Canal

CRUMLIN ROAD

Grand Canal

Harold's
Cross

REPUBLICAN FORCES

and ● Positions and outposts

Battalion areas (lines indicate maximum extent,
not a defensive perimeter)

BRITISH FORCES

and ■ Barracks and positions

–·–◄· Monday
◄——— Tuesday and Wednesday
··········► Thursday, Friday and Saturday

Troop movements

0		1/2		1 Mile
0	400	800	1200	1600 meters

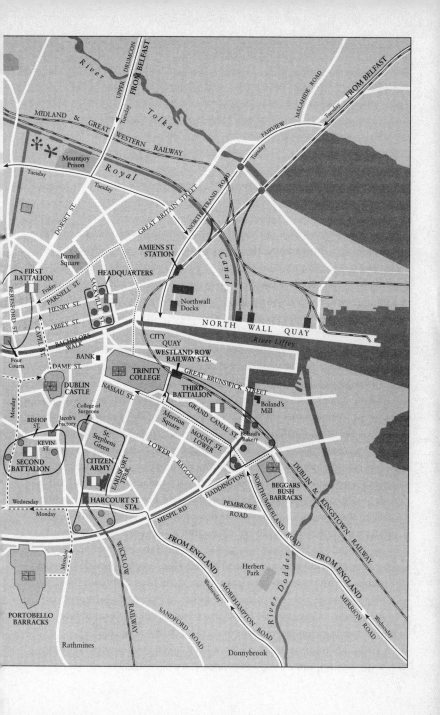

Preface

Invited to comment on one of Diarmuid Lynch's essays (which would be published posthumously in 1956 as *The I. R. B. and the 1916 Insurrection*), Bulmer Hobson sardonically replied, 'I have no wish to deter Mr Lynch from getting his particular distortion published. If this country ever does produce a historian', he added, 'his difficulties will have been made insuperable in advance.'[1] This was, perhaps, the embittered view of a man whose own contribution to the Irish revolution had – as we shall see – been effectively expunged from the historical record. But it was echoed twenty years later, on the fiftieth anniversary of the 1916 rebellion, by the eminent historian F. X. Martin, who knew as well as anyone what these difficulties were. Starting from the historical picture presented in the 1916 proclamation of the Irish Republic itself, Martin scathingly observed that 'at the very outset the pitch was being queered for the historians'. He went on to stress how much of the writing about 1916 in the succeeding half-century had been polemical and 'almost worthless to the historian'. Few of the participants – many of whom had been very young at the time of the rebellion – had published memoirs of their experience. The first professional historian to 'assess the rising in a comprehensive way', W. Alison Phillips in 1923, was also the last: no other academic has attempted the task since then.[2] Regrettably, Martin himself did not attempt it either, for all the depth and extent of his contributions as editor and reviewer. The nearest he came was the extraordinary 120-page review essay, '1916 – Myth, Fact and Mystery', a unique cocktail of information, assessment and research agenda.

Although impressive strides have been taken in contemporary Irish history writing since 1967, a surprising number of items on Martin's agenda remain blank. There is, to take one of the most striking of these, still no full-scale history of the Irish Volunteers; still no critical biography of many of the Volunteer leaders. There have been several excellent books about the rebellion, but it remains true that few academic historians have felt it worthwhile to fill the gaps. To do so is my main purpose in this book. In a sense I began work on it as long ago as 1969 with my first research on the Anglo-Irish war of 1919–21, and it has always been clear to me that if no other historian did so, I would have to try. That it has taken so long is due in part to the distraction of intervening research enthusiasms, but in part also to the problems of evidence so clearly identified by Professor Martin. Original documents on the pre-1916 Volunteer movement are thin on the ground; masses of them seem to have been buried just before the rebellion; many may still be laid up in attics across the country. Participants did publish accounts, but they trickled out in obscure and often ephemeral publications: he noted just how laborious it would be, for instance, to work through the 300-odd pieces relating to the rebellion which Piaras Béaslaí contributed to the *Irish Independent* between 1951 and 1956.

The biggest change in recent years has been the final release of the participants' accounts assembled by the Bureau of Military History, an organization about which Martin had some especially sharp comments to make. The BMH began in 1947 to gather material, principally in the form of 'witness statements', from all surviving participants, 'to form the basis for the compilation of the history of the movement for Independence'. Hundreds of statements were taken, but the 'Official History' of the revolution was never written. After the Bureau was wound up in 1957, the material, instead of being deposited in the National Library, disappeared into government archives. 'An official Iron Curtain descended cutting off the findings of the Bureau from all outsiders.'[3] Even Major Florence O'Donoghue, a pioneer member of the BMH, was refused access to material, as was Martin himself. This 'miser's hoard' was at last opened to the public in March 2003 and suddenly, instead of a few dozen accounts, we have many hundred. They suffer from all the problems to be expected in accounts written thirty years after the event, but they are a remarkable source nonetheless.[4]

Martin acknowledged that Alison Phillips, whose Unionist political standpoint certainly skewed the objectivity of his book, nonetheless brought to the subject the professional historian's sense of historical context – a 'proportionate view which few Irish writers and popular historians have been willing to recognize'. Setting 1916 in context is a crucial aim of this book, and the key context is of course the First World War, the memory of which was for many decades dimmed in Ireland by what Martin, again, memorably labelled the 'Great Oblivion'. It was, as he said, difficult then to 'find men and women who will acknowledge that they are the children of men who were serving during 1916 in the British Army' or other Crown forces – or even in the Irish National Volunteers.[5] This, perhaps, is where the biggest change has occurred since the 1960s. Ireland's participation in the war has come to be officially and popularly recognized, in books, commemorations and public monuments – a recovered memory that is a sign of wider changes in the public outlook. In a sense, though, this makes the evaluation of the rebellion – its justifiability in moral and political terms – a more complex issue than it has been since the end of the Great War. W. B. Yeats's perplexed question, 'Was it needless death after all?' was answered for two generations with a deafening negative; but now it must be heard again.

A note on terminology. I call the events of Easter Week a rebellion, though I am aware that this label has been disputed. Some republicans have always rejected its implication that the incumbent government was legitimate. This objection strikes others as obscurely legalistic. Possible alternative terms such as 'rising' and 'insurrection' have their merits, but my preference for 'rebellion' stems largely from the fact that it contains the term for its makers, and that term – 'rebels' – carries a charge of romantic glamour which was wholly appropriate to their minds. On a rather more trivial point, I have tried to use the most common form of the names of participants, which is sometimes an odd, partly Gaelicized, hybrid: thus Seán MacDermott, for instance, rather than John MacDermott or Seán Mac Diarmada. Padraig Mac Piarais remains Patrick Pearse, but Pierce Beasley becomes Piaras Béaslaí. I have also treated the widely used label 'Sinn Feiner' as a hybrid Irish-English word, and left the acute accent out of it – likewise, where the words 'Sinn Féin' are quoted from English sources which did not notice it. I have left the name of Dublin's principal street, the central scene of the 1916 street drama, in its official contemporary form as Sackville Street. I hope all this will not cause too much annoyance.

Over the many years I have been working on this subject I have run up many debts of gratitude; the biggest are to those beneficent organizations which intercede to provide precious time for research. My university had always been exemplary in the provision of sabbatical leave, but I am particularly indebted to the generosity of the Woodrow Wilson International Center in Washington, DC, and the Leverhulme Trust, without whose grant of a Major Research Fellowship this book would certainly not have been completed before the rebellion's centenary. Such – sadly rare – institutions are 'the one bright spot' (as was said of Ireland in a different context) on the horizon of contemporary academic life. Libraries and archives invariably do their best to make access to their precious holdings convenient and agreeable for researchers, but I would particularly like to acknowledge the dramatic changes not just in size and location but more importantly in helpfulness of service that have taken place in the Public Record Office, now officially renamed the National Archives (a renaming that may take longer to stick than did the extension of O'Connell's name from Bridge to Street) since I began research there in the 1970s. Researchers who live as far from London as I do can often feel that they are carrying a debilitating handicap, but the speeding-up of the PRO's operations has gone a long way to minimizing it. At the other end of the scale of physical resources, the Irish Military Archive in Cathal Brugha (Portobello) Barracks, Dublin, provides one of those rare hands-on archival experiences which can connect research with the vividness of real life. Working there has been hugely rewarding. I owe an extra special debt to my fellow historians George Boyce, Roy Foster and Theo Hoppen, and to Eve Morrison for sharing her unique knowledge of the Bureau of Military History material. Kate has put up with my steady descent into obsession with this book with wonderful good humour, and it is dedicated to her.

Charles Townshend
Keele, 2005

POBLACHT NA H EIREANN.

THE PROVISIONAL GOVERNMENT
OF THE
IRISH REPUBLIC
TO THE PEOPLE OF IRELAND.

IRISHMEN AND IRISHWOMEN : In the name of God and of the dead generations from which she receives her old tradition of nationhood, Ireland, through us, summons her children to her flag and strikes for her freedom.

Having organised and trained her manhood through her secret revolutionary organisation, the Irish Republican Brotherhood, and through her open military organisations, the Irish Volunteers and the Irish Citizen Army, having patiently perfected her discipline, having resolutely waited for the right moment to reveal itself, she now seizes that moment, and, supported by her exiled children in America and by gallant allies in Europe, but relying in the first on her own strength, she strikes in full confidence of victory.

We declare the right of the people of Ireland to the ownership of Ireland, and to the unfettered control of Irish destinies, to be sovereign and indefeasible. The long usurpation of that right by a foreign people and government has not extinguished the right, nor can it ever be extinguished except by the destruction of the Irish people. In every generation the Irish people have asserted their right to national freedom and sovereignty ; six times during the past three hundred years they have asserted it in arms. Standing on that fundamental right and again asserting it in arms in the face of the world, we hereby proclaim the Irish Republic as a Sovereign Independent State, and we pledge our lives and the lives of our comrades-in-arms to the cause of its freedom, of its welfare, and of its exaltation among the nations.

The Irish Republic is entitled to, and hereby claims, the allegiance of every Irishman and Irishwoman. The Republic guarantees religious and civil liberty, equal rights and equal opportunities to all its citizens, and declares its resolve to pursue the happiness and prosperity of the whole nation and of all its parts, cherishing all the children of the nation equally, and oblivious of the differences carefully fostered by an alien government, which have divided a minority from the majority in the past.

Until our arms have brought the opportune moment for the establishment of a permanent National Government, representative of the whole people of Ireland and elected by the suffrages of all her men and women, the Provisional Government, hereby constituted, will administer the civil and military affairs of the Republic in trust for the people.

We place the cause of the Irish Republic under the protection of the Most High God, Whose blessing we invoke upon our arms, and we pray that no one who serves that cause will dishonour it by cowardice, inhumanity, or rapine. In this supreme hour the Irish nation must, by its valour and discipline and by the readiness of its children to sacrifice themselves for the common good, prove itself worthy of the august destiny to which it is called.

Signed on Behalf of the Provisional Government,

THOMAS J. CLARKE.

SEAN Mac DIARMADA,   THOMAS MacDONAGH.
P. H. PEARSE,   EAMONN CEANNT,
JAMES CONNOLLY.   JOSEPH PLUNKETT.

G. R.

PROCLAMATION.

WHEREAS, in the City of Dublin and County of Dublin certain evilly disposed persons and associations, with the intent to subvert the supremacy of the Crown in Ireland, have committed divers acts of violence, and have with deadly weapons attacked the Forces of the Crown, and have resisted by armed force the lawful Authority of His Majesty's Police and Military Forces.   AND whereas by reason thereof several of His Majesty's liege Subjects have been killed and many others severely injured, and much damage to property has been caused.

AND, whereas, such armed resistance to His Majesty's authority still continues.   NOW, I, Ivor Churchill, Baron Wimborne, Lord Lieutenant-General and General Governor of Ireland, by virtue of all the powers me thereunto enabling DO HEREBY PROCLAIM that from and after the date of this Proclamation, and for the period of One Month thereafter (unless otherwise ordered) the CITY OF DUBLIN and COUNTY OF DUBLIN are under and subject to

MARTIAL LAW

AND I do hereby call on all Loyal and well affected Subjects of the Crown to aid in upholding and maintaining the peace of this Realm and the supremacy and authority of the Crown.   AND I warn all peaceable and law-abiding Subjects within such area of the danger of frequenting, or being in any place in or in the vicinity of which His Majesty's Forces are engaged in the suppression of disorder.

AND I do hereby enjoin upon such Subjects the duty and necessity, so far as practicable, of remaining within their own homes so long as these dangerous conditions prevail.

And I do hereby declare that all persons found carrying Arms without lawful authority are liable to be dealt with by virtue of this Proclamation.

Given at Dublin this 26th day of April, 1916.

WIMBORNE

GOD SAVE THE KING.

xxi

I

Revolutionism

*Let our generation not shirk its deed, which is to accomplish
the revolution.*   P. H. Pearse, 1913

When Patrick Henry Pearse stepped out of his newly established headquarters in the Dublin General Post Office, shortly after noon on
Easter Monday 1916, to read the proclamation of the Irish Republic,
he drew deeply on the history of Irish resistance to British rule – 'the
dead generations' from which Ireland received 'her old tradition of
nationhood'. To understand his famous words, we need to plunge
back into that historical deep. How far? From Pearse's own angle of
vision, the apostolic succession stretched back into prehistory and
legend. In his fierce, incantatory poem *Mionn* ('Oath'), he took it
back to 'the murder of Red Hugh' – the sixteenth-century chieftain
Hugh O'Donnell. In the proclamation of the republic he specified that
'the Irish people' had asserted 'in arms' their right to national freedom
and sovereignty 'six times in the past three hundred years'. This was
an impressive genealogy of revolt; but its apparent coherence disguised some significant variations among these outbursts of the
national spirit. How connected, how coherent, in fact, were such
struggles as those of the old Gaelic princes, Hugh O'Neill and Patrick
Sarsfield, the United Irishmen, or the Fenian movement of the 1860s?
In what sense were they conducted by 'the Irish people'?

  We may not need to follow Pearse all the way back to the sixteenth
century – though Irish nationalists routinely went much further, and
invoked 'eight centuries' of resistance to English rule; but we do need
to examine the system that had existed since the Union of 1801.

Ireland in the first century of the Union was certainly not an entirely quiescent place. Indeed many observers, especially English observers, regarded it as lawless even when the peace was not openly disturbed; its very quietness at times was ascribed to the paralysing grip of rural 'terrorism'. From this viewpoint, the countryside was honeycombed with secret societies, with names like Whiteboys, Rockites or Captain Moonlight, waging a perennial nocturnal war against the legitimate order – torching hayricks, crippling animals, sometimes firing a few shots into houses, usually preceded by bloodcurdling threatening letters. Their prime targets were landlords, land agents or tenants who had broken what some called the 'unwritten law' – in essence a prohibition on the eviction of long-established tenants. Very few landlords could be got at directly, but tenants who took over 'evicted farms', from which the former tenants had been ejected, were vulnerable to retribution. The existence of such secret societies was beyond dispute, though whether they were as ubiquitous as they loomed in the middle-class imagination was open to some doubt. The Royal Irish Constabulary (RIC), the armed police force that was the principal, and often the only, state agency throughout most of Ireland, put the actions of the secret societies in a special category of 'agrarian' crime, to distinguish them from ordinary criminals, and to show that ordinary crime levels in Ireland were remarkably low. But the effect of this was to point up the salience of 'public' crime, and to suggest a deep alienation from the law, at least the law of property. The journalists who christened the intensification of the agrarian struggle in 1879–81 the 'Land War' helped to talk up the sense of crisis. The tenants themselves tended to exaggerate the likelihood of eviction – a process more often threatened than carried through, but no less alarming for that – and so created a kind of reciprocal terrorism.

But did this all really signify a fundamental rejection of British 'law and order'? Did it, indeed, as Irish nationalists often contended, represent the struggle not just of peasants against landowners, but of the Irish people against an alien system? Was it, in fact, implicitly revolutionary? This was the picture drawn by Michael Davitt, for instance, in his hefty and imposing book *The Fall of Feudalism in Ireland* (1904), charting the dramatic history of the 'land war' of the nineteenth century. In this epic view, the word 'war' became more than journalistic hyperbole, rather a description of what was in effect an international conflict, an Anglo-Irish war. Yet, if so, there were sharp limits to the 'war aims' of the ordinary Irish people. By the time he published his book, Davitt had been made painfully aware that the Irish peasantry did not, as he had hoped, cherish a dream of replacing what he called 'landlordism' by collective ownership of the land. They wanted, rather, to become little landlords with exclusive ownership of their property – in other words, they preferred the British idea of property rights to the supposed old-Irish idea of common social property. Yet this was just one flaw in the image of national unity projected by nationalist writers like him. Davitt's own career, admittedly, read like an embodiment of that unity: moving from the Irish Republican Brotherhood, an elite secret society dedicated to armed insurrection, through the mass organization of the Land League, to constitutional politics as a member of the UK parliament. But while he could change shape or colour, these structures themselves proved much more resistant to such melding. Indeed their tendency was to fracture rather than to unite.

Irish public experience was deeply marked by the traumatic split between the great 'liberator', Daniel O'Connell, and his Young Ireland allies in the 1840s, which was followed by the humiliating collapse of the Young Irelanders' attempted rebellion in 1848, in the midst of the great famine. Some of the survivors took the path of secrecy and ruthless centralization to guard against any repetition of this: the result was the Fenian organization – the name colloquially given to the Irish Republican Brotherhood (IRB). This clandestine oathbound group set its face against the danger of political sell-outs, rejecting all participation in the British political system in favour of a commitment to 'physical force' to remove British rule. Built in a cellular masonic structure of 'Circles' commanded by 'Centres', unknown to each other and linked only through the organization's hierarchical system, at the apex of which was the Supreme Council, the IRB was committed to open battle against England (as it invariably called its enemy). Discipline was rigid. It did not, in principle, take part in the land war. The agrarian conflict, with its dismal round of intimidation, cattle-maiming and occasional assassination, in the Fenian view showed the seamy side of the nation – cowardly violence and clan greed rather than a fight for the nation's honour.

Though the organization undoubtedly saw itself as revolutionary – the first version of its title, indeed, had been 'Irish Revolutionary Brotherhood' – its political programme was sparse. It focused almost exclusively on winning Irish independence and establishing a republic, which it conceived as a one-step process; it showed little attraction to the kind of wider social reshaping that had marked the great French Revolution. If anything, its leaders were rather conservative. In spite of this, the IRB found itself at odds not only with those who preferred to follow O'Connell in attempting to exploit the parliamentary process, but also with the Catholic Church. Senior clergy were deeply opposed to secret oathbound revolutionary societies, and the IRB replied with a republican rejection of clerical interference in politics. Its anti-clericalism may have been mild by the standards of its French republican exemplars, but it represented a real antagonism in the Irish social context.[1]

The parliamentarians, for their part, dismissed 'physical force' as both immoral and self-defeating. Failed rebellions merely provoked further repressive laws, and the imbalance (actually widening as the nineteenth century went on) between the demographic and economic weight of the two countries meant that rebellion was bound to fail. Constitutionalism, based on 'moral force', could exploit the shifting balances of British politics to achieve, not perhaps outright independence as a republic, but effective self-government – 'Home Rule' – within the United Kingdom. The key advantage of this strategy, to its founders such as Isaac Butt, was that it could head off the most disastrous of all potential Irish splits: the separation of the Protestant north from the Catholic south. In the 1880s Butt's charismatic successor, Charles Stewart Parnell, brought the nationalist movement to a peak of unity and effectiveness by combining the land agitation with the parliamentary strategy, and by his aggressive style managed to bring the Fenians guardedly on board as well. But this 'new departure' came at a price. The ruthless discipline he imposed on his party, to avoid a repetition of past failures, established an authoritarian tendency that was to cast a baleful shadow into the next century. And the unprecedented extent of Parnell's power, seen by some as creating a virtual Irish state, was based on an accommodation with the Catholic Church.[2] His moment of apparent triumph, the election of eighty-six Home Rule MPs in 1886, a grouping which held the balance of power at Westminster, also witnessed the first violent manifestation of Unionist resistance in Ulster.

The heady unity of the 1880s was followed by a decade of splits. Parnell's own personal crash was one of the great British political scandals of the century, a product of his reckless defiance of Victorian public morality. It opened the way for a conservative religious assault led by the barrister MP Tim Healy, who attacked Parnell's long-term mistress Katherine O'Shea 'not merely as the adulterous wife of Captain O'Shea' but also as 'the carnal embodiment of English dictation'.[3] The political fallout of the venomous struggle between Parnellites and anti-Parnellites dangerously weakened the Home Rule project in the 1890s. Strangely, though, despite Parnell's desperate invocation of the 'hillside men' in his final election campaign, the constitutionalist disaster did not lead to a shift back to the primacy of the physical-force group. The IRB was equally, if less publicly, split and paralysed in the wake of the experiments of the 1880s. The IRB Supreme Council had for a long time, under the presidency of Charles J. Kickham, taken a more purist line than its more powerful, or at least better-funded American sister organization, the Clan na Gael. Kickham's IRB repudiated not only agrarian violence but also the policy of systematic, selective terrorism in Britain adopted by the Clan na Gael in the 1880s.

Terrorism was the chosen weapon of international anarchism, and the Fenians would have none of it – not officially, at any rate. They became, briefly, 'accidental terrorists' when they tried to rescue Fenian prisoners from Clerkenwell gaol in 1867, and succeeded only in wrecking the neighbouring tenements. But they succeeded in spreading alarm across the whole country. Even more resonant in Ireland itself was the attempted rescue of prisoners from a police van in Manchester, a fracas in which two policemen were killed. The would-be rescuers were executed, and elevated to the pantheon of separatist heroes as 'the Manchester Martyrs': their memory lived on. Significantly, despite the IRB's reluctance, the impact of this 'terrorist' violence on British opinion was dramatic: the 'Irish Question' moved from the margins to the centre of the political stage.[4]

Yet the IRB never returned to bomb-planting: and the American Fenians' efforts petered out ineffectually.

The nearest thing to a home-grown terrorist group to appear in Ireland was the shadowy Irish National Invincibles; far less substantial or enduring than the IRB, this ephemeral group carried out only one operation. All the same, that single operation, the assassination of the two most important members of the British government in Ireland in Phoenix Park in 1882, had a tremendous psychological impact. Together with the Manchester Martyrs, the Invincibles' drama became an enduring spur to later generations. In *Ulysses* (set in July 1904), James Joyce gleefully recounted the story of how Lady Dudley, walking home through Phoenix Park 'to see all the trees that were blown down by that cyclone last year', decided to buy a picture postcard. 'And it turned out to be a commemoration postcard of Joe Brady or Number One or Skin-the-Goat. Right outside the viceregal lodge, imagine!' For over a decade, however, revolutionary leadership lost its impetus, demoralized perhaps by interminable waiting for the right moment for rebellion. Open conflict broke out within the Irish-American Fenian organization, as the veteran organizer John Devoy denounced the terrorist methods espoused by his rival Alexander Sullivan. Fenianism remained wedded to the idea of open insurrection.

By the turn of the century, however, out of the debris of the great nationalist mobilization of the 1880s was emerging another basis for revolutionary action. A second 'new departure', less deliberate but more far-reaching than the first, emerged as 'physical-force' men began to take an interest in culture – not so much the high art of the Irish literary renaissance led by W. B. Yeats, which was also bursting on the scene at that moment, but *kultur* in the sense used by German nationalists to describe the skein of customs, folkways and ideas that created national consciousness. The key to this was language. Up to this time, Irish nationalists had not devoted much effort to inquiring into the nature of Irish identity; what made the Irish a people? Both the United Irelanders and the Young Irelanders had pretty much assumed that Ireland's claim to self-government and separation from Britain was self-evident, and did not call for systematic explanation.

The existence of the Irish language was seen as one among a number of special characteristics, and its precise importance was not measured – could not be safely measured, perhaps, by separatist leaders such as Wolfe Tone, Robert Emmet or Thomas Davis, all Protestants and English speakers. (Though Davis borrowed from the leading European nationalists of his time such as Giuseppe Mazzini the mantra that 'a people without a language of its own is only half a nation', he clearly did not grasp its full implications.)[5] Famously, Daniel O'Connell, who was a native Irish speaker (and a Catholic), treated the language as a colourful ghost of the past, and many Catholic middle-class Irish people followed his lead in making sure their children learnt English. The key popular evocation of nineteenth-century Irishness, Charles J. Kickham's bestseller *Knocknagow* (first published in 1873, and going into a cheap edition in 1887), evinced little fear of cultural imperialism. Indeed, considering that it was written by the leader of the IRB, its sentimental tolerance of the prevailing order is probably its most striking feature.

But the rapid decline in Irish-speaking that became obvious in the mid nineteenth century eventually began to ring alarm bells, as some nationalists (once again, Protestants took the lead here) began to sense that it might be irreversible unless it was halted immediately. The 'Gaelic revival' that followed was the work of two organizations. The first in point of time, the Gaelic Athletic Association, set out in 1884 to revive traditional Irish sports – a mission based on the contention that imported English games (like cricket or the 'soccer' that was then beginning its conquest of the world) were not 'racy of the soil' but alien to it, as the Archbishop of Cashel put it at the GAA's foundation meeting. The complex construction of Irishness in this assertion had revolutionary implications, and despite their unwavering commitment to a straightforward political project – an independent republic – the IRB instantly recognized that the GAA was a kindred movement. Like them it was 'separatist', the favourite Fenian self-description. An IRB presence at every level of the GAA organization was soon obvious even to the police. For the first time the secret brotherhood had an open, popular and peaceful frame of action. And for the first time, too, the 'politicization of sport' became significant. The GAA banned the playing of 'English' games by its members – a combative line which chimed with the policy of 'de-Anglicization' identified with the other key organization, the Gaelic League.

The foundation of the League in 1893 tapped into the cultural anxieties of a generation, and unleashed an unprecedented wave of enthusiasm for language learning. This project was, perhaps more than the GAA's, at first believed by many of its promoters to be non-political. Many language-revival enthusiasts were not only middle class, but in political terms very far from being separatists; some indeed were Unionists (like Standish O'Grady, whose revitalization of Ireland's heroic age – and the legendary hero Cuchulainn above all – was a seminal influence on the new nationalism). Douglas Hyde, the man who gave the League its keynote task of 'de-Anglicizing the Irish nation', never fully accepted the political implications of his warning that 'by Anglicizing ourselves we have thrown away with a light heart the best claim we have upon the world's recognition of us as a separate nationality . . . the notes of nationality, our language and customs'.[6] Though he could vehemently denounce 'the dirty English tongue' – echoing the pioneering eighteenth-century German philologist Johann Gottfried Herder (who called French 'that slime of the Seine') – it seems that like Herder he believed that culture could transcend politics.[7]

Cultural nationalism may have hit Ireland a hundred years late, but its effects were no less revolutionary for that. Irishness was to be redefined and, with it, the shape of the Irish nation.[8] The wave of enthusiasm for what was often called 'Irish-Ireland' was slow-building, however; it crested at the turn of the century for reasons that lay outside these concerns about identity. Three developments – the centenary of the 1798 rebellion, the outbreak of the Boer War, and (less headline-grabbing but equally epochal) the creation of local government authorities – combined to accelerate the process of nationalist reshaping. The '98 centenary, falling towards the end of a disastrous decade, concentrated the minds of nationalists of all stripes, whether constitutional, agrarian or separatist, and it proved – despite some embarrassing failures – to be a uniquely sharp spur to unified action. The memory of 1798 was not wholly unproblematic, as the well-known (if ambiguous) mid-century ballad 'Who fears to speak of '98' indicated. The political legacy of the United Irish movement's most potent ideologue, Theobald Wolfe Tone, a serious political

thinker, was less widely accepted than the simple heroism of his youthful successor Robert Emmet. Tone, a child of the Enlightenment and
admirer of the Jacobin republic in the French Revolution, aimed to
reconstitute Irish identity through eroding the separate traditions of
'Catholic, Protestant and Dissenter'. The secularization this envisaged
was less attractive than his simple slogan 'break the connection', with
its implication that independence would solve all Ireland's problems.
Emmet's failed rebellion of 1803 became an icon of romantic activism,
its incompetence ignored while the brutality of the British reaction was
played up.[9] (Emmet never got his tiny force out of its assembly point,
Thomas Street, towards his target, Dublin Castle; his hoped-for 2,000
insurgents had dwindled to 20 by the time they reached the end of the
street.) And if the test of successful commemoration was the erection
of Tone's statue, then the IRB failed badly: nearly seven years after the
anniversary, P. T. Daly was lamenting to John Devoy that the failure
to build the memorial – the result of inadequate fund-raising – was
'destroying us'.[10]

But there was much more to it than this. The impulse to do something to mark the centenary led the former Parnellite William O'Brien
to relaunch the land agitation through a new and highly effective organization, the United Irish League. By 1900 the UIL had become strong
enough to force the warring factions of the Irish parliamentary party
into a reunion, with John Redmond as leader. The following decade was
one of growing hope for the constitutionalists, culminating in their
achieving the balance of power at Westminster for a second time in
1910, with the introduction of a new Home Rule measure the following year. The party maintained its grip on formal politics, and its
authoritarian structure, but it was from now on to be constantly looking over its shoulder at the challenge of more radical separatist groups.

Just how sharp the challenge could be, a new generation of
journalists demonstrated. On the heels of the astonishing literary
renaissance of the 1890s followed a spate of high-energy newspaper
activity, spearheaded by remarkable individuals such as D. P. Moran
of *The Leader*, and Arthur Griffith, a serial editor who published a
succession of small news-sheets, starting with the *United Irishman* in
1899. The year was significant. Griffith had just returned from South
Africa, where he had become a self-taught printer, at the outbreak of

the second Boer War. The stocky, mustachioed incarnation of auto-didactic pugnacity, he was a natural polemicist: it was to be said admiringly, but not inaccurately, that 'an epigram by Griffith is much like a bomb from a Zeppelin'.[11] He immediately took the lead in opposing the war. Whereas in England such opposition ran into over-whelming and sometimes violent patriotic hostility, in Ireland public opinion was far more ambivalent. To be a 'pro-Boer' might be to be in a (possibly quite small) minority, but not to be a traitor; and the sheer range of anti-war activity made it credible to speak of a 'move-ment'. From the foundation of an Irish Neutrality Association by the nationalist celebrity Maud Gonne and the raising of relief funds by the Irish Transvaal Committee, through a swath of anti-recruiting campaigners, to the nationalist press's marked tendency to admire rather than execrate the military achievements of the Boer forces, the stirring of opinion was wide.[12] Most dramatic of all was the raising of two 'Irish Brigades' to fight in South Africa under the command of Arthur Lynch and Gonne's future husband, John MacBride. (The aid of a few hundred Irish miners was probably less valuable as military than as moral support to the Afrikaners.) Unionists depicted Irish pro-Boerism as an unrepresentative fringe tendency, though at the same time they could not resist the temptation of using it as further proof that Ireland was unfit for self-government. In this respect, the newly created local councils played an important role, giving a new authority to speeches and motions by nationalist politicians.

Out of all this rich mix of protest, Griffith wove a distinctive sep-aratist project which was to transform Irish politics. In 1900 he set up a loose political ginger group – not quite yet a party – under the name Cumann na nGaedheal – the first Irish political organization to adopt a Gaelic title. (Roughly meaning 'band' or 'league of Gaels', it set a precedent for later nationalist groupings both in its historicism and its avoidance of any attempt to translate the word 'party'.) He had no political ambition or capacity in the conventional sense: 'though he was a fluent and lucid speaker, he was never able to dominate and stir an audience and never looked as if he enjoyed facing one.'[13] Movements tended to form around him rather than through his direct leadership. But form they did, and repeatedly. A more focused National Council, established in 1903 by Edward Martyn and other

Griffithites, evolved two years later into the still more pungent, programmatic, and permanent Sinn Féin. (Another Gaelic title, but a modern coinage without the divisive dark-age echoes transmitted in the name of its predecessor, and indeed successor parties like Fianna Fáil and Fine Gael.)[14] In between, Griffith argued vigorously for a new attitude to the idea of independence – not just political, but economic and cultural; and a new political strategy to replace the parliamentarism of the constitutionalists. In a word, this was abstention: the withdrawal of Irish MPs from Westminster to establish a national assembly with or without British consent. Griffith modelled this on the way the Hungarians secured autonomy within the Habsburg empire in 1867, a process which he recounted in a gripping (if somewhat misleading) historical narrative, *The Resurrection of Hungary*. Even though many nationalists found his historical model inappropriate, if not irrelevant, his key idea was a truly powerful and revolutionary one. Sinn Féin – 'ourselves', sometimes rendered 'ourselves alone' – offered a method of national liberation which rested entirely on 'self-development', the self-mobilization of the Irish nation as a conscious entity. (Griffith himself will have been aware of the nineteenth-century Italian nationalist precedent, 'L'Italia fará da sé'.) The 1905 Sinn Féin policy declaration insisted on 'not looking outside Ireland for the accomplishment of their aims'.[15]

The Sinn Féin programme offered a smorgasbord of variously risky or risk-free ways of resisting, subverting or simply ignoring British rule. As one leading Sinn Féin writer put it in a 1909 tract, the Irish people 'need not obey, and they need not be governed, a day longer than they wish'.[16] The modern term for the Sinn Féin strategy would become 'civil resistance'. (Though the Arabic word *intifada* was not yet familiar to the Anglophone world, its meaning – shaking or sloughing off – would have fitted the Sinn Féin line well.) This was a programme with real claims to global relevance; Gandhi, for instance, acknowledged the influence of Sinn Féin on his own idea of passive resistance, *satyagraha*.[17] People could refuse to buy British goods, refuse to pay taxes, play English games, attend English plays, or indeed to speak English. But this empowering agenda also upped the identity stakes in a fateful way. It invoked, and required, a sense of Irishness much stronger and more coherent than earlier nationalist strategies had assumed. For self-reliance and self-sufficiency to work in this grassroots way, the self had to be much more sharply defined.

Griffith himself did not fully grasp this implication of his idea. His notion of nationality remained (as the name of his first newspaper indicated) the civic, territorial view of the United Irishmen and his Young Ireland hero John Mitchel, whose central idea was simple detestation of England. Never a fluent Irish speaker, Griffith habitually took a utilitarian, functional, rather than mystical view of what made the Irish a nation. You were Irish if you dedicated yourself to Ireland against England. For Griffith, the 'national spirit' manifested itself in practical activity – such as the organization of a 'patriotic children's treat' as a demonstration against the events arranged to mark Queen Victoria's visit to Ireland in 1900. Small actions like this could indeed have bigger echoes; Maud Gonne went on to turn the picnic committee into a permanent women's activist group, Inghinidhe na hEireann (Daughters of Ireland), which would mark the entire revolutionary generation.[18] Griffith left the IRB around this time, but, interestingly, remained ready to use physical force in defence of Maud Gonne. He went to prison for using his souvenir *sjambok* on a magazine editor who had insulted the actress-activist. When she caused a public drama by hanging out a black flag (actually half a petticoat on a broom handle) in protest against the new King Edward VII's visit to Dublin in 1903, Griffith led a rescue posse to liberate her besieged house from irate loyalists – the 'battle of Coulsdon Avenue'.

Griffith could not have written, as the Gaelic Leaguer Patrick Henry Pearse did, that for Ireland to lose its language would be worse than for it never to gain its political independence: for Ireland to be free yet not 'Gaelic' would be meaningless and disastrous. It was Pearse, more than anyone else, who forged the direct link between culture and politics. In the process, the notion of separatism underwent a vital change. Even though he was not inducted into the physical-force group until barely three years before he emerged as commander-in-chief of the republican forces in the 1916 rebellion, for fifteen years Pearse had been making an increasingly distinctive and influential contribution to separatist thought. He joined the Gaelic League in 1896 at the age of seventeen; the elder son of an Irish mother and an English father, a monumental mason. By the time he was co-opted on to the League's executive committee, Coiste Gnotha, two years later, he had already displayed what his biographer calls his 'natural didacticism' by urging a programme of talks and activities to increase the popular appeal of League meetings. He went quickly into print with *Three Lectures on Gaelic Topics*. In 1899 he became 'Conductor of the Competitions' at the League's annual gala, the Oireachtas, and Eoin MacNeill's assistant as editor of the League's journal *An Claideamh Soluis*. When he became editor in 1903 his position as chief ideologue of the language movement was cemented.

The vehemence of Pearse's view of the language question was noticeable at an early stage. He warned that if the Irish people allowed their language to die, they 'would go down to their graves with the knowledge that their children and their children's children cursed their memory'.[19] His early evaluation of W. B. Yeats, which he later regretted, showed his combative outlook. Suggesting that Yeats was 'a mere English poet of the third or fourth rank and as such he is harmless', he added, 'But when he attempts to run an "Irish" Literary Theatre it is time for him to be crushed.' None the less, for the first decade at least of his League career, he remained committed to reawakening the people by essentially literary means. Pearse was first and foremost an educationalist. His period of legal studies at the Royal University (in 1901, like O'Connell before him, he became a barrister) really formed an intermission between his work as pupil-teacher at the Christian Brothers' School in Westland Row, and his later series of efforts to establish a school of his own. Though his most acute biographer thinks that the Brothers had no marked effect on Pearse's emotional development, it is likely that they left their mark on his sense of nationality. The formation of collective mentality is an exceptionally difficult subject to measure with any accuracy, but one of the clearest findings of political-science analysis of nationalism in Ireland has been the strong correlation between attendance at Christian Brothers' schools and subsequent militant activity.[20] Harder to read, perhaps, is the influence of his early environment; it may be a slight exaggeration to say that his home in Great Brunswick Street was 'wedged between perhaps the two most notorious red-light districts in the city' (both 'Monto' north of the river, and Grafton Street to the west, were a fair distance away).[21] Speculation about the 'confusions of his sexual identity' on the basis of his youthful habit of roaming the streets dressed as a beggar woman or girl may be tendentious. But there is some force in the suggestion that he emerged as a 'stiff, shy and socially awkward' man – 'more comfortable with children than with most adults'.

Education was a vital issue for cultural nationalists. Pearse labelled the national school system established by the British government 'the murder machine' – chillingly evoking the nationalist fear of cultural genocide. Pearse believed implicitly that the Gaelic language had been deliberately undermined by official policy – a belief which had the encouraging corollary that the language could be revived by reversing that policy. He pitched enthusiastically into the League's battle for the compulsory inclusion of Gaelic (now increasingly called the 'Irish language') for matriculation in the National University, when it was established in 1908. It looked, indeed, as if his great life-work was as an educationalist; he set up, on a shoestring budget, a bilingual school, St Enda's (Scoil Eanna). He decorated its first location, Cullenswood House in Rathmines, with a mass of Gaelic-revival artwork, including a stained-glass panel of Cuchulainn with his legendary words, 'I care not though I live but one day and one night, provided my fame and my deeds live after me.' Maud Gonne donated an allegorical painting of a hooded Cathleen ni Houlihan (which the artist was later alarmed to find inspiring at least one of the pupils 'to die for Ireland').[22] When Pearse moved the school to grander accommodation, The Hermitage in the neighbouring south Dublin suburb of Rathfarnham, he moved his presiding spirit-hero forward in time: it had been the home of Robert Emmet's fiancée, and Pearse kept on display the block on which Emmet had supposedly been beheaded.

A perceptive critic has said that Pearse, a 'deeply divided man', responded to the Gaelic movement's idealization of peasant life because of its freedom from the complexities and anxieties of modern 'civilization'. This was a common, indeed an elementary tenet of modern nationalism, as preached all across Europe since the 1780s: in the nationalist view 'the people' are an organic being with a single spirit (*Volksgeist*, in the German model; Pearse preferred the word 'soul').[23] The natural and proper state of the nation was one of unity; division was a sign of corruption. The sense of threat and the fear of contamination were potent drivers of political romanticism. Nationalism (as distinct from the sense of nationality) is a modern ideology because it answers a need for rootedness generated by the dislocating effects of the modernization process.[24] It is a spell against the void of anomie, the loss of traditional identity. For many Irish nationalists, the threat to Irishness came not just from the foreigner, but from modernity itself.[25] 'England' was not just an unfriendly neighbouring superpower, but the incarnation of a materialism that was profoundly corrosive of spiritual authenticity. This Manichean view was propounded, for instance, in the widely read novels of Canon P. A. Sheehan, written around the turn of the century.[26] 'It is striking', Roy Foster has pointed out, 'how emphatically the voices of Irish-Irelandness identified English cultural norms with corruption.'[27]

In this respect (and in the laxity of his logic) Pearse was a nationalist like any other, but his nationalism had a unique inflection. William Irwin Thompson suggests that while 'the role of a rebel is very general, the way in which the role appears in the imagination of one man is very particular'. Pearse constructed, or discovered, special lineaments for the lone hero who would pass through exile to death in combat with the foreign enemy. 'Before Pearse fired a shot, he rehearsed the insurrection by writing a play about it.'[28] That play, The Singer, was written late in 1915 and never performed in his lifetime – 'and would scarcely have attracted much attention if it had been', in his biographer's view. (But 'if Pearse were dead, this would cause a sensation', Joseph Plunkett suggested.[29] And it has, indeed, been quoted countless times since his death.) At its climax the hero declares, 'One man can free a people as one Man redeemed the world.' Here, Thompson says, 'one sees quite clearly that for Pearse the rebel is the perfect imitation of Christ'. Or rather, Christ in the role of Cuchulainn, the defender of the race, a religious hybridization that was distinctly unorthodox – some would say heretical.[30] The Singer should not, any more than the rest of Pearse's writings, be read as a literal blueprint for rebellion. For one thing its hero, MacDara, went into battle unarmed; and while it is not clear that Pearse himself ever 'fired a shot', he would certainly carry weapons into the GPO when his rebel forces mobilized in 1916, and did his utmost to ensure that none of his followers lacked them.[31] What is clear is that, for all his eccentricity, and against all the odds, Pearse's sense of mission was strong enough to place him, ultimately, at the head of an army.

Pearse was undeniably odd, but he was also in an important sense a 'representative man'. His faith in the symbolic force of drama, in particular, was common currency at the turn of the century. 'Dublin was drama mad in every sense of the word', as one of the most admired actors of the theatre revival, Maire Nic Shiubhlaigh, put it.[32] The National Theatre, pioneered by Yeats and Lady Gregory, and initially excoriated by Pearse, emerged from among a constellation of smaller, more transient amateur companies. They staged a succession of 'national', which mostly meant nationalist, plays both in English (which even Pearse was prepared to write in) and Gaelic. Yeats and Gregory's *Cathleen ni Houlihan* (first performed in April 1902 by another small group, the Irish National Dramatic Society) was probably the most resonant of this genre: fusing the mythic character of Ireland itself with the historical events of the 1798 rebellion, its impact is hard to exaggerate. Its star, Maud Gonne, 'emphatically bridged the divide between theatrical representation and propagandist meeting' by declaiming her climactic speech to the audience rather than the cast.[33] The journalist Stephen Gwynn reeled home, 'asking myself if such plays should be produced unless one was prepared for people to go out to shoot and be shot'.[34]

Pearse made drama central to the life of his schools, and in 1911 staged a passion play at St Enda's which led some to foresee a real 'tradition of acting and dramatic writing in Irish'. But the script disappeared, and it was never re-staged. Gaelic drama remained a minority enthusiasm, maintained by little groups like Na hAisteori, run by Piaras Béaslaí. Most attention was engrossed by historical plays like *The Memory of the Dead* (another evocation of the 1798 rebellion) written by a Polish exile, Count Casimir Markievicz, whose dynamic and colourful wife Constance was the moving spirit of the Independent Dramatic Company they started after the play's successful run at the Gaiety Theatre. Edward Martyn's 'Irish Theatre' (also called the Theatre of Ireland), housed in premises provided by the Plunkett family, provided a stage for the Plunketts' son Joseph and Pearse's teaching colleague Thomas MacDonagh. These two, one quiet, delicate, almost effeminate, the other vivacious and assertive, became key figures in a drama movement that would merge naturally and seamlessly into political activism. Plunkett, a 'delicate child' whose formal education had been delayed by pneumonia, pleurisy and tuberculosis, was twenty-three years old when MacDonagh 'came to teach him Irish for his matriculation and stayed as a friend: they were inseparable'.[35] When Plunkett was sent to winter in Algiers, MacDonagh prepared his first volume of verse for the printer. (Plunkett returned at Easter 1912 to a bout of flu and a lung haemorrhage, but remained a fan of motorbikes, rowing and dancing, as well as taking a 'violent interest in everything intellectual, from physics and chemistry, colour photography and wireless to mysticism'.) MacDonagh, who came to Dublin from Munster to take a BA at the new University College, wrote in every genre – poetry, journalism, criticism and drama – and also tried his hand at painting in Paris. His first play, *When the Dawn Is Come*, begun in 1904, dwelt on the moral and political complexity of rebellion, and the role of the archetypal poet-patriot warrior. His journalism was characteristically shot through with the intolerant exclusivism of Irish-Ireland – as when he accused the Irish Women's Franchise League of 'coquetting with West Britain' by inviting an English suffragette leader to give a talk in Dublin.[36] But he was also a rising academic star: his MA thesis on Thomas Campion led to his appointment as a lecturer in literature at UCD in 1911, where he became a colleague of Eoin MacNeill.

The impact of the confrontational posture of the Gaelic League and GAA was almost certainly more divisive than they intended. 'In effect, the extremists confiscated the language, much as they had confiscated Gaelic games', one modern scholar notes. 'By doing so they identified the language and games with a particular political ideology'; the language 'was to become an ideological weapon . . . feared by Protestants and increasingly regarded as foreign and hostile'.[37] (The tendency to call Gaelic the 'Irish language' was a potent signal of this – perhaps subconscious – politicization.) Pearse steadily became clearer about the wider implications of the Gaelic revival. In 1913 he was to announce that the 'appointed work' of the Gaelic League was now done. 'To every generation its deed,' he declaimed in the apocalyptic style he had by then perfected. 'The deed of the generation that has now reached middle life was the Gaelic League: the beginning of the Irish Revolution. Let our generation not shirk its deed, which is to accomplish the revolution.'

Pearse became editor of the *Claideamh* at an epochal moment in Irish history. F. S. L. Lyons, the most authoritative of modern Irish historians, labelled the years 1903–7 'the watershed'. This is an acute and vital perception. Lyons listed a series of 'apparently random events' in 1907 including the introduction and withdrawal of the government's Irish Council Bill, the resignation of C. J. Dolan from the Irish Parliamentary Party (IPP) to contest his seat as a Sinn Féin candidate, the formation of the Joint Committee of Unionist Associations, the promulgation of the papal decree *Ne temere*, the death of the old Fenian John O'Leary, the return of the exiled Fenian dynamitard Thomas Clarke to Ireland, the outbreak of industrial conflict in Belfast, and the riots during the staging of *The Playboy of the Western World* at the Abbey Theatre.[38] As Lyons remarked, these occurrences probably seemed disconnected to contemporaries, but to the historian they combine to suggest 'a heightened temper, a sharper tone in Irish life, which foreshadows the onset of a period altogether different in character from what had gone before'.

Perhaps the most obscure event on Lyons's list, the return of Tom Clarke, was the most crucial to the evolution of separatism. Clarke's explicit reason was to prevent a repeat of the Boer War experience, when England next became involved in a major war. The prospect of a war between Britain and Germany was widely discussed in the USA, and this time Irish republicans must take the opportunity.[39] Clarke's return came in the middle of the first really energetic attempt since the IRB's foundation to reform and revitalize the old organization. This began, like some earlier nationalist initiatives, in Belfast, where Denis McCullough and Bulmer Hobson established the Dungannon Club in 1905. The ostensible object of this was to celebrate those icons of the constitutionalist movement, the Volunteers of 1782. But the icon was carefully chosen: the Volunteers were an armed militia whose success might be taken to offer some instructive lessons. McCullough and Hobson were both IRB men, both dissatisfied with the degenerate state of the organization. McCullough has left a vivid account of his induction into the brotherhood, a key moment in his life. On his eighteenth birthday, his father brought him to the side door of Donnelly's pub on the Falls Road, where he took the IRB oath in a back room. Like many young Gaelic enthusiasts, he was a total abstainer. 'I was disappointed and shocked,' he recalled, 'by the surroundings of this, to me, very important event.' Worse, perhaps, was 'the type of men I found controlling the Organization: they were mostly effete and many of them addicted to drink'.[40] He immediately set about reforming the organization.

His single-mindedness had a rapid impact, and he soon became Centre of his Circle – and ejected his father, among others, from it. On his own, McCullough might have found it impossible to make further headway; but he acquired, in Bulmer Hobson, an ally of quite exceptional abilities. The two of them were the same age (twenty-one), good-looking and charming, and – as one perceptive historian has said – 'with a frightening simplicity'.[41] Though Hobson was later to be almost written out of the nationalist story, he played a leading part – perhaps the leading part – in the mobilization of a credible Irish liberation movement in the decade before 1916. In so far as this became a process of militarization, there was a certain irony in this, since Hobson never entirely abandoned his Quaker unease about the use of violence – indeed his well-known conviction that a premature rebellion would be both immoral and disastrous would lead to his being held under arrest by the rebel organizers over the weekend before the 1916 rebellion broke out.

He was an unusual kind of 'physical-force man', but a dedicated revolutionary for all that. Born John Bulmer Hobson in Holywood, Co. Down in 1883, he had a fairly strict Quaker upbringing, maybe intensified by being sent as a boarder to the Friends' School in Lisburn (his father was a commercial traveller, often away from home). But he began to break away from this at an early age. As a thirteen-year-old he became a subscriber to the poet Alice Milligan's nationalist journal *Shan Van Vocht*, and he never looked back. The key to his nationalism was a powerful sense of place, and in this he was a true heir of the Young Irelanders – a lineage made clear in his first Dungannon Club manifesto: 'The Ireland we seek to build is not an Ireland for the Catholic or the Protestant, but an Ireland for every Irishman [*sic*], irrespective of his creed or class.' This was an entirely conventional assertion, of course, but by 1905 its emphasis on an inclusive identity of Irish birth was subtly different from the growing emphasis on exclusive cultural homogeneity.

Hobson was a born organizer. He set up the Ulster Debating Club in 1900 when he was barely seventeen years old; two years later he launched a youth group, the Fianna Eireann, in the Catholic Boys' Hall on the Falls Road, Belfast. He wanted it 'to serve as a Junior Hurling League to promote the study of the Irish Language', and the intimate link between sport and language, amounting in Hobson's mind to a synergy, was characteristic. He imbibed a pure strain of nationalism from two remarkable women, Alice Milligan and Ethne Carbery, and his commitment to language revival drove him on to establish a northern version of the Abbey Theatre in the form of the Ulster Literary Theatre in 1904. Despite his urban background, he accepted the Gaelic League idea that the true spirit of Ireland was rural; 'the city', he thought, had been 'a stumbling-block to the right intellectual and artistic progress of the country'. But still 'a certain characteristic temperamental and mental trend has been lent to the town by the country', and the Theatre was intended to 'locate' this. All this came close to a kind of ethnic exclusivism; yet his own embrace of this outlook showed him that it did not necessarily exclude Protestants, and he kept experimenting with methods of bringing the two traditions together in a common national movement.

At the same time Hobson's friendship with McCullough led him into the IRB, a strange destination for a Quaker. But it is clear enough that he never accepted the simple Fenian dogma of insurrection. He always insisted that the revised IRB constitution of 1870 fundamentally reorientated the organization, making rebellion dependent on securing public support. The Dungannon Club idea fitted with this, and it worked, quickly spreading across Ulster and then merging into Sinn Féin in 1907. It was under the Sinn Féin aegis that Hobson wrote one of the most influential separatist tracts, *Defensive Warfare*, subtitled 'a handbook for nationalists', and providing exactly that – a clear, step-by-step programme of civil resistance. Its headline slogan was simple: 'If Ireland is governed it is because the people obey. They need not obey.' Hobson's distinctively modern contribution lay in his recognition that the modern state's complex administrative machinery relies on the habit of acquiescence. If that habit were broken, the machinery would immediately be paralysed. The modern liberal state could not respond with naked coercive violence, and sensible precautions could defend people from many of its legal sanctions. 'You cannot prevent the oppressing nation from imprisoning men and women', but 'you can so distribute the loss over the whole, that it will never be a serious loss to any individual.'[42] Here, as later, Hobson was conscious that people were not eager to take on the government: they needed to be convinced that resistance could work.

In 1908 Hobson moved to Dublin, and there he met the remarkable Countess Markievicz, already a veteran of the national theatre movement, who was then trying to start up a 'rebel boy-scout organization' – a counter to the Baden-Powell corps, which had staged a big rally at Clontarf. They made an odd pair. Born Constance Gore-Booth of Lissadell, Co. Sligo – a 'big house' immortalized by Yeats – a debutante, married to a Polish count and with the energy of a minor force of nature, 'Madame' was an even more surprising separatist than the Quaker Hobson. Her enthusiasm and flamboyance could be taken for shallowness, but she became a tireless activist for both the women's group Inghinidhe na hEireann and the Irish labour movement. One of her fellow writers for the group's journal *Bean na hÉireann* (Irish Woman), Helena Molony, remarked that 'the greatest defect of her character was a childish love for the limelight'. But 'it never prevented her from doing good, hard, unpleasant work. It never seriously misled her.'[43] She 'brimmed over with enthusiasm', as Kathleen Lynn, a pioneering professional (one of Ireland's first women doctors), put it. 'Though you might think her fantastic, she was full of sound sense and quite practical.'[44]

She was not wealthy, unfortunately for the movements she backed, but she had enough resources to make a crucial difference in the early days, when even finding a meeting place could be a problem. Her first attempt to set up a scout group, the 'Red Branch Knights', failed after a disastrous summer camp in 1908, wrecked by a combination of abundant rain and lack of qualified instructors. But when she met Hobson in August 1909, she revived his interest in the organization he had founded and let drop. She hired a meeting hall in Camden Street, and a hundred or so youths came to the inaugural meeting of the reborn *Fianna Eireann* which Hobson chaired on 16 August. Some of them immediately tried to eject her and Helena Molony on the grounds that 'this is a physical force organization' and there was no place for women in it. After Hobson explained that she would be paying the rent, she was elected to the committee, of which he became president. Shortly afterwards, when Hobson returned to Belfast for a time, she took over as president (though she later came to think that he had quietly maintained his control). She was very much the public face of the movement, which grew stronger over the next few years, and which gave her her first opportunity to step forth in a quasi-military outfit of her own design. Although, as her first biographer noted, the scouts 'sometimes laughed at her accent and imitated her high shrill voice' – and also aimed a few kicks at her dog Poppet, as well as making off with her cutlery – 'many of these boys adored her without reserve'. She was well on her way to becoming a separatist icon.

The sense of revival sparked by these developments helped to lever McCullough on to the IRB Supreme Council, but there he ran into the organization's entrenched old guard, headed by Fred Allen and P. T. Daly. The resulting deadlock might have gone on for years, but for the influence of Tom Clarke, who adopted McCullough and, still more closely, Hobson as his political sons. Their key initiative, typically, was the launching of a new republican newspaper. After a flurry of resistance from the old guard, *Irish Freedom* began to appear in 1911, edited by Hobson (and with a regular *Fianna* column contributed by Markievicz). The final crunch came at a classic republican front manifestation, the 1911 meeting to commemorate Robert Emmet's birthday, in the Dublin Rotunda. Another young IRB radical, Patrick McCartan, wanted to propose a resolution deploring an intended visit by King Edward VII, though Tom Clarke at first told him that the 'Wolfe Tone Memorial Committee' had decided to forbid such resolutions as being too provocative. After some hesitation, Clarke changed his mind, triggering a showdown on the IRB Supreme Council: Allen was defeated, even suffering the indignity of having his own Circle eject him as Centre. This coup set the IRB on a course of activity more energetic than any since its early years.

According to McCartan's own account, what drove him to risk 'dashing my head against the stone wall of discipline of the IRB' was the speech given at the Emmet birthday meeting, one of the central events of the republican calendar, by Patrick Pearse. One sentence in particular gripped him: Pearse's intensely emotional charge that 'Dublin would have to do some great act to atone for the shame of not producing a man to dash his head against a stone wall in an effort to rescue Robert Emmet.' We should not read too much into this perhaps, but it was more than mere rhetoric. By 1911 Pearse was plainly becoming more openly militant; Emmet as rebel and as sacrificial victim had come to dominate his pantheon of national heroes. His violence may still have been more aesthetic than practical, but it is hard to disagree with William Irwin Thompson about its intensity. As he moved into middle age, his 'imagery showed an almost pathological lust for violence'. Thompson also found an increasing 'desperation', which 'reveals just how much was at stake for Pearse psychologically'.[45]

While he might have preferred to call it exaltation rather than desperation, Desmond Ryan, one of Pearse's senior pupils at St Enda's, was certainly struck by his highly charged state. At another republican meeting around this time, Ryan saw Pearse answer taunts that he was a moderate with a speech ending, 'Give me a hundred men and I will free Ireland!' As they left the meeting, 'Pearse's eyes burned and he talked all the way to the Rathfarnham tram at the Pillar, saying intensely: "Let them talk! I am the most dangerous revolutionary of the whole lot of them!"'[46] Pearse was not an orthodox republican, and the IRB – or at least the deeply orthodox physical-force man Tom Clarke – remained suspicious of him for some time to come. The Fenians would not, and maybe could not if they would, give him a hundred men. But in 1911 a dramatic crisis was beginning to break which would overturn the conventions of nationalist activism and bring that distant icon of the Dungannon Clubs, the Volunteer militia, back to life.

How formidable was the British power structure against which Pearse became so impatient to hurl himself? The 'foreign enemy' had been in control of Ireland, more or less, for over 700 years, but only for the last century had there been an effort to make Ireland an integral part of the British state. In 1801 the 'United Kingdom' was created, with the aim of reducing the sharp division between Irish Catholics and Protestants that had turned the 1798 rebellion into a vicious civil war. But though the UK possessed a single parliament, its administrative centralization was less complete. Irish laws were made at Westminster, but their day-to-day implementation was carried out by an 'Irish Executive' in Dublin which was markedly different from its supposed parent in Whitehall. Its titular head, the Lord Lieutenant and Governor-General of Ireland, came to be generally called the 'Viceroy', a title whose ambiguity emphasized Ireland's odd semi-detached – and perhaps semi-colonial – status within the UK. The Viceroy of course was a nobleman whose function was partly decorative – 'dignified' rather than 'efficient', in Bagehot's famous distinction – and the actual work of government was done by a team headed by his Chief Secretary and Under-Secretary. It was the Chief Secretary who spoke on Irish issues in the House of Commons; gradually his political status grew, and by the twentieth century he was more likely than the Viceroy to be a member of the British Cabinet. Their roles were now effectively reversed, yet because the Chief Secretary had to spend half the year in parliament, the division of functions became if anything more ambiguous than before.

The Chief Secretary from 1908 to 1916, Augustine Birrell, was widely admired – certainly by nationalists – as a humane, intelligent and sympathetic minister, on whom the label 'ruler' sat less comfortably than it had on some of his predecessors. Though he loathed the mailboat crossing of the Irish Sea, he liked Ireland (and professed to like the Irish), where he was a thoughtful and observant tourist. A sophisticated ornament of the Liberal front bench, he had a formidable legislative tally to his credit, including key steps such as the establishment of the National University, which had baffled governments for decades. Yet his sceptical temperament – sometimes verging on cynicism – compromised his capacity for resolute action. He was acutely conscious of how difficult it was to get his colleagues to take any sustained interest in Irish policy; this had been one of the most debilitating weaknesses of the Union from its very beginning. (A hundred years before, one Irish politician had glumly reflected that 'It is a dispiriting task to endeavour to interest the English parliament in the welfare of Ireland.') Revealingly, Birrell said of his role as Chief

Secretary in Cabinet, 'a jackdaw or a magpie could do just as well by crying out "Ireland, Ireland, Ireland!" at intervals in the proceedings.'[47]

The real ruler of Ireland was neither of these political appointees (who resided, incidentally, in elegant lodges in Phoenix Park), but the Under-Secretary, a civil servant who ran the administrative offices housed in Dublin Castle, the central symbol of British rule in Ireland. The structure and logic of these offices did not follow Whitehall's nineteenth-century evolution, and by the early twentieth century they had an antiquated look: an irregular jumble of boards very different from a British ministry, and very short on the 'efficiency' on which the London government prided itself. 'If the Irish system of government be regarded as a whole,' the Commission of Inquiry after the 1916 rebellion would conclude, 'it is anomalous in quiet times, and almost unworkable in times of crisis.' This Olympian view, however, was somewhat different from the view from lower down. Dublin Castle represented the overwhelming power of Britain. Its local agents, the RIC, characterized by the 1916 Commission as a 'quasi-military force' (the more common description was 'semi-military'), with a strength of some 10,000, were distributed across the country in small stations called 'barracks'. Trained in military drill and armed with cavalry carbines, this force's primary function was to preserve public order rather than to prevent crime. This was a perennial problem for the authorities. 'In England, the maintenance of good order and authority are preserved by a procedure which is almost automatic; in Ireland the machinery requires perpetual attention.'[48]

The practice of stationing constables outside the county of their birth, to prevent intimidation of their families, gave colour to the nationalist description of the RIC as an army of occupation. Its undoubted military deficiencies – by this time its drill was a gesture and its weapons training perfunctory – were not obvious to the ordinary people. The RIC was omnipresent: 'the eyes and ears of Dublin Castle'. With the exception of one place: Dublin itself. Although Dublin Castle housed the headquarters of the RIC and its political intelligence unit, the Crime Special Branch, the capital was, in sharp contrast, policed by a British-style unarmed force, the Dublin Metropolitan Police (DMP), 'also a fine body of men' in the view of the 1916 Commission. Most of them were more famous for their physical dimensions than their intelligence, but the DMP also ran a detective unit (G Division) whose shadowing of Fenian suspects had assumed legendary proportions. The potential weaknesses of this split system were obvious in face of 'political crime, which takes no notice of police districts, and which in the case of Ireland assumes an international complexion'.[49] In fact, the fissures in the British intelligence-gathering machinery were multiple. When, eventually, an informal audit was done, it noted that 'intelligence is obtained by no less than five public bodies, viz: the Admiralty, War Office (MI5), Irish Command, Royal Irish Constabulary, and Dublin Metropolitan Police'. The result was 'overlapping' and 'unnecessary expense' (the most serious problem, no doubt, from a Treasury perspective); but also a potentially dangerous lack of co-ordination. There was 'certainly a danger' that 'from lack of co-ordination the Irish Government may be the last Department to receive information of moment to the peace of Ireland'.[50] The British giant had feet of clay.

But perhaps the deepest weakness in the structure of the Union lay at the level of social psychology and ideology. The British state had, despite a century of existence, never fully incorporated its Catholic Irish subjects. British attitudes to Ireland were an odd mixture of bafflement, arrogance and ignorance. Isaac Butt made an important point when he wrote (on the subject of land law), 'Our misfortune is that English phrases are applied to relations that bear no resemblance to the things which the words describe in the English tongue.' (He suggested that if 'landlords' and 'tenants' in Ireland were called *zemindars* and *ryots*, the English would immediately see the problem and set about righting wrongs.)[51] A deep cultural difference was disguised by indifference. British rule was marked by a deep-seated, pervasive prejudice that was described by a perceptive French observer (a professor of French at University College, Dublin, in fact) as 'un mépris doux, tranquille, bienveillant, établi, inconscient, inné' ('A gentle, quiet, well-meaning, established, unconscious, inborn contempt').[52] This systemic informal discrimination was as visible in the police force, where 90 per cent of constables, but barely 10 per cent of district and county inspectors were Catholics, as it was in the legal profession.

Although it was almost completely instinctual, natural and invisible to Protestants, discrimination was unmistakable to others.[53] The burgeoning Catholic middle class at the turn of the century was pushing at these ancient barriers, and the legitimacy of the United Kingdom depended on 'giving them access to the spoils system of the political nation'.[54] This was a matter of real urgency, but there is little sign that British statesmen had any conception of this. It may be true that 'the extent to which Gladstonian Liberals tried to absorb Ireland was truly astonishing'. Yet it must be doubted whether the effort 'very nearly succeeded'.[55] British political culture, with its moderately secular, moderately meritocratic assumptions, trammelled their thinking along mildy optimistic, consensual lines. To seek out and confront underlying contradictions was not its style. Irresolvable conflict was alien to the British way. Peaceful progress was inevitable. But in Ireland, as in other European countries, progress had generated 'an excess of educated men' (not to mention women). This would feed the revolutionary generation: 'far more bourgeois, in the strict sense, than their Redmondite predecessors', and far more educated; socially mobile but with very recent rural social origins.[56] In principle, this group should have been the easiest to absorb into the British system; in practice it remained excluded. The impending crisis would show just how insensitive the British establishment was to Irish difference.

2

The Militarization of Politics

To drill, to learn the use of arms, to acquire the habit of concerted and disciplined action, is, beyond all doubt, a programme that appeals to all Ireland.

Manifesto of the Irish Volunteers, November 1913

That the authorities allowed a body of lawless and riotous men to be drilled and armed and to provide themselves with an arsenal of weapons and explosives was one of the most amazing things that could happen in any civilised country outside of Mexico.

William Martin Murphy, statement to Royal Commission, 1916

In 1911 Ireland, along with the whole United Kingdom, entered a protracted crisis that was to rewrite the script of Irish politics. By the time it was eventually choked off by an even bigger crisis, the outbreak of the Great War (in Winston Churchill's phrase, the 'world crisis') in August 1914, there were over a quarter of a million men enrolled in citizen militias in Ireland. A substantial minority of them were armed with modern weapons, and more of these were on the way. During the last major gun-running, in Dublin in late July 1914, three people were to be killed in a street battle with British troops; the first people to lose their lives in the crisis, and a grim omen for the future. Ireland had entered a confused and volatile state that was not yet civil war, but no longer peace.

The trigger for this crisis, the confrontation between the Liberal government and the Tory-dominated House of Lords over the 1909 'People's Budget', had no direct connection with Ireland; but the outcome of this clash had profound implications. The abolition of the veto power of the Upper House removed the obstacle that had wrecked Gladstone's project of Irish Home Rule. When the Prime Minister, H. H. Asquith, announced in late 1910 that a new Home Rule proposal would now be brought forward, he pitched the country back into the fierce conflict that had surrounded the first two Home Rule Bills in 1886 and 1893. But there was an important difference. While Liberal politicians had in the meantime done their best to forget about the whole issue, and Irish nationalists had descended into internecine conflicts, Unionists – especially in Ulster – had been carefully building their organizations in preparation for the next round of the fight. Then, as later, they were dourly pessimistic about the British government's commitment to the Union. So when the 'Third Home Rule Bill' was announced, it ran into a more vigorous reaction than even the first two had. As it turned out, the House of Lords was not the final barrier to Home Rule: an Ulster-based mass mobilization brought to bear not the discredited privilege of the aristocracy, but a claim of democratic self-determination that matched the Irish nationalists' own claim.

What would have happened if Home Rule had gone through? This is one of the great 'what ifs?' of Irish history, and indeed of British history. The entire twentieth-century relationship between Britain and Ireland would have been different, certainly. How different? Speculation, always risky, is unusually treacherous here because Home Rule as offered by Gladstone, and even by Asquith, was never a precise and unambiguous blueprint. Both sides of the argument stressed this. Parnell, the political leader who seemed to embody the Home Rule movement at its zenith, took care to point out that no one could 'set bounds to the march of a nation'; and exactly the same point was hammered home by opponents of Home Rule, who argued that an Irish parliament, even if it began like 'Grattan's Parliament' as a dependent body, would gradually enlarge its powers until Ireland became effectively independent. Gladstone offered Home Rule as a means of satisfying Irish aspirations within the framework of the United Kingdom, and – if Unionists had accepted this idea – it would have achieved Gladstone's primary aim, to 'pacify Ireland'.

So speculation about its possible impact, however treacherous, is irresistible.[1] It would have divided the Irish nationalist movement, no doubt, but no more than it was already divided. Hardline republicans would have denounced it, but many other nationalists outside the 'constitutionalist' movement would have come on board: Patrick Pearse certainly, and maybe Arthur Griffith, and even Bulmer Hobson. Home Rule would have made the 1916 rebellion, in any case improbable, impossible in anything like the form it took. Thus 1916 followed directly from the failure of Home Rule, and it is vital to understand why – and still more how – Home Rule was frustrated. In formal terms, it actually succeeded. In September 1914, the Government of Ireland Act would receive the royal assent, through use of the Parliament Act: it was law, though it was suspended until the end of the European war. Paradoxically, this apparent success, as we shall see, was to lead the Home Rulers to ruin. But it had already become quite clear by that time that the Act would never come into effect without what the prime minister called some 'special provision' for northeastern Ireland. 'Ulster' had opted out of Home Rule, and had threatened armed rebellion to do so. It was this armed threat that transformed and militarized the language of Irish politics as the Home Rule crisis unfolded.

'Militarism' is a strong word. As it was used in Europe at this time, notably by critics of the Prussian-German monarchy, it meant the saturation of the entire political and social fabric by military values. In the German 'Second Reich', for instance, military uniform – even that of a reserve officer – gave greater status than any other social attribute. This would never quite happen in Ireland – even in the crisis of the civil war. Though the word has been applied to Irish history in this period, it has usually been without precise definition.[2] Those, like the German socialist Karl Liebknecht, who had to confront the 'real thing' up close, insisted on the need for precision.[3] Merely putting people into military units, or uniforms, does not make them militarists. But the sudden emergence of large-scale military organizations to contest a political issue was a development that went far outside the normal conventions of liberal politics, and it is not misleading to call this 'militarization'. It happened because the intensity of this political issue stretched the tolerances of the liberal political culture to breaking point: the characteristic British values of reasonableness, compromise and non-violence seemed unable to cope with the passions evoked by the threat of Home Rule.[4]

Looking back, a century on, it may seem hard to grasp why Home Rule unleashed such passionate hostility. It was a cautious measure of devolution, and the degree of independence it offered Ireland was distinctly limited. (Ireland would not have defence forces, for instance, or the power to levy customs duties.) For Gladstone and his Liberal successors, its central purpose and justification was to strengthen the Union – not break it – by reducing Irish discontent to a manageable level. It was presented as heralding a wider scheme of devolution which would give the rest of the regions of the UK similar autonomous powers, so eliminating the sense of Irish 'exceptionalism' that had unbalanced British politics since the Union itself. Sadly, the force that might have made this prophetic scheme work, the demand for English self-government, was simply not present. UK federalism, sometimes called 'home rule all round', had many intelligent advocates, but it remained a fringe idea; ironically, it was the weakness of English nationalism that made it a political non-starter. Instead of welcoming Irish Home Rule as a way of making the Union work better, Unionists saw it as a secessionist challenge like that of the Confederacy in the American civil war. It would destroy the integrity of the state, and threaten Britain's global power.

It was the mutual incomprehension of these two views of Home Rule that made the resulting crisis so jarring. With the benefit of hindsight, the seriousness of Unionist opposition should have been absolutely clear by the time Asquith brought in the third Home Rule Bill. The first Home Rule proposal, in 1886, had witnessed the century's most destructive riots in Belfast, with the police becoming a prime target of loyalist anger, alongside the more familiar sectarian assaults on Catholics. By 1893, Unionists were threatening that resistance to Home Rule would take a military form if necessary. But these warning signs were ignored. The Liberal government, and still more the Irish Nationalist Party, dismissed these protests as bluster and bluff. Objections to Home Rule were dismissed as illegitimate, since Ireland had a right to national self-government; and also illogical, since the island of Ireland so evidently constituted a natural political, economic and administrative unit. Liberals took the view that resistance was a throwback to old sectarian hatreds, which would eventually give way to the forces of progress; nationalism had history on its side. It was a key part of the *Zeitgeist*. The third Home Rule Bill was prepared with no more attention to the idea of accommodating Unionist resistance than the first two had been. The government was almost comically unprepared for the storm it unleashed; the results, however, were tragic.

Even before the launching of the third Home Rule Bill in April 1912, the Unionist movement had initiated a massive and dramatic protest movement. This was effectively concentrated in Ulster, or more precisely the four north-eastern counties, where Unionists (and Protestants) were in a substantial majority. The resistance preparations, in fact, precipitated a split within Unionism itself, as 'southern' Unionists – a weak minority in numerical terms – could not contemplate direct action. They depended on stopping Home Rule dead at Westminster, an all-or-nothing strategy, whereas the northerners had a fall-back option – rescuing 'Ulster' from the wreckage, if necessary by cutting it off from the rest of Ireland. It was this focus on Ulster that became decisively sharpened by the last Home Rule crisis. When the Parliament Act removed the final barrier of the House of Lords' veto in 1911, Irish Unionism was already shifting its ground. A big rally at Craigavon in September 1911 was followed by a bigger one at the Balmoral showground on the day of the Bill's first reading in parliament, when 100,000 men marched past Sir Edward Carson and a fifty-foot Union flag, the biggest ever woven, was broken out. The Ulster Solemn League and Covenant was signed by half a million people on 28 September – 'Ulster Day'. The use of symbols like flag and covenant – loaded with potent Protestant historical significance – was highly effective political theatre, and the location of the demonstrations in Belfast rather than Dublin sent a signal whose meaning would become increasingly clear. Although Unionism's most charismatic leader, Sir Edward Carson, was a Dubliner, southern Unionists simply could not muster the street muscle to dispute the issue. At the end of 1912, the Ulster Unionist Clubs, many of whose branches had spontaneously begun to practise military drilling, moved to form a citizen militia, whose name said it all – the Ulster Volunteer Force (UVF).[5]

Much of this process had been instinctive; its driving force was the long-established tradition of popular Loyalist militancy embodied in the Orange Order. The Order had an up-and-down history stretching back to the eighteenth century; it had seemed to die out from time to time, and had sometimes been denounced by the Unionist leadership, sometimes co-opted by them. By the early twentieth century, Orange Lodges had become more respectable, with the gentry taking on the role of Lodge Masters, but their fundamental urge to direct action never entirely disappeared. Their 'walking' was a euphemism for military-style marching, confrontational in body-language and symbolism. So the footsoldiers of Unionism were always ready to take to the streets; the problem was what they might do there. Throughout the crisis, there was an evident tension between the restive, visceral energy of the grassroots loyalists and the political caution (containing a healthy dash of middle-class anxiety) of the leadership. It was the spontaneous action of an Orange Lodge contingent from county Tyrone at the September 1911 rally that launched the craze for military drilling, and local paramilitary militia units had been forming up for well over a year before the UUC belatedly started to enrol them in a single force. The purpose of this was clearly to control them at least as much as to encourage them. The Unionist leadership talked violence but soft-pedalled on the business of providing the weapons to turn this 'stage army' into a real military force. Contrary to the view taken (and still taken today) by nationalists, there seem to have been very few service rifles in the hands of the UVF, even in late 1913, more than two years after the force began to emerge.[6]

In formal terms, the UVF accepted men between the ages of seventeen and sixty-five who had signed the Ulster Covenant. Its total enrolment was limited to 100,000. Territorial battalions were formed, grouped initially into districts and subdivisions. Twenty battalions were raised in Belfast. In the summer of 1913, a number of former British officers (there were sixteen 'known to the police' by September) were recruited to inject leadership experience at the top; the most senior were General Sir George Richardson, who became commander-in-chief of the UVF, and Colonel W. Hacket Pain, who became chief of staff. They moved the force closer to the British army model, introducing county regiments. Belfast had four regiments, making up the Belfast Division. But when that impressive-sounding division, 10,390 strong, held a parade at Balmoral in October 1913, it was unarmed apart from fourteen modern Lee-Metford rifles, one carried by each battalion marker.[7] Everyone believed, of course, that they had more, but no one knew how many. The idea of displaying so few, we may guess, was that their opponents should believe they had 10,000. Nationalists asserted that 25,000 rifles were in UVF hands by the time the government eventually banned the importation of arms in September 1913. But we know that as late as January 1914 the Antrim UVF had only 150 British and 50 Italian service weapons for its 10,700 men, and that there were several heated confrontations between the rank and file and the UVF leadership over the failure to provide rifles in significant quantities. And in fact it was the relatively small number of the guns known by the authorities to have reached Ulster that made it difficult to decide how to react. The law did not provide fixed rules about the illegality of arms imports: as the Irish government's law officers noted, 'forty-five rifles might be satisfactorily accounted for, while 100,000 could bear no innocent explanation'. In mid-1913, the police were reportedly 'aware of' about 1,100 rifles that had been imported over the previous year.[8]

Nationalists charged (and still do) that the government's belated decision to prohibit the importation of arms was a way of giving the Unionists a head start. This says more about nationalist perceptions than about political realities; for the Liberal government the appearance of the UVF was an alarming and disorienting development.[9] The crisis was outrunning the political experience of 'liberal England' and its language of consensus. When the Conservative leader Andrew Bonar Law denounced Asquith's Cabinet as 'a revolutionary committee which has seized upon despotic power by fraud', he was raising the political stakes to a vertiginous level, and his party threatened to push them off the charts when it talked of using the House of Lords to veto the annual Army Act. Even in its reduced two-year suspensory form, such a veto would have created an unprecedented situation in which (theoretically, at least) the government could no longer control the armed services. Merely to hint at such an action was a kind of extremism that threatened to unhinge the long-established restraints of British political life. In these fraught circumstances the Liberals trod with even more than their habitual caution, weighing their words and actions with extreme care. What should they do about the paramilitary drilling craze? Drilling was outlawed under the Unlawful Drilling Act of 1819 – except where two magistrates authorized it to make people 'more efficient citizens for the purpose of maintaining their rights and liberties'. This loophole had been exploited to the full by Unionist magistrates since 1911. Sir John Simon, the Attorney General, argued that this was not 'lawful authority' when 'the whole proceeding is a seditious conspiracy'. The whole movement was a crime, and the JPs who 'gave such authority would be accessories to the crime'.[10] These were forceful words, but the government did not act on them for fear of pushing the situation into open conflict.

Moreover, Simon nerved himself to this tough line only after illegal drilling had been going on for two years. The procrastination of the authorities laid them open to the charge of partiality, but the painfully cautious tone of their deliberations suggests that this was true vacillation. When, for instance, in May 1912 the army's law officers looked into the possibility of 'calling to account' military officers who were known to have taken part in drilling in Ulster, they noted that these officers would probably have obtained legal authority (under 60 Geo.III cap.1), but this in itself 'would be an admission that the officers in question were training the persons assembled at the meetings to the use of arms, or at least in military exercise, movements or evolutions'. The question then was the purpose of this training. Since 'it cannot with any show of veracity be contended that it has a purely educational object, as in the case of the boy scouts', it must be either 'seditious resistance to constituted authority as has often been openly stated', or 'preparation for a political demonstration'. Either would be forbidden to serving officers. Again this was a muscular enough analysis, but its conclusion was distinctly limp – 'there would not seem to be any objection to asking those officers who have taken part in drilling . . . how they explain their conduct'.[11]

It is not clear whether even this cautious action was taken, but it is certain that officers persisted in this activity. Well over a year later, when some 200 members of the 'Enniskillen Horse' paraded through the town under their commander, the local magistrate William Copeland Trimble (editor of the implausibly named Unionist newspaper the *Impartial Reporter*), the police observed that this band of unofficial yeomanry, armed with 16 carbines and 143 lances, was inspected on Portora Football Ground by a regular officer, Major Viscount Crichton of the Royal Horse Guards, who complimented them on 'the work they did so well'. The Irish Attorney General then declared bluntly that 'these demonstrations of armed forces are highly criminal and in fact are acts of treason' – but immediately added, 'as regards the question whether the Police should take action, my answer is that the Police should not take any action in the matter as far as interfering with the demonstrations for the purpose of stopping them'; they should merely note the names of those involved. Six months later still, the military intelligence staff in Dublin put 'the tolerance of the Government towards the systematic drilling and arming which has been going on for nearly two years in Ulster' at the top of their list of outstanding issues.[12] All this was fully exploited by the Ulster Unionist leadership, who revelled in their impunity – none more so than Carson, who crowed in September 1913, as the UUC prepared to launch its 'Provisional Government' of Ulster, 'I am told that the government will be illegal. Of course it will. Drilling is illegal. The Volunteers are illegal, and the Government know they are illegal, and the Government dare not interfere.'

The UVF was the decisive spur to the militarization of nationalist politics. Whatever its limitations and internal tensions, and however short of arms it may have been, it impressed nationalists, maybe even more than it did the government. In early 1912 the Gaelic League activist Michael O'Rahilly (known to history by his Celticized title, 'The O'Rahilly') published a series of articles in the separatist paper *Irish Freedom* based on the proposition that 'the foundation on which all government rests in the possession of arms and the ability to use them', which went on to a detailed military history of the 1798 rebellion – 'the most recent occasion when any considerable body of Irish people appealed to arms'. This kind of history-lesson-cum-parable was a staple of the republican press, and his peroration – 'if you are serious in wanting freedom from British domination, get arms and be prepared to use them', was hardly as novel as his recent biographer maintains. The very first issue of the journal in 1910 had insisted that arms were 'the free man's first essential'. A series of articles called 'the Faith of a Fenian' declared that 'Ireland's national attitude towards all things English is war', while the journal's *Fianna* column (written by Constance Markievicz) assured its young readers that 'the history of the world proves that there is but one road to freedom, and that is the red road of war'. Freedom attained by 'oratory, logic or votes' was merely 'a more secure form of slavery. The freedom that is not worth fighting and dying for is not worth having.' Its second number reiterated the Fenian commitment to 'directly seeking to establish a republic by force of arms', mocking the idea of passive resistance ('endeavouring to find rose-strewn paths to freedom') as an attempt to avoid the old methods of 'secret conspiracy and armed rebellion'; and in September 1911 the journal indicted 'this generation' with the 'sin' of 'passing away – the first since Cromwell – without an armed denial of England's right to rule it'.[13]

The rhetoric was familiar – maybe over-familiar. 'We of the Wolfe Tone Clubs hold still that it is a greater and a better thing to lay up pikes, as Emmet did, than to lay up gold in banks or shares in profitable businesses.' O'Rahilly, however, was plainly not talking about pikes: 'Rifles can be bought by anyone who has the price of them': there were no longer any 'disarming Acts', and he suggested that 'a man who is dissatisfied with his form of Government, and has not got a rifle and 1,000 rounds of ammunition in a place where he can get them when he wants them, is only playing at politics'.[14] What was perhaps most significant about these articles in the IRB's newspaper was that their writer was not a member of the IRB (he followed the Catholic hierarchy's condemnation of oathbound secret societies). He may be placed in a semi-political grouping of what one historian described as 'constitutional separatists', who were rapidly becoming increasingly radicalized in the face of the Ulster challenge, and who were to play a pivotal role in the seismic political shift that was to follow.

The key figures in this were Eoin MacNeill and Patrick Pearse, both formerly supporters of Redmond, and both prominent Gaelic

Leaguers, and former editors of the League's journal *An Claideamh Soluis*. By 1912 Pearse was ready to welcome the Home Rule Bill with the public warning, 'Let the Gall [foreigner] understand that if we are cheated this time there will be red war in Ireland.' MacNeill was moving dramatically from his early categorical rejection of 'physical hostility' in the cause of nationality to warning, in March 1912, that the younger generation might justifiably go beyond constitutional methods to secure 'our rights'. O'Rahilly became editor of *An Claideamh Soluis* in mid-1913, and in the autumn he invited MacNeill to contribute an article urging nationalists to imitate the UVF. Taking his title, 'The North Began', from one of Thomas Davis's martial ballads about the Volunteers of 1782 ('The North began, the North held on / . . . Till Ireland rose and cowed her foes'), MacNeill built up a rather ambiguous and sophistical argument that the UVF were virtual Home Rulers, and that 'Sir Edward Carson has knocked the bottom out of Unionism.' The Ulster mobilization had certainly broken the unity of Irish Unionism, but in the process it had generated a vastly more formidable obstacle to Home Rule, a movement which could deploy the same rhetoric of democratic self-determination as the nationalists.

MacNeill, an Ulsterman himself, could not resist attacking Carson's policy and his loyalist followers, though: he called the Provisional government 'the most ridiculous piece of political histrionics ever staged', and strongly implied that the whole Ulster Volunteer movement was a pretence; 'the crowning sham' was the million-pound insurance fund that had just been announced. 'The real insurance fund for war', MacNeill lectured, 'is fighting material, and those who are in earnest about war will not devote a penny to any other sort of insurance.' His positive proposals were less trenchant, but he suggested that, since it was now clear that the British army could not be used to prevent the drilling and reviewing of volunteers, 'there is nothing to prevent the other twenty-eight counties from calling into existence citizen forces to hold Ireland "for the Empire"'. This argument was probably too subtle to convince most nationalists, but MacNeill had done enough to precipitate the process. He was aware that a 'Midland Volunteer Force' had already appeared – at least in the imagination of the pressmen of Athlone (some kind of drilling displays went on there, though probably on nothing like the scale suggested in the *Westmeath*

Independent).[15] In late October and early November, D. P. Moran's *Leader* had twice urged the starting of local companies, asking 'Why should not every Gaelic Athletic Club, for instance, turn out as Volunteers?' The idea was in the air. What MacNeill and Moran probably did not know was that steps had actually been taken in this direction by the IRB in its various guises, under the presiding genius of Bulmer Hobson.

Hobson's later fall from republican grace led to a fair bit of rewriting of the history of this crucial formative period, but there is no doubt that after he moved from Belfast to Dublin in 1908 his influence on the IRB grew steadily. When he became chairman of the Dublin Centres Board in 1912 he was the key organizer, and he fostered two key policies. He began preparing for a national military volunteer organization, and created a dedicated IRB circle for the reborn *Fianna Eireann*, the most definite military initiative taken so far. Even after he handed the presidency over to Markievicz, Hobson went on drawing the link with the IRB tighter, through protégés such as Con Colbert, Padraig O Riain, Seán McGarry and Liam Mellows, and (it seems) fixed the elections at each annual congress (*ard-fheis*). The *Fianna* programme – scouting, fieldcraft, and shooting – was unambiguously military. Con Colbert and Eamon Martin studied the British army manuals and started the process of training instructors. By the time Hobson proposed to the IRB Dublin Centres Board in July 1913 that a militia should be set up, he was able to bring in a substantial trained *Fianna* element to kickstart the process. Secret drilling began during the summer in the Irish National Foresters Hall in Parnell Square.

There can also be little doubt that Hobson was the IRB's leading strategic thinker at this stage. A member who was present at a general IRB meeting in Parnell Square in 1914 found himself sitting next to Pearse while Hobson expounded his prediction that there would be a major war within ten years, and that would give the IRB its opportunity. Pearse drove him home in his pony trap afterwards, and 'appeared doubtful whether Hobson was right'.[16] Pearse's own passage into the IRB was oddly long drawn-out, apparently being vetoed several times by some of the higher leadership – Charlie Burgess (Cathal Brugha) regarded Pearse's financial dealings as dishonest, and

Hobson said the same subsequently. (Many rank-and-file IRB men, however, seem to have been admitted without such high-level searching scrutiny.) A turning point seems to have come when the Supreme Council accepted Seán MacDermott's proposal that Pearse should give the Emmet anniversary address in 1911. This was a high-profile republican event, and Tom Clarke was almost as impressed by his performance as Pat McCartan. But opposition still persisted, and his appearance on a Home Rule platform in April 1912 confirmed the view that he was not a true separatist, his sanguinary threats to 'the Gall' notwithstanding.

About the same time, he had launched his own Irish-language newspaper, *An Barr Buadh* ('The Trumpet of Victory'), and kept it going for eight issues despite being effectively bankrupt. The series of political and economic articles he published in it still strayed from the republican line, though there also appeared his poem *Mionn* ('Oath'), opening with a mesmeric, quasi-liturgical incantation of the nationalist pantheon, and ending with an almost blasphemous embrace of physical violence: 'We swear the oaths our ancestors swore, / That we will free our race from bondage, / Or fall fighting hand to hand / Amen.'[17] Eventually, in November 1913, the week after MacNeill's article, he wrote the ultimate paean to armed rebellion. Since 'nationhood is not achieved otherwise than in arms', he was 'glad that the Orangemen have armed, because it is a goodly thing to see arms in Irish hands'. Once again there was an incantatory rhythm in his repeated references to arms. 'We must accustom ourselves to the thought of arms, to the sight of arms, to the use of arms' – but now the rhetoric went all the way to the shedding of blood: 'bloodshed is a cleansing and a sanctifying thing, and the nation which regards it as the final horror has lost its manhood. There are many things more horrible than bloodshed; and slavery is one of them.'[18] This last sentence was a familiar enough sentiment, perhaps, but the idea of the 'cleansing and sanctifying' power of bloodshed was much more unusual: here Pearse showed that he could speak simultaneously in both physical and symbolic terms.

Pearse finally joined the IRB by way of the Irish Volunteers, and this was itself evidence of the care taken by Hobson and his group to launch the Volunteer movement in a way that would maximize its cross-party support. MacNeill, in writing 'the North began', singled himself out as the natural public instigator, but undoubtedly the initiative and the impulse to the series of meetings leading up to the public inauguration of the Volunteers came from the IRB. It was Hobson's guarantee that he could provide a nucleus of reliable men to launch the movement that persuaded O'Rahilly to go to MacNeill with the project.[19] Twelve men from across the political spectrum were invited to the first meeting to form a steering committee, in Wynn's Hotel on 11 November. It is not clear exactly how the list was drawn up, or why some crucial invitations (including those to Eamonn Ceannt, Piaras Béaslaí and Seán Fitzgibbon) were not sent until the day before. What is clear is that over the next couple of weeks the committee expanded by a process beyond IRB control. Of the original invitees, one of the few nationally known figures, D. P. Moran, made his excuses, but several others were added at each of the next four meetings, until the Provisional Committee reached the unwieldy total of thirty. This procrastinating fortnight (the meeting place itself was rearranged three times into progressively larger spaces) allowed the Irish Transport Workers Union to get in first by creating its own militia, the Irish Citizen Army, on 23 November. But at last a manifesto for the Irish Volunteers was put together, and launched at the Rotunda Rink on 25 November.

The manifesto levelled the charge – at 'one of the great English political parties' rather than the Ulster Unionists – of aiming 'to make the display of military force and the menace of armed violence the determining factor in the future relations between this country and Great Britain'. Thus 'the people of Ireland' had either to 'surrender', and so 'become politically the most degraded population in Europe, no longer worthy of the name of Nation', or 'take such measures as will effectually defeat this policy'. The manifesto declared the object of the Irish Volunteers to be 'to secure and maintain the rights and liberties common to all the people of Ireland', so carefully skirting the issue that had generated the Ulster crisis, the refusal of some of those people to accept 'the name of Nation'. It argued for a Volunteer movement which would be permanent, 'a prominent element in the national life under a National Government . . . as a guarantee of the liberties which the Irish people shall have secured'. The basis for the organization was to be as wide as possible – its ranks would be 'open to all able-bodied Irishmen without distinction of creed, politics, or social grade' (though 'there will also be work for women to do').[20]

The terms of the manifesto represented something of a balancing act, designed to make it possible for Redmondite nationalists to join up, even though Redmond himself – ever suspicious of any rival movements, and ever anxious to avoid provocation – would or could not (as MacNeill appreciated) give a lead. Indeed, an initiative to raise volunteers in Belfast had already been quashed by Joe Devlin, who ran the nationalist party there. 'The two Johns and Joe' (Redmond, John Dillon, and Devlin), the party's controlling triumvirate, remained an awkward obstacle for those who wanted to move the Volunteers in a more confrontational direction over the following months. The party's own strong-arm organization, the Ancient Order of Hibernians (AOH), dedicated not so much to opposing loyalists as to crushing dissent within the nationalist movement, often undermined Volunteer recruiting. But the movement's biggest problem – and the biggest contrast with the Ulster movement – was shortage of funds. Although MacNeill might mock the UVF's million-pound insurance fund, it showed the readiness of wealthy backers to dig deep in their pockets (Craig and Carson each subscribed a staggering £10,000). The initial subscription list for the Irish Volunteers totalled £8 7s. 6d., with the biggest contributors – Hobson, MacNeill, O'Rahilly and seven others – giving a pound each. A somewhat larger donation by Sir Roger Casement at the end of the year provided a vital boost. But the Volunteers would have to be self-supporting, and one of the primary functions of the organization set on foot at the turn of the year was to gather individual subscriptions and remit enough funds to the centre to allow the establishment of a headquarters at 206 Great Brunswick Street (later 2 Dawson Street). Drill halls and training grounds could be prohibitively costly, but the clergy often provided significant aid – the Capuchin friars, notably, gave the Dublin Volunteers the use of Father Mathew Park (named, suitably for the puritanical new militiamen, after the great nineteenth-century temperance campaigner).

The structure of the Volunteers was amorphous at the beginning. The manifesto suggested that they would be enrolled according to the district they lived in; then, as soon as possible, 'the district sections will be called upon to make provision for the general administration and discipline, and for united co-operation', through an elective body to replace the provisional Committee. In Kerry, the Tralee Volunteers 'referred to the four Companies generally as the "Tralee Volunteers", rather than forming a battalion.[21] In Cork there was no battalion or brigade structure until 1915.[22] Early in 1914 a set of military instructions laid down a basic structure closely modelled on the British army's, with battalions consisting of eight companies, composed of two half-companies of four eight-man squads. Officers were to carry regular military ranks, non-commissioned and commissioned, from corporal to colonel.[23] But there was one big difference: they were to be elected. (After two months drilling, company elections were to take place, with only those who had attended 75 per cent of drills for those two months eligible to vote.) Their disciplinary powers were to be voluntary, and there was not even any form of attestation oath for recruits (the 'general instructions for forming companies' merely specified that those setting units up should 'let everyone clearly understand that the aim of the Volunteers is to secure and maintain the rights common to all the people of Ireland'). The motive force of the movement was enthusiasm. 'Each member', as the instructions said, 'must purchase his own uniform and his rifle.'[24] Companies needed to go out and buy copies of the British Infantry Manual, 1911, costing a shilling from Ponsonby's of Grafton Street.

This democratic element reflected the hybrid military-political inspiration of the Irish Volunteers. A distinctly unmilitary tradition of collective command was established through the 'battalion councils', eventually to be formalized in 1915. Most significantly, the IV did not follow the UVF's example of appointing a military man as commander-in-chief, despite Casement's urging the need for 'a general' and his proposal of General Kelly-Kenny. Eoin MacNeill's role as 'Chief of Staff' underlined the political as well as military logic of the movement.[25] Still, it proved true enough that, as the Volunteer manifesto claimed, 'to drill, to learn the use of arms, to acquire the habit of concerted and disciplined action' was 'beyond all doubt, a programme that appeals to all Ireland, but especially to young Ireland'. This popular military enthusiasm was certainly not confined to Ireland; it appeared in varying intensities across pre-war Europe.

But in the Irish case, it did not necessarily signify a military commitment. As one Volunteer organizer in the west said, 'the public in general certainly did not anticipate that the military form of the new movement was directed to military action'.[26]

Most likely, age made a difference here, as the manifesto implied. 'Young Ireland' was the most enthusiastic and militant element of the movement. The average age of the Volunteers before 1916 was probably a little higher than it would be afterwards, though the available records do not allow us to be certain of this. One survey (of Cork county Volunteers) suggests that the median age in 1916 was twenty-seven. But undoubtedly youth was a marked feature of the movement. What was perhaps more important than the average age was the clear sense of identity of a 'younger generation', if not quite a youth revolt. In the countryside this carried potent associations with deep-set traditions of ritualized rebellion by groups of young and unmarried men under names such as 'Wren Boys', 'Biddy Boys' or 'Straw Boys' – all 'boys' for short.[27] Combined with 'a simple but vibrant symbolism of resistance' – the memory of old rebellions – this ensured that 'Irish rural society was imbued with a sense of warfare.'[28] Nationalism may have been in a sense a pretext for this cocktail of recreation and male bonding, but ideology was a crucial factor in the self-definition and motivation of the Volunteers. Whatever social dynamics it might tap into, this was a movement whose rhetoric and imagery were highly politicized. This kind of 'militarism' can be seen as a vital agent of transition from tradition to modernity.[29]

Recruitment into the Volunteers was not as spectacular as the UVF's had been, though it reached 10,000 by the end of 1913, and steadily mounted through to the spring of 1914. Playing soldiers had novelty value, though its very novelty was a problem at the start. 'In Ireland we had no knowledge of military training', as one Dublin Volunteer noted; on principle 'we would not watch a company of British soldiers training on the barrack square; we would not even watch the changing of the guard at the Bank of Ireland.' As the self-confessedly puritanical Desmond FitzGerald, an organizer in Kerry found, the policy of enrolling anyone with or without military aptitude made it hard to impose standards. 'I tackled one man who seemed incapable of forming fours and asked him what was the matter. He replied, "Erra, the way it is, after all you said about keeping away from drink, I drank so much lemonade last Sunday in Tralee that I can do nothing with my feet."[30]

But in Dublin, at least, 'the ex-soldiers of the Dublin Fusiliers, Munster Fusiliers, Connaught Rangers . . . flocked to the drill halls and offered their services'. Military manners started to take hold: 'In a short time we were knocked into shape. We could hold our heads up; we could drill; we could march. We were taught what discipline meant and we knew how to obey orders.'[31] Learning the use of arms was more problematic, and actually getting a real rifle – the key ambition of every Volunteer – was an uncertain process. Energetic quartermasters such as Michael Staines, responsible for three companies of the 1st Battalion, 'collected one shilling per week from every Volunteer who wanted a Martini rifle and two shillings and sixpence from any Volunteer who wanted a Lee Enfield'.[32] The Tralee Volunteers – who unusually preferred to amass single-shot Martini Henrys (the type used by the RIC before the war), and got rid of their few Lee Enfields 'so as to have a uniform type of rifle as far as possible' – gave a rifle to any man who put down a subscription of five shillings.[33] Staines eventually secured a rifle for every man in his three companies, but not all were so successful. Though many had to make do with pistols, shotguns or even pikes, possession of a rifle was vital to the self-belief of Volunteers as a military force. It has been said, indeed, that 'the rifle was almost fetishistically central to the Volunteers' purpose and identity'.[34]

Uniforms were also a key signal of military credibility, and also took some time to sort out – the Uniform Sub-Committee did not report until August 1914, and was still undecided on vital accoutrements such as headdress. 'A considerable body of opinion favoured soft hats' (on the model of the Boer slouch hat), 'but it was found impossible to get a suitable hat of Irish manufacture.' Instead they decided, for Dublin at least, on a cap of rather puzzling design – 'a smart one somewhat after the Cossack style'. Some of the accumulated store of Gaelicist enthusiasm was funnelled into the Volunteers: the cap badge and belt buckles, for instance, evoked a prehistoric ancestry for the force with their sunburst symbols and 'FF' (Fianna Fáil) title. Possibly reflecting an ongoing debate about Ireland's true 'national colour', early IV membership cards were blue rather than green. A final ruling on the correct flag for Volunteer units to carry – a plain gold harp on a green ground – did not follow until May 1915. Pearse was still tinkering with all these questions at the end of that year.[35]

The 'work for women to do' promised in the Volunteer Manifesto also emerged rather slowly; and, when it did, rather controversially. Not until April 1914 was an inaugural meeting held (in Wynn's Hotel again) to establish a women's auxiliary organization, Cumann na mBan (League of Women). Though this was greeted enthusiastically – certainly by the Volunteers' womenfolk – its role was not to accelerate women's emancipation. It took from its president, the Gaelic Leaguer Agnes O'Farrelly, a conventional rather than revolutionary tone: members were not to take part in political discussions, nor (except in the 'last extremity') to take a direct part in military operations. Their task was to support the Volunteers. 'Each rifle we put in their hands will represent to us a bolt fastened behind the door of some Irish home to keep out the hostile stranger. Each cartridge will be a watchdog to fight for the sanctity of the hearth.'[36] Unlike the women's section of the Citizen Army, which was barely distinct from the main body (and was to see several of its members in combat during the rebellion), Cumann na mBan remained a separate and subordinate body. This came in for some sharp criticism from the small but vocal feminist grouping, notably Hanna Sheehy-Skeffington of the Irish Women's Franchise League (daughter of the Nationalist MP David Sheehy). The *Irish Citizen*, edited by her husband Frank, challenged the use of the term 'the people of Ireland' in the Volunteer Manifesto, and regretted that they 'had not the courage' to add the phrase 'without distinction of sex' whenever it occurred. Frank Sheehy-Skeffington went on later to tax his friend Thomas MacDonagh, in an extraordinary open letter warning of the incipient militarism of the Volunteer movement, with the deeper significance of its exclusion of women. 'When you have found the reason why women cannot be asked to enrol in this movement, you will be close to the reactionary element in the movement itself.'[37]

It was not just MacDonagh and Pearse, but the majority of the Cumann na mBan themselves, who missed the point of this critique.

They stoutly defended the independence of their organization, and repudiated any suggestion of subordination. They were not hand-maidens, but allies. Not only did they make an essential contribution to the military viability of the Volunteers, they embodied the inspiration of the movement; as Mary Colum put it, 'where the members of Cumann na mBan are the most numerous the spirit of the Volunteers is best'.[38] And vice versa, of course: one member of the Belfast Cumann ruefully recorded that 'it was impossible to obtain any central premises' for the group of thirty-odd women to meet, 'as our organisation was not popular or considered respectable in Belfast'.[39]

Though the IV was a national organization, it was in more than one sense centred in Dublin, and drawn principally (like the Fenians of the past) from the respectable working class. Despite the prominence of teachers in the leadership, professionals were probably under-represented in Dublin; shop assistants and clerks, who appeared to many observers to dominate the movement there, actually made up less than a fifth of the Dublin Volunteers who would be interned in 1916.[40] (They were, however, over-represented in relation to the national average – commercial clerks, for instance, by a factor of nine.)[41] Skilled workers, on the other hand, made up 40 per cent. Plumbers, painters, carpenters, bakers, tailors, machinists, fitters, electricians and 'artists' were as important to the life of the Volunteer companies as they were to the life of the city. In the provinces, unsurprisingly, the proportion of skilled workers was half the Dublin figure; but more surprisingly, farmers and their sons accounted for less than a third of the Volunteers interned. This social structure may have exerted an influence on the decisions to be taken – or not taken – in Easter Week 1916.

Dublin would continue to generate most of the movement's organizational energy. An organizer sent out from headquarters later in 1914 found that the great majority of provincial units 'existed only in name'. In the Bandon area of south Cork, for instance, only one man of independent means, William McDonnell, committed himself to the IV movement in 1914. 'Orange' Bandon (which nationalists tirelessly recalled had been the first Irish town to welcome Cromwell) had a strong Unionist community, but 'Loyalism was far less an obstacle than native apathy, so strikingly reflected in the almost total boycott of the Volunteers by prominent men in the town and countryside.' McDonnell's first task was educational. He found it 'amazing' how ignorant people were of the history of their country and indeed of their national identity. He had to 'bring home to them an understanding of their status as Irishmen, to show that the English occupation was mere usurpation, that under Brehon law no one could forfeit land . . . The impact of this information raised a new sense of pride and power.' But this took time.[42] Florence O'Donoghue, later a leading IRA officer and historian, recorded that even in mid-1915 the Volunteer organization in Cork city and county was barely holding its own: small groups started, worked for a time, relapsed into inactivity and disintegrated. In the extensive territory of West Cork, only two IV companies (Bantry and Ballingeary) had been established.

An essay contributed under the name 'Rapparee' (possibly by O'Rahilly), in the September 1913 issue of *Irish Freedom*, presented a military analysis of Emmet's rebellion, arguing that it came closer to success than was generally thought. Had Emmet's intended attack on Dublin Castle come off, he wrote, 'there is no doubt that the country would have risen like one man'. This argument may tell us more of the attitudes of the soon-to-be volunteers of 1913 than it does of the realities of 1803, but the essayist's insistence that succeeding separatist leaders had erred in ignoring 'the paramount strategical importance of the capital' was highly significant for the future. Early twentieth-century Dublin was, in the words of one historian, 'a city in distress', and in September 1913 was in the grip of an intense crisis.[43] A tramway strike which broke out on 25 August had spread into a full-scale showdown between the Irish Transport and General Workers' Union (ITGWU) under the leadership of Jim Larkin, and a coalition of employers led by William Martin Murphy, a pluralist proprietor in the modern capitalist mode, whose empire included the Dublin United Tramways Company as well as a national newspaper, the *Irish Independent*, and the Dublin *Evening Herald*. This 'bloodsucking vampire' (as he was characterized in the ITGWU's own paper, the *Irish Worker*) was determined to destroy what he called 'Larkinism'. By 22 September, 25,000 men had been locked out, and the city was paralysed.

This was a crisis not only for the livelihoods of Dublin workers but also for relations between Irish and British trades unions. It played a vital part, too, in the final unravelling of the great political movement of Irish nationalism as it had existed since the time of Parnell. Murphy represented the Catholic middle-class power-base of the parliamentary nationalist party, hostile from both Catholic and bourgeois stand-points to the menace of 'syndicalism'. That menace was, of course, vastly exaggerated by both the church and Murphy's press, but in the process of grinding down the resistance of the Dublin workers, he went some distance towards making it a reality. Now the vaguely syn-dicalist militancy of 'Larkinism' was focused in the shape of a work-ers' militia, set up at first as a bodyguard for Larkin and other labour leaders in their frequent confrontations with the hired strikebreakers of the Tramways Company. In October, Larkin was arrested for sedi-tious libel and conspiracy, and given a seven-month prison sentence. A wave of public protest impelled the government to release him after a fortnight, and at a big rally to celebrate his release on 14 November, his deputy, James Connolly, issued a dramatic call to arms: 'Next time we are out for a march, I want to be accompanied by four battalions of trained men with their corporals and sergeants.' A week later the Irish Citizen Army was formally announced. Larkin called it a 'new Army of the people, so that Labour may be able to utilise that great physical power which it possesses to prevent its elementary rights being taken away'.[44]

The ICA was a Dublin outfit through and through, confined by its proletarian base and the financial constraints of a union movement battered and bruised by the 1913 dispute. Even so, it was weaker than it might have been. Although several thousand were enrolled in November, after the end of the strike the roll shrank to less than a thousand, and few more joined over the following months despite the enthusiastic efforts of the army's chief organizer, Captain Jack White (the son of a British general). One key reason was the competition of the Irish Volunteers. The playwright and labour activist Sean O'Casey, Secretary of the ICA Council, found it 'difficult to understand why the workers chose to join an organisation which was largely controlled by their enemies rather than one which was guided and governed by the men who were their elected leaders'.[45] One of those who did join the ICA, Frank Robbins, was clear enough about the problem. He thought that while some workers might have stayed away for 'genuine reasons, such as shabby clothing and lack of proper footwear', the plain fact was that most workers did not sympathize with the army's purpose. 'The socialist ideals expressed in the constitution of the ICA were not understood by the workers, and where understood, were not acceptable.'[46] Unlike the IV, the ICA made no effort to dilute its revolutionary posture to widen its support. It suffered, too, from the inevitable fractiousness of the left. O'Casey became infuriated by Constance Markievicz's flamboyant posing and her 'bourgeois background'; he thought her sympathy for the workers a sham. Later in 1914 he tried to have her expelled from the ICA Council because of her close association with the Irish Volunteers, an organization 'in its methods and aims inimical to the first interests of Labour'. This internal squabble ended with O'Casey's own resignation, a real and pointless loss.[47]

In early 1914, as the ICA struggled to rebuild itself in the grim aftermath of the Dublin lockout, the wider Irish political crisis intensified. The atmosphere was thickening. Patrick Pearse, in the USA on a fundraising tour in February and March (extended because the St Enda's College Fund had failed to reach $1,000 by 21 March), was moving to a new level of military rhetoric. His exposure to the semi-hysterical Irish-American republican culture was a 'heady experience', and its effects were measurable. Impressed by the hardbitten old-style Fenians such as John Devoy and 'their romantic lust for violent resolution',[48] he found like many separatist visitors before him that the fiercer his rhetoric, the more ecstatic (and generous) was his reception. Haranguing an Emmet commemoration meeting in New York, he proclaimed:

Today Ireland is once more organising, once more learning the noble trade of arms . . . There is again in Ireland the murmur of marching, and talk of guns and tactics. The existence on Irish soil of an Irish army is the most portentous fact that has appeared in Ireland for over a hundred years: a fact which marks definitely the beginning of the second stage of the Revolution which commenced when the Gaelic League was founded.[49]

In March, moreover, the crisis in the British state was suddenly ratcheted up another notch. Events at the main military base at the Curragh turned into something entirely outside British experience, at least since the time of Cromwell – a crisis of civil–military relations. Though it is sometimes called the Curragh 'mutiny', it was not quite that – no orders were actually disobeyed.[50] But the government got into a dangerous fix by attempting to ensure that, if it did order the army to act in Ulster, the order would be obeyed. That there should be any question of this was itself a sign of how serious the situation had become. The Home Rule Bill was set to become law as soon as the two-year suspensory veto of the House of Lords expired, and since no political resolution of the Ulster issue had been reached, the threat of armed resistance seemed a real possibility. The government ordered troop reinforcements to be sent north as a precautionary measure, but the army was acutely aware that many of its officers were openly hostile to Home Rule. In a particularly ham-fisted manoeuvre, the War Office decided to offer Ulster-domiciled army officers exemption from action in Ulster (they were to be allowed to 'disappear' for the duration), while threatening that any others who refused to go there would not be allowed to resign but be 'cashiered'. When the General Officer Commanding (GOC) in Ireland put this option to the officers of the 3rd Cavalry Brigade at the Curragh, he found that most of them would rather lose their careers than risk having to oppose the Ulster rebels.[51] In the end, the government had to provide a guarantee that the army would not be used to enforce Home Rule in Ulster – a major political humiliation, which had an electrifying effect on nationalist opinion in Ireland. Even moderates began to wonder whether republicans were not right about British intentions. The viability of Home Rule looked more fragile than ever.

This shift of opinion hardened in the next month when the UVF ran nearly 50,000 rifles and 3 million rounds of ammunition into the Ulster ports of Larne, Bangor and Donaghadee. Quite apart from the military significance of the weapons, this carefully organized night-time operation was a striking demonstration of the expertise of the UVF general staff. The quality of the guns was perhaps debatable – many were old Italian rifles, barely serviceable – but from a nationalist viewpoint the size of the gun-running threatened to eliminate the possibility of any compromise solution to the Ulster crisis. And the inactivity of the police during the operation reinforced their suspicions of governmental partiality. For many nationalists this was the last straw. Recruitment into the Irish Volunteers, then going rather sluggishly, began to accelerate from its total of nearly 27,000 in April to over 130,000 by the end of May, reaching 180,000 in the summer.[52] This period even saw the appearance of some IV 'cavalry corps', reflecting the adhesion of wealthier farmers and even gentry. But burgeoning recruitment had its negative side, too. It increased the strain on the structure and logic of the inexperienced militia. The shortage of arms looked all the more obvious as bigger public parades with dummy rifles took place, so pressure to emulate the UVF increased: a tall order for the still penurious IV.

Moreover, 'the two Johns and Joe' suddenly took notice of what was going on in the national movement they were accustomed to directing. On 9 June, when Redmond issued a statement declaring that the parliamentary party now supported the Volunteer movement, it faced its first internal political crisis. Redmond's 'support' took the form of an assertion that the Volunteer executive committee was not fully representative, and should be enlarged to allow it (for which read – force it) to represent the party. This first clash between Redmond and the Volunteer founders, though less openly dramatic than the final split three months later, none the less clearly demonstrated the widening gulf between the old nationalist movement and the new. It was not only the republicans who bridled at Redmond's demand for effective control of the Volunteers; the independents led by MacNeill and O'Rahilly, in asserting that the Volunteers should remain uncommitted to any political party, demonstrated the same suspicion of 'politics' and the fear of a sell-out. Sir Roger Casement insisted that 'the Volunteers are the beginning of an Irish army, and every man must feel he is entitled as an Irishman to step into the ranks without being questioned as to his political opinions any more than as to his religious views'.[53] MacNeill, who had been fencing with the parliamentary leadership for three months on the issue (at one point, in mid-May, he told Gwynn 'my interview with the Party was like being examined before a Royal Commission'), consistently protested his commitment to Home Rule, but insisted on the need for the Volunteers to be seen to be independent. In the process he reiterated his own view of the reasons for establishing the IV – to 'show the Tories that the alternative to Home Rule was a policy of repression and coercion beyond any they had yet experience of', and 'show the Ulster minority that Nationalist Ireland could not be treated with contempt'. ('Their whole strength', he said, 'lies in the contempt inspired in them.') He himself had 'no personal ambition, no idea of doing other than support the Party'.[54]

O'Rahilly's own account bristles with anger at Redmond's aim of 'emasculating the movement', and his tactic of threatening to establish a rival volunteer organization. But as he pointed out, the Volunteer executive was in a bind that could not be known to its rank and file. The threat of splitting the movement was a very real one, and it came at a crucial juncture – 'the Provisional Committee had on the high seas at that very period their secret shipments of arms, and were already arranging those elaborate schemes for landing them which afterwards materialised at Howth and Kilcool'.[55] The executive offered Redmond a national election to form a new committee, but he insisted on the immediate addition of twenty-five of his own nominees. The IRB men on the committee stood firm against concession, with the exception of Hobson, for whom the overriding aims of bringing in the arms shipment and avoiding 'a disastrous, and indeed a fatal split' outweighed the obnoxious act of surrender to the parliamentarians. Hobson had expected this showdown for some time; he told McGarrity in May that the AOH and UIL were 'whipping up their members and getting them all to join. They will probably try to get control. And they can get it if they try – but not just yet.'[56] He argued that the concession would make little difference in practice, because Redmond's nominees could be kept away from real control of the Volunteers. His view swung the Executive vote in favour of compromise, but the crunch was painful. O'Rahilly told Béaslaí that after 'the surrender, I felt so utterly disgusted with myself that I wrote my resignation for the Committee and gave it to Padraig Pearse, who advised me not to send it'.[57] The tussle brought out the bitter unreconstructed Fenian in Tom Clarke, who had almost adopted Hobson as a son over the previous four years. He asked him, 'What did the Castle pay you?' – a terrible and dismal accusation. The two men never spoke informally again. Hobson resigned from the IRB Supreme Council and was even sacked by John Devoy as a contributor to the Gaelic American, his main source of income. Though Pearse urged McGarrity to reverse this, it was the beginning of the end of Hobson's career as a leading activist.

His greatest triumph, however, was still to come: little more than a month after the acceptance of Redmond's formal control of the IV, he organized the reception of the arms shipment – 1,500 rifles and 49,000 rounds of ammunition, bought in Germany. This was truly a decisive moment for the Volunteers, and not simply because of the sudden expansion of their limited armoury. In fact the rifles themselves, which O'Rahilly had purchased, were not hugely impressive; first-generation single-shot Mausers from the 1870s, they were in strictly military terms obsolete (like the UVF's, though unlike the UVF's they were in good condition). And, thanks to the desperate shortage of IV funds, there were few enough of them. Volunteer funds themselves would hardly have bought a dozen, and the Irish-American Fenians, traditionally eager (verbally at least) to raise money for guns in Ireland, remained suspicious of this newfangled open organization even before the compromise with Redmond. Although Devoy eventually sent $5,000, it did not arrive until late June, and the money that made the gun-running possible was subscribed by two sympathizers, Mary Spring Rice and Sir Roger Casement – both Anglo-Irish Protestants, like the two men who went to Hamburg to collect the guns, Darrell Figgis and Erskine Childers. Childers, and yet another sympathizer from outside the IV, Conor O'Brien, furnished the two small sailboats in which they were brought to Ireland.

In light of Childers' brilliant 1903 story *The Riddle of the Sands*, perhaps the first true modern spy novel, this extraordinary expedition was a striking example of reality imitating fiction. That book remains one of the most vivid of all celebrations of the art of coastal sailing, and Childers' own voyage likewise depended on a remarkable mixture of skill, nerve and luck. His little boat *Asgard* (a name drawn from the Norse mythic tradition that Tolkien would also tap into) was loaded with 900 rifles and 29,000 rounds of ammunition from a German tug hired by Darrel Figgis, off the Scheldt estuary on the night of 12 July. When Figgis announced that O'Brien had already taken the smaller half of the consignment (600 rifles and 20,000 rounds), Childers and his crew 'looked at each other. Could we ever take them?'

Well they might wonder. But 'fortunately, it was a warm, calm summer's night. For hours on end, in a lather of sweat, they loaded the big canvas bales, each done up in straw . . . until the *Asgard*'s saloon, cabin, passage and companion way were stacked high.'[58] Then the heavily laden boat had to be navigated through hundreds of miles of coastal waters regularly patrolled by the navy, often sailing close to big warships and once being nearly rammed by a destroyer in the dark. Astonishingly, the timing of Childers' arrival at Howth was perfect; the white yacht, with his wife Molly on deck wearing a bright red skirt as a recognition signal, came into view just as the first column of Irish Volunteers marched into the little port on Sunday 26 July.

This justified Hobson's calculated risk of arranging the landing so close to Dublin in daylight – making the unloading of the arms easier, but risking a challenging confrontation with the authorities. 'If we could bring them in in a sufficiently spectacular manner we should probably solve our financial problem and the problem of arming the Volunteers as well.'[59] He sent a section of Fianna ('the only body on whose discipline I could count') with a cartload of specially made wooden batons to form a defensive cordon. Although he may have expected that the police would turn a blind eye as they had at Larne, if they took action they would provide useful propaganda by confirming nationalist allegations of official bias.

Had the matter been one for the RIC, in fact, it seems likely that they would indeed have confined themselves to observation. But Dublin had its own police force, whose heads took the view that (in the words of the Commissioner of the DMP) 'a body of more than 1,000 men armed with rifles marching on Dublin, the seat of the Irish Government, constitute an unlawful assembly of a peculiarly audacious character'.[60] His deputy, Assistant Commissioner Harrel, took up Hobson's challenge, summoned military aid, and headed out towards Howth. He ran into the Volunteer column on the Malahide road, but his attempt to disarm it turned into a fiasco. The Volunteers dispersed across the fields and through the north Dublin suburbs, often hiding the guns with sympathetic householders, while Harrel was kept talking by Hobson, Darrell Figgis and Thomas MacDonagh. There was a brief melée when the police (disregarding Harrel's order to halt) charged, and 'some of our men fired revolvers and automatic pistols', slightly wounding two of the nearby troops. Hobson tried to stop this shooting, 'as at any moment it might provoke a volley from the soldiers', who were not more than thirty yards away from the dense column.[61] The policemen, tussling with the front of the Volunteer column, got hold of nineteen rifles – 'all of which were broken in the struggle' – but Maurice Moore, the IV Inspector-General, coolly went up to the Castle the next day and had the remnants returned to him.[62]

This tense, exhilarating confrontation was hailed as a second 'battle of Clontarf' by Volunteer propaganda, echoing the most famous of all Irish victories, the defeat of the Danes (and their Leinster Irish allies) by the Munster king Brian Boru in 1014. It gave a tremendous boost to the movement; for many Volunteers and Fianna boys the Howth landing was a defining moment in their lives. 'We cheered and cheered and cheered and waved anything we had and cheered again', recorded one of the Cumann na mBan there. 'To see and hear that was the best thing that ever happened to me in my life.'[63] The 'Howth Mausers', as they became known (though over a third of the whole shipment was run in by O'Brien to Kilcoole, about ten miles south of Dublin on the Wicklow coast, in a much lower-profile operation the following week) were big, heavy, and used large-calibre (11mm) ammunition. Their distinctive thump was to be one of the defining sounds of the 1916 rebellion. Certainly they pleased their new owners at first. Jack Plunkett, who paid fifteen shillings for his 1871 Mauser, plus another ten shillings for fifty rounds of ammunition, thought his rifle 'delightful'; 'the bore of the barrel was good, and when I saw repeated cleanings improve its polish I felt very proud'. He added a bayonet, making the whole thing about seven feet long. Even the ammunition was a work of art: 'it was in the original cardboard cases dated variously up to 1874. There was very little verdigris and when the beautifully made cartridges were all spotless and lodged in an enormous ammunition pouch I felt fit to meet an elephant – as, in fact, I was.' A company of men armed with these long weapons was, Plunkett thought, an impressive sight, and their length had one big virtue – they were very accurate. But still, for all their special German charms, many Volunteers tried to replace them with handier, more modern magazine rifles as soon as they could. Seamus Daly of the 2nd Battalion maintained that 'the boys never liked them', and opinions of their value in the rebellion were always to be divided.[64]

The bravado of the Howth operation was immediately rewarded with a public sensation. When the troops (of the 2nd King's Own Scottish Borderers) Harrel had requisitioned returned along the Liffey quays to their barracks, they were followed by a jeering and abusive crowd. 'The men were very excited after all they had been through', one of the junior officers said, 'and were difficult to keep in hand.' As they marched along Bachelors Walk, they were pelted with stones – something they seem to have been quite unprepared for. They halted to face down the mob; shots were fired, and three people killed (a fourth died later of injuries). An official inquiry, conducted by three senior judges, concluded that, although no order to fire had been given, the soldiers believed that one had. Major Haig had, however, ordered troops under his command to prepare to fire; he had just joined the column from the Dublin direction and was unaware that their guns were loaded. (The inquiry found this 'regrettable'.)[65] It has been suggested that he believed that they were loaded with blank, rather than live, ammunition (though this seems unlikely, as it would have flown in the face of well-understood military rules about 'aid to the civil power'). In any case, the result was a public relations disaster, aggravated when the commission of inquiry publicly rejected the reasoning of the Dublin police chiefs. It suggested somewhat airily that 'the possession of rifles may possibly have laid the Volunteers open to suitable proceedings taken under the Customs Acts'. But their armed assembly 'was not characterised by violence, crime, riot, disturbance, or the likelihood of any of these things'. The commissioners found it 'difficult to follow' the Assistant Commissioner's thinking, 'in view of his knowledge and long experience'.[66] This was a deadly condemnation: Harrel's police career was effectively ended, and his Commissioner, Sir John Ross of Bladensburg (a man of vast law enforcement experience stretching back to the land war) also resigned in protest.

The abortive attempt to prevent the Howth gun-running was seen by many nationalists as further confirmation of the authorities' bias towards the Ulster rebels: after all, no attempt, however feeble, had been made to stop the Larne operation, and the subsequent police investigation had been perfunctory. But the government's hasty disavowal of its over-zealous DMP minion showed that the real motive in both cases was a deep-set apprehension of any potentially provocative action. Nationalists might have seen things differently if they had been able to read an army paper drawn up at the end of March, even before the UVF gun-running. Here Irish Command launched an astonishingly direct attack on 'the failure of the Government to appreciate the true state of feeling in the North of Ireland, and its ignorance of the plans of the Ulster leaders'. The government's tolerance of illegal drilling, and its failure to establish any functional intelligence system, the army declared, had created a really dangerous situation. The RIC was undermanned, and its grasp of the Ulster threat was hamstrung by its 'political sympathies' – both the Unionism of its higher ranks and the Nationalism of its rank and file led to misreading the situation. The DMP was equally useless: 'the Police Intelligence in Dublin itself was poor, and it would appear that little trouble had been taken to gauge the situation in the city'. The RIC had no real 'secret service' capacity, in the military view – they had not tried to employ any intelligence specialists from England, or any women – and 'the civilian officials did not know what was going on'. The verdict was crushing. 'Although an extraordinary state of affairs has been in existence in the North for nearly two years, nothing out of the normal has apparently taken place in the routine of the Irish Executive.'[67]

The Under-Secretary, belatedly realizing how little information the government had, had asked Irish Command to set up an intelligence department on 20 March. The army warned, however, that this was perilously late to be trying to build such a delicate organization. Moreover – still raw from the Curragh incident – it pointed out that if it was itself too closely involved there was a risk that it might be 'brought again before the public', and the impression given 'that a system of military espionage has been set up by the soldiers'. Yet something had to be done, and quickly. It was vital that the police should be able (i) to prevent all further importation of arms into Ireland, and (ii) 'to honeycomb the various political organizations in Ireland with police agents'. There needed to be some system of co-ordination between the police and agencies such as the Coastguards and the Custom House, and 'no effort should be spared to attract a better class of men' to enlist in an Irish secret service. This should be done 'at once'.[68]

There is no sign that the Irish Executive took any steps to respond to this no-punches-pulled assessment. Its routine remained undisturbed; such military urgings no doubt appeared politically inept. At least one change took place over the next few months, however. The IV gun-running alerted the Inspector-General of the RIC to the transformation of the danger he faced. In mid-June he issued a sombre warning that 'the drilling and training to arms of a great part of the male population is a new departure which is bound in the not distant future to alter all the existing conditions of life'. He observed that 'in times of passion or excitement the law has only been maintained by force', and this had been possible because of the lack of organization of the opponents of the police. The future would be different. 'Each county will soon have a trained army far outnumbering the police, and those who control the volunteers will be in a position to dictate to what extent the law of the land may be carried into effect.'[69] This was a truly revolutionary situation; the limits of the possible had been broken.

Its implications became clear to the Chief of the Imperial General Staff too. He told Asquith in early July that there was no military plan to deal with the situation that would arise if the 200,000 men, 'systematically raised, trained and equipped on a military basis' in two opposing forces, should 'unfortunately come into conflict'. No plan could be prepared, he added pointedly, until the army was 'informed what policy the government proposes to adopt' in that eventuality. But what was certain was that 'in the event of a conflagration, the whole of the Expeditionary Force may be required to restore order'. This would 'probably involve general mobilization, placing Special Reserves troops in the ports, and assembling the Local and Central Forces now composed of Territorial troops'. The bottom line was that, in that case, 'we shall be unable to meet any of our obligations abroad'.[70] Beyond doubt, this had been noticed in Berlin as well, where it must have encouraged the German General Staff in the course it had already adopted, of forcing a showdown with the Entente powers. By the time the troops opened fire in Bachelors Walk, the German army was assembling on the Belgian frontier. The Irish crisis was about to be engulfed in a crisis of global scale.

3

England's Difficulty

*Redmond has been honestly Imperial in the war, but by going
as far as he has done he has lost his position in the country.*

Sir Matthew Nathan, November 1915

August 1914 was one of the decisive moments in the history of the
modern world, and it proved decisive in the history of Ireland as well.
Its transformative effect there was, however, indirect rather than
direct. All the European belligerent countries – and some neutrals too
– had to make significant adaptations to the demands of the war.
'Total war' would impose a stringent test of the viability of institutions
and assumptions. For some states, the stress of war triggered violent
political change, even social revolution. Ireland was technically a belligerent, and for the first year at least its experience of war was not
greatly different from that of the others. Irish recruits poured into the
mass armies created in response to the novel demands of trench warfare; those left at home, as everywhere, turned a blind eye to the grim
realities of that warfare (assisted in self-deception by a ruthless regime
of military censorship). From the start, however, a kind of mental neutrality could be sensed in the Irish public sphere, an absence of the
fierce spasm of patriotism which gripped the English. Probably few
Irish people were pro-German, in the way they had been 'pro-Boer'
at the turn of the century; many accepted the British view of Germany
as a menace to the liberty of western Europe, and the police plausibly
reported 'a general dread of German invasion'.[1] But few shared the
visceral loathing of 'the Hun' that erupted in British popular opinion.[2]

This was not surprising – not as surprising, maybe, as the British government's apparent confidence that Ireland would rally to its cause. For the Liberal Cabinet, the onrush of war was a heady experience, and not least because it instantly pushed the Irish problem from the centre of the political stage to the remote background. In July, Ireland was on the point of overwhelming the bulwarks of the British constitution; the failure of the last-ditch efforts to negotiate a Home Rule compromise in the Buckingham Palace talks, and the deadly affray on Bachelors Walk, led some to think the unthinkable – the possibility of civil war. In August, Ireland suddenly became almost invisible. When the Foreign Secretary, Sir Edward Grey, surveyed the gloomy global scene, he declared – incredibly enough – that the 'one bright spot' on the horizon was Ireland. As Canon Hannay, better known as the novelist George A. Birmingham, drily noted, this was 'the first time that Ireland had ever been hailed' as such: adding realistically, 'It will probably be the last.'[3] The Prime Minister's own relief was almost palpable. As early as 25 July, he told Lady Ottoline Morrell (with something more than the studied jocularity which he often affected in female company) that the Serbian crisis 'will take the attention away from Ulster, which is a good thing'; next day he wrote to another intimate female correspondent, Venetia Stanley, that the situation, 'the most dangerous of the last forty years', might 'have the effect of throwing into the background the lurid pictures of civil war in Ulster'. On 29 July he was talking of 'the coming war' putting 'the whole Irish business . . . into the shade'. It would be stretching the evidence to suggest that the Irish crisis impelled Britain into the world war, but it is inconceivable that it had no influence on the harrassed government leaders.[4]

It is clear enough that no doubts were expressed about Ireland's willingness to accept participation in the war. Far from being worried by the pessimistic report of the CIGS on the military threat of Irish nationalism, Asquith irritably dismissed it as an unwarrantable piece of political interference. The war enabled him to strike a deal with the Unionists, to withdraw their opposition to the Home Rule Bill on patriotic grounds, as long as its operation was suspended until the end of hostilities, and some as yet unspecified provision for the special treatment of Ulster was guaranteed. On this basis the Government of Ireland Act became law. Asquith assumed that this would be enough to ensure John Redmond's support for the war, and in this at least he was right.

Even before British military operations had begun, Redmond launched an initiative whose wisdom has been debated ever since. On 3 August he pledged Irish support for the war, and urged in the House of Commons that the defence of Ireland should be entrusted to the Irish Volunteers, so that all regular troops could be freed to march to defend France. Though he clearly expected Home Rule to be delivered, he carefully refrained from making any formal demand for it as the condition of Irish support for the war. In this he ignored the strong advice of Maurice Moore, who had urged four days earlier that 'if there is any hesitation on the part of the government in getting the King to sign the Home Rule Bill *immediately* the Irish reservists ought to be told not to join'. Moore insisted, 'this is the only pressure we can exert'.[5] It was clear enough to him that if the reservists joined up, the Volunteer organization would lose most of its military effectiveness for the foreseeable future. Redmond preferred to rely on British goodwill, and believed that if the War Office recognized the Volunteers as an official home defence force, it could go on being trained and supplied with arms. Even when it became clear that the War Office had no intention of accepting his offer, he went on to issue a public call on 16 September for recruits to an 'Irish Brigade' for service at the front. His thinking seemed to be that if distinctive Irish units could be formed within the British army, Irish Volunteers would be encouraged to join them. At the end of the war, Ireland would possess a national army with real military experience and credibility. Four days after this call, he went much further; in an apparently spontaneous address to a Volunteer review at Woodenbridge, Co. Wicklow, he seemed to commit the Volunteers to serve not just as a home defence force, but 'wherever the firing line extends'.

This pledge has been seen as a fatal miscalculation, from which the steady unravelling of his political power inexorably followed. We need, though, to recognize the positive dimensions of his strategy, and his genuine belief that a co-operative war effort could heal the divisions of the Home Rule crisis.[6] His speech did provoke a crisis, but his doom was sealed in the long run by British policy. The British response to Redmond's ideas was at best lukewarm. Beyond the rather odd decision on 6 August to revoke the prohibition on the importation of arms (which nationalists had seen as favouring the UVF), nothing concrete was done. Asquith would not have been sympathetic to the long-term objective of creating an 'Irish army' since this was expressly ruled out by the Home Rule legislation. The prospect of a nationalist-controlled army that might be used to enforce Home Rule in Ulster was even less appealing. The Prime Minister did see the need to demonstrate that Britain was making an answering gesture to Redmond's commitment, but by appointing Lord Kitchener to head the War Office (two days after Redmond's first offer) he involuntarily ensured that any such gesture would be minimal. At the Cabinet meeting on 11 August, Birrell formally proposed that the Volunteers should be recognized. Kitchener, in his second appearance as a member of the Cabinet, suggested that recognition should be the vehicle for reaching 'arrangement', by which he meant the postponement of Home Rule. Asquith seems to have needed nudging by Charles Hobhouse, the Postmaster-General, to quash this blatant piece of military politics: 'After some struggle with [Kitchener] and Churchill, the P.M. in reply to a direct question by myself agreed that recognition of the Volunteers in Ireland could not be made conditional, but must be immediate and complete.'[7] In fact, it never happened, and Asquith never pressed the matter.

Kitchener was a military technician whose political ideas were rudimentary. Making him a Secretary of State was one of the earliest signals of the war ethos that would compromise Britain's Irish policy for the duration. When John Dillon ill-advisedly – if not inaccurately – remarked during negotiations over Irish recruitment, 'I see clearly that you do not understand the country or the people', Kitchener brusquely retorted, 'Mr Dillon, I understand everything about Ireland.' This understanding amounted to a caricature of Tory prejudice. Even after he agreed to create a new Irish division, the 16th, and to open up one of its brigades for direct entry from the Irish Volunteers, Kitchener remained opposed to fostering its Irish identity by the kind of public symbols that Redmond believed to be vital to encourage recruitment. A recent biographer calls this a 'foolish lack of tact', but that fails to touch its malign destructiveness.[8] In so far as Kitchener offered any explanation for his obduracy, it was the fear of allowing politics to enter the army (a fear shared, certainly, by a number of less senior soldiers). Whether Asquith accepted this, or simply shirked a confrontation with the formidable Field Marshal, he never tried to instruct Kitchener about the potential importance of the issue for Anglo-Irish relations. From the start, therefore, it was clear that the 'war effort' would trump any political policy. Military logic, and military expertise, were in the ascendant, in a way unprecedented in British history.

Redmond believed he could carry Irish opinion with him, on the argument that the war was not a British imperial conflict but, as he put it at Woodenbridge, the 'defence of right and freedom and religion' (the last of these would probably have surprised many people in Britain). On the same day he wrote confidently to the president of the United Irish League in America that the Home Rule Act, which was due to receive the royal assent the next day, would neutralize 'Sinn Feiners and others of that kidney'; 'They really have no following in the country, and I anticipate that they will be immediately steamrollered by public opinion.'[9] There was certainly a strong dose of optimism in his hope that Irish participation would not only cement Home Rule, but also mend the widening breach between nationalists and Unionists. It was a gamble, and he was not unaware of the risks involved. As early as 6 August he was warning that if his offer to commit the Volunteers to the defence of Ireland was not taken up, 'the happiest opportunity in Irish history will be lost'. Two days later, he was pleading with Asquith to persuade (or order) Kitchener to take it up, saying that 'there would be such a wave of enthusiasm as would lead to a very large body of recruits' if he agreed. But if he did not, 'people will be disheartened and hurt'.[10] And on the ninth he warned Birrell directly that 'if the existing Volunteer organisation is ignored and sneered at and made little of, recruiting in the country will not go ahead'.

In fact, however, the government's sanguine – indeed complacent – expectation was at first borne out. Irish recruitment was not so far out of line with the national pattern as might well have been expected, or as is frequently imagined even now. In the first six months, 50,000 enlisted, and another 25,000 in the following six. The increasingly sharp fall-off that would set in from mid-1915 was paralleled in

Britain itself.[11] Though the statistics are treacherous, the most careful calculations suggest that the rate of recruitment in Ireland (outside Ulster) through 1914 and 1915 was about two-thirds of the British rate.[12] This gap was primarily due to Ireland's different social structure: Irish society remained predominantly rural, and across the whole United Kingdom recruitment was significantly higher in urban areas. Moreover, where Britain had a fairly youthful demographic profile, Ireland's population was ageing – at least until emigration was choked off by the war. Some statistics, such as the proportion of the Ulster Volunteer Force and the Irish Volunteers who volunteered for military service, reflected different age structures. There were, admittedly, striking regional variations within Ireland: Ulster matched the British rate, while Connaught consistently lagged behind Munster and Leinster.

Nearly half of all recruits came from the two militias, the UVF and Irish Volunteers. Though a higher proportion of Ulster volunteers joined up, this was partly due to the stricter age limits the force had imposed (limiting its membership to men of military age, where the IV accepted men up to the age of sixty-five). But the impact of the war on the two organizations was dramatically different. When Carson offered the UVF for military service, the War Office was more co-operative (though Kitchener started by handing out to Carson, too, a lecture on Irish politics). Of course, Carson made sure to trump Redmond's offer by attaching no strings, or demands for special status, to his own. All the same, UVF recruits were incorporated in an 'Ulster Division', the 36th, enlisting in sufficient numbers to carry across many of their familiar unit structures. Carson was free of the historical baggage and political threats that encumbered Redmond. General Richardson, the UVF Commander-in-Chief, explicitly – and recklessly – told his men that they owed a debt of gratitude to the British army for its support during the Curragh crisis. For most Ulstermen, support for Britain's war was a matter of patriotism pure and simple, and a chance to demonstrate the value of that 'loyalism' which many people in Britain had come to view rather quizzically during the Home Rule crisis.

For the Irish Volunteers, the war brought to a climax the internal struggle that had been festering since Redmond's semi-forcible takeover in June. The Redmondite nominees on the Provisional Committee included several party men who had been openly critical of the Volunteer movement; 'with one or two exceptions they acted as a solid block and turned the committee's meetings into a faction fight', according to Bulmer Hobson. Hobson, for his part, carried on as if the Redmond nominees were not there – appointing office staff, for instance, 'without their ever being aware that such things had been done'. The treasurer, O'Rahilly, contrived to keep the organization's books in such a way as to thwart Redmondite efforts to tap its funds. The balance within the movement began to shift, however, more markedly with the approach of war. 'All sorts of people who had never touched the national movement before' were drawn in, including the Earl of Meath and the Marquess of Conyngham. 'For a short period the Volunteers had the more or less active support of a very large number of titled people, and many untitled, whose respectability and steady adherence to Dublin Castle made them strange colleagues for people like us.'[13] A crunch was bound to come, but the split-line was by no means predetermined. The main dissident grouping, the pre-Redmond leadership, were united only in their distrust and dislike of Redmond. Pearse gave his view of the situation at length in a letter to Joe McGarrity a week after the outbreak of war. As an example of the problem, he described how the previous week the Irish Volunteer Dublin County Board had drawn up a resolution, for adoption by the Dublin Brigade battalions, expressing readiness to co-operate with Ulster for the defence of Ireland but refusing to support Britain in war against foreign nations with which Ireland had no quarrel.

Three out of five Dublin battalions adopted this unanimously and paraded in front of the Provisional Committee's office during a meeting and sent in a spokesman to convey the resolution to the Committee. The reply was to order the Dublin Co. Board to apologize and promise not to adopt resolutions dealing with matters of policy again on pain of suspension.

In Pearse's view, Redmond's capture of the Volunteers was 'absolute and complete'. His hope that the original members would act together and save the movement from capture 'has proved vain', and his own position was mortifying. 'I can never carry a single point. I am now scarcely allowed to speak. The moment I stand up there are cries of "Put the question" etc . . .'[14]

Pearse was clear where the blame lay – with Eoin MacNeill. 'He has the reputation of being "tactful", but his "tact" consists in bowing to the will of the Redmondites every time. He never makes a fight except when they assail his personal honour, when he bridles up at once.' He was prepared to admit that MacNeill was in a 'very delicate position', but insisted, 'he is weak, hopelessly weak'. And he could not resist adding, of his old Gaelic League senior, 'I knew that all along.'[15] (He told his pupil Desmond Ryan that MacNeill was 'a Grattan come to life again'.)[16] Certainly MacNeill's position bore strong hints of inconclusiveness. He wanted to keep the Volunteers free of 'political' control, but free to do what? He wanted them armed, but only as a kind of indirect threat, a means of ensuring that Home Rule would be secured, and power passed to – whom? In fact, to the nationalist party, of which he appeared to be so suspicious. The ambiguity of MacNeill's long-term strategy would ultimately have critical effects, but for now what counted was his suspicion of Redmondism. As Redmond pushed up the stakes of participation in the war, MacNeill began to dig his heels in. For Hobson, too, the argument with which he had swung the vote in favour of compromise with Redmond in June, that to risk splitting the Volunteer movement might be even worse, was neutralized by Redmond's commitment to the war.

The point of MacNeill's divergence from the party line on Home Rule can be quite precisely dated. On 15 August, writing to Roger Casement, he was generous enough about Redmond's initial gesture of solidarity with Britain, going as far as to argue that 'Grattan at his best would not have gone beyond what Redmond said, had he been faced with a similar situation.' But he went on to outline a radical plan of action to capitalize on the humiliation of Dublin Castle after the Howth fiasco. Arguing that the suspension of Assistant Commissioner Harrel, and the subsequent resignation of the Commissioner of the DMP, Sir John Ross of Bladensburg, had 'almost paralysed' the 'foreign regime', he held that 'if certain persons can be got to see the real state of affairs, all the King's horses and all the King's men will not set Humpty Dumpty up again'. His conclusion was dramatic – 'we could have effective self-government in a week without waiting for any enactment'.[17] On or about 17 August he went to see one of these 'certain persons', Joe Devlin, to propose a unilateral declaration of self-government by the Irish MPs. Devlin replied that 'it would be too great a responsibility'. MacNeill fumed, 'when this was the view of the youngest and most active and enterprising of the Party leaders, the case of the Party appeared to me to be altogether hopeless'.[18] No doubt MacNeill's proposal sounded too close to Arthur Griffith's ideas, and indeed it showed that (contrary to the common view of him) he did have an imaginative, even daring streak.

Redmond's Woodenbridge commitment presented MacNeill with the same dilemma he had faced over enlargement of the committee, but this time he opted to take a stand and split the movement. With twenty members of the committee, he issued a statement on 24 September denouncing the party leader's policy as 'utterly at variance with the published and accepted aims and objects' of the Volunteers. They declared 'that Ireland cannot, with honour or safety, take part in foreign quarrels otherwise than through the free action of a National Government of her own', and demanded that the Dublin Castle government be immediately abolished 'and that a National Government be forthwith established in its place'. The signatories included O'Rahilly, Pearse, Thomas MacDonagh, Joseph Plunkett, Piaras Béaslaí, Eamonn Ceannt, Seán MacDermott, and Liam Mellows. In Redmond's view, and that of the public, these were mostly minor, indeed obscure figures. Moreover, the immediate impact of their secession seemed to bear out Hobson's original pessimism, and Redmond's confidence.

The Irish Volunteer movement split with a muted bang and a drawn-out whimper. The precise number who adhered to the MacNeill line has never been certain; the British intelligence estimate, of some 13,500 out of 188,000, may well have exaggerated it. What is certain is that the overwhelming majority remained loyal to Redmond. In the typical view of one provincial newspaper, 'Mr Redmond and the Irish Party are the nearest thing to a government that we possess, and simple commonsense demands that they should have the controlling voice in the direction of the Volunteer force.' A few local companies, such as Tubbercurry in Co. Sligo, voted to support MacNeill; but even this one split up soon afterwards. 'We were drilling in the field and somebody spoke about how Redmond wanted us to go and fight for gallant Belgium', one of its members recalled. 'Captain Bernard Brady stepped forward and said "I never joined Redmond's Volunteers, I joined MacNeill's Volunteers and anyone who wants to fight for gallant Ireland step out here with me."' Five out of sixty followed him. (And, interestingly, the RIC men who were watching the parade followed them.)[19]

The process was repeated, in differing proportions, across the country. Many provincial units virtually disappeared. Even in Dublin, units adhering to MacNeill became weaker than they had been before the Redmond takeover. Though Captain Eamon de Valera, for instance, initially carried a majority of his Donnybrook Company, his muster of fifty men rapidly melted away after that. When it dropped to seven, 'Dev solemnly made us form fours' in a field opposite Donnybrook church, and 'told each of us to be a recruiting sergeant'.[20] What proved crucial for the future was, finally, not the numbers who now followed them, but the energy and commitment of leaders like de Valera. The core cadre of dedicated Irish-Irelanders almost all stuck to 'fighting for gallant Ireland', and their motive was ideological. De Valera, like surprisingly many 1916 leaders, was to join the IRB late; he had been (and would again be, after the rebellion) opposed to secret societies, which he believed caused division and uncertainty within the national movement – besides being anathema to the Church. Serious, some thought chilly, spare and tall, a mathematics teacher who looked the part, 'Dev' belied his exotic patronym. His Spanish-American parentage, and faint doubts about his legitimacy, must have affected his upbringing in his mother's home town of Bruree, County Limerick: 'no psychiatrist could forecast the outcome of such an inheritance and early environment', as his officially inspired biography later gnomically observed.[21] But one outcome was meticulous attention to detail, a trait that would have been immensely valuable in a staff officer – if the Volunteers had had any. In the event, though he was at one stage to be appointed adjutant to the Dublin Brigade, he would become one of a handful of front-line unit commanders.

Though sharp tussles took place here and there, the Volunteer divorce was mostly awkward rather than acrimonious. By mutual consent the two groups adopted different titles, the secessionists – who of course regarded themselves as the true originals – being 'Irish Volunteers' and the majority 'Irish National Volunteers' (INV). Though it is often suggested that the latter title was invented at the time of the split, in fact it had been in use by many units from early 1914 onwards. (The founding manifesto of the Cumann na mBan in April 1914 specifically declared its allegiance to the 'National Volunteers', and some units had started as 'Ladies' Irish National Volunteers'.) Titles were easier to share out than assets, but even the prized rifles seem to have been divided without direct conflict. Given that some companies still had few or none, the issue may not have arisen in many places; in some, there were charges that the INV actually stole guns from the IV. But on the whole it seems clear that the minority managed to hold on to a disproportionate number of the guns.

Both sections were damaged and demoralized by the split, and for several months it looked as if the minority IV – who were widely called 'Sinn Feiners' from this time onwards – would come off worst. Certainly they were unpopular, especially in the countryside. The Longford Volunteers, for example, 'more or less died out from 1914 to 1916', they were 'very much in the minority', and often denounced as 'pro-Germans'.[22] In Mayo, 'dry rot set into' the organization for almost a year.[23] Both sections suffered from the amorphous state of the whole force. The RIC, who watched it very carefully, reported in August that the Volunteers were 'making no headway in organization', and again in September that 'no progress whatever was made during the month in organization. The Force is not even formed into definite units.' Though this was perhaps a slight exaggeration, the Volunteer staff would have admitted its essential accuracy.[24] The police counted 'about 7,500 rifles of different patterns', but believed that reassuringly few had been brought in since the withdrawal of the proclamation against the importation of arms on 6 August. The crucial weakness of the INV, however, lay in the shortage of instructors since the reservists had rejoined the colours. 'Some county gentlemen with military experience who joined seemingly in the hope that it would in some way become affiliated with the Forces of the Crown, appear to have either resigned or ceased to take part.' The RIC's conclusion was crushing: 'It is a strong Force on paper, but without officers, and untrained, is little better than a huge mob.'[25]

Both sections had to start again more or less from scratch, and this soon proved to be an insuperable problem for the INV. Although Redmond remained bullish about its future, telling a gathering of 5,000 National Volunteers in Waterford on 11 October that he had secured a national headquarters building in Dublin, and intended to create a 'vigorous, intelligent, united and efficient organization' with a new journal, the *National Volunteer*, and £5,000 available for buying arms, local experience was quite different. The Party lost what little interest it had had in the Volunteer movement; resources ceased to flow into it. The local supply of arms, especially, dried up, despite Redmond's persistent efforts at national level. By November 1914 the police reported that the INV were 'steadily declining', and in February 1915 'still declining rapidly' to just over 142,000 nominal members. In April they were down to 134,000 and 'apathy is everywhere noticeable'. When Colonel Moore reviewed an INV assembly in Limerick in June, he had to explain at length why it was impossible to obtain rifles for them. Although large parades continued to be held – in January, successive assemblies of 250, 300 and 500 'armed Volunteers' drilled at Celtic Park in Belfast, while on Easter Sunday a parade of 20,000 took place in Phoenix Park – such manifestations of men who (as the RIC acidly noted) were demonstrably refusing to enlist began to appear rather unseemly as the war went on. In September, when the police estimated their number at 117,752 (of whom 5,492 had 'Sinn Fein' tendencies), Moore wrote bluntly, 'In my opinion nothing can be done with the Volunteers or anything like them; they cannot be trained, disciplined or armed; moreover the enthusiasm has gone and they cannot be kept going.' Even if some organization was kept alive, 'it will be no use for practical purposes against any army Orange or German'.[26]

The collapse of the National Volunteers presaged that of the Party itself, though this was less obvious. Its support for the war was gradually revealed to be a major political encumbrance. This was not just a question of public attitudes to Britain's war aims. The war remorselessly opened economic divergences between Britain and Ireland, which cruelly exposed the powerlessness of the party to protect Irish interests. The rapid rise in food and fuel prices, and the pegging of wages, had a disproportionate impact in Ireland, where unemployment and low pay were much bigger problems than in Britain. Some 78 per cent of Irish workers, as against 50 per cent of Scottish and 40 per cent of English workers, lived on less than £1 a week. The wage freeze was only one of a set of British policies which were widely viewed in Ireland as British exploitation. The virtual elimination of unemployment in Britain through the vast expansion of the munitions industry was not matched in Ireland, and the suction effect of British industry was denounced by nationalists as enforced migration; the withdrawal of housing grants had a particularly deleterious effect there; liquor taxation and licensing laws generated angry opposition. Even by early 1915, 'the Irish Party had become politically unconvincing and its popular power-base began to crumble'.[27] This was in spite of, or in a sense because of, the enactment of Home Rule: 'The very events which marked the Party's triumph were also the sources of its subsequent petrification.' After Home Rule was passed, the Party's position was awkward. The old programme and slogans were redundant, yet because the act was suspended the party had no definite role; while the threat or promise of amendment in relation to Ulster raised new fears of betrayal.

Constitutionalism passed into a kind of suspended animation – as a mocking ditty said:

> We've Home Rule now the statute book adorning,
> It's there to be seen by every mother's son;
> We brush the cobwebs off it every morning,
> For the constitutional movement must go on (and on, and on) . . .

In concrete terms, the Party had nothing to show for the struggles of the previous generation; yet it had cast its lot in with the British state. Its occupation had gone. And while it would be an exaggeration to say that the country passed under military government, the steady proliferation of regulations under the Defence of the Realm Act had the effect of paralysing such 'normal' political processes as had existed before. Redmond was given a chance to demonstrate his political clout when he was invited to enter the new coalition Cabinet as a minister without portfolio in May 1915. 'The ministry is about to be reconstructed on a broad national basis', Asquith told him on 18 May; 'I am most anxious that you should join.' It made no sense to refuse the invitation: Redmond was consigning himself to responsibility without power.[28] But rationality was irrelevant in face of the long historical memory of earlier sell-outs (the party had always been haunted by the ghosts of collaborators like 'Sadleir and Keogh'). His reply was inevitable: 'The principles and history of the Party I represent make the acceptance of your offer impossible.' Carson, on the other hand, was happy to accept. Asquith did not give up, telling Redmond, 'I attach more value than I can describe to your active participation in the new National Government', and asking him to take the issue to his party with this message. But once again, the answer was the same: the party 'unanimously endorsed' Redmond's decision.

By May 1915 Redmond must have had some inkling of just how wrong his initial hopes about the war had been. In his optimistic address to the Volunteers in Waterford in October he had set forth the beguiling fantasy of at least 100,000 well-drilled and well-equipped Volunteers marching through the streets of Dublin to assemble at College Green for the opening of the Irish parliament 'a few short months hence'.[29] When Home Rule was put on ice for the duration of the war, Redmond like many others assumed this could hardly be longer than a year. The inexorable protraction of the fighting and the receding prospect of any conclusion did more than anything else to corrode the Home Rulers' position. The escalating demand for manpower to feed Kitchener's mass armies locked Redmond into the role of recruiting sergeant, an image that would steadily undermine his public prestige. Caught up in the high-pressure British war effort, recruiting came to be the overriding priority in Irish party policy. The spontaneous gesture of solidarity became a draining commitment; the level of Irish recruitment became a kind of test of Redmondite credibility.

To begin with the test seemed to be triumphantly passed. In the early days, meetings in support of the war were immense gatherings, and the Redmondite MP Stephen Gwynn thought 'enthusiasm was unbounded'. Genuine sympathy with the suffering of Belgium meant that there was no need to work at organizing such things. 'All this time the Sinn Feiners were simply "snowed under" and were I think almost dumbfounded by what they saw around them. They held no meetings and *had no press*.'[30] In Gwynn's opinion, there were two main reasons for the gradual change that became noticeable in the spring of 1915: the realization that the war would be long, and the lack of English recognition of Ireland's contribution. Nothing could be done about the first, but the second was a real failure of policy. In February, when Sir Reginald Brade at the War Office (who cheerfully admitted 'I have no knowledge of Ireland') urged Redmond to get together with Carson to issue a joint appeal to buck up the 'distinctly languid' Irish recruitment, he was treated to an outpouring of resentment. Redmond reeled off statistics about Ireland's falling, ageing, agricultural population, and recited his offers to have the Volunteers defend Ireland, which had 'received no response either from Sir Edward Carson's friends or from the Government'. He reiterated his belief that if the two bodies of Volunteers were trusted with the defence of the country, under proper military drill and discipline, the result 'would unquestionably be that a large number would volunteer for the front'. But now there was worse: of the two Irish divisions, the 10th had been 'filled up with English', and the 16th had suffered 'various circumstances which had a chilling effect on recruiting'. The 16th's commander, General Parsons, had written a public letter asking 'the ladies of Ireland to work regimental Colours for him', but the War Office had brusquely refused to permit this imaginative gesture. A proposal for a divisional badge, simply consisting of the Irish coat of arms as it appeared on the royal arms, was also rejected. 'To this date no distinctive badge whatever has been supplied to the 16th Division', and the 'most mischievous impression' had been created that the War Office was 'hostile to the creation of a distinctly Irish Brigade or Army Corps'.[31]

There were certainly problems with the two Irish divisions. The 10th had been filled up with non-Irish drafts because it was persistently below strength. Even in the period of apparent public enthusiasm, actual recruitment, as we have seen, did not approach the UK rate. Only erratically did it reach the replacement rate for the Irish units. Explanations for this, then and since, have varied. The Inspector-General of the RIC, Sir Neville Chamberlain, struggling to reconcile his wish to believe that the Irish people were basically in favour of the war with the fact of sluggish enlistment, perhaps inevitably concluded that the explanation was simply cowardice. He managed to blame both the National Volunteers and the decline of volunteering: thus, in Galway,

the large majority of the nominal National Volunteers approve of Mr Redmond's pronouncement but only very few will enlist; a considerable falling off in drilling is due to the fear that they may be compelled to enlist for service at the front.[32]

In Queen's County (now Laois) in September 1914, the people 'regard [the war] with sympathetic interest, but more or less from a detached point of view; a powerful factor in the diminishing interest taken in drilling by the National Volunteers is the fear of being called out to serve in the war'. In King's County (Offaly), the country people were apathetic and ignorant about their responsibilities in the war; the existence of the Volunteers was 'a hindrance to recruiting'. Canon Hannay's analysis of the problem was more acute and more sombre. He saw the apathy of the Irish people in general as 'much worse than any which existed in England, because at the back of it was a vague feeling that to fight for the British Empire was a form of disloyalty to Ireland'. He argued too that speechmaking at recruiting meetings, however eloquent, was useless, because Ireland was 'less responsive to oratory than any other part of the British Isles' – a surfeit of fine speaking over a century and a half had deadened its sensibility. The problem, at root, was visceral anti-English feeling: 'smouldering, lacking public expression, but strong'.[33]

Part of the difficulty with the Irish military units was that the 10th was an Irish division in name (and in parentheses) only. It has been suggested that because the 10th Division was 'the least politicized of the three raised in Ireland', it could be thought 'the "purest" Irish response to the call of 1914'. It contained 'arguably the keenest, most willing Irish recruits, less concerned with maintaining the integrity of their pre-war Irish situation' than with getting to the front as soon as possible.[34] Its commander, Sir Bryan Mahon, was described in the divisional history as 'an Irishman without politics', but of course this meant he was a Protestant and an unthinking, not to say pig-headed conservative. In a word, he was a cavalryman. (In the Boer War he had led the flying column which had relieved Mafeking.) He naturally took a dim view of the Volunteers ('their usefulness is nil'). As his division was brought up to strength not only with Englishmen but also with drafts from the newly forming 16th, Redmond was so antagonized by the treatment of his cherished 'Irish Brigade' as to protest in public. But when it was sent into action, as part of the Gallipoli operation, he began to trumpet its ecumenical virtues, as a unit where Protestant and Catholic had 'combined for a common purpose', a symbol of Irish unity.[35] He hailed the division's landing at Suvla Bay on 6 August as 'the first time in history' that Ireland had 'put a national army in the field'.

Yet this 'turning point in the history of relations between Ireland and the Empire' was squandered by the British authorities. Beyond the vexed question of names and symbols, there was the simple matter of information. Irish people knew as little of the war as the British, maybe less; and the British army was dedicated to ensuring that this situation continued. The extraordinarily comprehensive system of military censorship was justified in the name of security, but went far beyond its requirements. Kitchener's ban on photography at the front sacrificed any possibility of conveying the reality of war to civilians, and if there was some method in this, it was surely madness to suppress reporting of Irish participation in gruelling military actions like Suvla. The reports that seeped out were damagingly negative. (Redmond fulminated privately of the 10th Division landing, 'Father Murphy actually heard the Colonel of one of our Battalions asking a stretcher-bearer if he had any idea where the enemy was!') The official silence was corrosive. Katharine Tynan's lament as 'blow after blow fell day after day on one's heart' with the growing casualty lists, hinted at the alienation of the key Home Rule constituency, the professional classes; 'For the first time came bitterness, for we felt that their lives had been thrown away and their heroism had gone unrecognised.'[36] The British army could presume much upon the tolerance of British opinion, but to do the same in Ireland was not safe.

The precise motives of those who enlisted are impossible to establish with any certainty. At the time, nobody seems to have asked; and it may be that Redmond's emphasis on recognition was not as crucial as he maintained. Recent historical research suggests that 'the decision to enlist in Ireland, both before and during the war, was influenced more by economic than political considerations', though one of the most perceptive researchers insists that 'this great collective sacrifice of life, and comfort, cannot be understood through the logic of economic rationality'. Wartime recruitment patterns remained remarkably similar to those before the war – 'tradition-bound and sporadic', as one local study puts it. The conclusion that the sluggishness of enlistment in much of Ireland 'had more to do with inadequate market research than political alienation' indicates that anti-recruiting activity may have been less significant than administrative inefficiency.[37]

From the autumn of 1915, Irish enlistment fell far below the 1,100 recruits needed each week to maintain the Irish battalions' reserves. Under pressure from Kitchener, Dublin Castle began to agonize over the figures (which were treated as confidential information, carefully kept away from the press) to establish the real total of single men who had not yet joined the forces. Estimating, on the basis of the 1911 census, that there had been 640,000 men of military age (475,000 of them unmarried) in Ireland in 1914, Dublin Castle suggested that 'after necessary deductions' there were about 100,000 men 'really available'. A series of recruiting drives had employed concentrated publicity techniques, sometimes to good but transient effect. By the beginning of February 1916 (when the weekly total fell to 314) the Under-Secretary was reduced to consulting the writer and mystic Æ (George Russell) about the kind of literature 'Ireland should be fed to secure an improvement in the recruiting atmosphere'. His office was frankly 'depressed' by their failure to stimulate the 'trickle' of recruits. They urged the military authorities to understand 'the difficulties of making an impression on a scattered population of conservative tendencies'.[38] Redmond's lieutenant, Stephen Gwynn, was more embittered. During the summer, he said, recruiting meetings had often been addressed by Protestant gentry whose own sons were still at home, and worse still by military speakers who more or less openly threatened their audiences. These men, not the Sinn Feiners, were the first to flourish the spectre of conscription – the issue which would destroy both the Irish Parliamentary Party and, in the long run, the British government in Ireland.

By the autumn of 1915, the threat of conscription was becoming an obsessional topic in rural Ireland. In this increasingly neurotic atmosphere, a damaging sequence of events set in train the unravelling of the Irish Party's long-established political control. At the centre of this process was the Irish Catholic Church. For the first year of the war, the clergy played a fairly positive part in the war effort; the police concluded at the end of 1914 that 'the Catholic Clergy throughout the country in general supported the policy of the Irish Parliamentary Party in relation to the war and recruiting'. One or two Catholic bishops showed an almost Anglican enthusiasm. There were some problems, though: 'recruiting advertisements on the theme "Save Catholic Belgium" raised the awkward issue of which group of belligerents was more deserving of Catholic sympathies on religious grounds'.[39] To make the issue more acute, the fighting had hardly begun before reports arrived of how the French military hospital authorities had required a wounded Irish soldier who had asked for a priest to sign a declaration (in French) that he was a Catholic and expressly demanded the sacraments. This aggravated raw Catholic memories of French republican anti-clericalism, and the bishops protested against 'this miserable French device'. French anti-clericalism was one of the objections raised by the odd few clergy who spoke publicly against participation in the war. The police carefully monitored these, and though their number doubled between late 1914 and late 1915, it remained relatively small (fifty-five individuals during 1915).[40] But when a few of the higher clergy began to speak out, the problem was dramatically enlarged. In July 1915, Cardinal Logue himself told an audience at an industrial exhibition in Dundalk that 'the government that killed their Irish industries, and forced the people to emigrate, were looking out for men to fight for them, and the men were not there to be got'. This combative line was greeted with cheers.[41]

On 28 July Pope Benedict XV's encyclical *Allorche fummo* denounced the war as futile and called on Christians to make peace. On the carefully chosen date of 4 August, the anniversary of Britain's declaration of war, Bishop Edward O'Dwyer of Limerick wrote to Redmond, declaring that 'the prolongation of this war for one hour beyond what is absolutely necessary is a crime against God and humanity'. He called on him as a 'Catholic Irishman' who 'by your wise and upright statesmanship before this disastrous war, deserved

well of your country', to follow the Pope's 'noble and Christlike proposal'. This initiative presented Redmond with an awkward dilemma.
Refusal would emphasize his 'recruiting sergeant' image at a time
when popular alienation from the war was growing – magnified
inevitably by these clerical interventions. Acceptance, however, would
play into Unionist hands by confirming the old 'Rome Rule' charge.
Redmond replied rather cursorily to the bishop's extensive argument
(ignoring his point about the economic damage caused by the war),
blaming the continuation of the war on German ambitions. If he was
at all worried by this clerical shot across his bows, he gave no sign of
it in November when a minor crisis brewed up at Liverpool docks,
where some 700 Irishmen were trying to take ship for America. This
first wave of conscription refugees was patriotically held back by the
Cunard and White Star lines, who refused to embark men they
thought should be at the front. A frisson of outrage ran through
Ireland. Redmond's effort to reassure the country that these ignorant
westerners' fear of conscription was groundless was torpedoed by his
concluding remark that it was 'very cowardly of them to try to emigrate'. This sentence may be regarded as the beginning of the end of
Redmond's political career.[42]

Bishop O'Dwyer's riposte was explosive. In a letter published in a
number of provincial papers (where it escaped the censorship imposed
in Dublin) on 11 November he powerfully fused human sympathy for
the 'poor emigrant lads' with a far-reaching political critique of
Redmondism. His first register was emotional: the treatment of 'poor
Connaught peasants' who wanted only to be left 'to till their potato
gardens in peace' should 'make any Irishman's blood boil with anger'.
Then he asserted in more political terms than any clergyman had so
far done that the war was nothing to do with them.

Their blood is not stirred by memories of Kossovo, and they have no burning desire to die for Serbia . . . Their crime is that they are not ready to die
for England. Why should they? What have they or their forebears ever got
from England that they should die for her?

Finally, he indicted Redmond directly as having betrayed his responsibility as national leader. 'In all the shame and humiliation of this dis-
graceful episode, what angers most is that there is no one, not even one

of their own countrymen to stand up and defend them.' And in a killer punch, he disputed even Redmond's claim to have achieved Home Rule: 'any intelligent Irishman' would see it as only 'a simulacrum of Home Rule, with an express notice that it is never to come into operation'.[43]

This really was a lethal blow, and it seems was intended as such. O'Dwyer's letter rapidly became an icon of separatist nationalism, circulated by handbills across the country. As J. J. ('Ginger') O'Connell, then rising to prominence as a member of the Volunteer staff, noted, it was a propaganda gift – 'a convenient length, and in the Bishop's customary manly and vigorous fashion': it 'had a terrific demand'.[44] By the end of the year the police had found copies in seventeen counties, and Dublin Castle had given up on the idea of prosecuting those who quoted it. The administration was reduced to hoping that in time the bishop's influence would wane. This was doubtful. Bishop Fogarty of Killaloe may have exaggerated when he wrote to O'Dwyer, 'the whole body of the people have rallied to you and your letter on the Emigrants. It has opened their eyes.' Anti-British clergy remained a small minority. But something far-reaching was happening.

Almost as soon as the split began to open up in September 1914, the authorities took to calling the breakaway group 'Sinn Fein' Volunteers. This was, on the face of things, a little odd, since Sinn Féin had played no direct part in the Volunteer movement, and MacNeill himself was not identified with Sinn Féin. In terms of doctrine, the two groups might have looked even further apart, since Sinn Féin was founded on the principle of passive rather than armed resistance. Arthur Griffith himself took at most a tangential interest in the Volunteers (though he had turned up in ordinary Volunteer uniform for the Howth gun-running); when the Volunteers were founded he insisted that in the circumstances 'we must work through the force of public opinion rather than through force of arms'.[45] But other 'Sinn Feiners' (as the bilingual popular label had it) were more closely involved. Enterprising IRB leaders were happy to use Sinn Féin as a vehicle for separatist activity. Hobson's brilliant pamphlet *Defensive Warfare*, published under the banner of Sinn Féin, was entirely compatible with Volunteer doctrine as it was set out in early 1914. The police label for the minority Irish Volunteers after October 1914 was not unperceptive. Most nationalists outside the party fold probably thought of themselves as in some sense 'Sinn Feiners'. The sad fact, from the separatist point of view, was that there were so few dedicated activists that they could hardly afford not to work together. Sinn Féin in 1915, indeed, was at a low ebb.

Griffith's key activity, journalism, was seriously constricted by the war. After a few anti-war issues, his paper *Sinn Féin* was placed under distribution restrictions, and in November it was closed down, along with *Irish Freedom*, the *Irish Worker*, and Terence MacSwiney's journal *Fianna Fáil*. Griffith naturally responded by launching another journal, and then another – so the short-lived *Eire-Ireland* and *Scissors and Paste* (a sardonic nod to the censor) both went the same way, to be followed by *Nationality* which appeared early in 1915.[46] Griffith's combative nature showed through all this, but even though British intelligence estimated the real circulation of *Nationality* at 8,000 rather than its nominal 4,500, his appeal remained to a minority. Still more restricted, though more fiercely separatist, was the little weekly *The Spark* (a single folded sheet), edited by Sean Doyle, launched in February 1915. This combined high-minded tracts by Pearse with virulent gutter-press scandal-mongering about the party and the Castle administration. Perhaps the most notable new journal of 1915, though, was produced by the only separatist group that could be said to be definitely outside the Sinn Féin umbrella – James Connolly's *Workers' Republic*, launched at the end of May. From the start it tirelessly urged not just separatism but revolution, in terms that middle-class nationalists found distinctly unsettling. Reading its articles 'of a rather advanced revolutionary character', Ginger O'Connell 'saw danger ahead on those lines'. He was certainly not alone in this.[47]

With Sinn Féin in the doldrums, the Irish Volunteers also struggled to rebuild their organization after the split. With never more than six paid full-time organizers – notably Robert Monteith in Limerick, Liam Mellows in Galway, and Ernest Blythe in Kerry – and in many places a persistent public hostility, the process was painfully slow. In Limerick, for instance, the small Volunteer contingent was pelted with garbage when it paraded before Pearse himself in May 1915. In Tipperary the police could see no sign of Volunteer activity throughout the year.[48] Seán Moylan recollected that in north Cork a Volunteer organiser, Tom McCarthy, arrived from Dublin and stayed a few months. He worked hard but he had the difficult task of convincing a people who, like myself, had never dreamt of fight, of the need or use of a Volunteer organisation, and his success was not great.[49]

'The work of an organizer', O'Connell noted,

was varied and not at all easy. It comprised getting together a group of men to form the nucleus of a corps, bringing this group into contact with headquarters, giving preliminary instruction, getting particulars of arma- ment, and generally doing a hundred and one jobs – and incidentally give the local RIC something to do besides read the newspapers and repair bicycle punctures.

O'Connell himself, the IV Director of Training, ran training camps and toured the country inspecting local formations. Organizers such as Mellows cycled astonishing distances in all weathers to gee up their constituencies. (The revolutionary role of the Irish-made 'Lucania' bicycle – a particular boon to Irish-Irelanders trying to boycott British imports – has not yet been fully appreciated.) In areas which could not be provided with organizers, and where units were slow to form, indi- vidual Volunteers were urged to get on their bikes and get together. 'Cyclists can rapidly concentrate on a given centre'; and they were encouragingly told that 'in Ireland cyclists can to a large extent replace cavalry' for scouting and outpost duty.[50]

Mellows faced particular difficulties in the winter of 1914–15, as an outsider and a townsman, in organizing a deeply rural area histor- ically embroiled in the – still ongoing – land conflict.[51] By the spring he was making some headway, but in July, along with Blythe, and Herbert Pim and Denis McCullough, he was served an expulsion order under the Defence of the Realm Act. (This required them to move to an approved place of residence in Britain.) As the *Irish Volunteer* fumed, Birrell had become 'the first English governor of Ireland since Oliver Cromwell who has assumed the power to trans- port Irishmen out of Ireland without going through the hypocritical sham of a judicial trial'. Alf Monahan took over from Mellows, and Blythe was replaced by Desmond FitzGerald; but Monaghan in turn was arrested in Belfast in October. These were real setbacks to the organization; the only consolation was that the expulsion orders were deeply unpopular, and produced a surge of public support for the Volunteers. In any case, in O'Connell's view training was more of a problem than organization. 'Any decent corps should organize its own neighbourhood', but the departure of the reservists in autumn 1914 had left a gap in the training programme that could not be closed. For this reason, some of the Volunteer leadership, quoting the analogy of the Boer commandos, were in favour of dropping formal military drill, and concentrating on shooting and fieldcraft. Here a significant difference of perspective began to appear. O'Connell disputed the Boer analogy, and 'placed no reliance whatsoever on untrained mass-enthusiasm'. He thought that while only a few drill movements should be prescribed, those few should be perfected.

Another persistent problem was that 'military rifles were impossible to get for love or money', but because of the almost superstitious awe in which they were held, men had no confidence in substitutes – though O'Connell himself, backed up by O'Rahilly, tried to argue that shotguns could be just as effective in the kind of conflict that was likely to occur. The hardest problem of all to overcome, O'Connell argued, was that very few IV officers were prepared to impose rigid discipline. Its root cause was the democratic way the movement had evolved. When Volunteer companies elected their officers, they 'commonly selected someone because he was popular or distinguished in some sphere or other'. Very often it was sport: unsurprisingly there was a close match between GAA and Volunteer captains, but even the best of these preferred sport to military training. 'It was a fact that the Volunteers did not receive from the GAA the help that they expected.'[52] Only the Fianna boys selected officers 'with the touch of iron essential for leadership', O'Connell thought. A desire for popularity is a crippling handicap in a military commander, and this defect was never really overcome. A uniform standard of command and training was never achieved. In fact, O'Connell thought that as time passed the divergence between the Dublin and provincial units became ever greater. The effect of this would be all too obvious in 1916.

But whatever the technical military weaknesses of the Volunteer movement, its political situation undoubtedly began to improve towards the end of 1915. Apart from drilling and training, its prime activity was campaigning against recruitment into the British forces, and this oppositional stance became noticeably less unpopular than it had been in the early months of the war. Resistance to conscription radicalized many like the champion Dublin hurler Harry Boland, a tailor's cutter whose first 'public intrusion into politics beyond the GAA' took place when he led a call for an anti-conscription conference at the Dublin Workingmen's Club and Total Abstinence Association.[53] A major watershed in public attitudes was the funeral of the irreconcilable Fenian terrorist exile O'Donovan Rossa in Dublin in August. This was the biggest nationalist manifestation since the funeral of Parnell, and Volunteers from all over the country assembled in Dublin. Even the moribund Mayo Volunteers, for instance, were revived by the heady experience of seeing the 'uniformed and armed parade'.[54] Besides providing an imposing demonstration, it set the Volunteers at the centre of an evolution in which it became clear that the Catholic clergy were ready to be identified with a large-scale celebration of the physical-force idea.

The shift in atmosphere and confidence in the autumn of 1915 is registered in a surviving fragment of the diary of Terence MacSwiney, second-in-command of the Cork brigade, who was appointed a full-time organizer in October. The situation in Cork was for a long time unpromising. One of the more active companies, at Lyre, started in August with about twenty men, and managed to add ten more by the end of the year. 'Local feeling was generally hostile or indifferent.'[55] In October the serious, anxious MacSwiney was still clutching at straws of comfort, such as the local Volunteer who 'astonished me by reciting a long passage from Davis on the right to bear arms – a good omen'. On the nineteenth he had extensive conversations at Derrincerrin in Kerry, noting that 'all men around would be against conscription – but as in other places not alive to danger. Never see daily papers and know nothing of what happens . . .' At the end of November, however, the Volunteers mounted a big parade in Cork city, with some 1,500 turning out, and MacSwiney exulted, 'sensational success. We are making history.'[56]

Even the police began reluctantly to admit that the 'Sinn Fein Volunteers' were at last making progress. Although they had failed to establish units in a number of counties, such as Carlow, Leitrim,

Longford and Sligo (though here the police surprisingly identified 237 'Sinn Feiners' within the INV), and were very weak in Roscommon, in the southern and western counties they were at least holding steady, and often growing – in marked contrast to the moribund National Volunteers. In the East Riding of Galway, for example, the police thought that 'a very large proportion of the people disapproved of the policy of the Sinn Fein party; but they were afraid to show their disapproval, having no confidence in either the will or the power of the Government to protect them'. If true, this was an ominous development indeed. In addition, the IV 'though small as regards membership, having only 292 at the end of the year, gained considerable ground owing to the activity of William Mellowes and local suspects'. In the West Riding, three branches of the INV 'went over in a body to the Irish Volunteers' in November. Sinn Féin ideas were 'spreading' in Tipperary; in Limerick the IV were 'very active' towards the end of the year, and 'a new movement was started to form branches in the Newcastle West and Abbeyfeale districts under the cloak of the Gaelic League by suspect Ernest Blythe'. In Cork the 'Sinn Fein Volunteers . . . began to assume an importance altogether out of proportion to their numbers.' Still, the Inspector-General of the RIC clung to the comforting notion that Sinn Féin was harmless because its 'prominent men are persons of no influence' in the traditional sense.[57]

The authorities' assessment of the threat represented by the Volunteers was not entirely complacent. At the beginning of the year, indeed, Dublin Castle had sounded a very serious warning.

It may without exaggeration be said that in the personnel of its Committee, in its Declaration of Policy, in the utterances of its leading representatives, in its opposition to the efforts of Mr Redmond to bring Ireland into line at the present National Crisis, and in its crusade against enlistment in the Army, the Irish Volunteer organization has shewn itself to be disloyal and seditious, and revolutionary if the means and opportunity were at hand.[58]

These were the accents of Major Ivor H. Price, Ll.D., a former RIC County Inspector who had been appointed by the War Office at the outbreak of the war as Intelligence Officer to Irish Command. Price carried prime responsibility for implementing the Irish part of the wartime censorship regime, the most systematic ever witnessed in

Britain. 'England's difficulty' here led directly to a dramatic increase in the power and activity of the state. But Price laboured under several handicaps, quite apart from his own limitations. Some were general: for instance, although the decision to construct a surveillance system was taken before the war, and the powers specified in the War Office's 1914 'War Book', even the chief press censor in England seems to have been unaware of this – the book was 'secretly buried in a safe belonging to another branch of the General Staff', and not found until after the end of the war.[59] Some were specific to Ireland. It is a striking fact that whereas MI5's postal censorship bureau in Britain was 1,453 strong by the end of 1915, its Irish counterparts in Belfast and Dublin consisted of five men each. Given that some 192 million letters were mailed in Ireland in 1914–15, and that, in late 1915, seventy-one censorship warrants were in force, it is not surprising that Price continually complained of overwork. It is not clear whether he was refused more staff, or why Ireland seems to have had such a low priority in the overall system.

Moreover Price, unlike MI5, interpreted his remit as the monitoring of all potentially subversive nationalist opinion, not just communication with the enemy. In technical terms this was extremely difficult, especially in Dublin where the mails were amazingly fast – routinely achieving same-day delivery. In spite of this, Price's system delivered a lot of information – almost too much, and he was driven at one point to sample his suspects' writing less frequently. 'A list of men and women under censorship in December 1915', one historian has written, 'reads like a *Who's Who* of advanced nationalism.'[60] But there were one or two important exceptions, most notably Pearse himself. As would become clear after the rebellion, Price had a very eccentric idea of the internal power structure of the 'Sinn Fein Volunteers', in spite of all the millions of words he had read.

The government's approach to press censorship also troubled Major Price. He was convinced that 'any man who knows Ireland knows that printed matter has a great deal of influence'. The Chief Secretary, however, took the opposite view. Birrell consistently responded to all demands for the prosecution or suppression of newspapers with a blithe dismissal of such rags as Griffith's *Scissors and Paste* as 'not worth powder and shot'. Although he sometimes suspected that 'the fatal disease' was 'there, deep buried in certain Irishmen and women', and that nothing would enlarge or reduce it, he also seems to have convinced himself that there was a steady (if painfully slow) growth of 'loyalty', which would be reversed if the government paid too much attention to 'speeches made by crack-brained priests and other enthusiasts'. He usually gave way in the end, because '*action* is forced on us by the feeling in England' and also by 'the danger of a real street row and sham rebellion in Dublin'.[61] In the process he worried his loyal, conscientious, workaholic Under-Secretary, Sir Matthew Nathan. Nathan had taken up his post shortly after the outbreak of war, having had no previous knowledge of Ireland (in itself an apposite comment on the government's attitude to Irish affairs). He was on a steep learning curve, but within two months he could tell Birrell that he was already tired of hearing the Sinn Feiners called 'an insignificant minority'. He also agreed with Price's view of the press: 'from my short experience of this country I believe Irishmen *are* affected by what they read and hear probably more than more phlegmatic peoples'. Sinn Féin's 'cleverly worded and insidiously scattered papers spread all over the country, and in the distribution of leaflets they and their American allies have the field practically to themselves'.

But Nathan was too loyal to his chief. He absorbed Birrell's deep ambivalence about the balance between suppression and provocation. In response to one military demand to shut down a 'seditious' newspaper, he argued that

the seizure of the printer's plant would probably be followed by a demonstration of armed Volunteers in Phoenix Park, violent speeches and all the other troublesome manifestations of ill-feeling which I am so anxious to avoid while the conscription question is still pending.

Like Birrell he saw his overriding task as being to keep the situation as quiet as possible, to prepare the way for the constitutional nationalists to take over when Home Rule was finally implemented.[62] Their caution often reflected the advice of IPP leaders such as Dillon himself, though Nathan had a sharper sense than Birrell of how vulnerable the Redmondite position was becoming. He noted perceptively as he watched the preparations for the Rossa funeral, 'I have an uncomfortable feeling that the Nationalists are losing ground to the Sinn Feiners and that this demonstration is hastening the movement.' A few weeks later he concluded that Redmond 'has been honestly Imperial in the war, but by going as far as he has done he has lost his position in the country'.[63]

Nathan had also realized quite soon that 'a good number of the lower officials' in government service were Sinn Feiners – 'and in this respect the Post Office has a bad pre-eminence'. A notable example was Patrick Sarsfield O'Hegarty, who combined the postmastership at Queenstown Co. Cork with presidency of the Munster IRB and membership of the Supreme Council. (Another was Austin Stack, the income-tax collector for Dingle and Caherciveen in Co. Kerry, also an IRB stalwart and Volunteer captain, who was sacked for being 'an advanced GAA man and pro-German'.) According to the head of the Irish Post Office, A. H. Norway, 'a high officer called on me to say that Hegarty must not remain at Queenstown, or indeed in Ireland', because he had been 'in very recent communication' with the German ambassador. When Norway acted to remove him to England, however, he ran into sharp resistance from the Post Office chiefs in London who had worked with O'Hegarty and 'were most indignant that any one could doubt his loyalty'.[64] This was of a piece with the 'light complacency' that Norway found everywhere about the danger of Irish subversion. He was one of those Englishmen with the simple conviction that 'the truth about the Irish is that they appreciate strength, despise weakness, and desire to be governed firmly and justly'. When he arrived in Ireland he had been alarmed to hear about possible IRB penetration of the postal service, but his efforts to find out more about the organization had met with bland reassurances from the police that it 'might be regarded as dormant, and in fact negligible'. He found Nathan 'not discerning, nor resolute'; the Under-Secretary once revealingly asked 'What is the use of contending against the stream of tendency?' When Norway protested 'That is fatalism', Nathan replied 'No, it is good sense.' Norway percipiently noted that Nathan's 'conception of loyalty was not to tell his political chief when he thought him wrong, but to help him in his policy'. In this he acted like a soldier rather than a top civil servant.[65]

Even Birrell was (or claimed to be) frustrated by another instance of the way Ireland was governed according to British public opinion. The ostensibly fearsome Defence of the Realm Act had brought in a kind of statutory martial law – not unlike earlier Irish Insurrection Acts – which offered the authorities the welcome prospect of trial without jury. (Irish juries were famously unwilling to convict in 'political' cases.) In March 1915, however, Lord Parmoor's amendment guaranteed a civil trial to British citizens for most breaches of the Defence of the Realm Regulations.[66] After this, prosecutions for serious offences under DORA in Ireland practically broke down. Major Price protested that 'in a capital offence there was no chance of conviction; it was useless to try a man except summarily, when possibly he might get six months' imprisonment'. Trial by local courts became farcical: in one recent trial by Cork magistrates, for example, 'the evidence was clear and absolutely plain, but the majority dismissed it'.[67] The attempt to use DORA powers to deport subversives was likewise hampered by deference to the 'Nationalist Press', which 'said it was a monstrous thing to turn any man out of Ireland'; as a result, 'we were a very long time before we attempted to turn out four men'. And only two of these were actually deported. England's difficulty was not the war, but the opposite: the difficulty of applying war measures in face of entrenched liberal traditions.

4

Ireland's Opportunity

If the German offensive timed for May comes off, the English
will be so much occupied that it is possible we could hold out
one way or another for anything up to three months. At the
end of that time the English would have to make peace.

Joseph Plunkett

The outbreak of war found the advocates of insurrection in a difficult
position. After a success unparalleled since the early days of
Fenianism, they faced losing control of the militia which had been
almost in their grasp. In mid-July 1914 Patrick Pearse gloomily
explained to Joe McGarrity in America how serious the Redmondite
takeover of the Volunteers was becoming for the IRB. They had feared
that Redmond would paralyse the arming of the Volunteers; now it
was clear that he wanted to arm them, but for the wrong reasons –
'not against England, but against the Orangemen'. The Volunteers
risked being turned into a sectarian militia. The Redmond nominees
on the committee were urging that 'those of us in the south and west
who have guns should send them north for use by the Catholics there
to defend themselves when the "massacre" breaks out. The whole
tone of the movement has changed.' The Unionists were armed, the
Redmondites were arming, but the Nationalists ('Sinn Feiners and
Separatists') remained unarmed. As Pearse wryly remarked, 'it will be
the irony of ironies if this movement comes and goes and leaves us –
the physical force men! – the only unarmed group in the country'.
What he wanted was guns: 'at least 1,000 to start with'.[1]

A month later the situation had become critical, he believed. Public enthusiasm for the war was dismayingly visible; in a sharply poignant betrayal, troops were even being played to the railway stations by Irish Volunteer bands, some of them bearing the name of Emmet himself.[2] Pearse still believed that the Volunteers 'are sound, especially in Dublin. We could at any moment rally the best of them to our support by a *coup d'état*; and rally the whole country if the *coup d'état* were successful. But a *coup d'état* while the men are still unarmed is unthinkable.' The guns they had got at Howth and Kilcool had mostly been 'stolen' by the Redmondites, he told McGarrity; only 400–500 were left in IV hands. But in any case they were little use – single-shot Mausers of 'a rather antiquated pattern' and large calibre – 'much inferior to the British service rifle and even to those which Carson's men have'. (The last assertion was debatable, but was well calculated to rile McGarrity.) Worse still, the ammunition O'Rahilly had bought had turned out to be 'useless' – explosive bullets 'which are against the rules of civilised war'. Once more he called on the Americans to send modern weapons, Springfield or 7mm Mauser rifles, 'at once and on a large scale'. He dangled before McGarrity the ultimate Fenian dream: 'a supreme moment for Ireland may be at hand'.[3]

Pearse's concern with technical military questions was a clear indication of the direction he was now taking. For him, an IRB man of less than a year's standing, and with no previous military experience or interest, it was the first year of world war that made him a 'physical-force man'. It pitched him to a position of pre-eminence in the command structure of the Irish Volunteers, and in the Supreme Council of the IRB. Most remarkably, it was to be Pearse, rather than the Fenian veteran Tom Clarke, who became President of the Irish Republic declared in April 1916.[4] In the process he also, incidentally, faced personal and professional disaster as St Enda's went to the verge of bankruptcy. The school, and Pearse's reputation, was saved by McGarrity and the Irish-American Fenians. But they still needed some convincing that Pearse had truly embraced separatism.

When he was demanding guns in August 1914, it was still for essentially defensive, reactive purposes. In October, after the split, he argued that the pared-down IV was 'infinitely more valuable' than the previous 'unwieldy, loosely-held-together mixum-gatherum force'. With some 150 companies, a 'small, compact, perfectly-disciplined, determinedly *separatist* force' would be 'ready to *act* with tremendous effect if the war brings us the moment' – and if only America would supply the guns. 'The spirit of our Dublin men is wonderful. They would rise tomorrow if we gave the word.' Five things, he said, could precipitate a crisis – '*the* crisis': a German invasion, the imposition of a Militia Ballot or conscription, a food shortage, an attempt to disarm the IV, or an attempt to arrest their leaders. 'If the chance comes and goes, it will in all probability have gone forever, certainly for our lifetime.'[5]

As his sense of urgency intensified, his language grew more heated. In November, at a Thomas Davis commemoration meeting (held outside rather than inside Trinity College because the Provost had banned it on the grounds that the speakers included 'a man called Pearse' – as well as W. B. Yeats) a new note appeared: Pearse exalted John Mitchel above Davis. The point, as Yeats noted, was that whereas Davis preached love of Ireland, Mitchel preached hatred of England.[6] The most violent – verbally – of the Young Irelanders in the 1840s, Mitchel had foreshadowed one of Pearse's key phrases when he wrote that there were 'far worse things going on than bloodshed'. Pearse went on to give some substance to his rhetorical flourish about 'rising tomorrow'. He drew up a plan, echoing Hobson's *Defensive Warfare* (in fact Hobson was probably its instigator) for a sequence of resistance activities building up into guerrilla warfare. In December this literary effort – and some determined personal lobbying – secured him the job of Director of Military Organization in the newly constructed IV 'headquarters staff'. This placed him alongside MacNeill as Chief of Staff, Hobson as Quartermaster General, O'Rahilly as Director of Arms, Joseph Plunkett as Director of Military Operations, and Thomas MacDonagh as Director of Training. (Eamonn Ceannt was added in late 1915 as Director of Communications, and Ginger O'Connell as Chief of Inspection).[7] His qualifications for the post were slender enough, but he had acquired a pivotal role, enabling him to place IRB men in key positions throughout the Volunteer organization. It also greatly increased his appeal to the American Fenians, and later in the summer of 1915 he used this appeal to save himself and his school from bankruptcy.[8]

The scheme of organization that he produced was modelled, like his own title, on British military practice, with one nominal difference that would serve to express Irish distinctness: the rank of colonel was replaced by the Teutonic-sounding 'commandant'.[9] Although the formal military organization was possibly less appropriate to the slender IV forces than it had been to the original Volunteer movement, in Dublin the notion of a brigade was not entirely absurd. The four Dublin city battalions, and the fifth in northern county Dublin, were substantial and reliable. Training and parades were well attended. The 1st was commanded by Edward Daly, Tom Clarke's brother-in-law, the 2nd by Thomas MacDonagh. The 3rd was given to Eamon de Valera, surprisingly perhaps, since he was not in the IRB. (He seems not to have joined until MacDonagh later appointed him Brigade Adjutant.) But Pearse took the precaution of subjecting him to a terse interview, to establish de Valera's readiness to obey orders without question. Eamonn Ceannt took over the 4th Battalion. Pearse himself, Plunkett, O'Rahilly and Hobson became 'commandants on the headquarters staff'. Pearse immediately assembled the four battalion commanders to discuss the feasibility of an insurrection the following September, on the basis of a plan prepared by an Advisory Committee. Finally, he put MacDonagh in overall command of the Brigade.

Pearse's determination to stage an insurrection during the war was already fixed. He believed, or persuaded himself, that the new Volunteer force was ready to join him in it. Whether he was right in this became an issue to be debated long into the future, but he was certainly not alone. On 9 September a rather odd meeting of separatists called by Tom Clarke, including some who were not in the IRB or the Volunteers, resolved to expand the IV, ICA, Fianna and Cumann na mBan, to assist a German invasion if it were launched in support of Irish independence, and to resist any attempt to disarm the Volunteers. More controversially, it reportedly decided to stage a rebellion before the end of the war, with the object of securing Ireland's right to a place at the peace conference. (This notion was quite widely accepted, and there were of course many small European national groups with the same aspiration. None of the others, though, had one of the leading Allied powers to block their way.)[10] This stratagem was only likely to work if Britain was defeated in the war.

But the majority of the Volunteer Executive remained explicitly opposed to armed action except in self-defence. MacNeill himself,

Hobson and O'Rahilly had made their positions clear. Hobson grounded his argument on the IRB's own constitution, as revised after the 1866–7 setback, which required that insurrection should have popular support. He maintained that all those he had sworn into the organization since 1906 had known this. Still, even Hobson's energetic efforts could not eliminate the appeal of the old republican nostrum, 'England's difficulty is Ireland's opportunity'. (Indeed, even Hobson himself veered once in 1915 into advocacy of insurrection, at least according to police reporters.) Immediately after the outbreak of war, the Supreme Council held one of its rare meetings and resolved in general terms to mount a rebellion, but the enthusiasts for insurrection – pre-eminently Tom Clarke and Seán MacDermott – were faced with the same problem as Pearse. They needed to keep their plans secret from their own colleagues, even those on the smaller IRB Executive (the Supreme Council's standing body) who, like Denis McCullough, accepted Hobson's interpretation of the Brotherhood's constitution. In early May 1915, MacDermott met one of the Supreme Council's representatives for England, P. S. O'Hegarty, in Liverpool, and told him that a military plan for a rising in Dublin had been drawn up. Shortly afterwards, MacDermott was arrested under the Defence of the Realm Act at Tuam, Co. Galway, where he was sentenced to four months' imprisonment with hard labour. It seems to have been Diarmuid Lynch, who stood in for him as secretary of the Executive, who proposed the establishment of a small planning committee to elaborate the plan. He felt that the 'Advisory Committee' which had drawn up the Dublin plan was too large for security. (And too big for IRB control – Le Roux's well-informed biography of Tom Clarke calls it a committee of the Volunteers rather than the IRB.) At the end of May a much smaller IRB 'military committee' was established: just three men to start with – Pearse, Plunkett and Eamonn Ceannt.[11]

This little group kept, or at any rate left, no written records. It did not really function as a committee, since the plan it drew up was never shown to the Supreme Council. (Lynch himself never saw either the Advisory Committee's plan, or the later version, though battalion commanders were clearly briefed on their part of it at an early stage.) We have only a hazy idea of how frequently it met. In September, however, it was enlarged to include Tom Clarke and the newly released

MacDermott. In January 1916 Connolly joined it, and finally in April MacDonagh was co-opted, bringing its membership to seven. (At some stage it came to be called the 'military council' – this may have happened retrospectively, when the IRB constitution was revised yet again in 1917 to include a military council.) Its planning procedure seems to have been simply to adopt a plan which Plunkett had worked out some time before. Whether, and how, the underlying logic of that plan was discussed, only its members knew. How far the plan extended beyond the original Dublin version to incorporate country-wide action has, ever since, been a matter for speculation. According to its penultimate recruit, James Connolly, only three copies of the final insurrection plan were made, and none of them survived. Tantalizingly, the Wexford RIC captured during Easter Week an 'old passbook' which they said contained a pencil copy of the plan.[12] It was produced at a local court-martial, but has never subsequently reappeared. Could it indeed have been one of the three copies, or did it indicate that there were more? This is one of the ways in which the decision to plan in secrecy produced problems, not just for the historian, but for the prospect of a successful rising.

Although we have no idea why Plunkett's ideas were so readily accepted, we can be fairly sure that they were dominant. Where did they come from? Plunkett had so far been even less in the public eye than Pearse and the other 'Sinn Feiners'. The son of a papal count, descendant of the Irish saint Oliver Plunkett, he was a Catholic poet of a deep dye; and an eccentric of the kind that the best families generate. His own creative work was suffused with his fascination with St John of the Cross and St Catherine of Siena, but he also played a more secular role as editor of the sixpenny literary monthly *Irish Review* between 1911 and 1914 – another of the journals snuffed out by the war. Its contributors included James Connolly, Arthur Griffith, W. B. Yeats, and Sir Roger Casement, as well as Thomas MacDonagh (Plunkett's tutor in the Irish language) and Plunkett himself, who wrote on 'obscurity in poetry'. Politically, he started out (like MacDonagh) as a Home Ruler – an adherent of the Young Ireland Branch of the Parliamentary Party, the ginger group centred around Thomas Kettle. All this changed at the end of 1913. Volunteering became the transformative experience of Plunkett's life. He gradually turned the *Irish Review* into the unofficial IV organ (a more interesting read than the *Irish Volunteer* itself), and when it sank he noted in his final editorial that 'our entire staff has for some time past been working full time and overtime (if such a thing is possible) in the Irish Volunteer organisation'. When Mrs Sidney Czira (the sister of his fiancée Grace Gifford, who wrote as 'John Brennan', and was secretary of the New York Cumann na mBan) met him in New York in 1915 she thought that this once 'taciturn, reserved' man now seemed outgoing and happy. He told her 'I am a different man since joining the Irish Volunteers.'[13]

When did Plunkett start planning the seizure of Dublin? And why? The answer to this seems to lie in a fusion of historical and theoretical thinking. As we have seen, Pearse, O'Rahilly and others drew from their persistent, indeed obsessive study of Emmet's abortive rising the belief that the capital city must be the epicentre of any future armed action. As the Volunteer movement grew in mid-1914, the idea of large-scale open fighting began to seem possible. But was it feasible to seize such a city with the shrunken forces of the post-split Volunteers? Here military theorists, in particular the high priest of modern military thought, Clausewitz, provided real encouragement. Despite his admiration for the strategic boldness of Napoleon, Clausewitz demonstrated at length that, in tactical terms, the defender was in a significantly stronger posture than the attacker. The development of rifled weapons since his time had only – as the Boer War, among others, had dramatically demonstrated – increased this defensive advantage. The defensive posture also offered a better chance of keeping the inexperienced Volunteers under control, and possibly also the moral advantage of forcing the enemy to fire the first shots (assuming that the defensive positions could be seized without violence).[14] Plunkett's plan also followed the Clausewitzian orthodoxy of the decisive battle as the hinge of all strategy. This was vital, because some of the Volunteer headquarters staff were convinced that the optimum strategy for a rising would be very different – not a sudden stand-up street fight but a dispersed, protracted guerrilla campaign.

When the Dublin Brigade went for a field day (at Stepaside) at Easter 1915, the divergence between the two approaches was obvious. The opposing sides in the manoeuvres were commanded by

MacDonagh and Pearse. The results were unimpressive, certainly to Ginger O'Connell – a student of both Clausewitz and the elder Moltke. Pearse's orders, O'Connell recorded, 'ran over four closely-typed pages of foolscap and prescribed the most minute details for the conduct of the attack, including the formations of attacking units at definite geographical points and the precise hour at which the assault was to be delivered'. None of these prescriptions, inevitably, 'were even approximated to'.[15] The fundamental problem, in O'Connell's view, was not so much the leaders' incompetence as their 'preconceived idea of an Insurrection' which imposed a strategic straitjacket on the Volunteers, instead of allowing them to adapt to the nature of the country and the people. Organizationally, this distorted the overall shape of the Volunteers, leading to the expenditure of disproportionate, and wasted, energy in the attempt to organize areas deemed strategically valuable, such as Kildare. O'Connell accepted 'that the most easily organisable districts might be remote from anywhere – "of no strategic importance" in fact. But he thought that the mere fact of having their men trained and armed would at once render them "of strategic importance".' They could operate in areas where the enemy would find it harder to exert his strength.

O'Connell was a man who worried at length about the real prospects for effective military use of the Volunteers. He thought, for instance, that it was pointless to look for examples to the French army, since they had 'thrown us over completely' (the implication is that some bid for support had been made, though if so the timing would seem to have been absurd). On the other hand, 'German discipline and general military spirit' were 'so rigid as not to be well suited to the Irish character – especially in a short service force like the Irish Volunteers'. In mid-1914, therefore, he told McGarrity, he was studying the Italian army as a possible model; later he looked to the example of the 'improvised militia' of Bulgaria in its war with Serbia in 1885. He also treated McGarrity to extensive discussions of technical military issues such as 'the improvisation of supply trains', since the most difficult problem facing an insurrectionary army was the securing of supplies. (This was something that, as we shall see, the military committee seems to have been rather relaxed about.) From O'Connell's standpoint, Pearse and Plunkett were merely playing soldiers.[16]

Did Plunkett's plan contain a theoretical argument for the defensive strategy, alongside its concrete proposals for defensive tactics? Some strategic discussion must have taken place, at least enough to convince the hard-headed James Connolly, who had some – albeit distant and low-level – military experience, that Plunkett was 'a brilliant military man'. Yet the judgement of one eminent historian, that Plunkett's plan 'could not be other than an amateur's effort, and that not of a gifted military amateur', if severe, is judicious.[17] Connolly did not join the military committee until January 1916, and some of his own military ideas were demonstrably wrongheaded. It may be from Connolly (who lectured widely to the Volunteers on the topic of street fighting throughout 1915) that the belief that the British army would not use artillery in Dublin emanated. This belief became a shared assumption among the planners. The sceptical Desmond FitzGerald was breezily assured by MacDonagh, for instance, that 'the British would not shell the city, as by doing so they would be injuring their own supporters'.[18]

MacDonagh also made clear to those in his confidence that O'Connell's cherished scheme of training camps was tolerated – 'on the grounds that they would do no harm, rather than that they would serve any useful purpose'. The Chief of Inspection's 'mind runs on country fighting, taking cover behind hedges and so forth', MacDonagh said. 'But all that means nothing. It would really be much more useful to be getting such things as the keys of buildings in Dublin, or instruction in street fighting.' It was Hobson, in the view of the Kerry organizer Alf Cotton, who was basically responsible for 'that trend in training which was evident from articles by O'Connell and O'Duffy appearing in the *Irish Volunteer*'. Hobson told Cotton that he and Pearse had 'hot arguments about the matter', Hobson arguing 'that gambling everything on one throw was not good tactics, and the adoption of guerrilla tactics would enable us to make a more sustained effort with better prospects of success'. Pearse had (so Hobson claimed) admitted the soundness of this argument, but said 'we must have a sacrifice'.[19] What was in dispute here was the concept of success itself. Pearse had put the issue squarely in one of his American talks in 1914. 'No failure, judged as the world judges these things, was ever more complete, more pathetic, than Emmet's. And yet he has left us a prouder memory than the memory of Brian victorious at Clontarf or Owen Roe victorious at Benburb.' Even, or especially, in death, Emmet had 'redeemed Ireland from acquiescence in the Union'.[20] For Pearse, gesture was all; the only question was how to make the gesture sufficiently striking.

Towards the end of 1915, the 'hedge-fighting' group seem to have believed that they were winning the argument. The umpire's report on the Dublin Brigade field day at Coolock in November noted how 'units became broken up in the close country', and suggested that 'this had impressed on all the need for special training in hedge-fighting'. It had also, encouragingly, made sure that 'the hopeless position of cavalry or guns in such country was manifest to everyone'. O'Connell's protégé Eimar O'Duffy triumphantly concluded (in an essay entitled 'Carnage at Coolock') that 'the most hopeful sign in these operations was the practical disappearance of thinking in army groups'. He thought that 'all would agree that in these sudden encounters at the turn of a road, a shot gun will be as good as a rifle, if not better'. To bolster this dose of pragmatism, O'Connell quickly published a series of articles on 'Hedge fighting for small units' in the *Irish Volunteer*.[21] But it is clear enough that these meticulous essays on fieldcraft were entirely irrelevant to Pearse, Connolly and Plunkett.[22]

Maybe the closest we can get to Plunkett's thinking is through the testimony of his sister Geraldine, who claimed to have heard, or been told of, many discussions within the military committee. Because 'the position was so desperate', she thought, 'it was very little use making plans for all Ireland until the measure of success of the Dublin plans could be ascertained'. Plunkett's objection to a rural campaign was partly based on his belief that this was what 'the English army' expected: rebellion would always 'take the form of marching out of Dublin to take to the hills'. Even 'high officers in the Volunteers had the same view', and 'Joe had a job with some of them to argue them out of it'. They 'were afraid of being caught like rats in a trap amongst the streets', and 'had a fantastic idea of the accuracy of big guns and of machine guns. They thought that they mowed you down.' According to her, Plunkett, backed by Connolly, eventually succeeded in overcoming these (all too accurate) objections.[23] How much his comrades grasped of the fighting in Flanders and Gallipoli cannot be

known. Geraldine saw no contradiction between her brother's determination on a stand-up fight in Dublin, and his hope that, if the
Germans were putting enough pressure on the Western Front – and
he evidently believed that a major offensive was due in May – 'we
could hold out one way or another for anything up to three months'.

The minds of the little committee were plainly mesmerized by the
physical and symbolic weight of their city. Their discussions must
have concentrated mainly on the selection and assessment of individual buildings for seizure and defence, and perhaps – though the final
selection does not do much to bear this out – on the possibility of
mutual communication and reinforcement. It is a remarkable fact that
we know nothing of the reasoning applied to this selection process.
We can, however, be fairly sure that the broad outlines were established right at the start, and very few changes made as a result of later
discussion or reassessment. Piaras Béaslaí records that the dispositions
for the 1st Battalion (occupying the area between Broadstone Station,
the North Dublin Union and the Four Courts) 'were in our hands early
in 1915 and were substantially the same as those we tried to carry out
in 1916'.[24] If so, the plan contained several puzzling choices and omis-
sions that have never been fully explained. Most obviously, why was
the rebel headquarters placed in the General Post Office? We have no
idea what appeal the GPO possessed, apart from its visually impressive location opposite Nelson's pillar on Lower Sackville Street,
Dublin's widest thoroughfare. It was, as one military analyst says, 'a
strong position but did not provide very suitable fields of fire'.[25] It was
awkwardly placed in relation to the other positions and, as the event
proved, unable to maintain communication with them or provide support. The committee's apparent decision not to attempt to occupy
Dublin Castle was fateful. In retrospect, the knowledge of how lightly
the Castle was garrisoned, together with its obvious symbolic significance as the historic centre of British power – it had been Robert
Emmet's objective – make the decision appear surprising. There is
some evidence that no such decision was, in fact, made. According to
Michael Staines, the Dublin Brigade quartermaster, Pearse fully
expected to set up his headquarters in the Castle: 'he never intended
to remain in the GPO', and on Easter Monday the news that the
Castle had not been taken 'caused consternation'.[26]

Another notable omission from the plan was Trinity College, whose sheer size has been offered as a reason for not attempting to occupy it. The strength of the Dublin Brigade makes this argument less than wholly convincing, at least as far as the original plan went. Militarily, there was no disputing that it was 'a natural fortress in the heart of the city', and it was to play a key role in the suppression of the rebellion.[27] Maybe its symbolic status as a bastion of the Protestant Ascendancy paradoxically suggested that it might be seen as a sectarian target. Another aspect is hinted at by one of Trinity's defenders: serious damage to the college would have been a 'national catastrophe'. (MacDonagh is said to have given a similar explanation for the refusal to occupy the Bank of Ireland, which had housed Ireland's last parliament.)[28] But most likely the planners thought that neither of these formidable structures could be seized without violence, and the same view may have been taken of the Shelbourne Hotel – a big, food-rich building which was to be spurned in favour of a militarily hopeless position in the open on St Stephen's Green. The point about all these speculations is that no reliable evidence of such assessments has survived.

Perhaps the hardest aspect of the planners' approach to explain is their apparent unconcern with some of their city's most striking topographical features. Dublin's key feature, militarily as well as scenically, is the fact that it is crossed by a fair-sized river, into whose notoriously polluted waters Connolly had consigned a coffin labelled 'British Empire' during the 1903 royal visit. The Liffey, which was navigable by seagoing ships up to the Custom House in 1916, and still busy with barge traffic (most famously the steam barges from Guinness's brewery), bisected the rough circle of planned rebel strongholds. It would have made communication and movement between them difficult, if this had been intended. If intercommunication was not intended, it might have made more sense to concentrate all the rebel forces on one side or the other: presumably the north side, where both the GPO and the Four Courts lie. It is hard to see that any of the three major positions taken on the south side had as much symbolic value as these. Though the Liffey was crossed by too many substantial bridges to be a really formidable military obstacle, because it was tidal its quay walls were very high. And even the immensely wide

O'Connell Bridge (whose name was then being colloquially extended to Sackville Street itself) would have been a logical focal point for defence, commanded by a very wide field of fire.[29] The river would have maximized the rebels' limited firepower. Central Dublin is also ringed by two canals, but again the planners do not seem to have considered using them as defensive lines, though all four of the major rebel posts in the southern part of the city were either on or close to the Grand Canal. The canals are punctuated by squat, thick bridges, often as wide as they are long, which could not have been demolished with the munitions then available, but which would still have limited and channelled any military countermoves. It was to be at one of these, in fact, that the most stunning rebel military success of the Dublin battle would come.

The precise form of the occupation of Dublin relates directly to what has been perhaps the most vexed question about the military committee's plan: whether it assumed that significant military action would be confined to the capital, or saw the Dublin action as an integral part of a countrywide rising. One of the most knowledgeable writers on the period, Florence O'Donoghue, has implied that these were mutually exclusive alternatives: 'a choice had to be made between the traditional pattern of a rising in the country, and the more daring and dramatic seizure and holding of the heart of the capital as a first blow'.[30] This seems like special pleading. There was no necessity for this choice, since the provincial units could not be brought to Dublin, and would have to fight 'in the country' if they were to fight at all. The two forms of action were not mutually exclusive, except perhaps in the minds of the military committee. Most of those who claimed to have seen the plan said that it did not extend outside Dublin (this was true also of the mysterious passbook captured by the Wexford police).[31] The most plausible explanation for this, though, is simply the persistent, indeed widening, discrepancy between the IV organization in the capital and in the provinces. Careful historical analysis of this issue suggests that there is very little evidence of 'any supervision or initiation of plans by headquarters staff for most areas in the country', and that though the planners did provide advisers to certain areas, 'no overall plan is discernible'. When all the provincial organizers were arrested or displaced in 1915, even this limited system broke down. The planners might have liked the idea of a national rising, but in practice they dealt with the forces they knew and trusted.

There was one, potentially dramatic, exception to this, and it lay outside Ireland. In April 1915, Joseph Plunkett set out for Germany, taking a route through neutral territories – Spain, Italy and Switzerland. After a twenty-three-hour train journey to Berlin, he was possibly fortunate (since his command of German was limited to a phrasebook he bought in Italy, which unsurprisingly did not contain the phrase 'foreign ministry') to reach the foreign ministry without being arrested as a spy, and thence meet up with Sir Roger Casement. Their object was to persuade the Germans that Ireland offered them a strategic opportunity big enough to justify sending an expeditionary force to support the Volunteer rebellion.

Casement's mission to Germany was one of the most exotic Irish nationalist responses to the war, and Casement's own exoticism – his Protestant Ascendancy origins, his homosexuality and manic-depressive personality, his international career, and above all its sensational denouement in a treason trial, have guaranteed him the repeated interest of biographers. His contribution to the Volunteer movement was, in the end, a marginal one. But for some time, his significance seemed much greater. Ireland was in a sense his last enthusiasm, at the end of a lifetime spent abroad in the British consular service, during which he became a liberal hero for his campaigns against the exploitation of the Putumayo and against Belgian atrocities in the Congo. He also acquired a knighthood, which may ultimately have become his death warrant when he was tried for treason in 1916. He returned to Ireland in search of a cause, and at first found mainly a cause for gloom. As he wrote to Maurice Moore from Galway in December 1913:

It is pathetic to see the fine strong handsome boys all burning to *do* something for Ireland, and to feel powerless to do more than talk. Galway appals me – its ruin and decay and the transatlantic mind of the people. Looking at Galway one feels Carson and Ulster must win![32]

But the launching of the Volunteer movement rapidly lifted him from deep gloom to feverish elation. As we have seen, his modest financial contribution was vital, and he himself became, at Moore's invitation, a tireless stump speaker at IV recruitment meetings. He exchanged lengthy letters with MacNeill about the movement's direction and purpose. His prestige peaked in mid-1914 when MacNeill sent him as 'accredited representative of the arms sub-committee' on a fundraising trip to the USA. Like MacNeill, he believed that the Volunteers could take no action unless they could get guns on a mass scale. He was lionized by the Irish-Americans (who, as he wryly noted, were 'mad for a Protestant leader') and a Philadelphia group christened him 'Robert Emmet'. More significantly still, he was taken seriously by the flintiest of the old Fenians, the Clan na Gael chief John Devoy.

At some stage, Devoy decided to back Casement in an attempt to get Irish prisoners of war in Germany to enrol in an 'Irish Brigade'. This project carried echoes of Devoy's own methods in the 1860s, when the Fenians set out to infiltrate the Irish regiments of the British army. The aim was to turn whole companies or even battalions into ready-made instruments for a Fenian seizure of power. The potential appeared dramatic, and although it was certainly not easy to suborn enlisted men who had taken an oath of allegiance to the British sovereign (and who were possibly the opposite of separatists), the failure of 'military Fenianism' was primarily due to the ruthless methods adopted by the army command to suppress it. It is perhaps surprising that the IRB never tried to repeat the exercise. Devoy, indeed, seems to have been particularly unenthusiastic about it, though he was keen on securing German political and military aid, and thought Casement might do some good as an ambassador.

Casement's mission depended on three vital assumptions: first, that the Germans would help Irish separatists to establish an Irish Brigade; second, that they would not simply exploit them; and third, that prisoners of war would join such a force in substantial numbers. There was some evidence for the first, in that the German government was clearly aware of the Irish republican movement, and, as soon as it became clear that Britain would enter the war, interested in the possibility that it could embarrass or weaken the British position. But from the very start there were ominous misunderstandings about what the potential Irish rebels wanted, and indeed about the nature of Irish politics. Casement might have been worried to know, for instance, that the German military attaché in Washington billed him as 'the leader of all Irish associations in America', and thought that he was 'ready to land arms for fifty thousand in Ireland with own means'.[33] But his optimism would probably have led him to discount such evidence that the Germans were no more adept on Irish issues than the British. He strongly believed at that point that a German victory would be good for Ireland and for the world.

Casement was not unaware of the likely difficulties in enlisting prisoners of war. Because 'the Irish soldier has a sense of honour and loyalty that is innate and must be reckoned with, he will not transfer his allegiance merely to better his condition, or to escape from imprisonment in Germany'. But he believed that most recruits had enlisted because of poverty and unemployment; at heart they were Irish nationalists and '*not* proud to be fighting England's battles'. He saw his task, once he arrived in Berlin on 31 October, as simply one of opening their eyes to reality, and telling the Germans where to send military aid. At first, all seemed to go 'splendidly'; the Germans 'will help in every way', he wrote on 2 November. Soon, though, it became evident that there were problems with his cherished idea of a German declaration of support for Irish independence, and also with the idea of raising an Irish legion. Von Jagow, the Foreign Minister, cautiously noted on the seventh that 'the military results would be small, possibly even negative, and it would be said that we had violated international law'.[34]

Eventually, on 20 November, Germany did issue a statement that, should it invade Ireland, it would do so with 'good will towards a people to which Germany wished only national welfare and national liberty'. This was far from the direct recognition the Fenians hoped for. The military authorities who had to make the arrangements for Casement to address Irish prisoners, and release those who volunteered to join him, were even less enthusiastic. In the event, very few – embarrassingly few – did so. Casement blamed this on ham-fisted German arrangements, beginning a long and dismal falling-out with his hosts. The German military insistence that Casement address the Irish prisoners *en masse* rather than meeting them individually looks so wrongheaded that it may have been intended – for whatever reason – to sabotage the project. When it became clear to Casement that there was no possibility of any German invasion, he began to recognize Germany's motives as utterly selfish. Ultimately, in 1916, he would ask 'Why did I ever trust in such a Govt as this – They have no sense of honour, chivalry, generosity . . . They are Cads . . . That is why they are hated by the world and England will surely beat them.'[35]

It was in the midst of this process that Plunkett arrived. He had no more success than Casement in drumming up recruits for the Irish Brigade, but together they prepared an extended (thirty-two-page) strategic appreciation of the military possibilities for a German intervention in Ireland. The Volunteer Headquarters Staff, they said, recognized that 'it would be impossible to bring any considerable military operation to a successful issue without help from an external source'. But they contended that the British forces in Ireland were far less formidable than their numbers – totalling 37,000 at that stage – might suggest. These forces, they said, consisted of many small, scattered garrisons and a few large training camps, 'not equipped for the occupation of the country, much less to resist invasion'. Plunkett and Casement proposed a German invasion on the western coast, at the Shannon mouth, which would support a mass rising of western Volunteers at the same time as Dublin was seized according to the military committee's plan. They suggested that 12,000 German troops, bringing 40,000 rifles for the local Volunteers, would be enough to turn Limerick into an 'impregnable' base and begin the process of unravelling British control.

Their essay deployed some perfectly plausible strategic thinking; such as their argument that the combination of wide river and a mass of straggling lakes made the Shannon area – 'the line Limerick–Athlone' – especially easy to defend by a relatively small force. But in its search for supporting evidence it drifted, inevitably perhaps, into an extended account of the French invasion of 1798. While it celebrated the achievement of Humbert's tiny force, it wisely downplayed the performance of the local Irish levies who joined him, and completely ignored the experience of the much larger expedition under Hoche which had failed to get ashore two years earlier. This history lesson, so obviously persuasive to Irish nationalists, was probably less so to the Germans. They were more likely to ponder the stupendous danger of an attempt to land and support an entire division after a 2,000-mile voyage through seas controlled by the British navy, and to ask how rapidly the weak British forces in Ireland could be reinforced. These issues did not figure in the appreciation. And the bottom line, that the task of overcoming the Irish–German force 'would tax the military and moral resources of Great Britain to the utmost', stopped short of promising outright victory.

Does the Casement–Plunkett 'Strategical Plan' provide, as has been argued, 'a unique insight into the attitudes, intentions and aspirations of the Military Council'?[36] Given the document's intended purpose, it is hard to avoid the conclusion that it contained a fair amount of window-dressing. It was designed to put the rosiest colouring on what were in many cases very remote possibilities. In some important respects it could be said to be misleading, as when it stated that the military committee had made plans for the destruction of British transport facilities at railway bridges, canals and viaducts. As we shall see, if any such plans existed they were sketchy in the extreme. And when, noting that 'the country is eminently suited to a kind of guerrilla or irregular war' (something that was, in fact, far from attractive to the German army), it declared that 'the training of the Volunteers was directed to that end', it was frankly disingenuous. We may wonder, too, whether its insistence on the need for German troops, not merely guns, reflected Casement's views rather than Plunkett's. This was a point on which Casement plainly diverged from the military committee's final plan; when he eventually returned to Ireland, it was in a despairing attempt to stop the rising because the Germans had refused to send troops. It would seem that Plunkett, on the other hand, like his fellow planners, was prepared to go ahead without them.

Were they prepared to go ahead without the guns either? This has always been a key question about the planners' 'attitudes, intentions and aspirations'. Was the rising expected to end British rule, or was it a 'bloody protest'? Without the guns there was no hope of the former outcome. The Casement–Plunkett document has been said to 'reveal the Military Council's plans as optimistic, and directed to achieving a military victory by overwhelming the British forces in Ireland'.[37] This may well be true. Pearse himself gave repeated evidence during Easter Week of his hope that the Germans would arrive in spite of everything, and his last letter to his mother confirmed this. It is hardly possible that Pearse lied to his mother, though he may have wished to reassure her that he had not, in effect, committed suicide (and brought hundreds of his subordinates out to risk their lives) in a hopeless enterprise. But Seán MacDermott was also heard, in Richmond Barracks after the surrender, to say of the Germans 'we were sure they would be here'.[38]

If the guns were indeed vital to the IRB planners, we might expect to find them making careful practical arrangements to deal with the formidable problem of landing and distributing them in the face of an alert British garrison. The military committee consistently called for the arms landing to be timed for the evening of the outbreak of the rebellion. Their reasoning (as with everything else, we can only guess) may have been that in order to mobilize sufficient Volunteer forces to cope with the arms landing they would have to forgo the element of surprise, and begin mobilization several hours ahead. In principle, the Casement–Plunkett document indicated that it might be possible to overwhelm or neutralize the weak British forces in the landing zone for long enough to get the guns ashore. Thus we might assume that the Cork, Kerry and Limerick Volunteers, at the very least, would have clear orders for this operation. Plunkett, after the surrender, maintained that 'everything was foreseen, everything was calculated, nothing was forgotten'. This makes it particularly surprising that no evidence of any such orders has survived, except in very vague terms which would be likely to – and in fact did – produce confusion and paralysis rather than rapid and decisive action.

An unusually careful attempt to assemble the evidence for a general plan was later made by Liam O Briain for the Bureau of Military History, on the basis of conversations with leaders before and after the rising, in Richmond Barracks, Wandsworth gaol and Frongoch internment camp. O Briain was certain that there was such a plan, though the information he picked up – from the planners themselves – was patchy. On the key issue of the arms landing, he heard two stories. On Easter Monday morning, Seán Fitzgibbon told him of the 'big job imposed on the Limerick battallion [*sic*] of engaging the British garrison there while the arms were transported across the river, and then sent forward in a seized train through Clare to Athenry'. But, while Fitzgibbon had been sent officially from Volunteer Headquarters on this mission, 'secretly orders had been sent to the IRB men there to keep Fitzgibbon (branded 'a talker' by MacDonagh)

moving around, to let him think he was in charge, but when the decisive moment came to take things out of his hands'. O Briain thought
that, as a result, Fitzgibbon's negative report to MacNeill on the
unpreparedness of the Limerick area may have been 'a little too black'
(albeit 'true in general'). Later, when the landing place was changed
to Fenit, the same responsibility fell on the Kerry Volunteers. (The
Kerry commandant, P. J. Cahill, told him in Frongoch that some 700
men assembled near Tralee on Easter Sunday for this operation.)[39]

Thirty years on, O Briain struggled to remember whether it was
from Seán T. O'Kelly, Michael Staines, or possibly 'the Galway men,
Larry Lardner or someone else like him' that he first heard talk of
Athenry as the 'all-Ireland base'. Exactly what this term signified is
hard to deduce. In Galway itself, 'the leaders seemed to have no plan
but to assemble a large number of men at one point and stay there'.
In Cork, Terence MacSwiney explained to him at length, the plan was
to assemble the brigade in the western hills to receive their portion of
the arms shipment – 'I *assume* in the neighbourhood of Ballyvourney
or Ballingeary.' (In fact it was to be Carriganimma – or Beeing; as we
shall see, MacCurtain and MacSwiney were extremely sparing in the
information they supplied to their own units about this plan.) This
suggested that not all the arms were to be sent to Athenry, though
there is no indication of how the division was to be made. The orders
for midland and Leinster areas were 'to move generally westwards
across the Shannon', while Ulster would be abandoned – its forces
would 'move to North Connacht and try to hold the northern end of
the Shannon'.[40]

On Dublin's part in the general plan, O Briain heard some illuminating comments. When Michael Mallin, the Citizen Army commander, was shown the plan, his reaction was akin to Ginger
O'Connell's: 'I said immediately, "Where is the alternative plan for use
when this one breaks down? This plan is far too clockwork and there
should be an alternative plan." But they had none.' Mallin found the
requirement for 'every movement of every group of our forces to dove-
tail into the movement of some other group' completely unrealistic.
There might, O Briain thought, have been a trace of class hostility in
the ICA man's assessment of the Volunteer leadership, but it is clear
from his comments that the planning for Dublin was at a different

level of detail than for the provinces. And it seems that it did 'break down'. O Briain 'always understood that it was never the plan to allow the Dublin brigade to be cooped up in the city, surrounded and forced to surrender'. Interestingly enough, he was convinced that Emmet's plan was to be followed quite precisely (he recalled Seán MacDermott insisting that 'it was no childish dream'), in that Dublin Castle was the keypoint of the strategy. The idea was that government would be 'paralysed by the seizure (and perhaps destruction) of Dublin castle', and the country aroused 'by this startling event, as nothing else could do it'. Then, 'After a few days the Dublin Brigade, if forced to do so, were to leave the city and beat a fighting retreat westwards – all the way to Athenry, if driven to it.' O Briain believed that 'it will be found that the companies and battallions [*sic*] of the Dublin Brigade had particular areas outside the city with which they were to familiarise themselves'. The 1st Battalion, for instance, oper-ated in northern Co. Dublin, with O Briain's own unit, F Company, at Finglas.[41]

If there was indeed such a plan, it would have borne out O'Connell's criticism of the planners' inexperience – indeed irrespon-sibility – since the attempt by a force like the Volunteers to carry out the most difficult of all military operations, a fighting retreat, would have been more disastrous than what eventually occurred in 1916. So, while his testimony that the planners did not intend to be 'cooped up' in Dublin is important (and is corroborated by Frank Henderson's memory of a 2nd Battalion briefing by MacDonagh in February 1916),[42] direct evidence of a coherent plan is still missing. Were meas-ures to be taken to obstruct the movement of British reinforcements into Dublin, for instance? O Briain thought that the Wexford Volunteers intended to 'prevent reinforcements passing through [Enniscorthy] to Dublin from Rosslare'. But this seems to have been a last-minute idea of Connolly's rather than a plan laid down by the military committee. It remains inexplicable that no instructions seem to have been issued to interfere with the landing or movement of troops at Kingstown. Various individuals testified to receiving orders to damage bridges and railway tracks leading into Dublin, but as we shall see few practical preparations for such action appear to have been made, and many of these instructions were to be changed or abandoned at the last minute. On the whole, the knowledgeable judgement made in the 1960s that 'on the evidence at present available, it would seem that the insurgents had no intelligible, or militarily speaking intelligent, blue print for an all-Ireland rising' still seems sound.[43]

The same could certainly be said of the Irish Citizen Army contingent, if only for the reason that it remained a tightly concentrated Dublin force. But in late 1915 (around the time the military committee was enlarged), this small element began to exert a heightened influence on the situation. It had always been explicitly revolutionary in a way that the Volunteers had not, but this was mainly a reflection of James Connolly's direct engagement, which was intermittent in the Citizen Army's first year of life. Though he had played a major part in its creation, Connolly took surprisingly little interest in its development, leaving the elaboration of uniforms, banners and military paraphernalia to Larkin and Markievicz. He spent most of the next year in Belfast, and only returned to Dublin when Larkin left for America in October 1914. Even then, his interest in the technicalities of military organization seems to have remained limited. In sharp contrast to most of the Volunteer leaders who were enthusiastic uniform wearers (MacNeill and Hobson were exceptions), he did not put on a uniform in public until Palm Sunday 1916.[44] He does not seem to have pressed for systematic enlargement of his tiny 'army', which never grew beyond 200–300 (from a low of 80, according to police estimates, in April 1915). He left the business of organization and training to Michael Mallin, a practical former soldier.

Connolly may well have preferred to keep the Citizen Army small, as a revolutionary vanguard. Its crucial quality, for him, was its commitment, and its readiness to take action at short notice. Though his talks on street fighting were always popular, Connolly's central contribution was his philosophical activism. The onset of war was a watershed moment for him; as one of his biographers puts it, he 'became a revolutionary nationalist'. The creed of international socialism was disastrously undermined by the patriotic reaction of the masses to the outbreak of war. 'What then becomes of all our resolutions?' Connolly agonized; 'all our protests of fraternity, all our threats

of general strikes, all our carefully built machinery of international-
ism. Were they all as sound and fury, signifying nothing?' Out of this
wreckage, all that could be salvaged was the historic opposition of
Ireland and the British empire. 'If you are itching for a rifle, itching to
fight, have a country of your own', he urged against Redmond's support for the war. 'Better to fight for your own country than for the rob-
ber empire.' National liberation became the only feasible path to
socialism. In the first issue of the *Irish Worker* after the outbreak of
war he wrote that 'Ireland may yet set the torch to a European conflagration that will not burn out until the last throne and the last capitalist bond and debenture will be shrivelled on the funeral pyre of the
last warlord.'[45]

The problem was that even the extreme nationalists were all
middle-class; their revolutionary ideas were, in Connolly's view, either
vacuous romanticism, or a mindless commitment to 'physical force'
without social content. War might be a grim necessity, 'forced upon a
subject race or subject class to put an end to subjection of race or class
or sex'. But it could not, he insisted in January 1915, be welcomed,
much less glorified. 'When so waged it must be waged thoroughly and
relentlessly, but with no delusions as to its elevating nature'; there was
'no such thing as humane or civilised war!'[46] Pearse's febrile exaltation of blood sacrifice, and his pious wedding of nationalism to
Catholicism, were equally repellent to Connolly. But despite this, he
moved closer to Pearse and his small coterie, for two reasons. Pearse's
increasingly explicit talk of rebellion seems to have convinced him that
some of the Volunteers were prepared to go beyond empty gestures
and romantic rhetoric. Also, despite his bourgeois background, his
legal training and his deference to the Church, Pearse had been genuinely shocked by the experience of the 1913 Dublin labour dispute,
and the immiseration of the working class that it revealed. After this
he showed an inclination towards a cautious socialism, which – however naïve – gave Connolly an inkling of hope that the Irish revolution might be more than simply a change of capitalists.

Connolly's concept of 'insurrectionary warfare' was spelled out in
his last journal, the *Workers' Republic*, which he set up in Dublin with
an abandoned printing-press in April 1915. Using – like the Volunteers
– a series of historical case studies, starting – unlike them – with the

Moscow rising of 1905 and ending with the Paris insurrection of 1848, he held that regular armies were 'badly handicapped' in urban fighting, and that 'really determined civilian revolutionists' could be victorious. 'Every difficulty that exists for the operation of regular troops in mountains is multiplied a hundredfold in a city', which he likened to 'a huge maze of passes or glens formed by streets or lanes'. Arguing that a street was a defile just like a mountain pass, he ignored the most obvious difference – that mountain passes are few and far between, while streets are multiple. To call them a 'maze', with the implication that there was only a single way through, could be dangerously misleading. Undismayed by the fact that the Russian and French workers had been mercilessly crushed, he maintained that an irregular force like the ICA could achieve military success through 'the active defence of positions whose location threatens the supremacy or existence of the enemy'.[47] He adopted the implicit assumption of the old Fenian adage, that the British state ('England' to all nationalists) would be weaker during a major war. Evidence that the reverse was the case – not just the vast expansion of the armed forces, but also the unprecedented DORA internal security regime – was set aside. (Michael Mallin reportedly believed that England would only have 1,000 men in Ireland 'fit to fight', a figure hardly credible from any viewpoint.)[48] In November Connolly alleged that whereas the old adage had once been heard on a thousand platforms, 'since England got into difficulties, the phrase has never been heard or mentioned'. In a style arrestingly close to Pearse's, he insisted that 'if Ireland did not act now the name of this generation should in mercy to itself be expunged from the records of Irish history'. And when Maeve Cavanagh, 'the poetess of the revolution' and Citizen Army stalwart, piously told him 'Righteous men will make us a nation once again', Connolly brusquely retorted 'Get anyone, anyone who will fight.'[49]

Connolly's well-publicized impatience seems to have instilled a new urgency into the military committee's preparations. Pearse's increasing public belligerence has often been attributed to his inner turmoil, or to the IRB's need to prepare the public mind. But it seems likely that the need to forestall unilateral action by the ICA became steadily more pressing in late 1915. Pearse deployed his formidable verbal skills both to legitimize the idea of insurrection and to persuade his audience that it was a real possibility. His reaction to the European war was suffused with that sacral view of patriotic death which Connolly found so cretinous. Even the little affray on the Dublin quays after the Howth gun-running provoked the exultant cry that 'the whole movement, the whole country has been re-baptised by blood shed for Ireland'. Contemplation of the Flanders battlefields and their dizzying casualty lists brought forth a more elaborate philosophy of violence. In December Pearse wrote (anonymously) in *The Spark* of the 'homage of millions of lives given gladly for love of country' as 'the most august homage ever offered to God'. It was 'good for the world that such things should be done'. His most febrile phrase, 'the old heart of the earth needed to be warmed by the red wine of the battlefields', suggested to one of his biographers 'a deranged view of the world'. And Connolly – to Pearse's dismay – contemptuously dismissed this article as the thinking of 'a blithering idiot'; 'We are sick of such teaching, and the world is sick of such teaching.' Yet it was not essentially different from Pearse's most successful piece of oratory, his speech at the funeral of O'Donovan Rossa in August, which Connolly had approved.

Many commentators suggest that Pearse was now beginning to look actively for a sacrificial death; one has proposed that his 'ritualistic courting of death and violence borders on the psychopathic'. He 'suffered severe psychological conflict which made the prospect of going out to die on Easter Monday 1916 seem attractive, even compelling'.[50] Even without invoking this pathological dimension, the 1916 rebellion has been commonly portrayed as a 'bloody protest' (in Pearse's own phrase) or even 'blood sacrifice'. Pearse certainly seems to have announced his intentions, through 'The Mother', who does not 'grudge / My two strong sons that I have seen go out / To break their strength and die, they and a few / In bloody protest for a glorious thing.' There was a Fenian model for Pearse's rhetoric, at least as presented in a late novel by Canon Sheehan, *The Graves at Kilmorna*, published in 1914. 'As the blood of martyrs was the seed of saints, so the blood of the patriot is the seed from which alone can spring fresh life, into a nation that is drifting into the putrescence of decay.'[51] The model Pearse first chose to hold up to his St Enda's acolytes, of course, was the hero Cuchulainn's careless embrace of death in battle; though after the move from Cullenswood House to the Hermitage he veered towards Emmet 'and the heroes of the last stand'. (He wondered whether it was 'symptomatic of some development within me'.)[52] 'Pearse and those who followed him to certain destruction, came to believe that their actions appropriated the transcendent power of the myth.'[53]

Yet we may wonder whether many, if any, of his co-conspirators shared this view. It is not at all evident that many saw themselves as risking 'certain destruction'. Though there were certainly others who, like Terence MacSwiney, called anxiously on God to 'teach us how to die', the event would prove that even such febrile rhetoric did not translate automatically into action.[54] The hope that one would 'not from danger swerve, in the sacred cause we serve,' was after all a convention of patriotic commitment. Readiness to die is not quite the same thing as the 'vertigo of self-sacrifice' that, as W. B. Yeats felt, made Pearse uniquely dangerous.[55] Even Plunkett, who was thought to be terminally ill, showed little sign of this sort of death-wish; he was about to get married, for one thing, and, as we have seen, entertained military fantasies of holding out for three months.

Pearse's oratorical gift was potent, and widely recognized. Patrick McCartan's experience of his passionate invocation of Emmet has already been quoted. Pearse delivered this kind of inspirational address at countless meetings across the country throughout the first year of the war. His words sounded rhetorical, but conveyed to many of his listeners a very definite message. At St Enda's, as one of his senior pupils put it, 'in his talks to his students, he always stressed that every generation of Irishmen should have a rising in arms. He stressed it in such a way that you felt impelled to believe that he did actually believe that there should be some attempt.'[56] The culmination of this was his astonishing performance at the Rossa funeral. In this he reaffirmed the apostolic succession of separatist nationalism to buttress his definition of freedom: 'it is Tone's definition, it is Mitchel's definition, it is Rossa's definition'. Ireland must be 'not free merely, but Gaelic as well' (an insistence that would certainly have puzzled Tone). Most crucially, just before his celebrated peroration, he declared that 'Life springs from death; and from the graves of patriot men and women spring living nations.' His peroration directly confronted 'the Defenders of this Realm' who thought they had pacified half of us and intimidated the other half. They think that they have foreseen everything, think that they have provided against everything; but the fools! the fools! the fools! – they have left us our Fenian dead, and while Ireland holds these graves, Ireland unfree shall never be at peace.

The tremendous impact of the funeral, and especially of this oration, has been amply attested. Richard Walsh in Mayo 'heard it recited on railway journeys to football and hurling matches'.[57] It was shortly after this that the military committee took the definite decision to launch a rebellion in the following six months. The extremism of the *Spark* article surely reflected this heightening tempo.

The decision to rise intensified the problem caused by the committee's determination to keep its preparations secret, not just from the authorities but also from the IV leadership. Its preparations fell into three broad categories. First, negotiations between the IRB and the Germans, via the Clan na Gael, for the shipment of arms from Germany to Ireland. Second, the briefing of selected local IV officers with the general outlines of the insurrection plan. Third, devising a way of mobilizing the Volunteers without alerting the authorities.

The first process went on for several months, starting from Plunkett's visit to Berlin. Casement's attempt to enrol an Irish brigade had stalled at the derisory total of fifty-six, and the motivation of even this weak company was dubious. In October Captain Robert Monteith, one of the few properly qualified IV military instructors, who had been working in Kerry, was sent to join Casement and try to give the force some military credibility. In the maw of the great German military machine, however, Monteith's own credentials became considerably less impressive than they seemed in Kerry. Casement was dismayed by the contempt shown towards Monteith, and the growing realization that the Germans had abandoned (if they had ever entertained) any idea of invasion. They would only send a consignment of second-rate rifles, with little interest in what became of them. Though Monteith made real improvements in the 'Brigade', it was plainly an embarrassment to the Germans. Casement, increasingly convinced that a rising without German participation would be a catastrophe, shifted to the idea that the Brigade should be sent to join the Turkish army trying to 'liberate' Egypt. This proposal was put to the men on 3 December, but only thirty-eight consented to it.

Casement himself was marginal to the arms negotiations that went on between the military committee and the Germans, by way of Devoy and McGarrity. On 1 March 1916, Monteith was summoned to Department IIIb of the German General Staff to be told that Devoy had sent a message announcing the date of the rebellion. The German Admiralty proposed that 'between April 20 and 23 in the evening two or three fishing trawlers could land about 20,000 rifles and 10 machine guns with ammunition and explosives at Fenit Pier in Tralee Bay'. They noted that 'unloading has to be effected in two or three hours', and asked for confirmation that the necessary steps could be arranged.[58] Shortly afterwards, Monteith found that a single vessel would be sent – the ship that would be known to history as the *Aud*.

Although the evidence is imprecise, it seems clear that the second process, of briefing selected local officers, had also been going on for several months before the eventual rising. In September 1915, while reviewing a Volunteer parade in Limerick, Eoin MacNeill accidentally heard of instructions issued by Pearse to some commandants to make certain 'definite military dispositions in event of war in Ireland'.[59] He was disturbed by this, but, unfortunately for the historian and for his own reputation, he did not make any sustained effort to uncover the secret network he had stumbled on. More surprisingly, neither did Hobson, who was certainly more aware of the insurrectionist element in the IRB and better placed to investigate it. (According to some, Hobson's view of the feasibility of rebellion at this time was more ambivalent than his later writing claimed.) When MacNeill was in Limerick in September, the military committee was still following Plunkett's proposal to land the German arms there. Shortly afterwards, though, Pearse sent Diarmuid Lynch to assess the landing arrangements, with the idea of shifting them to Ventry in county Kerry. Lynch made an extended tour of the IV units along the west coast, and found the Kerry Volunteers under Austin Stack to be strongly in favour of Fenit, which had a deep-water quay and a light railway line to Tralee (originally built to import Indian corn). As we have seen, the Germans accepted this alteration happily enough.[60]

Why the IRB did so is harder to say, since it committed the fate of the venture to a local chief whom the Supreme Council had 'many times mooted' removing from office before the war for laziness. According to P. S. O'Hegarty, neither Michael Crowe nor his successor as Munster Divisional Representative, Lynch himself, 'could get him to do anything'; 'but there was nobody else on offer'.[61]

The third issue, the method of mobilizing the Volunteers for action, seems to have been resolved at a very early stage. According to Diarmuid Lynch,

the Military Council was faced with the problem – how, without disclosing either its own existence or its purpose to the IV Executive, could the numerous Battalions of the countrywide Volunteer organisation be successfully launched into action – each at a time and place to suit the insurrectionary plans?

He thought that the 1915 Easter manoeuvres 'furnished the basis for a solution'.[62] The basis was probably laid earlier still. Shortly after the September 1914 separatist meeting, it appears that a full mobilization of the Dublin brigade and the ICA was planned with the intention of occupying the Mansion House and defending it by force if necessary, to prevent a recruiting meeting to be addressed by both Redmond and Asquith on 24 September.[63] The plan was abandoned, but its underlying idea re-emerged. When the military committee decided to use the Easter 1916 manoeuvres as the means of getting the Volunteers 'out', it set up the final crisis of its shadowy game with MacNeill and Volunteer headquarters.

In Diarmuid Lynch's account, the 'Secret Instructions for I.V. Comdts. (IRB Men)' were only given to him in early January 1916 by Pearse at St Enda's. Nothing was written down; he was to convey them orally to the Cork, Kerry, Limerick and Galway commandants. Pearse 'outlined the positions which these Brigades were to occupy' in the Easter weekend manoeuvres, 'viz: Cork to hold the County to the south of the Boggeragh mountains – left flank contacting the Kerry Brigade which was to extend eastwards from Tralee; Limerick was to contact the Kerry men on the south and those of Limerick–Clare–Galway to the north'. Whether these instructions modified or merely confirmed those which MacNeill had accidentally discovered three months earlier, and how the 'secret instructions' differed from the formal orders for the manoeuvres, Lynch does not say. In the event, he was confined to Dublin by an 'Enemy Alien' order (Defence Regulation 14B), and his mission was cancelled. But things were moving. That month the Supreme Council held what turned out to be its last meeting before the rebellion, to approve Seán MacDermott's motion that 'we fight at the earliest date possible'. (The President, Denis McCullough, remained in the dark about the precise planning process.) At the same time MacNeill was at last preparing to make a stand against the insurrectionists on his headquarters staff.

In response to the warlike urgings of the *Workers' Republic*, the Volunteers' Chief of Staff invited Connolly to a meeting in January, at which Connolly frankly stated that he intended to mount a rising soon. While MacNeill contented himself with writing a letter to Pearse, warning against premature action, Pearse and the military committee took more direct steps. Connolly's famous 'disappearance' has often been portrayed as a kidnapping, during which he was persuaded to fall in line with the IRB plans. It seems more likely, as Connolly's ITGWU colleague William O'Brien suggested, that the conversation was consensual. Connolly was not the kind of man who would take kindly to kidnapping, though when he reappeared after his brief disappearance he resolutely refused to speak about what had happened.[64] Desmond Ryan, who was close to Pearse, noted that he also 'said nothing about a kidnapping or anything like that'. It had been an intense encounter, clearly: Pearse told him 'there seemed to be a terrible mental struggle going on in Connolly', until at last 'with tears in his eyes he grasped Pearse's hand and said "God grant, Pearse, that you are right."' Pearse soberly reflected, 'Perhaps Connolly is right. He is a very great man.'[65]

At Volunteer headquarters, Pearse managed to stifle MacNeill's challenge by reading his letter out at a meeting in the Chief of Staff's absence. MacNeill then called a special meeting for which he drew up a more substantial memorandum, a closely argued analysis of the arguments for and against insurrection. This sombre document, which lay forgotten from the day of that meeting until the 1960s, showed that MacNeill was – unsurprisingly – well aware of the impulse to rebellion, and that he was also a better historian than his fellow nationalists who drew so heavily on Irish history for their inspiration.

For MacNeill, the insurrectionists were people who took refuge in 'ready-made arguments' and 'a priori maxims' because they 'did not find themselves able to think out anything better'. He highlighted three such 'formulas': 'it is essential that Ireland should take action during the present war', 'Ireland has always struck her blow too late', and 'the military advantage lies with the side that takes the initiative'. The first was unprovable, the second historically wrong (Irish failures had been primarily due to inadequate preparation) and in any case irrelevant, and the third was 'a sort of magic spell' which disguised the fact that the real initiative would ultimately lie with the over-whelmingly powerful British forces. Why were these formulas so attractive?

To my mind, those who feel impelled towards military action on any of [these] grounds are really impelled by a sense of feebleness or despondency or fatalism, or by an instinct of satisfying their own emotions or escaping from a difficult and complex situation.

This was a shrewd thrust, and MacNeill followed it by insisting on the need for patience, for both moral and practical reasons. The Volunteers might be a military force but they were 'not a militarist force'. The 'reproach of the former Volunteers' (of 1782), he added, 'is not that they did not fight but that they did not maintain their organisation till their objects had been secured'. He stressed, too, that the situation was better than it might look. The new Volunteer move-ment had effectively transformed it; 'England' could no longer rule Ireland 'normally by what are called peaceful means'. The government was afraid to suppress the Volunteers, because it was 'convinced that it would lose more than it could gain by moving its military forces against us'. Only a failed insurrection would 'create a special oppor-tunity for it' to do so. And he insisted that anyone who thought an insurrection could succeed had simply failed to grasp the huge discrep-ancy between the Dublin and provincial Volunteers. He urged the activists to deal with the real world, not fantasy. They must get the people on their side first, and not indulge in 'the vanity of thinking ourselves to be right and other Irish people to be wrong' – even in purely military terms it was 'a factor of the highest importance to be able to fight in a friendly country'.

We have to remember that what we call our country is not a poetical abstraction, as some of us, perhaps all of us, in the exercise of our highly developed capacity for figurative thought, are sometimes apt to imagine . . . What we call our country is the Irish nation, a concrete and visible reality.[66]

This dose of professorial wisdom would certainly have been as unwelcome for its patronizing tone (MacNeill spoke of 'childish illusions', and ponderously insisted that 'there is no such person as Caitlin ni Ullachain or Roisin Dubh or Sean-bhean Bhocht, who is calling us to serve her') as for its minatory message. In the event, the insurrectionists never saw or heard it. At the meeting, Pearse immediately 'denied in the most explicit terms having any intention to land the Volunteers in an insurrection, and reproached the rest of us for our suspicious natures', Hobson recorded. MacNeill backed off, and slipped his memorandum into a drawer. Pearse's victory carried a price; the Chief of Staff's opposition to an insurrection would, two months later, express itself in a vastly more dramatic and disruptive manner.

5

To the Brink

*On the way [to Carriganimma] my uncle asked me, 'Do you
expect to come back today?'*

Patrick O'Sullivan, Easter Day 1916

In a sense, the rebellion was in train from the moment shortly after
the outbreak of war when the IRB Supreme Council resolved to act
before the war ended. When the Council met again in Clontarf Town
Hall in mid-January 1916 to fix the date, its decision to fight 'at the
earliest possible moment' was a formality. Later that month Connolly
told Cathal O'Shannon 'that a definite date had been fixed for the
rebellion, and that MacNeill would not be in a position to interfere'.
The message announcing that armed action would begin on Easter
Sunday reached Devoy in New York 'on or about February 5',
brought by an IRB courier. (Unhelpfully, 'it was in a cipher that I did
not know, and was neither dated nor signed'.)[1] A second courier,
Plunkett's sister Philomena, arrived with a duplicate a week later. (She
also brought a set of codewords, including 'Fionn' for a mishap, and
'Aisling' for the arrival of the requested German submarine in Dublin
bay; this has been interpreted as evidence that the military committee
were unaware that radio contact with the German ships would be
impossible.)[2] Ostensibly, the decision to rise was driven by fear of
British action to suppress the Volunteers, but there was no firm evidence that such action was imminent. If there had been, the choice of
Easter Sunday would hardly have met the case. The real calculation
was probably that the Easter 1915 precedent would make the mobilization look like a routine exercise. The three-month delay allowed

plenty of time to make arrangements with the Germans, though as the committee was to demonstrate in April, it took a very optimistic view of the speed with which such arrangements could be made and altered. It also gave time for another trial mobilization, on St Patrick's Day, which might well have provoked the government into repressive action. So indeed might the increasingly widespread discussion of the impending event, not only throughout Ireland but as far afield as Berlin and Rome.

In one of the more mysterious events of a confused period, Joseph Plunkett's father, Count Plunkett, had an audience with the Pope in early April. He delivered a letter purporting to come from Eoin MacNeill, 'President of the Supreme Council of the Irish Volunteers', informing the Pope that 'we have an effective force of 80,000 trained men, and the people, the Catholic nation, is with us'. The letter added that not only German assistance but also a big shipment of arms from America was promised. The war offered the chance 'to obtain the freedom of rights and worship for our Catholic country'. The insurrection would begin 'in the evening of next Easter Day'. The terminological confusion (mixing Volunteer and IRB titles), and the invocation of MacNeill (who later, plausibly, denied any involvement in this), suggest that this message was at least garbled, if not concocted by the eccentric papal count himself. Repeated references to religious identity, potentially very injudicious if they had become public, do not fit the Fenian pattern. The statement of available forces was frankly dishonest. While it is hard to believe that Plunkett would have deceived the Pope, it is also hard to believe that the letter was composed by either the IRB or the Volunteers. It has been suggested that the military committee was trying to 'pre-empt the hierarchy's condemnation' of the rising.[3] But it may also be that Plunkett (not for the first or last time) acted on his own initiative, or his son's. (A few days before the rebellion, Joe Plunkett told Eoin MacNeill 'he had received a message direct from Rome to the effect that the Pope had sent his blessing to the Irish Volunteers', and to MacNeill in particular.)[4] In any case, one statement in the letter was absolutely accurate: the date of the rebellion. The Pope knew more about what was going on than did Eoin MacNeill.

So, it is certain, did others. There is wide testimony that rank-and-file Volunteers felt that action was imminent. Frank Henderson recalled a series of lectures at which the Dublin Brigade officers 'were gradually brought to the realisation that there would be a rising soon'. About three months before Easter, Thomas MacDonagh 'told us definitely that there was going to be a rising'.[5] Many others recalled a growing excitement, or 'a tenseness which made us anticipate that we may be in a fight at short notice'.[6] Some of this testimony should perhaps be discounted; it has been suggested that 'plans to resist conscription were later attributed, as plans for a rising, to the men who actually brought one about', and that 'more substance than they deserve has been accorded to these vague and shifting schemes'.[7] But the intensification of preparations was unmistakable. Large numbers were involved in manufacturing more or less primitive munitions in workshops all across the country. The dramatic St Patrick's Day mobilization on 17 March, when some 1,400 Volunteers assembled in Dublin and 4,500 in the provinces, was a further clue. The centre of the capital was taken over in what could easily have been a dry run for a rising: 'The Dublin Brigade, practically fully armed, uniformed and equipped held that portion of Dame Street from City Hall to the Bank of Ireland for over an hour, during which no traffic was allowed to break the ranks of the Volunteers, Citizen Army and Cumann na mBan.'[8]

For Todd Andrews, then a fifteen-year-old schoolboy and eager 'camp follower of the Volunteers', it was his 'most thrilling experience'. Here, 'with Eoin MacNeill, bearded, smartly uniformed and wise-looking at their head, was the reincarnation of the glamorous army of 1779'.[9] We can only guess how many still thought that all this was a show – like Casement himself, whose reaction when the Germans belatedly gave Monteith training in the use of the explosives they were sending along with the old Russian rifles was one of denial. (As his biographer notes, he 'hardly seems to have thought of the rifles as dealing death: they were symbolic or at worst defensive'. Explosives were less ambiguous, however; Casement thought that the Volunteers could 'refuse' them when they were unloaded.)[10] But the men of Michael Brennan's Meelick company in Clare could have harboured few illusions after their commander advised them that day 'if an attempt is made to seize your arms, use them, and not the butt ends but the other ends of them and what is in them. Some of you may not like to commit murder, but it is not murder.'[11]

The sense of imminent action intensified during Holy Week. (Although, curiously, Plunkett's other sister Geraldine had arranged her wedding for Easter Sunday; she thought that the rebellion would come in the first week of May because 'Joe had learned from Bethmann Hollweg that a German offensive was planned for that time.' She was 'dumbfounded' when her fiancé received his mobilization orders on Saturday.)[12] On 15 April, Pearse told a meeting of the Dublin Brigade council that nobody who was afraid of losing his job should come out on Easter Sunday.[13] On Palm Sunday the Dublin Volunteers held route marches, and though 'nobody said anything definite, we realised that something unusual was approaching. The excitement was intense.'[14] Volunteer meetings were held every evening, and on Wednesday Thomas MacDonagh was reported by the police as ordering his battalion to bring three days' rations that weekend. 'We are not going out on Friday, but we are going out on Sunday. Boys, some of us may never come back.' On Thursday MacDonagh, who usually gave his battalion 'an encouraging little speech, a few compliments on our efficiency' after a parade, addressed them at some length. He 'reminded us we were standing on historic ground in Clontarf where Brian Boru had defeated the Danes in 1014. Easter was the time of the battle of Clontarf.' More directly, MacDonagh warned them that 'when big things happen like this, there is very often confusion of ideas; you may get an order over the weekend, and I want every man to obey it implicitly'.[15]

Despite these preparations, however, all the military committee's planning came unstuck at the last minute. Secrecy had been seen by the IRB as vital to success, but it carried a price. In the week before Easter Sunday, three events – the end of Casement's project, the so-called 'Castle Document', and MacNeill's 'countermanding order', came together to derail and almost destroy the rising.

The IRB's January message to Devoy contained a request for a 'shipload of arms' to be sent to Limerick quay between 20 and 23 April. This may possibly have been aimed at the Irish-Americans, but because, as Devoy recorded, all the Clan funds had been expended, he sent the message on to the Germans. 'We have decided to begin action on Easter Saturday. Unless entirely new circumstances arise we must have your arms and munitions in Limerick between Good Friday and Easter Saturday. We expect German help immediately after beginning action. We might be compelled to begin earlier.' On 10 February the German Embassy telegraphed this with the note that 'the Confidential Agent will advise them if at all possible to wait, and will point out the difficulties in the way of our giving help'.[16] In particular the Germans, then at the height of their submarine warfare campaign, were understandably resistant to the request that they send one of their hard-pressed U-boats to make an attack around the River Liffey. Their first proposal, as we have seen, was to send 20,000 rifles with 10 machine guns, ammunition and explosives in 'two or three steam-trawlers'. Their 10 March telegram included the stern injunction that success in landing the arms 'can only be assured by the most vigorous efforts'.

Shortly afterwards they decided to use a single 1,200-ton cargo ship, the former Wilson Line *Castro* (built in Hull in 1911), which had been seized in the Kiel Canal on the outbreak of war and recommissioned in the German navy as SMS *Libau*. They eventually gave way to Casement's insistence that they provide a U-boat to take him back to Ireland – in direct contravention of Devoy's unambiguous instruction that he stay in Germany. Under the command of a reserve lieutenant, Karl Spindler, the *Libau* sailed from Hamburg on 30 March through the Kiel Canal to Lübeck, where it was disguised as a similar-sized Norwegian steamer, the *Aud*. On 10 April Spindler set out through the Skagerrak on his perilous voyage. Without a radio, his orders were to arrive in Tralee Bay on the 20th, and rendezvous off Inishtooskert Island with the U-boat carrying Casement and Monteith. Remarkably enough, he arrived on time (at least, according to the colourful account he published after the war). To do this, he had to survive not only hurricane-force winds, but also the attentions of several British auxiliary cruisers. Since there is strong evidence that the Admiralty knew all about Spindler's mission, it is an interesting question why the British allowed him to reach Tralee Bay. One investigator has proposed a Machiavellian motive: it would have been good propaganda to have had a comparatively insignificant cargo of second-rate arms landed by the Germans as proof of enemy involvement. This hazardous gamble would have been strange, though not inconceivable.[17] Even more extravagant is the suggestion that the Admiralty intelligence chief, Captain Hall, was happy to see a rebellion take place, since it would trigger a full-blown repressive policy in Ireland.[18] But it is curious that the Commander-in-Chief of Western Approaches, Admiral Bayly, based at Queenstown near Cork, claimed to have told the Irish Executive directly about the arms ship, and got no response. Oddest of all, perhaps, a careful survey of survivors in the 1960s showed that local people had seen no military or naval defensive preparations in the Fenit area.

Casement and Monteith, with a sergeant from the Irish Brigade, Julian Beverly – a particularly dubious ornament of a dubious outfit – sailed out of Wilhelmshaven on the U20 (the submarine that had sunk the *Lusitania*) on 12 April. After a day and a half it turned back with mechanical problems, and the three were transferred to U19 (commanded, by coincidence, by Captain Weisbach, who had been torpedo officer on the U20 when it sank the *Lusitania*). Monteith had used the day's delay to try out the collapsible dinghy in which they were to land, spraining his right wrist in the process. On 15 April they set out again, to endure six days in the cramped and bilious conditions of a fighting submarine. Just why Casement was doing this has never been wholly clear. According to Monteith's attractive memoir *Casement's Last Adventure* (denounced, predictably enough, by one of their German comrades as 'not just very inaccurate but more or less fiction'), Casement told him that it was his duty to stop the rising, since the Germans were not prepared to provide real military aid.[19] Monteith, who seems not to have known of Devoy's urgent wish to prevent Casement returning to Ireland, agreed with this. But one of Casement's last letters shows him shifting his view dramatically: 'the impending action in Ireland', he wrote to Count Wedel on 2 April, 'rests on very justifiable grounds' (the government's determination to smash the Volunteer movement and impose conscription). 'I will very gladly go to Ireland with the arms and do all I can to sustain and support a movement of resistance based on these grounds.'[20] Captain Weisbach, who 'developed a great admiration for Casement' – still an imposing figure, even when seasick and shorn of his fine beard for the voyage – remembered his Irish passengers singing patriotic songs and breaking out a big flag (of Casement's design). This was indeed a strange item to be carrying on such a mission, along with the Zeiss binoculars, flashlights, Mauser pistols and cyanide capsules with which the Germans had supplied them.

On the afternoon of Friday, 14 April, with the *Libau/Aud* hove to near the Arctic Circle because Spindler was slightly ahead of schedule, John Devoy was greatly surprised to see Philomena Plunkett walk into the *Gaelic American* office with a peremptory message from the military committee. 'Arms must not be landed before midnight of Sunday, 23rd. This is vital. Smuggling impossible. Let us know if submarine will come to Dublin Bay.' Devoy passed the message on, but seems not to have been told that there was no radio contact with Spindler. Nor does he seem to have wondered what was meant by the remark about 'smuggling'. Is it possible, despite subsequent denials, that the military committee had really hoped until this point that the arms could be got ashore secretly?[21] From this point, the IRB's response to the German demand for 'the most vigorous efforts' is wrapped in obscurity.[22]

Spindler, his nerves strained no doubt by the weather and his brushes with the Royal Navy, dropped anchor off Inishtooskert Island in Tralee Bay on the afternoon of Thursday 20 April. To his great disappointment, 'no pilot boat came and there was no evidence on shore of any preparation to receive us'. Just after midnight, Captain Weisbach brought U19 to the rendezvous point a mile north-west of Inishtooskert. The *Kriegsmarine* had, it seemed, done its bit with distinction. But U19 searched for at least two hours without finding the *Libau*. Next day, Good Friday, was 'a wonderful spring day'; yet neither boat, apparently, could see the other. According to Spindler's account of his position, this was impossible. Weisbach, however, judged Spindler a bad navigator, and later analysis supports him. The *Libau* was probably at least seven miles from the rendezvous point. Even so, the passivity of the Volunteers ashore was weird. Spindler cruised around the bay (he claimed to have come within 600 yards of Fenit pier at one point), showing the pre-arranged signal, a green light, but nobody saw or answered it. The pilot saw a ship on the evening of the 20th and again the next morning, but did nothing.[23]

Spindler's account may be unreliable, but it surely remains true that 'maritime minded people in Fenit might have been expected to become curious about a strange ship hanging around Tralee Bay'.[24]

On 17 April Austin Stack had presided as usual over the weekly meeting of the Tralee Battalion council. Unusually, according to his biographer, no minutes of this meeting survive. A week earlier he had announced that 'he was arranging for the battalion to spend the Easter holidays in camp and hoped to have full details for the next meeting'. On the 12th, he sent his deputy commandant Paddy Cahill to Dublin to a meeting with Pearse 're arrangements'. Two weeks earlier, Cahill had gone to Dublin to receive from Seán MacDermott two signalling lamps to communicate with the arms ship. For reasons unknown, he failed to bring them back to Tralee. Still more puzzlingly, Stack never explained to him, or anyone else, the 'detailed plan which he had' – so his biographer thinks – 'prepared for the landing of arms at Fenit and their distribution'.[25] Cahill, as a good IRB man, naturally did not ask about it. No copy of the plan survived. Stack took the trouble to go to Cahirciveen to brief one of his IRB men who worked at the Valentia telegraph station on how to send the news of the rising to America. But it did not occur to him to set a watch on the coast at the time originally arranged for the arms landing. The explanation offered by Florence O'Donoghue, who dismissed any suggestion 'that a small party might have kept a lookout, disguised as fishermen or otherwise' as 'quite unrealistic' because the RIC was too vigilant, does not seem entirely convincing.[26]

Stack's great test came early on Good Friday morning. He was having breakfast with Cornelius (Con) Collins, who had just come down from Dublin to take charge of the wireless arrangements, when he was told that two strangers had arrived at his father's shop and wanted to see him urgently. They did not go there for an hour, but then Collins immediately recognized Monteith, and got the news that Casement had landed somewhere north of Fenit during the night. (Monteith and Bailey had walked from Banna Strand into Tralee, but did not know exactly where they had landed; Casement had collapsed on the beach after the dinghy had overturned in the surf.) Stack and Collins set off to find him, driving as far north as Ballyheigue and eventually running into a group of RIC searching the dunes at Banna Strand.

Casement had already been arrested at 'McKenna's fort'; the police had no idea who he was, though the collapsible boat was clearly hard to explain. Stack and Collins headed off, followed by an RIC man on a bicycle, until they ran into another RIC patrol at Causeway, which arrested Collins and took him into the police station. In an almost farcical scene, Stack then pulled out his pistol and went into the barrack to rescue him. Inexplicably, not only was he not arrested – though he was of course very well known to the police – he succeeded in getting Collins out, with Collins' gun obligingly returned into the bargain.[27] (Together with the fact that the RIC County Inspector who interrogated Casement at Tralee asked him why on earth he had not shot the constable who arrested him, this may make us wonder how the force would have coped with any serious rebel activity.)

Later that day Stack convened a conference at the Rink in Tralee to brief the Volunteers on the Easter mobilization. During the meeting he received confirmation that Casement was being held in Ardfert RIC barrack (he was transferred to Tralee in the evening). His reaction was to break his silence and announce that the rising would begin on Sunday, but to argue, against those who wanted to go and rescue Casement, 'that he had given a solemn injunction that no shot was to be fired' before the rising. This was an odd argument from a man who had, only a few hours before, carried out an armed assault on a police station. As it turned out, this was to be Stack's only armed action of the rebellion. He was finally arrested in the early evening when he again went – apparently at Collins' request – to the police barrack where Collins was being held after being re-arrested. We do not know why Collins should have issued this highly irregular request, and Stack's reasons for deciding, in effect, to give himself up, have never been explained.[28] Both ended up in the barrack at Tralee where Casement was being held overnight, before he was taken rapidly out of Ireland and rushed over to London. The failure to rescue Casement, and the suspicion that the police had been led to his hiding place on Banna Strand by local inhabitants, would haunt not only Stack himself but also the local community for generations.[29]

A small but poignant disaster in Kerry later on Friday evening seems, in retrospect, to encapsulate the aura of doom hanging over the whole reception plan. Seán MacDermott and others had devised a plan to seize equipment from the wireless station at Cahirciveen and reassemble it in Tralee, 'to establish communication with the arms ship and submarine from Germany'.[30] Five men sent from Dublin, including a wireless specialist, Con Keating, were met by two cars in Killarney; two of them travelled in the first, and three in the following car. The second car took the wrong turning in Killorglin and plunged in the dark off Ballykissane pier into Castlemaine harbour. Although the driver survived, the three, Keating among them, were drowned. The leading car halted a few miles west of Killorglin, and when the following car's lights failed to appear, the remaining group abandoned the mission and returned to Dublin.[31]

The maritime phase of the rebellion ended on 22 April. Spindler had spent the previous day drifting south-westwards past the Blasket Islands, shadowed by two British armed trawlers, and wondering if he should start commerce-raiding operations in the Atlantic. Towards 6 p.m. he was finally rounded up by two 'Flower' class sloops, which he identified, bizarrely, as cross-channel steamers. (It was an error that was of a piece with a string of mis-statements in his racy account, culminating in his encounter with a 'whole swarm' of British warships.) They escorted him towards Queenstown, where he scuttled his ship at 9.28 a.m. on the 22nd. As a final touch of vainglory, he claimed thereby to have blocked the entrance to Cork harbour.

The news of Casement's arrest arrived in Dublin at a time when the military committee's efforts to keep Eoin MacNeill from interfering with the mobilization were delicately poised between success and failure. The most remarkable of these efforts had been made on Wednesday that week, when, at a meeting of the Dublin Corporation, Alderman Tom Kelly rose to read out a document purporting to have been leaked from Dublin Castle. It listed 'precautionary measures sanctioned by the Irish Office on the recommendation of the General Officer Commanding the Forces in Ireland'. All members of the Sinn Fein National Council, the Central Executive, General Council, and County Board of the Irish Sinn Fein Volunteers, Executive Committee of the National Volunteers, and Coisde Gnotha Committee of the Gaelic League, were to be arrested. The inhabitants of Dublin were to be confined to their houses 'until such time as the Competent Military

Authority may otherwise permit or direct'. Pickets were to be posted, and mounted patrols 'continuously visit all points' on the accompanying 'Maps 3 and 4'. Finally, various premises were to be 'occupied by adequate forces' – Liberty Hall, 6 Harcourt Street (the Sinn Fein office), 2 Dawson Street (the Volunteer Headquarters), 25 and 41 Rutland Square (the Gaelic League and Irish National Foresters) – while others were to be 'isolated'. These included the Archbishop's House, Drumcondra; the Mansion House on Dawson Street; 40 Herbert Park (O'Rahilly's house), Woodtown Park (MacNeill's house) and 'Larkfield', Kimmage Road (Count Plunkett's house); and St Enda's College, Rathfarnham. This document, published next day in *New Ireland*, caused a sensation. The paper's editor, P. J. Little, had received it from Rory O'Connor and passed it to Tom Kelly. The original was said to be in code, and to have been spirited out of Dublin Castle by a sympathizer. Little (who later became Minister for Posts and Telegraphs in the 1930s) believed then, and maintained for the rest of his life, that it was genuine.[32] So, more importantly, though more briefly, did Eoin MacNeill, who exclaimed 'the Lord has delivered them into our hands!' This was exactly the kind of repression he had long expected, and believed would justify armed resistance by the Volunteers. He immediately issued a general order for all units to 'be prepared with defensive measures', with the object of preserving 'the arms and organisation of the Irish Volunteers'. Local commanders were to 'arrange that your men defend themselves and each other in small groups so placed that they may best be able to hold out'. MacNeill was careful to remind them that 'Each group must be provided from the outset with sufficient supplies of food, or be certain of access to such supplies.' (This might sound obvious, but as the eventual Easter mobilization would prove, was all too easily overlooked.) There can be no doubt that the Chief of Staff was in deadly earnest at this moment. He signed the order with yet another chivvying injunction – 'This matter is urgent.'[33]

But was it? Many people found the language and the policy of the 'Castle document' quite plausible (though the maps and annexes with their name lists never emerged). Others had doubts, however. Naturally the authorities brusquely denounced it. Even on the other side, a number of people wondered whether the government could envisage such a pointlessly provocative action as surrounding the house of the Archbishop of Dublin, a well-known opponent of republicanism, or arresting the leaders of the moribund Redmondite Volunteers. Insiders soon came to think that the document had been concocted by Joseph Plunkett. 'Forgery is a strong word,' as Desmond Ryan wrote, 'but that in its final form the document was a forgery no doubt can exist whatever.'[34] Plunkett, 'on the basis of what he knew or could surmise of the precautionary measures drawn up by the military authorities', had constructed 'a ruse of war to create an atmosphere for the rising'. Its purpose was 'to deceive Eoin MacNeill, the rank and file of the Volunteers, and the Irish people in general'. In particular the naming of the INV as a target was intended to bring the constitutional nationalists (of whom P. J. Little was one) into line.

Ryan was right to say that 'in its final form' the document was a forgery, a judgement echoed by academic historians as well, but it seems that the scepticism may have been overdone.[35] Little's enduring belief in its genuineness had some basis. Seán MacDermott himself swore to it a few hours before his execution; telling the priest who spent the evening with him that 'it was an absolutely genuine document'.[36] Grace Gifford, Plunkett's fiancée, remembered sitting on his bed at Larkfield House writing it down as he deciphered it, using a code sheet that was later found in his field pocket book (picked up in Moore Street following the surrender, and now in the National Library). She was 'quite certain' that it had come out of the Castle, smuggled out in pieces by a sympathetic official, Eugene Smith. Smith's own testimony (long delayed for fear of losing his pension) confirms this in essence: the document was 'practically identical with that read out by Alderman Kelly, except that it did not state that the operations suggested were authorised by the Chief Secretary'. It was a despatch from General Friend to the Irish Office in London, detailing precautionary measures in the event of conscription being imposed. So this was not a plan for imminent action, but it was a real plan: Smith said that even the notorious reference to Ara Coeli, the archbishop's house, which was taken by many as proof that the document was a forgery, was in the original.[37] Though Plunkett certainly 'sexed up' the document, he did not make it up; this was a real leak. As Grace Plunkett sagely reflected, 'You cannot be too careful when the Civil Service is composed of Irish people.'[38]

The common nationalist denunciation of the document must have gratified the military committee, but it was soon followed by a disastrous collapse of unanimity. MacNeill had been on his guard ever since the confrontations with Connolly and Pearse in January and February, though, as he later explained to Hobson, 'I had great reluctance to show mistrust and preferred to rely on the assurance I had received.' But in early April he once again became convinced that he was 'not in the current of all that was going on'. He called a meeting of the Volunteer Staff at his house 'to arrive at some definite understanding'. At this meeting, on 5 April, according to Hobson, 'Pearse explicitly repudiated the suggestion that he or his friends contemplated insurrection or wanted to commit the Volunteers to any policy other than that to which they were publicly committed.' He and the staff agreed to a written instruction that, apart from routine matters, no order would be issued without MacNeill's counter-signature. Next day, MacNeill received a letter from a Chicago Irish-American, Bernard MacGillian (posted a month earlier but delayed by British military censors), warning him on the basis of 'absolutely reliable information' of a plot 'to deluge Ireland in blood'. The plotters were aiming to discredit Redmond at any price, using the Volunteers as their tools. For the time being, MacNeill ignored this. The 'intense tension' of Holy Week persuaded him to issue his Wednesday general order warning of 'a plan on the part of the government for the suppression and disarmament of the Irish Volunteers', and instructing them to resist disarmament by force if necessary. On Thursday, Hobson and others took these orders out to provincial units.

About 10 p.m. that evening, however, Ginger O'Connell and Eimar O'Duffy told Hobson that companies in Dublin were receiving orders for the Sunday manoeuvres which could only mean that they were being used as a cover for insurrection. The three of them went to MacNeill's home in Woodtown Park, got him out of bed, and went over to St Enda's with him. The long-delayed confrontation between MacNeill and Pearse finally took place around midnight, when Pearse admitted for the first time that a rising was planned, and MacNeill said he would do everything in his power – short of informing the authorities – to prevent it. Pearse bluntly told him that the Volunteers had always really been under IRB control, and told Hobson that he was bound to accept the Supreme Council's decision. Hobson rejected this, going back to his theory that a rising (at least one in circumstances Hobson disapproved) would contravene the IRB constitution. After this stand-off, the MacNeill group retired to Woodtown Park to draft three orders. The first directed that 'all orders of a special character issued by Commandant Pearse with regard to military movements of a definite kind' were 'hereby recalled or cancelled'; all future special orders were to be issued by the Chief of Staff alone. The second empowered Hobson to issue orders in MacNeill's name, and the third gave O'Connell overall authority over the Volunteers in Munster.[39] The Munster officers were instructed to 'report to Commandant O'Connell as required by him on the subject of any special orders which they had received and any arrangements to be made by them in consequence'.[40] O'Connell took the first available train to Cork, while Hobson set about circulating the orders (and copies of the 'Castle Document') across the country.

In the meantime, the military committee launched a damage-limitation exercise. MacNeill was roused from his bed again at 8 a.m. on Friday by the arrival of Seán MacDermott, with the news that 'a ship of arms from Germany was expected at that very time'. MacNeill, suitably impressed, replied, 'Very well – if that is the state of the case I'm with you.'[41] He went downstairs to find that both Pearse and MacDonagh had also arrived. They all had breakfast together, but 'there was not much said', MacNeill recorded, because they were all 'looking forward to an immediate rising in arms'. What did he mean by this rather surprising phrase? His biographer suggests that it can be explained by another order he wrote on the 21st: 'Government action for the suppression of the Volunteers is now inevitable and may begin at any moment.' Volunteers were to be on their guard, and to ignore the 'worthless' government statements denying the Castle Document. But his orders indicated that he was gearing up not for a 'rising' so much as for guerrilla resistance on the lines preferred by the 'hedge-fighting' group. MacNeill said that Joseph Plunkett called on him later to ask if he 'was prepared to sign a proclamation', but when MacNeill asked what its terms were, Plunkett 'told me no more about it'.[42] MacDonagh believed that MacNeill had 'abdicated' as Chief of Staff and transferred his authority to Pearse and MacDermott, while

MacDermott claimed that MacNeill had endorsed orders recalling O'Connell and instructing local commanders to 'proceed with the rising'.[43] Like so many others, this order has disappeared, though the reply of Cork Volunteer commander Tomas MacCurtain was preserved: 'Tell Seán we will blaze away as long as the stuff lasts.'[44]

All these uncertain happenings provided the basis for the belief (fostered by Constance Markievicz among others) that MacNeill had agreed to a rising, and even signed the proclamation of the republic. It seems clear, though, that he was still being fed the minimum information calculated to keep him on side. At the same time, the terms MacNeill himself used for the kind of action he was expecting were ambiguous. He recorded that on Saturday the emergency seemed to recede, and he agreed with O'Rahilly and Seán Fitzgibbon 'that the rising ought to be prevented'. By 'rising' he seems to have meant a purely defensive resistance, though it was an odd choice of word. When he read the news of the discovery of Casement's collapsible boat on the Kerry coast he thought 'that the situation was beyond remedy – though I was ready to take part in the rising I did not see the least prospect of success for it'. In the notes he made for his lawyer after his arrest in May 1916, he said he had seen MacDonagh and Plunkett in his house on Saturday morning and 'dissuaded them. They were a bit shaken but not convinced. They undertook to consult their friends further (Pearse, Connolly, etc.)' and arranged 'to meet me again in Dublin at Rathgar'.

At last, on Saturday afternoon, the scales began to drop from MacNeill's eyes. Yet another visitation, this time O'Rahilly bringing Seán Fitzgibbon and Colm O Lochlainn (who had met Fitzgibbon at Limerick on his way back from the disastrous Cahirciveen expedition), revealed that the arms ship was lost, the Castle Document a forgery and, finally, that Hobson had been placed under arrest. For the last time, MacNeill dashed with the others over to St Enda's. Pearse was 'in a very excited state', according to O Lochlainn, and told him 'We have used your name and influence for what they were worth, but we have done with you now. It is no use trying to stop us.' When MacNeill said he would forbid the Sunday mobilization, Pearse retorted 'Our men will not obey you.' Even now, it took MacNeill some hours longer to come 'to the conclusion that these persons intended to have their own way'.

Only at midnight, after a final meeting with MacDonagh (his colleague at UCD), did MacNeill draft a curt order to all units: 'Volunteers completely deceived. All orders for special action are hereby cancelled, and on no account will action be taken. Eoin MacNeill, Chief of Staff.' A group of senior staff officers left to take the order out into the country – O'Rahilly, the only one who habitually drove his own car, extravagantly took a taxi to Cork and on through Kerry and Tipperary to Limerick. MacNeill went to the *Irish Independent* office to place a slightly modified version in the Sunday paper.

This was a disorienting torrent of events. Hobson's arrest by his comrades of the IRB Leinster Executive, on the orders of MacDermott and the military committee, at the Volunteer Headquarters in Dawson Street on Good Friday afternoon was particularly remarkable.[45] The conspirators seem to have believed that he was more likely than MacNeill to take effective action. He was certainly 'the only one given this dubious honour', as one historian has noted – a tribute to his continuing influence and knowledge. It was also a decisive moment in that longer process which has been called the 'disappearance' of Hobson, his elimination from the Irish nationalist story. By 1935, when MacNeill was asked which of the 1916 leaders had used 'Bulmer Hobson' as a pseudonym, 'as far as the general public was concerned, he had disappeared as completely as if he had been executed with the rebel leaders'. More so, one might well say, since his reputation has never recovered. (In fact he was at some mortal risk from his captors, according to the Dublin IRB Centre in whose house he was held. They were apparently so 'annoyed by being out of things' once the rising began that 'they were even suggesting he should be executed and dumped on the railway line at the back of my place'. Hobson, for his part, was, unsurprisingly, 'inclined to be obstreperous, protesting against his arrest'.)[46] Hobson himself later claimed that 'they were very nice to me', and that his arrest was 'almost a relief' because matters were taken out of his hands.[47] He was liberated on Monday evening by Seán T. O'Kelly, but rehabilitation was a different matter. 'Ireland could ill afford', as has been said, 'to lose the services of so capable and devoted a son', but his freezing out was 'a mystery, a whodunnit', which could not be explained on policy disagreements alone.[48] There were personality clashes too, not least with MacDermott ('deadly sly'); it is plain that Hobson was self-confident to the point of arrogance, and intolerant of dissent. But so was Griffith. Pride played a part, clearly. Though it is true that Hobson 'did not retire voluntarily from national affairs', he certainly preferred to avoid justifying his position to the survivors of the fighting. The air was never cleared. The IRB for its part seems to have considered putting Hobson on trial after the rebellion; but Michael Collins took avoiding action with the argument that this could only be done 'by his peers', who were all dead.[49]

Bulmer Hobson's detention showed the lengths to which the conspirators would go – and were now forced to go – to neuter the 'hedge-fighting' group. They had risked a fateful conflict of authority, and on Easter Sunday morning their chickens came home to roost. When the 'countermanding order' appeared on the news-stands in the *Sunday Independent*, the military committee had already assembled at Liberty Hall. As the 'Provisional Government', the seven had now signed the Proclamation of the Irish Republic, which was being printed (with type obtained from an English master printer in Stafford Street) on the presses of the *Workers' Republic*.[50] With typical reckless impetuosity Constance Markievicz grabbed one of the first copies off the press and rushed out to declaim it to the passers-by in Lower Abbey Street. In the same spirit she flourished her pistol when she heard of the countermanding order, and told Connolly 'I'll shoot Eoin MacNeill.' Connolly and the Provisional Government reacted more thoughtfully. Tom Clarke urged that they go ahead that evening as planned. 'If the rising was delayed until Monday, the men in most places would be demobilised and unable to do anything, as the British military would by then be on guard.'[51] But Pearse, despite his bullish assertion to MacNeill that the Volunteers would not obey him, preferred to wait till next day. The others agreed. Even MacDermott, to Clarke's distress, 'voted against me'.[52] And the impatient Connolly, whose own force was unaffected by the countermand, also accepted the delay. This may have been a serious error; the turnout on Sunday was much larger than the eventual muster for rebellion on Monday. Pearse's earlier confidence was more justified than his last-minute caution.

MacNeill's published order was unambiguous in intent, though it was gnomic about its reasons. 'Owing to the very critical position', all orders for Sunday were 'hereby rescinded, and no parades, marches, or other movements of Irish Volunteers will take place'. In an effort to trump Pearse's insubordination, MacNeill added almost pedantic-ally, 'Each individual Volunteer will obey this order strictly in every particular.' The military committee, for its part, decided to issue two separate orders. The first confirmed the cancellation of the Sunday manoeuvres; the other ordered the start of operations at noon on Monday. The point of the first, according to Diarmuid Lynch, was 'to obviate the possibility that units outside Dublin might start operations before the Dublin Battalions could occupy their allotted positions on Easter Monday', and also – should the British 'become aware' of it – to allay their suspicions. Neither of these reasons seems very convinc-ing, unless it was believed that the second order (sent out overnight) would be less likely to come to British attention. What is clear is that the two orders risked magnifying the confusion outside Dublin, and the evidence suggests that they did just that.

In most accounts of the rising, including those by participants such as Diarmuid Lynch and Desmond Ryan, Easter Sunday is written off as a day of rueful inaction. They give the impression that the counter-mand, duly confirmed by Pearse, was obeyed, and that no mobiliza-tion took place.[53] This may have been true for the leaders, but was clearly not true for all their subordinates. In Dublin and across the country, many Volunteers headed off to the manoeuvres, cheerfully unaware of either MacNeill's or Pearse's order. James Crenigan, for instance, joined some 200 of the Fingal (5th) Battalion of the Dublin Brigade at Saucerstown. Harry Colley of F Company, 2nd Battalion – MacDonagh's own unit – took his three rifles to Father Mathew Park, where he found 'a number of the various companies of the 2nd Battalion assembled'. Seamus Daly outdid him, lugging no fewer than six rifles and four big parcels of revolvers on the tram to the park. (Some DMP men he passed on the way, evidently impressed by this arsenal, cheerily said 'Well, James, you are going to have a great field day today.')[54] The pavilion at the park had become a large arms depot. Colley's First Lieutenant, Oscar Traynor (who, according to his commander, Frank Henderson, had come up with the bright idea of printing mobilization slips for the whole battalion), asked him how many rounds he had for his revolver. 'He went to the pile of .32

ammunition and dipping his hands into it said "take that – you'll want it. It will be all hand-to-hand fighting we'll have at first.'"[55] Colley was eventually 'demobilised again by Captain Tom Weafer on information from Miss Ryan (MacNeill's secretary) that only the ICA were out'. This left the 2nd battalion with the task of guarding the arms depot (which included 'a good deal of 1st battalion and GHQ equipment', plus explosive and electrical equipment, Frank Henderson recalled). Since the 'police spies were very active that Sunday night while our men were on guard, there was a lot of noise with both sides tramping about, and I got very little sleep that night'.[56]

Liam Tannam of E Company, 3rd Battalion, took a robust view of the countermand, telling some members of his company he met on the way to Mass not to obey any order that did not come directly from him. As a result, he assembled fifty-eight out of his sixty-three men in Oakley Road around 3 p.m. A quarter of an hour later, 'a white-faced young fellow, sweating and panting', pedalled up on a bike, with a letter from Eoin MacNeill addressed to Father McMahon of Rathmines, authenticating the countermand. Tannam sent him back with the message that he would only obey orders from his immediate superior (i.e. Eamon de Valera) and drew his men up with their flag (3ft by 2ft, 'with a harp') in front. Just then Captain Ffrench-Mullen, a 4th Battalion officer (whose sister, Madeleine, was a prominent Cumann na mBan activist), rode by in full uniform on his bike, and shouted 'the whole thing is off'. 'Not as far as I'm concerned', Tannam robustly replied. Ffrench-Mullen said that Eamonn Ceannt had just demobilized the whole of his battalion, so he could take it as official. Tannam still refused, and only demobilized when his brother rode up with MacDonagh's order, countersigned by de Valera, closely followed by MacDonagh himself and both Pearse brothers on their way home. He sent his men off around 3.45 p.m. with orders 'to be ready for a sudden mobilisation', and went home himself 'bitterly disappointed, and thinking here is another case of conflicting orders'.[57]

Outside Dublin, many Volunteers had still more strenuous, and much more anti-climactic experiences. Over 1,000 men of the Cork Brigade, for instance, assembled in various places across the county. Many, but not all, seem to have had instructions to meet at Beeing or Carriganimma.[58] It was while the Kilnamartyra Company was marching towards Carriganimma that Patrick O'Sullivan's uncle posed the searching query, 'Do you expect to come back today?' Like many others, O'Sullivan had not thought about this, but was not entirely surprised.[59] Twenty-nine of the Ballinhassig Company mobilized at Raheen Cross; some had been told that their aim 'was to get arms that were to be landed' but they 'were not to tell anyone else in the Company of this. We were afraid that they would not turn out if they knew.'[60] Con Collins, of D Company of Cork City IV, paraded at the station with thirty-eight others to take the train to Crookstown, and marched from there to Macroom. There, Seán O'Sullivan 'told us the exercises had been cancelled. He said it was the intention to go to Carriganimma, where other men were to meet us, but that owing to the downpour of rain no arrangement could be made for the men to camp out that night.' It might endanger their health and make them unfit for 'more important work later on'. All the Corkmen remembered the terrible weather of Easter Sunday. After a beautiful spring morning came 'one of the wettest days we could remember'. When the assembly at Beeing was finally dismissed around 5 p.m. by MacCurtain and MacSwiney – 'in uniform with high red boots' – 'everybody was thoroughly saturated . . . faces were coloured green where the dye from their hats had run onto them'.[61] 'Never such rain fell', as Tim O'Riordan of Castlelack told Kathleen McDonnell.

The train brought us back to Crookstown. Every man had to buy his own ticket. We made a long stop at Crookstown, and another at Scariff. It was 4 o'clock or so by the time we got back to Castlelack. We brought with us an amount of rifle ammunition belonging to the Cork Volunteers. When the order came to disband, they were not prepared to return to Cork with it and it was to be cast away.[62]

What was the impact of MacNeill's 'countermanding order' on the rebellion? The traditional separatist verdict was unambiguous: it was disastrous. This view was established straight away in Liberty Hall, when Tom Clarke fulminated that MacNeill had ruined everything, and Markievicz brandished her pistol, swearing she would shoot him.[63] Pearse's final communiqué, on the Friday of Easter week, spoke of the 'fatal countermanding order' which had prevented the original plans from being carried out. In time, and in the light of the rebellion's impact, even hardline republicans came to take a slightly different view. Diarmuid Lynch proposed that the 'untoward experiences' of Holy Week had been 'Providential in more than one respect'. Causing the Dublin rising to stand out in heroic isolation had been a blessing in disguise. Many recognized that one of the countermand's inadvertent effects had been to confirm the authorities in their belief (stimulated by the capture of Casement) that the rising had been called off. But there was general agreement that the order's effect had been significant.

By contrast, the first serious historical evaluation of its impact offered a rather different perspective. The traditional view was based on Tom Clarke's anguished cry. 'Our plans were so perfect, and now everything is spoiled.' Only if the plans had indeed been perfect would the countermand have been disastrous. But a systematic examination of the situation in the provinces, by Maureen Wall, argued that the plans were so sketchy that the countermand could not have decisively affected their viability. The basic problem, on this view, was the secrecy of the military committee's work, and the scrambling of the chain of command caused by the selective briefing of trusted officers. 'Absolute secrecy maintained by a tiny group of men, who were relying on the unquestioning obedience of the members of a nationwide revolutionary organization, was bound to defeat their object of bringing about a revolution, except in Dublin where these men were, in fact, in a position to control events.' It was 'useless' to put IRB men in key positions without letting them know of the existence of the military committee, or of the deep divisions in the higher leadership of the Volunteers.[64]

Can Wall's stark verdict that 'Eoin MacNeill's countermand stopped no Volunteer, who was anxious for war, from participating in the Rising' be sustained? Was laying the blame on him perhaps an example of the kind of search for scapegoats often found in 'versions of Irish history' which tried to simplify circumstances that were complicated or 'too painful to contemplate objectively'?[65] The assertion that the military committee's command structure was too fragile to bear the weight that Pearse placed on it is persuasive; and it is of course true that there was nothing to stop anyone coming 'out' in Easter week. (Some who had never even joined the Volunteers did so.)

But, as often happens with such necessary correctives, 'revisionist' assessment may have swung too far in the opposite direction.[66] Even with a shortage of service weapons, the numbers mobilized on Sunday were capable of mounting more extensive operations than would occur on Monday. In a sense – and as many critics later charged – the Sunday mobilizers had been brought out under false pretences; but that is not the same as saying they did not accept the idea of a rebellion. The evidence suggests that they did not feel duped by the mobilization plan. But while turning a field-day into a war was, as the planners had calculated, almost easy, turning out in the cold light of a weekday might be much more difficult. On Monday, only those who were indeed 'anxious for war' would turn out. It seems clear enough that the 'countermand' had dramatic effects.

Ironically, the military committee's efforts to keep their plans secret may have deceived their own IV comrades more effectively than they did the 'foreign enemy'. The British authorities were bombarded with warnings about the approaching rebellion. The last and most accurate came at the end of Holy Week from a police agent codenamed 'Chalk', who reported 'Professor MacDonagh's' orders on Wednesday evening: 'We are not going out on Friday but we are going out on Sunday.'[67] Crucially, however, they did not want to believe such warnings. When the rebellion broke out, they were taken completely by surprise. This was a classic instance of intelligence failure: caused not by a lack of information, but by the blinkered view of those whose job was to interpret it. We need to grasp the reasons for this, because without it the rebellion would, almost certainly, never have happened.

On 10 April 1916, just two weeks before Easter week, Major Price submitted a report (unavoidably delayed, 'owing to pressure of work') to his commander, Major-General Friend, on the state of the country. He outlined the main reasons for the faltering of military recruitment, including a generalized public dislike of military service, and the 'lukewarm' attitude of the clergy, as well as the 'persistent and insistent' Sinn Fein anti-recruiting campaign. Most of his report was taken up with his analysis of the 'Sinn Fein Volunteers', now totalling some 10,000 with 4,800 rifles, revolvers and shotguns.[68] Large caches of home-made bayonets and grenades had been recently found. The conclusions he drew were mixed. There was 'undoubted proof that the Sinn Fein Irish Volunteers are working up for rebellion and revolution if ever they got a good opportunity'. At the same time, 'the mass of the people are sound and loyal', and there were encouraging signs that 'popular feeling is turning against the Sinn Fein Party'. So how serious was the situation? Was immediate action required? Perhaps the key point in Price's analysis was his assumption that 'of course, these Sinn Feiners could never expect to face trained troops successfully'. This perfectly rational assumption left a German invasion, which could undoubtedly be 'enormously assisted' by the Volunteers, as the only significant military threat.[69]

If Price did not quite allow the government a way out, he diluted the urgency of his advice by its oblique phrasing – 'It is a question of high policy whether the time is not ripe for the proclamation and disarmament of this hostile anti-British organisation before it is given an opportunity to do more serious injury.' The 'high policy' people (who never saw this report, in fact) had of course repeatedly decided that the time was not ripe. Through the autumn and winter of 1915–16 Birrell and Nathan had endured a buffeting by the Unionist peer Lord Midleton, a big Cork landowner and former secretary of state for war, who persistently demanded decisive action. Birrell repeatedly argued that to attempt to suppress Sinn Féin 'would probably result in shooting, and divide the country' in the midst of war. 'Strong measures when effective', he lectured the exasperated Midleton, 'are the best of all measures and the easiest, but if ineffective do no good but only harm.'[70] To put down the Volunteers would be 'reckless and foolish'. The implicit pessimism of this analysis sat oddly with his bravado, as when he declared 'I laugh at the whole thing.' Midleton dissented: 'I told him frankly that I thought he was pursuing a dangerous course.'

But Nathan loyally accepted his chief's conviction that though Ireland was 'in a rotten state' and 'ripe for a row', it was without leadership; the only danger was of isolated terrorist attacks rather than a full-scale uprising. This was in spite of his own belief that the situation (in late November 1915) was 'bad and fairly rapidly growing worse'. As a soldier himself, he was plainly unsettled by the increasingly grim view taken by the military authorities. Not long after his arrival in Ireland, he was treated to a heavyweight interview with Kitchener, who told him that Ireland was 'in a state of festering rebellion'. By February 1916 the Irish commander-in-chief was calling for the suppression of the Volunteers, and the commander-in-chief of home forces, Lord French, pressed this course on Birrell, whose response was only to repeat his belief that public displays of troops marching about with bands would have 'a good effect'. Nathan noted that 'strong measures – or the appearance of them – are being put on the file for the time being, I am sure rightly'. That Nathan had some inkling of how mistaken Birrell's optimism was can be seen from a revealing private reflection in March. 'The press is always attributing base motives and sinister schemes to my country', he wrote to a friend, 'and the more truly Irish the newspaper the more violent its abuse of England.' This was not surprising perhaps, but the syndrome went further. 'The casual acquaintance does not hesitate to speak his mind, as he would say freely, on the subject of English wickedness, and I have dined as a guest with friends who have made this the main topic of conversation intended to entertain me.'[71] Nathan clearly wanted to see this as merely an odd, if upsetting, quirk of the Irish character; but it was really a crucial political fact.

Though their confidence waxed and waned, Birrell and Nathan held on to the belief that the only likelihood of a rising would come from a premature attempt to suppress the Volunteers, and that even a consistent campaign against the subversive press might boomerang on the authorities. In response to a demand by the West Kerry MP for the suppression of the openly disloyal *Kerryman*, Nathan 'pointed out that it would be difficult to justify the suppression of papers in the country if such as the *Workers Republic* published in Dublin were allowed to go on'. And suppressing them, he said, 'would involve a whole sequence of events probably leading up to coercion' – so 'could not be contemplated except as part of a very big question'.[72] Very big questions, naturally, were not in contemplation. When the Volunteers published a manifesto in the Dublin *Evening Mail* on 27 March, its editor, Henry Tivy (a Unionist of 'fairly sound judgment though warped by strong political bias', Nathan thought), protested, 'Let me stake my reputation to you and General Friend that although there is a possibility of isolated outrages and even assassinations here and there, there is none whatever at present in any part of Ireland of what is called a general "rising".'[73] Ten days before the rebellion, Lord Midleton 'took Mr Tivy's view that the public should know all about the [subversive] movement, because that might lead to its suppression'. So Nathan once again patiently 'explained the other aspect of the case' – the danger of giving 'currency to seditious talk and exaggerated boasts' of the Volunteers by publication in the 'better class of newspapers'.

The feasibility of rebellion was repeatedly weighed up, sometimes with ambiguous results. In mid-1915 the police had information 'from two sources' that 'a large number' of Volunteer leaders were anxious to start an insurrection. A motion proposing immediate insurrection had, they thought, been put to the Volunteer Executive by Bulmer Hobson, and only defeated by the casting vote of Professor MacNeill. Although the details of this were certainly garbled, the fact that there was talk of rebellion was plain. But, like Major Price, the police were looking for definite signs of German intervention, and could not find them. Like everyone else, the police gave out mixed messages: in September 1915, the Inspector-General opined that 'the Sinn Fein leaders do not command either followers or equipment sufficient for insurrection', but in December the RIC Special Branch sounded a more worrying note. The development of the Irish Volunteer movement was 'now a matter deserving serious attention on account of its revolutionary character'; it was 'thoroughly disloyal and hostile to the British government', was 'apparently now on the increase and might rapidly assume dimensions sufficient to cause anxiety to the military authorities'. Still, as late as 10 April 1916, Nathan told General Macready at the War Office that although the Volunteers had been 'active of late, I do not believe that [their] leaders mean insurrection, or that the Volunteers have sufficient arms to make it formidable if the leaders do mean it'. In the early stages of the war, the danger of a German invasion was taken seriously enough for the Admiralty to send a group of naval officers disguised as American tourists on a yacht, the *Sayonara*, to cruise the west coast. (No other agencies were told of the undercover operation, and the yacht was arrested several times by naval patrols.) Coastal communities were placarded with warning notices telling the inhabitants to evacuate their homes in event of an invasion. But in January 1915 the yacht patrol was stood down, having found nothing; and – incredibly, perhaps – no further military steps were taken to prepare against any possible landings in the west.

The Irish government's quietist consensus was increasingly disturbed by the Viceroy, Lord Wimborne, who saw his main task as to stimulate recruitment. He had taken personal charge of the new recruiting organization, the Department of Recruiting for Ireland, set up in October 1915 to replace the unsuccessful CCORI, and grew more and more worried by the spread of seditious propaganda. Arriving in April 1915, he was annoyed to find himself outside the loop of governmental decision-making, and battled for months to break out of the invisible barrier constructed around his office in the time of his predecessor, Lord Aberdeen, whom Birrell had held in contempt. In early March 1916 he finally persuaded Nathan to forward daily police reports to him ('but not with a view to inviting my opinion').[74] He began to press for the tightening up of security measures. When he found, for instance, in March 1916 that deportation was again being discussed, he pointed out that it had been tried before without success, and demanded to 'know what different methods of enforcement are contemplated to make the order effective'. He found the police reports defective, complaining 'I can't understand how the night manoeuvres in Dublin were omitted from the police report summary', or 'why it is that we are left to learn from the press this morning of the arms seizure in Cork. Surely we should have daily reports from the police of any Sinn Fein activities, and action of this kind should not be undertaken without the cognizance of the Executive?'[75]

Wimborne was far from incompetent, but he was a political lightweight. A former Liberal MP (and cousin of Winston Churchill), he had been sent to the House of Lords in 1910 to bolster the Liberal minority. He came to the Lord Lieutenancy after a few months on the staff of the nascent 10th Division at the Curragh. His appointment did nothing to demonstrate that the British government was seriously engaging with the critical situation in Ireland. He continued to hold court in the traditional Viceregal manner. Lady Cynthia Asquith, then involved with Wimborne's private secretary Lord Basil Blackwood, was a guest at the Viceregal Lodge in early 1916, and provided a brilliant vignette of 'His Ex' and 'Queen Alice', a couple who took themselves just a little too seriously. (Travelling at the end of January, Lady Cynthia echoed Birrell's distaste for the Holyhead–Kingstown crossing: 'most unpleasant – there wasn't any sensational amount of motion but it must have been very well chosen, anyhow it carried its point . . . I got off feeling very green and plain.') One of her main objects became to avoid an invitation to Wimborne's private sitting room. 'It is very oriental, the way he stalks out of the room followed by the woman, whom he returns at his leisure to the drawing room.' He astonished her not just with his 'terrible way of flapping his furry eyelids at one', but also with his declaration that 'he had read everything worth reading'. He 'had the audacity to talk of his poverty', while '"Queen" Alice was outraged the other day when someone estimated her annual dress expenditure at only £10,000.' Yet this pompous would-be proconsul was the only member of the Irish executive with a positive agenda. Lady Cynthia wryly observed the gulf between him and the Chief Secretary, when Wimborne asked him to visit a shell factory. Birrell was puzzled – 'Shells? Shells? What shells?' He was thinking of the beach, not the war.[76]

Though the authorities might well have been alarmed by the big Volunteer parades on St Patrick's Day, they preferred to focus on the fact that 'only' 1,817 of the 4,555 who turned out in the provinces were armed, less than half of these with rifles. (So the RIC estimated, though the DMP did not count the weapons of the 1,400 who mustered on College Green in Dublin). They drew comfort from the unenthusiastic attitude of the spectators. Again, on 30 March, when a big rally outside the Mansion House to protest against the deportation of Blythe and Mellows 'was followed by disorderly conduct during which traffic was held up and two policemen were fired at', they noted that while violent language was used, 'the conduct of the persons attending was not disorderly'.[77] Crucially, perhaps, the well-informed source 'Chalk' reported on the 31st that the 'Genreal [sic] Mobilization for next Sunday has been cancelled . . . as they appear to be afraid of being disarmed in a body'.[78]

In late March, at a War Office meeting between Wimborne, Birrell and Kitchener to discuss recruiting, Wimborne raised the question of reinforcing the Irish garrison. Again, on the 23rd, senior Irish government officials conferred with Lord French at the Horse Guards to discuss the desirability of transferring one or more reserve infantry brigades from Britain to Ireland. French was happy with this in principle, but pointed out that it would delay training, might complicate draft-finding, and could entail other complications. The civil officials evidently did not press the point firmly enough to ensure that anything happened. Wimborne himself kept quiet about his real reasons for wanting the transfer – 'that we had not enough troops in Ireland in case of internal trouble' – because he thought it undesirable to say this 'at the Conference, before the people who were there'.[79] The leisurely pace of governmental preparation remained untroubled. No significant military reinforcements appear to have been sent; although on 6 April General Friend finally responded to Birrell's hints about 'some display of military force in the City', saying he would see if he 'could arrange for the Dublin Fusiliers, the RIC and some of the Cavalry to be more in evidence'.[80] The government also planned a bigger role for the part-time Volunteer Training Corps. On 22 April Nathan suggested to Colonel Edgeworth-Johnstone, the head of the DMP, that their uniform 'has now been made sufficiently familiar to the public for men in it to be employed on quasi-military duty without exciting much comment'. As ever, the prime need was to avoid excitement.

As ever, too, Wimborne was the only senior official ready to risk provoking opposition. On that day, Easter Saturday, the government's situation perfectly demonstrated its inner contradictions. The Chief Secretary was in London, where he had attended a Cabinet meeting and decided to stay for Easter. When the news of the sinking of the *Libau/Aud* arrived in Dublin, General Friend, amazingly, decided to follow his example. This left Nathan and Wimborne to interpret the mixed messages emerging from the multiplicity of meetings and journeys by 'suspects' across the country on that weekend of suppressed drama. They acted true to type. Both of them thought that Casement's arrest and the loss of the German arms meant that the rebellion was off. (Nathan wrote to Birrell on Saturday, 'the Irish Volunteers are to have a "mobilisation" and march tomorrow but I see no indications of a "rising"'.) But Wimborne seized on the opportunity these events provided to strike at Sinn Fein. Late on Saturday evening he urged immediate action. When Nathan came to see him at 10 a.m. next morning, however, it was only to propose a raid on Liberty Hall and 'two other minor Sinn Fein arsenals'.

The pretext for this was that 250 lbs of gelignite stolen from Tullagh Quarry had been taken to Liberty Hall. Wimborne supported Nathan's suggestion, writing to Birrell 'Nathan proposes, and I agree, that Liberty Hall, together with two other Sinn Fein arsenals – Larkfield Kimmage and the one in Father Matthews [sic] Park, should be raided tonight.' But he added that he had 'strongly urged him at the same time to put his hand on the ringleaders'. The evidence was 'now sufficient for any measure we think desirable'. Wimborne wanted 'to implicate as many of the [sic] Sinn Fein as I can with the landing – invasion, in fact. It has changed everything', and justified a major policy shift. Nathan, who plainly assumed that the Kerry events had provided a breathing space, insisted on waiting for Birrell's reply. Nothing was done until 6 p.m. that evening, when Nathan returned to the Viceregal Lodge with the acting military commander, Colonel Cowan. They discussed the feasibility of raiding Liberty Hall, and Cowan stressed that it was by no means an easy operation; it would need 'a gun' (i.e. an artillery piece) which would have to be brought from Athlone. 'Time was short for adequate preparations to ensure success.'[81]

Wimborne was by now seething with impatience. He cancelled a planned trip to Belfast, and convened another conference at 10 p.m. on Sunday evening, bringing Nathan and Cowan together with the DMP Commissioner and Major Price. There he argued that extensive preparations for a raid on Liberty Hall would be a waste of time; by the time they got in they would probably find an empty building. (It is hard not to suspect that this would have suited Nathan quite well.) What really mattered, Wimborne insisted, was to arrest the leaders: '60 to 100' should be taken that very night. Edgeworth-Johnstone said that such a programme of arrests was feasible, but Nathan predictably objected that it would be illegal; arrests on the grounds of hostile association required approval by the Home Secretary. Wimborne argued that the prisoners could be remanded until this approval came through – he was quite prepared 'to sign the warrants and take full responsibility for possible illegality'. Nathan still temporized, and the conference ended with a decision to abandon the Liberty Hall raid and wait for the DMP Commissioner to draw up a list of 'prominent suspects'.

As Nathan was leaving the meeting, Wimborne, according to his own account, once again urged on him 'in the strongest possible language the need for immediate and vigorous action, and again offered to take all responsibility'. Nathan's reaction to this display of Viceregal uppishness can be well imagined. Nothing would happen until the next day; even the 'minor arsenal' at Fr Mathew Park was to be left alone, if not in peace. (Yet to raid that would surely not have required artillery.) And, ironically, Wimborne himself now backed away from his earlier determination to call for immediate reinforcements from the Curragh and Athlone, for fear that 'any military activity would arouse the suspicion of the men we had in view and lead to their absconding'. On Easter Monday, instead of garrisoning the capital, the army would go off to the races.

6

The Battle of Dublin I:
to the Barricades

It was on Easter Monday the boys got the call
To join their battalions in park, glen and hall.
In less than an hour they were out on parade;
They were true men tho' few in the Dublin Brigade.

There was much work to do in getting things right,
But the old and the young were all anxious to fight.
Every man worked hard at his own barricade,
And rifles rang out from the Dublin Brigade.

Anon: 'The Dublin Brigade'

One of the frustrated would-be rebels of Easter Sunday was Aine Heron, who assembled with a group of Cumann na mBan first-aid workers at Blackhall Street in the evening. (Earlier in the day she had been cooking extra food for the manoeuvres when her – non-Volunteer – husband looked up from his Sunday paper to tell her not to bother; when he explained about the countermanding order, she replied sharply, 'Who would mind the *Independent*?') She had packed twenty-four hours' rations and a waterproof coat along with her first-aid kit. The women were confident that what was going on was more than an exercise. As they discussed the situation, they 'all agreed that it would be impossible to put off the rising, as never again would the people be brought to the pitch of enthusiasm they were now at'.[1] In Dublin, at least, this may have been true. Even a day's delay had drastic consequences. How the mobilization would have worked out if it had gone to plan on Sunday can only be guessed at. What is beyond doubt is that when the process finally began on Monday morning, it produced near-chaos. Units assembled in fragments, individuals set off on random paths, capricious orders and counter-orders were issued by a baggy collection of commanders. Most had little idea what was happening, and even those who thought they knew what they were doing often found that they were doing the wrong thing. All this could hardly have been further from the precisely planned insurrection of Pearse's imagination. Amazingly, out of it all, emerged the most potent military action ever mounted by Irish rebels.

The experience of Seumas Kavanagh, of the 3rd Battalion, was typical. He was a 'mobilizer' – each mobilizer being responsible for seven or eight men. (The 2nd Battalion idea of printed slips seems not to have been shared.) On Saturday he had bumped into his company lieutenant, Simon Donnelly, who had taken him to the Volunteer HQ at Dawson Street to help parcel up documents for removal. In case he did not grasp the significance of this, Donnelly also advised him to go to confession. He spent most of Sunday 'walking the city' in disappointment after the countermanding order; like many, he slept in on Monday morning. He was roused by a Volunteer named Doyle who told him that the company was to mobilize at Earlsfort Terrace at 10 o'clock. 'I pointed out to him that it was by now 10.15. He was rather excited and said, "That is the order I got."' Kavanagh rushed out, mobilized his first man in Redmond Hill, then went on to Aungier Street to see the battalion quartermaster, James Byrne. To his dismay, Byrne informed him that he was going to the races at Fairyhouse. 'What will the battalion do?' Kavanagh asked. 'They are depending on you.' Byrne casually said they would have to shift for themselves. When they finally assembled at Earlsfort Terrace, it turned out that the company commander had also decided to absent himself, so Simon Donnelly had to take charge. They marched down to Mount Street Bridge, where Kavanagh was put under the command of Mick Malone. With a small group he began to fortify the Schools on Northumberland Road, just across the bridge. Only after they had spent much time and effort sandbagging the building did it dawn on them that it was totally unsuitable: set far back from the road, and surrounded by high hedges, it had 'no military value'.[2]

Liam Tannam, captain of E company of the 3rd Battalion, had

been summoned to see Pearse on Saturday, and told that his force was to mobilize in Beresford Place (outside the battalion area). No reason for this seems to have been given. He protested that the size of his company area – stretching from Leeson Street, just inside the Grand Canal, out as far as Goatstown – would make it more sensible for him to mobilize in his own area and march his company in to Beresford Place. Pearse saw the point of this, though he does not seem to have offered any explanation for the last-minute change in mobilization plans. On Sunday, as we have seen, Tannam's company mobilized at Oakley Road at 3 p.m., but made no move towards the city before demobilizing. On Monday, like so many others, he slept in, and was only awoken by 'a rapping on the door' of his home in Wilton Terrace at 10.30. 'A man named Stephenson was there with an order that "E" Company was to parade at 10 a.m. at Beresford Place. "Look here," I said, "you are handing this to me at 10.35." "It can't be helped," he said, "you are to do the best you can."'[3] Tannam had clearly had no idea that he might be remobilized that day, and never found out why the mobilization order was left so late. He launched into the laborious process of rounding up his men once again, and by midday had assembled about twenty-five of them. He sent them on under the command of Paddy Doyle while he went on looking for others. Doyle was on his way in to the city when he was met by 'a couple of men of the 3rd battalion' somewhere near Holles Street, who advised him to take the men to Boland's bakery. Doyle asked for a direct order from the battalion commandant; Eamon de Valera, already worried about the weakness of his force, was only too relieved to issue it. So Pearse's last-minute change of plan was itself casually changed.

The experiences of Kavanagh, Tannam and Doyle were repeated across the city. Frank Henderson, who had spent a disturbed night at 2nd Battalion's arms depot in Father Mathew Park, 'was just beginning to get to sleep between six and seven o'clock in the morning when a message came from Tom Hunter, Vice Commandant, asking me to provide him with a number of cyclists, I think he said at ten o'clock that morning'. Henderson refused – he only had a couple of cyclists in his company, and he 'did not attach any importance to the message'. Thinking it was 'merely routine', he went back to sleep. This was just one of many unplanned, unexpected shifts in the Volunteers' preparations. Two hours later, while Henderson was still in bed, Hunter turned up in person to instruct him to parade his company with all arms on St Stephen's Green at ten o'clock. When Henderson protested that this would be impossible in the time available – an hour or less – Hunter merely said 'Do your best, and get as many men as you can.' Only at this point did Henderson grasp that things were serious, and 'proceeded to set the mobilization scheme in motion'. His own account of what followed provides a vivid sense of the dislocation of earlier plans.[4]

Henderson headed back home 'to get ready', and on the way mobilized several of his men. (Traynor's printed slip system seems to have been used up on Saturday.) This was quite time-consuming, as some of them lived as far away as Dominick Street, Goose Green and Dollymount. He next received a written order, signed by James Connolly, calling for a reliable man for a special job. After a display of deliberate pedantry, asking 'who is James Connolly?' – since MacDonagh had specifically told them only to follow orders from their immediate superiors – he found a message from MacDonagh on the back of Connolly's order, telling him to comply with it. Connolly had, unknown to the Volunteers, been appointed 'Commandant General' with overall military command of the IV and ICA in either the Dublin area or the whole of Ireland (witnesses differ on this). Henderson detailed a Volunteer for the job, which turned out to be the attack on the Magazine Fort in Phoenix Park. Clearly this operation was not, as many have thought, part of a long-prepared plan intended to launch the rebellion, but a last-minute improvisation. The same seems to be true of a surprisingly large part of the eventual battle plan.

Henderson and Hunter decided to send half the company over to Stephen's Green, keeping the rest to guard the stores. The Headquarters' view, provided by Diarmuid Lynch, suggests that those of the 2nd Battalion 'who responded earliest to the Monday morning mobilisation were sent to Commandant MacDonagh; those who reported later were ordered to convoy the military and medical supplies stored there to the GPO'.[5] Why, for one thing, were these stores not sent to the 2nd Battalion's own positions? Lynch's characteristic suggestion of deliberate intent is rather different from

Henderson's picture of himself, his brother Leo, Oscar Traynor and Thomas Weafer debating what to do next after sending half their men on to Stephen's Green (not itself a 2nd Battalion position). 'There was a certain amount of indecision about what was to be done.' Traynor was the only one in favour of 'proceeding immediately into town'. Henderson, as a non-IRB man, 'felt myself in a rather difficult position'. In the end he urged that Weafer, as the senior officer present, should decide what to do. Weafer then went off to find Connolly, while the rest of his command 'were to demobilise in small groups and go to certain houses', about six apiece, spread across Fairview and Summerhill. Henderson sat tight, though Traynor decided to go off, first to the Magazine Fort and then on to the GPO.

Only after another half an hour did Weafer's order to re-mobilize arrive, and the force was collected once again – minus half a dozen or so who either made themselves scarce or could not be located. The lorry driver had also 'got timid', and a replacement had to be found. At last a column 80–100 strong, including men from three different 2nd Battalion companies, as well as some from 1st Battalion, formed up to take the lorry-load of stores into the city. A Fairview curate, Father Walter MacDonnell, blessed them before they finally moved off, about 3 o'clock in the afternoon. They crossed the Tolka Bridge and were moving down Ballybough Road towards Parnell Square and Sackville Street when they ran into a group of British troops at the Grand Canal bridge. A sharp encounter fight followed.[6] Henderson, who was in charge of the rearguard, retreated to the Tolka Bridge and took over a Gilbey's wine store. His men had already been dismayed to find themselves pushing past a flow of refugees coming from the city centre, and now they added their mite to the flood by ejecting an old lady and her daughter who lived above the shop (an experience which dented the romantic self-image of young Volunteers such as Harry Colley). Colley had just come across with Harry Boland from a Citizen Army outpost in the Wicklow Chemical Manure Company's offices a couple of hundred yards away, where they had found themselves under the command of an irascible ICA officer, Vincent Poole. This post had apparently been set up on Connolly's orders, rather than in accordance with the prepared plan; even the compact Citizen Army, which had not been directly affected by the countermanding order, seems to have been infected by the weekend's confusion.

Henderson's command spent the rest of the day on the lookout for Weafer's force, but never made contact with it again. Several conferences were held, and the question of their line of retreat (probably one of Ginger O'Connell's contributions to Volunteer thinking) was discussed at some length. 'We had a general line of retreat made out, although it would be very difficult to say where we would eventually get to if we had to retreat from the position.'[7] Fortunately the fleeting British military presence in the area vanished as fast as it had materialized. Weafer, without apparently contacting Henderson, marched on with the battalion stores to the GPO, where he arrived around 4.30 in the afternoon. Henderson had to wait another twenty-four hours before he received any orders.

All this welter of uncertainty contrasts sharply with what may be called the official IRB picture, as drawn by Diarmuid Lynch, of the 'tense but serene' scene at Liberty Hall, where the military committee and some of the Volunteers and Citizen Army men and women who would come to be known as the Headquarters Battalion 'quietly attended to final details'. This serenity may seem surprising in light of the fact that, as Lynch noted, because the 'muster was far short of normal, none of the prearranged positions could now be manned adequately to ensure a prolonged defence'. It might be expected that the leaders would be urgently trying to adapt their plans to make the best use of their reduced forces. If any such discussion did take place, Lynch kept quiet about it. His fatalistic comment, 'No matter, the die was cast', suggests rather that the planners assumed that nothing could be done. This would fit with Connolly's oft-quoted remark to his ITGWU comrade William O'Brien, 'Bill, we are going out to be slaughtered.' This pessimism was uncharacteristic of him, and as we shall see he did, in his capacity as the newly appointed commander of the Dublin area, alter a number of dispositions. But he does not seem to have tried to exert control over the battle as a whole. His attention stayed focused on the situation at the end of his street.

The march of the headquarters group from its assembly point in Beresford Place, outside Liberty Hall, down Abbey Street and into

Sackville Street, was short but significant. An eclectic mix of units, totalling some 150 on Lynch's count, 'some inadequately armed', moved off at about 11.50. Onlookers assumed that this was a route march like dozens of others they had seen over the last couple of years. The police clearly thought the same. Even when they arrived in front of the Imperial Hotel, and Connolly issued the order to wheel left and charge the GPO the situation still appeared playful. Once inside, they had to deal with the bafflement of post office staff and bank holiday customers, one of many scenes of disbelief that played out across the city that morning. Only the threat of violence gradually persuaded people to obey orders to leave, and in some places the violence went beyond threats.

Once the GPO was occupied it began to act as a magnet to the many Volunteers who had missed their unit assemblies and who were crisscrossing the city, either as individuals or in groups, looking for someone in authority. The most celebrated individual to turn up was the O'Rahilly, immaculately uniformed, at the wheel of his prized De Dion automobile. (He had spent all of Saturday night and Sunday carrying MacNeill's orders to stop the rising around the country, but was deeply wounded by the rebels' decision not to tell him of the Monday mobilization.)[8] The original garrison of 150 steadily expanded until it became by far the largest concentration of rebels in the city. As with all the other units, however, its exact size was never precisely known. Later jokes about the tens of thousands who claimed to have been in the GPO indicate the kind of difficulty involved, since no muster seems to have been held at any stage during the week. The most careful subsequent calculation, by Diarmuid Lynch (whose aim was to pare down the standard figure, while also demonstrating that Desmond Ryan had pared it down too far), put the total garrison of the GPO area at 408, at least 120 more than the next largest concentration in the 1st Battalion (Four Courts) area.[9] They were not all in the GPO itself, of course; immediately after the occupation, groups were sent out to take over a string of premises on both sides of lower Sackville Street – the Imperial Hotel, Clery's department store, the shops facing O'Connell Bridge (Kelly's and Hopkins'). An elaborate attempt was made to set up a radio station in Reis's store, using equipment taken from the Wireless School. Eventually the whole street from Henry Street to the river was occupied, and we should perhaps call the position 'Sackville Street' rather than 'the GPO'. It was unquestionably a strong position in one sense; the British forces never even considered trying to assault it directly. Whether it was a well-chosen position in relation to the other garrisons is, as will be seen, more questionable.

But whatever its military value, the GPO was an impressive stage for the political drama that the military committee, now the Provisional Government of the Irish Republic, had prepared. The sheer expanse of Sackville Street around the focal point of Nelson's Pillar provided maximum exposure for key symbolic acts such as unfurling the flags which would make an indelible impression on everyone who saw them. Although there was to be plenty of dispute about exactly which flag hung on which corner of the GPO – and who hung them there – there was no mistaking their significance. One was the tricolour (designed on the French model, possibly by a Frenchman), introduced in 1848 by the would-be revolutionaries of the Irish Confederation, and by now the generally accepted symbol of the republican move- ment. Interestingly, though, its careful colour-symbolism, setting the white of peace between green and orange, was often read as the ear- lier green–white–gold made famous by Robert Emmet. (Pictures of him in 'his cocked hat and feathers, his green and gold and white uni- form as Commander-in-Chief of the forces of the Irish Republic', were to be seen 'in the humblest cabins of the land' throughout the century after his death.)[10] The new tricolour would take time to be understood; the fact that white and gold are the papal colours would be a fruitful further source of misreading. A Trinity student from Belfast described the tricolour hung from the College of Surgeons as 'quite a pretty one, the colours being green, white and orange. I can't understand why it was orange, but perhaps they call it yellow!'[11]

The other flag raised on the GPO was a one-off creation – master- minded, inevitably, by Constance Markievicz – using the traditional golden Irish harp on a green ground, with the words 'Irish Republic' painted in gold. The material was, allegedly, an old coverlet ('of a bed that Larry Ginnell used to sleep in'), dyed green; her gold paint had hardened and had to be thinned with mustard.[12] The harp itself was (it need hardly be said) of a variety specifically approved by Pearse. A third symbolic flag was raised a little later, but Connolly chose to fly the elaborate 'starry plough' banner woven for the ICA – a superb piece of (apparently anonymous) design – not on the GPO, but over the road on the Imperial Hotel. This was the most glittering asset not of the British state but of the ITGWU's bitterest enemy, William Martin Murphy, and Connolly plainly derived intense satisfaction from seeing the socialist banner atop this palace of capitalism.

The other key symbol of the rebellion, and equally enduring, was Pearse's proclamation of the republic. Even the production of this resonant document on Connolly's run-down machine, against the clock and with inadequate stocks of type, was a minor epic of printing.[13] (In fact, the job was not completed until Monday morning, so without the countermand the proclamation would not have been available to launch the new republic.) At its head, the Gaelic title 'Poblacht na hEireann' did take priority, though once again the text was rendered in English (presumably, like the choice of English for the legend of the 'Irish Republic' flag, to assist understanding). Not that this seems to have assisted the public reception of the document when Pearse stepped out into the street to read it to the modest crowd of onlookers shortly after noon. As Lynch gruffly noted, 'the few cheers that greeted this epochal announcement furnished an index of the denationalised state of Ireland after the era of Parliamentarianism'. (Few even remembered where Pearse stood as he read it; the most common memory had him standing 'on the steps of the GPO', yet there were no steps; one or two writers speak of 'the low step' – presumably the doorstep; others again put him on a plinth set up in the middle of the street near Nelson's Pillar.)

It has been suggested that 'on this of all occasions his magnetism for once ebbed from him'.[14] What is certain is that his audience was the worst he had faced since he had become a star public speaker; yet he treated it to one of his finest verbal evocations of the spirit of national struggle. Reproduced countless times, and still serving as the title deed of Irish republicanism (not least in the literary works of Gerry Adams), the terms of the proclamation were a kind of distillation of nationalist doctrine, a kind of national poem: lucid, terse, and strangely moving even to unbelievers. Addressing 'Irishmen and Irishwomen' in 'the name of God and of the dead generations' from which Ireland 'receives her old tradition of nationhood', the proclamation set out the mystical separatist belief that Ireland 'through us, summons her children to her flag and strikes for her freedom'. The female personification of the land, and the ethnic community as a kinship group, were the fundamental currency of romantic nationalism. The Provisional Government of the Irish Republic proclaimed that the republic was 'a sovereign independent state', and guaranteed 'religious and civil liberty, equal rights and opportunities to all its citizens'. It would 'cherish all children of the nation equally, and oblivious of the differences carefully fostered by an alien government'.

Seven men signed the proclamation as the Provisional Government. Two of them were not in the GPO during Easter week; it is not clear whether the other five took any action in their governmental role, or whether any of them were given particular administrative roles. The general view (following the announcement in the single issue of *Irish War News* published on Tuesday) is that Pearse became 'Commanding [*sic*] in Chief of the Army of the Republic and President of the Provisional Government'.[15] Tom Clarke's widow, however, always maintained that Clarke had become President, and this certainly would have followed standard IRB thinking. Some others agree with her contention, but the issue is a murky one, and the general lack of concern with it tells its own story. It is certainly significant that both civil and military supremacy was vested in Pearse – who became a kind of generalissimo – and that the military function was given primacy. Connolly and the other government members seem to have seen their function as exclusively military. Seán T. O'Kelly, who was in and out of the GPO all week (to the annoyance of some of its garrison), records that he was asked by Seán MacDermott – in what capacity he did not say – to act as 'Civil Administrator of the Government of the Republic' with a group of others, including William O'Brien, Alderman Tom Kelly, and Hanna Sheehy-Skeffington. What lay behind this intriguing proposal is hard to tell. O'Kelly laconically notes that he 'heard nothing more of the matter', and that the project was evidently not proceeded with.[16] There was no attempt even to adumbrate the political structure of the new Irish state. The contrast with the later Sinn Féin action when the republic was re-established in January 1919 is very striking, and it is this perhaps more than anything else that marks the 1916 rebellion out as a Fenian rather than a Sinn Féin manifestation.

A long shadow was to be cast by the title chosen for the congeries of forces mobilized on Easter Monday, the Army of the Republic. A new composite name clearly had to be found for them, and this was neutral enough. But colloquial usage soon rendered it as 'Irish Republican Army', a more loaded label – with obvious IRB echoes. (This formula would, of course, eventually be permanently adopted by the Irish Volunteers in 1920.) Here was another key title coined casually and lacking a Gaelic equivalent – the IRA's Irish-language title remains 'Oglaich' (Volunteers). Most of the available energy of the army and its commanders, naturally, was expended in sandbagging the occupied buildings and enjoying the heady rush of action. Connolly, who brought with him his doughty secretary Winifred Carney, and her typewriter, set about dictating a stream of orders (nearly all of which, sadly, have been lost).[17]

When Connolly's main body marched off to Sackville Street, a much smaller ICA detachment was already heading towards an area of far greater historic, and indeed strategic, significance. Its commander, Captain Seán Connolly (no relation), was one of the Citizen Army's most glamorous figures, a leading man in theatre groups such as the Liberty Players and National Players. (He had just starred as Robert Emmet in a production of Mangan's play, which also featured two of the ICA's women stalwarts, Helena Molony and Marie Perolz.)[18] At noon he arrived with about thirty men in front of the gates of Dublin Castle, the symbolic – and indeed actual – seat of British rule in Ireland. His actions from this point form one of the central, representative mysteries of the 1916 rebellion. As it happened, some of those British rulers had just gone into conclave; Major Price, the army's chief intelligence officer, met Sir Matthew Nathan at 11.45, and they were joined soon afterwards by the head of the Post Office, Arthur Hamilton Norway, who had just walked across from the GPO, which he had left a few minutes before Pearse and Connolly arrived. Moments after midday, they heard a shot at the gate of Upper Castle Yard. Price had a moment of insight: 'They have commenced!'

They had – but what? They had indeed shot the unarmed DMP

constable who formed (as the later commission of inquiry was to repeat, with puzzlement, several times) the only guard on the Castle gate. Despite using a dud grenade – the first of many such failures of the home-made munitions laboriously manufactured over the previous months – they had overwhelmed the six soldiers quietly brewing up their lunch in the guardroom.[19] When Major Price ran into the yard blazing away with his revolver, he was the Castle's last line of defence. He prudently retreated; and so, more strangely, did Captain Connolly's men. After what Diarmuid Lynch calls 'an encounter with the enemy' – an odd phrase for such a complete success – Connolly ordered the occupation of the *Daily Express* building across the road, and also of City Hall. He seems to have had no idea that the whole garrison of the Castle amounted to 'a corporal's guard', and that even in Ship Street Barracks immediately behind the Castle there were no more than twenty-five troops. Two questions suggest themselves: why did he not know this, and, had he known, would he have acted differently? The first question raises one of the big puzzles of 1916. Although some of the buildings occupied may have been reconnoitred in the period before the rising, this was quite an unsystematic process, and no intelligence section had been set up by either the ICA or the Volunteers. The rebels had neglected to grasp the most elementary advantage available to insurgent forces, local knowledge; they were as much in the dark as their opponents.

The second question is usually answered by the assertion that it was in any case never the intention of either James or Seán Connolly to capture the Castle, however weak its garrison. If this was indeed the case, it is still difficult to explain. Not only was the Castle's location vital, but the persistent and widespread belief that the core of the 1916 plan was to follow the example of Robert Emmet showed that its overwhelming symbolic importance was fully grasped by the planners. And, as has been remarked, the defensive strength of the government centre was not only physical: for the British it 'would not have been as seemly to have shot or burnt the intruders out of the Castle as it was to shoot and burn them out of the GPO'.[20] The argument (made also about the equally vital location of Trinity College) that these extensive buildings would have needed large garrisons, might have held good on Monday, but seems strange in view of the forces available to the original planners, which were surely adequate. Even with the force available, Dr Kathleen Lynn, who arrived to give medical attention to Connolly and took over command when he died, wondered why the ICA men had allowed British troops to move into the Castle Yard. (Her guess was that they were demoralized by the early death of their leader.)[21] If the original plan was hastily adjusted to exclude the Castle, why were so many of the available forces placed in buildings such as the GPO and Jacob's factory rather than at the truly vital points?

Seizing the Castle would have been an ambitious undertaking, but the project of pinning its garrison down was not much easier. And the choice of City Hall for this purpose, whether on James Connolly's instructions or Seán Connolly's initiative, was not a good one. Its roof, in particular, with its elegant open balustrade, proved to be a death trap; Seán Connolly himself was killed up there within a few hours of taking over the building. In fact, the ICA garrison held City Hall for barely twenty-four hours before the British military reinforcements in the Castle launched a counter-attack. By mid-afternoon on Tuesday all the three rebel positions at the top of Parliament Street had been retaken. A member of the Trinity College Officers' Training Corps (OTC), looking out up Dame Street, saw 'men in successive waves rush across the street from the City Hall towards the *Express* offices'. There was an hour of intense gunfire, with 'plaster and powdered brick flying in showers' from the façade of the *Express* building. In Trinity they still thought that the rebels had captured the Castle, and that they were witnessing their expulsion.[22] Then it all went quiet. The trained troops of the Curragh mobile column showed that big buildings were not, in themselves, enough.

At the same time as Seán Connolly's company set off from Liberty Hall for the Castle, the main ICA force, commanded by Michael Mallin – who had been given the Volunteer rank of commandant on Saturday – also headed southwards across the river. Some 100 strong, and accompanied by a number of Cumann na mBan and Fianna, they passed several defensible, strategically located buildings (the Custom House, the Bank of Ireland, and Trinity College included) on their way. Frank Robbins noticed the clock on another of these, the Ballast

Office on the corner of Westmoreland Street and Aston's Quay, show-ing 11.55 as they went by. Lustily singing popular tunes such as 'the Peeler and the Goat' (apparently without intending to provoke the police), they swung on up Grafton Street to reach St Stephen's Green soon after midday. Once there, Robbins' section pushed on to take over Harcourt Street Station, while the rest set to building barricades.

But the process of constructing the barricades, mainly using com-mandeered cars and drays, led to the first clashes with 'civilians', some of whom resisted the seizure of their vehicles. A St John's Ambulance volunteer, W. G. Smith, passing through the Green, witnessed the sudden change of atmosphere after the killing of an elderly man who had been warned several times to stop trying to remove his lorry from a barricade near the Shelbourne Hotel. Smith had been mystified by the appearance of the rebel force. 'Many of them were mere boys, in fact only about one in ten was a man.' He was struck by the fact that 'they had a great many young girls, ranging [in age] from about 13 to 20, furnished with haversacks, evidently acting as *vivandières* to their Army'. The onlookers seemed to be 'taking it as rather a joke'. But the effect of the shooting on the crowd at the corner of Merrion Row was 'awful . . . Women began to shriek and cry and kneel down to pray in the street, and the *vivandières* with the rebels began crying and screaming and wringing their hands, to be told by the rebels to go home.'[23] Lilly Stokes, who walked into the Green from Dawson Street, described the barricade as made up of 'a big dray (its horse shot dead close by), a side car, two motors and a big laundry van, out of which the baskets had fallen, their contents lying about'. Like Smith, she thought that the trenches at the park gates 'were chiefly manned by children – lads of 16 or 17'.[24]

The writer James Stephens watched the building of this barricade outside the Shelbourne Hotel. He had just heard from a bystander in Merrion Row, near his office, that 'the Sinn Feiners have seized the city', and like many others his instinctive reaction was to run to the Green to see what was happening. As he came up to the barricade,

a loud cry came from the park. The gates opened and three men ran out. Two of them held rifles with fixed bayonets. The third gripped a heavy revolver in his fist. They ran towards the motor car which had just turned the corner, and halted it. The men with bayonets took position on either side of the car. The man with the revolver saluted, and I heard him begging the occupants to pardon him, and directing them to dismount. A man and woman got down.

Their chauffeur remained in the car, and was told

to drive to the barricade and lodge his car in a particular position. He did it awkwardly, and after three attempts he succeeded in pleasing them . . . He locked the car into the barricade, and then, being a man accustomed to be commanded, he awaited an order to descend. When the order came he walked directly to his master, still preserving all the solemnity of his features. These two men did not address a word to each other, but their drilled and expressionless eyes were loud with surprise and fear and rage. They went into the hotel.[25]

This was a revolt – or was it revolution? The curious Stephens spoke to the man with the revolver, who was 'no more than a boy, no more certainly than twenty years of age, short in stature, with close curling red hair and blue eyes – a kindly-looking lad'. To Stephens,

this young man did not seem to be acting from his reason. He was doing his work from a determination implanted . . . on his imagination. His mind was – where? It was not with his body. And continually his eyes went searching widely, looking for spaces, scanning hastily the clouds, the vistas of the streets, looking for something that did not hinder him . . .

His answer to Stephens' question, 'What is the meaning of all this?' suggested perhaps a less metaphysical reason for the 'ramble and errancy' in his eyes: 'We have taken the city. We are expecting an attack from the military at any moment, and those people' – he indicated knots of men, women and children clustered towards the end of the Green – 'won't go home for me. We have the Post Office, and the railways, and the Castle. We have all the city. We have everything.'[26]

Stephen's Green was a transport hub for the south-eastern approaches to the city centre, and the idea of closing it certainly made sense. But where Seán Connolly had followed too literally James Connolly's promise to 'fight from the rooftops', Mallin ignored it altogether. Instead of establishing posts to cover the barricades from the tall buildings overlooking them – especially the Shelbourne Hotel –

Mallin's force set about digging rifle pits inside the railings of the park. The reasoning behind this has never been clear. Guests in the hotel, an epicentre of the Ascendancy lifestyle, now packed to the rafters for the Fairyhouse races, peered out in some bafflement at the strange goings-on. 'Disappointingly little was to be seen. The thicket inside the railings screened the insurgent troops – green uniforms merged into the bosky shadows: here the glint of a rifle barrel, there the turn of a head in a bandolier hat were spotted from time to time.' Finally, Countess Markievicz, resplendent in her Citizen Army uniform, began to march up and down, gun on shoulder, in full view of the hotel. This caused something of a sensation, as Elizabeth Bowen later wrote, 'for lady colonels were rarer then than now'.[27] As she went on parading for some time after British troops started to occupy the hotel, the head porter thought that 'the Countess took unfair advantage of her sex'. Not, perhaps, for the last time.

'Madame' was widely believed by the spectators, and subsequently, to have been in command of the Stephen's Green force – an impression her behaviour did nothing to contradict. Her role, however, was ambiguous. According to Dr Kathleen Lynn, the ICA's medical officer (who had set out in her car with Markievicz to distribute medical supplies), she had been planning to drive around all the rebel positions – a function which may sound self-indulgent, though as will be seen it could have been vital – but she never got beyond Stephen's Green.[28] Mallin, it seems, asked her to stay, first as a sniper and then as his second-in-command; perhaps another sign of his lack of confidence. She spent the day going 'round and round the Green, reporting back if anything was wanted, or tackling any sniper who was particularly objectionable' (with what weapon, she did not specify).[29] Who was responsible for the decision to occupy open ground – whether it was part of the original plan or an improvisation – is still a matter of argument. But here, as at City Hall, the penalty for miscalculation was heavy and rapid. Easter 1916 was to be remembered as a week of brilliant spring sunshine, but Monday was different: the weather did its best to give the Citizen Army a taste of Flanders trench life. During a rainswept night, British troops entered the Shelbourne by its Kildare Street door, unheard and unopposed by the garrison on the Green, and at daybreak opened fire with a machine-gun from the roof. Only the lush vegetation (though less prolific then than it is today) saved Mallin's force from ghastly casualties. But it was immediately obvious that their position was untenable. By noon most of them had taken refuge in the College of Surgeons on the western side of the Green – a strong building, even if not much more than half the height of the Shelbourne, and, unlike the latter, absolutely empty of life-sustaining resources.

The College had been occupied on Monday afternoon, in a way that told its own story about the ineffectiveness of the Citizen Army's more advanced positions. Two groups (nearly half of Mallin's whole force) had pushed south from the Green; Captain Richard McCormick with twenty-five men (Frank Robbins among them) was supposed to control or destroy the railway line from Harcourt Street Station. Seven more men went all the way down to the Grand Canal and occupied Davy's pub overlooking Portobello Bridge. This was a position well chosen to dispute the crossing into the city of the troops in Portobello Barracks just across the canal, particularly if it had been supported by a few other posts, however small. But it was abandoned after a very brief assault – in fact, before it was actually assaulted – and McCormick's force also abandoned the attempt to control the railway within a couple of hours. By early afternoon they were back in Stephen's Green. Frank Robbins with a scratch group of a dozen (four ICA and eight others, including Markievicz, Mary Hyland and Lily Kempson of Cumann na mBan) was sent to search the College. Mallin had information – a rare piece of reliable intelligence, as it turned out – that it housed a substantial arsenal belonging to Trinity College OTC.[30] The idea seems to have been to bring the weapons out to the force on the Green, but by the time the fifty rifles were eventually found, the Green had been abandoned, and guns were needed less than food.

The same thing happened to the other outposts pushed towards the canal down Leeson Street. Liam O Briain, a 2nd Battalion man who had no idea where his company 'would be positioned in case of active service' decided to join the Stephen's Green force on his way home to collect his rifle and ammunition. ('If you want to fight, isn't this place as good as any place for you?') On Monday evening, standing in the three-foot-deep trench, the result of several hours' digging, by the

Leeson Street gate, he was ordered to 'fall in'. After making a somewhat unmilitary joke he was sent off in a mixed group of twenty
under the command of an ICA officer to garrison the houses covering
the canal bridge at the end of the street, where they stayed overnight
on the roof. Early next morning, the redoubtable Margaret Skinnider
appeared in the street below with orders from Mallin for half the force
to fall back to the Green, and some while later she returned to order
the rest back too.[31] The reason for this was not clear to O Briain. (Or
to Laurence Nugent, a roving observer, who noted that 'there was no
threat of attack' when this post was evacuated.)[32] Was it lack of numbers? The advance of the Crown forces from the south had not begun,
so there was no way of knowing which route they would take, and
the outposts might have been vital. Twenty men there, or even ten,
might have had a dramatic effect. The reason usually given for the failure to occupy the Shelbourne, lack of numbers, seems unconvincing
there too. The ICA had not been affected by the countermanding
order, and turned out pretty much in full strength at Liberty Hall.
Unless a last-minute decision was taken to divert men to the GPO, it
is hard to see how any original plan could have supposed that Mallin
would have had a larger force than he eventually did. If such a decision
was in fact made, it proved a costly one.

The positions taken up by the four city battalions of the Volunteers –
or three of them at least – were more straightforward. The 1st
Battalion went into action close to its mobilization area, in Blackhall
Street. Piaras Béaslaí, its vice-commandant, later estimated the
turnout at less than a third of its full strength; one of those who turned
out counted 250 men.[33] Its zone of operations was large, extending
from the Four Courts on the river Liffey, northwards to Cabra on the
Royal Canal. The original intention seems to have been that these
northern posts would link up with the 5th Battalion outside the city
in county Dublin. (Béaslaí heard later from Thomas Ashe, in Lewes
gaol in 1917, that his instructions were 'to arrange some system of
cooperation'. Ashe had sent a messenger to contact 1st Battalion at
Cross Guns Bridge, but found nobody; clearly Béaslaí himself knew
nothing of this plan.)[34] A key point in the centre of this area was
Broadstone Station, where the line from Athlone – the army's artillery

depot – terminated. On Monday, however, the northerly deployment was seriously compromised. Although a strong company (B Company, with some sixty-five men according to Jerry Golden) was sent up to Cabra Road, Broadstone Station was bypassed. At noon, after formally announcing that the republic had been proclaimed, Daly marched his main force through North King Street into Church Street, where they occupied a series of premises and set up barricades. Jack Shouldice commanded a group of about twenty at the crossing of Church and King Streets, dominated by Reilly's pub, which he fortified with sacks of flour and meal taken from the Blanchardstown Mills shop on the opposite corner of the junction.[35] Although the North Dublin Union was occupied, no attempt was made to take control of Broadstone Station just beyond it. At this stage, though Daly had announced that they were going into action (and a handful of his men had decided against it), many still had no information about the battalion's plans, or the reasons for building barricades. Daly set up his headquarters first in North Brunswick Street, and later in Father Mathew Hall near the northern end of Church Street. At the southern end, on the river, some of his men occupied the Four Courts.

It was on the Liffey quays that the first clash with British forces took place, but this was not the immediate counter-attack that most of the rebels – commanders as well as rank and file – seem to have expected at any moment on Monday. A convoy of five lorries bringing ammunition to the Magazine Fort in Phoenix Park was moving along Ormond Quay, escorted by a squadron of lancers. (This proceeding smacks more of Birrell's repeated requests for military displays in Dublin than of real protective action; although they were carrying rifles rather than lances, they had only been issued with five rounds of ammunition each.) After being allowed to pass along the quays from O'Connell Bridge, they were fired on by the Four Courts garrison. The ensuing panic and confusion must have been a gratifying sight to the apprehensive Volunteers; horses reared and plunged as the wagon drivers tried to steer their vehicles into a laager, and the cavalrymen hastily dismounted and ran in all directions looking for cover. Most of them ended up pinned down in Charles Street until Thursday, where their main problem was not direct fire but the starvation of their horses. (One of their lances became a flagstaff for a small republican tricolour, propped up in the middle of the King Street–Church Street crossing.) Lancers were also seen by B Company which had to run the gauntlet of a 'fusillade of rotten cabbages, oranges, apples etc.' from a crowd of 'separation women' – the wives of soldiers, dependent on the 'separation allowance' paid by the War Office, and thus fiercely loyal to the government (for the duration at least) – in Phibsboro Road on its way to take up positions around the railway bridge on the North Circular Road.[36] But the Volunteers took cover in the garden of St Peter's Church, and the cavalry passed by before turning south on their way to Sackville Street. This northern outpost of 1st Battalion was already dangerously isolated, however, and would come under serious attack the following day.

The battalion's main positions remained undisturbed for the next couple of days. But there was a significant exception. D Company, commanded by Seán Heuston, did not mobilize with Daly's main force. It was the northernmost unit, and mobilized near Mountjoy Square – not far, in fact, from the battalion's intended northern front at the Cabra Road. But instead of taking up positions there, Heuston took his men due south, through Parnell Square and down Sackville Street towards Beresford Place. His first lieutenant, Seán McLoughlin, recalled that 'we did not march or take up military formation; we just strolled across'. But 'everybody was carrying arms' – Lee-Enfields with 100 rounds of ammunition each – and he himself had 'a small handbag containing .303 ammunition'. At Beresford Place they met up with some of the 'Kimmage garrison' (McLoughlin called them the 'refugees'; the Company second lieutenant, Dick Balfe, recalled 'the London Irish waiting under the loop line arches, with a queer assortment of arms of all sorts, including pikes'). After a conference with Connolly they were sent on across the river. They set off barely twenty-five strong, this time 'in rather ragged military formation', across Butt Bridge, and around midday caught a Kingsbridge tram. Only as they sat together in the back of the tram did Heuston tell his Lieutenant that they were going into action: 'I am afraid we are on our own, at least for the beginning.' Finally, when they got to Queen Street Bridge, Heuston announced to his company that they were going to seize the Mendicity Institute. Perhaps not surprisingly, 'some of them were astonished'.[37]

The Mendicity garrison is usually described as one of Daly's ouposts.[38] But it is clear that Daly did not put it there, and it had not figured in the original plan. Heuston seems to have come under Connolly's direct orders, and to have communicated direct with HQ rather than with Daly as long as communications could be maintained. This was not to be for long, because the Mendicity was the only rebel post which could even indirectly dispute the free movement of British reinforcements from Kingsbridge Station into the centre of the city. It was in fact a key position; but why had it not been occupied by Daly's force just across the river, rather than by a unit which had to come by a long detour from the northern side of the battalion area? Why, indeed, was it not occupied by the 4th Battalion, responsible for the area south of the river? Dick Balfe heard Connolly tell Heuston that a 1st Battalion company (D) had been detailed to occupy it, but its captain had decided to obey MacNeill. But if Connolly realized belatedly that there was a dangerous gap in the centre of the rebel positions, we may wonder why did he not do more to plug it by establishing a post which could directly close the route along James's Street and Thomas Street to the Castle. Why not, indeed, occupy Guinness's Brewery (as, curiously, Connolly's own communiqué of 28 April was to claim)?

South of 1st Battalion, Eamonn Ceannt's 4th Battalion also deployed on quite a narrow front, though it is not clear whether its original plan was more extensive. The battalion mobilized at Emerald Square, just north of Dolphin's Barn, where a little over 100 had assembled by 11 a.m. About half an hour later they moved off down Cork Street to occupy two main posts, the South Dublin Union and the distillery in Marrowbone Lane. Ceannt's group moved along the branch of the Grand Canal which extended to James's Street Harbour by the Guinness Brewery, reaching the Rialto Bridge at noon. They entered the SDU by its southern gate. This rambling mass of buildings, covering fifty acres and extending north nearly – but not quite – as far as the junction of James's Street and Stevens Lane, certainly formed a substantial obstacle to the movement of British forces. (Seumas Murphy, the battalion adjutant, remembered Ceannt earlier 'describing with enthusiasm how from the South Dublin Union we could control or stop the troops entering the city from Richmond Barracks'.)[39] But it could not, and did not, prevent the movement of reinforcements arriving at Kingsbridge Station. The sheer size, and the odd nature, of the SDU complex presented big problems to Ceannt's force. This walled community was the country's biggest poorhouse, with 3,000 destitute inmates, its own churches, stores, refectories, and two hospitals with full medical staff. Ceannt was taking a daunting responsibility in turning it into a battleground. His force was never large enough to attempt to hold the whole perimeter, and was soon fighting a shifting struggle against the troops who immediately began to advance from the barracks in the west. No effort seems to have been made to evacuate the inmates, who became embroiled in the increasingly intense mêlée. (Whether removal – even if feasible – would have been a nastier fate is open to question.)

Immediately behind the canal was a much more compact stronghold, Jameson's Distillery on Marrowbone Lane. Bob Holland of F Company arrived there around 3 p.m. after a series of adventures of the kind replicated by many Volunteers across the city. Originally detailed by Con Colbert to watch the entrance to Wellington Barracks on the South Circular Road while the battalion mobilized, he went on at midday to Colbert's post, Watkins' brewery in Ardee Street. There he ran into a 'very rowdy crowd of women of the poorer class' who were assaulting the main gate in protest against the 'Sinn Feiners' who had gone in and beaten up the caretaker. After a fruitless attempt to get the occupiers to open the gate, he wandered off, and bumped into his fellow-Volunteer brother who was bringing a heavy cartload of guns, ammunition and tinned food to the post. He persuaded him not to try to get past the irate women, and the two of them took the cart back up Cork Street and parked it in a yard at Dolphin's Barn, before making their way back 'down Cork Street at top speed, running', to the sound of gunfire from the canal area, to Marrowbone Lane. They found the force in the distillery 'in good spirits' (presumably not, being good Volunteers, John Jameson's own), filling a large vat with fresh water in preparation for the siege. There seemed, Holland thought, 'to be more women than men in the garrison'. They turned out to be from the Gaelic League branch where Holland had been at a *ceilidh* the evening before. Since he was proficient with all the main kinds of rifles used by the Volunteers, he was given two and posted in one of the huge grain storerooms with a commanding view out to the west.

I had grand observation of both north and south sides of the canal banks, along the back of the South Dublin Union as far as Dolphins Barn bridge . . . I could see over all the roofs of the houses in that area and in the distance a portion of the James's Street section of the South Dublin Union.[40]

With one of the women, Josie McGowan, loading his assorted rifles (one Lee-Enfield and one Howth Mauser) in turn, he was to exploit this position for the next four days of fighting.

Not all the 4th Battalion garrisons were so effective. Just to the north of the Union, across Mount Brown, part of C Company had occupied Roe's Distillery. This seems to have been intended as an out-post to strengthen the northern defences of the SDU, but it was a building with many problems. Only three storeys high, it did not command the Union grounds, and was itself overlooked by the Royal Hospital at Kilmainham – the location of the headquarters of the British army in Ireland – a mere couple of hundred yards away. The rear entrance of Roe's was at Bow Bridge, which carried the road to the Royal Hospital across the Cammock stream. It was a bridge too far; even before the military response began, local people came out in force to oppose the garrison's attempt to put up a barricade on it. 'The women shouted jingo slogans, while the men started to pull down the barricade.' The Volunteers of C Company, like others elsewhere in the city, had the unpleasant experience of starting their revolution by hand-to-hand fighting with ordinary Dubliners; they had to go at them with clubbed rifles, and laid out two before the rest dispersed. Once British troops began to fire on their building, its limitations became more apparent. Its windows were either too high to see out of, on the upper floor, or too low for safety. In the early evening, the second-in-command recalled, 'Larry O'Brien rushed over from the side building and told us that the grain was ready to burst into flames.'[41] Most of the garrison dashed in to move it, ending up exhausted; then an attempt to bolster the walls of the yard with grain-filled sacks was driven back by enemy fire. Much of this might have been predicted, perhaps. But, strangely, repeated efforts to get in touch with the garrison over the road in the Union failed. Mount Brown, open to British fire from the west, was a deadly barrier. Patrick Egan spent a long time gazing out at the depressing sight of what seemed to be three dead Volunteers in the field across the road; a fourth, mortally wounded, struggled vainly to raise his water bottle to his mouth.

Egan felt, nonetheless, that the garrison was quite secure in the building. British gunfire became more desultory on Tuesday, and no direct assault came. He was taken aback when Captain Tommy McCarthy announced in the afternoon that the position was untenable, and rejected Egan's suggestion that, if so, they should try to cross the road into the SDU. In fact, several of the garrison had already decamped. This realization only dawned slowly on the men upstairs; Larry O'Brien felt 'an uneasy quiet seemed to settle over the building'. He then found that 'the section manning the top floor was the only one left. For some reason that has never been explained satisfactorily, the building had been evacuated without any notification to the section holding the top.'[42] With no officer left, the men had 'an informal conference', and decided to try to get over to the Marrowbone Lane garrison.

Eamon de Valera's 3rd Battalion was the south-east Dublin unit. Its headquarters, and central mobilization point, was in Brunswick Street, close to Westland Row Station. But its area was extensive, socially as well as physically. ('No greater contrast could be imagined', one observer wrote, 'than between the squalid slums of Ringsend and the stately and fashionable houses in the Mount Street area.')[43] Two of its companies mobilized as far west as Earlsfort Terrace, while E Company mobilized out at Oakley Road. Like the others, the battalion's mobilization on Monday was disappointing. As we have seen, C Company ended up without its captain; so did A Company; and the whole battalion mustered fewer than 130 men. Uniquely among battalion commanders, de Valera specifically refused to allow women to join the muster. The Cumann na mBan group assembled in Merrion Square expecting to receive orders from him never did. He drew in his reduced forces closer to his operational headquarters, in Boland's Bakery at the bridge on Grand Canal Street, which he occupied around 12.30. He told his men that this would be the main route into

Dublin of any British reinforcements that might arrive via Kingstown. Still, he tried to cover some of the wider deployment originally envisaged for his battalion – especially northwards towards the Liffey at Ringsend (where Boland's mill was), and westwards to Westland Row Station and railway works. Southwards, only one of the canal crossings, at Lower Mount Street Bridge, was covered, by a very small group detached by Simon Donnelly as he took his company in from Earlsfort Terrace to join de Valera's main force. The Baggot Street crossing was left undefended.

De Valera's positions were carefully chosen. Joe O'Connor, the first lieutenant of A Company, who had to replace his absent captain in charge of its feeble muster, records that de Valera had briefed them 'in very great detail' at a battalion council on Good Friday evening. He was 'able to tell each Company Captain where he would enter on to his area, and what he would find to his advantage or disadvantage when he got there'. O'Connor was 'amazed at the amount of information the Commandant had accumulated and how thoroughly he understood about the position each Company was to occupy'. His own company was to control all the level crossings on the railway line from Grand Canal Quay to Kingstown, and 'dominate' Beggars Bush Barracks. B Company was to take over Westland Row Station, and send a party up the line to Tara Street Station where they were to link up with the 2nd Battalion who would be in charge of the Amiens Street Station area. C Company would occupy Boland's bakery and dispensary building, together with Roberts' builders yard and Clanwilliam House; barricade the canal bridges at Grand Canal Street, Mount Street, Baggot Street and Leeson Street, where they should join up with the 4th Battalion and/or the Citizen Army. D Company was to be based at Boland's mill, and control the section between the bakery and the quays. F Company was to occupy Kingstown harbour. (E Company, which came from St Enda's school, was specially detailed to form part of Pearse's HQ force.)[44]

Much of this ambitious plan was curtailed on Monday, notably the intended links to the north and west, and the occupation of Kingstown. As we shall see, though, the abandonment of this last objective continued to haunt the battalion commander. The impact of the botched mobilization soon became clear to O'Connor as he brought his reduced company into the Boland's area. He halted his men at Great Clarence Street and told them they were going into action 'for the glory of God and the honour of Ireland'; on hearing this news, one of his small band decamped, though fortunately at the same moment another turned up to take over his equipment. His group occupied a terrace of houses at the junction of South Lotts Road and Grand Canal Street, while others entered the railway workshops, climbing over the wall from a disused cart by the road (in the process, one shot himself in the leg). Now O'Connor was reluctantly appointed battalion vice-commandant, a worrying result of the shortage of officers. The battalion's position was a cause for concern. Simon Donnelly noted that 'the railway was a very vulnerable position to hold as it ran practically right through our headquarters, and had the enemy got possession of it our area would have been cut in two'. To prevent this, B Company after barricading and locking up Westland Row Station, moved 300 yards down the line and dug a 'fairly deep trench, dominating the situation generally'.[45]

Part of 3rd Battalion's task was to 'dominate' Beggars Bush Barracks, but evidently de Valera's extended reconnaissance of his area had not revealed that the barracks were practically empty. (Its main occupants were from the army catering corps.) There was only a handful of troops there (with seventeen rifles), and the only force that appeared on the scene to fulfil the rebels' expectation of an immediate military riposte was a unit of the Irish Association of Volunteer Training Corps, part-time reservists, many of them lawyers, doctors and other professional men, and many above military age. (The Irish Rugby Union, for instance, had its own contingent.) The 'Gorgeous Wrecks', as they were unofficially dubbed, wore civilian clothes with armbands emblazoned 'GR' – Georgius Rex; they had recently become a fairly familiar sight on the Dublin streets, where Nathan had been cautiously employing them on guard duties. On Easter Monday they had been on exercises in the Wicklow hills, where they had heard of the rebellion in the early afternoon, and were cautiously making their way back to their depot at Beggars Bush in two columns. The smaller of these came under fire from the Mount Street Bridge outposts in Northumberland Road. As Simon Donnelly tersely put it, they were 'unfortunate enough to pass our posts and of course had to be dealt with'. They were either unarmed or carrying rifles with no ammunition; four were killed and several wounded before the rest managed to scramble into nearby houses. The larger column, nearly 100 strong, managed to get into the barracks, where they formed the only garrison, and eventually opened fire on the rebel outposts.

The mobilization of the 2nd Battalion presents the biggest puzzle. Its recruitment area, as we have seen, was north-western Dublin, with its depot at Father Mathew Park out beyond the Royal Canal. Strategically, this area was certainly as important as the other three battalion areas. Amiens Street Station was the terminal of the line from Belfast, and it was down this line that some of the first significant British reinforcements were to come. The area also had great symbolic significance as the site of the battle of Clontarf, something of which Thomas MacDonagh, the battalion's commander, was as we know intensely conscious. It seems clear from de Valera's instructions to his own battalion that the original plans anticipated the occupation of Amiens Street by the 2nd Battalion, and it is likely that they envisaged the main strength of the battalion operating like 1st Battalion as a shield for the republic's headquarters. In the event, however, a very different deployment took place.

As we have seen, part of 2nd Battalion spent Monday and Tuesday of Easter week in somewhat uncoordinated (and, at least to one company commander, unexplained) movements along the road from Father Mathew Park to Parnell Square. One section stayed at Ballybough and Annesley Bridges on the Royal Canal, while another went on to join the headquarters force in Sackville Street. Henderson sent out cycle scouts as far north as Malahide to look out for advancing Crown forces, and these reported on Tuesday afternoon that troops were moving down the Malahide Road towards Fairview, and down the Swords Road towards Drumcondra. On Monday evening, or Tuesday, 'acting on GHQ orders', Henderson's force sent men with explosives to demolish the Great Northern railway line as it crossed the 'sloblands' east of Fairview. Strangely, however, the chosen group, including Harry Boland and Harry Colley, was completely unprepared for the task: 'none of us knew anything about gelignite'. Colley was already so tired that he tore his thigh badly in trying to climb over the barbed wire fence at the foot of the railway embankment.[46] Thus another long-planned project fell victim to last-minute improvisation. At some point on Tuesday evening, Connolly seems to have ordered this northern outpost group to fall back to Sackville Street. Lynch's explanation of this move is that 'the Republican positions at Fairview and Annesley Bridge were becoming encircled by overwhelming forces of the enemy', who were already in control of the Amiens Street–North Strand sector.[47]

Certainly British moves here were significant, which underlines the fundamental importance of 2nd Battalion's area.[48] Yet the main body of the battalion had left its area entirely and marched off south of the river. As the ICA force arrived at St Stephen's Green at midday, they could see MacDonagh's men parading on the west side of the Green in front of the College of Surgeons. Peadar Kearney of B Company (the composer of what was fast becoming the Volunteer national anthem, 'A Soldier's Song') felt 'orphaned'; he and one comrade were the sole representatives of a company which a week before had mustered close on 200 men. MacDonagh was joined by Major John MacBride, the legendary Boer War Irish Brigade leader newly appointed his vice-commandant. (Indeed MacBride, who had for years been marginal to the separatist elite, seems simply to have appeared on Monday because he heard that something was going on.) His sudden promotion was certainly due to his military reputation, rather than his intervening experience as a water bailiff for the Dublin Corporation, or his famous drink problem which set him apart from the puritanical new republicans. It came too late for him to acquire Volunteer uniform; he turned out in an immaculate suit (complete with white spats and malacca cane). He and MacDonagh led their force off westwards down Cuffe Street to Bishop Street, where they entered the imposing mass of the Jacob's factory building. Again, they had to face some popular resistance as they did so, especially in trying to set up outposts in the Liberties, one of Dublin's most notorious slum districts. Kearney, set to building barricades in Blackpitts and New Street, thought that the aggression of the 'separation women' was 'easily the worst part of Easter week'. In any case he doubted the value of barricades there – 'a futile business, but apparently part of Sunday's plan and based on our keeping communications open . . . had 4,000 men taken the field'.

Placing MacDonagh's main force in Jacob's factory suggests an intention to dispute the movement of troops from Portobello Barracks into the city. If this was the aim, however, the occupation of a single building, however strong, was not the most promising method. (Paradoxically, indeed, the very strength of the Jacob's building would sharply limit its effectiveness for this purpose.) There were plenty of ways around it. A series of small outposts might have been much more effective. This was something the rebels were to learn by experience, but even in the original plans there was some provision for such tactics. The occupation by a ten-man ICA detachment of Davy's pub overlooking Portobello Bridge (now the Portobello Hotel) had great potential. The seizure of the building, led by one of Davy's disgruntled cellarmen (felicitously named James Joyce), now transformed into a proletarian fighter, is one of the emblematic revolutionary scenes of the rising.[49] But the garrison gave away its position by firing on a lone officer, and soon came under heavy fire as, in what the press called 'one of the most exciting of the events of Easter Monday . . . strong reinforcements, with machine guns, were rushed up' from the nearby barracks, 'to the accompaniment of hearty cheering of the crowds on the Rathmines road' (no doubt including a few of Davy's regulars).[50] When, after an hour or so, the troops rushed the bridge and broke in the plate-glass windows of the pub, they found that 'the rebels had made good their escape'.

After the evacuation of Davy's pub – which had not in any case been under MacDonagh's command – there were no prepared rebel posts along the whole length of Camden and Richmond Streets. MacDonagh's outposts in Blackpitts, New Street and Fumbally Lane were withdrawn on Monday evening before any contact with the enemy. ('Late that night we were withdrawn to Jacob's', one member of F Company wrote, adding laconically, 'after that I enjoyed a very quiet week'.)[51] The barricades 'were in a dangerous position and no useful purpose was being served', one garrison member noted; 'they were attacked on all sides by civilians'.[52] Early on Tuesday, when the expected British attack on Jacob's had failed to materialize, MacDonagh had second thoughts and sent out two small parties to occupy shops in Camden Street, but these once again withdrew after a sharp exchange of fire with advancing troops. The garrison of Jacob's factory itself totalled no fewer than 185. Soon after they took over the vast building, some of them got the chance to open fire on a group of soldiers passing the end of Bishop Street as they went down Redmond's Hill. Several were wounded; but this was almost the last the garrison saw of the enemy. Most of them stayed in the biscuit-filled mausoleum for the rest of the week, waiting for an attack that never came.

The rebels who went out to do battle on Easter Monday morning may have been marching into the unknown, but they shared one expectation: that the British military response would be rapid and hard. This may have influenced their choice of positions and procedures in ways that cannot be exactly clarified. The handful of encounter fights that happened at odd intervals on Monday sustained this apprehension. But it was a mistaken belief. Like a number of other assumptions, it was the product of a surprising ignorance of the strength and location of the Crown forces. At midday on Monday, there were just 400 troops in 'immediate readiness', out of a total of 120 officers and 2,265 soldiers. At the Castle there was a guard of just 6; in Ship Street Barracks beside it, some 20–25. An unknown number of officers had gone off to the big race meeting at Fairyhouse. The most notable absentee was the GOC Irish Command, Major-General Friend, who had gone to London for a long weekend. He had not returned for the urgent meeting on Sunday to discuss the arrest of leading republicans, and he only found out about the rebellion when he went in to the War Office on Monday. His deputy, Colonel H. V. Cowan, maintained nonetheless that the military response was unaffected. There was 'no delay owing to officers being away'; the thirteen headquarters staff on duty were 'ample' to deal with the situation; the troops themselves had not been given Bank Holiday leave, and were all in barracks.[53] Still, he admitted that they were taken by surprise. No special orders or dispositions had been made to deal with the Volunteer manoeuvres on Easter Sunday. The military authorities still assumed that the capital was safe; 'the chief anxiety was outside Dublin'. The rebels had certainly seized the initiative. (Both Cowan himself, and the commanding officer of the Dublin garrison, Lt. Col.

Kennard, were out of their offices when the news broke, leaving Kennard's adjutant to take on the rebellion.) The army's response would be instinctual.

7

The Battle of Dublin II:
the Counterstroke

*I find no tendency at present to be afraid of strong action. I
have no doubt it will come when we have shot a few people.*

Brigadier-General Byrne, 28 April 1916

On Easter Monday morning, the total military force immediately
available for action was 400, in the shape of an 'inlying picquet' of
100 troops at each of the four principal barracks (Richmond,
Marlborough, Royal and Portobello). Surprisingly, perhaps – it
would certainly surprise the Royal Commission of Inquiry – no special orders or dispositions had been made for the expected
Volunteer manoeuvres on Sunday. The rebel mobilization on
Monday was observed by the police, but (as on Sunday) they seem
to have reported nothing. Certainly no word came to the military
barracks until after midday. While Eamonn Ceannt's force was
occupying the South Dublin Union, they could hear a band playing
in Richmond Barracks. 'They don't know yet', Ceannt remarked
around 12.15, a moment before the band fell silent. The army's first
stab at an explanation for its surprise was that the 'Sinn Feiners had
collected quietly in Dublin', possibly in the guise of Bank Holiday
trippers.[1] The situation was distinctly embarrassing, if not alarming. Dublin Castle was virtually undefended, and the overriding priority was to make it safe. The inlying picquets sallied forth in the
direction of the Castle. (Incidentally, apart from the 6th Reserve
Cavalry Regiment in Marlborough Barracks, all these units were
Irish: the 3rd (Special Reserve) Battalion of the Royal Irish
Regiment in Richmond, the 10th Royal Dublin Fusiliers in Royal

Barracks, and the 3rd Royal Irish Rifles in Portobello.) All soon ran into some kind of resistance.

The most spectacular of these early encounters handed an easy triumph to the rebels. A force of lancers was sent out from Marlborough Barracks to investigate the vague report of rioting in Sackville Street. Diarmuid Lynch suggests that at 1.15 p.m. 'Glad tidings flashed through the GPO: "The horsemen are coming!" . . . As they neared Nelson's Pillar Republican volleys were unloosed. The surviving Lancers hastily retreated. No mere "riot" this, but war!'[2] Three were killed and one fatally wounded; for the rest of the week a dead horse lay where it had fallen. Lynch was right to see this little affray as a potent symbolic drama. (In the history of war as well as Anglo-Irish relations, cavalrymen were still reluctant to learn the lesson of their obsolescence in modern battle.)[3] The brief fusillade announced that Britain's Irish policy had failed.

The reconnaissance of the infantry units was less reckless, however. The first 100 men of the RIR from Richmond Barracks, soon joined by another 200, quickly overwhelmed the small group that Ceannt had posted at the western end of the South Dublin Union grounds. Their commander, Colonel Owens, sent forces around both sides of the Union, to the Royal Hospital on the northern side and along the canal to the south. Throughout the afternoon there was fierce fighting as Ceannt's men, quickly becoming veterans in close-quarter combat, held on to their positions in the main buildings. After nightfall, though, Colonel Kennard, the Dublin garrison commander who joined the Richmond force when he could not get back to his headquarters, took 86 of the RIR to Ship Street Barracks and thence into the Castle. The Dublin Fusiliers picquet from Royal Barracks had already arrived. They had come under fire from the Mendicity Institute as soon as they started to advance down Ellis Quay, but worked their way around and rushed across Queen Street Bridge under cover of machine-gun fire; after that their movement along Watling Street, Thomas Street and High Street was unimpeded. Some 130 of them were in the Castle by 2 o'clock.

At about the same time, 50 men of the picquet from Portobello also arrived. It had taken them about an hour to work their way along Richmond and Camden Streets, after a brisk assault on the rebel outpost at Davy's pub on Portobello Bridge. They had come under fire from two small outlying posts of MacDonagh's force, and from Jacob's factory itself at the junction with Bishop Street. But they seem to have found a way round via New Street, despite the outposts there and in Fumbally Lane. So when Kennard reached the Castle, he had a garrison of around 300, and could go over to offensive action against Connolly's force in City Hall. On Monday afternoon and evening, a few other defensive movements took place. The troops who ran into the Volunteers of the 2nd Battalion under Weafer and Henderson in Ballybough Road were moving to secure the North Wall and Amiens Street Station. Here, as elsewhere, the rebels, expecting an instant military assault, were puzzled by the disappearance of the troops. As elsewhere, the army's priorities were different. At St Stephen's Green, the first aim was to get reinforcements into the Shelbourne, which as we have seen was done on Monday evening.

Trinity College, which was never directly threatened by the rebel forces, had its own small OTC garrison – students with a few hours' part-time military training, with a sprinkling of regular officers and NCOs. Only eight were in the college at midday; the commanding officer, Major Tate, was on leave in the country and could not get back. It was the college's Chief Steward who locked the front gates, while Corporal Mein of the OTC closed the Lincoln Place gates, issued a rifle and 50 rounds of ammunition to each member of the guard, and gave orders: should there be 'an attack in force', the garrison would retire to its HQ in the pavilion, and take up defensive positions already prepared on the balcony. The closest rebel forces were just over the road in Westland Row Station and on the railway viaduct, which overlooked the college sports field, and there was good reason to anticipate an attack – the college was, as the OTC's Adjutant pointed out, a key position. 'Had the rebels taken the College on the first or second days of the rising, it would have been exceedingly difficult to dislodge them,' since the buildings were 'of a most substantial character, and heavy artillery would have been required' to retake them. (This would, as he thoughtfully added, have been 'a National Calamity'.) The Bank of Ireland would also have been at risk.[4] As it was, a trickle of OTC cadets and regular officers on leave drifted into the college during the afternoon; Captain

Alton arrived to take command at 3 p.m., and by 7 he had a garrison of 44.

Overnight, the military authorities gradually got their act together. Reinforcements were summoned from the Curragh and Belfast. The first 150 men of the composite battalion sent from Belfast arrived at Amiens Street on Monday night. Colonel Cowan at last called for the artillery from Athlone. Generals began to appear on the scene. The key arrival was Brigadier-General W. H. M. Lowe, commander of the 3rd Reserve Cavalry Brigade at the Curragh. The first trainload of his troops reached Kingsbridge Station at 2.15 a.m. Lowe arrived at 3.45, and the whole Curragh Mobile Column of 1,600 was in Dublin by 5.20. Shortly afterwards it was followed by the 25th Irish Reserve Infantry Brigade of around 1,000. Lowe took over command of the capital from Kennard immediately, and launched the operations that would define the shape of the battle over the next five days: the establishment of a central axis of communication running from Kingsbridge to the North Wall and Trinity College, followed by the cordoning off of the main rebel positions. No copy of his general plan has survived – a curious echo of the situation on the other side – and Lowe may have been improvising. Some contingency plan (in military parlance a 'defensive scheme') for Dublin must have been drawn up by the Irish Command staff earlier, but it may well not have anticipated anything like the eventual situation. What is certain is that General Friend, who dashed back by destroyer overnight and arrived at Kingstown around 9 a.m., made no attempt to modify Lowe's orders.[5] Lowe retained operational command until he took the surrender of the rebels at the weekend, although he has remained a somewhat shadowy figure, overshadowed certainly by the new commander-in-chief who was to appear on Friday. (His obscurity was compounded by the fact that the Royal Commission, perhaps surprisingly, did not see fit to call him as a witness.)

But if the military command recovered its poise, the civil authorities were in disarray. Easter Monday did not quite decapitate the Irish government, but it took it apart in an unprecedented way. For several hours, the Under-Secretary – effectively the head of the administration – was cut off in Dublin Castle, and even after he regained his freedom of movement he chose to stay there. The Chief Secretary, of course, was in London. This left the Lord Lieutenant in splendid viceregal iso-lation in Phoenix Park. Wimborne's position was an interesting one. His increasingly urgent warnings and exhortations of the last few weeks had been dramatically borne out; after long frustration in his bid for a real governmental role, he was now suddenly presented with an historic challenge. The atmosphere in the Viceregal Lodge was electric; according to Wimborne's private secretary, 'his Ex simply *swilled* brandy the whole time'; in 'superlatively theatrical' style he 'insisted on his poor secretaries using the most melodramatically grandiloquent language down the telephone – standing over them to enforce his dictation: "It is His Excellency's command . . ."'[6] But what commands could he usefully issue? Naturally he called for military reinforcements – not for the first time, and not, in the circumstances, extravagantly. He penned a personal letter to the secretary of the War Office asking for a brigade to start at once, with two more to be held in readiness. Things were serious; the wires to the Curragh had been cut, and he hardly overdramatized in saying that 'the situation is not in hand and we have no news from the provinces'.[7] Taking no chances, he sent the letter by hand – it arrived in Whitehall just after 9 a.m. on Tuesday morning, about the time that Friend was disembarking at Kingstown.

Wimborne's next action was less restrained: he declared martial law in Dublin. Did he try to consult the Castle's law officers before he did this? Or did he, as seems likely, simply assume that he had no alter-native? (The Attorney General told the Royal Commission that he did not see either the Lord Lieutenant or the Under-Secretary at any time during the week.)[8] Civil administration had unquestionably collapsed. After three DMP constables were killed in the first moments of the rebellion, the police were taken off the streets. The Commissioner then 'had them put in plain clothes' and sent out 'scouting; they sent in a stream of information about the movements of the rebels', but this was hardly a substitute for their normal law-enforcement function.[9] In effect, the civil law was paralysed. Wimborne's action probably seemed mere common sense, albeit no doubt quite exhilarating after the frustrations of the preceding weeks. All the same, it was far from unproblematic, and it would cast a long shadow. Martial law was pro-foundly abhorrent to the English liberal outlook, and it had only ever been used in modern times in distant parts of the empire. Even in Ireland, it had not been declared since the early years of the Union – in the wake of the 1798 rebellion – and a variety of alternative legal powers had been found to deal with the various armed challenges to British rule in the nineteenth century. Where it had been used recently, as during the South African war, it had raised the spectre of militarism and led to serious judicial complications. The legal doctrine of martial law in English jurisprudence was dangerously unclear. And in 1916, of course, the government already had what might have been called a form of statutory martial law in the shape of the Defence of the Realm Act. This gave very large powers to military tribunals to try cases of collusion with the enemy – a charge which the rebels had, by trumpeting in the proclamation of the Republic their 'gallant allies in Europe', openly embraced.

There was a real danger that the declaration of martial law would antagonize moderate Irish opinion without delivering any real benefits to the authorities. The danger was clear enough to the Chief Secretary, who took the hated crossing to Dublin for the last time in mid-week, and penned an urgent appeal to the Prime Minister not to extend martial law outside the immediate zone of fighting.[10] But Birrell's influence was shattered, and the Cabinet took the decision to do so in his absence. This was a very serious step, much less easy to explain than the Viceroy's instinctive action. Whereas Wimborne had been all too conscious for the last year of the limitations of DORA, the Cabinet had no such experience. In normal times, Liberal ministers would have hung on to the principle of legality. But 1916 was a very abnormal time. The war had shifted the balance of power within the executive; if it had not eclipsed the principle of civil supremacy, it had hugely enhanced the mystique of the military authorities. The army's view, as the incoming Irish Commander-in-Chief was soon to make clear, was that the rebellion had been permitted by the weakness of the civil government. Such weakness would now end. When the Cabinet declared martial law across the whole of Ireland for an indefinite period, and placed Ireland under a military governor, it was sending a deliberate signal. The suppression of the rebellion, by whatever means, was the overriding priority.

*

On Tuesday, Friend assessed the situation to be 'that of Civil War'; he estimated the strength of the rebels at 2,000. By 4.20 p.m. the number of troops available had risen to 3,000, but 'the arrival of the reinforcements from England is anxiously awaited'. His plan was that the Belfast reinforcements would 'move into the City from the N.E. by Amiens Street', while the brigade from England would move in from Kingstown by the two roads nearest to the coast, 'clearing the suburbs as they go'. A battalion was to land directly at North Wall. He noted that 'in the remainder of Ireland, everything appears to be quiet'. It was also significant that in Dublin 'the mob did some looting but do not appear to be concerned in the rebellion'.[11] This did not lead to the conclusion that countermeasures might be less vigorous, however. Lowe's orders to the troops arriving from England set the tone of the next phase of operations. The reinforcements were to set out from Kingstown immediately after breakfast on the 26th, their objective being 'to clear the country of rebels between the sea and the Stillorgan, Donnybrook and Dublin roads'. According to present information, 'it is improbable that resistance will be met with south of Donnybrook and Ballsbridge, but from these points increasing opposition may be expected'. The orders were explicit on how to deal with such resistance: 'every road and lane must be traversed by patrols', machine-guns, 'which will prove of great value in street fighting, should be carried close to the head of each column'. Crucially, 'the head of the columns will in no case advance beyond any house from which fire has been opened, until the inhabitants of such house have been destroyed or captured'. Moreover, 'every man found in any such house whether bearing arms or not, may be considered as a rebel'. The chilling undertone of this order was softened by the information that the rebels formed only 'a very small proportion of the population'. 'It must be impressed on all ranks that the householders and inhabitants of this country are with very few exceptions loyal in their support of the Empire.' A large proportion had friends and relations serving in the army. The houses fortified by the rebels had 'in every instance been seized by force from their lawful owners, and care should be taken that property be not damaged to a greater extent than is necessary'. But the orders went on to spell out the necessity for the 'hunting down' of 'these outlaws.'[12]

This dramatic, even lurid vocabulary was a symptom of the shock the rebellion had administered to a complacent establishment. The army's determination to crush the rebels was natural, but it also received the blessing of statesmen who had been wrestling for years with the recalcitrant complexity of the Irish problem. Throughout Tuesday, the situation remained obscure. In one of the week's many odd developments, the troops who had captured most of the South Dublin Union area on Monday and were preparing to assault the garrison of the main buildings on Tuesday, were pulled back 'for some extraordinary reason' (in the view of the regimental history) to Kingsbridge Station, where they were held – despite the protests of their commander, Colonel Owens – until Wednesday. It has been suggested that the reason was simply that the Castle was now safe, but it is clear from military reports that there was a real worry about the security of military headquarters itself. (This persisted through the week. On Wednesday afternoon the 178th Brigade received a message that 'Irish Command was being heavily attacked and asking for help.' Even after two reinforcing brigades had been brought to Kilmainham on Thursday, they 'were nervous lest the place should be rushed at dawn'.)[13]

The optimism of military reports rose and fell by the hour. In the evening, it was reported that the Bank of Ireland had been taken by the rebels, and earlier reports that the rebels had been cleared from Stephen's Green and the Corporation Buildings were contradicted. More worryingly, 'some disquieting rumours from country districts' came in, with reports of a rising in Galway. 'Rebels said to hold Gort, Galway road and probably Crusheen Railway Station (Clare).'[14] Some of the small police stations in Meath, Clare and Galway were reported captured. There was relief that the big munitions factory (Kynoch's) in Arklow was secure and its guard reinforced. But communication between Longford and Dublin was cut off. Friend's central objective was an attack on the main forces of the rebels in Sackville Street; but 'this main attack will not be delivered till the English troops arrive on the south side of the Liffey, at Trinity College and Dublin Castle.' He had wired for the rest of the 59th Division to be sent, not because he thought it would be needed for this attack but 'military occupation of the disaffected districts and thorough disarmament of the rebels therein will be necessary even after the rebellion in Dublin has been thoroughly crushed'.[15]

Even before the main military advance could be prepared, two ominous events announced the manner of military repression. By the early evening, four eighteen-pounder field guns had arrived from Athlone and were brought into Trinity College. The OTC garrison was relieved at the same time by troops of the Leinster Regiment with two machine-guns, but six Trinity Cadets went out in mufti to dig gun emplacements in Tara Street 'under most trying circumstances', and went on to act as ammunition porters.[16] It proved impossible to remove enough of the densely packed cobblestones to sink proper emplacements for the recoil of the heavy guns, and the local residents were sceptical of the explanation given for the excavations – drain repairs. On Wednesday morning two guns were finally brought out regardless. On the river nearby, HMS *Helga*, a fishery protection vessel (usually described as a 'gunboat', but technically an 'armed yacht') currently serving on an anti-submarine patrol duty, had come up from Kingstown on Tuesday afternoon, and sent a few three-inch shells into the republican position at Boland's.[17] (De Valera reportedly ran around shouting 'Hurrah! Rotten shot!' before coming up with the idea of diverting the gunners' attention to an empty distillery just north of the bakery by hanging a republican tricolour on it.) Early on Wednesday morning, the *Helga* lay off Sir John Rogerson's Quay and opened fire on Liberty Hall. The shelling was fairly ineffective at first, but then the eighteen-pounders joined in. 'At the first report every pane of glass in the street was shattered, and even in Trinity College the solid buildings seemed to quake under those who were lining the parapets.'[18] Liberty Hall was steadily reduced to a burnt-out shell. Whether the army believed it to be garrisoned is not clear – Friend reported that 'the Headquarters had evidently been previously removed' – but its prime importance was probably symbolic. The *Irish Times* pointed out with grim satisfaction, 'for many years past Liberty Hall had been a thorn in the side of the Dublin Police and the Irish Government. It was the centre of social anarchy, the brain of every riot and disturbance.' The bombardment itself was also symbolic. Liam O Briain's comrade in the College of Surgeons, the ICA man Bob de Coeur, regaled him with Connolly's maxim that if the British were ever compelled to use artillery in 'the second city of the empire', they were doomed. O Briain 'was not in the mood to argue the proposition. But', as he reflected, 'was it an absurd one?' Any attempt by the government to dismiss the rebellion as a minor street affray would henceforth be an uphill task.

The second event overnight was a more tragic demonstration of what martial law might mean. Shortly before 8 p.m., the junior officer in command of the military picquet occupying Davy's public house at Portobello Bridge, with orders 'to defend my post, but to avoid a conflict if possible', saw a small crowd approaching.[19] They were following Francis Sheehy-Skeffington, one of Dublin's best-known eccentrics, some of them shouting his name. Skeffington, a radical pacifist and feminist (who had adopted his wife Hanna Sheehy's surname, and was something of a trial to her father, a Redmondite MP), had been one of the strongest critics of what he called the 'militarism' of the Irish Volunteer movement.[20] On Tuesday he had printed some leaflets condemning looting, and was trying to arrange a public anti-looting organization. As usual he attracted a crowd of admirers and detractors, and it was this – in a situation where the police had disappeared and martial law had been proclaimed – that led Lieutenant Morris to arrest him and take him into custody in Portobello Barracks. The situation inside the barracks was disorganized; the commanding officer of the garrison (3rd Royal Irish Rifles) was on sick leave, and his deputy Major Rosborough had (in the words of the commission of inquiry) 'under his command many officers and men who were unknown to him, but of whose services he was glad to avail himself in the restoration of order'. The three young officers in charge of the guardroom 'arranged among themselves spells of duty, and it was not clearly established which of them was in actual charge when Mr Sheehy Skeffington was brought in'.

The atmosphere in the barracks was, to say the least, exciting. It was 'full of refugees from almost every regiment and corps in the British Army, all home on leave for Easter'.[21] One of these, Monk Gibbon of the Army Service Corps, was in 'the mood of a boy scout who has been served out a rifle and told that the game he has been rehearsing as a happy recreation is now to be played in real earnest'.

The troops were trigger-happy. 'If someone started a rumour that a sniper was firing into the barracks from a church spire across the canal, half the men in the compound rushed for their rifles and started blazing away . . .'²² Rumour, inevitably, was rife. 'Various alarming rumours were current as to an impending attack on the barracks, and both officers and men thought that they were in serious peril, which could only be averted by the taking of strong measures' – so at least suggested Sir John Simon's commission of inquiry in its effort to understand what followed.²³ What followed was, however, all but incomprehensible.

Captain J. C. Bowen Colthurst, an Irish Rifles officer with fifteen years' experience – not one of the Easter week blow-ins to Portobello – decided to lead a raiding party up to Harcourt Road to search the premises owned by Alderman James Kelly (a tobacconist, and a Unionist – whom Colthurst may have confused with Alderman Tom Kelly). As he took his party, a junior officer and forty men, out of the barracks he demanded that Sheehy-Skeffington be taken with them as a hostage. As if his 'extraordinary and indeed almost meaningless procedure' was not odd enough, he told Skeffington to say his prayers and, when he refused, Colthurst had his troops remove their hats while he said one of his own devising: 'O Lord God, if it shall please thee to take away the life of this man forgive him for Christ's sake.'²⁴ If his men were baffled or even alarmed by this proceeding, they seem to have put it down to the extremity of the situation and the existence of martial law. Just outside the barrack gate, in Rathmines Road, Colthurst challenged a passing youth by the name of Coade: telling him that martial law was in force, he shot him dead without awaiting a reply.²⁵ Again his junior officer and men stood by. He took his party on across Portobello Bridge, leaving Lt Wilson with half the force in charge of Skeffington, with orders to shoot him if Colthurst's party were 'knocked out'. The rest went on to Kelly's shop, which they rushed after throwing in a grenade, and seized two men they found there, Thomas Dickson and Patrick McIntyre. Colthurst then took all three of his prisoners back into the barracks.

According to his own account, Colthurst spent the night scrutinizing the documents he had seized at Kelly's shop and those that Skeffington had been carrying. He came to the conclusion that 'these three were all very dangerous characters'. At 9 a.m. he went to interrogate them, and, deciding that the guardroom was not a suitable place, had them taken out into the yard. He told the officer in charge of the guardroom, 'I am taking these prisoners out and I am going to shoot them as I think it is the right thing to do.'[26] Seven troops with loaded rifles followed them out, and Colthurst ordered them to shoot the three prisoners. He gave two explanations of his action. Later on Wednesday, he reported to his commanding officer that 'the yard was a place from which they might have escaped' – in fact it was surrounded by high walls – 'and as I considered that there was a reasonable chance of the prisoners making their escape I called upon the Guard to fire upon them'.[27] On 9 May, after he had eventually been placed under arrest, he offered a somewhat different explanation. 'I was very much exhausted and unstrung after practically a sleepless night, and I took the gloomiest view of the situation and felt that only desperate measures would save the situation.' Now he described his prisoners as 'leaders of the rebels' and 'desperate men'; 'I felt I must act quickly, and believing I had the power under martial law, I felt, under the circumstances, that it was clearly my duty to have the three ringleaders shot.'[28]

Colthurst's own motives are perhaps not the central issue here. He was certainly 'half-cracked', as Monk Gibbon put it, if not clinically insane as he was later found by a court martial. (Though 'to do him justice', as one of his puzzled juniors recalled, he 'seemed completely fearless'.) The real question raised by this gruesome incident is why he was not challenged or restrained sooner. What did Major Rosborough do when Colthurst reported that he had shot three prisoners? Rosborough ordered that Colthurst was 'only to be employed on the defences of Portobello Barracks, and not outside'.[29] But in fact he stayed at large. On Thursday, Hanna Sheehy came to Portobello looking for her husband, accompanied by her sister, the wife of another political celebrity, Tom Kettle MP. (Their brother, incidentally, was a lieutenant in the Dublin Fusiliers.) Colthurst nonetheless roundly accused them both of being Sinn Feiners, and had them bundled unceremoniously out of the barracks. Hanna Sheehy only found out on Friday, through the father of the youth Coade, who got into Portobello through the good offices of a priest and saw Skeffington's corpse lying beside his son's, that Skeffington was dead. That evening,

Colthurst appeared at her house with an armed raiding party to search for incriminating material. It seems that none of his superior officers was concerned to restrain him, and had it not been for the presence in Portobello of a rather different maverick, Major Sir Francis Vane, no further action might have been taken by the authorities. Vane was establishing an observation post just down the road in the tower of Rathmines Town Hall at the time of the shootings, but as he made his way back to the barracks he was heckled by bystanders with shouts of 'Murderer! Murderer!' His awkward inquiries and protests would ensure that Colthurst was court-martialled, and crucially bolster public demands for an inquiry. It was the start of a slow-burning public relations disaster for the army – and indeed for the Union.

The reinforcements summoned from England began their advance into Dublin at 10.35 a.m. on Wednesday. Two infantry brigades were sent, the 176th and 178th, part of the 59th North Midland Division. The four battalions of the 178th arrived at Kingstown from Watford at about 10.30 p.m. on Tuesday night. They had lost one of their four Lewis guns in the process of embarkation at Liverpool, and disembarkation in the dark 'was a regular nightmare', as the Brigade Major, Captain Arthur Lee, recorded. They had left all their 'bombs' (grenades) back in Watford. Each brigade was made up of two battalions of the Sherwood Foresters, and as Lee noted, 'most of our "men" were merely boys, Derby Recruits, who had been in uniform about 6 or 8 weeks. They had not fired their musketry course and many had never fired a rifle.' They had not been issued with rifles until just before they started out, and then, with the army's characteristic wit, had been given Mark VI ammunition to go with Mark VII rifles. Just before they set off, they were ordered to send a company with two of their remaining Lewis guns down to Arklow 'where there was trouble.' In Kingstown itself, though, 'all the streets were thick with people clapping and cheering us', apart from the 'spy element' which Lee found easily recognizable 'by their stupidly lowering faces'.

The brigade moved, as ordered, in two columns of two battalions each, along the two roads closest to the coast. It was a fine spring day, and the road took them through 'a prosperous and beautiful suburb, whose luxuriant and in some parts almost tropical gardens make the chance visitor think of the Riviera'.[30] Many of the soldiers, indeed, at first assumed they had been brought to France. The inland force, the 2/5th and 2/6th Battalions, 'reached Kilmainham and Kingsbridge without opposition', as Friend reported, but the two battalions on the coastal road, the 2/7th and 2/8th, 'continuing towards Beggars Bush ... were strongly opposed at the Canal crossing'. In fact they had gone past Beggars Bush and were presumably aiming to reach Trinity College by way of Mount Street when they ran into the outposts of the 3rd Battalion in Northumberland Road. They were pressing on into the centre of Dublin after receiving an alarming appeal for help from Irish Command and revised orders not to 'delay to search houses more than is necessary for their safe progress'. They had already experienced some fire shortly after midday in the vicinity of Carrisbrooke House, but the troops had dispersed quickly and returned fire. The rebels who had been supposed to garrison the house had decided to take up other positions, and eventually went home. (According to Seumas Grace it was 'prematurely evacuated by 14 men under orders of a Blackrock officer'.)

A certain amount of 'casual firing' continued, with 'stray bullets coming from all directions past the end of St Mary's Road'. The next combat was very different, however. When Malone and Grace in No. 25 Northumberland Road opened fire, the effect was devastating. The 2/7th Sherwoods were walking up the road in column of fours with their officers out in front. All hit the ground while they tried to locate the source of the firing – very difficult as the sound of gunshots echoed around the neighbouring houses. Malone was 'the crack shot of the 3rd Battalion with the Mauser automatic', and his position, in a bathroom at the side of the house, was brilliantly chosen. (Grace remembered Malone calling him in to look at it – 'one look was sufficient'.)[31] From there, and also from Clanwilliam House, a substantial Victorian town house block facing across the low hump of Mount Street Bridge with a clear view down Northumberland Road, the soldiers appeared hopelessly confused. As they tried to crawl en masse towards the building they believed to be their objective, the school, they presented an almost absurdly immobile target. Officers, such as Captain Dietrichsen, the Adjutant of the 2/7th (until recently a lawyer in Nottingham), who tried to get the troops to move, were instantly shot down.

A near-unimaginable disaster loomed for the battalion as the little rebel garrisons, soon gaining the confidence of veterans, fired into the khaki mass as fast as they could load their eclectic collection of rifles and pistols. The Martini rifles in Clanwilliam House gave trouble – it became increasingly hard to eject their cartridges.[32] Malone's 'Peter the Painter' automatic, on the other hand, was stunningly effective. But why did the British troops not find an alternative route into Dublin? The batallion commander, Colonel Fane, had already reported as early as 2.45 that he was holding Baggot Street Bridge, which was undefended. Yet five hours later his men were still struggling with the rebel posts in Northumberland Road. Instead of moving on into Dublin, the brigade received direct orders from Lowe to overwhelm the posts around Mount Street Bridge. The brigade commander, Colonel Maconchy, who had come forward to assess the problem, walked back to his headquarters in Ballsbridge – 'not a very nice walk' as he recorded – and explained to Lowe by telephone that this could not be done without significant casualties. He deliberately asked whether the situation was serious enough to require that the position be taken at any cost; the reply was 'to come through at all costs'.[33] The persistent shortage of grenades was eventually remedied around 5 o'clock. No. 25 and the schools were finally rushed and carried by grenade assaults (notably the so-called 'hair brush bomb' – Hand Grenade No. 12, one of the early mechanical grenades, with a throwing handle shaped like a hairbrush) and a supply of fresh troops, the 2/8th Battalion, which was brought through to relieve the exhausted and demoralized 2/7th.

Malone was killed some time after 5 p.m., but even in the thick of a full-scale attack, Grace was able to make his escape from the back of No. 25, where British troops had supposedly been working their way around the rebel positions for several hours. (He was eventually captured on Thursday in an outhouse in Haddington Road, after the owner informed the army.) The schools were taken around 8 p.m., shortly after 178th Brigade had sent an urgent request for another battalion 'at least' to be sent up from Kingstown. The Clanwilliam House garrison continued to fire across the bridge, but as troops concentrated along the canal side the balance of firepower inexorably shifted. The troops were firing from most of the houses in Percy Place, and James Doyle 'could see the soldiers coming from the Baggot Street direction crawling along the ground behind the stonework of the railings along the canal'.[34] By dusk, when a final assault across the bridge was ordered, Clanwilliam House had become a 'perfect inferno', its curtains shredded, mirrors, chandeliers and ornaments shattered, plaster fallen in 'and almost every square foot of the walls inside was studded with bullets'. Most dangerously for the garrison, the stairways began to collapse. The 'wild cries of assault outside, combined with the unceasing rattle of the musketry, made an incredible din'. A mile away, at the other end of the battleground, Captain Lee thought he heard cheering as the final assault went in, led personally by Colonel Oates. But Maconchy told him it was the cries of wounded men – 'the first time I heard it – a horrible sound – something between a "wail" and a "shout" or "cheer"'.

Did Lowe insist on a frontal assault because he had not understood the nature of the combat? Or was there some idea that in any case military honour had to be satisfied? Why would this take precedence over the need to get forces into the centre of the city as rapidly as possible? It is impossible to say.[35] What is certain is that the Sherwoods' casualties were potentially catastrophic. The 178th Brigade had to be withdrawn and sent around next day via the South Circular Road to Kilmainham. In the process the whole column nearly bolted when some random rifle fire broke out. 'It *was* tragic', one of the brigade officers wrote of the Mount Street fight.

You must remember all their officers and men came from Nottingham and the Retford–Newark–Worksop district, and they all knew each other and each other's parents and relations, and to see their lifelong pals shot down beside them by their own countrymen (as Irish men were then considered) *was* a shock.

They were 'completely flummoxed' by the whole situation and disoriented by being pitched into a civil war.[36] Had they, in the end, won a victory, however costly? Maconchy walked up into Mount Street with Lee to survey the captured territory, and found the streets crowded with people 'all of a good class', clapping and cheering. Lee only saw one prisoner, with a nasty bayonet wound in the neck, but he became convinced that he was not an Irishman. 'I don't think we killed less than 500 of them', he wrote later, 'and I don't think they were genuine Irishmen at all. I think they were paid mercenaries, the scum of the earth, gaol birds and hired for the job.' Though he added reasonably, 'I may be wrong.'[37]

If the army's tactics of reinforcing failure in the struggle for Mount Street Bridge were strange, the failure of the rebels to reinforce their successful outposts may seem equally difficult to understand. The headquarters and main force position of the 3rd Battalion was barely 200 metres away from this ferocious fight. The trenches dug by A Company around the railway bridges over South Lotts Road and Bath Avenue overlooked Haddington Road and the murderous junction with Northumberland Road. But de Valera seems to have made no attempt to intervene in support of his outposts, or to adjust their dispositions. Malone himself decided to send home two of his three comrades, who were 'just boys', before the fighting broke out; but he got no reinforcements. The substantial force in Carrisbrooke House melted away without any apparent reaction at headquarters. Donnelly sent four men (including Tom and James Walsh) to reinforce Clanwilliam House in response to an urgent request from George Reynolds during the afternoon. But at 5.30, while the outposts other than No. 25 were still fighting on, Donnelly ordered the group he had placed in Roberts' builders yard to fall back to Boland's bakery.[38] Clearly de Valera – like all the rebel commandants – was expecting an assault on his main position, and a couple of stray encounters close to the bakery with troops trying to work their way round Beggars Bush to outflank the Mount Street Bridge positions probably convinced him that it was imminent. His misreading of the situation was not surprising, though it showed how hard it was for many inexperienced commanders to adapt their plans in face of reality.

De Valera's political reputation was made by his status as the sole surviving battalion commander of Easter week, and by the reflected glory of 'the Irish Thermopylae'. The nature of his subsequent career – excoriated by many as the cause of the bitter civil war in 1922 – made it likely that his performance here would be controversial. In fact, criticism was surprisingly muted until the 1960s, when Max Caulfield's vividly detailed account of the rebellion included testimony from members of the 3rd Battalion indicating that the Commandant showed increasing symptoms of strain during the week. Caulfield's picture – as interpreted by one of de Valera's less sympathetic biographers – was of

a man on, or over, the threshold of nervous breakdown. Eyewitnesses recalled seeing a tall, gangling figure in green Volunteer uniform and red socks running around day and night, without sleep, getting trenches dug, giving contradictory orders, and forgetting the password so that he nearly got himself shot.[39]

This image brought an indignant rebuttal by Simon Donnelly, who went as far as to accuse Caulfield of misrepresenting his own testimony. In Donnelly's view Caulfield's 'account of events in the sector with which I was concerned is so distorted that it is almost impossible to know where to start in pointing out the errors'. He repudiated in particular the suggestion that de Valera had not trusted his own men.[40] He argued that men could not have been spared from Boland's bakery to reinforce the Mount Street Bridge outposts without unduly weakening the other positions, and pointed out that there had in fact been supporting fire from the railway workshops. He suggested that Caulfield's witnesses were either political opponents of de Valera, or men who had not been able to understand the whole situation.

Yet Donnelly's own account of Easter week, defiantly entitled 'Thou Shalt Not Pass', showed that he himself had been puzzled and anxious about some of his commander's decisions. At midnight on Monday de Valera had ordered him to take a party of four or five men down the railway line to 'scout towards' Kingstown, a job that Donnelly 'didn't altogether like as I knew it was rather ticklish and the men fairly nervy'. But he got his force together, 'and we were just about to start when the Commandant changed his mind, much to the relief of those going on the expedition'. Donnelly himself drew a picture of de Valera as hyperactive – 'a real live wire from the first moment we entered our position: he was forever on the move, ignoring danger, and to my mind taking unnecessary risks'. By Friday he was clearly worn out, but refused to rest until 'he was prevailed on eventually' (a faint suggestion of physical pressure?) and 'retired to an office he was using in the Dispensary'. But 'after a few hours he was on the move again, anxious about a hundred and one different things'.[41] One of the guards Donnelly posted outside the office, Sam Irwin, put this rather differently. When de Valera awoke, 'it took a number of officers to restrain him, I don't know what he wanted to do but I recall he was gesticulating and talking nonsense. I was only a boy of 18 then, and the whole incident wasn't very reassuring.'[42]

Donnelly's account also bears out one of Caulfield's most controversial revelations – the effect on the Boland's garrison of de Valera's unexplained decision on Friday night ('for some reason known to himself') to take them all up on the railway embankment. For the first time they could see the fires engulfing the centre of the city. A 'great number' of them were unnerved, and one officer 'lost his head and fired at a Volunteer standing near me', and had to be clubbed to the ground (by Donnelly himself) with a revolver butt. Donnelly did not understand why de Valera had issued his original order, since the railway was hardly a strong position (it was only fifteen feet above the level of the bakery itself). Then, 'after some time the Commandant apparently altered his plans and we were ordered to reoccupy the Bakery'. This was a fairly hazardous course by that stage, since the troops might well have moved in. The whole incident spread bafflement throughout the battalion.

De Valera's hyperactivity may have been a personal trait, but his inexperience was common to all the senior Volunteer commanders. Indecisiveness was often a result, as they tried to grasp the real nature of the battle they had so often fought in their imaginations. The nearest kin to de Valera in this respect was perhaps his neighbouring Commandant, Thomas MacDonagh. One of his students had heard him say that 'the most romantic experience of his life was marching along the Dublin road carrying a rifle after the gun-running at Howth'. Now, immured – for reasons still unclear – in the gloomy pile of Jacob's factory, he faced a daunting task in keeping up the morale of his beleaguered garrison. There were spasmodic dramas, as when the British troops tried to set up a machine-gun post in Digges Street and were 'literally blown out of it' ('a dozen Howth Mausers could always do that', Peadar Kearney recorded).

But most of the time, the British sniped, day and night, and often 'raced up and down Aungier Street in improvised armoured cars', creating the maximum psychological disturbance. Sleeplessness was aggravated by hunger. Jacob's was packed with biscuit and cake, a treat which soon palled: 'a couple of meals of Jacobs best gave the sweetest toothed member of the section a feeling of nausea when they saw an "Oxford lunch"'. Soon Kearney 'began to notice that aching void which compels the mind to dwell on bacon and eggs and such things . . .'. There was 'absolutely no authentic news' to be had; just rumours of German invasion, rumours of provincial Volunteers flocking to Dublin, rumours of annihilation, 'each rumour more fantastic than the last'.[43] MacDonagh moved around the vast spaces of the factory in his immaculate uniform, trying to encourage his men; but most of his interventions were more demoralizing, as he persistently sent out small parties on missions to the neighbouring garrison in Stephen's Green, often picking tired men at a moment's notice.

In the end, nothing could disguise from the garrison the fact that it was unable to affect the battle raging around it. The high towers of the factory, from which 'most of the city could be seen through field glasses', seemed to offer a commanding position to Volunteer snipers, who could 'pick off soldiers moving about in Portobello Barracks beyond the Grand Canal'.[44] But as the week went on they also offered a dispiriting view of the growing inferno north of the river. Maire Nic Shiubhlaigh, in charge of the garrison's small Cumann na mBan group, was up there on Friday evening, watching the GPO and its surrounding streets 'blazing fiercely'. 'There were huge columns of smoke' and 'all around, through the darkness, bombed-out buildings burned . . . the whole city seemed to be on fire. The noise of artillery, machine-gun and rifle fire was deafening.[45] None of that artillery fire was directed at Jacob's itself, however – uniquely among the main rebel posts; it was not enough of a nuisance.

Most of the garrison commanders had to deal with the fact that, instead of the immediate assault at bayonet point that they first expected, they had to sit immobile while the British troops gradually tightened the cordons around their strongholds, deluging them with machine-gun and artillery fire. The experience of the 4th Battalion in the South Dublin Union and Jameson's Distillery, however, was more dramatic. After the troops of the Royal Irish Regiment who had put in the initial attack were inexplicably withdrawn to Kingsbridge, there was a period of calm. But on Thursday, when the reinforcements from Kingstown had come across to the western side of the city, the attack intensified again. The fighting, at very close range, was grim enough to satisfy the goriest fantasies of hand-to-hand combat. The comparatively small garrison of the Union was energized by the leadership style of Ceannt and his Vice-Commandant, Cathal Brugha. One of the garrison remembered Ceannt as 'always cool and cheerful', while Brugha was the most silent member of the garrison, sitting for hours cleaning his automatic pistol during the quieter periods, but 'always composed and contented'. One of their officers, Douglas Ffrench-Mullen, displayed the classical soldierly (and Anglo-Irish) virtues when he was wounded, saying 'Do you know, I believe I've been hit – I feel very hot about the leg.' And 'he smiled as if he was very happy', James Coughlan of C Company thought.[46] The close-quarter fighting produced more ghastly results; one of the garrison slowly went insane as he obsessed over his guilt in causing the death of a comrade by offering him a light across a window. Brugha himself, who made a point of being in the front of every action, had to be taken out of the Union by some of its medical staff on Friday with a mass of wounds, twenty-five in all. Still, the position held, and the marksmen in the distillery were able to fire effectively on the attacking troops as they tried to work their way up from the Rialto direction. Bobby Holland had a strong sense that they were winning. The 'odd stragglers' who came into the distillery during the week told them that all the troops that landed at Kingstown had been eliminated, and they were only 'mopping up the crowd that came down from Belfast'. Holland's group believed this, because the soldiers they had killed belonged to many different regiments:

We have seen their cap and collar badges. The Notts, the Derbyshires [actually both part of the Sherwood Foresters], the West Kents, the Berks, the Wiltshires, the Royal Irish Rifles, the Dublin Fusiliers, the 4th and 5th Hussars, the 17th Lancers, South Irish Horse, Iniskilling Fusiliers, Liverpool Rifles, and several others, so we thought there could not be many more left.

The reasoning was attractive, if flawed.

*

In fact, the main concentration of troops was employed from Tuesday onwards north of the river, establishing the cordon from Kingsbridge to Amiens Street Station and the North Wall. The outer cordon around the North Circular Road was completed by Tuesday evening. The only resistance was met at the Cabra Road railway bridge, and quite swiftly dispersed. Indeed one military train was sent early on Tuesday by the Loopline to the North Wall, 'passing by Old Cabra Road to Glasnevin, then along by Royal Canal . . . Clarke's Bridge at Summerhill, under the Great Northern Railway, without attracting the attention of the Volunteers'.[47] The eastern military HQ was set up at Amiens Street Station, barely 800 yards from the GPO. In the process, the Volunteer 2nd Battalion outpost commanded by Frank Henderson came under increasing pressure from these military movements, and during the evening Connolly ordered it to come into the Sackville Street area (where its first experience of action was to be fired on by the trigger-happy garrison of the Imperial Hotel; two men were wounded before Connolly himself ran out into the street to stop the firing).[48]

In the end, as one military historian has stressed, 'the fact that there was no strong insurgent post in the north-eastern part of the city would have momentous consequences'.[49] For the time being, however, an intermediate strategic stage remained to be completed, and the military attempt to establish an inner cordon was more dramatically contested. Moving around to the north of the GPO along Parnell Street, troops were quickly in control of Capel Street, but only slowly became aware of the defensive positions of the 1st Battalion. This proved to be the most vital, strategically, of all the republican positions, and in the course of the fighting Ned Daly emerged as perhaps the shrewdest tactician among the rebel commandants.

The 1st Battalion's outpost at the Mendicity Institute had not, of course, been positioned by Daly, and seems not to have been in contact with him as the British assault intensified on Wednesday. 'Clearly Heuston regarded his connection with Daly's battalion as severed and looked to Connolly as his superior officer.'[50] Connolly sent Heuston a reinforcement of twelve men direct from the GPO on Tuesday – easily the most substantial attempt to redeploy republican forces made anywhere in the course of the battle. Still, it is (as Hayes-McCoy sagely observed) 'not clear what Connolly hoped ultimately to accomplish at the Institution'.[51] He was only loosely in touch with Ceannt's forces further west; his reference to their occupation of Guinness's brewery in his famous Friday general order seems to have been a genuine misconception. (Guinness's had become a key British post.) His grasp of the military advance from the west may have been equally imprecise, and he seems to have been surprised that Heuston managed to hold out until Wednesday. His short stand became one of the scattered mini-epics of Easter week. As the military fire intensified, Heuston believed that some 400 troops were surrounding the Institute, some working their way to within twenty feet of its windows. The messengers he sent to Connolly found that the GPO was already cut off, and with his garrison 'weary, without food and short of ammunition' he decided to surrender. As in other posts at the end of the week, this decision was contested by some of his men, and it is possible that he might have fought on. His post was not one that the troops had to capture at any cost, and they never tried a direct assault.

The 1st Battalion positions north of the river remained fairly comfortable until Thursday. Jack Shouldice, in command at Reilly's, noted that 'the fighting in the early part of the week mostly consisted of sniping from elevated posts like the top of the Malthouse, the roofs of Reilly's and adjoining houses'.[52] Indeed the worst threat they faced was of their own creation. On Wednesday Daly was casting about for ways to strengthen his position. A belated attempt to seize Broadstone Station to the north was abortive, but the near-empty Linenhall Barracks (held by forty unarmed men of the Army Pay Corps) just north of King Street were successfully taken over. So was the nearby police Bridewell. But full occupation was impossible, and 'to prevent its reoccupation' Linenhall Barracks was set on fire. (It is not clear if this was Daly's decision or a spontaneous initiative.) The result was uncomfortably spectacular. 'During Wednesday night it lighted up the streets with a murky glow', and it steadily spread into Bolton Street, where 'large barrels of oil were tossed into the air and exploded, and a cloud of stifling smoke shrouded the district'.[53] The brightness of the streets seems to have persuaded Daly to abandon a plan to attack the troops gathering in Capel Street, and the fires were still burning so brightly on Thursday night that Daly was able to convene an open-air meeting of his battalion officers at the junction of Church Street and King Street to discuss their increasing isolation. The military cordon along Capel Street had cut Daly's force off from the GPO, and he was in effect surrounded. Like the rest of the battalion commanders he had run out of options other than preparing more buildings for defence and strengthening barricades.

The long-awaited attack finally materialized early next morning as one of the improvised British armoured trucks rumbled into Bolton Street to deposit troops of the South Staffordshire regiment near the junction with North King Street. They had a short dash to seize the municipal technical school. The difficulty of attacking an occupied street, with many mutually supporting posts, had led to a primitive technical evolution.

A couple of motor lorries were obtained from Guinness's brewery; the engines were covered with iron plates, and old boilers were placed on the lorries. The lorries backed up to a house at a street corner. The men from the boilers crashed open the door with crowbars, rushed in and upstairs to the windows, from which they got command of the street.[54]

The intention was to throw another cordon out along King Street to envelop the Four Courts, where the main positions of the 1st Battalion were thought to be. In fact, King Street was so strongly held that even with the aid of armoured vehicles, progress had to be disputed yard by yard and from house to house in fighting of unprecedented intensity. In the end, the troops could only get forward by using the same methods as the defenders, boring through the inside walls from house to house. In the process, a number of occupants died, and were buried in their own cellars: victims of random gunfire, according to the troops, shot deliberately by the soldiers according to their relatives.[55]

As the positions in King Street became untenable during the day, Daly decided to pull back his headquarters to the Four Courts on Friday evening. He may have left this move dangerously late, since it was by then a daunting task to move his men back down Church Street – a task made more difficult and dangerous by Daly's own barricades. From this point, things could only get worse. The atmosphere inside the vast building was not cheerful; three days of watching the city burn had a traumatic effect, and at least one member of the garrison went mad and had to be handcuffed to a bed.[56] Daly was effectively cut off from his men who held out in the shrinking King Street battleground. Reilly's, its garrison reduced to seven or eight 'wearied-out and almost stupefied' men, was evacuated early on Saturday morning, and 'the whole of the fighting became concentrated along fifty yards of Upper Church Street'.[57]

The killing of civilians in North King Street was perhaps inevitable in fighting of such claustrophobic intensity. The incoming British commander-in-chief, General Sir John Maxwell, had some justification for his later assertion that 'the number of such incidents is less than I expected, considering the magnitude of the task'.[58] But it seems impossible that the troops were unaffected by their original orders, and he himself stoked up the atmosphere of retribution soon after his arrival in Dublin on Friday. This may, indeed, have been his principal contribution, since he arrived too late to influence the course of the fighting, and in any case General Lowe was specifically left in operational control after Maxwell's arrival.[59] Maxwell's appointment was above all a loud warning of the government's attitude to the suppression of the rebellion. Ireland certainly needed a formal commander-in-chief – Friend had been arguing this for a long time – and Friend had probably ruled himself out by his unfortunately timed absence. But it was a significant step from this to the appointment of a military governor. This was clearly intended as a signal that the most resolute steps would be taken, though it also signalled the eclipse of civil government and 'politics' generally.

Much would hinge on the quality of the officer chosen for this highly charged role, and the choice was constricted by the demands of the 'real' war on the Western Front and in the Middle East. The first general considered, for example, was Sir Ian Hamilton, tainted by the failure of the Gallipoli operation. He was ruled out (regrettably, since he was notably intelligent – maybe too intelligent to be a field commander) because the Prime Minister thought that damaging Irish memories of Suvla Bay would be revived. Maxwell was another general in enforced semi-retirement after a period in Egypt, and it seems that his main qualification for the job was his complete lack of any previous contact with Ireland – 'no past record', as Asquith characteristically put it. (It is clear, though, that Kitchener thought highly of his efficiency, and possibly also of what his biographer called his 'insight into and sympathy with racial characteristics', his 'strong common sense', and his 'imperturbable good humour'.) Maxwell's orders were to 'take such measures as may in your opinion be necessary for the prompt suppression of the insurrection', and his first act was to issue a proclamation asserting that 'I shall not hesitate to destroy all buildings within any area occupied by rebels.' Interestingly, this phrase stuck in one officer's memory as 'to raze Dublin to the ground'.[60]

Though one officer with the troops in the western part of the city thought that 'the rebels were really little other than fugitives even on the 28th April', the situation was still somewhat uncertain. One of the officers who arrived with Maxwell at the North Wall around 2 a.m. on Friday 'found Dublin like a "blazing furnace" – the whole of Sackville Street was on fire & the buildings along & at the back of Eden Quay – there was vigorous musketry fire going on on both flanks, fortunately not directed at us!' He added, 'it did not look as if the situation was "well in hand"!'[61] There was nobody to meet them, moreover, though eventually Cowan 'turned up – very uneasy – did not know what to do with us'. After a makeshift night at the Royal Hospital, Maxwell went over to the Headquarters at Parkgate and thence to the Viceregal Lodge where he found Wimborne and Birrell. 'The former seemed rather disconsolate at having his power taken away'; more surprisingly, the latter seemed 'quite prepared for vigorous action'. Maxwell's Deputy Adjutant General, who drafted the proclamation, found 'no tendency at present to be afraid of strong action', though he grimly added, 'I have no doubt it will come when we have shot a few people.'

Maxwell's crucial operational decision was to refuse any negotiations short of unconditional surrender. This had a vital effect as the army closed with the main republican positions in Sackville Street from Wednesday onwards. Late on Wednesday afternoon the 3rd RIR, which had been brought across from Kingsbridge via Trinity College, was reconnoitring Upper Sackville Street using the first of the improvised armoured trucks. Henry Street, the northernmost rebel position, was swept by fire from the west, and the men on the roof of the GPO came under fire from a machine-gun on the roof of Jervis Street Hospital. From this point movement between the GPO and its outposts became difficult. Connolly had taken considerable trouble in establishing and inspecting these posts, though his exact idea of their role remains unclear. All their garrisons followed the same instructions to fortify windows, make loopholes in external walls, and break communicating holes through the internal walls. When Connolly went over on Wednesday afternoon to inspect the garrison in the block running from Prince's Street to Abbey Street (including the Metropole Hotel and Eason's bookshop), under the command of Oscar Traynor, he struggled to get through one of the holes, and grumbled 'I wouldn't like to be getting through that hole if the enemy were following me with bayonets.' Traynor stiffly 'reminded him that these holes were built according to instructions issued by him in the course of his lectures'.[62] Across Sackville Street in the post between North Earl Street and the Imperial Hotel, Captain Brennan-Whitmore (a Wexford IV officer) complained that the ICA men were the worst instructed in loopholing – they had made the outer side of their holes wider than the inner, and had to rebuild them all.[63]

All accounts testify to the heavy labour involved in the effort to fortify these posts. Different floor levels and wall thicknesses made the job of breaking through arduous and frustrating – 'really heart-breaking work', Brennan-Whitmore called it. The garrisons were exhausted and often hungry by the time the artillery bombardment began. This certainly compromised their military effectiveness. For instance, Frank Henderson – who was fortunate enough to have half a dozen skilled builders to cut through the walls of his post in Henry Street – found one of his sentries in the Coliseum early on Thursday morning, 'standing in the window with his head resting on the outer sill, fast asleep'.[64] The anticipated infantry assault never materialized. Connolly seems really to have believed that the authorities would rather sacrifice the lives of their soldiers than destroy property – a reading of British culture in which modern socialist thinking was compounded by traditional Irish nationalist assumptions.

As the barrage intensified, the outposts were gradually withdrawn. In the most exposed of them, 'Kelly's Fort' overlooking O'Connell

Bridge, the garrison had 'had plenty of chocolate to eat, but little else' when firing began on Wednesday. (Not a shot had been fired at them until that morning.) Most of them, like Joe Good, were Londoners from the 'Kimmage Garrison', a group the Plunketts had taken under their wing and given facilities at their Kimmage house. (Michael Collins, a Corkman-cum-Londoner who had become Joe Plunkett's aide-de-camp, called them 'the refugees' – i.e. from conscription.) They were armed only with shotguns, and their attempts to reply to the growing crescendo of fire – including 'what seemed to be a pom-pom' – were ineffective.[65] 'Also, with every blast from a shell our views were obscured, even from each other, by clouds of dust and falling plaster.'[66] They had no idea whether the outpost over the road in Hopkins and Hopkins was still there (in fact it was), and Good volunteered to dash back to the GPO for instructions. As a stranger to Dublin, he had only a hazy idea how to get there. In Abbey Street, however, 'which was – amazingly – deserted', he got directions at a pub, where 'there were men still drinking pints'. (They sagely warned him to beware of 'them milithary in Capel Street'.) When he finally got to the GPO he found the rest of his group already there, only to be told by their commander, George Plunkett, that they should not have evacuated their post. They made an effort to return, but gave up in face of withering fire.

Back inside the GPO, Good found the garrison 'to my mind unduly optimistic'. They were buoyed up by repeated rumours that provincial Volunteers were coming to relieve the capital. Good, who was 'desperately hungry, not having had a real meal since Sunday', found the attitude of Desmond FitzGerald, in charge of rationing supplies, infuriating. Since he 'only had supplies for ten days or thereabouts', FitzGerald was very stingy with them.[67] (He allowed himself, however, to be overruled by one or two officers he respected – notably Michael Collins, 'the most active and efficient officer in the place'.)[68] To Good – and, to be fair, to FitzGerald himself, who was sceptical of his leaders' optimism and acutely aware of his unpopularity – the ten days were a fantasy: 'I was bemused by the general attitude of security.' Only the steadily encroaching fires eroded it. Frank Henderson went up on the GPO roof on Thursday evening, after delivering his routine report to Connolly, 'and found that we were practically surrounded by fires'. Shortly afterwards, even the Henry Street garrison was withdrawn into the GPO. By Thursday night the whole of Sackville Street seemed to be blazing. Everyone who witnessed the growing inferno was awestruck by its terrifying beauty. Returning to duty after tea on Thursday, Dick Humphreys was 'appalled at the stupendous increase the fire has made. The interior of our room is as bright as day . . . Reis's jewellers shop is a mass of leaping scarlet tongues of light . . . A roaring as of a gigantic waterfall re-echoes from the walls.'[69] 'The roaring of the flames, the noise of breaking glass and collapsing walls was terrific', Henderson recorded. 'The flames from the Imperial Hotel and from Hoyte's drug and oil stores at the corner of Sackville Place were so fierce that they almost touched the walls of the GPO, and we could feel the heat of them.' The heat was 'so great that men had to be employed to keep the window fortifications drenched with water to prevent the sandbags and sacks going on fire'.[70] When an oil-works in Abbey Street caught fire,

a solid sheet of blinding death-white flame rushes hundreds of feet into the air with a thunderous explosion that shakes the walls . . . Followed by a thunderous bombardment as hundreds of oil drums explode . . . millions of sparks are floating in an impenetrable mass for hundreds of yards around.

The morning after was more dispiriting, however: 'all the barbaric splendour that night had lent the scene has faded away, and the pitiless sun illuminates the squalidness and horror of the destruction.'[71]

On Friday morning, the women of the Cumann na mBan were ordered out of the GPO. They did not go quietly. In fact Pearse had to quell a near-riot, and looked so nonplussed that Seán MacDermott had to back him up. But the message to the rest of the garrison was unambiguous: the end was near. Nothing was left but an exhausting and increasingly desperate struggle to contain the fire spreading through the building. The GPO was not directly hit by a shell until about noon, and serious fires did not begin until about 3 p.m. But they then spread with overpowering velocity; 'when one fire was nearly subdued a fresh shell would start another at a different point', wrote the Headquarters Battalion quartermaster.[72] Combustible stores and ammunition were taken out into the courtyard. ('Everyone seems to consider it his duty to give orders at the top of his voice', Humphreys irritably noted.) Military options had run out. This was dramatically symbolized when Connolly was carried in on Thursday afternoon with wounds in his left arm and left leg. 'The leg wound is serious as it caused a compound fracture of the shin bone', Joe Plunkett carefully noted in his field pocket-book.[73] All week Connolly had been ubiquitous: inspecting posts and barricades, dictating orders to his imperturbable secretary Winifred Carney ('calmly click-clacking away, as though accustomed to working in this martial atmosphere all her life'), chivvying the garrisons and leading sorties in person. This recklessness surely reflected the frustration of his expectations about the nature of the battle. His ghastly wound came not from a direct shot but a ricochet, one of the commonest and most disorienting effects of street fighting.

With Connolly crippled and fires spreading down through the GPO itself from the roof, Pearse took the decision to abandon the building. But what was to happen next? Nobody seems to have had any idea (O'Connell's strictures on preparing a line of retreat had clearly cut no ice here). Eamonn Bulfin thought that 'nobody seemed to be in charge once we left the GPO; it was every man for himself'.[74] 'One wondered at the plans', Joe Good mused as they stumbled out into Henry Place and O'Rahilly called for 'twenty men to follow him in a charge with rifles and bayonets'. They were under fire from their own men in a whitewashed house nearby, and 'who or what he was going to charge was not clear'. Eventually O'Rahilly drummed up some followers and led them across Henry Street into Moore Street. 'I heard the burst of fire, then the sound of running feet, then the sound of one man's feet, then silence.'[75] O'Rahilly, moving spirit of the Volunteers, who had spent the week fretting over his suspicion that the rebel leaders thought he had tried to stop the rebellion to save his own life, and who still 'could not be satisfied that a real justification existed for leading those young men out to die', was mortally wounded.[76] The intermittent narrative of Plunkett's pencil-written diary petered out in staccato notes.

> Signal to Imperial
> Cut way to Liffey St
> Food to Arnotts
> Order to remain all posts unless surrounded
> Barricades in front

Henry St

Food[77]

Next day his pocket-book was found lying in the street by a waiter from the Metropole Hotel.

8

The National Rising

In these moments one felt a free man. We were soldiers of the
free Irish nation. A yoke seemed lifted from our shoulders.

Seán MacEntee

More than once during the siege of the GPO, Pearse gathered the garrison in the main hall, climbed on to a table, and delivered an extempore (or possibly more carefully prepared) morale-boosting speech. These addresses presumably reflected the continuous discussions among the leaders – Pearse, Connolly, MacDermott and Plunkett – that their followers observed.[1] On Thursday, 'a glorious day' with 'a burning sun and cloudless blue sky', yet one when 'the everlasting wait for the unexpected is terribly nerve-racking', Dick Humphreys thought, Pearse's address was a welcome distraction. His message was uplifting and unambiguous. 'The country is steadily rising, and a large band of Volunteers is marching from Dundalk to Dublin.' Barracks were being raided throughout the country; 'Wexford has risen and a relief column to march on Dublin is being formed.' The garrison's reaction was equally definite – 'a deafening outburst of cheering'. Pearse had 'put new vitality into the men which three days of uncertainty and suspense had rather dispersed'.[2] Whether Pearse really believed that such relieving forces were on the march, and – equally – whether his audience could (had they thought about it) really have believed that their ill-armed provincial comrades could fight their way through the surrounding military forces, it is impossible to say. The power of the belief clearly overwhelmed doubt. It was by the standard of this exalted hope that the actual performance of the provincial IV units in Easter week would (perhaps unfairly) be judged. It was unimpressive, on the whole, and subsequent histories have tended if anything to make it even less impressive. If not relegated to a footnote, the provincial rising has been treated as a kind of afterthought to the battle in Dublin.[3] At best it was, in the words of its first historians, 'somewhat amorphous'. The exception is the fight at Ashbourne on Friday, which was not only the most decisive success of any rebel action during the week, but also a forerunner of the methods to be adopted in a later and very different republican insurgency. Ashbourne was certainly important, for both these reasons, but so – for different reasons – was the wider attempt at a rising throughout Ireland.

Interestingly, Pearse's invocation of relieving forces did not include those closest to the city, the Dublin Brigade's 5th Battalion, operating in northern County Dublin. The reason for this may become apparent. In the days before its brilliant success at Ashbourne, this force – generally known as the Fingal Battalion – gave a demonstration of the improvisatory aptitude needed to fight a guerrilla campaign. In what would soon become recognizable as a classic guerrilla pattern, it started out weak, ill-armed, inexperienced, and without any clear idea of how best to operate. It had never been a full-sized battalion, at best reaching company strength. Something like 120 men turned out for the Easter Sunday mobilization, but barely half that number – almost all from the battalion centre at Swords – on Monday. Joe Lawless, who later became a professional soldier, disapprovingly recalled them as 'just a number of individuals and no useful tactical formation'.[4] In this, paradoxically, may have lain their salvation. They had only twelve or fifteen modern service rifles (.303 or 9mm), ten to twelve Howth Mausers, and a dozen single-shot Martini carbines, with around 100 rounds of ammunition apiece. Nearly half were armed only with shotguns. The force was short of transport for its supplies: the battalion commandant, Thomas Ashe, had a motorcycle, and the former commandant, Dr Richard Hayes, brought his two-seater Morris Oxford. (Hayes had resigned the command to Ashe shortly before Easter, owing to pressure of work in his medical practice, and had become battalion adjutant.) Crucially, however, all those who mobilized had bicycles. The force had real mobility; but where was it to go? Its leaders instinctively looked to the Dublin Brigade for orders.

Ashe knew in advance that he should disrupt communications, and on Saturday had detailed Charlie Weston to blow up the Great Northern Railway bridge at Rogerstown Viaduct. (Weston had asked if he could lay the charges on Saturday night at low tide, but Ashe refused.)[5]

They mobilized at Knocksedan, a few miles from Swords, in response to an order brought from Pearse by Mollie Adrian of Cumann na mBan – 'Strike at one o'clock today.' Pearse had also sent orders, as Hayes recalled, to 'move to Finglas, hold the main road there, and ambush or fire on any enemy officers returning from Fairyhouse races'. Unfortunately, none appeared, and the attempt to blow up the railway line at Rogerstown was 'only partially successful'.[6] Weston had to set out with 40 lb of gelignite but without the quarrymen from Lusk who were to have assisted him, and found the tide flowing so strongly around the pillars of the viaduct that it was impossible to place charges there. He put them between the girders of the bridge, but only succeeded in causing minor damage to the track. Another group sent out at midnight to wreck the line at Blanchardstown was also 'not entirely successful'. As the battalion bivouacked overnight at Finglas, things did not seem to be going too well. Next day, they got worse. Ashe sent Mollie Adrian into Dublin to report his situation. He may, anticipating the arrival of reinforcements from Skerries and the northern part of the country, have exaggerated his numbers. She came back with an order from Connolly to send forty men to the GPO. As Hayes noted, he was 'very disappointed' with this order, since he had been hoping for a significant transfer in the opposite direction. Ashe did his best to comply, sending twenty men under the captain of the Swords Company, Mick Coleman, into the city.[7]

He was left with barely forty men. A few 'stragglers from the city' seemed a poor compensation. (One of these was Jerry Golden, who had been urged by his commander at the Phibsboro outpost to fall back to Daly's main position, but preferred to go north to join the Fingal battalion. Five or six others went with him.) But an officer who arrived around midday after 'having been unable to get in touch with his own unit in the city' – oddly, perhaps, in view of the ease and frequency of movement around the city at this point – proved to be a real asset. This was Richard Mulcahy, 'known already to the other members of the battalion staff', as Joe Lawless (son of the battalion quartermaster, Frank Lawless) noted. 'It was soon apparent to everyone that his was the mind necessary to plan and direct operations.' Interestingly, his own unit, 2nd Battalion, had clearly not picked this up: it had sent him on an ill-prepared sabotage mission to Howth Junction, whence he decided not to return to the city.[8] Lawless judged him 'cool, clear-headed and practical, with a tact that enabled him virtually to control the situation without in any way undermining Ashe's prestige as commander'.[9] Ashe himself was an inspirational figure: good-looking, artistic and pious, 'courageous and high-principled, but perhaps in military matters somewhat unpractical'.[10]

On Wednesday, things began to look up. Ashe (possibly inspired by Mulcahy) reorganized his column into four roughly equal sections. Each day one was to have responsibility for foraging and defending the camp, while the other three went out on 'the daily raid or other mission', carefully spaced between advance and rearguards. By happy accident, he had happened upon what would be an ideal guerrilla 'flying column' size. Early on Wednesday morning Ashe's three fighting sections arrived in Swords. Charlie Weston, in command of the first section, was ordered to occupy a row of houses facing the RIC barracks, while others rushed the Post Office and smashed the telegraphic instruments. The police, apparently taken by surprise, immediately complied with Ashe's demand that they surrender. Five carbines were taken, and Weston broke the iron shutters of the barracks with a sledgehammer. The haul of ammunition – a mere twenty rounds – was disappointing, but more important was the commandeering of a Kennedy's Bakery van full of bread: food and motor transport all in one. The van driver stayed with the column for the next day, receiving ten shillings for his trouble. The column moved on to Donabate, where it deployed to cut the railway line. 'A few shots were fired at a man on the railway who refused to halt', to the intense annoyance of Mulcahy, who castigated the waste of ammunition and the warning given to the police by the firing. The alerted RIC at first refused to surrender their post, but did so when Weston's section rushed the door with a pickaxe and sledgehammer after a fire-fight of about ten minutes, in which one of the police was wounded.[11]

Next day the column moved to the northern edge of the county to repeat the process in Garristown. But war, and especially guerrilla fighting, is a reciprocal learning process. The rebels had so far been given freedom to move about in security, and the police seemed to be making no effort to respond to their threat. At Garristown, they took the elementary step of abandoning the small barrack and falling back to reinforce the post at Balbriggan to the east. Ashe found only one unarmed man, and no weapons, at Garristown. He responded by upping the stakes in his raid on the post office: so far, his men had scrupulously taken no money, but now they decided to treat the post office funds as 'spoils of war'. Mulcahy gave the postmaster a receipt, but accompanied it with a revolutionary declaration – 'this money is no longer of any value'. Ashe also had to cope with a potentially serious crisis of morale. 'Some of the men were grousing that the Volunteers in the country had not risen.' He paraded his battalion in a field and addressed them, insisting that although the rest of the country had not yet risen, they would rise. His force needed to keep going, but any of them who wanted to leave were free to do so. Three or four (including a couple whom Weston regarded as potential troublemakers) did. The clincher, though, came when Ashe called on all his men to kneel so that a priest, Fr Kavanagh, 'the son of a Fenian' as Ashe explained, could give them his blessing. Here was the 'Catholic people' in arms. Almost as vital for morale, 'food was good this day and we had plenty of eggs and butter'.

On Friday, the force set off again, this time with new orders from Dublin (brought by the redoubtable Miss Adrian, who was in and out of Dublin all week until Thursday) to cut the railway line at Batterstown, about ten miles from their position, and 'generally to create any diversion that might impede troops from moving to the city'. On the way they were to take the RIC barrack at Ashbourne. As they came down to the Slane–Dublin road at Rath Crossroads, they ran into two RIC men, who were taken prisoner after a scuffle. They could see the police manning an elementary barricade (merely planks on boxes, presumably designed to halt road traffic) outside the barrack, and sent the prisoners down with Paddy Holohan under a flag of truce to negotiate a surrender. They did not come back, and Weston's section was sent to work its way to the front of the barrack

1. 'The North began': the UVF struts its stuff, January 1914.

2. Molly Childers and Mary Spring Rice aboard the *Asgard* with the shipment of Mauser rifles, July 1914.

3. Irish Volunteers carrying the rifles back from Howth, 25 July 1914.

4. The crowd of mourners crossing O'Connell Bridge on 29 July 1914, following the funeral procession for those killed in the Bachelor's Walk shooting.

5. The Irish Citizen Army parading in front of Liberty Hall in 1915.

6. Sir Roger Casement with John Devoy in New York, 1914.

7. Thomas J. Clarke, President of the Supreme Council of the Irish Republican Brotherhood.

8. James Connolly, leader of the Irish Citizen Army, and commander of all republican forces in Dublin in April 1916.

9. Patrick Pearse, the Irish Volunteer Director of Organisation, President of the Provisional Government and Commander-in-Chief of the Army of the Republic in April 1916.

10. Sean MacDermott, the most tireless of all republican organizers.

11. The warrior aesthete: Grace Gifford's sketch of her fiancé Joseph Plunkett in Volunteer uniform.

12. Are you looking at me? Constance, Countess Markievicz, in characteristically combative pose.

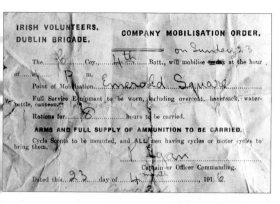

13. Mobilization order for the 4th Battalion of the Irish Volunteers on Easter Sunday 1916.

14. The 'Starry Plough', the Citizen Army flag raised over the Imperial Hotel during Easter week 1916.

15. Waiting for the counterattack: Irish republican forces inside the GPO, Easter week 1916.

16. 'Soldiers are we' : two men of the GPO garrison show off their eclectic mix of clothing and equipment (the bayonet carried by the Volunteer on the left is for a French Lebel rifle, a surprising rarity in Ireland).

17. Into captivity: Eamon de Valera marching at the head of the 3rd Battalion after the surrender.

Der Aufstand der Sinn-Feiner in Irland.
Die Connel's Brücke mit der City von Dublin, wo die heftigsten Kämpfe stattgefunden haben.

18. The war zone: a German image of the ruins by O'Connell Bridge after the 'Aufstand' (insurrection).

19. 'Conky' and the 'Gorgeous Wrecks': General Sir John Maxwell inspecting the Volunteer Training Corps shortly after the rebellion.

20. Resistance commodified: postcards of de Valera and other rebel leaders sold widely after the rebellion.

IRISH REBELLION, MAY 1916

ED. de VALERA
(Commandant of the Ringsend Area).
Sentenced to Death;
Sentence commuted to Penal Servitude for Life.

21. Incarceration: Irish internees in Stafford gaol, May 1916.
Michael Collins is under the cross.

under cover of a low bank, and launch an attack. Dr Hayes with another section worked their way around the rear. After some fairly heavy firing, two men lobbed canister grenades at the door. As so often, one was a dud; the other missed its target but exploded by the wall, and seems to have demoralized the garrison, who now agreed to surrender.

Just at this moment, a new police tactic materialized. A motorized column fifty-five strong, in seventeen cars, came down the road from Slane looking for the guerrilla marauders.[12] Its exact objectives are still unclear. (According to one of the RIC men in the column, 'the Marchiness [sic] of Conyngham who lived at Slane Castle was afraid the rebels were going to attack Slane and it was she who forced the County Inspector to go towards Dublin to meet them'.)[13] But the Volunteers were so intent on the barrack attack that the leading car got within 200 yards of the attackers before it was spotted. There was some mutual alarm and confusion as the rebels opened fire and the police scrambled out of their cars. The police in the barrack reconsidered their decision to surrender. Ashe seems to have considered retreat – a superficially reasonable idea, since the police column was estimated to be around 100 strong. Mulcahy, however, evidently understood how perilous and possibly suicidal a fighting retreat in face of superior numbers would be, and responded to the scout's estimate with calculated bravado: 'It doesn't matter if there are a thousand, we'll deal with those fellows.' He sent Weston's section forward to the crossroads to pin down the head of the police column, while the main force worked its way around to their rear. 'I do not know how long we were in position at the crossroads', one of Weston's section wrote. 'It is impossible to reckon time under such circumstances. Some of our fellows say we were there a couple of hours.'[14] For this time, six or seven men held down the whole police column. There was a fair degree of confusion on both sides, not surprisingly, and much of the evidence is contradictory.[15] But the Volunteers were clearly fortunate in their opponents, who showed no desire to come at them, and in the countryside around them. It was flat, with high banks and thick hedges that 'prevented any extended view beyond the length of a field except along the main road'.

Mulcahy led the outflanking manoeuvre in person, picking up Joe

Lawless's section, which had been apprehensively watching stray bullets kicking up the dry clay of a ploughed field in front of them. 'The example of Mulcahy walking unscathed across it encouraged us to move across at once at the double and without seeking the shelter of the fences.'[16] It was a simple, classical manoeuvre whose outcome depended on the skill and alertness of the two sides. The Volunteers had been surprised, but, as Lawless saw, the police even more so; they had no idea how big a force they had run into. Mulcahy's plan nearly came apart after an hour or so of fighting. Joe Lawless's section, in the field east of the police convoy, came under fire from the north. At that moment he ran out of ammunition, and when he made his way back to the Garristown road he found Ashe and Hayes in urgent conference about the sudden increase in firing from the north, which seemed to indicate more police reinforcements. They were on the point of ordering a general retreat (indeed Charlie Weston's section had already been ordered to retreat from their crucial position at the crossroads) when Mulcahy appeared. He testily explained – to Lawless's 'considerable discomfiture' – that 'the force we had thought to be enemy reinforcements and exchanged shots with, were in fact our own fourth section, under my father, who had come up from the camp at Borranstown'.[17]

Fortified by this, and occasional police surrenders bringing vital supplements of ammunition, the rebel column hung in. Maybe the Volunteers' fieldcraft training paid off here; the police certainly had none, and when they found themselves outflanked they began to panic. Their commanding officer, County Inspector Gray, was disabled early in the fight (mortally wounded, he died a fortnight later), and his deputy, District Inspector Smith, was killed. Their initial decision to stop the convoy rather than driving into the attackers was fatal if they were not prepared to follow it with a determined attempt to outflank the rebels. Mulcahy continued to dominate proceedings: Weston heard him call on the police to surrender with the ferocious threat, 'If you don't we will give you a dog's death!' The police nerve finally broke when Mulcahy led seven men with fixed bayonets in a charge down the Slane road.[18] The police began to stream down the road to give themselves up at the crossroads, and shortly afterwards the barrack garrison (which had not fired a shot since offering to surrender) also surrendered. Two of Ashe's men had been killed, and five wounded in the five hours of fighting; the RIC lost eight dead and fifteen wounded. (The first to die, Sergeant Shanner, 'a bad one who had been very tough on the men', may have been shot by his own men.)[19] In the circumstances, this was a brilliant triumph. It is not surprising that, as they made their way back to camp, the little battalion 'felt ready now for anything that might come', as Weston said. 'We had gained great confidence in ourselves', and felt 'we were a match for any force that we might meet.' (Michael McAllister, though, recognized that the police had been very badly led and had shown no initiative.) There were problems: the involvement of the base section in the fighting meant that commissariat arrangements had broken down, and 'food was poor'. On Saturday the column moved to a new camp near Kilcallaghan, still waiting for orders from Dublin. When news finally came, it would, of course, be bad indeed.

By the time the Fingal battalion secured its dramatic victory, the general rising in which Ashe so fervently believed had proved stillborn. Only his nearest neighbours were really still in business. All week, the Fingal men had expected to join up with the Meath and Louth Volunteers, and it remains unclear why this did not happen. The Louth Volunteers certainly took the field. Dan Hannigan (Donal O'Hannigan) had been given command of the area at the beginning of April with an ambitious task, to 'knock into shape' the local units and prepare to keep open communications between Dublin and the west. There was a fair bit of local enthusiasm – personified in the leading spirit of the Dundalk separatists, Paddy Hughes – but as Seán MacEntee said, 'there was not one of us who knew in a practical way anything about military matters'.[20] The new temporary commander was sent in response to a direct request to Seán MacDermott when he delivered the Robert Emmet Commemoration lecture in Dundalk on 16 March. Hannigan, a cooper by trade, was 'master of everything that a competent regimental sergeant-major should know about the role of the combat infantryman', had 'immeasurable energy, physical stamina, and outstanding ability to get things done'. He succeeded in turning 'our somewhat amorphous corps' into 'a cohesive, organic unit within a couple of weeks'.[21] There were still glitches in his preparations, though. When he was being briefed by Pearse at St Enda's, he was introduced to Seán Boylan, who had raised the Dunboyne Company, and was to come under his command. Boylan, however, 'did not hear from O'Hannigan again until after the rebellion had started, although I expected to do so'. (When mobilization began on Sunday, it came as a 'complete surprise' to be told by Seán Tobin from Volunteer HQ that he, Boylan, was also responsible for the mobilization at Tara.)[22] On Monday, thinking everything was off, he went with his brother to Fairyhouse races.

Hannigan and MacEntee started mobilization after early Mass in Dundalk on Easter Sunday, 'cold and squally with passing showers of rain'. Unlike every other Volunteer unit, the Louth battalion did not demobilize in response to MacNeill's countermand. The Dundalk contingent was over 160 strong when it moved off around 9.30 a.m. towards Ardee. Hannigan left MacEntee in Dundalk to seize some forty rifles which had been held by the local IV executive committee ever since the split; he would have to wait until 7 p.m. when the rebellion was timed to start, before doing this. Hannigan himself planned to pick up the Ardee company together with another collection of Redmondite rifles, before moving on to the (highly symbolic) main mobilization point at Tara. (Hannigan had objected to Pearse that Tara was 'a very inconvenient place', but was told that it was 'all-important for historical reasons' – it was the coronation place of the old High Kings of Ireland – and Pearse 'wanted the proclamation of the republic read there'.) The Drogheda Volunteers were to go direct to Tara, as were those from Kells under Garry Byrne. However, not all of this area was fully organized. 'South Armagh were not expected to do anything, and no allowance was made for them.'[23] Hannigan succeeded in getting forty-eight Lee-Enfields from the house where they were deposited (passing a guard of four amiable RIC men at the door), and 3,000 rounds of ammunition from another depot. He headed off towards Slane. In the meantime, however, MacEntee had at last heard of the countermanding order, and dashed off to find his commanding officer. He arrived at Ardee – 'as peaceful and unruffled as any small Irish town on a Sunday. The same quiet stillness, the same few, unhurrying townspeople, the same couple of policemen lazing at the barracks door.' He caught up with the column just outside Slane, to find that Hannigan (who was of course well aware of Pearse's secret command arrangements) would not accept the countermand without a direct confirmation from Pearse himself.

Unfortunately, the first despatch rider he sent (with a motorcycle) failed to return, and so did two he sent out later on bikes. Finally, in the middle of a ghastly night, with rain 'pouring down in wild spates drenching us through and through', and 'the men beginning to grumble at our inactivity, sensing a hitch', MacEntee himself volunteered to go into the city. He left a brilliant description of his epic bike ride to Drogheda with Tom Hamill that night.

There was a strong head wind blowing, beating the heavy rain into our faces and almost blinding us. Our raincoats were soaked, and streams of water poured off them and down our legs and ankles. The mud, thin and liquid, was inches deep on the road, and as our wheels splashed through it, they cast up a lavish spray that no mudguard could intercept.

It was 'impenetrably dark' at first, though slowly 'shadows began to creep together and the long, slow curving outlines of the low hills became apparent against the foreglow of the coming dawn'. As they approached Drogheda, where they hoped to catch a train, the rain slackened, but MacEntee faced 'the steep hill which leads to the station . . . a climb to break your heart' with only a few minutes left. After collapsing on to a train, he eventually arrived at Liberty Hall and met Connolly and Pearse before they set out for the GPO.[24] He missed his return train and did not manage to get back until early Monday evening, by which time Hannigan's force was reduced to twenty-eight men. He had taken his column back towards Dundalk (shadowed by a force of sixty RIC) at 3 a.m., and had allowed all the men who wanted to go to their jobs on Monday morning to leave. (They were to 'stand to and await further instructions at their homes'.) After marching for hours through a deluge, 'hungry, tired and very wet', it is perhaps not surprising that many chose to go home.[25] When they reached Lurgan Green, MacEntee drove up in a car he had commandeered, with a despatch from Pearse. 'Dublin is in arms. You will carry out your original instructions.'[26] Hannigan immediately announced to the inhabitants of the village that the republic had been declared, and called on the dozen policemen in the town to surrender. They did, and he went on to stop and arrest two groups of British officers passing by in cars. At Lurgan Green (according to later court martial testimony) 'a man called Patrick McCormick, a farmer, came towards Sergeant Wymes, who had been following the party throughout, and accused MacEntee of having wounded him in the hand with a revolver'. MacEntee spiritedly declared, 'I did it as a matter of duty. Ireland is proclaimed a Republic, and you must stand or fall by that fact.'[27] As with Mulcahy and Ashe's action, there was an electric sense of liberation. 'In these moments one felt a free man', as MacEntee recalled. 'A strange feeling of independence and exhilaration possessed me. No more taking cognisance of British authority . . . We were soldiers of the free Irish nation. A yoke seemed lifted from our shoulders.'[28]

Hannigan's force held up another two cars in Castlebellingham, where he also captured ten unarmed RIC men. Here MacEntee (according to the witnesses at his trial later) assembled twenty men and told them, 'See that your revolvers are properly loaded and be ready to obey me.' Another passing car was stopped, and an officer, Lieutenant Dunville, ordered out and made to stand with the police against the barrack railings. A fracas broke out in which Dunville was wounded, and Constable McGee shot dead. (Charged with murder later, MacEntee affirmed that 'the constable received no abuse from him, and he lamented his death; the constable was his fellow-countryman, discharging his duty'.) After this flurry of action, MacEntee once again took off for Dublin, and spent the rest of the week in the GPO. Hannigan's column now had 'more arms than we had men for', ten cars, two horse traps, an outside car and a wagonette, and although some of these disappeared mysteriously as he moved on to Dunboyne, he was joined there by a group of sixteen men under Seán Boylan. It was too late, though, to find the Tara force, which (despite having an organizing officer, Garry Byrne, specially appointed from Dublin) suffered the general confusion of Sunday. Some thirty men had mobilized, but 'had to keep more or less under cover', and after hearing of the countermand from Boylan at midnight, Byrne had sent them home on Monday.[29]

On Tuesday Hannigan received his first direct order from Connolly – 'Commandeer transport and move your men to Dublin where they will be rested and armed before being sent into action.' This order – totally at variance with the extensive and elaborate instructions that Pearse had given to Hannigan (and also to Boylan) before the rising – suggested that Connolly either misunderstood the situation of the battalion, or failed to grasp its potential (unless its purpose was to supply the basis for Pearse's assertion in the GPO that a large band of Volunteers was marching from Dundalk to Dublin).[30] Hannigan and his officers decided it could not be complied with, and set about trying to organize a junction with Ashe's force. They moved out in the direction of Dublin and took over a big house (Tyrrellstown House) near Blanchardstown, which proved burdensome to guard.[31] There they seem to have run out of ideas, merely scouting the area and waiting from Wednesday to Saturday for Ashe to arrive. (Seán Boylan's brother believed that the contact with Ashe was betrayed by 'a Bad One'.)[32] Finally a message from Ashe proposed a meeting in Turvey on Sunday morning, but by the time Hannigan got there, he found that Ashe had surrendered.

The mobilization in Ulster was, not unexpectedly, more short-lived. There was a robust republican tradition in Belfast, but the Volunteer movement was naturally conscious of operating in a hostile environment – and not just that of Unionism. Joe Devlin, with the 'unparalleled personal loyalty' of his Hibernian followers, had taken over control of the Belfast Volunteers at the time of the split – despite Denis McCullough's 'futile effort to state our point of view'.[33] The 'Sinn Fein' Volunteers remained fragmentary, and their rebellion plans centred on moving westwards. Pearse had told McCullough that 'the northern Volunteers were to assemble in the Dungannon area, join the men of Tyrone, all march to Galway and join up with Liam Mellowes and his men there'. McCullough found, however, that the Tyrone men 'refused point blank to take the orders' at a meeting on Good Friday.[34] The Tyrone commander, Patrick McCartan, seems to have taken the view that the strategic orders were unfeasible (even before the countermand). The same was to happen, McCullough claimed, on Sunday: he told the Tyrone leaders 'that if they would not undertake to get their men moving and ready to start with mine for Connaught in the morning, I would order my men back to Belfast and disband them there'. Joseph Connolly had so little faith in his comrades' capacity that he 'preferred to take my chances under reasonably reliable leadership', and decided to go to Dublin that day.[35] There was quite a substantial gathering at Coalisland, but the arrival of the countermanding order simply compounded the existing leadership dispute. McCullough was clearly at sea; 'worn out in mind and body', on his own account he 'could not face the responsibility of keeping' the 'hundred or so men and boys that I had brought to Tyrone' there, 'in country and amongst people of whom I had no knowledge'.[36] Cathal McDowell disputed the countermand, announcing (belatedly perhaps) that Pearse had recently told him not to obey any orders except his own, but after a conference between McCullough, Herbert Pim and Patrick McCartan they decided to obey it.[37] 'Although McCullough was much my senior', Manus O'Boyle recorded, 'I remember pointing out to him that we were being led into a death trap by returning to Belfast.' He replied that orders had to be obeyed.[38] When the captain of the Blackwaterstown company arrived in Coalisland he found the Tyrone men occupying a hall near the square; some were cooking and others eating a meal. The Belfast men were 'formed up in military order on the square', and 'soon after we arrived they marched out of the town'.[39] The sixteen men of the Benburb Company, communication specialists proudly sporting their equipment of bikes and pistols, found themselves ordered to 'act as an escort to a body of Belfast Volunteers through a hostile local area' on their way to Cookstown to get the train back to Belfast.[40] McCullough paid for their tickets personally.

This was not quite the end of the story, at least as far as the police were concerned. The County Inspector of Tyrone reported that 'on Easter Monday and the day following, McCartan and several other scouts were out . . . making the final preparations for the rising in Tyrone which was fixed for Wednesday 26 April'. Without revealing the source of this information, he said that the rebel plan was to capture the RIC barrack and the post office at Beragh and then move on to Omagh and 'seize the police barracks, post office, county court house and military depot'. Their aim was 'to cut telegraph wires, blow up the bridges and otherwise impede communications of the police and military'. In the picture drawn by the Inspector, it was only the vigilance and activity of the police on 25 April – their 'influence with all loyal persons being exercised to the full' – that scotched this ambitious plan.[41] This may be – McCartan himself left no account of this phase among his rather full recollections – but a more likely cause of paralysis was something else referred to by the County Inspector: 'in case of necessity, large contingents of the M.V. [misprint for U.V., i.e. Ulster Volunteer] Force would have been placed at the disposal of the military authorities or the constabulary in Omagh'. Indeed, many members of the UVF 'did voluntary unofficial scouting work around Omagh, Beragh, Sixmilecross and other parts of the district'. The rebels would, in effect, have had to operate in enemy territory.

In Westmeath, the hinge of Pearse's imagined grand strategy, nothing seems to have happened. Only seven of the seventy Volunteers in Tyrrellspass, for instance, turned out on Monday, and 'the story was the same everywhere. The countermand had done its work and the boys stayed at home.' Even when they

heard of fighting in Dublin, they were confused and did not know what to do. Militarily they could not do anything. They were disorganised and the element of surprise was gone. To have attempted to take a post or hold a village would have been a useless sacrifice.[42]

In the west, however, where the midland and Ulster forces were supposed to be heading, the mobilization was distinctly more substantial. In Liam Mellows, Galway had an energetic and dedicated organizer, though not perhaps a brilliant one. (Mattie Neilan's careful choice of words – 'a sincere, competent trainer' who 'conveyed to the men some of the fire and spirit of the Volunteer movement' – hints at his limitations.)[43] His force was psychologically prepared. In March, he had told his deputy, Alf Monahan, to 'impress upon the men that there might be trouble', so 'when the word of the Rising came it was no surprise'. On Easter Sunday morning, 'all Volunteers went to the Altar'.[44] Mellows himself had been deported in 1915, along with Ernest Blythe, and was living in Leek, Staffordshire. In his absence, the brigade commander, Larry Lardner, seems to have got wind of dissension among the Volunteer leadership in Dublin, after two visits to Hobson for guidance. By Easter Saturday his officers came to the conclusion that he was 'funking it'; Frank Hynes found him in distress. 'I'm nearly out of my mind between all the rumours I was told in Dublin.'[45] Mellows escaped from England and entered the country via Belfast, but did not succeed in making contact with the senior brigade officer until Monday evening. The Sunday mobilization was erratic. (Monahan heard that one company only received Pearse's confirmation of the countermanding order as they were taking up positions around the local RIC barrack on Sunday night.)

Their problem was not simply the countermand, but also the failure of the Kerry arms landing. When the brigade finally received Pearse's mobilization order on Monday, they raised a very respectable force, estimated by many at around 1,000 men across the county. But they were plainly uncertain what to do with it. The original plans (which Pearse unhelpfully ordered them to implement) were based around the reception and distribution of some 3,000 rifles, followed by a strategic movement to 'hold the line of the Shannon'. Without the rifles, this vague directive seemed even more impractical than it might originally have been. One obvious line of action, which seems in any case to have been part of the original plan, was an immediate attack on as many RIC barracks as possible. This offered the possibility not only of 'liberating' large areas of the county, but also of seizing significant quantities of arms and ammunition (though RIC stations were often poorly provided with the latter). In Galway city, George Nicoll (who 'seemed to know more about what they intended to do in Dublin than the rest of us did') had a plan to occupy the post office. But 'it was too late to do anything as the RIC and military were already alerted'.[46] After a few desultory efforts on Tuesday morning, the idea of attacking police barracks was abandoned in the rest of the county. Monahan's explanation of this – that the element of surprise had been lost, allowing the police to abandon their weaker posts to concentrate in the stronger ones – may seem convincing.[47] But it is surely at odds with his main argument, that the original plan depended on the arms landing: that certainly would have alerted the police, if nothing else.

Late on Tuesday, Lardner and Hynes took their force of around 300 men from Athenry to meet Mellows at Oranmore, and 'leave it to him to decide what was best to do'. Mellows assembled all the available forces in the area at the Department of Agriculture and Technical Instruction's experimental farm outside Athenry. The north Galway contingent never appeared; they assembled, but were told that 'Tuam was occupied by RIC fully armed and that it was impossible to do anything under the circumstances'.[48] Still, there were over 500 men (Hynes thought 600), including 'many who had not been in the Volunteers at all' but joined in for the fight, with 35 rifles and 350 shotguns. Hynes thought that the provision of grenades was sadly inadequate, though the brigade quartermaster, John Broderick, perhaps naturally held that 'we had a good supply'.[49] 'All were in the best of humour and full of pluck', according to Monahan; food was plentiful and the local people were generous in supplying bread and milk. Bullocks were 'commandeered and slaughtered'; the 'girls of Cumann na mBan' did the cooking, and 'the fragrance of Irish stew' pervaded the camp. The main kinds of operations for the next few days were patrols sent through the countryside to disrupt communications. The RIC were in evidence; the DATI farm had been the subject of extended agrarian dispute, and had its own police post. The companies that marched over from Galway city and Castlegar were fired on as they approached. But though Brian Molloy counted 'thirteen cars of police and troops', they suffered no casualties.[50]

After this clash, on Wednesday, Mellows moved his camp to Moyode Castle, still continually sending out 'small bodies of Volunteers on bicycles and in motors'. But in spite of many rumours of marching British troops and artillery, they did not come into contact with any military forces. Why the castle was chosen is unclear, since Monahan thought it was 'not a good place to put in a state of defence'.[51] But in any case, defence was a fatally passive option. Mellows seems to have had no other ideas, however. He held repeated convocations of his brigade council to discuss the situation. Several of the officers were evidently rattled by the repeated rumours of a big military force nearby.[52] 'The wisdom of continuing the fight was questioned by some', and twice, on Thursday and again on Friday ('in deference to the views of those officers who favoured disbandment'), Mellows put the question to a general vote of the garrison. A majority voted to soldier on, but on Friday some 200 decided to quit. As more definite reports came in of a large military force at Attymon,

Mellows decided to move on again, with the idea of linking up with the Volunteers further south in Limerick. At Lime Park, midway between Ardrahan and Gort, they were joined by a clergyman with information that the Dublin rebels had given up. Father Fahy told them the rest of the country had not risen, and 'a large body of marines was at that moment coming in pursuit of them and would certainly overtake them in a matter of hours'.[53]

The column's last move was to Tulira Castle, a residence of the National Theatre patron Edward Martyn, and also the place where what the police called the 'Galway Secret Society' – an agrarian terrorist group – had been formed by members of the National Invincibles in the 1880s. It was still in business in 1916, and this was one of the most consistently 'disturbed' areas of the west.[54] None of this, however, seems to have helped the rebels now. At Tulira Father Fahy renewed his pressure on Mellows to disband, and yet another conference of the brigade's fourteen officers was held. Mellows responded with a desperate appeal – more a confession of faith.

I brought out the men to fight, not to run away. If they disband now, they will be shot down like rabbits without a chance of defending themselves. I refuse to disband them. I hand over command to anyone who wants it. I haven't slept for three nights. I'm going to sleep here until the soldiers come.

He said he would fight as long as he could, 'then they can do what they like to me'.[55] Alf Monahan immediately declared that he would stay with him, but urged instead that 'the better armed section of the force' should 'take to the open country and carry on a guerrilla fight'. The majority of the officers dissented; many seem to have been overwhelmed by a sense of responsibility to the rank and file. 'The general feeling of the meeting was that it would be merely slaughter to venture the weak Volunteer force in the west' against the strong British forces. When Mellows refused to communicate this view to the men, Father Fahy went out of the meeting and did so personally, advising them to break up as quietly as possible.[56] Slowly and emotionally, the column disbanded.

Clerical intervention also choked off the less substantial mobilization in Mayo. The Volunteer pioneer and Howth veteran Darrell Figgis had gone 'back to the people' on Achill Island. There peace reigned until Tuesday, 'a day of unimaginable beauty', when the news from Dublin arrived.

Voices rose up from the land, where the spring work, long delayed by a bad winter, was in full swing. Voices of men, voices of women, and the barking of dogs flowed over the land pleasantly. It was not strange that the mind found some difficulty in recognizing the meaning of this tale of war that came like a stream of blood violently across the peace and beauty of the day.

Gradually a group of Volunteers assembled and improvised a plan to cross to the mainland to meet up with 'the men from Castlebar, Westport and Newport'. They 'hoped to take the police barracks at these places by rapid strokes before dawn, and beyond that we did not trouble to inquire'. On Thursday, however, a message arrived that 'the priest in Castlebar (where nearly all the rifles were on which we relied) had refused to allow the men there to make any move'. The mobilization spontaneously halted. Figgis reflected that 'the priest was a wise man' – 'nothing we could have done would have been the slightest use'.[57]

If the failure of the Kerry arms landing contributed to the uncertainty of the Galway rebels, it was obviously central to the experience of the Volunteers in Kerry itself, and also in Clare and Limerick. All of these were intended to concentrate round the intended route of the arms into Limerick, and assist their distribution from that point; although it is doubtful that the planning was quite as clear-cut as is suggested in, for instance, Desmond Ryan's famous account *The Rising*. Here, as elsewhere, the secrecy of the military committee's preparations generated a risk of misunderstanding or confusion. For instance, the planned arms landing was only revealed to the Limerick brigade commander, Michael Colivet, at a very late hour. For months before Easter 1916, Colivet was working on the first set of instructions he had from Pearse, involving the movement to 'hold the line of the Shannon'. Like many provincial brigades, Limerick was a somewhat sketchy unit. The eight battalions under Colivet's command (one in Limerick city, three in Limerick county, and four in county Clare) averaged no more than 200 men apiece, and 'only the city battalion could be said to be reasonably well armed'.[58] Colivet was reportedly 'somewhat amused' by

Pearse's talk of holding the Shannon line, pointing out that his force would be stretched out to one man per 300 yards. Still, he had no other instructions until the Tuesday before Easter, when Seán Fitzgibbon arrived with new orders to deal with the arms landing. The new orders 'differed so much from the original instructions' that Colivet went up to Dublin to talk directly to Pearse about them. In the end, he was faced with the task of drawing up the details of a new plan at less than a week's notice.[59] The experience of Charlie Wall, the founder and commander of the Drumcollogher Volunteers, was equally surprising. On 16 April he was invited to a meeting with an officer from the Limerick brigade staff and another from Dublin, and asked if he was willing to join the IRB. He was sworn in on the spot, and immediately told that he had been given command of the West Limerick sub-area. He was to mobilize at Glenquin Castle on Easter Sunday, and board the train carrying the arms shipment on its way from Abbeyfeale to Newcastlewest. He was enjoined 'not to divulge any plans', only to give orders for three days' rations and full equipment to be brought by each man.[60]

Those who were not vouchsafed this kind of instruction were left in a state of real confusion. One of Colivet's battalion commanders, Liam Manaha of the Galtee battalion, also went up to Dublin, on the Thursday before Easter, after hearing rumours of imminent military action. He naturally went to Volunteer HQ, where Hobson and O'Connell confidently told him that nothing special was going on. Only by accident did he bump into MacDonagh, who brusquely said he should not be in Dublin, but on the alert in Ballylanders: there was 'an immediate danger of raids and arrests'. Asked, naturally enough, why the staff at Volunteer HQ had not told him this, MacDonagh simply said 'They are not in it.' When Manahan got home he issued orders for the Sunday manoeuvres, and found that some of his officers were opposed to carrying arms because of the risk that they might be captured. On Sunday, Manahan at first ignored the countermanding order and went ahead with some field exercises, but in the early evening his cautious officers pointed 'to the weariness of the men, and stated their opinion that prolonged night marching in the bad weather would only dishearten their followers'. Section by section, his battalion disbanded and went home.

The news of the disaster at Ballykissane pier, the failure of the arms landing, and the arrest of Casement and Stack, had a paralysing effect on the senior officers in all three counties. (Alf Cotton, who might have taken control of the situation, was held in Belfast under a DORA order.) In Mannix Joyce's picturesque phrase, the 'fatal countermanding order was like the snapping of the cord of a powerfully bent bow just as the arrow was about to be shot'. When Colivet received Pearse's message on Monday calling on him to 'carry out his orders', he held a brigade council, which came to the conclusion that since the orders all focused on the arms shipment they could no longer be carried out. It does not seem to have occurred to them simply to revert to the plans they had made before they heard of the arms operation. The rank and file, of course, had no information to go on. In Clare, 'Tosser' Neilan of the Ennistymon company ruefully recalled that although his 'bosom pal as well as his comrade in the IRB' had 'received an order of some kind, he did not mention anything about it, even to me'.[61] Clare was not quite quiescent; the Ennis district and the area around the railway line to Limerick 'remained in such a disturbed condition that measures were taken to put Limerick in a state of defence against attack from the Clare side'.[62] But nothing happened. The whole of the south-west seemed paralysed. Mark Kenna of the Churchill Spa company in Kerry (in the planned arms landing area) had 'no information of any kind'. At the Sunday mobilization in Tralee, he noted that the Dingle company marched barefoot the thirty-two miles from Dingle to Tralee on Sunday, and back again on Monday.[63]

One or two, like Eamon O'Connor, captain of C Company in the Tralee battalion, who was shot in the leg when a Volunteer dropped a loaded revolver on Friday night, and who spent Easter week in hospital, may have been glad to have been invalided out. For many, the burden of inaction became an increasingly guilty one. Colivet, in particular, disputed the conclusions of a committee of inquiry set up by the IV Executive in 1917 to investigate the failure of Limerick, Kerry and Cork to take military action during Easter week. (The committee broadly exonerated the Limerick brigade, but in rather negative terms – 'we do not see that any good purpose will be served by any further discussion of this matter'.) Colivet wanted an affirmation in direct terms, rather than pious generalities, that his action had been the only one possible in the circumstances. This he never got. In Limerick, it seems uniquely, the impact of the 1916 fiasco was to be long-drawn-out: two disputing factions formed, becoming two new Volunteer battalions which stayed separate until 1921.[64]

The atmosphere of guilt was to settle most heavily over Limerick's southern neighbour, Cork. Cork City Battalion would be the only Volunteer unit to issue its members with a commemorative certificate attesting that they had participated in the rising.[65] Whether it provided much of a salve to their consciences it would be hard to say. Of course, its primary intent was to assert that the ordinary rank and file bore no responsibility for what happened, or failed to happen, and that they were indeed ready to take the same risks as their comrades elsewhere. The (unstated) implication is that they were let down by somebody. For their leaders, there was much to explain. Cork was a reasonably strong brigade. Its commander, Tomas MacCurtain, and his deputy, Terence MacSwiney, were dedicated and hardworking officers. In the months before Easter 1916 they put their forces through a vigorous training programme. Ginger O'Connell conducted an officer selection course in the headquarters at Sheares Street in Cork. By this time Cork was reckoned (at least by itself) to be 'the best-organised county in Ireland', officered by the 'old hard core of the Irish-Ireland movement'.[66] In the days before the Easter Sunday mobilization, the senior officers – 'in a very serious mood' – stayed in the Volunteer Hall day and night.[67] They were aware of problems within the Dublin leadership. On Good Friday, O'Connell arrived with a commission to take command of all Volunteers 'south of a line from Wexford to Kerry inclusive'. His arrival was quickly followed by another message, from Seán MacDermott, saying that all differences at HQ had been resolved, and that they were to carry out the 'original plans'. After a meeting of the brigade leaders, 'great satisfaction was expressed that agreement had at last been reached between all parties at Dublin Headquarters'.[68] In this belief they were mistaken, but it indicated a predisposition to take the MacNeill line on Sunday.

When the brigade mobilized on Sunday, the city battalion was below strength. (A later count numbered the parade at 221.)[69] One of them thought that 'an indefinite rumour got round on Saturday night that something serious was contemplated, and this resulted in many not turning up'. MacNeill's stern warnings about the gulf between the Dublin and provincial Volunteers were amply confirmed here. Those who did turn out marched off to Capwell Station and took the train to Crookstown (the cyclist section, and a few individuals with their own bikes, such as Liam de Roiste, went by road). The plan was to move on to meet up with other units at Carriganimma, about half-way between Cork and Fenit, but information was sparse, and most of the Volunteers seem to have had no idea where they were going. The points of concentration, also including Kealkil, Inchigeela and Millstreet, had it seems been 'determined by higher authority', not by the Cork brigade commanders, and their main purpose was related to the expected movement of the arms landed in Kerry.[70] The total number mobilized was around 1,200. O'Connell, however, did not reappear, and when the countermanding order was received by MacCurtain and MacSwiney they set out to inform their widely dispersed forces in a car which broke down on the way. They were still on the road at midday on Monday, when, to the puzzlement of the rest of the brigade staff in Cork, 'a Miss Peroze' (i.e. Marie Perolz) of the Dublin Cumann na mBan arrived on a motorbike with a note from Pearse, saying 'We go into action at noon today. PHP.' The note was written on the flyleaf of a small pocket diary, and their puzzlement was increased by the fact that it was not a military order, and was initialled rather than signed. (Certainly Pearse's other notes to provincial forces had been much more definite, and included the phrase 'carry out your original orders'.) This was the first of 'nine separate dispatches' to arrive in Cork over the next few days.[71]

Con Collins of D Company found 'considerable confusion' in the Hall on Monday; 'none of the senior officers were there'.[72] A messenger sent by train with Pearse's message failed to find MacCurtain and MacSwiney, who got back to Cork at 8 p.m. on Monday evening. The general belief at that stage was that the rumoured Dublin rising was the work of the Citizen Army, possibly because the GPO garrison had set out from Liberty Hall.[73] MacSwiney's sister Mary gave voice to a common Volunteer prejudice when she indignantly asked 'was a fine body of men like the Irish Volunteers to be dragged at the tail of a rabble like the Citizen Army?' MacCurtain and MacSwiney decided to sit tight in Sheares Street and wait for clearer instructions. In Seán O'Hegarty's view, 'the evil of "dual control" seemed to exclude everything else from their minds'.[74] MacSwiney was to be found gloomily pacing the floor of the Volunteer Hall hour after hour, deep in Thomas à Kempis' *The Imitation of Christ*. But others began to think that something should be done. Riobard Langford thought that 'the younger officers particularly wanted to fight, and were resentful of the waiting policy adopted by the leaders'. Eithne Ni Suibhne and her sister were 'completely puzzled. How could it be that there was a rising, and the Cork Volunteers apparently ignorant of it and inactive?' The official MacSwiney line was (as his sister Mary later wrote) that Cork 'as everyone knows, is built in a hollow surrounded on every side by hills', and the Volunteer HQ was 'directly under one of the enemy's big guns all the week' . . . 'all egress was impossible'.[75] But one local Volunteer, Donal O'Callaghan, insisted that 'the Volunteers could easily have been got out of the city; he had walked up to the top of the Western Road with his rifle under his coat and was not interfered with'. The brigade leaders were arguing that the level of military and police activity in the city made any Volunteer action impossible. O'Callaghan, however, judged them (perhaps a little cruelly) 'three incompetent men in a state of blue funk'.[76]

Meanwhile, the Cork Volunteers 'held themselves in readiness' at home. Men went back to work on Tuesday. On Wednesday, Liam de Roiste's teaching duties were to take him to Inishannon. He was one of those who fumed, 'there has been something like blundering, or confusion, in Cork Oglaich affairs. It has now come to the situation of every man acting on his own judgment.' Before leaving Cork he went to HQ to ask if he could do anything useful on his travels. He found MacSwiney, 'very serious, very perturbed and strained-looking', who asked him to find Tom Hales and tell him to take no action. De Roiste had heard of the Hales of Ballinadee, noted local activists ('bad boys' in police parlance), but never met them. On yet another rainsodden night, after several wrong directions down unlit country paths, he found their house. (This episode in itself was not a good advertisement for the brigade's communication system.) Tom Hales was fretting, and shortly after de Roiste gave him MacSwiney's evidently unwelcome message, his brother Seán also returned from a trip to Cork with the same instructions. 'It will be as in '98 when Wexford fought and got no help.' Their mother gloomily added another historical perspective: 'the weather is always against ye'.[77]

The inactivity of the 'bad boys' (who would come into their own in a later guerrilla campaign) shows how hard it was to respond to the confusions and frustrations of Easter in the provinces. Tom Hales had been given command of the west Cork battalion by MacCurtain on 19 April. His own Ballinadee company had mobilized 48 strong on Sunday, with 12 Mausers and 8 Lee-Enfields. (The Clogough company, by contrast, had only one Mauser, 3 'old rifles', 25 shotguns, and a Spanish revolver. They brought 12 pikes with nine-foot ash handles, made by Thomas Collins of Clashmore.)[78] They met up with the city battalion at Kilmurray and were placed under the command of Seán O'Sullivan, who led them on into Macroom. Just outside the town, MacCurtain came by in a car, and without getting out gave some instructions to O'Sullivan. After he had gone, the senior officers talked about the possibility of a fight. O'Sullivan said, 'The most we could do would be to create a moral effect.' They held a discussion about the prospect of going on to the concentration point at Carriganimma. 'It was raining fair hell at the time', and O'Sullivan persuaded his officers that 'the enemy had refused action that day by not interfering with our march'. Hales and Chris O'Gorman were the only officers opposed to the decision to return home. At home, Hales received no orders until Friday, when he was told to send two carts into the city to bring out the city battalion's rifles; the carts were sent but returned empty. He had a visit from Michael McCarthy of Dunmanway, who said 'What is left of us are willing to fight', and went on to see Seán O'Hegarty in Ballingeary to propose that they join up for an attack on the RIC post in Macroom. But McCarthy returned in pessimistic mood: 'he said he feared any attempt then would be hopeless. Things had gone too far and we would have no chance.' Even the pugnacious Hales was forced to agree.[79]

The fate of Cork's rifles was the last straw for many of the battalion's members. From Tuesday onwards the brigade leaders were under sustained pressure from the Lord Mayor (understandably anxious to avert open fighting in the city) and local clergy to negotiate with the military authorities to surrender their arms. The Assistant Bishop, Daniel Cohalan, repeatedly taxed them with the awful responsibility of taking military action in a hopeless situation. Eventually MacCurtain allowed him and the mayor to broker an elaborate deal whereby the arms could be placed in the care of the mayor or the church and not confiscated by the government. They were to be given back to the Volunteers after the crisis had passed. The whole business was to be kept out of the papers, and the RIC County Inspector apparently undertook to 'check the indiscreet zeal' of any policemen who wanted to take the matter further. Unfortunately, according to Cohalan's account, the Volunteer leaders missed the deadline set by the military authorities (midnight on Monday 1 May). Then, in a 'breach of faith' that 'created a bad feeling and very dangerous excitement in the city', the Volunteer leaders were arrested. Finally, to the Assistant Bishop's dismay, the rifles were seized on the evening of Wednesday 3 May.[80] It was this murky process that triggered the demand for an official Volunteer inquiry into the performance of the Cork Brigade, eventually headed by Cathal Brugha in 1917. (In March 1918 the committee of inquiry produced the verdict that, while the confusion of Easter week was so extensive that the Cork leaders could not have acted other than as they did, the surrender of arms at any time without a fight was 'to be deprecated'.) After a short retirement in Reading gaol, MacCurtain and MacSwiney returned to command of the brigade.

In Cork the only shots fired in anger were to be fired by the brothers Kent of Bawnard, near Fermoy, resisting arrest the following week; one of them, Richard, was killed in the affray and another, Thomas Kent, became the only non-Dublin Volunteer to be executed.[81] 'Rebel Cork' had the sour taste of failure. The Munster rising ended, as Liam de Roiste reflected, 'with heart-burnings, disappointments, and some bitter feelings. The hour had come and we, in Cork, had done nothing.' The same, just as surprisingly, could be said in Kilkenny, where Ginger O'Connell ended up spending the week in a similar stew of uncertainty. About a fortnight before Easter, Cathal Brugha had arrived at the Volunteer headquarters in King Street to issue orders that the Kilkenny company was to move via Borris, Co. Carlow, to join up with the Wexford forces at Scallop Gap on the county border. Captain O'Connell was to be 'in command of all units in city and county, and all orders for the carrying out of operations were to be taken from him, and this would hold when we linked up with Wexford at the Scallop Gap.'[82] When the local commander, Thomas Treacy, objected that they only had about twenty-five guns (including pistols) for some sixty men, Brugha told him that they would be able to pick up 'sufficient arms and ammunition for all the available men' from Dr Dundon in Borris. It seems, however, that soon after this visit, Peter de Loughrey was sent up to Dublin to consult Eoin MacNeill about the planned rising. MacNeill 'said the first he knew of it was when a few more lads from other parts of the country went to him on the same mission'. They then agreed that Kilkenny would not rise without a direct order from him.[83]

The Sunday mobilization saw 'all available officers and men' on parade (only two of the latter having forgotten to bring their rations), only to be dismissed at 2 p.m. with orders to reassemble at 8 p.m. Meanwhile, the 'officers in the know' discussed the situation. At 10 p.m. O'Connell arrived from Dublin with confirmation that everything was 'off'. But they still collected guns from Borris on Monday. Was O'Connell tempted to put all those months of careful training and preparation to some use? If so, he seems to have kept quiet about it.

As there was no clear word of what was happening beyond the news that trickled through about the fighting in Dublin, Captain O'Connell arranged to have a dispatch sent to Limerick to find out how the position stood in Munster and generally, as there were all sorts of rumours afloat.[84]

This was on Tuesday. O'Connell clearly could not envisage taking action on his own. Not until late on Wednesday did the message return that Limerick was 'not out'; O'Connell then ordered a 'mobilization' at 8 p.m. to discuss the situation. To one of the Kilkenny Cumann na mBan who saw some of the leaders debating at de Loughrey's shop, it seemed that 'Peter [de Loughrey] was in great distress, and my reading of his mind was that Commandant O'Connell restrained them from going out to fight, while Peter and the others were anxious to do their part'.[85] Indecision prevailed; the same process was repeated the next day – when once again there were no absentees from the muster

– with the same result. Only on Saturday evening was the mobilization finally called off (but 'there was no surrender of arms in Kilkenny'). O'Connell was arrested – or some said gave himself up – on 3 May, shortly before a large military force arrived to carry out a further series of arrests (Treacy and twenty-five others were taken on 5 May).[86]

To those with an intense awareness of history – this meant all separatists – the failure of Munster left, as in 1798, the main responsibility for the national rising to Wexford. Pearse's phrase 'Wexford has risen' was a resonant one. Its encouraging effect on the GPO garrison was visceral. And Wexford – at least, Enniscorthy – had risen. But the process was fragmentary. As elsewhere, the countermanding order 'put us in a profound quandary, literally we did not know what to do'. On Monday, the leaders, headed by Robert Brennan, shuttled around trying to get information. According to the Brigade Adjutant, Seumas Doyle, J. J. O'Connell arrived and 'asked us not to do anything until he found how matters stood in the counties which were to have co-operated with us'.[87] This presumably referred to O'Connell's whole group of southern brigades. He disappeared until Tuesday night, when he returned 'weary and dejected and assured us that if we struck we would do so alone'. This pessimism was odd, especially since his messenger to Limerick had not (as far as the Kilkenny men knew) yet returned. In any case, even if an open fight was out of the question, O'Connell was a vocal apostle of 'hedge fighting', and the vice-commandant of the Wexford brigade, Paul Galligan, seems to have been a keen student of his writings on guerrilla tactics.[88] Robert Brennan wrote in his well-known memoir *Allegiance* that the Wexford men received a despatch saying that under no circumstances would Kilkenny turn out. (After it was published, the Kilkenny survivors 'held a meeting and no one knew anything of such a despatch'.) On Tuesday, Volunteers had begun to gather in Enniscorthy – a company from Ferns, for instance ('the only company that came intact'). So forces were available for some kind of action; as many as 600 according to some observers.

Inevitably, as if commemorating Wexford's epic 1798 history, they occupied Vinegar Hill, and 'exchanged shots with the police' from its slopes. They were weakly armed, however, and decided that even an attempt to attack the RIC barrack was impossible: instead they tried to starve it into surrender, because 'we needed their arms and ammunition very badly'. On Wednesday, they had 'difficulty in restraining some of the men who wanted to march on Dublin'.[89] That day, Galligan received orders from Connolly to cut the railway line from Rosslare to Dublin, and this impelled him to attempt to mobilize a larger force. About 100 men assembled to occupy the town on Thursday. The Athenaeum in Castle Street was taken over as a headquarters, and the tricolour flag flown. The Volunteers paraded through the town 'to impress the people'.[90] But no direct move on the railway line seems to have been made, and eventually on Saturday Galligan called for volunteers for a march to Dublin. He set off with forty or fifty men and got as far as Ferns before he himself was injured in a car crash. The column, according to press reports, ran into 'a train containing a few soldiers' at Camolin, just north of Ferns, and 'believing them to be the advanced guard of a force coming up from Arklow, retreated precipitately'.[91] They eventually trickled back to Enniscorthy, to find the inevitable deputation of clergy and businessmen urging the Volunteers 'to accept what, in their estimation, was inevitable'.[92] Here, though, the Volunteers held out until two of them, Seumas Doyle and John Etchingham, had gone to Dublin, conducted by the local military commander, Colonel French, to get confirmation of the surrender order direct from Pearse in Arbour Hill.[93]

Although French, in command of troops in south-eastern Ireland, was absolutely punctilious in his communications with 'the Rebel Officers at Enniscorthy', it is not clear how seriously the military authorities took the threat posed by the attempted rising in the provinces. The Earl of Midleton, an important Cork landlord, who was by now a disgruntled 'Southern Unionist', but who had serious ministerial experience, was convinced that only an instant military response prevented a major uprising. 'But for prompt measures taken by Sir Lewis Bayly, all the south would have risen.'[94] Dublin military headquarters seems to have been somewhat less impressed. After 'some disquieting rumours from country districts' were reported on Tuesday, the situation clarified. Most of Ireland was quiet, but there had been 'risings' in Meath, Clare and Galway and some 'small police stations captured'. The disruption of telegraphic communication briefly worried the Senior Naval Officer at Galway on Wednesday, but small troop reinforcements were deemed adequate to maintain security. On Thursday the threat appeared to be growing; no fewer than 1,500 rebels were reported at Athenry, and said to be 'contemplating moving on Galway'. A warship 'shelled and dispersed a column of rebels on Tuam Road on the 26th', and the Admiral at Queenstown (the commander of the Western Approaches, the senior commander outside Dublin) 'considers state of affairs at Galway serious'. In fact he advised the local military and police commanders against attacking the rebels when they occupied Moyode Castle, 'as the small force available would have made it improbable that the rebels could be captured, and want of success would have had a bad effect locally'.[95] A force of 100 marines was sent from Queenstown to Galway, where they arrived on the morning of the 27th, but the garrison remained in a defensive posture. At the same time the rebel seizure of Enniscorthy railway station was reported, and one or two isolated incidents elsewhere: Killarney was 'disturbed', and there was 'an attack on Clonmel'. Next day, rebels were 'holding Enniscorthy and three miles round'; they had blown up railway bridges north and south of the town. In Wicklow, 900 rebels were 'moving from Gorey towards Arklow'. The Galway rebels were reported, however, to be 'retreating south'. None of these developments led to a significant military response until a mobile column consisting of 60 cavalry, 1,000 infantry, two field guns and a howitzer, was sent from Queenstown to Wexford on Friday 'to relieve Enniscorthy'. Otherwise the main call was for cavalry 'to deal with bands of rebels at large in the country'.[96]

The provincial rising may not have amounted to an emergency, but it was enough to justify the extension of martial law across the whole country, and ensured that the suppression of the rebellion would eventually reach far beyond Dublin. As General Friend ('that amiable person', as Arthur Griffith sardonically called him) argued on Wednesday, when news from the country was still 'very meagre', 'military occupation of the disaffected districts and thorough disarmament of the rebels therein will be necessary, even after the rebellion in Dublin has been thoroughly crushed'.[97]

9

Surrender

*I still feel as if it was a nightmare – only the ruins of Dublin
prove it to be no dream.*

Susan Mitchell, May 1916.[1]

On Wednesday, Captain Brennan-Whitmore paused on a tour of
inspection of his posts in the Imperial Hotel to take stock of the wider
situation. He was one of the few Volunteer officers with some military credentials, and was perhaps sorely missed that week by his own
unit, the Ferns Company in Wexford. He had 'sought to impress on
the general staff time and again', and once on Connolly himself, that
'we had no effective reply' to the most likely British military plan.
Now the military were clearly carrying it out: 'they were occupying
strategic points, and drawing a ring of fire tighter and tighter around
us'. The longer the republican forces fought as they were, 'the more
desperate our position became. We were simply in a ring of steel from
which there were only two avenues of escape – death or surrender.'
No member of his garrison, he believed, feared death. But 'surrender
was hateful'.[2] Undoubtedly many rebels felt the same. Many had
resigned themselves to fighting 'to the last man' or the last round of
ammunition, and some at least may have relished the prospect. Pearse,
however – the rhetorician of 'blood sacrifice' – decided on unconditional surrender. The decision was significant; it may indeed be that
but for the surrender 'there would hardly have been executions, as the
Volunteer leaders would probably have died in action'.[3] Pearse's reasons are worth exploring.

The simplest reason, perhaps, was the uniquely perilous situation of the Headquarters Battalion. While the other main rebel posts had not yet come under either direct assault or serious artillery bombardment, and so remained sanguine about their chances of continued resistance, Pearse's own force had been forced into a fairly chaotic evacuation of the blazing ruins of its positions. Its strategic options had by this time been closed off. The cautious Brennan-Whitmore had realized as early as Thursday that even withdrawing across the street into the GPO would be 'hazardous in the extreme'. He still felt that 'if I could slip my little force through the British lines, which did not seem to be continuous to our rear, and if we could reach open country, we could achieve some real purpose'. But being a Wexford man he had no idea where to go. 'I inquired what was the nearest open country to our rear and was promptly told Fairview.' To him it was no more than a name.[4] He formed his group up in three sections and set out, but his front section quickly became separated from the rest and lost their way. They came under fire and two of them were wounded. Even the Dubliners did not know where they were, and as he said, 'there was not much use trying to reach some ill-defined area if you did not know from where you were setting out'. They took shelter in a building in a hostile area, 'full of "dependants' allowances" women' (usually termed 'separation women'), and eventually they were betrayed to the military forces and captured.

Whether Pearse himself entertained the possibility of a breakout we do not know. It would have fitted with the sort of ideas he had been sharing with his friends in the weeks before the rebellion. But the desperate reality of the retreat into Henry Street and Moore Street was probably different from his expectations. And, crucially, Connolly (whose crippling wound certainly influenced Pearse's thinking) had never been attracted to the prospect of escaping to the countryside. Both of them came to the conclusion that the rebellion, whether or not it had reached the limits of its military potential, had at least achieved enough for the time being. On Friday both had issued communiqués which, as it turned out, were their final manifestos. The tone of Connolly's general order suggested that resistance could go on for some time – 'Courage, boys, we are winning', it concluded – but it stressed the significance of what had already been done. 'For the first time in 700 years the flag of a free Ireland floats triumphantly in

Dublin city.' Pearse's was more sober on the immediate prospects: 'We are completing arrangements for the final defence of Headquarters, and are determined to hold it while the buildings last.' But this was transcended by a highly personal vindication. Of the 'Soldiers of Irish Freedom who have during the past four days been writing the most glorious chapter in the later history of Ireland', he said, 'Let me, who have led them into this, ask those who come after them to remember them.' 'If they do not win this fight, they will at least have deserved to win it. But win it they will, although they may win it in Death.' They had already 'won a great thing. They have redeemed Dublin from many shames, and made her name splendid among the names of Cities.' Ultimately, 'if we accomplish no more than we have accomplished, I am satisfied that we have saved Ireland's honour'.

The surviving Headquarters forces in Moore Street were at the end of their endurance, after a week with little sleep and inadequate food. Dr James Ryan, in charge of the medical unit, had lost his remaining supplies in Moore Lane, and had no more morphine for Connolly. While he was changing Connolly's dressings about midday on Saturday, Connolly told him that Pearse had gone to arrange surrender terms. Looking out of the window, Ryan 'saw a sight I shall never forget. Lying dead on the opposite footpath of Moore Street with white flags in their hands were three elderly men.' They had left their houses as the fires approached, and been cut down by machine-gun fire. 'Seán MacDermott came over to the window and pointed to the three dead men and said something like, "When Pearse saw that we decided we must surrender to save the lives of the citizens."'[5]

According to Connolly, Pearse surrendered to save the lives of the rank and file. (Connolly thought that 'the leaders would all be shot but the rank and file would go free'.) But the British commander did not offer terms. One of Maxwell's earliest decisions was that he would only accept unconditional surrender. When Pearse was brought in to see him on Saturday afternoon, he told him that the rebels must 'throw themselves on our mercy'; all prisoners would be dealt with under the Defence of the Realm Act. A laconic set of interview notes has survived, and gives us a vivid sense of this moment:

Pearce 3.30 p.m., 29–4–16
– no conditions
– personally unconditionally
– wants no more bloodshed. followers
– go back and surrender unconditionally
– all arms and ammn given up – & throw themselves on our mercy
– all people bearing arms
– necessary to send to all rebel centres
– written authority
– ordinary men lay down their arms – save their lives

Maxwell seems to have indicated he 'had no doubt that British Govt may exercise clemency for rank & file as is possible'; and told Pearse that 'a great deal would depend on the celerity of the general surrender'.[6]

This vague threat certainly increased the pressure on the republican command to ensure that all their forces surrendered as soon as possible. This was not an easy task. As the notes suggest, it was necessary to send written orders to all units. Pearse immediately drafted a general order (signed at 3.45 p.m.) to the 'Commandants of the various districts in the City and Country . . . to lay down arms', so as 'to prevent the further slaughter of Dublin citizens, and in the hope of saving the lives of our followers now surrounded and hopelessly outnumbered'. This was taken to the Red Cross post in the Castle where Connolly had just been carried across from Moore Street by a special party of four bearers and three officers. ('Connolly was a heavy man', as one of them recalled, 'and the four worn-out men carrying him were quite unable to do so without help.')[7] He countersigned it – with a curious retraction from his position as commander of all Dublin forces – 'for the men only under my command in the Moore Street district and for the men in the Stephen's Green command'. (That is to say, for the Citizen Army only; and did he think the women were going to fight on, or had he just returned them to the sidelines?) The order was finally taken back, by the Cumann na mBan nurse, Elizabeth O'Farrell, who had first gone out with a white flag to begin the surrender talks, to

Moore Street, with the army's special instructions on how to perform the surrender.

Right away she ran into a problem that would recur in amplified form over the next twenty-four hours. Grim as their position might seem, some of the Moore Street fighters found surrender more repugnant. They may have been 'hotheads', as Max Caulfield called them, though in the light of their recent battering this seems unlikely. More likely they had grasped that they were much less exposed and vulnerable than they had been in the GPO, and could impose a heavy cost on any enemy attempt to root them out. They had stumbled on a more flexible and resilient form of urban warfare, the use of ordinary street houses rather than big isolated buildings. Artillery could still take effect – Eamonn Bulfin watched a house in lower Moore Street collapse 'like a pack of cards'.[8] But the military effect was much more limited (in this case the garrison had already shifted to another house), while the collateral damage, and the likely political damage to the government, would be much greater. According to a member of Oscar Traynor's section, 'we were so confident that at least the fight could have lasted a while longer to give time for the country at large to reach Dublin'.[9] They had to be argued out of their determination to fight on by, ironically, the flintiest Fenians in the leadership, Clarke and MacDermott. Clarke said he was satisfied that the fight would ensure that Ireland was 'all right in the future'. MacDermott, showing signs of intense strain, admitted that they had been 'outclassed'. Not until evening could the force be assembled, something less than 200 strong, and marched out, carrying a white flag, following the precise British instructions, through Henry Street 'around the Pillar to the right-hand side of Sackville Street' (seen from the Parnell statue, presumably, rather than the rebel positions). They were to march up to within 100 yards of the troops lined up near the statue, 'halt, advance five paces and lay down arms'.

This was a crushing moment for men who had just experienced, like Seán MacEntee, the exhilarating sense of liberation from British authority – 'a yoke lifted from our shoulders'.[10] Now that yoke was thumpingly replaced. The brief illusion that they would be treated as prisoners of war was soon shattered.[11] The disarmed men were herded on to the strip of grass outside the Rotunda and kept in the open for the night (the Cumann na mBan and ICA women, something of an embarrassment to the military authorities, were given shelter). Unsurprisingly, perhaps, no arrangements had been made to house them. Joined by prisoners from 1st Battalion, eventually some 400 were crammed on the little lawn; 'we were lying on top of one another'.[12] They were the object of good-humoured contempt from some of the troops, and more malevolent harassment from the officer, Captain Lee-Wilson, who rolled out from a session at the bar to take command of the prisoners after midnight. Oscar Traynor was one of many who witnessed 'all sorts of indignities being inflicted on our leaders, principally Tom Clarke and Ned Daly'. Bulfin remembered a British officer 'threatening to shoot the lot of us', and saw Michael Collins stand up to him. 'This [Plunkett] is a very sick man – will you leave him alone.' Only at 9 a.m. on Sunday morning were they marched back down Sackville Street and along the quays to Richmond Barracks.

After delivering the surrender order to Daly, nurse O'Farrell seems to have been given the rest of the night off. The garrisons south of the river awoke to a strangely quiet Sunday morning, and no doubt some must have suspected what the cessation of the artillery bombardment signified. Even so, O'Farrell's reception by the three battalions was mixed. Whether on British suggestion or her own initiative, she went first to Boland's bakery (oddly, Joe O'Connor recalled her as Agnes Farrell of Cumann na mBan). De Valera did not know who she was, and refused to accept the order unless it was signed by his immediate superior, MacDonagh. O'Farrell went off to find him, but in the meantime several of the 3rd Battalion officers confirmed her identity, and de Valera told O'Connor to gather the garrison together. There was clearly resistance to the idea of surrender – at least one officer started to gather volunteers for a last-ditch stand – and it appears that de Valera took the decision on his own. He told his assembled force that the whole garrison might 'leave by the railway and proceed home quietly, but this would not fulfil the terms of the surrender'.[13] As soldiers they must obey the order. 'I obeyed the orders of my superiors in coming into this fight; I will obey the orders of my superiors to surrender and I charge you all to observe the same discipline.' It seems that most if not all of 3rd Battalion accepted this. They formed fours and marched out of the bakery gate along Grand Canal Street, up Grattan Street to a barricade manned by Sherwood Foresters, where they piled arms. They were held overnight in the show grounds of the Royal Dublin Society at Ballsbridge (then in military use as a remount depot) before being moved on to Richmond Barracks on Monday.

If de Valera had waited for MacDonagh's confirmation, he might have been waiting some time. MacDonagh, who was, all witnesses agree, showing symptoms of intense strain ('careworn and dishevelled', in Peadar Kearney's view), greeted O'Farrell not by disputing the authenticity of Pearse's order, but its legitimacy. He said that it might have been written under duress, and that in any case he was not bound to obey the order of a prisoner. He was persuaded by two Capuchins, Fathers Aloysius and Augustine, who had been working for some time to secure a ceasefire, to talk to General Lowe, and they arranged a meeting on the corner of St Patrick's Park at noon.[14] For over an hour MacDonagh stalled (they started out standing, and ended sitting in Lowe's car), but eventually he agreed to recommend surrender. A truce was arranged until 3 p.m. so that he could go back to Jacob's, and then go on with the Capuchins to persuade the 4th Battalion to surrender.

MacDonagh's arguments to his men were distinctly low-key. 'Boys, we must give in,' Bob Price remembered him saying; 'We must leave some to carry on the struggle.' To the indignant Volunteers who shouted 'We won't surrender to be shot like dogs', he replied sadly, 'They may shoot some of us, but they can't shoot us all.'[15] The atmosphere of suppressed hysteria in the Jacob's factory after the frustrating days of inaction welled up into open dispute. Seamus Hughes made a 'fiery speech', saying that by surrendering they would be offering their leaders as a sacrifice: it would be 'better to die with guns in our hands than to face the firing squad'. Others, including Michael O'Hanrahan and Bob Price, reasoned that by holding out they 'were inviting the destruction of the factory by incendiary shells, and also of the surrounding thickly populated area'. Was a breakout a possibility? Price thought that 'if we left Jacob's we could only reach the country in two's and three's and our prospects of getting together again were well-nigh hopeless'.[16] The garrison was on the brink of disintegration. Kearney thought there was 'a confused feeling that something had been done behind their backs'; Thomas Pugh of B Company remembered 'terrible confusion'. Price saw 'men, old in the movement, seeing their dearest hopes dashed to the ground, become hysterical, weeping openly, breaking their rifles against the walls'.[17] In these 'chaotic conditions' MacDonagh instructed him to take charge of marshalling the garrison; and 'with some difficulty' he succeeded in getting them out through the New Bride Street gate.

It is clear that MacDonagh's own military judgement was no longer entirely accepted, and a key part in restoring some control was the appearance of Major MacBride, still immaculately attired (looking to Kearney as if he had just 'walked out of a drawing-room'). The old veteran accepted that the fight was over for the time being. 'Liberty is a sweet thing', he advised. 'Any one of you that sees a chance, take it. You may live to fight again. If it ever happens again, take my advice and don't get inside four walls.'[18] Eventually military habits prevailed: 'by a series of parade-ground manoeuvres, the arms were laid down and the men formed up in column of route'. Price was 'really proud of my Volunteers then. All their movements were carried out without a hitch, and proved a credit to their training.' They marched down Lord Edward Street, through Thomas Street (where Emmet had been executed) and on to join the other prisoners in Richmond Barracks.

In the Jameson distillery, morale remained high on Sunday morning. Adequate stocks of food had been commandeered, dinner was being prepared, and a ceilidh was planned for the evening. About 4 p.m. Rose McManners, Vice Commandant of the Inghinidhe branch of the Cumann na mBan (and chief cook to the garrison) heard cheering at the front gate, greeting the arrival of MacDonagh and Father Aloysius. MacDonagh was 'hatless and unarmed, and looked old, weary and ill', another garrison member thought; 'something in his appearance told me the worst had happened'.[19] The mood darkened rapidly. After making some refreshments for the priest, McManners saw MacDonagh leave in tears, 'great commotion' among the garrison.[20] Finally, around 7 p.m. Eamonn Ceannt and William Cosgrave walked over from the South Dublin Union, together with General Lowe, to confirm the surrender arrangements.[21] When the garrison surrendered, one of them counted forty-four, all ranks, marching out of the Union with all their weapons – still loaded – to deposit them in the Iveagh Baths in Bride Street.[22] Rose McManners and the other twenty-one women in the Marrowbone Lane garrison marched out behind the men, singing the 'Soldier's Song', picking up discarded rifles and pistols (and carrying the latter right into Richmond Barracks, since no female searchers were available).

When O'Farrell brought the order to Mallin's post, he sent a note to MacDonagh, presumably asking what he was doing; but seems to have got no reply.[23] On Saturday afternoon 'a dismaying rumour' of surrender was already in circulation at the College of Surgeons. Frank Robbins walked round there from his post in South King Street, passing a large crowd of civilians on Stephen's Green who confirmed that Pearse had surrendered. He heard that Mallin was planning a break-out, 'to fight our way through the British net to the Dublin hills, where the struggle would be carried on along the lines of guerrilla warfare'. One officer suggested that all men in uniform should try to get civilian clothes, a suggestion Robbins found incredible until he actually saw some of his comrades 'rigged out in the fashion suggested' on Sunday morning. Then he too went and commandeered a tweed suit (several sizes too large) before going back to the College. When he got there he was struck by 'the atmosphere of gloom that had settled over the place since the previous day'. Men and women who had been 'gay and light-hearted were now crying. The general feeling seemed to be that something terrible was going to happen.' His first thought was that perhaps the British were about to attack, but then Mallin and his staff appeared to announce the surrender; 'anyone who desired could leave'. A few did so. The rest watched Mallin lower the tricolour and raise the white flag. 'It was apparent that at that moment the act of surrender was a greater calamity than death itself. Men and women were crying openly with arms around each other's shoulders.'[24]

When Constance Markievicz surrendered she lost her composure briefly (according to Alfred Bucknill, then a Deputy Advocate General in the army), 'We dreamed of an Irish Republic, and thought we had a fighting chance.' Then 'for a few moments she broke down and sobbed'.[25] She kissed her automatic pistol before handing it over, a theatrical gesture that may have betokened defiance or distress. But the appearance of British troops transformed the atmosphere again, Frank Robbins thought. Depression was swept away by 'a new spirit of independence, hope and exaltation'; 'we were satisfied that all things that were possible to do had been done'. A 'manly part' had been played 'for the vindication of our principles', Robbins felt. 'We had nothing to be ashamed of.' They might have failed, but 'others had failed before, and they had not been ashamed or afraid of the consequences. Why should we?'[26]

Had they, indeed, failed, or had they, as Pearse and Connolly maintained, succeeded? In military terms, they had been defeated, but had they put up the best fight they could, and was it enough? Some of the weaknesses of the planning for the rebellion have been mentioned earlier, and they were apparently aired immediately after the surrender when hundreds of captured men found themselves crammed 'cheek by jowl' with their senior officers in Richmond barracks. 'Their fighting activities appeared so haphazard', one later wrote, 'that many doubted anything in the nature of a prepared blueprint.'[27] The failure to seize the Castle, the Bank of Ireland and Trinity College, due to 'inexplicable neglect' or the lack of initiative of local commanders, were thought to have 'robbed the insurgent cause of an influential morale boost'. The secrecy of planning had the obvious, large-scale effects we have observed; but it also had many more trivial – if irksome, and maybe dangerous – ones. Liam Archer was so convinced that 'when we were going out we would be going into the countryside and not the city streets, I had shod my boots with studs (numerous and highly polished)'; as a result, 'when I found myself on the asphalt and the stone steps, I was sliding all over the place'.[28] Perhaps the most fundamental handicap the rebellion's planning imposed on the republican forces was, as Brennan-Whitmore says, to hand the initiative so completely to the authorities. The limitations of the rebel strategy were scathingly criticized by some of their opponents – Major Raymond Savage Armstrong noted that 'of course the fools never attacked Kingsbridge & there was the only telegraph in Dublin working & of course the most important' (i.e. to the Curragh).[29] The scope for commanders to adapt and respond to British movements was extremely narrow. This may, in one sense, have been for the best, since the commanders were so inexperienced. Certainly, if there was a military genius lurking in the republican ranks, he or she was not given much opportunity to demonstrate their talents.

But it remains surprising that so little was done to counteract the inevitable dislocations caused by the second mobilization. One veteran thought it 'questionable whether in the confusion of improvisation any rational redisposition was attempted'.[30] After midday on Easter Monday, no effort seems to have been made even to encourage men to join their own units, rather than the first force they happened to bump into. No doubt units, painfully conscious of their weakness, were happy to pick up extra bodies from almost any source (the GPO garrison famously welcomed two Swedish sailors who had presumably grown tired of neutrality). But the mingling of strangers must have compromised the discipline and effectiveness of some forces, at least. Archer, again, reflected on the force he commanded at the junction of Church Street and St Mary's Lane:

I had a mixed collection on my barricades, many of whom I did not know. Only the minimum could be relied on to remain at their posts. Others wandered around the area seeking food or their 'pals'. This was particularly bad at night and called for frequent inspections. Sleep being impossible during the day I do not recall getting more than about four hours' sleep between Monday and Thursday.

He realized 'in retrospect that we should have organised sentries' tours of duty, rest points, etc. But we were very ignorant.' And much of the 'wandering' could have been prevented if there had simply been enough food available.[31]

Such efforts as were made to provide mutual support seem to have been spontaneous – as when a force of eighteen men from the under-employed Jacob's garrison were sent out in an 'attempt to provide relief for the Mount Street garrison'. After making their way down Leeson Street and Fitzwilliam Street, they came under fire at the corner of Lower Mount Street and Merrion Street. They kept the fight up for half an hour, and then made their way back across Stephen's Green.[32] This support operation was more than de Valera's own force attempted, admittedly, but it was too little too late: the expedition set out on Thursday, by which time the Mount Street Bridge positions had already fallen, and the troops they ran into were probably those who had broken through there. In general, communication and co-operation between posts seem to have been a lost cause; 'difficulties in keeping contact routes with outlying garrison centres had become insuperable as early as Wednesday'.[33]

The testimony of survivors was almost entirely uncritical of the senior officers, at least for many years afterwards. Probably the most famous exception was Michael Collins, who roundly denounced the military arrangements as 'bungled terribly, costing many a good life'. He also grumbled that a rebellion was not 'an appropriate time for memoranda couched in poetic phrases, or actions worked out in similar fashion'.[34] This anti-aesthetic view marked the distance between two revolutionary generations – though Collins was barely younger than Joe Plunkett. But Collins never criticized Plunkett or any other leader directly. Connolly's performance seems to have been universally praised – Collins saw 'an air of earthy directness about him' and 'would have followed him through Hell had such action been necessary'. (He doubted if he would have followed Pearse, however – 'not without some thought anyway'.)[35] Still, Connolly was indirectly indicted by Collins' most damning verdict, that while the rebellion 'seemed at first to be well-organised, [it] afterwards became subjected to panic decisions and a great lack of very essential organisation and co-operation'. It is certainly hard to assess whether the stream of orders Connolly issued had any significant effect on the shape of the battle. (One of the handful that survive, to the officer in charge of the Reis-Dublin Bread Company position on 25 April, offered a paragraph of instructions on preparing defences and communications, and explained the location of neighbouring posts – and also the likely direction of enemy attack. But it gave no idea of the strength of these posts, or any prioritization of defensive tasks. If it was followed by any other orders, they did not survive.)[36] Desmond Ryan, while calling him 'the brain of the revolt', said nothing about his decisions – indeed pictured him as almost immobile, 'vigilant and taciturn' in the GPO, except when he went out on his ill-fated (and surely irresponsible) sortie 'into a flaming, ruin-starred and death-raked street'.[37] His fixed ideas seem to have persisted: he continued to insist, for instance, that 'a few men were not enough to hold a building'. Of course he did not know what had happened at Northumberland Road and Mount Street Bridge; that was just the problem.

Nobody else at headquarters, including the IRB's most admired military thinker, Joe Plunkett, seems to have tried to exert any influence on the fighting. Plunkett was, of course, a sick man – perhaps terminally ill. Even his fiancée, who seemed convinced that (contrary to the widespread assumption) he did not have TB, saw that he was 'wretched looking' on Sunday, and he entered the GPO wearing a blinding white throat bandage from a recent operation. The field pocket book he scribbled pencil notes in during the week does not hint at any attempt to direct the battle. He, Pearse, MacDermott and Clarke conversed several times a day about the justification of the rebellion, but their outlook seems to have been fatalistic. At times, Plunkett's generally unfailing charm may have run dry. One Volunteer returned from a reconnaissance mission on Wednesday and 'gave my report to Plunkett – it was a verbal one. I told him about the troops in Trinity College and the *Helga* etc. All he said was, "Why didn't you put it in writing?"'[38]

The only senior officer to come in for any direct criticism – and only belatedly – was the only one to survive beyond May 1916, Eamon de Valera. A sharp public exchange of views by two of his 3rd Battalion veterans in the mid-1960s led to a pungent assessment of his command methods. Noting that there were 'only less than eight casualties' among the hundred-strong garrison of Boland's, Sam Irwin tartly observed 'That wasn't much of a fight, but it wasn't the fault of the men. They weren't put into the position to fight.' In his view, 'Any trained corporal in today's army would have disposed the troops of Boland's garrison to better effect than de Valera.' But Irwin took some of the sting out of this criticism by accepting that it applied to all the republican forces. 'Nobody officers or men knew what they were about.'[39] An exaggeration no doubt, but the general point was valid. Most of the commanders had reconnoitred the positions they were to take up – de Valera was assiduous in this – but their reconnaissance of their opponents was almost negligent.

There has also been little critical assessment of rebel military techniques, such as the ubiquitous barricades – one of the most striking and enduring symbols of the rebellion. Joe Good paid tribute to their variety and ingenuity: the barricade constructed 'with the entire stock of a bicycle warehouse', for instance (one is bound to wonder whether better military use could not have been made of these). 'The most delightful of all was a barricade of clocks. At last I saw a use for those horrible marble clocks, like the ones inside the entrance to a bank.'[40] But what were the barricades for? It is interesting that Plunkett himself, according to his sister, never intended the barricades to form part of the rebel defences – 'simply to interrupt communication for the enemy, and enable us to cross the street', he told her.[41] If so, he certainly never told the rank and file, who were often uncertain what to do with them. Though their construction efforts were very varied, Connolly at least conveyed the strong impression that the barricades should be defensible. Some barricade commanders saw him try to tear their constructions apart (Brennan-Whitmore smugly revealed that he had wired his pieces of furniture together). Connolly reserved his highest praise for the barricade put across Abbey Street by the exemplary Captain Tom Weafer, who did not use furniture – in fact he punctiliously supervised the careful placement of the manager's furniture in the basement of the Hibernian Bank on the corner of Abbey Street – but huge rolls of printing paper from the printshop of the *Irish Times*.[42] It was a formidable obstacle, until a stray artillery shell hit the *Irish Times* building and the rolls of paper caught fire, carrying the fire across to the other side and rendering all the posts in Abbey Street untenable. This was, in fact, the cause of the greatest swathe of destruction in Dublin.[43]

There was greater readiness to criticize the failure to seal Dublin off completely from outside communication. The most obvious case in point was the Crown Alley telephone exchange, which was totally unguarded on Monday. ('Ineptitude' or 'some lunacy of bad planning' left it alone, in the view of one.) It seems clear that the original plan took account of this, and indeed that Connolly made quite extensive arrangements for groups of saboteurs to cut communications around the city.[44] On the day, however, nothing happened. Piaras Béaslaí believed that 'at the last moment this was entrusted to a supplementary squad'; the reason for its failure was 'not clear'.[45] Since these were primarily Citizen Army projects, they should not have been affected by the countermand confusion. One explanation, that the Crown

Alley detachment simply failed to turn up, is not impossible, but it does not explain why Connolly did not check up on the situation and take steps to rectify it.[46] Seán Byrne of 1st Battalion was told some time before the rising 'that a special squad was being formed to deal with communications', and 'plans were to be prepared immediately for cutting communications so as to isolate the city'. On Saturday, though, he was assigned to surveying police barracks, and when he mobilized on Monday and was sent by Daly to 'cut the western trunks', he only succeeded in bringing down a telegraph pole on Broome Bridge level crossing with the aid of a bridge demolition party that happened to be nearby.[47] A similar party at Cabra Road railway bridge was given the task of breaking the bridge with a cobbler's hammer and a coal chisel.[48] Mulcahy was sent with an ad hoc group of ICA men to cut the telegraph cables at Howth Junction; but there seems to have been no co-ordination, and when they had done this job, they were 'unclear as to what to do next'.[49]

The attempt to establish a radio station was an imaginative idea whose failure, again, must be attributed to inadequate planning rather than the dislocation caused by the Sunday postponement. 'Might have been managed, Joe, it really might', lamented Joe Good's fellow electrician Johnny 'Blimey' O'Connor on Thursday, after the destruction of Reis's Chambers where the Atlantic Telephone Company's wireless school had been housed. O'Connor's team had reassembled some dismantled equipment to the point where they could tap out a few messages, but power failures prevented them from getting the system fully operational. 'We might have been the first insurrectionists to proclaim a new republic anywhere in the twentieth century', as Good wistfully reflected.[50]

The organization of ammunition supplies was, as we have seen, irregular. In military terms, the rebels 'had no supply system and could only carry on fighting as long as their first line ammunition lasted'.[51] Some posts had munitions in abundance, while others ran out; and there was no general system for monitoring or redistributing stocks. The quality of war *matériel* was inevitably variable. The homemade munitions whose laborious manufacture had consumed so many man-hours in the months before the rebellion, were by general consent unsatisfactory. Matthew Connolly of the ICA was handed bombs made from milk canisters, weighing 5 lb, with instructions to strike the sulphur cap on a wall or stone, count three, then throw.[52] These grenades in particular, bulky and unreliable in operation, proved more of a liability than an asset. (Examples of actions in which they were successfully used are rare.) The function of the pikes that many Volunteers carried remains hard to decode. They clearly formed a link with traditional images of rebellion (as immortalized in such ballads as 'The Rising of the Moon'), and had featured prominently in the St Patrick's Day manifestation in Dublin. 'Special pike exercises' had featured in the Volunteers' 1915 training programme, but just what they were is not clear. (The programme also included instruction for company and half-company commanders in 'Communications, Ammunition supply, how maintained', and 'Special duties in addition to superintending their commands when the Company is acting as part of a larger force'; but no participants recalled details of these either.)[53] On Easter Monday, Andrew McDonnell of E Company, 3rd Battalion, was ordered to stop a tram outside de Valera's headquarters in Great Brunswick Street armed only with his pike, and not surprisingly found this far from easy.[54] After Monday morning, the pikes seem never to be mentioned – what happened to them remains a mystery. The visually impressive home-made bayonets for shotguns were never used, fortunately perhaps – those made at Kimmage 'would have bent against three-ply wood' – though they may have bolstered morale. Home-made shotgun shells were probably more useful. A British officer who broke one apart in front of the prisoners at the Rotunda was impressed: 'Look at this bally cartridge', he shouted to Captain Lee-Wilson, 'it has five bullets, each of which would kill a bally elephant.'[55]

The grave allegation that the rebels actually used some of the dum-dum ammunition that had arrived with the Howth shipment still hangs in the air. It was famously aired in Seán O'Casey's 1926 play *The Plough and the Stars*, where a British sergeant says that one of his men had died with 'an 'ole in front of 'im as 'ow you could put your fist through, and 'arf 'is back blown awoy! Dum-dum bullets they're using.' O'Casey was reporting a fairly common allegation. No rebels admitted to it, though since it was universally regarded as a heinous war crime, it would have been surprising if they had. Such evidence as there is remains in the nature of hearsay. The wife of one St John's Ambulance Brigade volunteer, for instance, recorded in her diary that her husband 'had a terrible time out all night with the ambulance' on Friday: 'the Sinn Feins fired on them even when they had Sinn Fein wounded. The Sinn Feins are using soft-nosed bullets.'[56] Strangely, despite the propaganda value the charge possessed, the military authorities seem to have made no systematic effort to investigate it, or even to prove that dumdum ammunition had been found in rebel positions.

Ammunition supply was always bound to be problematical, because of the sheer variety of weapons amassed by the rebels. No such problems, however, need have affected supplies of food. The planners of the rebellion had weeks, if not months to prepare, and in Dublin they had the resources of a major city – their own city. Yet food shortages turned out to be the biggest difficulty for many if not most rebel units during Easter week. 'We failed to discover any planning arrangements to ensure adequate food supplies.'[57] Even in the GPO, where there were ample stocks, the garrison went hungry as we have seen, because of an over-cautious rationing policy. Elsewhere food supplies were extraordinarily erratic. After the men had used up the rations they were instructed to bring with them at mobilization (while some had been instructed to bring only twelve hours' rations, no doubt a number of others who had more, like Thomas Young in the Ardee Street brewery, 'ate my 48 hours' rations in 10 minutes'), many had no idea where to get food.[58] Some had plenty of luck; in Marrowbone Lane, for instance, they were able to ambush a messenger boy with ten chickens on Wednesday, and a stockman with three calves the next day. Bob Holland, a butcher, was in his element. Later, as their head cook triumphantly noted, they captured a 'load of cabbage'.[59] Others rapidly lost any kind of balanced diet – Joe Good in Kelly's, for instance, had 'plenty of chocolate to eat but little else' for two days or more.[60] Things were even worse in Jacob's factory. 'Despite constant foraging', one of the Cumann na mBan cooks wrote, 'no food suitable for hungry men could be found . . . Eventually one of the girls found a gross or two of slab cooking chocolate.'[61] Some of their limited supplies were taken over to the College of Surgeons, where 'girls were fainting for want of food'.[62] All of this seems incredible in an operation that had been planned for well over a year, taking place in a major city where (despite the war) there were no food shortages. It must give some colour to the suggestion that the planners did not expect to hold out longer than their initial rations would last.

Medical services were better organized, thanks to the eagerness of the Cumann na mBan and ICA auxiliaries to find a role more dignified than that of cooks and coolies. Every major garrison seems to have had a medical unit, several with a doctor (the most active of these, Kathleen Lynn, ended up taking command at City Hall after Seán Connolly's death, and negotiating the surrender of the Citizen Army garrison). Even so, it is clear that many of the arrangements were made at the last minute. Molly Reynolds was at Stephen's Green when 'Margaret Skinnider arrived and said there were no women in the GPO and she had been sent to look for volunteers for that post.' When they got there, O'Rahilly had to take them all around the huge building 'to select the most suitable place for a casualty station'.[63] The group attached to 1st Battalion set up a first-aid post in the Priory in Dominic Street, but were quickly expelled from it by the Prior (Aine Heron lost her treasured waterproof in the debacle). They were then left in limbo. 'The Rising was in full swing, but we were left without any direction and just hung about marking time', until eventually they drifted across to join the Sackville Street forces. Around 6 p.m. some of the women received definite orders – presumably from Daly – 'brought by a dispatch rider on a bicycle, that we were to go home, as our services would not be required'.[64] Only on Tuesday evening did some of Heron's group finally go back to the 1st battalion in the Four Courts.[65] And then Heron was turned into a messenger, sent by Joe McGuinness to tell his wife to destroy all the Battalion papers kept at his house in Gardiner Street. She never got back to the Four Courts.

This peripheral tasking was the experience of most of the women in the rising, despite their enthusiastic prominence at the outset. When Seán MacEntee went into Liberty Hall on Monday morning, 'a group of girls, gay and happy, came running past me, almost tumbling over in their excitement'. The '*vivandières*' at Stephen's Green likewise impressed onlookers. But while Eamon de Valera was the only commander to exclude women from his garrison, the others had quite clearly not planned on including them. Daly, as we have just seen, ignored his Cumann na mBan contingent, and Mallin's co-option of Markievicz was a last-minute improvisation. The experience of Mary Walker (Maire Nic Shiubhlaigh), one of the brilliant stars of the Dublin theatre scene, the favourite actress of Pearse and MacDonagh – and also a Cumann na mBan stalwart – is instructive. Some months before the rising, she had left the city to work in a small town several miles away, where she set up a new Cumann na mBan branch, but lost contact with the Dublin organization. Though she was in Dublin in Holy Week, making up first-aid kits at Volunteer HQ in Dawson Street, her unit was given no orders for Easter. She had arranged informally, as a family friend of Eamonn Ceannt, to join his 4th Battalion on mobilization, but despite spending the whole of Sunday in his home, she arrived on Monday to find the house empty, and no information about where the battalion was assembling. Only by accident, on her way along the South Circular Road, did she stumble on the gunfight at Davy's pub, and met up with a small group of women who decided to make their way to Jacob's factory. When this ad hoc unit arrived there they had to run the gauntlet of the 'huge crowd of poorly-dressed men and women . . . shouting and screaming and waving their fists', and talk their way in past the Volunteer guard. Only then did she meet up with MacDonagh. 'My God, it's Maire Walker! How did you get in?' was his reaction. 'We haven't made any provision for girls here.' Finally the group of women was assigned to cooking duty in a room buried deep in the sepulchral gloom of the great factory, where they spent a frustrating week. ('Our isolation and periods of inactivity were not pleasant; there was an eeriness about the place, a feeling of being cut off from the outside world.')[66]

Not until Monday evening, when two Cumann na mBan representatives got into the GPO to vent their frustration on Pearse and Connolly, was a formal mobilization order belatedly drafted for the women's groups. In all, it has been calculated that sixty Cumann na mBan and thirty ICA women eventually took part in the rebellion, all the former being restricted to cooking, nursing and messenger work.[67] For many, mere participation was excitement enough, but for some it was a big let-down. The willing Marie Perolz of the Citizen Army, who made two journeys to Cork in the days before the rebellion ('and I would crawl on my knees to do it all again', she wrote at the age of '71 or 72'), was stationed as a messenger on College Green. 'Said Mallin with his heavenly smile, "Is that dangerous enough for you?" I felt very proud.' But afterwards she 'had a bitter feeling, as I did not take part in the fighting'.[68] A few women did fight, nearly all of them in the ICA garrisons in City Hall and on Stephen's Green. One, Margaret Skinnider, was seriously wounded in combat near the College of Surgeons. (She seems to have been more upset about the ruin of her elegant uniform, a personal gift from Markievicz, than by her wounds.) Margaretta Keogh of Cumann na mBan was killed in the College. But in most commands they were kept out of harm's way, or even – as in de Valera's – out of the garrison altogether. Brennan-Whitmore, leading his break-out attempt, had no compunction about using trickery and force to disembarrass himself of the four 'gallant young ladies' who were determined to stick with his men. ('Our respect for their gallantry and devotion would not permit us to drag them into some horrible situation.')[69] Many no doubt had a similar experience to that of Pauline Keating with the Cumann na mBan in the Four Courts kitchen, when a Franciscan priest came in to remind them of their proper duties. 'We thought we were heroines, but when he had finished with us we thought we were all criminals.'[70] The emancipation offered by the rebellion was not wholly illusory, but it was tantalizingly brief.

Women made a distinctive, but more reactionary, contribution on the other side too. The violence, verbal and physical, of the 'separation women' made its mark on many of the idealistic revolutionaries. When Aine Heron's Cumann na mBan *sluagh* (troop) was swinging across from the GPO to the Four Courts, they ran into a disagreeable obstacle. 'I felt scared for the first time. There was a crowd of drunken women who had been looting public houses. They called all sorts of names at us, but were too drunk to attack us.' Still it was 'a shock to us, and we marched away as quickly as we could'. This sort of behaviour, disturbingly common in the Sackville Street area, was also a shock to the high-minded Pearse himself. When he decided to surrender, it was in part to protect the citizens of Dublin from themselves as well as from the British fire. The rebellion had created a weird, almost unimaginable situation for the ordinary population. 'All the usual routine of life had ended and it was hard to believe that it had ever been', as one acute observer wrote. Traffic had ceased, shops, cinemas and theatres had closed, the post had stopped, even 'the very clocks on the public buildings had stopped because there was no one to wind them up'. The tramways came to a halt on Monday, and even street lighting (already reduced by a cash-strapped Dublin Corporation) was cut off. Works closed down, and wages dried up; banks closed too, but even people with money found it hard to buy food. 'In short, life during those brief fierce days was completely revolutionized. Dublin had a sample of real war conditions.'[71]

In much of south Dublin this situation remained a curiosity, but in the tenements north of the river its impact was catastrophic. The decision of the DMP Commissioner to take his policemen off the streets of the entire city had dramatic results.

Now a horrible procession poured into the streets, mainly women and girls, shoeless, hatless, with filthy faces, with tangled, matted hair flying loosely in the wind, with dirty shapeless darkened dresses . . . They came out into the streets in crowds, shouting, shrieking, yelling . . . Ordinary shutters were useless against this throng. They started with stones and sticks, a breach would be made, the door would be forced in.

If the shopkeeper tried to resist 'they would beat him and down him without mercy'. Once inside, they took everything they could carry, and even things they could not. F. A. McKenzie watched women dragging a sack of rice into the roadway.

They had no means of carrying it away. They tore it open. They yelled madly and started to caper round it. Then, catching hold of handfuls of rice, they threw them up in the air, laughing like mad folk.[72]

Many people, including the dismayed rebel garrisons themselves, witnessed the bizarre and destructive saturnalia. Eamonn Bulfin thought that the spectacular firework display set off by boys in the middle of Sackville Street, with a huge pile of fireworks taken from Lawrence's, was 'one thing that will stick in my mind forever'.[73] Brennan-Whitmore saw the process turn from this 'spirit of mischief' to an 'insensate passion for wanton destruction'. This was not only 'maddening' but 'dangerous in the extreme' when the mobs 'took to setting the looted premises on fire to cover their depradations'. He would have taken action to 'make an example of' some looters, but for explicit orders from Connolly not to interfere with ordinary citizens.[74] When Desmond FitzGerald asked Pearse 'were those caught looting to be shot, he answered "yes". But I knew he said it without any conviction.' And when, some time later, 'a prisoner was actually handed over to me charged with looting', Pearse, asked for instructions, replied 'Ah, poor man, just keep him with the others.'[75]

Some Volunteers did try to halt the looting, but they found it a Sisyphean task. When one detachment of the 2nd Battalion arrived outside the GPO from Fairview, 'crowds of people were looting the shops, and a lot of us dropped on our knees with rifles "at the ready" – some fired, at what I do not know. The panic was spreading'; but then 'Connolly came out of the Post Office and marched up and down the road. "Steady, we are going to have a good fight." He quelled the panic.'[76] But the looting went on. Other republican forces, presumably ignoring Connolly's instructions, took action that definitely interfered with citizens. In Henry Street, whose shops were as attractive as Sackville Street's, one garrison poured water from the roof on to looters in the street below, and at least one post commander (in Williams' store) arrested several of them.[77] None of this stopped the looting. The army barely tried, though under martial law they might have shot looters on sight. 'With the looting they don't seem inclined to cope', wrote one housewife living between Stephen's Green and Redmond's Hill on Thursday. (On Friday her husband got a group of residents together 'to seek the military authorities and try to get some protection for the shops'.) Another citizen, whose 'blood boiled' at the 'appalling sights', thought it 'a mystery why the military allow such fearful looting'.[78] In the vacuum of authority ('I have not seen a policeman since last Monday') it was left to the citizens themselves to cope, perhaps by forming vigilante groups. Frank Sheehy-Skeffington seems to have been trying to do just that when the army demonstrated where its real priorities lay.

How bad, altogether, was the looting? Other journalists present in the city suggested that 'in view of the opportunity which the rebellion presented, the amount of looting was comparatively small'. Outside the Sackville Street district, 'the behaviour of the crowds was in general remarkably orderly'.[79] It is clear, though, that looting – maybe less intensive – extended further south. Alfred Fannin found that around his Grafton Street pharmacy on Friday 'the streets were full of straw and rubbish from the looting of the street'.[80] (The eventual tally of police prosecutions for looting ran to 425, with 398 convictions.)[81] It is clear, too, that the fighting and especially the fires drew sizeable crowds throughout the week. People 'followed the military operations with a close interest that often came near to foolish recklessness'. Dick Humphreys, looking out from the GPO on Wednesday morning, was impressed by the 'ever-inquisitive crowd' in D'Olier Street and on O'Connell Bridge, 'right between the two firing parties'. Only as the firing began to hot up towards 10 a.m. did they 'drift away'.[82]

Beyond looting and sightseeing, though, the public's reaction to the rebellion was not easy to gauge. We may not be able to get far beyond Frank Henderson's laconic comment that 'the attitude of the civilians towards us was mixed'.[83] (His subordinate Harry Colley, however, was more specific: 'the people [in Fairview] were good, but some of those in Clontarf were not'.)[84] Around the GPO, as it happened, there was a lot of hostility. Pearse 'knew that those who had been out about the streets on various errands came back and reported that the people were ready to attack them'.[85] Dick Humphreys, who was sent out across the river with O'Rahilly's car to gather provisions, met with 'mixed receptions from the amazing number of citizens who still throng the streets' in Ringsend.[86] In many areas, the response of the citizens was pure puzzlement: they simply had no idea what was going on. Some assumed that it was an invasion, like the woman in Westmoreland Street who told Humphreys that 'a corpse of Germans has landed in the Park'. At Jacob's factory, 'Only this evening [Thursday] a woman was heard imploring her daughter – a volunteer nurse – to come home', one witness recorded. The daughter's robust reply was 'No mother, here I shall die!' As the diarist noted, 'This spirit seems to animate them all, they expect to die, but so far no one has been able to tell me what they are sacrificing their lives for.'[87]

John Dillon was to ground his denunciation of the military regime on the assertion that this was the first Irish rebellion in which the government had had the majority on its side. This was certainly true of the middle class, in the view of Wells and Marlowe: they 'generally treated the troops as their deliverers from a regime of anarchy', whereas 'the attitude of the lower classes was more complex and uncertain'.[88] People with marked Unionist sympathies, such as A. M. Bonaparte-Wyse, naturally sensed 'a very menacing tone among the lower classes', and believed that 'the sympathies of the ordinary Irish are with Sinn Fein'.[89] But the workers tended to keep quiet. We inevitably know more about the reactions of middle-class people, most of them letter-writers and many of them diarists, such as Elsie Henry who fastidiously noted that 'The cleanest and best buildings are destroyed, the miles of slums are intact.' It was particularly annoying that 'the GPO had just been done up'.[90] (George Bernard Shaw made the same point from the opposite political angle when he dismissed the GPO as 'a monument of how dull eighteenth-century pseudo-classical architecture can be', and said 'its demolition does not matter. What does matter is that the Liffey slums have not been demolished.')[91] The extent of destruction of commercial premises in the Sackville Street area was certainly impressive. One journalist listed 34 in Lower Sackville Street (including the Imperial Hotel and the Metropole), 39 in Upper Sackville Street, Sackville Place and Henry Street (ranging from the Coliseum Theatre to 'The World's Fair 6½d Stores'), 48 in Lower and Middle Abbey Street (including Wynne's Hotel, where the Volunteer movement had been founded), 28 in Earl Street and Eden Quay, and three or four dozen more in the surrounding streets – damage amounting to £241,870, out of a total of £2.5 million for the whole city.[92]

John Dillon was in Dublin at Easter, but he stayed in his house all week for fear of 'a bullet in the head' – a perhaps exaggerated caution, as James Stephens and many other observers demonstrated. (The Kilmallock Lady's husband's 'curiosity or excitement' was a continual anxiety – 'every sound he hears he must rush into the street'. But movement in many areas was fairly safe. Although Alfred Fannin was told on Tuesday morning that it was 'madness to attempt to get into town', he reported later that evening that 'none of our people had any difficulty in getting in to or from business although shooting was going on in Stephen's Green. A great deal of the shooting is aimless.') Stephens in particular was keen to get a sense of his fellow-citizens' attitude, and went around constantly listening. He did not find any easy answers. 'There was a singular reticence on the subject', he found in mid-week. 'Men met and talked volubly' – of course – 'but they said nothing that indicated a personal desire or belief.' There was a deep thirst for news ('or, rather, rumour'), but the main view was simply one of 'astonishment at the suddenness and completeness of the occurrence'.[93] The only judgements he heard were from women – who 'knew they had less to fear' – and these were not just unfavourable, 'but actively and viciously hostile to the rising'. From the 'best dressed' to the 'dregs', Stephens heard a single refrain: 'They ought all to be shot.'

He did, however, notice one reaction which – in retrospect – was extremely significant. By Wednesday evening, the belief was growing that the Volunteers might hold out far longer than anyone imagined to be possible. (Alfred Fannin was obviously surprised that on Tuesday evening, 'after 36 hours rebellion, the rebels hold nearly all the points they have taken'.) 'The idea at first among the people had been that the insurrection would be ended the morning after it began. But today, the insurrection having lasted three days, people are ready to conceive that it may last forever.'[94] This did not imply approval, but it was the beginning of respect. Stephens sensed 'almost a feeling of gratitude towards the Volunteers' for 'holding out for a little while, for had they been beaten on the first or second day, the city would have been humiliated to the soul'. The labour leader Thomas Johnson, who was trying to return to Dublin via Belfast, found a similar reaction in Drogheda on Thursday: 'no sign of sympathy with rebels, but general admiration for their courage and strategy'.[95] This was tapping into a deep historical well; for, as Stephens wrote, 'being beaten does not greatly matter in Ireland, but not fighting does matter. "They went forth always to the battle, and they always fell." Indeed, the history of the Irish race is in that phrase.'[96]

A Cumann na mBan messenger stuck at Mallow Station, trying to get back from Killorglin to Dublin, heard a rumour run through the would-be passengers that the military had 'mown down the Volunteers in front of the GPO'. One of them turned to her 'to console me, saying "It is only the Sinn Feiners that were killed." This enraged me and I turned on them.' Soon, 'first one and then another began to murmur, and the little crowd began to argue and take sides. That was the first public expression of any sympathy I experienced.'[97] The process of opinion formation was beginning. On the face of things, there was certainly a possibility that people might – as Dillon desperately urged – be kept on the side of the government and the parliamentary nationalists. It is clear that the nature of the military reaction to the rebellion would be crucial to its ultimate impact on the future of Ireland and of the United Kingdom. The surrender was just the start: the atmosphere was darkening. One civilian diarist heard, from a colonel of her acquaintance, an instructive story about the negotiation of the surrender in Cork by General Stafford, 'a dug-out R. E.' (Royal Engineer) in command of the troops at Queenstown (Cobh, military headquarters for the Cork area). 'He declared he would suppress it without bloodshed and did so. Not only he, but his staff too, expected to be covered with medals. They were retired instead.'[98]

IO

Punishment

You are letting loose a river of blood . . . It is the first rebellion that ever took place in Ireland where you had the majority on your side. It is the fruit of our life work . . . and now you are washing out our whole life work in a sea of blood.

John Dillon, House of Commons, 11 May 1916

In purely military terms, the rebellion was suppressed with some efficiency. Perhaps it was true that, to the mind of Stephens's Dubliners, survival for more than a day was a rebel triumph. But in the circumstances, hamstrung in the preceding months by political caution, and wrongfooted by the tangled events of Holy Week, the army's performance was not unimpressive. The forces immediately available, which only barely outnumbered the rebels, were pushed instantly to key points, and within twenty-four hours it could already be said that the military challenge had been neutralized. Within forty-eight hours the rebellion was consigned to an increasingly hopeless 'last stand'. It should be remembered that the British army – in common with practically every army in the world – had no experience of urban warfare. The battle of Dublin was an extremely rare military phenomenon; as one observer noted, 'for a parallel to this form of fighting in a big city, one has to go back to the days of the French Revolution, or the Commune in Paris'.[1] A British officer who later wrote on the rebellion judged that 'to be in some parts of Dublin then was in many ways a worse experience than being in France or Flanders'.[2] Despite the difference of scale, it posed the same kinds of military problems as Stalingrad – or Fallujah, where the 'insurgents' were similar in number to the Dublin rebels (though the citizens had largely escaped before the assault began).[3] There can be little doubt that the rebels could, if they had not concentrated their forces as they did, have created an extremely difficult military situation.[4]

General Maxwell's allegation that the rebels 'mixed with peaceful citizens' in order to ambush the troops may have been misleading, but his assertion that 'I cannot imagine a more difficult situation than that in which the troops were placed' was fair enough.[5] His biographer amplified this point:

In fighting of this sort the soldier sacrifices much of what discipline and training have taught him, manoeuvre is a dead letter, and, man for man, the civilian with a rifle to his shoulder and a wall or barricade in front of him is fully, if foully, a match for the professional soldier.[6]

The minor military disaster at Northumberland Road and Mount Street Bridge, though it stemmed in part from some of the deep-set military weaknesses that were to be displayed on an epic scale two months later at the Somme, also reflected the lack of an urban warfare doctrine. It caused a disproportionate share of the week's military casualties. Overall, however, these were perhaps surprisingly small: 106 killed – 17 of them officers – and 334 wounded.[7] (Crown fatalities were thus about twice those of the rebels, broadly in line with Clausewitz's hypothesis.) In the same week, at Hulluch on the Western Front, the 16th Division had lost 570 dead and over 1,400 wounded.[8]

But, of course, in a civil conflict of this kind, 'purely military' terms are irrelevant, if not actually misleading. As soon as the limits of the rebel threat had become clear, the methods used to suppress the rebellion became a political as much as a military issue. The fear of German invasion would naturally persist, and as French wrote to Maxwell on 29 April, 'that is what we must be prepared for'; but he prefaced this by saying 'I do not think there is much chance (now) of a German landing on the West Coast.' That much had been clear by the 26th, indeed. If the government was going to exert some political control over the process of suppression, this was the moment to begin. But instead, the Cabinet reconfirmed Wimborne's proclamation of martial law and extended it across the whole country, most of which had remained entirely peaceful – a proceeding without any authority in common law.[9] The politicians were not entirely oblivious to potential problems. On Thursday Birrell sent an urgent warning against this extension, and on Friday morning the Cabinet spent some time thinking about it.[10] Asquith apparently remarked that 'there was no danger in the situation' by then. Lloyd George, who cannot have forgotten the bruising tussles over the use of martial law in South Africa, warned the Cabinet that 'the whole of Ireland might be set ablaze' by the 'unconsidered actions of some subordinate officer'. But Sir Nevil Macready, the Adjutant General, who was called over from the War Office to advise, suggested that 'it was better to risk overstepping authority than to delay action'. To limit the risk, all the Cabinet heavyweights – Bonar Law, Balfour and Curzon – weighed in to help draft an instruction advising Maxwell to tell his officers that the powers exercised under the proclamation of martial law 'are not to be put in force except after reference to yourself, unless urgent local circumstances necessitate immediate action, and that otherwise the ordinary machinery of the laws will continue to operate'.[11] But this was really only a rephrasing, rather than a restriction, of the standard doctrine of martial law (and, as Bonar Law pointed out, did not really meet Birrell's objection).

We have already seen the ferocity of the language used in military orders issued before Maxwell's arrival. He certainly did nothing to temper this; his boast to French on the 30th that 'any holding out tomorrow in Dublin will be blown off the face of the earth' was almost a caricature of gung-ho military machismo. There was a wide sense during Easter week that an alien kind of militarism was in the ascendant. Many Dublin citizens, even those most hostile to the rebellion, found the army's style alarming: 'this is true Germanism', thought one indignant loyalist who was aggressively ordered away from his front window by a soldier brandishing a 'heavy revolver'.[12] The Cabinet's reaffirmation of martial law contributed powerfully to this. In practical terms, as Maxwell was soon to discover, it had little meaning; but together with the formal appointment of Maxwell as 'Military Governor' it sent (as it was meant to) a resonant signal. Ireland was under military rule. Asquith himself was reported to be content for the army to get on with its task. French assured Maxwell on 1 May that the Prime Minister was 'very pleased with it all'.

What 'it all' amounted to at this point was the fulfilment of Asquith's public assertion that the government's 'paramount duty' was 'to stamp out rebellion with all possible vigour and promptitude'. On 30 April, Maxwell and Lowe laid out a plan for the final mopping-up of rebel forces in Dublin, based on 'expanding the existing cordon so as to comprise a wider field'. They set up two area commands, under Colonel Maconchy north of the river and Colonel Portal south of it, with four sub-areas. Each of these consisted of a brigade of infantry, two field guns, and two armoured cars. 'The general idea' was for each sub-area commander 'to gradually overcome the rebels in his area by "feeling his way" and by ascertaining through every possible means the location of rebel strongholds'. They were also to distribute the C.-in-C.'s proclamations, and 'carry out rigourslly [sic] the punishments provided therein'. A mobile column held in reserve at the Castle would be available 'should it be necessary to instigate any encircling movements within sub areas'.[13] Sporadic resistance did in fact continue in Dublin for several days after Pearse's surrender, particularly in the Ringsend area, so these operational arrangements were not excessive.

Maxwell's next moves, however, would be less politically palatable. On 2 May he sent Kitchener a despatch which made clear that he blamed political weakness for the outbreak of the rebellion, and hoped that 'politicians will not interfere until I report normal conditions prevail'. Though he had 'said the rebellion is crushed, I have not said more than that, and there is still work to be done'.[14] He was 'disarming all districts that have broken out in actual rebellion – house to house search', and he intended to arm the DMP with the captured weapons. ('Had they been armed', he said, 'I don't think the Dublin rebellion would have broken out.') Of the rebels, he concluded that 'at the last moment the bulk of the rank and file were jockeyed by the leaders into active rebellion. But they have all been playing at rebellion for months past and therefore deserve no pity.'[15] A few days later he reiterated to the Chief of the General Staff that 'although this rebellion is crushed, it is folly to suppose that all danger is over'. He added an interesting interpretation: 'it is in the Irish character to loudly proclaim loyalty, and such protestations are pouring in, but this in my opinion is a reason we should be all the more watchful'. It would 'never do to be caught on the hop again'.[16] Others were even more suspicious than Maxwell. One of MI5's 'private correspondents' who had been stranded at Malahide during the rebellion reported that 'the bulk of the people were merely waiting for the slightest sign of success to join the rebellion', and MI5's director suggested that 'if the truth were known this feeling is very general and it is very hard to draw the line where Sinn Feiners and Redmondites part'.[17] All these were danger signals that might have caused some worry to the government, had it known of them.

On 3 May, the garrison commander at Queenstown was informed that 'now that the rebellion in DUBLIN and elsewhere has been crushed the GOC-in-C intends to arrest all dangerous Sinn Feiners'. This category was to include 'those who have taken an active part in the movement although not in the present rebellion'.[18] To do this, the country was divided into three areas, the north (Ulster and County Louth), the country 'south of a line running 5 miles north of the railway Ennis–Limerick–Clonmel and a straight line from there to Arklow', and 'the remainder of Ireland'. In the southern area, placed under the Queenstown commander, 'small columns consisting of Infantry and Mounted Troops should be sent to various Centres and gradually the whole district worked through', in co-operation with the police. In the central area, more substantial mobile columns were set up at Longford, Athlone, Kilkenny and Castlebar. Each of these consisted of two companies of infantry, a squadron of cavalry, and an eighteen-pounder gun; an armoured car ('useful to round up outlying bands if any such exist', Maxwell thought) was added to each on 5 May.[19] Lowe was instructed that 'great care should be taken to collect as much evidence as possible with regard to the part each arrested Sinn Feiner has taken in the rising', and told that 'any Sinn Feiner who actually resists arrest may be dealt with on the spot by Court Martial'.[20]

Maxwell told a number of people that 'after he had finished with Dublin, he would deal with the country'; but even though this policy had been adumbrated by General Friend as early as the second day of the rebellion, its exact point was never entirely clear. It was intended in part, as the accompaniment of heavy artillery indicated, as a show of force designed to encourage loyal subjects and overawe disaffected nationalists. The standard cordon-and-search technique used ('a sudden encircling of disloyal areas by the cavalry, while the infantry systematically drives the enclosed area section by section') was thought successful in this. Lowe later reported that the appearance of troops in areas where they had 'not been seen for some time past and in some cases never', had had an 'excellent moral effect'.[21] (Birrell, it will be recalled, had repeatedly asked for ostentatious displays of military force before the rebellion, and been repeatedly fobbed off.) In terms of concrete results, however, such as disarmament, the columns were less productive. Maxwell told Kitchener that '*all* arms will have to come in before I can rest assured that there is no chance of another outbreak'. But although a fair number of arms were captured (just over 2,000 rifles by early July), he had to recognize that the quantities left in nationalist hands were 'impossible to estimate'.[22] (The local commander in Limerick, for instance, noted that in one village only a couple out of over twenty guns had been handed in: 'they are known to be there but their owners have concealed them'.)[23] He contented himself with arguing that 'the number of rifles in the hands of Sinn Feiners and Nationalists known to the police seems small, and even if doubled is negligible from a military point of view'.[24] Full disarmament could only be achieved by house-to-house searches, which seem to have been ruled out on the quasi-political grounds that, as Lowe warned, they would 'exasperate the populace'.

If the number of guns collected was inadequate, the number of 'Sinn Feiners' arrested – 3,430 men and 79 women – was much more impressive. Unfortunately, this haul was to generate more problems than seem to have been anticipated. Although the original military instructions had stressed that 'great care should be taken that men who are merely strong Nationalists should not be confused with Sinn Feiners', and that 'the dividing line between the two should be generously on the side of the Nationalists', the issue of who was a 'dangerous' Sinn Feiner proved to be a tricky one. On 6 May Maxwell reiterated the 'importance of arresting only dangerous Sinn Feiners, the object being to secure the leaders of the movement and those who are known to have taken (or have borne arms with intent to take) an active part in the rising'.[25] He sent a stronger warning signal on

14 May, noting that 'in some districts Sinn Fein followers have been arrested who cannot be considered as leaders exercising dangerous influence'. He made clear that the only people to be arrested were 'A. men against whom there is evidence to try by Court-Martial on a charge of having taken part in rebellion. B. Those known to be inciting others to retain arms or to resist authority and whose continued presence is considered likely to lead to further bloodshed.'[26] Maxwell himself, however, took the MI5 line that it was virtually impossible to distinguish between Sinn Feiners and Redmondites, and so, evidently, did some of his subordinates. When, for instance, the northern column raided the houses of nationalists in Omagh without consulting the police, the result was to 'give rise to a very bitter and hostile feeling amongst a very large section of the Nationalist population who were hitherto stongly opposed to the Sinn Fein movement in all its forms'.[27]

When the Prime Minister sprang a visit to Ireland in mid-May, he went to see the prisoners in Richmond Barracks. He found that they were 'for the most part, men and lads from the country, who had taken no part in the Dublin rising', and concluded that many of them 'ought never to have been sent to Dublin. A process of "combing out" should be at once set on foot.'[28] A few days later, Irish Command assured the War Office that they were 'doing all in their power to expedite' the process of 'combing out "innocents" with vigour'. They had taken on a leading Dublin barrister, and hoped to get through about 150 cases a day.[29] (In fact, 1,424 of the 3,430 men arrested were released within a fortnight.) But by this time, the whole policy had come under acute scrutiny. John Dillon had made several private efforts to persuade Maxwell of the unwisdom of – as he wrote on 8 May – 'instituting searching and arrests on a large scale in districts in which there has been no disturbance'. On 11 May he took his complaint into the open in a blistering speech in the House of Commons. 'Would not any sensible statesman think', he asked, 'he had enough to do in Dublin and other centres where disturbance broke out, without doing everything possible to raise disturbance and spread disaffection over the whole country?' Describing the effect of military searches in Limerick, Clare and Mayo, he charged that 'you are doing everything conceivable to madden the Irish people' and turn friends into enemies of the government. 'If Ireland were governed by men out of Bedlam you could not pursue a more insane policy.'[30]

Dillon's fierce invective found ready echoes in the nationalist press in Ireland. The military authorities soon had to threaten even the *Freeman's Journal* (no admirer of Sinn Féin) with 'immediate action' under DORA for criticizing the military regime. They accepted that 'the suppression of the rising inevitably entailed the regrettable arrest and detention of a number of persons who neither encouraged nor took part in the rebellion', but press comments 'dwelling upon and emphasising in flamboyant and incendiary language' such cases of hardship and injustice could only have 'a prejudicial effect on the peace of the country'. Maxwell held that 'if Dillon had not made that unfortunate speech I think things would have very nearly got back to normal' by the 20th; but, as it was, 'he has provoked a good deal of racial feeling'.[31]

The Home Secretary, Herbert Samuel, soon faced the tricky problem of how to deal with the burgeoning mass of Irish prisoners. Maxwell had addressed the issue as soon as he arrived in Dublin, by which time some ninety prisoners had already been taken. Initially, 'Sir John was very keen to try everybody "under military courts" held under martial law', according to his DAG, Joseph Byrne, 'but I persuaded him against this.' Byrne held that the Defence of the Realm Regulations were adequate, and, more importantly, 'will not raise any difficulties afterwards'.[32] Maxwell proposed to French on 28 April that 'in cases where clear evidence is not immediately available, or trial is not desirable, to send the accused out of the country to suitable internment camp. I suggest vicinity of Holyhead.'[33] Two days later, by which time he had some 600 in custody, he confirmed that he was 'sorting them out keeping only those I intend to deal with here'.[34] One of his early ideas, that some of the prisoners should be 'allowed to expiate their crime by serving the Empire as soldiers' (he thought they 'might usefully garrison such places as Sollum and elsewhere'), received short shrift from the War Office.[35]

Then the beautiful simplicity of the military mind began to run into the tangle of the law. During the first week of May, the Irish Law Officers, the Irish executive's chief legal advisers, began to consider the implications of the wholesale despatch of captured rebels and arrested suspects to England. Many had been 'taken red-handed either as the result of the storming of certain strongholds or capitulation and surrender', and the rest had been rounded up on the basis of 'a strong suspicion of complicity'. Unfortunately, proper records had not been kept, and even with those taken red-handed it was 'fairly certain that it would be practically impossible to ascertain either the particular overt acts alleged against them or even the names of the particular military officers or men by whom they were made amenable'. For the rest, there was nothing against them beyond suspicion. It would be 'practically useless to bring them back to Ireland with a view to being disposed of by Courts Martial'; yet it would be 'dangerous and disastrous' to allow them to return free to Ireland. So what was to be done with them? They might be tried under DORA in England. But that would involve 'the great expense and delay of collecting' the materials needed to convict them. And, thanks to the Amendment Act, they could exercise the right to elect to be tried by the ordinary courts. If they were held until they could safely be taken back for civil trial in Ireland, such trials would mostly 'prove abortive owing to the sympathy, apathy and cowardice of the jurors'; and worse, would destroy the prospect of pacification by 'keeping alive in an aggravated form the burning embers of the recent conflagration'. The Law Officers advised drafting a new DOR Regulation, combining elements of DRR 14 and 14B, but specifically dealing with the rebellion.[36]

By the time the Home Secretary addressed the problem in mid-May, there were nearly 1,600 Irish prisoners in England. They had overflowed the ordinary military prisons, and many were being held in 'certain civil prisons lent for the purpose by the Prison Commissioners and temporarily certified by the War Office as military prisons'. Housing them was one problem, but now that the outbreak had been completely suppressed, there was a possibility that they might apply for writs of habeas corpus; and it was 'not clear what valid answer there would be'. In Home Office language, this was a shrieking alarm bell. Samuel reiterated for his Cabinet colleagues the problems outlined by the Irish Law Officers, though he did not favour their solution. Special legislation might be difficult to pass through parliament, and a new regulation 'would be open to the grave objection of being ex post facto legislation'. He proposed to stick to Regulation 14B, allowing the internment of enemy aliens. But how could Irish men and women, who were indisputably British citizens, in law if not in their own aspirations, be classified as enemy aliens? Samuel suggested that the phrase 'hostile origins or associations' in the Regulation could cover the rebels because of 'the known connection of the Sinn Fein movement with Germany'. This might be proved by the landing of Casement and the attempted arms landing, and 'by the passage in the rebels' proclamation which refers to the Irish Republic's "gallant allies in Europe"'.[37] This was not entirely promising, however, and Samuel added that, as his colleagues were aware, Regulation 14B had already been attacked as a breach of civil liberties. 'These criticisms will probably become more widespread if the procedure is now applied to this large body of persons, particularly since their connection with Germany is only indirect.' Given 'the importance of the issue involved', Samuel asked for a Cabinet decision.

In spite of these drawbacks, the Cabinet approved the use of Regulation 14B to legalize the detention of the rebellion prisoners. This meant that, as the Regulation stipulated, there would be an Advisory Committee to which prisoners could 'make representations' that they had been wrongly imprisoned. (Not appeals as such, since the committee was not bound by judicial rules.) In the case of the Irish prisoners, the Advisory Committee, chaired by Justice Sankey, did not wait for representations, but set about interviewing the lot in order to push ahead with 'combing out' of the 'innocents'. Sankey would eventually release all but 579 of the detainees on the grounds that they were not dangerous – in other words, should never have been arrested. This was a swingeing indictment of the police intelligence services on which the army had relied in making its sweep. (Maxwell was guilty of some naivety, perhaps, in believing the assurances he had from 'the RIC and Police that no Sinn Feiners can escape them'.) It would not be the last.

Maxwell's decision to send the untried prisoners out of Ireland landed the government with a troublesome problem. His treatment of those he did not send out, however, became a much more serious one. On 2 May, chafing against the advice he had been given not to 'deal with them under Martial Law' he told Kitchener that he hoped nonetheless 'to get through with the Courts Martial'. He planned to have three courts sitting simultaneously, and to 'be through with this part in a week to ten days'. The first courts were sitting as he wrote. (Their Presidents had immediately 'begun to raise legal difficulties', but he hoped to get over these.)[38] The first batch of rebels were sentenced to death later that day, on a charge of 'waging war against His Majesty the King, with the intention and for the purpose of assisting the enemy'.[39] They were Patrick Pearse, Tom Clarke and Thomas MacDonagh. The three were taken from Richmond Barracks to Kilmainham gaol, a grim disused prison nearby, and shot in the yard at dawn on 3 May. The government suddenly took note. The Prime Minister summoned Lord French and 'expressed himself as "surprised" at the rapidity of the trial and sentences'. French 'pointed out' (as he reassured Maxwell) 'that you are carrying out your instructions exactly and correctly and in strict accordance with Military and Martial Law'. Asquith apparently 'quite understands', but asked French 'to warn you not to give the impression that *all* the Sinn Feiners would suffer death'.[40] The Prime Minister, a famous procrastinator (and a lawyer), was plainly ill at ease, and well he might be (since neither military nor martial law was involved in the trials, French was hardly taking him seriously). Yet while he was also already preparing his political damage-limitation exercise, he did not yet see the need to intervene directly.

In French's view, the fact that three rebel prisoners had also received 'much less severe sentences was evidence enough' of Maxwell's sensitivity, and Asquith agreed to leave him 'to his own discretion'. But he sent a telegram directing that 'no sentence of death on any woman, including Countess Markievitz [*sic*] should be confirmed and carried out without reference to the Field-Marshal Commanding in Chief and himself'. Even in the case of men, Asquith added, 'the greatest care should be taken that the extreme sentence is not carried out except on proved ringleaders or persons found to have committed murder'.[41] Over the next two days, another five men were executed (Ned Daly, Willie Pearse, Joe Plunkett and Michael O'Hanrahan on the 4th, followed by John MacBride on the 5th) and five more sentenced to death (Eamonn Ceannt, Seán Heuston, Con Colbert, Michael Mallin, and Thomas Kent). Now the politicians jumped. At midnight the Adjutant General, Macready, telegraphed Maxwell. 'PM has told me to impress upon you the necessity of avoiding anything which might give rise to a charge of hasty procedure or want of due care and deliberation in confirming sentences.' Asquith made clear his view that 'anything like a large number of executions would excite a swift revulsion of feeling here', and 'sow the seeds of lasting trouble in Ireland'. He said he had no reason to doubt that justice had been done, 'but desires that you weigh thoroughly the points I am bringing to your notice for future guidance'.[42] Although he concluded by assuring Maxwell that 'there is no intention to hamper your freedom of judgment or your initiative', this was a heavy political warning. The general was haled before the Cabinet to explain his policy, the ministers stressing once more that no woman should be executed. Once he gave them that assurance, however, he was again left to his own discretion 'subject to a general instruction that death should not be inflicted except upon ringleaders and proven murderers', and an urging that the executions should be brought to a close as soon as possible.[43]

In fact, the most doubtful cases – notably Pearse's younger brother (who as he said at his trial was no more than an aide-de-camp) – had already been despatched. Colbert, Ceannt, Mallin and Heuston, executed on the 8th, had held independent commands, and Thomas Kent (executed at Cork on the 9th) was convicted of killing a policeman. About the two last 'ringleaders', James Connolly and Seán MacDermott – eventually convicted on 9 May – there was not likely to be much doubt. Although Asquith sent a final instruction on the 10th 'that no further executions are to take place until further orders', he allowed these to go ahead. Neither was there any doubt of the impact of even this limited programme of military justice. As early as 3 May, John Redmond protested to Asquith that 'if any more executions take place in Ireland, the position will become impossible for any Constitutional Party or leader'.[44] Two days later the London *Daily Chronicle* carried a leader arguing that the executions should have stopped after 3 May. Of the four men executed on the 4th, only one (Plunkett) was a signatory of the Proclamation, and the killing was beginning to look like private vengeance.[45] 'The feeling is becoming widespread and intensely bitter', John Dillon told Maxwell on the 8th. 'It really would be difficult to exaggerate the amount of mischief the executions are doing.'

In case the C.-in-C. thought such views prejudiced, he heard a similar opinion from a very different source the same day. The Viceroy (who knew that in the public mind he would be held responsible for the policy, and nobody would believe he was 'without influence') protested that the execution of 'three comparatively unknown insurgents' meant that 'in the popular estimation nearly a hundred others are liable to the same penalty with it will be held in many cases more justification'. Although he accepted that Maxwell did 'not mean to create this impression', Wimborne felt 'bound to tell you that it exists and is capable of producing disastrous consequences'. As if aware that words were the only influence he had left, he poured them out: 'I must respectfully urge you in the most serious manner' that public opinion would not support further executions 'of any save perhaps one or two *very prominent* and deeply implicated "insurgents"'. A public statement 'of a reasoning character' by Maxwell was 'urgently needed to allay the feeling aroused by this morning's action and to define the limits of your contemplated policy'.[46]

This extraordinary intervention pointed up just how completely the civil government in Ireland had been superseded by the military. Birrell had already resigned, taking Nathan with him on 5 May. Wimborne himself resisted, since unlike the others he felt vindicated rather than condemned by the outbreak, but Asquith had decided to take out the whole Irish Executive.[47] (For one heady day, Wimborne thought he had survived, writing to Maxwell that 'I am for the present head of the Irish Executive.')[48] The result was a yawning political vacuum. The damage this might inflict was suggested in Dillon's highly charged Commons speech on 11 May. In terms seldom if ever heard in parliament, Dillon reiterated and amplified the warning he had issued to Maxwell; now less a warning than a cry of despair. 'You are washing out our whole life work in a sea of blood.' 'What is poisoning the mind of Ireland, and rapidly poisoning it, is the secrecy of these trials and the continuance of these executions.' Thousands of people in Dublin 'who ten days ago were bitterly opposed to the whole Sinn Fein movement and the rebellion, are now becoming infuriated against the Government'. Dillon asked the Prime Minister directly to stop the executions: 'this series of executions is doing more harm than any Englishman in this House can possibly fathom'. The men being executed were not guilty of murder, as the government said; they were 'insurgents who have fought a clean fight, a brave fight, however misguided'. By this time Dillon's speech had opened up an all too familiar ethnic (or as Maxwell said, racial) gulf. As the English MPs heckled him, Dillon became passionate. 'It would be a damned good thing for you if your soldiers were able to put up as good a fight as did these men in Dublin.' He was 'proud of their courage, and if you were not so dense and stupid, as some of you English people are, you could have had these men fighting for you'. What they needed was 'not a Military Service Bill', but 'to find a way to the hearts of the Irish people'.[49]

What may have struck Asquith most uncomfortably was Dillon's denunciation of military rule. 'You have swept away every trace of civil administration in the country', he alleged with perhaps pardonable exaggeration. The only guarantee of civil liberty left was 'the well-known high character of Sir John Maxwell' he said, adding sharply, 'I confess I never heard of him before in my life. I refuse, and the Irish people will refuse, to accept the well-known high character of Sir John Maxwell as the sole guarantee of their liberty.' The MPs were outraged, but Dillon went on, 'I say deliberately that in the whole of modern history, taking all the circumstances into account, there has been no rebellion or insurrection put down with so much blood and so much savagery as the recent insurrection in Ireland.'

Maxwell certainly believed that he was following the injunction (frequently repeated both by him and by the Prime Minister) to execute only the 'ringleaders' of the rebellion and those guilty of 'cold-blooded murder'. But nobody undertook to define the term 'ringleader', and the Courts Martial were given no usable definition. The evidence presented to these tribunals was, it is fair to say, slapdash. Willie Pearse, for instance, who on no plausible definition could have been called a ringleader, was convicted on the basis of the testimony of a captured officer of the Royal Inniskilling Fusiliers in the GPO that 'I know that William Pearce was an officer but do not know his rank.'[50] He was tried alongside three others, and though all four were condemned to death, only Pearse's sentence was confirmed by Maxwell. Admittedly Pearse was the only prisoner to plead guilty. But it remains hard, as it was for Wimborne, to grasp the logic of Maxwell's selection process. Immediately after confirming the sentences on Connolly and MacDermott, Maxwell sent Asquith a wire classifying all the cases under three headings: '(a) Those who signed proclamation on behalf of provisional Government and were also leaders in actual rebellion in Dublin. (b) Those who were in command of rebels actually shooting down troops, police and others. (c) Those whose offence was murder.'[51] He placed Willie Pearse in category (b), though the worst thing he could find to say about him was that he 'was associated with the Sinn Fein movement from its inception'. Also in category (b) were Daly, MacBride, Colbert, Mallin, Heuston and O'Hanrahan. Only two of these were battalion commandants, and though four battalion commanders were executed, one was not. Eamon de Valera, most famously, escaped death for reasons that are still not clear, while the sentence on O'Hanrahan was justified by nothing more than the statement that he had been 'employed at the office of the Headquarters of the Irish Volunteers', was 'one of the most active members of that body', and had been 'arrested in uniform and armed'.[52] Dozens of others would have fulfilled these criteria. (Indeed, since O'Hanrahan had been in the Jacob's garrison, he was less likely than most to have been involved in any fatal action.)

The simplest explanation, of course, is that the inconsistencies were due to the irregularity of the available evidence. As Maxwell noted, 'naturally we have to depend largely on police reports'. He had to weigh the need for solid evidence against the need for despatch. That he was not blind to the political ramifications of the military trials was clear in two particularly tetchy cases. The first was that of Eoin MacNeill. Maxwell told French on 4 May that he was 'a little perplexed what to do about this man McNeill, he is no doubt one of the most prominent in the movement'. Though Maxwell accepted that 'he did try and stop the actual rebellion taking place when it did', Maxwell evidently wanted to convict him, and reflected gloomily, 'the priests and politicians will try and save him'.[53] Many soldiers took the view that the countermanding order was a ruse to put the authorities off guard, and believed that MacNeill was ultimately responsible for the rebellion; but the absence of any direct evidence was a big problem. The steps taken to secure a conviction speak volumes about the weakness of the British system in Ireland. While the soldiers might be forgiven for their vague assumption of MacNeill's responsibility, it was more surprising that the chief intelligence officer, Major Price, was convinced of it. When MacNeill went to military headquarters to try to secure an interview with Maxwell, Price excitedly gripped his arm and declared 'I am arresting you on the charge of being a rebel.' His interrogation of MacNeill revealed a farrago of misinformation that would have been laughable had its implications not been so serious. 'Price made a number of statements', MacNeill recorded, 'designed to convey the impression that he was in possession of much inner knowledge.' The actual impression, however, 'was distinctly the contrary. In fact, in view of the open character of the Volunteer organization, the ignorance shown by the Intelligence Department was surprising.'[54]

Maxwell received political direction as early as 3 May that 'one of the leaders in particular, John McNeile [sic], an ex-professor, should not be shot without reference here'. Why he was singled out in this way is not clear, but the injunction was not necessary. There was no question of shooting MacNeill, though his case raised awkward problems: Maxwell reported after two weeks that 'the Law Officers advised me that to hold MacNeill's trial in public would have a most serious effect and would cause danger to the public safety'. As late as 23 May, his law chief was grumbling that 'the McNeill trial is taking longer than we thought, but I hope it will be finished tonight'.[55] When at last MacNeill was sentenced to life imprisonment, it was on comparatively trivial charges – eight separate charges of attempting to spread disaffection, and four of acting in a way likely to prejudice recruiting. All the same, Maxwell sent the proceedings to Asquith with the suggestion that 'we ought to make a great deal of them public'. He believed that the evidence proved that if the arms shipment had got through, MacNeill would have backed the rebellion and it would have been much more formidable.[56]

The Markievicz case raised a different set of issues. During the rebellion, as Maxwell reported, seventy-four women surrendered or were arrested. From the start, the soldiers were uncomfortable with them. Most of those who surrendered, including the emotional Countess Markievicz, were quietly spirited away in motor cars rather than being forced (or permitted) to march into detention with the men. Special prison accommodation was found for them. Maxwell fretted about 'all those silly little girls', and as soon as the capital courts martial were done with, he sent a legal officer to sort them out. William Wylie, a barrister and 2nd Lieutenant in the Trinity College OTC, who was serving as a junior Assistant Provost Marshal with the 177th Brigade during Easter week, had been co-opted by Maxwell's Deputy Advocate-General, Byrne, to conduct the prosecution of the leading rebels. The day Connolly and Ceannt ('the most dignified of any of the accused') were executed, Wylie went to interview the 'girls' in Richmond Barracks. 'I wisely got the C.-in-C. to give me a chit; the officer in charge turned out to be a major of the old and peppery kind who did his damnedest first to keep me out and second to keep the girls in.' Wylie found the process of interviewing them 'really amusing. Some of them began by being truculent and ended by being tearful. Others reversed the process.'[57]

With an effortless display of masculine superiority, he sent the great majority home, 'putting back' a few who were 'older, better educated and real believers in a free Ireland'. Maxwell reported to London on 11 May that he had released sixty-two of them with a caution, and detained eighteen 'prominent and dangerous' women, whom he had placed 'in the female portion of Mountjoy prison where they can receive suitable attention'. He proposed to deport eight of these, including Kathleen Lynn, 'B. Lorerench Mullen' (Madeleine Ffrench Mullen), Helena Molony and Winifred Carney (whose deadliest weapon had been her typewriter). But this turned out to be harder than he thought. After three weeks of negotiations with the Home Office, he decided to release another five (including Ffrench Mullen), and deport only seven. But it was made clear to him that the Prime Minister 'did not desire these deportations to be carried out'. He explained again at the end of May that 'in view of their sex I considered that it would be desirable that they should be granted their liberty, but at the same time I could not allow them to be at large in this country'.[58] On 5 June he was still waiting for arrangements to be made to receive the rest in England – Countess Plunkett was to be deported under DRR 14B to Oxford, Kathleen Lynn to Bath, and five others (Winifred Carney, Marie Perolz, Helena Molony, Breda Foley and Ellen Ryan) to Aylesbury.[59]

None of these, of course, was quite so 'prominent and dangerous' as the colourful Constance Markievicz, the only woman to be court-martialled. Like everything else about her, her trial was a sensation. Wylie, the prosecuting officer, noticed the court president, Brigadier-General Blackader 'getting out his revolver and putting it on the table beside him' as she was called in. Her theatrical spirit was catching. What followed was less edifying, at least according to the rumour that reached Elsie Mahaffy, the daughter of the Provost of Trinity College. 'All her "dash" and "go" left her' – 'she utterly broke down, cried and sobbed and tried to incite pity in General Blackadder [sic]: it was a terrible scene – the gaunt wreck of a once lovely lady.'[60] Where the rumour started we can only guess. It may have been with Wylie himself. In a private memoir written for his daughter during the Second World War, Wylie recollected that Markievicz had 'curled up completely'.

'I am only a woman, you cannot shoot a woman, you must not shoot a woman.' She never stopped moaning the whole time she was in the Court room . . . We were all slightly disgusted. She had been preaching rebellion to a lot of silly boys, death and glory, die for your country etc., and yet she was literally crawling. I won't say any more, it revolts me still.[61]

Unsurprisingly, none of this appeared in the formal record of the trial, where she was recorded as stating, 'I went out to fight for Ireland and it doesn't matter what happens to me. I did what I thought was right and I stand by it.' Some historians regard Wylie's account as a malicious fabrication – though, if so, his motive is obscure.[62]

But no matter how she had behaved, the question was whether she should share the fate of her male comrades. The soldiers took a robust view: Maxwell thought her 'bloodguilty and dangerous'; she was 'a woman who has forfeited the privileges of her sex'. Although she had 'a following who see something to admire in her', or perhaps because of that, 'we can't allow our soldiers to be shot down by such like'. French told him, 'Personally I agree with you – she ought to be shot.'[63] But for Asquith and the Cabinet this was an impossibility. From the start they reiterated their insistence that no woman should be executed, and the court martial, while finding her guilty and sentencing her to death, accordingly recommended mercy 'solely & only on account of her sex'. Maxwell commuted her sentence to penal servitude for life.

*

In the final count, Maxwell commuted all but fifteen of the ninety death sentences handed down by his courts martial (replacing them by prison sentences ranging from six months to life).[64] He strove to be just, and believed that the whole trial process had been fair. He maintained to Redmond on 12 May, 'I am giving everyone all opportunities of proving their innocence.'[65] This must be doubted. One or two capital sentences were delayed by a few hours while the police sought witnesses requested by the accused, but the speed of the trial process rested on the absence of any defence counsel. Wylie objected to this at the outset, and also urged that the trials should be held in public, but the Attorney General, James Campbell, sent him off with a flea in his ear. 'He wouldn't hear of it, said he would give them no public advertisement, that he wouldn't be satisfied unless 40 of them were shot.' Wylie declared that he 'would defend them to the best of my ability and bring out every damn thing I could in their favour'. The absence of a formal defence was normal procedure in military courts, but this was unlikely to improve the public image of the process. There was a suspicion – amply borne out by the evidence presented to the courts martial – that secrecy was imposed to cover the weakness of the cases made by the prosecution.

Interestingly, when Maxwell prepared a political dossier to explain his decisions, he included a lot of intelligence material that had not been offered in evidence to the courts. He also redrafted several times a public statement of the fundamental justification for his policy. This was that 'the gravity of the rebellion', its 'connection with German intrigue and propaganda', and the resulting 'great loss of life and destruction of property' made it 'imperative to inflict the most severe sentences on the known organizers of this detestable rising and on those commanders who took an active part in the actual fighting'. It was hoped that 'these examples will be sufficient to act as a deterrent to intriguers and to bring home to them that the murder of His Majesty's liege subjects or other acts calculated to imperil the safety of the Realm will not be tolerated'.[66] The deliberate adoption of ponderous legal language (an earlier draft read more simply, 'We hope to deter by these examples & make the intriguers realise that we will not tolerate murder of loyal subjects, or any acts against the safety of the Realm') may have indicated a certain unease.

Whether or not she feared death, Markievicz surely expected to be condemned. Pearse certainly did, and so did MacDonagh (though Wylie thought his death 'particularly unnecessary'). Indeed many, not just the leaders, feared the worst. As they marched to Richmond Barracks the surrendered rebels were treated to lurid warnings about the digging of mass graves. But some seemed oddly optimistic. Joseph Plunkett himself wrote to Grace Gifford, 'I have no notion what they intend to do with me, but I have heard a rumour that I am to be sent to England.' No doubt Plunkett was trying to reassure his fiancée, though in these extreme circumstances deception would hardly have been kind. He may well have been genuinely uncertain; as he remarked to her, 'We have not had one word of news from outside since Monday 24th April, except wild rumour.' His verbal style was certainly relaxed; he went on conversationally, 'Listen, if I live it might be possible to get the Church to marry us by proxy – there is such a thing but it is very difficult.' He ended 'I am very happy.' The outcome of this was to provide the rebellion with its great romantic icon, the wedding of Plunkett and Gifford in the chapel at Kilmainham gaol a few hours before his execution. This would make her a nationalist heroine, with her own 'instant traditional' style ballad ('God bless thee, Grace Plunkett, thy faithful devotion / Has won the great heart of a Nation to thee . . .').[67]

Grace had just converted to Catholicism: she claimed to be uninterested in politics – though she had been present at the foundation of the Inghinidhe, she was not an active member of Cumann na mBan – and it was their shared religious enthusiasm that brought her and Plunkett together. Their relationship had a chummy rather than romantic feel. In the week before the rebellion, she did not visit his house. On Easter Saturday, the day before they were due to be married (alongside Plunkett's sister Philomena), she heard nothing from him about the impending jolt to their plans. On Sunday she did not see or apparently hear from him. Though the intention was that 'I was to go out with them in the Rising, I did not.' Thirty-three years on, she could not recall why. During Easter week she had two notes from him, one from the GPO, the last from 'somewhere in Moore Street'. He does not seem to have tried to dissuade her from going to the GPO, and she does not seem to have thought of trying to do so. When she eventually felt drawn (by a psychic force) to visit him in Kilmainham, she was 'never left alone with him – even after the marriage ceremony' (though the guards thoughtfully removed his handcuffs while he was in the prison chapel). She rejected the widely reported tale that they had been left together 'for a few hours'.[68] When she returned on the evening before his execution, 'a man stood there with his watch in his hand, and said "Ten minutes"'. To her annoyance, 'Min Ryan and Father Brown were allowed to stay a long time with Sean MacDermott' that evening. But she seems, on her account, to have left without making a fuss.[69] According to one of the military guards, she was smiling.

James Connolly's situation was different from the rest: seriously but not fatally wounded, he posed an awkward question for the authorities. Should they wait until he was well enough to be shot? Maxwell avoided such grim irony by his absolute insistence that he be tried. When Wylie demurred, Maxwell said 'The court can be convened in the hospital.'[70] Absurdly enough, Connolly was found 'not guilty' on one of the two charges brought – 'attempting to cause disaffection among the civilian population'. There was no political consultation. It later transpired that 'nothing was known in London' of Connolly's wounded condition until a question was asked in parliament. His execution 'was a purely local affair'.[71] But the impact of the ghastly execution procedure, in which Connolly had to be propped up in a chair in order to be shot, was more than local, and it was not short-lived. The politicians' lack of interest in Connolly's fate, in sharp contrast with the concern for MacNeill, raises interesting questions about their grasp of the situation.

By the time Asquith arrived in Ireland on 12 May, serious political damage had already been done. And while executions could be suspended, other damaging proceedings would linger on. Two key events began to be seen as defining the nature of the military regime. Dillon launched his 11 May tirade by pointing out that the Prime Minister 'never heard anything about' the shooting of Frank Sheehy-Skeffington until the end of the first week of May.

A more lurid light on military law in Ireland could not possibly be imagined than that a man is to be shot in Portobello Barracks – it must have been

known to at least 300 or 400 military men, the whole city of Dublin knew it
... and the military authorities turn round and say they knew nothing whatever about it until the 6th of May.

Dillon charged that nothing would ever have come out 'if Skeffington
had not been one of the leading citizens in Dublin'; Dubliners could
hardly be blamed for believing that 'dozens of other men have been
summarily shot in the barracks'. These 'horrible rumours' were 'doing
untold and indescribable mischief'.[72]

The killing of Sheehy-Skeffington raised two grave issues. One was
the behaviour of Bowen-Colthurst, which seemed to confirm the worst
fears about how martial law powers could be abused by local military
officers. (Maxwell, demonstrating the 'insight into racial characteristics' that had recommended him to Kitchener, said in mitigation that
Colthurst was 'a hot-headed Irishman'.) The other was the tardy
response of the higher military authorities, which looked suspiciously
like a cover-up. The authorities in turn faced two issues. The first was
what judicial procedure to apply. Though few soldiers (apart from the
eccentric Sir Francis Vane, whose reward was a sudden lack of military employment) showed much remorse for Skeffington's death, none
questioned the illegality of Colthurst's action.[73] The problem was that,
in the opinion of the Judge Advocate General's office, even if he was
on active service, he could not be tried by a military court for a criminal offence committed in the UK. On 19 May, two days after this
opinion was reached, a high-powered legal conference was convened
in London by the Lord Chief Justice, with the Solicitor-General and
the Director of Public Prosecutions present as well as the Irish
Attorney-General and Maxwell's legal chief, Brigadier Byrne. They
decided that a new DOR regulation should be drafted to permit civil
offences to be tried by court martial. While it was being drafted, however, Tim Healy started another alarm by drawing the government's
attention to Section 162 of the Army Act, 'from which we were somewhat concerned to learn', as the DPP told Byrne, 'that a trial by court
martial would not be a bar to a second trial in a Civil Court'. Since
the Law Officers said that to leave 'such a contingency even remotely
possible' was 'not to be thought of', the draft had to be adjusted again
to obviate this.[74] It was sent to Dublin for promulgation on 22 May.

Unfortunately, when the Lords Justices of Appeal in Ireland saw it, they were unimpressed. They could 'find nothing to authorise the King to interfere with the trial of any offence, except an offence against the Regulations', nor could they find any authority to make a regulation depriving the civil courts of their power to deal with all offenders against the criminal law.' Murder was very definitely a criminal offence. As James Campbell, the Irish Attorney-General, pointed out, this would mean that the new regulation was *ultra vires* 'in so far as it seeks to exclude the jurisdiction of the civil courts in cases of persons subject to Military Law who are to be tried for offences *other than* offences against the Regulations'. Things looked bad. But he concluded more encouragingly after 'the fullest consideration' that the Regulation was not really necessary after all 'for the Skeffington trial and similar cases'. They could be tried under the existing provisions of the Army Act either by general court martial or field general court martial.[75] In effect, Campbell simply reversed the original Judge Advocate's opinion. Then the English Law officers came to the same conclusion, though by a significantly different route, holding that 'the main object of the regulation is to prevent the jeopardy which would be caused to the public peace and safety by a civil trial'. The Irish Law Officers' opinion that 'the delay, excitement and popular agitation which would result from a civil trial of this case would possibly lead to disturbance' was decisive.[76]

Now at last the court martial could go ahead; but this was just the beginning of the problem.[77] Asquith had insisted from the start that because of 'the exceptional character of the Skeffington case, the interest and anxiety which it excites in Parliament and elsewhere', the 'Court Martial proceedings should be open to the public and press'.[78] But his hope that this would 'make clear that it was adequately and impartially dealt with' was not borne out. Hanna Sheehy-Skeffington's solicitor, Henry Lemass, told John Dillon that the court martial was unacceptable: they were permitted to attend it, but not intervene. 'We fear this Court-Martial may be construed as fulfilment of the Prime Minister's promise to hold a full public inquiry.' At best it might serve as a preliminary hearing, 'enabling us to elucidate what happened after the arrest of Mr Skeffington, as to which we are absolutely in the dark'.[79] After the court martial found Colthurst guilty but insane,

Lemass bombarded Asquith and Maxwell with complaints about the inadequate evidence presented to it.[80] Asquith grasped the damaging potential of the whole issue, and a Royal Commission of Inquiry was set up in August, chaired by Sir John Simon.

This concluded that the problem lay in the misunderstanding of martial law. Simon reiterated that the proclamation of martial law did not 'in itself confer upon officers or soldiers any new powers'. Yet Colthurst had clearly thought it did, and he was not alone; tellingly, 'the young officer who was left at Portobello Bridge while Captain Bowen-Colthurst went forward' (to attack Alderman Kelly's shop) had seen 'nothing "strange" in the order that he was to shoot Mr Sheehy-Skeffington in the event of anything happening' to Bowen-Colthurst's party. Simon gravely insisted that 'the shooting of unarmed and unresisting civilians without trial' was murder, whether martial law had been proclaimed or not.[81] Predictably enough, Hanna Sheehy-Skeffington was unimpressed by what was 'largely a white-washing report'. Although it was 'valuable for its strictures on mar-tial law', she thought, 'it does not fasten the blame on the real culprits, the military authorities'.[82] Certainly the authorities would have been relieved by Simon's acceptance that Major Rosborough was not at fault in failing to prevent the murders, or in failing to place Bowen-Colthurst under arrest afterwards. This aspect of the case had been their primary concern.[83]

The formidable Mrs Skeffington remained a thorn in the side of the authorities, pursuing her demand for the two large trunks, attaché cases and portfolios (containing Sheehy-Skeffington's papers), and the stock of household linen that Bowen-Colthurst had removed in his armed raid on her house in Ranelagh on Friday evening. She raised the question of the financial value of her husband's manuscripts, and insisted to Dillon that the whole issue must continue to be pursued. 'It was taken for granted by everyone that there would be a debate in Parliament in connexion with the infamies of Martial Law as revealed in the Report.'[84] Even without this, the memory of the Portobello killings remained a potent source of anti-government feeling. Yet the army may have done worse things still in Easter week. Whether or not Bowen-Colthurst's plea of insanity was accepted, the authorities could plausibly portray him as a rogue individual. The allegation that several civilians had been summarily killed in North King Street suggested a much wider indiscipline, perhaps even a deliberate policy of exemplary violence.

The charge that thirteen innocent civilians had been shot out of hand by troops of the 2/6th South Staffordshire regiment during the fighting in North King Street was addressed by Maxwell in his first full report on the rebellion, on 26 May.

No doubt in districts where the fighting was fiercest, parties of men under the great provocation of being shot at from front and rear, seeing their comrades fall from the fire of snipers, burst into suspected houses and killed such male members as were found.

It was 'perfectly possible' that some were innocent, but, he maintained, they could have left their houses had they so wished; and 'the number of such incidents that have been brought to notice is happily few'.[85] Allegations were being 'most carefully enquired into', but Maxwell held that 'under the circumstances the troops as a whole behaved with the greatest restraint'. The defensive tone was unmistakable; and Maxwell privately told Kitchener that there were 'one or two other cases' to be looked into.[86] French did his best to reassure Maxwell that '"regrettable incidents" such as those you refer to are absolutely unavoidable in such a business as this', and he agreed that 'the only wonder is there have been so few of them'. 'You must not think too much about what goes on in Parliament', French added with feeling; 'We soldiers have always to put up with that.'[87]

The military court of inquiry into the North King Street killings opened in late May, a week or so before the Colthurst trial. But considerably less care and resources were lavished on these proceedings, and it soon became clear that no steps had been taken to prevent military witnesses from being posted out of Ireland in the interim. Within these limits, there seems no reason to doubt that the courts – presided over by the commander of the 177th Brigade, Colonel Maconchy – were conducted with reasonable care.[88] But Maconchy was naturally loyal to his subordinates; he thought 'the South Staffords a quiet and very respectable set of men' and his conclusion, that no direct responsibility for any of the deaths could be apportioned to any specific soldier, did not look entirely convincing.[89]

Maxwell's verdict was predictably more pugnacious: in the case of the two men killed at No. 177, for instance, he concluded that 'the responsibility for their death rests with those resisting His Majesty's troops in the execution of their duty'. In the case of the four men killed at No. 27, he impatiently noted that 'the women concerned have been given every opportunity of identifying the men they allege were last seen with these four men. They cannot do so.' He concluded that he could 'obtain no evidence that soldiers killed these four men', and 'no evidence as to who buried them in the yard'.[90] Surprisingly, Asquith, himself a lawyer, told the House of Commons in July that he 'had himself read the evidence taken by the courts of inquiry, and was of opinion that further enquiry would not be likely to lead to any different result'.

We now know that the Prime Minister had significantly different advice on the question of responsibility – an evaluation that went to the heart of the military regime in Ireland. Sir Edward Troup, the senior Home Office civil servant and a veteran of many disputes about military aid to the civil power, prepared a careful assessment of the military inquiry proceedings for the Prime Minister's benefit. Although he took the view that the majority of verdicts could be sustained (usually because of the lack of reliable evidence of any kind), in one case – that of James Moore – there was no doubt that 'if the evidence were published there would be a demand that [Sergeant Floods] should be tried for murder'. In other cases it seemed 'that the soldiers did not accurately distinguish between refusing to make prisoners and shooting immediately prisoners they had made'. There was no evidence that the soldiers were 'exasperated or reckless', rather the problem was that they 'had orders not to take any prisoners, which they took to mean that they were to shoot anyone whom they believed to be an active rebel'. 'The root of the mischief', Troup concluded, was this order: in itself it may have been justifiable, but 'it should have been made clear that it did not mean that an unarmed rebel might be shot after he had been taken prisoner: still less did it mean that a person taken on mere suspicion could be shot without trial'. His advice was unequivocal: it would be 'undesirable' to publish the evidence. Though it had been 'fairly and carefully' taken, 'there are many points that could be used for the purpose of hostile propaganda, and I have no doubt its publication would be followed by a strong demand for a further inquiry'. And 'nothing but harm' could come of this.[91]

The issue of publication of the capital court-martial proceedings would smoulder on into 1917. Asquith himself promised in parliament that they would be published, and in mid-November 1916 the government repeated that arrangements were being made to do this. But when the military legal authorities were asked to provide the copies, they stalled.[92] The Adjutant General, Macready, suggested that since the lives of witnesses would be in jeopardy if their names were made public, 'the whole matter is one for decision by the cabinet'. Asquith clearly still felt that his pledges were 'too definite to get out of', but thought that the names of witnesses at risk could be omitted from the published records.[93] But Macready had unerringly touched a sensitive nerve. After Lloyd George replaced Asquith as prime minister, the government responded to repeated parliamentary questions by saying that the whole issue was 'a question of policy'. The military legal authorities stepped up the pressure to maintain secrecy. They argued that publication would imply that Maxwell had been wrong to hold the trials in camera, and would certainly betray the understanding on which witnesses had testified, even if it did not actually endanger their lives.[94]

The War Office also admitted that some of the evidence was 'extremely thin', while other parts would not play well in public (in Ceannt's case, for instance, the record showed that one of the witnesses summoned – MacDonagh – was 'not available as he was shot that morning').[95] General Macready then raised the stakes even higher. 'The inevitable result of publication' would be that nationalists would 'urge that the sole reason for trial in camera was that the authorities intended to execute certain of the Sinn Feiners whether there was evidence against them or not'. In his 'humble judgement', this argument 'would be extremely difficult to meet successfully'. And Macready, who would have been military governor of Ulster if the March 1914 crisis had broken (and who would later direct the attempt to suppress the IRA campaign in 1920–21), added a still more ominous warning. Such publicity would make any 'successful and hasty suppression of rebellion' in the future much more difficult, and indeed 'I doubt that any general officer would consent to undertake the repression of rebellion without the assurance that in all cases where he might deem it necessary to administer justice in secrecy that such secrecy should be maintained.'[96]

The political vacuum of May 1915 was also to linger on, with baleful consequences. After Birrell and Nathan resigned, followed more reluctantly by Wimborne, the Irish Executive was paralysed. 'In my humble judgment', Maxwell told French (with doubtless the same humility as Macready), 'the Government of Ireland is rotten from A to Z.' Its mainstay, the RIC, was 'a farce – a magnificent body of men certainly, but singularly out of sympathy with the people'. There was 'too much reporting & nothing happening, because no one has authority to act on even trivial things'.[97] Asquith sprang his visit to Ireland on the night of 11–12 May in part because he could not find anyone to succeed Birrell as Chief Secretary. He had immediately cast about among his Liberal colleagues such as Montagu and Runciman, none of whom wanted the job. (Montagu pleaded 'his own Jewish race, his lack of physical courage and interest in the Irish race'.)[98] Simon was unavailable. Asquith fought shy of Unionist pressure to install Walter Long, a former Chief Secretary and a persistent influence on Unionist thinking about Ireland. He had toyed with a return to the nineteenth-century pattern by installing Lord Crewe as Viceroy with a Cabinet seat and 'some underling' as Chief Secretary, but Redmond was against it. He sent over a new Under-Secretary, Sir Robert Chalmers, to get a grip of the administration.

But he was 'in despair for a Chief Secretary'.[99] He decided to take the job on himself for the time being, and the visit to Ireland gave substance to this. But the problem was not just the limited pool of political talent. Asquith agreed that the whole structure of the Irish government was rotten. The Viceroyalty had 'become a costly and futile anachronism', and he had 'come very clearly to the conclusion that no successor ought to be appointed' to Wimborne. The 'fiction of the Chief Secretaryship', another key part of the problem, would also 'disappear'. 'There must', Asquith insisted on 21 May, 'be a single Minister controlling and responsible for Irish administration.'[100] Such reconstruction needed time, however, and he also launched the classic mechanism for buying it, a Royal Commission of Inquiry. Some inquiry into the causes of the rebellion was of course inevitable, but the Royal Commission chaired by Lord Hardinge that began its hearings on 18 May (while Asquith was still in Dublin) embraced a comprehensive review of the administrative system. 'Such deep ignorance I never heard as they displayed', noted an observer who attended one of the hearings in the Shelbourne Hotel.[101] The Commission was clearly taken aback by the extensive evidence of the Irish government's supine tolerance of the armed militias. Its report, published on 26 June, held that 'the main cause of the rebellion' was that for several years Ireland 'had been administered on the principle that it was safer and more expedient to leave the law in abeyance if collision with any faction of the Irish people could thereby be avoided'. While it avoided direct criticism of the police, it sharply identified the weakness of the intelligence system. Its judgement on the 'Irish system of government' as a whole mirrored the Prime Minister's: it was 'anomalous in quiet times, and almost unworkable in times of crisis'.[102] Yet immediately after the commission's report, Asquith restored the old system. At the end of June he finally appointed a new Chief Secretary, Henry Duke, a Unionist fellow-lawyer; and next month he allowed Wimborne to return as Viceroy. Futility and fiction were thus both restored. Maybe this was intended as a caretaker regime, but it is hard to avoid the conclusion that he was too tired, or too distracted by the war, to carry through his intention of serious reform.

For three months, therefore, Maxwell remained – or appeared – the effective ruler of Ireland. At the time, Asquith seems to have seen little wrong with this situation. 'On the whole – except the Skeffington case – there have been fewer bad blunders than one might have expected with the soldiery for a whole week in exclusive charge', he noted quite cheerfully. During his visit he confined his intervention to the settlement of compensation claims and the demand to comb out the innocent prisoners more energetically. Compensation was of course a major political question. The former Treasury Secretary, Sir Robert Chalmers, took a robust view of the issue – 'personally I would not concede anything whatever' – but seems to have found Asquith's ruling in favour of *ex gratia* grants acceptable. On 16 May the government accepted 'the same liability as would have fallen on insurance companies if the risk had been covered by policies in force at the time of the recent disturbances'. (Looting might be 'deemed to be burning', but 'no consequential damages of any kind' would be covered.) Chalmers was alarmed, however, when Herbert Samuel followed Asquith to Dublin and seemed to be more flexible than the prime minister. (Chalmers gratuitously opined that 'Jews are at a discount here and 'Erb will be viewed with suspicion among the warm-hearted Irishry' – adding 'I hope no more Cabinet ministers are en route.') Privately he warned that 'this is a big thing and the C of Ex [Chancellor of the Exchequer] may be let in for millions beyond what has been conceded, if the PM is not firm in upholding what he approved.'[103] We may note that one small segment of this threatening mountain was a claim by the Norwich Union Insurance Society for the £500 they had paid out on Frank Sheehy-Skeffington's life policy.[104]

Asquith tackled the issue of the detainees by his visit to Richmond Barracks. In a rather odd public relations exercise (exasperated Unionists like Lord Midleton were much less polite about it) he fraternized amiably with the suspected rebels, and issued a bizarre instruction that they should be given the best food possible, 'regardless of expense'. As a result they got a better diet than the troops guarding them. (This provoked 'some grumbling' among the Sherwood Foresters.)[105] One of the prisoners cheerfully wrote that they were 'better off than at the Gresham [Hotel]', adding 'I have never spent a more enjoyable holiday in my life.' Another fondly recalled 'eggs and ham for breakfast, tins of jam, genuine butter and porridge (if anyone liked it). For dinner roast beef or perhaps mutton and plenty of vegetables (far more than we could eat), more bread, jam, butter and tea.' Carrying their meals from the cookhouse to their quarters they were 'besieged by hungry soldiers begging hunks of cheese or bread or anything that could be conveniently handled'.[106] Asquith evidently enjoyed his time in Ireland; he was pleasantly surprised to find little if any hostility. 'I myself went one day partly on foot through a considerable crowd, and was received . . . with remarkable warmth.'[107] He allowed himself to think that a rosier future could be secured by more frequent royal visits to Ireland. The viceroys, even with the best of intentions, had been 'incapable of evoking and stimulating the latent sense of personal loyalty and devotion which is inherent in the Irish temper and character'. Indeed, he immediately went to see the king and got him to agree 'to arrange for an annual residence of himself, the Queen, and the Court in Ireland'.

Such a sanguine view would very soon come to look implausible. Optimism was waning even in the week after Asquith returned to England. Though Maxwell thought that the PM's visit 'has done a lot of good', he added that 'things would have got very nearly back to normal' – if only 'Dillon had not made that unfortunate speech'.[108] Ministers started to worry about the situation in the USA, where criticism of the army's repressive methods was sharper than in Ireland itself. Asquith suggested that Maxwell give an interview to an American journalist explaining his policy. (The practised Maurice Bonham-Carter, the PM's private secretary, explained to the general that the 'interview' was 'almost a matter of form 10 minutes or a quarter of an hour just to give the journalist some slight acquaintance with his subject'. The 'substance of what is wished to appear' would take the form of a written statement 'which he will translate into his own words'.)[109] Maxwell duly explained that the courts martial had been 'absolutely fair', and the officers acting as judges 'in all cases inclined to leniency'. If any innocent people had been arrested, this was because 'suppressing a rebellion must be quick. The greater the delay, the greater the loss of life and property.' The army had done its duty, and deserved praise rather than blame. Even before the interview could be published, however, the War Office was beginning to feel uneasy. 'From secret sources', wrote Colonel Brade on 8 June, 'we are receiving much evidence to shew that there is a strong public opinion against our methods of handling the Irish rebellion.' This was fostered by 'our own silence as to the actual facts, coupled with the publication of the proceedings of the Court Martial on Sheehy Skeffington'. Brade worried that the language of the official despatches so far 'looks as though we were glossing over a bad record'.[110]

11

Transformation

*The greatest result of the Rising is the complete and amazing
revival of Irish nationality. We have been asleep . . . now we
have awakened to the knowledge that we really are a separate
nation.*

   'Moira Regan's Story', *New York Times*, September 1916

*The reaction in popular feeling upon the repression of the
rebellion has altered the relations of the extremists to the general population.*

   H. E. Duke, Chief Secretary for Ireland, September 1916

> *I write it out in a verse –*
> *MacDonagh and MacBride*
> *And Connolly and Pearse*
> *Now and in time to be,*
> *. . .*
> *Are changed, changed utterly . . .*
>   W. B. Yeats, 'Easter, 1916'

Although General Maxwell has not received a good press, he cannot
be held entirely responsible for British policy. Nor can he be seen as a
mere unthinking soldier. While it may be strictly true that he was 'a
junior general of no great reputation', as one historian says, he was
highly regarded by Kitchener, so 1916 was a double blow to his career.
The Irish imbroglio, together with Kitchener's death, shrank Maxwell's
prospects. Until then he was reputed an extremely competent

commander, something of a wit, and a passable Egyptologist. William Wylie, a legal high-flyer who was 'cross examined for an hour or so' by Maxwell after dinner every night while the courts martial were in progress, thought him 'a clever man, broadminded and open to argument'. He retained a vivid memory of him, 'leaning forward over the table slinging questions, like a boxer slinging left and right hooks'.[1] Maxwell's jutting presence (his slab of a nose had earned him the nickname 'Conky') can still be felt in the heavy-inked, muscular penmanship of his correspondence.

Two letters he wrote in mid-May give a sense of his thinking. Replying to one of those who urged him to use clemency, he asked: 'When Dublin is still smouldering and the blood of the victims of this mad rebellion is hardly dry is this the moment for clemency to win the rank and file?'[2] For him, the question was plainly rhetorical. Any thought of treating the rebels as soldiers who had fought a 'clean fight' was ruled out by the belief that they had killed policemen, soldiers and civilians 'in cold blood'.[3] (There was, in fact, a widespread allegation that they had 'fought dirty', not only using dumdum bullets but even using their hostages as human shields – 'apt pupils of Germany'.)[4] Maxwell was concerned with the guilt or innocence of the ordinary Volunteers, not with the possible political effect of punishing them. He was, certainly, not entirely blind to the latter. Shortly afterwards, when Mrs Pearse asked that the bodies of her sons be released for burial, Maxwell entered a clear-eyed objection. 'Irish sentimentality will turn these graves into martyrs' shrines'; annual processions would be made to them, 'which will cause constant irritation in this country'.[5]

In any case, as he curtly added, 'the Prime Minister should know that the bodies of all the executed rebels are buried in quicklime, without coffins, in the Arbour Hill Prison grounds'.[6] Did he think that this would prevent them from being turned into martyrs? Here, perhaps, we may see the limits of his 'insight into racial characteristics' that Kitchener prized. When public opinion began to bridle, he was puzzled. As early as mid-May, the RIC was reporting 'a significant sign in a sudden unfriendliness or even hostility towards the police' in places throughout Ireland; throughout Leinster 'popular sympathy for the rebels is growing', while the 'labouring and shop-boy class' of Dublin were showing 'sullenness'. In Munster, too, 'sympathy among all Nationalists is becoming intensified in favour of the rebels arrested or sentenced'.[7] Early in June Maxwell alerted Asquith to

a growing disposition to demonstrate on every possible occasion in favour of Sinn Feinism or Republicanism. At masses for the repose of the souls of executed rebels, at the arrival or departure of released or deported suspects, on their return to their native towns, are [sic] all seized upon to demonstrate.

Sinn Féin badges were being more frequently and openly worn. These might be 'little things in themselves but if permitted will shortly embarrass the police'. He was particularly bothered by 'the extremist ladies' who, with the priests, were 'difficult to handle'.[8] Next week he saw an even more alarming symptom – a demonstration by the congregations of several churches on both quays of the Liffey, where requiem masses had been said for the rebel leaders. They 'joined up spontaneously and marched in procession waving small Irish Republic flags', past the Castle and Trinity College. 'It appears they "booed" at officers and soldiers', he noted, adding 'we cannot allow these things to go on.'[9] He showed a typically English exasperation in telling Asquith's private secretary, 'the Irish are impossible people . . . even if they were to get Home Rule there will always be a large number "agin the government" whatever it may be'.[10]

But if he was beginning to grasp the scale of the problem, he was reluctant to attribute it to his policies. In mid-June he drew up a much more systematic report on the situation, starting from a history of 'what is now known as Sinn Feinism' and the paralysis of the authorities before the rebellion. He maintained that 'the first results of the punishments were good'. The 'majority of the people' had 'recognized that these were not excessive and were just'. But then 'a revulsion of feeling had set in – one of sympathy for the rebels'. Why? He blamed not his policies, but 'misrepresentation' of them. His list of those responsible for this – politicians, the press, priests – would be familiar to many a soldier. But why they had been so successful in suggesting that 'the leaders were murdered or executed in cold blood without trial, that people have been deported who took no part in the Rebellion, that the military have been harsh, unjust and oppressive etc.', he seems to have been at a loss to understand. He was baffled by the public's lack of 'sympathy for the civilians, police or soldiers who were murdered or killed in the Rebellion'.[11] He was also mystified by his own negative image. His status as military governor was particularly vexatious. 'A grievance is manufactured because martial law has been declared. All public bodies spend their time in passing resolutions protesting against it.' This was due to 'confusion of thought', with people thinking that the Defence of the Realm Regulations were the same as martial law. 'The fact remains that no one in Ireland has been hurt by martial law, because it has not been enforced.'[12]

This phantom grievance spoke volumes about the British response to the rebellion. Asquith himself had clearly seen as early as 19 May that, since there was 'no single case in which it has been or is likely to be necessary to resort to what is called "Martial Law" . . . there is no adequate ground for its continuance'.[13] Any lawyer brought up in the English legal tradition would have said the same. And yet a week later Asquith's government proceeded to extend its application indefinitely. Asquith told the House of Commons that it was 'a precautionary measure', and none of his fellow lawyers there disputed either the legality or the political wisdom of this. The real motive was perhaps revealed by the Irish Law Officers' opinion that the extension 'could be done without any risk of serious complaint'. Martial law was not necessary, they agreed, because of the proclamation suspending the right to civil trial. 'But undoubtedly the average citizen has an extraordinary belief in the magic term "Martial Law"', and its continuance would 'bring home to loyal and law abiding people a great sense of security and safety', while 'the very indefinite knowledge of its powers spreads terror amongst the disaffected'.[14] So this was to be conscious state terrorism, a dramatic divergence from the anti-militarism that had been so persistent a feature of English political culture. It would have been a very odd reading of English history indeed that could have portrayed martial law as having some magical charm; the 1916 regime testified to the dislocating double impact of world war and rebellion.

Rather more familiar was the wilfully crude division of the people into 'loyal' and 'disaffected', ignoring the majority to whom martial law might be neither encouraging nor terrifying, but merely irritating or offensive. The government deliberately risked incurring all the odium of martial law without getting any of the benefits it might provide in terms of rapid, decisive action. When Maxwell tried to head off the complaints of the Tipperary Nationalist MPs about martial law by pointing out that 'nothing had as yet been done under it', he found that 'that is what seems to excite them, and made them state that by having it hanging over their heads we were creating Sinn Feiners!!'[15] The double exclamation marks vividly attest his bafflement. To Walter Long he grumbled, 'Apparently you and other Cabinet Ministers think I have some definite powers!' But that was a 'wrong conception': 'I am not Military Governor of Ireland, though some seem to think I am, so I have no authority to interfere with the machinery of civil government.' He had hoped that the Prime Minister would make some reference to his powers in his statement to the House of Commons, but he did not. 'An idea is prevalent that I have been entrusted with greater powers than is the case', he told Asquith on 17 July. 'I am now of the opinion that my position must be regularized.'[16] It never was. Though the nominal 'martial law' regime would persist into the autumn, Asquith gradually distanced himself from it.

The regime had its supporters. In mid-May over 700 businessmen in Dublin and other cities petitioned the Prime Minister against 'any interference in the discretion of the Commander-in-Chief during the operation of Martial Law'.[17] The *Irish Times* notoriously gave voice to a certain strain of Unionist enthusiasm, insisting on 1 May that 'the surgeon's knife has been put to the corruption in the body of Ireland, and its course must not be stayed until the whole malignant growth has been removed'. A week later it scoffed that 'much nonsense is likely to be written in newspapers and talked in Parliament about the restrictions of Martial Law in Ireland. The fact is Martial Law has come as a blessing to us all.' For the first time in many months Dublin was 'enjoying real security of life and property'.[18] But a dangerous sign of the political damage it might be doing came during the week the Prime Minister was in Ireland. Though Maxwell worried about the priests, most of them were at this stage very cautious in taking an attitude to the rebellion. But two of the exceptions, Fr Thomas Wall of Drumcollogher and Fr Michael Hayes of Newcastlewest in County Limerick, led the general into a jarring confrontation. He told their bishop that they were 'a dangerous menace to the peace and safety of the Realm', and invited him to remove them from their parishes. If he thought that this was a diplomatic way of avoiding an open conflict with the clergy, he was spectacularly wrong. The bishop was Edward O'Dwyer, whose response Maxwell might well have predicted if he had studied recent history.

Bishop O'Dwyer first agreed to conduct an inquiry, asking Maxwell to provide evidence against the two priests. But it transpired that the key piece of evidence against Fr Wall was that on 14 November 1915 he had read out O'Dwyer's own letter about the Irish emigrants in Liverpool.[19] The bishop considered his response for five days and then, on 17 May, he let rip. Describing the two suspects as 'excellent priests, who hold strong national views', but had not 'violated any law, civil or ecclesiastical', he drew a contrasting image of Maxwell himself – a 'military dictator', whose proceedings were 'wantonly cruel and oppressive'. He contrasted the treatment of the Jameson raiders in South Africa ('if ever men deserved the supreme punishment it was they') with that of the rebels. The British had interceded to save the lives of the African 'buccaneers', but 'You took great care that no plea of mercy should interpose on behalf of the poor fellows who surrendered to you in Dublin. The first information we got of their fate was the announcement that they had been shot in cold blood.' O'Dwyer then turned his fire on 'the deporting of hundreds and even thousands of poor fellows without a trial of any kind', which he called 'an abuse of power as fatuous as it is arbitrary'. His verdict was damning: 'your regime has been one of the worst and blackest chapters in the history of the misgovernment of the country'.[20] The bishop's judgement that the executions had 'outraged the conscience of the country' was not intended to remain private, and the letter was quickly leaked and published as a pamphlet.

It has been suggested that Maxwell took O'Dwyer on deliberately, in an effort to bring the Hierarchy into line on the guilt of the rebels. If so, this was one of the most serious of his miscalculations. O'Dwyer was not the first bishop to express reservations about Maxwell's policy – on Sunday 14 May both Bishop Hoare of Ardagh and Clonmacnoise and Bishop Fogarty of Killaloe had preached against 'vengeance'[21] – but this confrontation cemented his influence with the younger clergy and accelerated a shift in public opinion that was already under way. It was a shift that would have epochal consequences. Its exact course is not easy to chart, however. 'The consensus among historians', it has been suggested, 'is that an initially hostile public opinion was transformed by the executions into retrospective support for, and romanticisation of, the rebels.'[22] This exaggeration had the attraction, for some, of suggesting that both the rebellion and the British reaction were mistaken. The evidence for it stemmed in part from a tendency (led by Unionists, but colluded in by some rebels themselves) to play up the hostility shown towards the deportees on their march across Dublin to the cattle boats that conveyed them from the North Wall to Holyhead. There was undoubtedly some display of open anger, but there was also plenty of evidence of sympathy. The truth is that there was never a general condemnation of the rebellion. James Stephens framed his verdict in carefully negative terms: 'the country was not with it.'[23] That was not to say the country was against it. Like a number of other observers, the Canadian journalist Fred McKenzie saw a marked division on class lines. 'In the better parts of the city', there had been open and strong sympathy with the troops, 'but what I myself saw in the poorer districts . . . rather indicated that there was a vast amount of sympathy with the rebels, particularly after they were defeated'. The fundamental cause of sympathy, in his view, was disarmingly direct: one woman who was cheering the rebel prisoners told him, 'Shure and aren't they our own flesh and blood?' McKenzie's conclusion was equally succinct. 'I for one am strongly convinced that the British Government would have been well advised to exercise much greater leniency towards the rebel leaders.'[24]

Sensitive Unionists, like the journalist Warre B. Wells, grasped the problem immediately. In a kind of public letter to the English people (like nationalists, he knew who the 'British' really were), he tried to show how Maxwell's policy looked to ordinary Irish people:

I am not asking you to regard the executions of the rebel leaders, the sentences of penal servitude, the deportations, announced baldly day after day without publication of the evidence which justified the infliction of the capital penalty, from behind the closed doors of Field Courts-Martial, from the point of view of their justice, or even of their expediency. I am simply inviting you to endeavour to understand their effect on that Irish public which read of them 'with something of the feeling of helpless rage with which one would watch a stream of blood dripping from under a closed door'.[25]

He thought that the government had completely misjudged the public relations side of its response. At the start, presumably to reassure British and Allied opinion, it 'made no attempt to explain the real gravity of the Rebellion, but inspired the English press to treat it merely as a sort of street riot on an extensive scale'. (Wells undoubtedly had direct experience of this spin-doctoring, as did a number of other journalists.) But this 'inevitably threw into disproportionately high relief' the punishments eventually imposed. The government might, he suggested, have mitigated the effect of this by publishing all the evidence, but it chose not to do so.[26] (The loyal Wells almost certainly had no idea how little formal evidence the government had.) Another thoughtful Anglo-Irishman, Æ, emphasized the damage done by persisting in repressive action. 'You see it is not the shooting of 50 or 1000 people moves public opinion, but the treatment of one person isolated & made public.' The government ought not, he thought, 'to leave such matters in the hands of policemen like Price' (who had, 'for an intelligence officer', given 'the most ludicrous evidence' to the Royal Commission).[27] And the recently converted Grace Plunkett, who seems to have accepted her new husband's execution stoically enough, fiercely instructed Asquith on the impact of the sentences (of ten years each) imposed on Count Plunkett's other two sons: they had created 'bitterness among *all* Catholics that is fast becoming dangerous'.[28]

There is ample testimony to the impact of the executions; and to the magnification of that impact by the slow-drip sequence of the secret trials and dawn fusillades (the irony being that it was precisely British legalism that forbade trying them by 'drumhead court martial', or simply shooting them without trial). Whether opinion was 'transformed' from hostility to sympathy – the most common view – or, as has recently been suggested, 'crystallised' (meaning that a latent sympathy was solidified), the available evidence is too subjective and fragmentary to demonstrate conclusively.[29] Newspapers, never a wholly reliable guide to public opinion, were at this point under unusually energetic restraint by military censorship, and the DORA regime came down heavily on any public expression of support for the rebellion.[30] But beneath this suppressive veil something was happening; it could be sensed – to take just one example – in a Westmeath cinema. 'On July 17 when pictures of the rebellion were shown at the Mullingar

Cinema Exhibition, a section of the audience hissed the soldiers and cheered the rebels.' As the police report laconically noted, 'The manager did not produce these films again.'[31] By August, Maxwell noted helplessly that the police reports were 'full of the doings of the priests all over the country. Their sermons . . . fan the feeling of sympathy amounting to martyrdom for the killed rebels.'[32] Towards the end of the summer, 'seditious' views began to break through more frequently, and Maxwell grumbled more and more about the inadequacy of the censorship system. (He wanted 'a selected civilian who is if possible a literary man or journalist' to be given charge of it.)[33] As so often, America provided the conduit for this material. In September, for instance, a Mullingar newspaper ran a series of 'Tales of the Rebellion' that particularly bothered the authorities. 'Moira Regan's Story', culled from the *New York Times*, was an open celebration of the rebellion's success in awakening Ireland's national spirit. 'I felt that evening when I saw the Irish flag floating over the Post Office, that this was a thing worth living and dying for. I was absolutely intoxicated.'[34]

The public mood change had two key components. The first, as we have seen, was condemnation of the military proceedings. The second, equally crucial, was a re-evaluation of the rebels themselves. In June the Inspector-General of the RIC observed that 'public sympathy' had been 'stimulated by the sale of photographs of the rebel leaders, and letters written by some of them on the eve of execution, together with mourning badges of green and black ribbon'. (He added cautiously that 'it was not considered advisable' to interfere with the sale of these mementos.)[35] Children led the way with these displays, according to one intelligence report – 'mourning badges were first in possession of children attending school, and distributed through their agency'.[36] Wearing of Sinn Féin badges became 'very general, but chiefly by young people'. The public re-evaluation was more than a matter of recognizing the rebels as 'our own flesh and blood'. What happened was well described by one 'impressionable boy of sixteen years' in Drogheda. 'People started to say: these men, poets, teachers, labour leaders, men respected in every walk of life, could not be, as they were told, irresponsible hare-brained adventurers, rainbow-chasers and hooligans.'[37] As James Stephens reflected of the leaders, 'in my definition they were good men – men, that is, who willed no evil'. No person living was worse off for having known Thomas MacDonagh, for example. And most of Ireland's intellectual elite had known him, even if not all had admired him. Ireland's greatest writer, W. B. Yeats, worried that 'I know most of the Sinn Fein leaders & the whole thing bewilders me for Conolly [*sic*] is an able man & Thomas MacDonough [*sic*] both able & cultivated.' (Pearse he had 'long looked upon as a man made dangerous by the Vertigo of Self Sacrifice', who had 'moulded himself on Emmett [*sic*]'.)Even his sharp-tongued sister Lily, who at first dismissed the rebellion as 'childish madness' and mocked the rebels (saying of MacDonagh that he was 'clever and hard and full of self-conceit'), soon turned her fury against 'this horrible work . . . this shooting of foolish idealists, not a vicious man amongst them' ('except perhaps MacBride', she could not resist adding). Soon afterwards she was fuming, 'We [Ireland and England] can never understand each other.'[38] For Yeats himself, in 'Easter 1916', his public meditation on the significance of the rebellion (composed during the summer of 1916 but not published until the following year), the rebel leaders had been 'all changed, changed utterly'.

One characteristic of the rebels that began to be emphasized – though not, of course, by Yeats – would have a steadily increasing significance: their religion. With the exception of Casement (who in fact embraced Catholicism before his execution) none of the known leaders was a Protestant. And while it was fairly well known that Tom Clarke was an anti-clerical Fenian, and MacDonagh a sceptic who had had long arguments with Joe Plunkett about the truth of revealed religion, the view of the rebels as good Catholics began to put down deep roots. 'Reports of the extraordinary piety of the rebels before, during and after the insurrection were soon in circulation.'[39] Manifestations ranged from the charming (if slightly disturbing) tale of the little girl who began praying to 'Saint Pearse' in a shop to persuade her mother to buy her a new hat, to the more resonant story that a priest giving Con Colbert the last rites before his execution had asked him to intercede in heaven to obtain an 'intention'[40] – with successful results. These were perhaps straws in the wind; one substantial marker of demotic Catholic attitudes, however, was the decision of the *Catholic Bulletin* to run a major series of articles called 'Events of Easter Week', from July onwards. The tone of these articles was, if not yet hagio-graphic, certainly respectful.

The Hierarchy was still a long way from any such identification with rebellion, but its position was beginning to shift; in particular, its trad-itional alliance with the constitutional nationalists started to crumble. Here the government once again played a key role in subverting its Irish allies. Its one and only attempt at a political initiative in the wake of the rebellion proved even more ill-advised than its endorsement of martial law. In his May report to the Commons, Asquith pointed to 'the strength and depth, and I might almost say without exaggeration the universality, of the feeling that we have now a unique opportunity for a new departure for the settlement of outstanding problems'. There should be 'a joint and combined effort', he added not without redundancy, to 'obtain agreement' on the future government of Ireland.[41] He announced that the Minister of Munitions, Lloyd George, was to undertake a 'mission of peace and reconciliation', to reopen negotiations about implementing the Home Rule Act. Unionists naturally castigated this move as a concession to violence, and the government never really succeeded in denying this charge. The main reason for the mission seems to have been the sense that 'Allied opinion', especially in the Dominions, and above all in America, was showing alarming signs of bridling at the military repression of the rebellion. Was there a real window of opportunity for a settlement? If by 'new departure' he implied some kind of readiness to compro-mise, Asquith would not have had to look hard to see distinct limits, on the Unionist side, to the 'universality' of this feeling. Clearly a good deal of faith was placed in the former Chancellor's negotiating skills. Lloyd George would have been Asquith's top candidate for the Chief Secretaryship, had he not already become too big for the job. The Chief Secretaryship was unappealing, but the lure of settling the Irish Question was a strong one. And to begin with Lloyd George did seem to make real progress, using his preferred technique of negotiating separately with the two parties. As before the war, the key point was the exclusion of 'Ulster' (more precisely, the six north-eastern counties): this had to be sold to the Nationalists as temporary, and to the Unionists as permanent.

It is often thought that the negotiations broke down when these contradictory undertakings became known, but the situation seems to have been more complicated. It is clear that Devlin, at least, believed that the two 'legitimate views of the same proposal' were not necessarily contradictory, and 'may be easily cleared up afterwards'. Redmond discovered that Carson had received what looked like a written guarantee of permanent exclusion, but Lloyd George had phrased this with cunning ambiguity ('at the end of the provisional period Ulster does not, whether she wills it or not, merge with the rest of Ireland' – in other words, a new arrangement would then be devised).[42] What really torpedoed the negotiations was not Lloyd George's deceptions but Unionist intransigence. In late June, a group of hardliners – Walter Long, Lord Lansdowne, and Lord Robert Cecil – dug in their heels. Cecil bludgeoned the cabinet with a viscerally Tory insistence that the Nationalist leadership could not be trusted with power while the war lasted. Dillon had proved by his 'disastrous speech' that he was 'a convinced enemy of this country'. This was just 'the latest expression of the ingrained Irish hatred for the British connection'. And Cecil asked whether, in any case, the Redmondites really had political legitimacy in Ireland: 'for all I know they would have as little Irish prestige as Castle government itself'. This was cruel – but cruelly prophetic. Cecil charged that Ulster had been pushed into negotiations by an exaggerated alarm about 'serious American and Colonial complications'. He accepted that 'if we tried to set up again Castle government, we should have to face a considerable outcry in the United States which might become formidable'; but if Home Rule was granted 'while withholding executive powers till after the war', this problem could be averted. This would mean keeping martial law in force for the duration.[43]

Hardline arguments like this confronted Asquith and Lloyd George with a grim dilemma. They almost certainly believed that an Irish settlement would assist the war effort – Lloyd George was particularly alarmist at this time, holding that the Irish-American vote could 'break our blockade and force an ignominious peace on us, unless something is done, even provisionally, to satisfy America'.[44] This was certainly the view of one of the Foreign Office's most trusted informants, who reported as early as 5 May that, whereas before the rebellion 'it would probably have been true to say that 25% of the Irish were actively pro-German and 75% were more or less pro-Ally', after the first executions 'one hundred per cent of the Irish are now actually anti-British'. Any idea of 'a rapprochement between the United States and Great Britain . . . may now be abandoned. The Irish will see to it that there will be nothing of the kind for fifty years to come.'[45] Mass protest meetings were held throughout the country, and thousands rallied in San Francisco, Boston, Providence, Buffalo and other cities. In New York, a meeting in Carnegie Hall on 14 May spilled out beyond the hall's 5,000 capacity, with an estimated 20,000 in the streets outside.[46] All thinking Americans, the Foreign Office was told, regarded the executions as a far worse blunder than the German 'murder' of Nurse Cavell. (The Germans certainly believed this, exulting that England's 'incredible folly . . . has altered the whole war situation in our favour'.) The ambassador in Washington wrote that 'the Irish here . . . have blood in their eyes when they look our way'. All this admittedly cut little ice with many ministers and officials, who saw the Irish-Americans as a lost cause in any case, and (rightly) thought that their influence would not decide US policy. But even sympathetic Americans were sending warning signals – Theodore Roosevelt wrote, for Lloyd George's benefit, in early June, 'I wish your people had not shot the leaders of the Irish rebels after they had surrendered . . . It would have been the better part of wisdom not to exact the death penalty.'[47] The most Anglophile US newspapers were plainly shocked by 'the image of savage repression'.[48]

But Asquith and Lloyd George were also acutely aware that if they pushed a settlement through they would certainly break up the Coalition Cabinet. This was a more immediate threat than the potential alienation of the USA. Once again, there would be no 'coercion of Ulster'. The Home Rule negotiations drifted into another month of inconsequential haggling over the issue of postponement, and the equally fraught question of Irish representation at Westminster. At the same time, the Cabinet was debating the fate of Roger Casement – sentenced to death on 29 June for high treason, after a trial which became notorious for the government's attempt to smear him with rumours and leaks of his homosexual 'Black Diaries'. Casement's fate was inevitable in the atmosphere of war emergency; and, however it might look in Ireland and abroad, it seems that in a technical sense he had a fair trial.[49] Though there was 'much doubting in the cabinet – among a few', according to the Home Secretary, most ministers accepted that 'his reprieve would let loose a tornado of condemnation, would be bitterly resented by the mass of the people in Great Britain and by the whole of the army, and would profoundly and permanently shake public confidence in the sincerity and the courage of the Government'.[50] Awkwardly for the Cabinet, the US Senate passed a resolution on 29 July urging clemency 'in the treatment of Irish political prisoners'; the fierce American public reaction to the May executions had been followed by an intense campaign for Casement's reprieve. The government's attempt to maintain that he was not a political prisoner did not play well there, and the eventual decision to execute him triggered a new wave of popular indignation.[51] As Roy Jenkins later observed, 'there can be few other examples of a Cabinet devoting large parts of four separate meetings to considering an individual sentence – and then arriving at the wrong decision'.[52] The fact that these meetings were taking place at the height of the biggest battle ever fought by the British army, on the Somme, makes the case even more remarkable – though it may help to explain the outcome.

A few days before Casement was hanged, Redmond finally accepted that all hope of a settlement was over. For Asquith it was a political embarrassment (though Lloyd George escaped largely unscathed). The chief casualty of this fiasco, however – as of 1916 more generally – was the Irish Party. Its larger hope that participation in the war would 'unite us all' may always have been too optimistic; the evidence suggests that while shared war experience at the front sometimes eroded old prejudices, it could just as often reinforce stereotypes (notably, of course, in wartime, the 'fighting Irish').[53] In any case Unionists back home remained resolutely unimpressed by Nationalist sacrifices. But the summer of 1916 created, through the shattering experience of the battle of the Somme, an enduring image of Ulster sacrifice to counterpoint that of the smoking ruins of Dublin. On 1 July – by deadly coincidence the 'true' date of the battle of the Boyne – the 36th Division lost a third of its strength (over 5,000 men) killed, wounded and missing in its assault on Thiepval Ridge. Ulster folk memory immediately seized on the significance of the Division's 'war-cry "No Surrender"', their 'sacred shibboleth'.[54] The 16th Division also fought, at a later stage in the three-month battle, but its political members were already painfully conscious of the double-edged blow to their great aspiration. Thomas Kettle, who had built up the most far-sighted case for Irish participation in the war, faced his death – at Guinchy in September – with the grim realization that his country would disown him. The Dublin rebels would 'go down in history as heroes and martyrs, and I will go down – if I go down at all – as a bloody British officer'.[55]

To keep wavering Nationalists in line through the compromising Lloyd George negotiations, Redmond had to draw deeply on his diminishing political capital. Particularly draining were his attempts to secure the Catholic Church's assent to the exclusion proposal. The bishops, especially of the northern dioceses, were 'violently opposed' to exclusion, because of 'the perilous position in which religion and Catholic education would be placed' in the six counties. On 19 June, Bishop McHugh of Derry bluntly told Redmond he would rather stay under British rule for the next fifty years than accept Lloyd George's proposals. Thus it was without the party's key allies that Redmond faced a crucial Nationalist conference – 776 delegates, including 130 priests – in Belfast on 23 June. He had to play the desperate card of threatening resignation to secure a vote of 425 to 265 in favour of accepting the proposals. One of the senior clerics whom Redmond persuaded to support him had spoken the previous week against 'the proposed mutilation of our country'.[56] The Church was moving to a position of outright opposition to the party.

This still did not necessarily mean a movement towards Sinn Féin. Sinn Féin itself was in disarray in the wake of the rebellion. A number of historians have suggested that the immediate use of the label 'Sinn Fein Rebellion', primarily by the press, reflected a misunderstanding of the situation. Clearly, Sinn Féin as an organization played no part in planning or staging the uprising; and equally clearly, Sinn Féin's ideas had always stressed the primacy of civil resistance over violence. But, as we have seen, the attraction of the Sinn Féin label for the minority Irish Volunteers (and not only in the eyes of the authorities) was irresistible. Sinn Féin members were targeted in the early

May round-ups (Griffith had already got himself arrested, knowing that imprisonment would be a key part of any future political credentials). The organization was crippled, but its ideas enjoyed a revival. The rebellion sparked a surge in public curiosity about the movement; there was a sudden run on pamphlets that had been lying around for years. Sinn Féin's relationship with the rebellion was nicely explained by one of its early historians. The failure of the rebellion, he wrote, in a sense confirmed Sinn Féin's scepticism about physical force. 'Sinn Féin with its policy of self-reliance, of distrust of all policies of reaching freedom by an acknowledgement of subjection [i.e. constitutionalism], offered the means of realizing what the Rising had failed to bring nearer.' But Sinn Féin had to change its programme: 'offering the constitution of 1792 it had failed to carry with it more than a few doctrinaire enthusiasts: agreeing with the constitution which the leaders of the Rising died for, it might (and did) carry the country with it'.[57]

Even so, this would be a slow process. The Volunteer organization was equally flattened; 'all the real brains of the organisation are dead or locked up'.[58] The leaders who had avoided arrest were in hiding, like Patrick McCartan (lying low in a cousin's barn near Carrickmore), and looking for hopeful signs. McCartan thought that 'the people generally do not condemn the "rebels" but blame them for starting too soon' (in this, by coincidence, they followed McCartan's own belief that the rebellion was premature). Though he was less impressed by Dillon's May speech than the British, he thought it 'on the whole quite good and manly' (but, as he acidly added, 'the Irish will out, even in a butler'). This was a gloomy time; 'sometimes I almost envy the men who were shot or have been sent to penal servitude, for they know nothing of the fate of the poor fellows who were not responsible, and the worries of their fathers and mothers'.[59] It was to be the prisoners who formed the focus for the movement's gradual revival. As in previous agitations, like 1848 and 1867, it was not long before prisoners' aid societies began to be formed. Petitions calling for a general amnesty were in circulation within weeks of the rebellion, and Maxwell complained that (as usual) the priests were 'foremost in promoting subscriptions for the families of those who suffered, and for the families of deported rebels'.[60] The Lord Mayor of Dublin launched a fund, while the Volunteer Dependants' Fund ('got up by widows of excuted rebels', Maxwell contemptuously noted) drew money from insurance schemes taken out before the rebellion to compensate Volunteers who lost their jobs (augmented by quite substantial sums from the Volunteer leaders just before the rebellion began). The IVDF had disbursed over £5,000 by the time it merged in August with the still larger National Aid Association Fund (which had given out nearly £10,000). Contributions 'poured in from every quarter, from Unionists and Home Rulers as well as from republicans'; by the autumn the society was spending £1,200 to £1,400 a week.[61]

These groups formed a link to the deported prisoners, whose incarceration became a key aspect of the rebellion's ultimate impact.[62] It was a strange experience for these respectable clerks, minor officials and teachers. For several days after the surrender, most of them were disoriented. Conditions in Richmond Barracks were hard (in the fortnight before Asquith's visit, at least), and the surrendered rebels were soon moved on to worse ones. When Bob Holland was marched down to the North Wall, 'there were very few people on the streets. We could hear the advance guard of soldiers giving orders to clear the streets – "Get in and close those windows."' At North Wall they put out to sea crammed into dirty, foul-smelling cattle boats, without rations; 'almost everyone vomiting under these conditions'. From Holyhead they were taken by train to two prisons, Knutsford and Stafford. At Stafford, some disgruntled locals who were aware that their local regiment had been fighting in Dublin, staged a hostile reception. There was no such confrontation at Knutsford, but the prison regime was extraordinarily punitive. Oscar Traynor laconically recorded that 'we were treated in a rather brutal fashion'. For nearly a month he had neither bed nor bedclothes. Liam Tannam struck lucky, getting the condemned cell – 'larger than the others'. But he 'could not eat the prison food for a few days . . . The diet was practically starvation diet and the meat I believe was horse flesh.' Sentences of solitary confinement were freely handed out for any breach of prison rules – such as speaking to another prisoner. Holland was kept for two weeks in virtual darkness:

I thought a hundred times I would go mad – then I would wish to be mad, anything to replace the hunger and loneliness and darkness. I was sorry I had not been killed in the fight. I was glad that others had been executed – they had been relieved of prison torments.[63]

In Stafford, where Frank Henderson wound up along with Michael Collins and Seán MacEntee (who was soon swept back to Ireland to face a court martial for murder) a similar regime of solitary confinement was imposed, though the military guards 'with one or two exceptions, were very decent men'.[64] Collins suffered from 'the dreadful monotony, the heartscalding eternal brooding on all sorts of things, thoughts of friends dead & living, especially those recently dead, but above all the time, the horror of the way it refuses to pass . . .'[65] In both gaols, however, after a month the regime was, for no apparent reason, suddenly lightened; the prisoners were not confined to their cells, and were allowed to talk. The reason may have been the process of 'combing out the "innocents"' by Judge Sankey's Enemy Aliens Advisory Committee. The influx of detainees was threatening to swamp the English military prison system. By 3 May, over 500 men had been brought to Knutsford and nearly 300 to Stafford. Over the next fortnight another 260 were sent to Stafford, 650 to Wakefield, 250 to Wandsworth, 200 to Glasgow, 40 to Woking and 59 to Lewes.[66] Early the following month further groups were brought over to Wakefield, Wandsworth and Knutsford.

Eventually the majority were moved to a specially emptied military prison camp (recently used for prisoners of war) at Frongoch in Wales – 'situated most picturesquely on rising ground amid pretty Welsh hills', Michael Collins reported to his girlfriend. But 'up to the present it hasn't presented any good points to me', as it rained all the time, and the cold was 'not pleasant, even now'. 'We sleep 30 in an 'ut (this is the regulation name) the dimensions being 60 long, 16 wide and 10 foot high in the middle. Not too much room to spare!'[67] But men who had 'had enough of high walls, cold cells and clanging doors' in grim penitentiaries like Knutsford, were generally pleased with the healthy lifestyle of the camp – including frequent route marches, providing good exercise, mental relaxation, and enjoyment of the countryside. Frank Robbins got his first proper shave for two months from James Mallon (who subsequently traded as 'The Frongoch Barber' in a shop on Eden Quay).[68]

In late June the laborious process of bringing batches of detainees back to Wandsworth and Wormwood Scrubs for interrogation by Sankey's committee began. One of them who was (as he thought) 'tried' by the committee grumbled about the waste of money and effort involved in bringing hundreds of men to London, 'whereas the committee of six could have come to Wales'.[69] The Home Secretary worried about how to ensure that 'it should not be said that Irishmen were being tried by an almost wholly English tribunal.' To this end he added an Irish judge to the committee, though he made clear that the tribunal was not a judicial one.[70] It began work on 16 June by discussing its terms of reference, not agreeing on these until the 22nd. Eventually, after interviewing Brigadier-General Byrne on the 23rd it discussed seventy-three cases of detainees from County Cork over the next couple of days, then went on to interview the RIC County Inspectors from Galway on the 28th before dealing with the seventy-one Galway cases. On the 30th it dealt with five women from Lewes gaol. After that its work rate stepped up. It held twenty-one sittings between 3 July and 28 July, several times disposing of more than 100 cases in a day (which, as Sankey grumbled, involved sitting from 10 a.m. to 9 p.m.). It was 'exacting and anxious' work, occasionally involving 'great trouble with the prisoners, many of whom were insolent and defiant, and some refused to answer any questions'. Sankey blamed this on the military guards, who allowed the prisoners to talk to each other, and thus be got at by 'agitators'.[71]

Sankey would eventually liberate 69 per cent of the detainees he saw, though unfortunately we do not know what criteria he used, or how searching his inquiries were.[72] (Much of the Aliens Advisory Committee records were 'quite wrongly' destroyed during the next world war.)[73] From the detainees' own accounts, it seems that Sankey's main concern was to ask them whether they had gone out knowingly to rebel on Easter Monday, or had been unaware of what was planned.[74] Robbins, like many others, found his interview mildly farcical. 'Judge Sankey addressed me by my christian name and opened the conversation rather surprisingly. "Good day, Frank. Won't you sit down?" I did so and thanked him.' Then, after some discussion about his exact whereabouts on 24 April, he was asked what he was doing in Liberty Hall.

My answer was, 'Guard duty and helping in the making of munitions.'

Judge Sankey then said to me, 'Frank, you are down here as having the occupation of a driller. Tell us what that means.'

I replied, 'That is the designation of my trade in the Dublin dockyard.'

'I thought it meant that you were drilling holes in soldiers,' said Judge Sankey with a wry smile. At this there was a general laugh.

His next question was in the form of a suggestion that I had been forced to take part in the Insurrection. I replied 'That is not so.'

He then suggested that I did not take an active part in the shooting, that I was probably attached to the Red Cross. I told him that that was not so, as I did not know anything about Red Cross work. He then wanted to know whether I had fired many shots, and my reply was that they were uncountable. He then asked, 'Do you think you killed or wounded many of His Majesty's soldiers?'

To which I replied, 'I could not say, being at the other end.' This reply was followed by more general laughter.[75]

Sankey seems to have conducted his inquiries without obtaining any expert advice on Ireland, though he did learn that a number of the detainees belonged to the Irish Republican Brotherhood, 'which is a somewhat dangerous society', he reported. By the time he finished his last hearing on 28 August, he had heard a total of 1,846 cases and recommended release in all but 573 of them.[76] Frank Robbins was one of those released.

The process of liberating the 'innocents' brought its own problems. In principle, it was a public admission that they had been unjustifiably detained, and the authorities were immediately made aware that Irish opinion saw the releases not as an act of generosity but as a confession of error. They also found that the releases could excite Sinn Féin demonstrations: to stop these, Dublin Castle had to ask that the Home Office should arrange for the released internees to arrive at Kingstown in the early morning, not the evening.[77] Once the programme of releases was complete, public attention focused on the 500 men still held in Frongoch. The camp, under the command of a 'dug-out' colonel, F. A. Heygate Lambert, became a testing ground for the organizational strength of the interned Volunteers. After some disagreement about the propriety of co-operating with the British authorities, an informal three-man general council, or 'Civil Government of the Irish Republic', which had assumed authority over the inmates, was replaced by a prisoner-of-war-style Military Staff. J. J. O'Connell became Commandant, with Brennan Whitmore as Adjutant (and semi-official historian), and five others including a Provost Marshal and Quartermaster. Elaborate and strict regulations were drawn up. In effect, 'the Military Staff raised Frongoch Camp into a Military Academy'.[78] O'Connell wrote approvingly of the 'militarization' fostered through camp life. When half the staff group were swept off to Reading gaol in mid-July, O'Connell was replaced by Michael Staines as commanding officer.

Lambert – 'a very tactless man' in Henderson's opinion, nicknamed 'Buckshot' by the internees – faced awkward problems inside and outside the camp.[79] It seems unlikely that he actually announced that 'he would have discipline in the camp even though it was filled with nothing but dead bodies', but his approach was clearly heavy-handed.[80] The attitude of his prisoners gradually deteriorated. In his view (and notwithstanding Sankey's efforts), 'a large proportion of the prisoners were harmless and ignorant men, led away by other unscrupulous and disloyal men, with whom they were perforce interned'. The Volunteer organizers echoed this; from their point of view, internment represented a quantum leap. 'The widespread and indiscriminate arrests', O'Connell wrote, 'ensured that men from every single area were roped in, in considerable numbers. Men who had never been Volunteers before Easter 1916 became Volunteers during internment by force of association with the others.'[81] Until October prison discipline was satisfactory, Lambert thought, but in September a dispute flared up over the orders given to prisoners to empty the 'ashpits' – i.e. latrines – not just their own but the guards' as well. The ashpit strike was followed by a hunger strike, and the contest left the prisoners 'very pleased with themselves for having, as they think, defeated His Majesty's Government'.[82] Lambert asked for some RIC to be sent in to assist him – 'they would probably know the ringleaders whom I have not so far been able to identify'. Then an ill-judged intervention by the War Office, an attempt to find a number of men who were avoiding conscription, had catastrophic effects. The increasingly uppish and confident prisoners spontaneously protected the draft-dodgers (of whom there were, according to Brennan Whitmore, 150 in the camp) by refusing en masse to answer the roll-call – an offence for which Lambert transferred several hundred to the 'South Camp' – a set of disused distillery buildings.

Here conditions were clearly worse than in the North Camp, and a sustained campaign of public complaint was launched. As Lambert grumbled, 'a large amount of time and labour' was taken up 'in answering the false accusations made against the conduct of the camp by two Irish MPs'.[83] At least four inquiries into conditions were ordered by the authorities; the first three, in July and August (two by a Home Office representative, the third by a specialist sanitary inspector of the Royal Army Medical Corps), pronounced the camp accommodation and facilities adequate. The last, however, which took place after the moving of the 'nameless' prisoners to the South Camp, noted that they were 'full of grievances, surly, truculent, disobedient' – adding fastidiously that they were also 'apparently averse to a high standard of cleanliness'.[84] By December the confrontation had become intense. The strain of constant criticism drove the camp medical officer – publicly accused of refusing medical treatment to the refuseniks – to drown himself in the nearby river. Col. Lambert's angry statement that the prisoners had hounded Dr Peters to his death with a campaign of lies was itself indignantly denounced as 'monstrous' by the Honorary Secretary of the Prisoners' Committee – Michael Collins.[85]

The growing prominence of this hugely effective organizer was an important sign of the longer-term effect of the Frongoch phenomenon. Collins, then twenty-six years old, had a brisk approach to practical problems, a vast capacity to store and order information, and brimmed over with energy and charisma. He was a revolutionary hero in the making, but his rise was not wholly uncontentious. When the men in the South Camp were separated from the existing system of prisoner organization, they had to start a new one.

One party thought ranks as they existed during the fight should be adhered to, and the prisoners organised and commanded as far as possible by officers. The other party succeeded in having a committee appointed to run the camp, this committee being entirely composed of members of the IRB.

This 'other party' was of course led by Collins, who was by this time ready to step into one of the vacancies on the IRB Supreme Council that the rebellion had created. Liam Tannam, although an IRB man, 'sided with the military idea and came in conflict with Collins over this'.[86] He would not be the last to do so.

It was Collins who put together what was published by the Cork Branch of the Irish National Aid and Volunteer Dependants' Fund Association as an impressive-looking 'Official Report' on the ill-treatment of the Frongoch 'prisoners of war'. This painted a grim picture of the rat-infested old distillery stores in which the South Camp inmates were housed, the miserable rations on which they had to survive, and the brutal nature of the prison regime. The camp was 'absolutely unfit for human habitation', the inadequate diet was producing an outbreak of skin disease, and the Commandant was continually adding further punishments, such as forced route marches, to the already oppressive conditions. The report hammered its message home (it had a section on 'Food', one on 'Brutality', and one on 'Conscription', followed by 'More Brutality' and 'Conscription Again') with an account of the hunger strike of those who refused the roll-call.[87] It was claimed to be 'signed by 360 men'; though Gerald Boland and Oscar Traynor refused to sign what they called a 'lying statement', despite being carpeted by the camp council for their obduracy.[88]

Certainly, Collins's charge at the end of the report that 'the Party' was uninterested in the release of the prisoners, while predictable, was far from true. As the Commandant testily observed, Irish MPs – most actively Alfie Byrne – were persistent visitors and critics. Byrne exploited his status as an MP to the maximum (Brigid Martin of Cumann na mBan, one of two women internees in Lewes gaol, remembered the amazement of the wardresses when he appeared, to take the prisoners out to strawberries and cream at the Lyons corner house. They 'did not know what to make of it. MPs were looked on by them as marvellous beings.')[89] Other Irish MPs also pounced on the issue of the detainees as a way of venting their frustration against the government. Over twenty parliamentary questions about conditions in Frongoch were tabled in the autumn, causing some exasperation to the usually even-tempered Home Secretary, Herbert Samuel. The fate of the deportees and convicts was central to the speech with which Redmond launched the most serious parliamentary debate on Ireland since the rebellion, on 18 October. In this he called Asquith to account for promising a complete reconstruction of the Irish government, and failing to provide anything but apparently endless martial law. 'England, fighting for the small nationalities of Europe, is maintaining by martial law a State Unionist Government against the will of the people.' The policy of deportations had been 'a terrible and fatal blunder'. Though he may have blunted the force of his assault by returning yet again to the failure of the military authorities to help Irish recruitment by recognizing Irish units – instancing the case of 300 men of an Irish reserve regiment who 'the other day were put into kilts and sent to a Highland regiment' – he chose the terms of his motion with a canny eye on British sensitivity to overseas opinion. 'The system of government in Ireland is inconsistent with the principles for which the Allies are fighting in Europe.' His demand for the immediate abandonment of martial law, and the recall of General Maxwell, was a resonant challenge.[90] And it had its effect.

12

The Politics of Militarization

*Every vote you give now is as good as the crack of a rifle in
proclaiming your desire for freedom.*

Eamon de Valera, East Clare, July 1917

It could hardly be denied that the current Irish administration, such
as it was, had a 'Unionist' cast. A month after Walter Long pressed
the urgent need for 'the presence of a strong, capable and courageous
Chief Secretary', Asquith finally gave the job to Henry Duke, a
straightforward if uncharismatic Unionist.[1] Long's parallel demand
that Maxwell's position should be 'regularized' and 'clearly defined'
was more blatantly ignored. Long wanted Maxwell to be 'given
authority over the police force'. This, as the future would show, was
a far-sighted response to the complex challenge of modern insurgency,
but it was (not for the last time) too unorthodox for the government
to contemplate. After Duke's appointment, Maxwell's position actually became less clearly defined than before, and his influence was
steadily eclipsed. By September Asquith was thinking of replacing
him, but as usual found reasons for delay. Wimborne reported to
Duke that it would be 'difficult to place him elsewhere – unless he were
to be retired, which would imply condemnation very injurious to us
and him'.[2] Nonetheless, when Duke led for the government in
response to Redmond's censure motion on 18 October he seemed to
be defending Maxwell, at least by arguing that no less stringent punitive policy could have been implemented. The rebellion had been serious, he insisted: it was misleading to portray it as 'an affair of some
hundreds of men who might have been treated as a negligible factor'.

At the same time he suggested that the resistance movement was marginal enough to be defeated: 'rooted amongst foolish, desperate and criminal people in various parts of Ireland'. And it could be defeated, but not by Redmond's 'easy prescriptions'. 'When a man is ill of fever, you do not give him a spoonful of water to cure him.' 'Is an amnesty the treatment for that state of things?' Duke (like Maxwell before him) rhetorically demanded.

Duke justified the continuance of martial law as simple common sense – a view he, as a lawyer, cannot have been wholly comfortable with. He airily dismissed Redmond's argument (reinforced later in the debate by some English Liberal MPs) that the Defence of the Realm Act gave all the powers necessary, even though as we have seen such an argument had been accepted within the government, and even the military, from the outset. He had more trouble disposing of Redmond's charge that the Irish administration had become Unionist in complexion – an attack, as he well understood, not so much on himself as on the Attorney General, James Campbell, whose appointment had outraged the Irish Party. The only non-Unionist Duke could point to in the Irish executive was Wimborne, and his assertion (against shouts of 'What power has he?') that the Lord Lieutenant – the title Viceroy was deliberately dropped at this stage – 'is able to take an active interest in the process of administration' was fairly disingenuous.[3]

All this was a limp end to the excited speculations that had been aroused by Asquith's visit in May. Immediately after his arrival, 'the most astonishing rumours' had been floated about rapid and dramatic reform of the Irish government. Intense press speculation had focused on the idea of a National Council 'to help in the Government of Ireland', and names of likely members had been canvassed.[4] Asquith indeed committed himself on paper to fundamental reform, but soon seems to have run out of enthusiasm. William Pitt's famously English adage about not repairing your roof during a thunderstorm no doubt reasserted its relevance, and it is not hard to see how the demands of the war ultimately distracted energy from awkward problems that could be classed as marginal. Herbert Samuel, who also discovered an enthusiasm for Irish affairs, also seems to have lost it again soon afterwards. The inability either to reconstruct the system – abolishing the

Lord Lieutenancy as Asquith had indicated – or, failing that, to appoint a substantial political figure to the Chief Secretaryship, meant a return to the familiar policy of drift. Sir Robert Chalmers, who devoutly hoped that no more Cabinet ministers would take an interest in Ireland after Samuel's visit, was unlikely to provide a substitute. Clearly, he and the Prime Minister had far-reaching discussions during the Lloyd George negotiations, extending to the education system and including reconstruction – or at least amalgamation – of the police forces. Chalmers was reported to be 'anxious that under the Provisional Government in the 6 Counties nothing should be done to prejudice the chances of future union with the rest of Ireland', so wanted education to stay 'national' until 'the final fate of the country is decided after the war'.[5] The Royal Commission may have taken the wind out of the issue of police reform: though it pointed to the problems caused by the dual system, it carefully exculpated the police from responsibility for the rebellion, and indeed heaped praise on them. The project would have been difficult, since the RIC was an armed gendarmerie and the DMP an English-style unarmed force. But in the end, Chalmers recommended against amalgamation on financial and legal rather than organizational grounds. (Among other things, the running of the DMP depended on a contribution from the Dublin rates.)[6] Treasury caution prevailed. The post of RIC Inspector-General survived, to be occupied eventually by Maxwell's former DAG, Brigadier-General, Joseph Byrne. By October it was evident – to foreign observers at least – that the 'provisional regime' had lapsed back into the old regime.[7]

The government comfortably survived the division on Redmond's censure motion, but quickly made some major concessions. Maxwell was recalled within a fortnight. Unionists were dismayed, but Duke coldly explained that 'it was unnecessary and useless to keep him there as an irritant'.[8] (Despite Asquith's delaying compunction, he became GOC Northern Command, a post which could only be construed as demotion.) Then, in December, immediately after Asquith himself was displaced by Lloyd George in a political coup, Duke announced that the internees would be released before Christmas. In the last letter he sent to Asquith as Prime Minister, Redmond again insisted that the release of the prisoners was 'of the most vital and far reaching importance to the general interests of the Empire and the successful conduct of the War'.[9] An effort to make them declare that they would play no part in politics was abandoned, and their release was unconditional. The effect in Ireland was electrifying. Welcoming festivities were organized all over the country – the wide net that Maxwell had cast in May and June now enlarging the political impact of the concession. Whatever the government intended by the gesture, its effect was perverse. 'Instead of exciting gratitude', the Inspector-General of the RIC grumbled, the release 'appears to stimulate resentment'. The men seemed 'unsubdued by internment', and their release was 'by ignorant country folk regarded as proof that they were interned without any just cause'.[10] The releases began a hesitant revival of separatist activity, and a historic reorientation of Sinn Féin.

The internees had of course had time to give plenty of thought to future strategy; Collins, above all, had grasped the need to construct a much broader political front than the old Volunteer organization. His first step on that path, in February 1917, was to become Secretary of the Irish National Aid Fund – an appointment made by Tom Clarke's widow, who saw Collins as the natural successor to Seán MacDermott. Collins was not yet a dominant influence in Sinn Féin, or even the IRB, but he had the vision and the restless energy to exploit the shifting public mood. His use of the Aid Fund as a vehicle for rebuilding the IRB was just one facet of his natural instinct for organizational activity. During the spring he played a key part in moving both the Volunteers and Sinn Féin towards political action, first backing Joseph Plunkett's father when he stood in February as Sinn Féin candidate in the North Roscommon by-election. Here was an outlet for the still unfocused energy of local separatist groups, like the big torchlight procession at Gurteen on 5 February, where the crowd carrying a 'yellow, white and green' flag was lit by twenty men carrying 'lighted sods of turf on poles'.

Count Plunkett's victory opened up the possibility of a dramatic reinvention of the separatist movement. He was a political oddity, and a maverick even in a Sinn Féin which, the hostile *Freeman's Journal* said with some justification, 'remains a mystery'. Only reluctantly did he accept the key commitment to abstention from the Westminster parliament. Though he had suffered in the post-rebellion repression – he was sacked from his post as Director of the National Museum of Science and Art, and deported under a DORA order to Oxford – most of his political credibility stemmed from his being the father of a rebel leader. It was a short step from this to electing an actual rebel. When the South Longford seat fell vacant in May, Collins proposed to put up Joe McGuinness, then in Lewes gaol. Eamon de Valera, the acknowledged leader of the prisoners, thought the idea of standing for parliament 'extremely dangerous from several points of view', and McGuinness himself, an IRB stalwart, was not keen on it. Thomas Ashe, however, now President of the IRB Supreme Council, argued that in the new conditions standing for parliament was 'not giving recognition to the British parliament but giving the people an oppor-tunity to support Irish freedom'.[11] Collins and Ashe showed that although they were in many ways old-style IRB men – which de Valera was certainly not – they possessed a new kind of adaptability. The slo-gan 'Put him in to get him out' became a legendary mantra of the new Sinn Féin strategy. And though McGuinness's very narrow victory did not immediately secure his release, it staggered the Irish Party. After the shock of North Roscommon where the Party had been caught off guard (thinking Plunkett a joke candidate), Dillon had taken personal charge of the campaign. He reported to Redmond, 'We have the bishop, the great majority of the priests and the mob – and four-fifths of the traders of Longford.' If they were beaten in spite of all this, 'I do not see how you can hope to hold the party in existence.'

The Lewes prisoners naturally became, after the Frongoch men were released, the central focus of separatist agitation. Like the detainees, they had endured a protracted phase of hard treatment in various prisons before ending up under a fairly easy-going regime in Lewes gaol, which allowed them to develop, as in Frongoch, a highly organized structure of political education-cum-recreation.[12] Their contacts with the movement at home intensified, and the prison leadership turned into a kind of provisional government in exile. For the British authorities, the same question arose as had arisen with the detainees: would the conciliatory effect of an amnesty outweigh the pernicious consequences of letting them return to political activity?[13] Lloyd George's new administration had already shown itself inclined to risk a conciliatory gesture, and the Prime Minister was still acutely conscious of the need to demonstrate to the Dominions and the USA that real political progress was being made. Surveying the world situation immediately after Lloyd George took over as Prime Minister, the influential Cabinet Secretary Maurice Hankey suggested that 'one of the greatest services that could be rendered to the Allied cause would be a settlement of the Irish question'. Still, it was not until the Nationalist MP T. P. O'Connor forced the issue back on to the House of Commons order paper in March 1917 that the War Cabinet got around to confronting it once again. Then it came up with the classically British device of a commission of inquiry, to consider how far the Home Rule Act should be modified to permit its application as soon as possible. But after an abortive attempt to get the Dominions to nominate representatives for the commission, the idea stalled once more. In April the USA finally entered the war on the Allied side, thus stilling the most alarming fears about Irish-American influence. But American participation brought with it the commitment to national self-determination which was the keystone of President Woodrow Wilson's 'Fourteen Points' for the postwar settlement. This was more encouraging to Sinn Féin than to the British government. At last, in mid-May, Lloyd George sent Redmond and Carson a letter offering the alternative of immediate application of Home Rule with the conditions established during the 1916 negotiations, or 'a convention of Irishmen of all parties for the purpose of producing a scheme of Irish self-government'.[14]

The Irish Convention would hold its first meeting on 24 July, and continue to deliberate until April 1918. In retrospect it looks like a cross between a will-o'-the-wisp and a giant red herring, and even at the time there were plenty of those who dismissed its chances of reaching any new 'scheme' that had not already been tried and found wanting in the negotiations of 1912–14 and 1916. But some were optimistic, arguing for instance that 'the soberising influence of the rebellion and its results' had 'taught Irishmen that their aim should not be so much to snatch at a temporary makeshift', as to reach 'a permanent settlement which would give peace and form a basis for a united regenerative movement'.[15] No doubt there were many, foremost among them the Convention's maverick chairman, Sir Horace

Plunkett – relishing his return to the centre of the political stage – who believed that a new formula could be found. But the minimum condition for success was that 'all parties' should take part. (More, of course, would be needed, and the Ulster Unionists were to display an all too familiar lack of interest in compromise.) Sinn Féin was offered five seats, but refused to participate unless the Convention's terms of reference allowed it to recommend the complete independence of Ireland; it also demanded that the Convention be elected on universal suffrage, and that Irish 'political prisoners' should be treated as prisoners of war.

Sinn Féin's refusal was not seen as fatal, because the party was regarded as a transient phenomenon, a political flash in the pan which would become irrelevant if a mainstream solution was reached. For many English observers, the Convention was a way of buying time for Sinn Féin to die away. But there was ample evidence that it would have the reverse effect: Sinn Féin's encroachment on the power-base of the Irish Party was serious and possibly irreversible. Time was not on the side of moderation. It was 'agreed on all sides', the army reported, 'that the number of people professing Sinn Fein sympathies is vastly greater now than it was a year ago'.[16] The Convention had two significant effects on the actual situation. First, it led to a soft-pedalling on the enforcement of DORA regulations. 'For reasons of broad policy, the police had to act with special discretion' during the summer. Although 'political considerations must not be allowed to interfere with the maintenance of public order', the Cabinet was told, 'the whole civilized world should see that every facility was being given to the Convention'.[17]

Then, on 17 June, the government announced the unconditional release of the 'political prisoners'. The declared intention was to 'create a favourable atmosphere' for the negotiations. It certainly created an atmosphere. The public welcome was 'immense, nothing seen like it in Dublin before . . . When the convict train got in to Westland Row everyone lost their heads. We were carried off our feet . . .'[18] The army thought that the public demonstrations were 'marked by a display of disloyalty and spirit of insurrection of such a nature as to have a disturbing effect on the peace of the country', and warned that 'if the present lawless spirit is allowed to remain unchecked, a situation may be created which will render a collision unavoidable'.[19] Military demands for the complete suppression of meetings and demonstrations, however, were neutralized by the republican decision to contest elections. Two of the released prisoners immediately followed McGuinness into election battles. In East Clare in July, the senior surviving 1916 commander, de Valera, emerged as a serious political figure. He demonstrated an acute awareness of the complications involved in conducting a revolutionary movement without alienating the 'all-important support of the clergy'.[20]

His stump speeches mixed threatening with reassuring messages. On the sensitive issue of physical force, he declared that since the rebellion had saved 'the national soul of Ireland', 'another Easter Week would be a superfluity'. But 'although we fought once and lost, it is only a lesson for the second time'.[21] If they were to eliminate physical force from their programme, 'John Bull could kick us as much as he liked.' As time would tell, this ambiguity could become congenial to the higher as well as the lower clergy. But a menacing tone was never far from the surface. Addressing a huge crowd in Dublin after the Clare victory, he roused furious cheers with the assertion that 'the people of East Clare had told the world that their ideas were the ideas of the men of Easter Week', and that Clare had 'set up a lasting monument to the dead'.[22] 'Let it be your dead bodies they will conscript', he told an audience in Callan on 5 August; and two months later at Inagh, 'If you cannot get arms get that old useful weapon at close quarters – the seven-foot pike.'[23]

De Valera also began to elaborate the political formula that would offer Sinn Féin a distinctive (yet also usefully ambiguous) platform for the future.

We want an Irish republic, because if Ireland had her freedom, it is, I believe, the most likely form of government. But if the Irish people wanted to have another form of government, so long as it was an Irish government, I would not put in a word against it.

The following month, the election of W. T. Cosgrave (a pioneer Sinn Féin member of the Dublin Corporation, and veteran of the South Dublin Union fighting in 1916) for Kilkenny city catalysed the rebuilding of the Volunteer movement there. As in many places, it had been paralysed by the mass arrests in May 1916, and even after all the detainees were released little progress had been made until the stimulus of the 'reorganising drive' led by Dublin headquarters in early 1917. But from then on the old structure was quickly revived, with the vital addition of press support in the form of the *Kilkenny People*, which became a 'holy horror' to enemies of the Sinn Féin movement (until it was closed down under a DORA order).[24] Volunteers were 'the driving force of Sinn Fein', and played a visible role as stewards at the hustings, also preventing 'intimidation or interference with voters' at the polling stations. The election victory accelerated the movement's momentum – 'now companies were founded in districts where previously the Volunteer movement did not exist'.

While the Convention began its long-drawn-out discussions, the growing network of Sinn Féin organizers stepped up their efforts to bring all separatists under the umbrella of the reinvented movement. Collins had an energetic co-worker among the newly released Lewes prisoners in Harry Boland, who played a prominent part in expanding the IRB and turning it into 'an efficient instrument of central control'. In their brisk, impatient hands the old organization 'seems to have lost much of its sociability', in the view of Boland's biographer, 'becoming little more than a network for distributing instructions, organising Volunteer companies, and acquiring arms'.[25] Collins was certainly aware of the limitations of secret-society activity, which he blamed for the frustration of the rebellion plans. Now the Volunteers and Sinn Féin were pushed forward in tandem. The East Clare election saw the first aggressive reappearance of Volunteers on the streets in support of de Valera, creating an atmosphere of suppressed violence. 'Almost every young man carries a revolver', the RIC County Inspector reported, and the police were systematically crowded out.[26] Clare was a traditionally 'disturbed' area, but even in Wicklow, at the opposite end of the agitational spectrum, where the RIC obligingly returned to the Volunteers the rifles that had been seized after the rebellion, the movement accelerated. 'In every district where I got a Sinn Féin cumann [branch]', the local leader recorded, 'I saw that I got a Company of Volunteers. We soon had sufficient Companies to form two Battalions.'[27] Recognizing the East Clare victory as an event of 'cardinal significance', Lord Wimborne characteristically noted that on the night of the poll there had been 'sinister disturbances' in Ennis, and an armed attack on a police barrack at Ballybunion in county Kerry in which one of the attackers was killed. This was a 'premature ebullition' which he hoped might 'elicit no immediate imitation', but there was unquestionably 'a serious menace in the movement'.[28] Even the cautious Henry Duke, noting that Sinn Féin Clubs were inclined to adopt names like 'Casement', 'MacDonagh', 'MacDermott', or indeed 'The Pike', saw that 'all the active spirits in the movement resort when they have the opportunity to some kind of incitement in favour of ultimate armed action' – if only by coded flourishing of hurley sticks.[29]

Though the fusion of physical-force and civil-resistance activity was not new in Irish politics, the gradual absorption of the ideas of Griffith and Hobson enabled Sinn Féin to create a more sophisticated synthesis than any of its predecessors. It was effectively symbolized in two events in the autumn of 1917. On 25 September Thomas Ashe died under clumsy force-feeding in Mountjoy gaol. After being arrested for making a seditious speech in July, and convicted by a court martial under DORA, he had refused to accept his criminal status, and gone on hunger strike. His death was a volcanic moment: Ashe was an iconic figure who combined revolutionary glamour with fervent religiosity. He had unique prestige as the most successful military figure of the rebellion; the miniature epic of Ashbourne was transformed into a kind of Clontarf. His poetry, most famously his patriotic prayer-poem 'Let me carry Your cross for Ireland, Lord', marked him out as Pearse's most authentic successor. Above all, his funeral became a focal point for all the dissident forces that were multiplying in Ireland sixteen months after the suppression of the rebellion.

It was a triumphant piece of separatist street theatre.[30] Under the careful direction of Richard Mulcahy, now bringing a new professionalism to the organization's staff work, Volunteers formed a huge procession stretching from the city centre to Glasnevin cemetery, and a firing party discharged a volley over the grave. Collins delivered a two-sentence oration whose brevity must have been in deliberate counterpoint to Pearse's impassioned speech at the Rossa funeral. 'Nothing additional remains to be said. The volley which we have just heard is the only speech which it is proper to make above the grave of a dead Fenian.' Most remarkably, the avowedly 'Fenian' funeral was accompanied by a Catholic bishop. This was an alarming portent for the authorities. Ashe's 'death and funeral', according to the army, 'have resulted in an outburst of popular sympathy, of which the utmost use has been made by the Sinn Fein leaders in all parts of the country'. Uniforms had been worn in public, arms carried openly in processions, and 'there is every indication of careful organisation of the dangerous and disloyal elements'.[31] Duke admitted that 'this most unfortunate event' had 'created the greatest possible stir throughout the country'.[32] Assessing the situation in the wake of Ashe's funeral, Maxwell's successor, Sir Bryan Mahon, painted a sombre picture. The organization of the Sinn Féin movement was 'becoming more perfect, and their followers are exhibiting discipline to a degree which is perhaps the most dangerous sign of the times'. It was 'a changed state of affairs', and though another armed rebellion was unlikely, sporadic outrages were on the cards, and there was a very real danger of a passive resistance movement – perhaps including industrial action such as a railway strike.[33] (Here the general was unusually prescient, even if the strike would wait until 1920.)

The fusion of military and political action was cemented in October when the Sinn Féin national convention (*Ard-fheis*) and the Volunteer convention were held back-to-back, and effectively created a single movement. For the time being, the momentum lay with the political side. Sinn Féin assembled 1,700 delegates (the majority under forty years old) representing some 1,200 local branches. This total, roughly equalling the number of Catholic parishes, and about as many as the parliamentary party itself, established it as a truly national party. The *Ard-fheis* marked the crucial accommodation between the old, monarchist, passive-resistance persuasion personified by Arthur Griffith, and the new republican tendency represented by de Valera. Griffith, who had never relished this kind of political fight, stood aside and allowed de Valera to assume the presidency of both Sinn Féin and the Volunteers by acclamation. He also accepted the two-stage reformulation of the movement's aim: to achieve recognition of Ireland as a sovereign independent republic, then to allow the people to adopt by referendum 'their own form of government', a formula which closely resembled de Valera's template in the Clare election. There was a politic muting of hardline attitudes. Significantly, an attack on Eoin

MacNeill led by Countess Markievicz and Helena Molony, on the grounds of the countermanding order, seems not to have impressed the delegates. (The women's group found the convention a disappointingly unfriendly environment; the movement had not responded to Sheehy-Skeffington's strictures on its sexism.)[34] MacNeill, supported by de Valera and Seán Milroy as well as Griffith, received the largest personal vote to the twenty-four-strong executive.[35]

Griffith made clear that de Valera's credentials for leadership were not only that he had been a leader of the rebellion, but that he had 'the mind and capacity that Ireland will need at the Peace Conference – the mind and capacity of the Statesman'. It was the growing belief that the postwar international settlement – brokered by America – would deliver Irish independence, that gave Sinn Féin credibility. The parliamentary party, on the other hand, hobbled by the Irish Convention, could not even offer a clear vision of Home Rule as an attainable goal. Its commitment to the war may already have doomed it; and there was a grim symbolism to the death of Redmond's widely admired younger brother Willie in the Battle of Messines in June – a battle in which both the Irish and the Ulster Divisions fought side by side, 'the closest the army came to creating John Redmond's dearest hope'.[36] Messines, 'the first completely successful single operation on the British front', would remain a poignant image of the war that might have been.

Short of proscribing Sinn Féin – a course that was now being toyed with, in fact – there was not much the government could have done to negate its impressive display of unity and practicality. The case of Ashe, however, was different: the policy that led to his rearrest (within weeks of his release, but on a far less serious charge), and also his treatment in prison, lay at the discretion of the authorities. Duke, ruefully noting that his death was 'a very great misfortune', admitted that 'I ought perhaps to have foreseen the conflict which would arise between the prisoners and the prison authorities.'[37] The potential impact of his martyrdom (something Maxwell himself had certainly been attuned to) seems not to have concentrated any minds in the restored Castle administration, much less in Whitehall. Duke, an upright and well-meaning administrator, showed that he could give out conflicting messages with the best of his predecessors, alarming liberals with the threat of martial law while exasperating Unionists by his meticulous legalism. (His instructions to the army in July 1917 ran to ten points, whose 'guiding principle' was intended to be 'a distinction between opinion uttered in speech and the overt acts generally to which mischievous opinions and evil advice are intended to lead'.)[38] Inconsistencies abounded: the authorities were tough on 'seditious' songs, like 'Who fears to speak of Easter Week', which were spread across the country at Sinn Féin concerts, and often intervened to ban these popular entertainments. But the display of portraits of executed rebels in shop windows, which was seen as equally dangerous, had been let alone for so long that 'interference now would cause much irritation and probably increase disaffection', so nothing was ever done about it.[39] Duke's use of DORA in 1917 has been described as 'almost inconceivable foolhardiness' and 'astonishing obtuseness'. The best that has been said of it is that it was 'fairly successful in containing political violence', but the main reason for this was that the Volunteers themselves were moving deliberately slowly towards any more open confrontation.[40] Indeed, the death of Ashe was catastrophic in terms of longer-term containment, since it energized a whole cohort of Volunteers.

The regime was still impaled on the corrosive contradiction between the image and the reality of military power. Like Maxwell before him, Mahon complained that the position was 'anomalous'. The country could not be said to be under martial law, though the normal administration of the law had been 'seriously modified' by DORA. 'The civil authorities remain primarily responsible for the preservation of law and order, and are not controlled by the military authorities in matters of policy.' Sentences imposed by courts martial under DORA could be 'modified by the civil powers on political grounds', and often were. The inevitable result of such adjustments was to create the impression that the civil and military authorities were 'following divergent policies'. Worst of all, the situation 'threw on the military authorities all the odium of a military dictatorship, where they do not enjoy the power'.[41] This mixing of messages was all the more surprising in light of Duke's initial conviction that 'subordination of an impartial administration of the law to political expediency' had led to a 'universal feeling of distrust in the integrity of the legal process in Ireland'. This had been a key component of the 'misgovernment' which had culminated in the rebellion. But in 1917 the Solicitor General was still insisting that 'the real test of whether a prosecution should be undertaken is not whether the offence deserves to be punished, but whether the prosecution serves any good purpose'.[42]

By the end of the year, the government had lost this luxury. It was unable to disarm the Ulster Volunteers for fear of provoking a strike in the northern munitions factories.[43] It was unable to prevent defiance of the law against drilling. The Cabinet was told in November that governmental authority 'was being openly defied'. If troops were used to put down drilling, 'bloodshed would undoubtedly ensue'. The Foreign Secretary went as far as to propose that tanks be brought in to 'bring home to the Sinn Feiners the perilous nature of their behaviour'. But Duke glumly concluded that the only thing was for the police 'to keep their heads up' and not be 'overawed by superior force'.[44]

Only one thing could have done more than this confused regime to foment opposition – the imposition of conscription. The threat never went away during 1917, but Duke was (inevitably) cautious about the possibility of carrying it through. Responding to Lord Milner's bullish – and very British – insistence in February 1917 that Irish resistance could and should be overcome by firmness, and that Ireland would be better for 'the improvement of the men drilled', Duke protested that without an immediate grant of Home Rule, conscription would mean 'some bloodshed now and intensified animosities later'. It would also destroy the parliamentary party.[45] He was firmly backed by Lord Wimborne – certainly no dove on the issue of recruitment – and by the newly appointed Inspector-General of the RIC, Brigadier-General Joseph Byrne (formerly Irish Command's legal chief). The issue was shelved for a year, but on 21 March 1918 the stunning German breakthrough on the western front brought it to a head. This was the most intense crisis of the whole war: it seemed to be the final emergency that would remove all remaining limits on conscription in Britain. Continued Irish exemption became intolerable to British public opinion. Only desperation can explain the politically disastrous steps taken by the government over the following couple of months.

As it happened, Lord French, the Commander-in-Chief of Home Forces, was on a tour of inspection in Ireland when the German offensive began. He came back to assure the Cabinet that only a small increase in the Irish garrison would be needed to enforce conscription. Taking Milner's cue, he argued that two-thirds of the Sinn Feiners could be turned into good soldiers if they were removed from the pernicious influence of their leaders. His belief in the transforming power of military discipline – and in the shallowness of Sinn Féin – was to survive for the duration of the war, with baleful consequences for British policy. The majority of young Irishmen were subjected to 'the terrorism of a few self-seeking hotheads', he insisted as late as October 1918. 'Place them in suitable surroundings, and they are just as easily aroused into imperial enthusiasm as, in the contrary case, they are filled with hatred and anger by a few crafty sedition-mongers, or young priestly fanatics, amongst whom alone they live.'[46] Against this view, Duke continued to protest that conscription would be an arduous, violent process with doubtful results: 'we might almost as well recruit Germans'. Sir James Campbell advised that Sinn Féin was no longer composed solely of extremists, but had support across the community, including many of the clergy. (And not just 'young priestly fanatics'.) More surprisingly yet, Sir Edward Carson advised that 'the result of conscription in Ireland would be such that its introduction is not worth contemplating' – unless it was absolutely necessary to secure wider compulsion in Britain.[47] In spite of this, Lloyd George not only accepted French's view, but gave him Wimborne's job. More than that, he was allowed to revive the title of Viceroy and construct a new administration in which he had real executive power.

All this was a propaganda gift of dizzying proportions to Sinn Féin: not only conscription – or at any rate a Military Service Bill to permit it – but also the return of a 'military governor', and then, in May, the arrest of Sinn Féin leaders under a trumped-up 'German Plot'. These oppressions were exploited with urgent energy by the increasingly efficient Sinn Féin organization, which could now claim to have seen off Henry Duke. Duke's final reports were extraordinarily pessimistic; in March he saw real signs of insurgency beginning: 'nightly visits of armed and masked men to houses in lonely districts in search of arms', even some attacks on police.[48] The mobilization against conscription crystallized the wide nationalist front which had been in gradual formation since 1916. The Irish Party walked out of the House of Commons, an action which had precedents in its own history, but which now looked like a vindication of Sinn Féin's abstentionism. The adhesion of the clergy was cemented when an anti-conscription resolution adopted by an all-party rally at the Dublin Mansion House on 16 April (the day the Military Service Bill passed its third reading) was endorsed by a meeting of the Hierarchy at Maynooth. A deputation from the Mansion House proposed to the bishops that a pledge (drafted by de Valera) 'to resist conscription by the most effective means at our disposal' should be taken by people in every parish. The bishops' reformulation was more guarded but hardly less decisive in political terms: 'We consider that conscription forced in this way upon Ireland is an oppressive and inhuman law, which the Irish people have the right to resist by every means that are consonant with the law of God.' What this limitation would mean in practical terms remained obscure, but an indicative exchange of views took place between de Valera and Cardinal Logue over lunch. When the Sinn Féin leader spelled it out that 'no matter who decided anything, the Volunteers would fight if conscription was enforced, and they had no use for passive resistance', the Cardinal replied, 'Well now, Mr de Valera, when I talk about passive resistance, I don't mean we are to lie down and let people walk over us.'[49]

In organizing the 300 or more anti-conscription meetings that took place (according to police figures) during the week ending Saturday 20 April, the clergy were at least as active as Sinn Féin. And clerical influence was no longer likely to contain extremism. When the pledge was signed outside parish churches across the country that Sunday, the Inspector-General of the RIC noted that some men were refusing the clerical version 'as restricting their right to use arms'.[50] The situation could hardly have been more serious for the government. Its reaction was to allow French to attempt to arrest and intern once more all the Sinn Féin leaders. The sweep was carried out on 16 May, but although at least seventy were arrested, the organization's impetus was barely checked. (Michael Collins, among others, evaded arrest.) The problematic nature of the alleged German plot was made clear to the Prime Minister by the new Chief Secretary, Edward Shortt: 'we do not pretend that we can prove that each individual taken has been in active personal communication with German agents, but we know that someone has', and each of the internees had said or done something 'which gives ground for the suspicion that he or she is in it'.

Lloyd George's support for this policy is hard to comprehend. At a critical juncture he gave power to a soldier who would take the view that 'every day that has passed since I became Viceroy of Ireland has proved more clearly the unfitness of Ireland for any form of Home Rule, now or in the immediate future'. Admittedly, Lloyd George might have appointed French under the impression – quite justified by French's behaviour during the prewar Home Rule crisis – that the Field-Marshal was a Home Ruler. But if this was simply a misunderstanding, it would not explain why he allowed French to assume greater powers – albeit refusing his brusque demand for at least two months of pure military rule – and why he also brought Walter Long back to the centre of the Cabinet's Irish policy-making in mid-1918. Long was, again, a Home Ruler of sorts – but the sort of Home Rule he favoured was the complicated federalism of 'Home Rule All Round', which had never been a viable project, and was by now a dead duck as far as Irish nationalist opinion was concerned. Strangest of all, this most assertive of prime ministers never challenged the self-proclaimed expertise of French and Long on Irish affairs. 'There was no penetrating inquiry into their views, no scepticism about their qualifications.'[51] It is hard not to conclude that he himself was never a Home Ruler, and that his preferred role model – one he was to spell out several times in the following years – was Abraham Lincoln. He would, if necessary, fight to preserve the Union.

A fight, certainly, he would get. During the winter of 1917–18 the economic impact of the war, rising food prices and unemployment, offered fertile ground for the government's opponents. Sinn Féin had exploited the increasing food shortages to display its practical administrative skills, while a new outbreak of agrarian agitation, probably as uncongenial to the new national leadership as it had ever been, nonetheless magnified the local position of the Volunteers. (Richard Mulcahy, now Chief of Staff in the reconstituted GHQ, cagily admitted that 'individual Volunteers including officers found it difficult not to be involved in agitational movements'.)[52] In the west, certainly, there seems no doubt that a major reason for Sinn Féin's dramatic growth in 1917–18 was its embrace of the cause of land redistribution. After the last serious agrarian disturbances, the 'Ranch War' in 1904–8, the Parliamentary Party had tried to bank down the fires of rural conflict because 'disorder' was bad publicity at Westminster. Thus Sinn Féin was able 'to outflank the IPP on the land question' during the war.[53] In Galway, the police warned in early 1918 that 'a new phase of Sinn Fein' as 'an agrarian movement for the forcible possession of lands' would 'bring many young men into the movement, which had no attraction for them before'.[54] The drastic reduction of emigration during the war raised land hunger to a new pitch, and the scale of agrarian action could be formidable. As early as July 1916 Maxwell had to send an entire battalion of infantry to Roscommon, where the police were being overwhelmed by large-scale cattle drives near Ballinasloe. By March 1918 'a bitter and aggressive feeling' was reported to be 'gradually and generally manifested towards the police' in the midlands as well as the south. In Clare, 'a state of utter lawlessness existed', and 'cattle-driving was general'. Crowds many hundreds, even thousands, strong 'assembled to carry out well-organised [cattle] raids, utterly regardless of the presence of the police'.[55]

The conscription crisis found the Volunteer organization poised to focus and exploit the new level of public militancy. Raids for arms became commonplace. The organization's national military structure became more systematic. Ernie O'Malley, who became an organizer in several midland counties, detailed the preparations to resist conscription: 'committees and subcommittees worked on transport and food supply; statistics were compiled . . . We skirmished and manoeuvred through towns and the countryside followed by police. Officers were arrested and at once replaced . . . gun cartridges were collected and refilled.'[56] A new 'General Headquarters' staff was far more energetic and professional than its predecessor before 1916. Its newspaper, re-founded under the title *An tOglác*, immediately adopted a more warlike tone than the old *Irish Volunteer*. In October, the veteran Volunteer organizer Ernest Blythe penned an article entitled 'Ruthless Warfare', more menacing than anything seen so far. Against the 'atrocity' of conscription, Blythe urged, 'we must decide that in our resistance we shall acknowledge no limit and no scruple'. Anyone, civilian or soldier, who 'assists directly or by connivance in this crime against us should be killed without mercy or hesitation'. Thus:

the man who serves on an exemption tribunal, the doctor who examines con- scripts, the man who voluntarily surrenders when called for, the man who applies for an exemption, the man who drives a police car or assists in the transport of army supplies, must be shot or otherwise destroyed with the least possible delay.

A new kind of insurgency, very different from the war of which Pearse had dreamed, was emerging.[57]

When the Great War at last ended, conscription had still not been implemented. But as with so many other parts of its Irish policy, the British government reaped all the political damage of the threat with- out achieving any concrete result. W. B. Yeats must have reflected the bafflement of many when he wrote to Lord Haldane just a month before the end of the war:

I read in the newspaper yesterday that over three hundred thousand Americans have landed in France in a month, and it seems to me a strangely wanton thing that England, for the sake of fifty thousand Irish soldiers, is pre- pared to hollow another trench between the two countries and fill it with blood.

He urged 'Englishmen' – the Scot Haldane presumably included – to listen to his friend Lady Gregory, who 'knows the country as few know it' (and who lived in that deeply 'disturbed' area of Craughwell in Galway). She was convinced that, when troops came to enforce conscription, 'the women and children will stand in front of the men to receive the bullets'. If this was alarmism, it reflected the reality, 'a return to that sense of crisis which followed the Rising', better than a British government that (Yeats protested) was 'rushing into this busi- ness in a strangely trivial frame of mind'.[58]

Thanks in part, at least, to Lloyd George's policies, the Irish Party which had worked for so long to achieve Home Rule within the frame- work of the Union was effectively wiped out at the end of 1918. The outcome of the December general election, in which Sinn Féin won all but six of the former 'Nationalist' seats, was an astounding reversal of the prewar political balance. It was not a mandate for renewed rebellion, certainly: Sinn Féin candidates tended to stress the primacy of peaceful methods, rather than invoking the memory of 1916. What Sinn Féin 'stood for' remained unclear to many. The *Irish Times* was not alone in saying 'Sinn Fein has swept the board, but we do not know – does Sinn Fein itself know what it intends to do with the victory?'[59] What was clear was that this victory had been directly determined by the 'conscription crisis' and the reversion to military government. The conscription issue had run like a dark thread through the whole history of Ireland's war experience. The terms in which the issue was put in the spring of 1918 – of 'equity of sacrifice' – seemed unanswerable in England. But such terms had become irrelevant in Ireland, and because of this the Union could not survive if the threat of conscription became a reality. Those Volunteer leaders who, like MacNeill and Hobson, had argued against rebellion, had always rested their case on this fundamental point. They believed that English necessity would inevitably drive the government to alienate Irish opinion. In this way, they thought that a unifying crisis like that of 1918 would have happened whether or not the republicans had come out to do battle at Easter 1916. Were they, in the end, proved right?

EPILOGUE:

The Rebellion in History

I had no idea that any public event could so deeply move me
– & I am very despondent about the future. At this moment I
feel that all the work of years has been overturned.

W. B. Yeats, 11 May 1916

On 21 January 1919, the victorious Sinn Féin general election candidates who were at large (36 out of 69 were in prison) assembled in the Dublin Mansion House as the independent parliament of Ireland, Dáil Éireann. For the next two and a half years, an attempt to establish an alternative state structure under the leadership of Eamon de Valera and Arthur Griffith was accompanied by a guerrilla campaign fought by the Irish Volunteers. The Irish Republican Army, as the organization became generally known, continued to be led from Dublin, where its headquarters were dominated by Richard Mulcahy and Michael Collins, but it also flourished – by contrast with 1916 – in the countryside, above all in Munster. Rebel Cork recovered its fame, Tomas MacCurtain was assassinated by RIC 'Black and Tans', and Terence MacSwiney matched Thomas Ashe in conducting the most epic of all republican hunger strikes. In July 1921 a truce was negotiated, followed by longer negotiations for a political settlement. The establishment of the Irish Free State in 1922, however, was a deeply contested process; men and women of 1916 took opposite sides over the terms of the Anglo-Irish Treaty that created it. A year of civil war was the start of a long struggle to bring political reality into line with the aspirations of the 1916 rebels. The anti-Treaty IRA remained, on and off, ready to return to violence against Britain itself, the six counties of partitioned Northern Ireland, and the twenty-six counties of the Dublin-governed state that they regarded as a British puppet. There was a wide sense that the Irish revolution was a *révolution manquée*. History had not gone quite according to plan. Had 1916 been betrayed, or was it – perhaps – itself a cause of this disappointment?

In the immediate aftermath of the rebellion, W. B. Yeats and Augusta Gregory registered its impact on that Ango-Irish intellectual elite which had so often been at loggerheads with the Gaelic enthusiasts of the Volunteers. The 'work of years' that Yeats was concerned about was the 'bringing together of classes, the freeing of Irish literature from politics'. Lady Gregory's mind, too, was 'filled with sorrow at the Dublin tragedy, the death of Pearse and McDonough [*sic*], who ought to have been on our side'. But she had a clear perception that 'the leaders were what is wanted in Ireland – a fearless & imaginative opposition to the conventional & opportunist parliamentarians'. Yeats was struck by Maud Gonne's reaction: 'tragic dignity had returned to Ireland'. As early as 11 May he was 'trying to write a poem on the men executed – "terrible beauty has been born"'.[1] The poem took longer than he, or at any rate Gonne, expected; he worked on it through the summer at her house on the Normandy coast (where, from time to time, he could hear the distant echoes of artillery from the Somme). He finished '1916' at Coole Park, Lady Gregory's home in Galway, in late September, and circulated it to a private audience as 'Easter, 1916'. Maud Gonne's response to this extraordinary poem was interesting. It was not worthy of him, '& above all it isn't worthy of the subject'. She, like many, was hoping for a poem 'which our race would treasure & repeat', and found a creation that despite its 'beautiful lines' was not 'a great WHOLE . . . which would have avenged our material failure by its spiritual beauty'.[2]

What made it hard to recognize this as a great public poem was in part its meditative inwardness: Yeats was visibly wrestling with the re-evaluation of the rebel leaders, and though he ended with an almost 'Davisite' celebration – 'Now and in time to be, / Wherever green is worn' – the refrain 'a terrible beauty is born' remained ambivalent. And from Gonne's viewpoint, the poem was verging on anti-nationalist, especially its wonderful central section, in which Yeats counterposed the rigidity of republican thinking ('Hearts with one purpose alone . . . Enchanted to a stone') against the endless changing of the real world (the 'living stream'). Worst of all, perhaps, it obliquely challenged the rebellion's validity. Yeats stopped short of saying that the real situation had been 'changed utterly'; it was only the memory of the rebels that had. Indeed, his final stanza gave expression to what may be called the 'revisionist' view: 'Was it needless death after all? / For England may keep faith . . .' – in other words, concede Home Rule. From a republican standpoint this was absolutely heretical – a reversion to the constitutionalist trust in British generosity. 'Easter, 1916' has been well called 'the first work of revisionist poetry, revisionist history, revisionist literary criticism'.[3]

By withholding publication of the poem for several years, Yeats initially opted out of what F. X. Martin called 'the rally of the literary men', one of the key modes of cementing the rebellion's place in national history. Though some who rallied, notably Bernard Shaw, were major literary figures, the stature of others might sometimes be debatable. One influential work, *The Memory of the Dead*, produced in 1917 by 'Martin Daly' (Stephen McKenna), was a quasi-hagiographical monument to nine of the men killed in Easter Week. Another, *The Soldier's Story of Easter Week*, published by Brian O'Higgins in 1925 but written in 1917, celebrated the rebellion as 'a spiritual victory over selfishness, expediency and compromise and materialism'. After 1925 it was never out of print, and together with a clutch of similar products it exerted a cumulative influence on the popular reading of the rebellion – what Martin called the 'faith and fatherland' interpretation. The dead 1916 leaders underwent a steady process of secular sanctification, at the expense of their human qualities and frailties: the pinnacle of this process was perhaps the famous 1932 biography of Pearse by Louis Le Roux, a Breton author writing in French. First published at Rennes, it was immediately translated by Pearse's pupil Desmond Ryan (who had himself written a short, celebratory study, *The Man Called Pearse*, in 1919). Something about the saintly image projected by this work had the effect of preventing any further attempt to evaluate Pearse until the 1970s. It was curious, too, that after the small spate of journalists' accounts published immediately after the rebellion, no participant, or historian, wrote a comprehensive history of it until Desmond Ryan did so in the late 1940s.[4]

By comparison, the 'revisionist' response got off to a faltering start. The former opponents of insurrection, admittedly, tended to keep quiet – notably Hobson and MacNeill (who never tried to vindicate his countermanding order, and whose tersely argued memorandum did not become publicly known until long after his death). O'Connell, perhaps less surprisingly, also refrained from open criticism. Not so, however, Eimar O'Duffy, who committed his long wrestling with the issue to paper in the form of a semi-autobiographical novel, *The Wasted Island*. Like so much of the earnest literary output of Sinn Feiners at this time, this was full of 'hours and hours of talk and arguments' between differing nationalist groups 'that are, for all their point and wit, like formal debates'.[5] O'Duffy chose a form which did not carry a single thesis, but the pessimism of his title made its own comment – and there was special force in one of his characters' view of the rebellion: 'This'll give the English just the chance they want, to grind us back into the mud we're barely rising from.' Another replies, 'Good God! A hundred more years of slavery. The blind idiots!' One can certainly imagine Hobson expressing such sentiments, and the fact that the novel was finished after Sinn Féin's election victory and the establishment of Dáil Éireann in 1919 indicates that O'Duffy did not place much hope in the second round of the Anglo-Irish war. (This despite the fact that under Mulcahy and Collins, who also condemned – though not on paper – the military conduct of the rebellion, a form of fighting much closer to the guerrilla model espoused by O'Duffy and O'Connell was then being adopted.)[6]

The second fight, which led to the Anglo-Irish Treaty and the establishment of the Irish Free State, had the effect of stilling re-evaluation of 1916 for many years. The anti-treaty republicans of course took their stand on the rightness, indeed the holiness of the rebels, but even their fiercest opponents incorporated the rebellion in the Free State's political genealogy. (This was not easy in principle, since it risked enshrining the very political violence that the Free State was denouncing as undemocratic during the civil war. It was especially hard for those like Griffith who – unlike his Free State colleagues Collins and Cosgrave – had not only not been 'out' in 1916, but who had been consistently opposed to violence even during the 1919–21 conflict.) Denying it was not a political option for anyone unprepared to alienate mainstream opinion. Only a maverick like Sean O'Casey could face the outrage caused by an attempt to portray the absurd, destructive and pointless aspects of the rebellion. *The Plough and the Stars* (1926) did just that, and despite its 'overpowering' quality – in the view of Lady Gregory, no mean judge of drama ('I felt at the end as if I should never care to look at another; all others would seem so shadowy to the mind after this') – it provoked a public furore. The uproar at the Abbey Theatre was so violent that Yeats, defending the play from the stage, was able to mime a speech and then go off to a newspaper office to write what he might have said. Hanna Sheehy-Skeffington's charge that the drama's claimed realism was 'morbid perversity' that 'held up to derision and obloquy the men and women of Easter Week' was a comparatively mild protest, but nonetheless effective. O'Casey's dyspeptic perspective – he would have called it honesty – was not endorsed by any significant public figure for almost half a century.

Participation in the rebellion, or at least the ability to suggest it, became a key part of every nationalist politician's résumé. Eoin MacNeill remarked to Bulmer Hobson during Easter week that 'we would have no political future if we were not arrested'. This was certainly true for Hobson himself (who had the unenviable distinction of being the only IRB man arrested by the republicans rather than the British). It may not have been true for everyone – Kevin O'Higgins was a spectacular exception – but the Free State's first political generation was dominated by 1916 veterans – Cosgrave and de Valera leading, with a cohort of lieutenants such as Mulcahy, MacEntee and Oscar Traynor. In the Fianna Fáil party, especially, which called itself 'the republican party', and which under the leadership of Eamon de Valera and his successors was the main party of government after 1932, the challenge 'where were you in 1916?' became an all too familiar put-down. And starting from the chilling invocation of the dead by hardline republicans during the debate over the Treaty, Irish political life tended to confirm what Yeats recognized in his fatalistic poem 'Sixteen Dead Men' (written in 1917), the power of martyrdom to prohibit compromise – 'who can talk of give and take . . . while those dead men are loitering there?' Political logic could not 'outweigh/MacDonagh's bony thumb'; indeed, political discussion was pointless, because only the conversation of the dead – 'bone to bone' with their 'new comrades', the heroes of the past – really mattered.

The fiftieth anniversary of the rebellion began a process of unravelling these stifling pieties. The public celebration of this event showed, admittedly, that Pearse's original prorities still prevailed. The reinforcement of 'Irish' identity took precedence over the preservation of a 'united Ireland'. The planners of 1916 had shown little if any interest in the risk of alienating northern Unionist opinion, and the possibility that their action might cement the partition of the island. The 1966 celebrations were similarly self-referential (if not solipsistic), even though the republic had fallen some way short of fulfilling the original vital aim that Ireland be both free and 'Gaelic', for which unity had been sacrificed. The festival was accompanied by 'a colourful crop' of popular 'faith and fatherland' accounts of 1916.[7] But the anniversary produced some good histories as well, most notably Max Caulfield's vividly detailed *The Easter Rebellion*, even though academic historians still confined themselves to collections of essays rather than full-scale studies.[8]

It also led some serious thinkers to reassess the rebellion's place in the title deeds of the Irish state. (We should note, since it is often suggested that 'revisionism' was provoked by the revival of IRA terrorism, that in 1966 the IRA was in disarray, and the belief in north–south détente was stronger than it had been at any time since 1921.)[9] Eoin MacNeill's withering assessment of the insurrectionists had recently been discovered (in 1961), and caused a degree of public interest rare if not unique for an academic journal publication. In 1966 Garret FitzGerald, son of Desmond FitzGerald, and a future prime minister, approached the problem from the angle of the Fine Gael politicians who had always had to handle the 1916 legacy gingerly. In a typically unostentatious essay he assessed the validity of the basic justification for the rebellion: the rebels' belief that 'without a gesture such as the Rising the spirit of Irish nationality and the sense of national identity would flicker out'. Cautiously airing the counterview that 'the gains thus secured were offset by losses' – above all, partition – he admitted that 'it would appear more logical to have given the maintenance of national unity priority over the speedy attainment of independence'. History had sadly demonstrated that once the political unity of Ireland was broken, it would be extremely hard (even perhaps impossible) to restore it. So the postponement of independence, 'even for a couple of decades, would have been a small price to have paid to avoid Partition'. But FitzGerald backed away from this conclusion, using his father's memoirs (still unpublished at that time) to argue for an acceptance of the cultural anxiety that had impelled the rebels to act. This, he said, called for an effort of imagination, because 'the very success of 1916 has weakened our understanding of why its leaders felt that the Rising was needed'.[10]

Francis Shaw and Conor Cruise O'Brien, however, pushed much more aggressively the contention that 1916 was a mistake. Shaw, a Jesuit, wrote his essay 'The Canon of Irish History – A Challenge' for the same issue of *Studies* in which FitzGerald's article was published, but the editors withheld it until 1972. (Whatever the reasons for this, it had the effect of launching the argument at the height of the IRA's renewed Northern Ireland campaign, reinforcing the impression that it was a response to terrorism.) It was certainly strong meat for a culture which had made a long and patient effort to absorb the 1916 legacy – to the point where inveterate Unionist institutions such as the *Irish Times* could celebrate the anniversary, and the Provost of Trinity College had hung a copy of the Proclamation on the wall of his study. Fr Shaw unleashed a head-on assault not only on Pearse's justifications for the rebellion, but also on the essence of his nationalist doctrine. The argument that Irish national spirit was dying away before 1916 was wholly wrong, he contended. Far from having lost their way, the Irish people knew very well where they were going, and were well on the way there. Home Rule was not only a realistic and achievable goal, but it answered the history of Irish national thought more accurately than did the separatist ideal of the republic. This was serious 'revision' indeed – the argument that an accommodation with Britain was natural, right and proper to the Irish, the polar opposite to the 'faith and fatherland' insistence on the absolute rejection of any connection. Shaw bolstered it with a blistering denunciation of Pearse's version of Irish nationality (which he sardonically labelled the 'new testament'). Its 'most potent ingredient was hatred of England'; it was 'essentially a gospel of hate'.

Pearse's claim to ground it in Christianity was specious, indeed blasphemous; of Pearse's equation in 'The Coming Revolution' of the people with Christ – 'the people itself will perhaps be its own Messiah, scourged, crowned with thorns, agonized and dying . . . for peoples are divine' – Shaw suggested 'it is hard to imagine anyone reading those words today without a shudder'.[11] And his key argument was that 'the people' had rejected the rebellion, without realizing it, in the way they lived. 'The ideals which inspired it have not worn well; they have been quietly but firmly side-stepped by the Irish people.'

Conor Cruise O'Brien rested his evaluation of 1916, provocatively, on a quotation from Lenin: 'The misfortune of the Irish is that they rose prematurely, when the European revolt of the proletariat had not yet matured.' O'Brien took the MacNeill/Hobson argument that conscription would have radicalized Irish resistance, and gave it a global reach. Not only could Ireland have mounted a real revolution in 1918, but it could have triggered the European revolution that never was. Irish troops in the British army would have mutinied, and the mutiny would have spread to the French and (here an uncharacteristic note of caution entered) 'it might' have spread to the German army too. The Irish rebellion then could have been the 'pin in the hands of a child' that could, in Connolly's phrase, have 'pierced the heart of a giant' – European capitalism.[12] This whole argument, of course, was unlikely to be attractive to those who never wanted a 'real' revolution in the first place – and this would include many Sinn Feiners and more Volunteers. But its premise was powerful: the mobilization that would have happened over the conscription issue would have been more spontaneous and far-reaching, and less divisive, than the process of responding to the rebellion.

The quarter-century between 1966 and the 75th anniversary of the rebellion in 1991 witnessed some of the farthest-reaching social transformations in modern Irish history. As the *Irish Times* journalist Kevin Myers wrote, there could be 'few more astonishing examples of the change in the political culture of the Irish Republic than the Dublin Government's decision to have such muted celebrations' of the anniversary.[13] Official activity was limited to a small military ceremony outside the GPO, attended by President Mary Robinson and

Prime Minister Charles Haughey; for the rest, the celebration was a gala of poetry readings and parades which 'could be mistaken for normal Easter high jinks'. The most pressing reason for the striking contrast with 1966 was the fear of giving aid and comfort to the IRA – an acknowledgement, in fact, of how successfully republicans had appropriated the 1916 legacy. (Or, as one anonymous source was quoted as putting it, 'we have allowed the very noble and honourable tradition which produced Easter 1916 to be hijacked by a conspiracy of thugs'.) The reason had not changed, but had become more acute: 'The Irish government find themselves venerating those who used violence in 1916 while denouncing those who do so today.'[14] At the same time, the ambivalence of 1991 also reflected a shift of priorities, from traditional nationalism to a wider Europeanism – and indeed an embrace of the materialism thought by nationalists to be so alien. When the IRA attempted to transform the view that Pearse would once have had from the GPO, by blowing up Nelson's Pillar in 1966, the space was eventually filled (at the city's millennium in 1988) by what Dubliners called 'the floozy in the jacuzzi' (officially the 'Anna Livia Millennium Fountain'), a somewhat louche representation of the Liffey in female form. The Christian millennium would in turn see this displaced by a more chaste giant needle; it would also see the other side of O'Connell Street occupied by an Ann Summers sex supermarket.)

There was also a re-evaluation of the rebellion itself, often blamed (as Myers noted) on 'the triumph of revisionist historians who regard the 1916 rising as a deeply anti-democratic conspiracy which cast as much darkness across Irish history as it did light'. This may perhaps have exaggerated the power of historians, most of whom were still impressed by the resilience of the traditional interpretation. In 1991, indeed, a vigorous wave of anti-revisionist argument (launched within the profession by Brendan Bradshaw and outside it by Des Fennell)[15] crested with a Field Day publication, *Revising the Rising*, notable for a fierce assault by Seamus Deane on Roy Foster's historical writing.[16] Focusing on a paragraph in Foster's *Modern Ireland* (1988) dealing with the negative impact of the 1916 rebellion on Ulster Unionist perceptions of nationalist Ireland, Deane asserted that 'revisionism' was not a genuine attempt to write value-free history but a politically loaded project; an anti-nationalist, in fact Unionist, project. This perception lay at the heart of the storm over 'revisionism', since nobody could really dispute the proposition (earlier made by Foster under the banner 'we are all revisionists now') that all historical research necessarily 'revises' the understanding of the past. Nor, surely, could many of their critics really think that historians believed they were producing wholly objective, 'value-free' interpretations. What 'revisionism' was about – not just in Ireland, but also in countries such as Italy whose *risorgimento* was the stuff of legend – was a preparedness to correct the distortions involved in the creation of national foundation myths. These myths are politically vital to the process of nation-building, but there has to come a time when, to complete the process of national emancipation, their elisions and fabrications are recognized, and less flattering aspects of the story can be confronted. In place of a linear, teleological story of national liberation, there needs to be awareness of the complexity out of which an alternative story could have emerged. To brand 'revisionism' as promoting any particular political view was simply to miss the point.

Admittedly some of the history written after 1966 was strikingly iconoclastic. The pre-eminent example was surely the first biography of Pearse to be published since that of Le Roux, by Ruth Dudley Edwards in 1977.[17] This brilliant study was far from hostile to him, but it was widely read as such; simply by treating Pearse as a human being rather than a secular saint it seemed guaranteed to outrage the mainstream view. Heightening the image of Pearse as a man tortured by inadequacy and failure drawn by William Irwin Thompson a decade earlier, and naturally enough – at least for the world outside Ireland – speculating about his sexuality, it nourished a much more complex image of the rebellion's motives and methods. Yet Ruth Dudley Edwards was still unusual among historians in tackling the shibboleths of 1916. Apart perhaps from James Connolly, no other rebel leader was subjected to full-scale re-evaluation in this way, and in Connolly's case the evaluation remained primarily political rather than personal.[18] The rebellion itself remained an unappealing topic for historians.[19] Even in a 500-page *Military History of Ireland* published in the mid-1990s, barely a single page was devoted to the rebellion; and here it was curtly dismissed as 'reckless, bloody, sacrificial and unsuccessful'. The rebels made 'no serious attempt to occupy sites of either strategic or symbolic importance', instead 'ensuring . . . horrific damage to civilians, shops and houses'.[20]

The stress on the conspiratorial, undemocratic, and destructive nature of the rebellion was only part of the re-evaluation. The most challenging 'revisionist' proposition was the argument that all the most important objectives of national liberation – including some, such as 'unity', that were lost as a result of 1916 – could have been achieved without bloodshed and violence. In a sense this was a restatement not only of MacNeill's and Hobson's objections to insurrection, but of the constitutionalist, 'Redmondite' commitment to negotiation. It derived its force from a hard-headed comparison of what was finally achieved in 1921 with what Britain was offering before the violence began. How wide, really, was the gap between these? The key gain, undeniably, was the formal British recognition of 'Dominion Status' – the favourite parallel at the time was the status of Canada – which put the Irish Free State in a category that had not been envisaged in the Home Rule discussions. Though republicans denounced the Free State as a puppet regime, there was also a strong argument that its institutions, and in particular its constitution, were 'essentially republican'.[21] And though republicans argued that its 'independence' was a sham, which could be withdrawn any time Britain chose, it is clear in retrospect that for Britain there was no going back. The centuries-long attempt to dominate Ireland by force was over. But alongside such gains was the equally undeniable fact that the Irish polity consisted of twenty-six counties, just as it would have done under Home Rule. It could be argued that the gains were achieved not by the unmandated violence of 1916 but by the popular mandate of 1918, a product of the war in general rather than the rebellion in particular, while the setback – partition – was not mitigated but actually made worse by the rebellion.

Almost forty years after his 1966 essay, Garret FitzGerald returned – as an elder statesman with long experience of government – to the questions he had raised, and came to the same conclusions.[22] But he did so in part by taking 'the national revival of 1916–21' as the process at issue. Though he found it 'very doubtful' that 'without 1916' Irish independence could have been achieved within a reasonable time (which he, characteristically, took to be time enough to allow Ireland to grow into the contemporary post-national world), he assumed that 1916 and 1918 were part of the same process. Yet the argument that the decisive national mobilization would have happened in 1918 with or without the 1916 rebellion remains a powerful one. Opposition to conscription was the key motive for the expansion of both Sinn Féin and Volunteer membership during the war. At the individual level, it may be asked whether without conscription Michael Collins (to take one notable example) would have returned to Ireland from London at that point. At the institutional level, no other cause could have brought the Catholic Church so firmly into the Sinn Féin-led national front. And on the face of things, at least, it could be argued that the 1916 rebellion made the imposition of conscription – and hence the dramatic upsurge of national unity in 1918 – less rather than more likely.

The problem with any such assessment is that of all 'counterfactual' historical argument: we cannot know what 1918 would have been like if 1916 had not happened. The potent effect of martyrdom is obvious, for instance, but we may be sure that a rebellion was not necessary to create martyrs – Thomas Ashe was killed by the routine incompetence of British administration. What the rebellion surely did was to shift the horizons of possibility, both at the subliminal and the practical level. It has been well said that 1916 was above all a public drama, an astonishingly effective piece of street theatre. It was costume drama, staged by dramatists in a 'drama-mad' city. In this sense Michael Collins missed the mark when he complained that it had 'the air of a Greek tragedy'. That was, above all else, its point. The occupation of the GPO was open to criticism in military terms, but 'as an act of dramatic symbolism it was an inspired choice, since it cut across the main street of the capital city, paralysing communications and forcing everyone to take notice'.[23] Even if it fell too soon because of military miscalculations by the planners of the rebellion, the manner of its fall – the awesome Wagnerian inferno of smoke and flame – etched an indelible image on the public memory. (Neil Jordan's imposing re-creation of the scene at the opening of his film *Michael Collins* has eloquently re-established this.) Not all the posts chosen, admittedly, were equally inspired, but the symbolic effect of the rebellion by the middle of Easter week was to burst the limits of what could be imagined. It was not, it transpired, necessary to seize such obvious symbols as Dublin Castle to show that the established order was upheld by psychological as much as physical means.

Collective psychological processes often work in an occult way that makes precise analysis difficult. Whereas it may not be hard to grasp the impact of such high-profile events as the execution of the 1916 rebels, it is harder to explain some of the lower-level shifts which nonetheless vitally contribute to political reconfiguration. An example, not entirely at random, is the adoption of Peadar Kearney's 'A Soldier's Song' as the virtual 'national anthem' of the new separatist generation in 1916. Why should this ballad, which in some ways fell lamentably short of the standards demanded, not just by high artists like W. B. Yeats, but by the Irish-Irelanders who dismissed his cultural elitism, have turned out to give such accurate voice to the mood of the hour? What distinguishes it from the dozens or hundreds of 'come-all-ye's' it so closely resembles? Certainly not the banality of its sentiments or its unreconstructed 'poetic' English language. Apart from a few stock Irish phrases, as has been pointed out, 'there is little about it stylistically to distinguish it from T. D. Sullivan's "God Save Ireland" composed in 1867' (the Parliamentary Party's unofficial anthem), 'nor indeed from Thomas Davis's "A Nation Once Again"'. The diction and sentiments of all three stem from the world-famous 'Moore's Melodies' of the early nineteenth century.[24] It evokes an epoch where 'slaves' battle against 'despots' for the destiny of an Ireland that is archaically rhymed with 'sireland'. It is impossible to say why this number was so spontaneously adopted by the rebels of 1916 – so firmly that it would later see off the Free State government's attempt to turn 'God Save Ireland' into the official national anthem. But it is clear that music played a major role in focusing radical nationalist enthusiasm in the wake of the rebellion. The surge of 'Sinn Féin concerts', at which the 'Soldier's Song' featured alongside established favourites such as 'The Green, White, and Gold', and new numbers such as 'Sinn Féin Amháin', seems to have replaced the pre-war craze for theatrical drama.[25] A skein of such subterranean processes was tightened through the rebellion into a new collective self-definition.

The abruptness of the change can of course be exaggerated, and in the traditional story it very definitely was. But there seems little doubt that the rebellion not only quickened the pulse of the separatist movement, but transformed its physical identity. The Sinn Féin movement as reconstructed in 1917 was obviously a mass movement in a way it had never been before – partly thanks to the British reaction. Ginger O'Connell, never an enthusiast for insurrection, admitted that the 'one solid national gain' from the rebellion was that the revival of separatist activity afterwards 'would largely meet with the approval of the country'.[26] The movement was also demographically changed. As 'a wave of new recruits flooded in', one recent historian notes, the emerging movement 'was not only much larger but also vastly more energetic and ambitious'. The flood of recruits added not only youth, but adolescence: a shift that was psychologically as much as statistically significant. This was the organization that was able to capitalize to the utmost on the conscription crisis. The Hobson–Markievicz Fianna cohort would of course have matured in the four years of war with or without the rebellion, but the unique political prestige of that action gave them the status of a revolutionary cadre. The rebellion launched the creation of a new political class. The conflict between Sinn Féin and the old Parliamentary Party can be said to have 'constituted a battle between two political cultures'.[27] In Galway, for instance, while only a tenth of Sinn Féin officials in 1918 had been members of the UIL at the beginning of the war, over 40 per cent had taken part in the rebellion. These vying leadership groups were ideologically distinct: 'their conceptions of what an independent Irish state would be like were very different'. But they were socially distinct as well: 'for the first time, the lower social orders and the young took their place among the local political elite'.[28]

This is not to deny that the 'independent' Irish state that emerged in the crucible of civil war was intensely conservative, or that it was persistently menaced by a threat of political violence. The civil war itself, and the longer-term, more diffuse violence of the IRA, have often been attributed to the prestige of the republican purism sanctified by the 1916 leaders, whose repudiation of compromise can be seen as deeply hostile to the values of liberal-democratic politics. Certainly that is how it was painted by Kevin O'Higgins, the Free State's Minister for Justice during the civil war, which he stridently portrayed as a conflict between democracy and militarism. But even though this argument was endorsed by the Catholic Church, it can be (as it perhaps was by O'Higgins) overstated. O'Higgins himself was assassinated by the IRA. Yet this does not prove that Pearse, or indeed the purist Fenians, Clarke and MacDermott, were anti-democratic. They were ready to act without majority support – this was the reason for their conflict with Bulmer Hobson – but in this they were hardly different from any revolutionary insurrectionists of the nineteenth or the twentieth century. They were, as was said of Hobson too, people of almost frightening simplicity. But so was the great socialist insurrectionist Auguste Blanqui, so was Garibaldi, and so, in this sense, were Fidel Castro and Che Guevara. Most 'liberation struggles', indeed, have been violent, and though many have not been followed by stable democratic systems, Ireland's performance in this respect was impressive.

The most damaging legacy of the Great War period was not political violence as such, but the finalization of partition. It was this that made 'normalization' difficult if not impossible. The leaders of the rebellion were undoubtedly guilty of failing to grasp the contradiction between their desire for an 'Irish Ireland' and their assumption that the island must form a single political unit. The rebellion played a part in cementing partition, but it is not easy to argue that its part was decisive, or that the Irish-Irelanders were unique in their error. The constitutional nationalists had only awoken reluctantly and belatedly to a realization that 'Ulster' was a problem they could not dismiss as an absurdity or a product of British manipulation. By 1911 the damage done by three decades of what Protestants saw as 'Catholic triumphalism' could not be quickly repaired. Redmond's recognition of this fact spurred his desperate hope that a common participation in the war effort could preserve the hope of unity. The sincerity of the parliamentarians' commitment cannot be doubted, and its outcome – the death of many leaders like Willie Redmond and Tom Kettle, and ultimately the death of their party itself – was in the strict sense more of a 'Greek tragedy' than the rebellion. And not only did their efforts end in disaster, but the very memory of Irish service and death in the war was then effaced through the 'great oblivion'. The slow, cautious restoration of this memory has been a vital part of the collective adjustment since the 75th anniversary of the rebellion.

In the central space of St Stephen's Green park, commemorative busts of Constance Markievicz and Tom Kettle stand quite close together, but angled so they do not quite see eye to eye. Kettle's memorial, planned in 1927, was held up for ten years by the refusal of the commissioners of public works to permit the phrase 'Killed in France' to appear on the inscription. The phrase finally accepted, 'Killed at Guinchy 9 September 1916', remains somewhat inscrutable. (By whom? Why?) The main National War Memorial, also delayed until the late 1930s, was consigned to 'public invisibility' by being placed at a considerable distance from the centre of Dublin, at Islandbridge.[29] But these gentle slights are receding into the past. Though it has never been fully completed, the Islandbridge memorial, like Armistice Day, has finally begun to be incorporated in the official calendar of the Irish government. And in 1998, the construction of an 'Island of Ireland Peace Tower' on Messines Ridge represented a striking attempt to reassert the aspirations of the Great War volunteers. It may never be possible to reconcile the Battle of Dublin with the Battle of the Somme, yet both may perhaps be contained by a more capacious understanding of the past.

Notes

PREFACE

1. Hobson to Colonel Dan Bryan, 18 February 1947, B[ureau of] M[ilitary] H[istory], W[itness] S[tatement] 652, Irish Military Archives, Dublin.
2. F. X. Martin, '1916 – Myth, Fact and Mystery', *Studia Hibernica*, 7 (1967), pp. 9, 31.
3. Ibid., p. 107.
4. There is a perceptive evaluation in Diarmuid Ferriter, '"In such deadly earnest": The Bureau of Military History', *Dublin Review*, 12 (2003), pp. 36–65.
5. Martin, '1916', p. 68.

I. REVOLUTIONISM

1. Charles Townshend, *Political Violence in Ireland. Government and Resistance since 1848* (Oxford 1983), pp. 24–38.
2. Emmet Larkin, 'Church, State and Nation in Modern Ireland', *American Historical Review*, 80 (1975).
3. Frank Callanan, *T. M. Healy* (Cork 1996), p. 311.
4. Townshend, *Political Violence in Ireland*, pp. 158–66.
5. F. S. L. Lyons, *Culture and Anarchy in Ireland 1890–1939* (Oxford 1979), p. 32.
6. Tony Crowley, *The Politics of Language in Ireland 1366–1922* (London 2000), pp. 182–8.
7. Donal McCartney, 'Hyde, Moran and Irish Ireland', in F. X. Martin (ed.), *Leaders and Men of the Easter Rising* (London 1967), p. 46. This is not to suggest that Hyde actually read Herder, though he certainly read Grimm. Dominic Daly, *The Young Douglas Hyde* (Dublin 1974), p. 141.

8. D. George Boyce, *Nationalism in Ireland* (3rd edition, London 1995), pp. 238–42.

9. A process illuminated in Marianne Elliott, *Robert Emmet: the Making of a Legend* (London 2003).

10. Timothy J. O'Keefe, 'The 1898 Efforts to Celebrate the United Irishmen: the '98 Centennial', *Eire-Ireland*, 23 (1988), p. 72.

11. *Arthur Griffith. A Study of the Founder of Sinn Fein* (anonymous) (Dublin n.d. [1917]), p. 8. He wrote 'lucid and vehement prose derived partly from Swift and Mitchel, but mainly from a natural talent which owed nothing to any formal study of syntax or grammar'. Seán Ó Luing, 'Arthur Griffith and Sinn Féin', in Martin (ed.), *Leaders and Men of the Easter Rising*, p. 56.

12. See Patrick Maume, *The Long Gestation. Irish Nationalist Life 1891–1918* (Dublin 1999), pp. 28ff. for an illuminating survey.

13. Ernest Blythe, 'Arthur Griffith', *Administration*, 8 (1960), p. 37. Blythe notes that time and again Griffith 'seemed deliberately to avoid being put at the top'.

14. Variously rendered in English as 'warriors of Ireland' or 'soldiers of destiny'; 'league' or 'band of Gaels'.

15. Shaw Desmond, *The Drama of Sinn Féin* (London 1923), p. 116.

16. Bulmer Hobson, *Defensive Warfare. A Handbook for Nationalists* (Belfast 1909).

17. For the international perspective see Richard Davis, *Arthur Griffith and Non-violent Sinn Féin* (Dublin 1974), pp. 91–8.

18. Margaret Ward, *Maud Gonne. Ireland's Joan of Arc* (London 1990), pp. 61–8. But as Ward shows in *Unmanageable Revolutionaries. Women and Irish Nationalism* (London 1983), esp. ch. 7, the mark proved to be less pervasive than Gonne and her fellow activists hoped.

19. *Fainne an Lae*, 19 November 1898, quoted in Ruth Dudley Edwards, *Patrick Pearse. The Triumph of Failure* (London 1977), p. 29.

20. There is a comprehensive analysis of the Brothers' educational methods in Barry M. Coldrey, *Faith and Fatherland: the Christian Brothers and the Development of Irish Nationalism 1838–1921* (Dublin 1988). See especially ch. 6 on the teaching of Irish history.

21. Sean Farrell Moran, 'Patrick Pearse and the European Revolt against Reason', *Journal of the History of Ideas*, 1 (1989), p. 629.

22. Edwards, *Patrick Pearse*, p. 117.

23. For a critical analysis of Pearse's political ideas, see John Coakley, 'Patrick Pearse and the "Noble Lie" of Irish Nationalism', *Studies in Conflict and Violence*, 62 (1983), pp. 119–34.

24. For a lucid survey see, e.g., Josep Llobera, *The God of Modernity* (London 1994), especially part II.

25. Tom Garvin, 'Priests and Patriots. Irish Separatism and Fear of the Modern, 1890–1914', *Irish Historical Studies*, 25 (97) (1986), pp. 67–81.

26. On Sheehan's *Luke Delmege* (1901) and other works see Patrick O'Farrell, *Ireland's English Question* (New York 1971), p. 230.

27. R. F. Foster, 'Marginal Men and Micks on the Make', in *Paddy and Mr Punch. Connections in Irish and English History* (London 1993), p. 299. Nowadays some cultural critics prefer to speak of 'deformation'. Cf Seamus Deane, *Strange Country. Modernity and Nationhood in Irish Writing since 1790* (Oxford 1997), pp. 49ff.

28. William Irwin Thompson, *The Imagination of an Insurrection. Dublin, Easter 1916* (New York 1967), p. 118.

29. Edwards, *Patrick Pearse*, p. 262.

30. Pearse's heterodoxy has been pointed out by various writers from J. J. Horgan to Francis Shaw; on Cuchulainn, see Sean Farrell Moran, *Patrick Pearse and the Politics of Redemption* (Washington, DC, 1994), pp. 158–60.

31. See the argument of J. J. Lee, 'In Search of Patrick Pearse', in Mairin Ní Dhonnchadha and Theo Dorgan (eds), *Revising the Rising* (Derry 1991), pp. 126–7.

32. Maire Nic Shiubhlaigh (as told to Edward Kenny), *The Splendid Years* (Dublin 1955), p. 140.

33. Ben Levitas, *The Theatre of Nation. Irish Drama and Cultural Nationalism 1890–1916* (Oxford 2002), p. 67.

34. R. F. Foster, *W. B. Yeats: A Life*, vol. I (Oxford 1997), pp. 261–2.

35. Geraldine Plunkett, 'Joseph Plunkett: Origin and Background', *University Review* 1 (12) (1958), p. 40.

36. Johann A. Norstedt, *Thomas MacDonagh. A Critical Biography* (Charlottesville, VA, 1980), pp. 52–5, 67–8.

37. Tom Garvin, *Nationalist Revolutionaries in Ireland 1858–1928* (Oxford 1987), pp. 98, 85.

38. F. S. L. Lyons, 'The Watershed, 1903–7', in W. E. Vaughan (ed.), *Ireland under the Union, II, 1870–1921* (*A New History of Ireland*, vol. 6) (Oxford 1996), p. 111.

39. L. N. Le Roux, *Tom Clarke and the Irish Freedom Movement* (Dublin 1936), p. 73.

40. B[ureau of] M[ilitary] H[istory], W[itness] S[tatement] 914 (Denis McCullough), Irish Military Archives, Dublin.

41. F. X. Martin, 'McCullough, Hobson and Republican Ulster', in *Leaders and Men of the Easter Rising* (London 1967), p. 99.

42. Hobson, *Defensive Warfare*, p. 25.

43. Sean O'Faolain, *Constance Markievicz* (London 1934), p. 78.

44. BMH WS 357 (Kathleen Lynn).

45. Thompson, *Imagination of an Insurrection*, p. 77.

46. D. Ryan, *Remembering Sion* (London 1934), p. 111.

47. *Royal Commission on the Rebellion in Ireland*, Minutes of Evidence, 1916, Cd. 8311, para. 549.

48. Ibid., para. 969 (Evidence of Sir David Harrel). Harrel added 'I think it may truthfully be said that the Irish Courts of Petty Sessions are not always exemplary illustrations of the administration of justice.'

49. *Royal Commission on the Rebellion in Ireland*, Report, 1916, Cd. 8279, para. 5.

50. 'Report on the Organisation of Intelligence in Ireland, September 1916', I[mperial] W[ar] M[useum], French MSS 75/46/12, quoted in Eunan O'Halpin, 'British Intelligence in Ireland', in Christopher Andrew and David Dilks (eds), *The Missing Dimension. Governments and Intelligence Communities in the Twentieth Century* (London 1984), pp. 60–1.

51. *The Irish People and the Irish Land* (1867), quoted in Deane, *Strange Country*, p. 70.

52. Sylvain Briollay (pseudonym of Roger Chauviré), *L'Irlande Insurgée* (Paris 1921), pp. 120–1.

53. Senia Paseta, *Before the Revolution: Nationalism, Social Change and Ireland's Catholic Elite, 1879–1922* (Cork 1999).

54. R. F. Foster, *Modern Ireland 1600–1972* (London 1988), p. 291.

55. Robert Colls, *Identity of England* (Oxford 2002), p. 96.

56. Garvin, *Nationalist Revolutionaries*, pp. 53–6.

2. THE MILITARIZATION OF POLITICS

1. Alvin Jackson, however, is pessimistic about what he calls this 'high-risk strategy'; 'it is just conceivable that a stable, pluralist democracy might have swiftly emerged', but more likely that it would have been followed by 'a delayed apocalypse'. 'British Ireland: What if Home Rule had been enacted in 1912?' in Niall Ferguson (ed.), *Virtual History* (London 1997), pp. 226–7.

2. But compare the argument implicit in David Fitzpatrick, 'Militarism in Ireland 1900–1922', in T. Bartlett and K. Jeffery (eds), *A Military History of Ireland* (Cambridge 1996), pp. 379–406.

3. Karl Liebknecht, *Militarism and Anti-militarism* (1907; English translation, Cambridge 1973), ch. 1.

4. See Charles Townshend, 'Militarism and Modern Society', *Wilson Quarterly* (Winter 1993), pp. 71–82; George Dangerfield, *The Strange Death of Liberal England* (London 1936).

5. A. T. Q. Stewart, *The Ulster Crisis* (London 1967) provides the most substantial account of this process.

6. See the recent reassessments by Tim Bowman: 'The Ulster Volunteer Force and the Formation of the 36th (Ulster) Division', *Irish Historical Studies*, 32 (2001), pp. 498–518; and 'The Ulster Volunteers 1913–14: Force or Farce?', *History Ireland*, 10 (2002), pp. 43–7.

7. 'The Movement in Ulster', Cabinet Confidential Print, 22 October 1913, WO 141 26.

8. NA, Crime Branch Special 23.

9. It is no accident that when the Attorney General addressed the arms issue it was in a paper entitled 'Power to Prevent Importation of Arms, &c, into Ulster', CAB 37/117.

10. Memorandum by Sir John Simon, 'Illegalities in Ulster', 29 November 1913, CAB 37/117.

11. Opinion by W. LeFanu, 17 May 1912, WO 141 26.

12. County Inspector, Enniskillen, to Inspector-General, RIC, 17 October 1913, WO 141 26; Opinion by Attorney General, 5 November 1913, NA, Crime Branch Special 23; Irish Command Intelligence Section, Memorandum on the Situation in Ireland, 31 March 1914, WO 141 4.

13. *Irish Freedom*, nos. 1, 2, 11 (November 1910–September 1911).

14. Aodogan O'Rahilly, *Winding the Clock. O'Rahilly and the 1916 Rising* (Dublin 1991), p. 84.

15. F. X. Martin's view (following that of O'Rahilly) that the Force was 'a hoax' is contested in Oliver Snoddy, 'The Midland Volunteer Force 1913', *Journal of the Old Athlone Society* (1968), pp. 39–44.

16. BMH WS 296 (Harry Nicholls).

17. Translation by Ruth Dudley Edwards, in her *Patrick Pearse. The Triumph of Failure* (London 1977), pp. 161–2.

18. P. H. Pearse, 'The Coming Revolution', *An Claideamh Soluis*, 8 November 1913.

19. O'Rahilly specified 50 men; Hobson said he had 500. F. X. Martin (ed.), *The Irish Volunteers 1913–1915* (Dublin 1963), p. 24.

20. Manifesto of the Irish Volunteers, *Volunteer Gazette*, December 1913; reprinted in F. X. Martin (ed.), *The Irish Volunteers 1913–1915. Recollections and Documents* (Dublin 1963), pp. 98–101.

21. BMH WS 114 (Eamon O'Connor).

22. BMH WS 90 (Con Collins).

23. Irish Volunteers, Military Instructions for Units, 1914, Hobson MSS, NLI Ms 13174.

24. Irish Volunteers, General Instructions for Forming Companies, 1914, loc. cit.

25. For an interesting if flawed attempt to set the Volunteers in international perspective see Jock Haswell, *Citizen Armies* (London 1973).

26. *Memoirs of Desmond FitzGerald*, ed. Fergus FitzGerald (London 1968), p. 39.

27. Peter Hart, 'Youth Culture and the Cork I.R.A.', in D. Fitzpatrick (ed.), *Revolution? Ireland 1917–1923* (Dublin 1990), pp. 15–20.

28. Eoghan Davies, 'The Guerrilla Mind', in Fitzpatrick (ed.), *Revolution?*, pp. 44–6.

29. Cf. the pioneering argument of Morris Janowitz, *The Military in the Political Development of New Nations: An Essay in Comparative Analysis* (Chicago 1964).

30. *Memoirs of Desmond FitzGerald*, pp. 37–8.

31. BMH WS 907 (Laurence Nugent).

32. BMH WS 284 (Michael Staines).

33. BMH WS 114 (Eamon O'Connor).

34. Peter Hart, 'Paramilitary Politics in Ireland', in *The IRA at War 1916–1923* (Oxford 2003), p. 98.

35. P. H. Pearse, 'The Irish Flag', in Martin (ed.), *The Irish Volunteers*, p. 132. Report by Uniform Sub-Committee, 12 August 1914, NLI Ms 13174. See also Pearse's holograph notes on 'Uniforms and Equipment', 13 October 1915, Thomas Johnson MSS, IMA CD258/3.

36. *Irish Volunteer*, 18 April 1914.

37. Francis Sheehy-Skeffington, 'An Open Letter to Thomas MacDonagh', *Irish Citizen*, May 1915, reprinted in O. Dudley Edwards and F. Pyle (eds), *1916: the Easter Rising* (London 1969), pp. 149–52.

38. Margaret Ward, *Unmanageable Revolutionaries. Women and Irish Nationalism* (London 1983), p. 97.

39. BMH WS 180 (Kathleen [Murphy] O'Kelly).

40. Peter Hart, 'The Social Structure of the Irish Republican Army', in *The IRA at War 1916–1923*, Table 13, p. 124. Farmers and their sons formed 38 per cent of the population, but only 29 per cent of the 497 non-Dublin Volunteers interned in 1916. Unskilled or semi-skilled workers formed 16 per cent of the non-Dublin and 36 per cent of 872 Dublin Volunteers interned; skilled workers 19 and 40 per cent respectively (the figures for shop assistants and clerks were 15 and 18 per cent).

41. Another statistical analysis of the 1916 arrestees, using slightly different occupational categories, confirms the heavy over-representation of 'general labourers'. Stein Larsen and Oliver Snoddy, '1916 – a Workingmen's Revolution?' *Social Studies*, 2 (1973), Table 5, p. 385.

42. Kathleen Keyes McDonnell, *There is a Bridge at Bandon. A Personal Account of the Irish War of Independence* (Cork 1972), pp. 18, 22.

43. Joseph V. O'Brien, *'Dear, Dirty Dublin'. A City in Distress 1899–1916* (Berkeley, CA, 1982), ch. 8.

44. R. M. Fox, *The History of the Irish Citizen Army* (Dublin 1943), p. 46.

45. Sean O'Casey, *The Story of the Irish Citizen Army* (Dublin 1919), p. 10.

46. Frank Robbins, *Under the Starry Plough. Recollections of the Irish Citizen Army* (Dublin 1977), p. 34.

47. Jacqueline Van Voris, *Constance de Markievicz in the Cause of Ireland* (Amherst, MA, 1967), pp. 140–1.

48. For the effect of the US tour, see Dudley Edwards, *Patrick Pearse*, pp. 184–97; and Sean Farrell Moran, *Patrick Pearse and the Politics of Redemption* (Washington, DC, 1994), pp. 141–4.

49. 'Robert Emmet and the Ireland of Today', Emmet Commemoration in the Academy of Music, Brooklyn, NY, 2 March 1914, *Bodenstown Series*, no. 1, quoted in W. A. Phillips, *The Revolution in Ireland 1906–1923* (London 1923), p. 81.

50. Charles Townshend, 'Military Force and Civil Authority in the United Kingdom, 1914–1921', *Journal of British Studies*, 28 (3) (1989), pp. 269–70. For a long view of the incident's significance, see Hew Strachan, *The Politics of the British Army* (Oxford 1997), pp. 112–17.

51. There is a level-headed account in Elizabeth A. Muenger, *The British Military Dilemma in Ireland. Occupation Politics 1886–1914* (Lawrence, Kansas, 1991), ch. 7.

52. Bulmer Hobson, *A Short History of the Irish Volunteers* (Dublin 1918), p. 93.

53. Ibid., p. 105.

54. MacNeill to Gwynn, 20 May 1914, Redmond MSS, NLI Ms 15204. There is an extended account of the Redmond–MacNeill manoeuvring in Michael Tierney, *Eoin MacNeill: Scholar and Man of Action, 1867–1945* (Oxford 1980), pp. 124–55.

55. The O'Rahilly, *The Secret History of the Irish Volunteers* (Dublin, 1915), p. 7.

56. Hobson to McGarrity, 18 May 1914, in Sean Cronin (ed.), *The McGarrity Papers* (Tralee 1972), p. 42.

57. O'Rahilly to Béaslaí, n.d. [June] 1914. Béaslaí MMS, NLI Ms 33917.

58. Andrew Boyle, *The Riddle of Erskine Childers* (London 1977), p. 191.

59. Bulmer Hobson, 'Foundation and Growth of the Irish Volunteers, 1913–14', in Martin (ed.), *The Irish Volunteers*, p. 33.

60. Sir John Ross of Bladensburg to Under-Secretary, 27 July 1914. BL Add. MS 49821, ff. 71–86.

61. Hobson, *Short History of the Irish Volunteers*, pp. 155–6.

62. Hobson, 'Foundation and Growth of the Irish Volunteers', p. 39.

63. Cesca Chenevix Trench's journal, 31 July 1914. Private possession, courtesy of Anthony Fletcher.

64. Plunkett papers, NLI Ms 11397; BMH WS 360 (Seamus Daly). As against the view of some that the Howth Mauser's heavy recoil made it difficult to use, others stressed the value of its accuracy, which made it 'a really excellent weapon' for sniping. M. Staines and M. O'Reilly, 'The Defence of the GPO', *An tOglác*, 23 January 1926.

65. *Report of the Royal Commission on the Landing of Arms at Howth on 26th July 1914*, 4 September 1914. Cd. 7631. The commissioners were Lord Shaw of the Court of Appeal, and two members of the Irish King's Bench.

66. Ibid.

67. Memorandum on the situation in Ireland on the 31st March, 1914, prepared in the intelligence section of the General Staff at Headquarters, Irish Command, WO 141 4, pp. 1, 4, 3, 6, 8.

68. Ibid., pp. 11, 9.

69. Cd. 8279, p. 7.

70. CIGS to Sec. of State for War, 'Mobilization arrangements in the event of disturbances in Ireland', 4 July 1914, WO 32 9569.

3. ENGLAND'S DIFFICULTY

1. Inspector-General RIC, Monthly Report, August 1914, CO 904 94.

2. As, equally, in France. See Stephane Audouin-Rouzeau and Annette Becker, *14–18, retrouver la Guerre* (Paris 2000), ch. 5.

3. James O. Hannay, 'Ireland and the War', *The Nineteenth Century and After*, 77 (August 1915), p. 394.

4. Cameron Hazlehurst, *Politicians at War, July 1914 to May 1915* (London 1971), ch. 1.

5. Moore to Redmond, 31 July 1914, Redmond papers, NLI Ms 15206.

6. This is argued by, e.g., J. J. Lee, *Ireland 1912–1985* (Cambridge 1989), p. 21. There is a persuasive re-evaluation of his strategy in Paul Bew, *John Redmond* (Dundalk 1996).

7. Charles Hobhouse, *Inside Asquith's Cabinet* (London 1977), p. 181.

8. George H. Cassar, *Kitchener. Architect of Victory* (London 1977), pp. 218–19.

9. Denis Gwynn, *The Life of John Redmond* (London 1932), pp. 416–17.

10. Redmond to Asquith, 8 August 1914, NLI Ms 15165.

11. Taking the figure for the first six-month period as 100, those for the next two were 50 and 40 in Ireland, 50 and 39 in Britain. P. Callan, 'Recruiting for the British Army in Ireland during the First World War', *The Irish Sword*,

17 (1987), pp. 42–56.

12. David Fitzpatrick, 'The Logic of Collective Sacrifice: Ireland and the British Army, 1914–1918', *Historical Journal*, 38 (4) (1995). Cf. the slightly different – but generally congruent – statistics in Keith Jeffery, *Ireland and the Great War* (Cambridge 2000), p. 7.

13. Bulmer Hobson, 'Foundation and Growth of the Irish Volunteers', in F. X. Martin (ed.), *The Irish Volunteers 1913–1915* (Dublin 1963), p. 51.

14. Pearse to McGarrity, 8 August 1914, NLI Ms 17477.

15. Ibid.

16. BMH WS 725 (Desmond Ryan).

17. MacNeill to Casement, 15 August 1914, Michael Tierney, *Eoin MacNeill* (Oxford 1980), pp. 146–7.

18. MacNeill memoir in ibid., p. 147

19. Newspaper quotation from *Sligo Champion*; Michael Farry, *Sligo 1914–1921. A Chronicle of Conflict* (Trim, Co. Meath, 1992), pp. 44, 45.

20. Liam Tannam, quoted in Joost Augusteijn, *From Public Defiance to Guerrilla Warfare* (Dublin 1996), pp. 51–2.

21. Earl of Longford and T. P. O'Neill, *Eamon de Valera* (London 1970), p. 472. See also Owen Dudley Edwards, *Eamon de Valera* (Cardiff 1987), pp. 26–7.

22. BMH WS 606 (James Flood).

23. BMH WS 400 (Richard Walsh).

24. J. J. O'Connell, who started work as an organizer in January 1915 (and joined the General Staff later that year), made several tours of inspection and found very few organized units. Holograph memoir, NLI Ms 22114.

25. Inspector-General RIC, Monthly Report, September 1914, CO 904 94.

26. Moore to Redmond, 24 September 1915, NLI Ms 15206.

27. Tom Dooley, 'Southern Ireland, Historians and the First World War', *Irish Studies Review*, 4 (1993), p. 8.

28. J. J. Lee, *Ireland 1912–1985* (Cambridge 1989), p. 23.

29. Thomas P. Dooley, 'Politics, Bands and Marketing: Army Recruitment in Waterford City, 1914–15', *The Irish Sword*, 18(72) (1991), p. 211.

30. Stephen Gwynn, Notes on Recruitment, n.d. [1916], NLI Ms 15262.

31. Brade to Redmond, 21 February 1915, and reply, 24 February, NLI Ms 15261. The argument was repeated in July, in correspondence with General Sclater.

32. IG RIC Reports, CO904 94–5.

33. Hannay, 'Ireland and the War', pp. 397, 400.

34. Jeffery, *Ireland and the Great War*, p. 41.

35. Terence Denman, 'The 10th (Irish) Division 1914–15: a Study in Military and Political Interaction', *The Irish Sword* 17 (1987), p. 21.

36. Quoted in Jeffery, *Ireland and the Great War*, p. 44.

37. Tim Bowman, 'The Irish Recruiting and Anti-recruiting Campaigns, 1914–1918', in B. Taithe and T. Thornton (eds), *Propaganda. Political Rhetoric and Identity 1300–2000* (London 1999), pp. 223–38; Pauline Codd, 'Recruiting and Responses to War in Wexford', in D. Fitzpatrick (ed.), *Ireland and the First World War* (Dublin 1988), p. 20; Fitzpatrick, 'The Logic of Collective Sacrifice', p. 1030.

38. Æ recommended Patrick McGill, Francis Ledwidge, Stephen Gwynn and Canon Hannay. Nathan to Magill, 15 February, and Kelly to Nathan, 25 February 1916. File on preparation of *Report on Recruiting in Ireland* for F. M. Earl Kitchener (Cd. 8168, 13 January 1916). Joseph Brennan papers, NLI Ms 26191.

39. David W. Miller, *Church, State and Nation in Ireland 1898–1921* (Dublin 1973), p. 313.

40. 'List of Clergymen who have come under notice owing to their disloyal language or conduct during the year 1915', Judicial Division, Chief Secretary's Office, Intelligence Notes, 1915.

41. Miller, *Church, State and Nation*, p. 313.

42. Jerome aan de Wiel, *The Catholic Church in Ireland 1914–1918* (Dublin 2003), pp. 69–72.

43. Miller, *Church, State and Nation*, p. 317.

44. NLI Ms 22114.

45. *Sinn Féin*, 20 December 1913.

46. For a comprehensive account see Virginia E. Glandon, *Arthur Griffith and the Advanced-Nationalist Press in Ireland, 1900–1922* (New York 1985), ch. 6.

47. The leading Volunteer organizer in Wexford, Brennan-Whitmore, 'entirely agreed with me, and said he would use his personal authority as far as possible to limit and confine the damage likely to be done by spreading such ideas. He shared with me – and with many others, as will appear later – a fear that the Irish Volunteers might become a revolutionary, and not a military body.' NLI Ms 13168.

48. Augusteijn, *From Public Defiance to Guerrilla Warfare*, pp. 48–9.

49. *Seán Moylan in his own words*, Aubane Historical Society (2003), p. 16.

50. 'How to Help the Volunteer Movement', IV Circular (produced by Lord Midleton for the Royal Commission, 1916), Cd. 8311, p. 115.

51. C. D. Greaves, *Liam Mellows and the Irish Revolution* (London 1971), pp. 72–7. See also the accounts of Thomas Hynes (BMH WS 714) and Thomas 'Sweeny' Newell (BMH WS 572).

52. O'Connell memoir, NLI Ms 22114.

53. David Fitzpatrick, *Harry Boland's Irish Revolution* (Cork 2003), p. 36.

54. BMH WS 400 (Richard Walsh).

55. BMH WS 72 (John Cahalane).

56. Diary, 17, 19 October, 28 November. O'Donoghue MSS, NLI Ms 31139.

57. RIC Reports, CO 904 98.

58. Chief Secretary's Office, Note on Irish Volunteers, 8 January 1915, NA, D/T S. 14049.

59. Ben Novick, 'Postal Censorship in Ireland, 1914–1916', *Irish Historical Studies*, 31 (123) (1999), p. 344.

60. Ibid., p. 346.

61. Birrell to Nathan, in Leon Ó Broin, *Dublin Castle and the 1916 Rising* (London 1966), pp. 40–41.

62. As he advised the Galway RIC County Inspector, 'the only thing to do is to act from day to day keeping the country as quiet as possible during the war'. Bod[leian Library, Oxford], MS Nathan 469.

63. Ó Broin, *Dublin Castle and the 1916 Rising*, pp. 53–5.

64. O'Hegarty had been delighted by the freedom he had been given at work in London. 'I found that my colleagues and superiors expected an Irishman to be unusual and not to be bound by rules and regulations.' Stereotyping could have its benefits. BMH WS 840 (Patrick Sarsfield O'Hegarty).

65. A. H. Norway, 'Irish Experiences in War', in K. Jeffery (ed.), *The Sinn Féin Rebellion as They Saw It* (Dublin 1999).

66. Colm Campbell, *Emergency Law in Ireland 1918–1925* (Oxford 1994), pp. 9–10.

67. Royal Commission Report, Cd. 8311, para. 1343.

4. IRELAND'S OPPORTUNITY

1. Pearse to McGarrity, 17 July 1914, McGarrity MSS, NLI Ms 17472.

2. BMH WS 695 (Thomas McCrave).

3. Pearse to McGarrity, 12 August 1914, NLI Ms 17472.

4. Though Clarke's widow Kathleen always hotly disputed that this had happened. See ch. 6 below.

5. Pearse to McGarrity, 19 October 1914, NLI Ms 17472.

6. For a strong critique of the role of hatred in Pearse's nationalism, see Francis Shaw, 'The Canon of Irish History – A Challenge', *Studies* (Summer 1972), esp. p. 125.

7. General Council resolution, 6 December 1914, *Irish Volunteer*, 19 December 1914.

8. R. Dudley Edwards, *Patrick Pearse. The Triumph of Failure* (London

1977), p. 239, notes that 'his utility to the IRB was based wholly on his public reputation, for he had little to offer as a counsellor or organiser. Bankruptcy would finish him.'

9. The original holograph of Pearse's scheme of organization is, remarkably, preserved (in both English and Irish language versions) in the papers of Thomas Johnson, IMA CD 258/3. O'Connell, inevitably, thought the scheme over-elaborate if not dysfunctional, Ms memoir, NLI Ms 22114.

10. Maureen Wall, 'The Background to the Rising', in K. B. Nowlan (ed.), *The Making of 1916* (Dublin 1969), p. 166.

11. Louis Le Roux, *Tom Clarke and the Irish Freedom Movement* (Dublin 1936); BMH WS 26 (Patrick Sarsfield O'Hegarty); Diarmuid Lynch, *The IRB and the 1916 Insurrection* (Cork 1957), p. 25.

12. *Royal Commission on the Rebellion in Ireland*, Minutes of Evidence, Cd. 8311, p. 83 (County Inspector J. R. Sharpe).

13. BMH WS 909 (Sidney Gifford Czira). She was also a regular contributor to *Bean na hÉireann* under the name Sorcha Ni Annlain.

14. This was perceptively suggested by Maureen Wall. There is no evidence, however, that the planners were anxious in advance about the discipline of the Dublin Brigade – if anything the reverse. Even the ever-fretting Ginger O'Connell was fairly confident on this score.

15. NLI Ms 13168. In fact, Pearse's orders to Eamonn Ceannt (4th Battalion) only ran to two handwritten notebook sheets; but MacDonagh's did cover five foolscap pages. Both highly atmospheric documents have been preserved in BMH CD 94/1/4-5.

16. 'The fact is both Pearse and MacDonagh, and Plunkett also, believed that the art of war could be studied in books without any trouble being taken to fit the book theories to material facts.' O'Connell, holograph memoir, NLI Ms 22114.

17. F. X. Martin, 'The 1916 Rising – A *Coup d'état* or a "Bloody Protest"?' *Studia Hibernica*, 8 (1968), p. 112.

18. Fergus FitzGerald (ed.), *Memoirs of Desmond FitzGerald* (London 1968), p. 79.

19. Ibid.; BMH WS 184 (Alfred Cotton).

20. P. H. Pearse, 'Robert Emmet and the Ireland of Today' (talk given at the Brooklyn Academy of Music, 2 March 1914), in *Collected Works of Padraic H. Pearse* (Dublin 1922), p. 69.

21. *Irish Volunteer*, 20 November 1915. O'Connell's series included 'The Nature and Varieties of Cover', and 'Ambushes'.

22. O'Connell noted the 'very marked animus' against the precocious O'Duffy among the Volunteer general staff, on the grounds of his 'OTC manner'. O'Connell's attempt to get O'Duffy appointed as trainer for the

Volunteer NCOs was only reluctantly and belatedly acceded to. Memoir, NLI Ms 22114.

23. 'When [the others] found that this was not so they were terribly surprised.' Geraldine Plunkett to Richard Hayes, 15 October 1947, BMH WS 29. She continued to hold that General Friend 'would not have bombarded Dublin', and attributed the use of artillery to Maxwell – in defiance of chronology, since artillery was first deployed three days before Maxwell took command.

24. BMH WS 261 (Piaras Béaslaí).

25. Colonel P. J. Hally, 'The Easter 1916 Rising in Dublin: the Military Aspects. Part I', *Irish Sword*, 7 (29) (1966), p. 326.

26. BMH WS 284 (Michael Staines). Sean Heuston's brother was one of those who became convinced that the GPO was never intended to serve as HQ. See, e.g., BMH CD 309/1 (Rev. J. M. Heuston).

27. The judgement of Lt. A. A. Luce, an RIR officer on sick leave who became part of the Trinity garrison on 24 April. TCD Ms 4874/2/1.

28. MacDonagh told Tom Slater (BMH WS 263) that 'the Bank of Ireland was not to be entered on account of its historical associations'.

29. Hally, 'Easter 1916 Rising . . . Part I', p. 319, judges the Liffey 'a good obstacle, and its bridges could become major defensive points'.

30. Florence O'Donoghue, 'Plans for the 1916 Rising', *University Review*, 3 (March 1963), p. 3.

31. Joseph O'Rourke of the 2nd Battalion is unusual in suggesting (BMH WS 1244) that the original plan was to move the Dublin Volunteers westwards by train, and that this was only changed in Holy Week, when 'something went wrong', and 'we were told we would have to take public buildings in Dublin and proceed with street fighting. But even to the last we clung to the idea that the first plan was going through.'

32. Roger Casement to Maurice Moore, 11 December 1913, Moore MSS, NLI Ms 10561.

33. Franz von Papen to Foreign Office, 9 August 1914. Reinhard Doerries, *Prelude to the Easter Rising. Sir Roger Casement in Imperial Germany* (London 2000), p. 46. This meticulously edited collection of documents from the German archives provides a revelatory view of German official thinking.

34. Gottlieb von Jagow to Arthur Zimmerman, 7 November 1914, in Doerries, *Prelude to the Easter Rising*, p. 58.

35. Notes by Casement, 6 February 1916, New York Public Library, Maloney Collection of Irish Historical Papers, Box 2.

36. Michael Foy and Brian Barton, *The Easter Rising* (Stroud 1999), p. 18.

37. Ibid.

38. BMH WS 6 (Liam O Briain)

39. Ibid.

40. Ibid.

41. Ibid. It is a pity that the BMH does not seem to have followed up his suggestion that 'it would be interesting to obtain statements from surviving old D[ublin] B[rigade] officers as to the areas in the county they were to occupy in case of active service.'

42. MacDonagh 'said the fight would start in the cities, that after about a week we would be driven out of the city and we would take to the country, where we would put up a great fight for some time, but that eventually we would have to capitulate', M. Hopkinson (ed.), *Frank Henderson's Easter Rising* (Cork 1998), p. 33.

43. F. X. Martin, '1916 – *Coup d'état* or "Bloody Protest"?' p. 110.

44. O'Casey was bitterly opposed to uniforms, which workers could not afford to buy; his final clash with Markievicz was partly over this issue.

45. C. Desmond Greaves, *The Life and Times of James Connolly* (London 1972), p. 352.

46. Ruth Dudley Edwards, *James Connolly* (Dublin 1981), p. 127.

47. 'Street Fighting', *Workers' Republic*, 24 July 1915; see also 5, 12, 19 June; 3, 10, 17 July 1915. Austen Morgan, *James Connolly* (Manchester 1988), p. 164.

48. BMH WS 382 (Thomas Mallin).

49. BMH WS 258 (Maeve Cavanagh).

50. Sean Farrell Moran, 'Patrick Pearse and the European Revolt against Reason', *Journal of the History of Ideas*, 1 (1989), pp. 639–40.

51. Patrick O'Farrell, *Ireland's English Question* (New York 1971), pp. 231–2.

52. Maureen Murphy, '"What Stood in the Post Office / With Pearse and Connolly?": the Case for Robert Emmet,' *Eire-Ireland*, 14 (3) (1979), p. 142.

53. Moran, 'Patrick Pearse and the European Revolt', p. 639.

54. T. J. MacSwiney, 'Before the Last Battle', UCD P48b/327.

55. R. F. Foster, W. B. Yeats. *A Life*, vol. 2 (Oxford 2003), p. 46.

56. BMH WS 497 (Eamonn Bulfin).

57. BMH WS 400 (Richard Walsh).

58. Nadolny to Foreign Office, 1 March 1916, in Doerries, *Prelude to the Easter Rising*, p. 17.

59. E. MacNeill, Memorandum No. 2, in F. X. Martin, 'Eoin MacNeill on the 1916 Rising', *Irish Historical Studies*, 12 (47) (1961), p. 247.

60. Lynch, *The IRB and the 1916 Insurrection*, pp. 29–30; John Devoy, *Recollections of an Irish Rebel* (New York 1929), p. 462.

61. BMH WS 26 (Patrick Sarsfield O'Hegarty).

62. Lynch papers, NLI Ms 5173.

63. Piaras Béaslaí, *Michael Collins and the Making of a New Ireland* (Dublin 1926), vol. 1, pp. 46–7.

64. BMH WS 1766 (William O'Brien).

65. BMH WS 725 (Desmond Ryan).

66. E. MacNeill, Memorandum No. 1, February 1916, in F. X. Martin, 'Eoin MacNeill', pp. 236–9.

5. TO THE BRINK

1. John Devoy, *Recollections of an Irish Rebel* (New York 1929), p. 458. Even more oddly, the courier, Tommy O'Connor, was carrying the cipher key with him.

2. Florence O'Donoghue, 'The Failure of the German Arms Landing at Easter 1916', *Cork Historical and Archaeological Society Journal*, 71 (1966), p. 60.

3. Jerome aan de Wiel, *The Catholic Church in Ireland, 1914–1918* (Dublin 2003), p. 84.

4. Michael Tierney, *Eoin MacNeill* (Oxford 1980), p. 202, calls this a 'fantastic intimation'.

5. M. Hopkinson (ed.), *Frank Henderson's Easter Rising* (Cork 1998), pp. 32–3. It is not clear whether MacDonagh was addressing only the 2nd Battalion.

6. BMH WS 34 (Patrick O'Sullivan).

7. Tierney, *MacNeill*, pp. 181–2.

8. BMH WS 1035 (Seán Cody).

9. C. S. Andrews, *Dublin Made Me* (Dublin 1979), p. 85.

10. B. L. Reid, *The Lives of Roger Casement* (New Haven, Conn., 1976), p. 348.

11. Cd. 8279, q. 1939, p. 85.

12. BMH WS 29 (Geraldine Dillon).

13. Mulcahy papers, UCDA P7/D/18, quoted in Maryann Valiulis, *Portrait of a Revolutionary. General Richard Mulcahy and the Founding of the Irish Free State* (Dublin 1992), p. 12.

14. BMH WS 398 (Brigid Martin).

15. Wednesday report in Cd. 8279, p. 8; Thursday in BMH WS 360 (Seamus Daly).

16. *Documents Relative to the Sinn Fein Movement*, Cmd. 1108 (1921).

17. John de Courcy Ireland, *The Sea and the Easter Rising* (Dublin 1966), p. 18.

18. Eunan O'Halpin, 'British Intelligence in Ireland', in C. Andrew and D. Dilks (eds), *The Missing Dimension* (London 1984), p. 60, notes that Hall refused Casement's request to publish his appeal to abandon the rebellion.

19. The denouncer was Joseph Zerhusen, a Hamburg merchant and reserve officer in the 5th Garde Grenadier Regiment, a sympathizer (he had lived in Liverpool 'and had the luck to get to know several influential Irishmen there and finally married an Irish lady of true Irish parentage') who had been anxious to transfer into the Irish Brigade. He was supported by an NCO of the Brigade who wrote 'I only wish the "boys" themselves were half as keen.' Reinhard Doerries, *Prelude to the Easter Rising* (London 2000), pp. 125–6.

20. Casement to Wedel, 2 April 1916. (TS copy) WO 141 19.

21. Interestingly, Monteith, the only man involved in the arms negotiations on the Irish side who had some military expertise, had indicated to Joe McGarrity that bringing arms in surreptitiously was not only possible, but preferable. McGarrity's diary, 20 August 1915, NLI Ms 17551.

22. The most careful attempt to clarify it is O'Donoghue, 'Failure of the German Arms Landing', pp. 49–61.

23. Narrative in *An Phoblacht*, 13 September 1930.

24. Ireland, *The Sea and the 1916 Rising*, pp. 15–17. Spindler's own story lost nothing in the telling in his well-known book *The Mystery of the Casement Ship* (Berlin 1931, an enlarged translation of his original *Das Geheimvolle Schiff* of 1921). He even painted a set of pictures showing his idiosyncratic version of the topography of the Kerry and Cork coast.

25. J. Anthony Gaughan, *Austin Stack. Portrait of a Separatist* (Dublin 1977), pp. 45, 48.

26. O'Donoghue, 'Failure of the German Arms Landing', p. 58. Possibly his allusion to 'local conditions' in this context indicates that the local people were not co-operative – a more dangerous problem.

27. BMH WS 117 (Maurice Moriarty).

28. Gaughan's detailed narrative (*Austin Stack*, pp. 61–2), based on Paddy Cahill's account, suggests 'the only plausible reason' as being that 'he wished to ensure that the British forces would not be placed on the alert'. But Gaughan admits that 'few people would find this convincing'. Desmond Ryan (on the basis of Stack's own account in the *Kerry Champion*, August–September 1929) thought that 'his successful bluffing of the police earlier in the day had thrown him off his guard'. *The Rising* (Dublin 1949), p. 240.

29. See Lucy McDiarmid, 'Secular Relics: Casement's Boat, Casement's Dish', *Textual Practice*, 16 (2) (2002), pp. 277–302.

30. Desmond Ryan, *The Rising*, pp. 112–14, argues that the Ballykissane tragedy 'destroyed the insurgent plans to establish wireless communications', though the *Libau* had no radio, and it is not likely that they would have been able to make contact with U19. He may be on stronger ground in suggesting that its psychological impact was to 'paralyse Kerry'.

31. There are several detailed accounts of the incident among the BMH Witness Statements, such as that of the owner of the fatal automobile (a Briscoe), John J. Quilty (WS 516).

32. P. J. Little, 'A 1916 Document', *Capuchin Annual* (1942), pp. 454–62. Little renewed his argument against Ryan's interpretation in the *Sunday Press*, 7 May 1961, and again in the Dublin *Evening Press*, 28 July 1961.

33. Circular order by E. MacNeill, 19 April 1916, Terence MacSwiney MSS, UCD P48b/364. Very few copies of this order appear to have survived. MacNeill's own papers do not seem to contain one, but Terence MacSwiney kept his.

34. Ryan, *The Rising*, p. 68. Ryan enlarged on his critique in reply to Little in the *Sunday Press*, 21 May 1961.

35. F. X. Martin, after a very careful analysis, also called the document a forgery, 'concocted' by Plunkett and MacDermott; '1916 – Myth, Fact and Mystery', *Studia Hibernica*, 7 (1967), pp. 119–21.

36. 'Although it was his last night on earth and he spoke with great conviction, I found great difficulty in believing it', BMH WS 729 (Mgr Patrick Browne).

37. Smith maintained, however, that the document contained no reference to maps or lists; and, more puzzlingly, that it was not in code. BMH WS 334 (Eugene Smith).

38. BMH WS 257 (Grace Plunkett).

39. F. X. Martin, 'Eoin MacNeill on the 1916 Rising', *Irish Historical Studies*, 12 (47) (1961), p. 260.

40. Diarmuid Lynch, *The IRB and the 1916 Insurrection* (Cork 1957), p. 50.

41. According to Lynch, his words were less collusive: 'In view of that, the fight is inevitable and we are all in it', ibid., p. 51.

42. Martin, 'Eoin MacNeill on the 1916 Rising', p. 249.

43. Dr Jim Ryan delivered this order to Terence MacSwiney in Cork at 6 a.m. on 22 April: 'Comdts. McCurtain and McSwiney are to proceed with the rising and Comdt. O'Connell is to go forthwith to Waterford as per previous instructions.'

44. Ryan 'took that to mean the stuff they had on hands. He certainly said nothing about holding out until arms and ammunition would come from Germany', BMH WS 70.

45. Other accounts (e.g. Hobson himself in the *Irish Times*, 6 May 1961) suggest that he was summoned to a meeting of the Leinster Executive in Phibsboro, and arrested there.

46. BMH WS 798 (Martin Conlon).

47. Leon Ó Broin, *Revolutionary Underground* (Dublin 1976), p. 173.

48. Martin, '1916 – Myth, Fact and Mystery', pp. 88–9.

49. BMH WS 409 (Valentine Jackson).

50. BMH WS 705 (Christopher Brady). Brady, the *Workers' Republic* printer, supervised the production of 2,500 copies of the proclamation.

51. Kathleen Clarke (ed. Helen Litton), *Revolutionary Woman*, p. 76.

52. L. N. Le Roux, *Tom Clarke and the Irish Freedom Movement* (Dublin 1936), p. 208.

53. The first 'insider' account to do this was Francis P. Jones, *History of the Sinn Fein Movement and the Irish Rebellion of 1916* (New York 1917).

54. BMH WS 360 (Seamus Daly).

55. BMH WS 1687 (Harry Colley).

56. Hopkinson (ed.), *Frank Henderson's Easter Rising*, pp. 39–41.

57. BMH WS 242 (Liam Tannam).

58. BMH WS 43 (Tim Buckley, James Murphy) has the Clondrohid Company at Carriganimma. The Macroom Company (5th Battalion) was there (BMH WS 93, Dan Corkery). The Castletownroche Company was at Beeing, as was the Lyre Company, though John Cahalane claimed that 'no men from other [i.e. neighbouring] districts turned out on Sunday', BMH WS 72.

59. 'We had no definite information as to what the purpose of the parade was, but for some weeks before that there had been a tenseness which made us anticipate that we may be in a fight at short notice', BMH WS 34 (Patrick O'Sullivan).

60. BMH WS 138 (Jerome Crowley, Maurice Healy, Timothy O'Riordan).

61. BMH WS 22 (Charles Cullinane); BMH WS 63 (Sean Butler, David O'Callaghan, Michael O'Sullivan).

62. Kathleen Keyes McDonnell, *There is a Bridge at Bandon* (Cork 1972), p. 51.

63. BMH WS 705 (Christopher Brady).

64. Maureen Wall, 'The plans and the countermand', in K. B. Nowlan (ed.) *The Making of 1916* (Dublin 1969), p. 218.

65. Ibid., pp. 233–4.

66. In particular, the fact that Wall does not consider the abortive Sunday mobilization seriously skews the balance of her assessment.

67. DMP Detective Dept. report, 23 April 1916, PRO CO 904 23.

68. Cf. the (improbably precise) police count of 1,886 rifles and 2,570 shotguns in the provinces, in addition to 800 rifles in Dublin. Chief Secretary's Office, Dublin Castle, 'The Sinn Fein or Irish Volunteers and the Rebellion', in B. MacGiolla Choille (ed.), *Intelligence Notes 1913–16 Preserved in the State Paper Office* (Baile Atha Cliath 1966), pp. 221–38.

69. Cd. 8311, para. 1346.

70. Birrell to Midleton, 25 February 1916. Leon Ó Broin, *Dublin Castle and the 1916 Rising* (London 1966), p. 65.

71. To N. Bailey, 12 March 1916, Bod, MSS Nathan 466.

72. Nathan to O'Donnell, 16 February 1916, Bod, MSS Nathan 469.
73. Tivy to Nathan, 27 March 1916, Bod, MSS Nathan 478.
74. Cd. 8311, para. 770.
75. Wimborne to Nathan, 15 March 1916, Bod, MSS Nathan 478.
76. Lady Cynthia Asquith, *Diaries 1915–18* (London 1968), pp. 125–31.
77. Cd. 8311, para. 14.
78. DMP Detective Dept. report, 31 March 1916, PRO CO 904 23.
79. Cd. 8311, para. 738.
80. Bod, MSS Nathan 481.
81. Cd. 8311, para. 807.

6. THE BATTLE OF DUBLIN I: TO THE BARRICADES

1. BMH WS 293 (Aine Heron).
2. BMH WS 208 (Seumas Kavanagh).
3. BMH WS 242 (Liam Tannam).
4. M. Hopkinson (ed.), *Frank Henderson's Easter Rising* (Cork 1998), pp. 41–51.
5. Diarmuid Lynch, *The IRB and the 1916 Insurrection* (Cork 1960), p. 160.
6. There is a good account of the fighting in Leinster Avenue in BMH WS 288 (Charles Saurin).
7. Hopkinson (ed.), *Frank Henderson's Easter Rising*, p. 48.
8. His nephew, Dick Humphreys, left an affectionate picture of the car and its owner in NLI Ms 18829.
9. Diarmuid Lynch MSS, NLI Ms 11125.
10. Michael MacDonagh, quoted in Marianne Elliott, *Robert Emmet: the Making of a Legend* (London 2003), pp. 182–3.
11. *Belfast Evening Telegraph*, 5 May 1916.
12. Mrs Macken's account to Eamon de Valera, de Valera papers, UCDA P150/467. Robert Walpole, however, who claimed to have been given the flag by Connolly to hang from the GPO roof, believed that it was made in Fry's Poplin Factory, Cork Street, and painted (at Markievicz's house) by Theo FitzGerald. BMH WS 218 (R. H. Walpole and Theo FitzGerald).
13. Only 1,000 copies were printed, not the 2,500 Connolly had wanted. Shortage of type meant that the text of the proclamation had to be run off in two halves (which did not quite fit together) on Connolly's stock of cheap poster-sized paper. Several letters in the headings had to be adapted with sealing wax, as is knowledgeably explained by John O'Connor, *The Story of the 1916 Proclamation* (Dublin n.d. [1986]).

14. F. X. Martin, 'The Evolution of a Myth – the Easter Rising, Dublin 1916', in Eugene Kamenka (ed.), *Nationalism: the Nature and Evolution of an Idea* (London 1973), p. 59.

15. *Irish War News*, 25 April 1916.

16. Seán T. O'Kelly, '1916 before and after', NLI Ms 27692.

17. See Chapter 7 below.

18. BMH WS 273 (Margaret Keogh).

19. James Stephens, *The Insurrection in Dublin* (Dublin 1916), pp. 18–20.

20. G. A. Hayes-McCoy, 'A Military History of the 1916 Rising', in K. B. Nowlan (ed.), *The Making of 1916* (Dublin 1969), pp. 264–6, is the most careful evaluation of the failure to take the Castle.

21. BMH WS 357 (Kathleen Lynn).

22. 'Inside Trinity College', by One of the Garrison, *Blackwood's Magazine*, July 1916, reprinted in Roger McHugh (ed.), *Dublin, 1916* (London 1966), pp. 158–74.

23. Autograph narrative of W. G. Smith, NLI Ms 24952.

24. 'The Personal Experience of Miss L. Stokes, 11 Raglan Road, Dublin, during the Sinn Fein Rebellion of 1916', *Nonplus*, 4 (Winter 1960), p. 12.

25. Stephens, *Insurrection in Dublin*, p. 26.

26. Ibid., p. 27.

27. Elizabeth Bowen, *The Shelbourne. A Centre in Dublin Life for More than a Century* (London 1951), pp. 155–6.

28. BMH WS 357 (Kathleen Lynn).

29. Presumably the big automatic pistol that became her trademark. J. Van Voris, *Constance de Markievicz in the Cause of Ireland* (Amherst, MA, 1967), p. 189.

30. Frank Robbins, *Under the Starry Plough* (Dublin 1977), pp. 94–6.

31. Liam O Briain, 'Saint Stephen's Green Area', *Capuchin Annual* (1966), pp. 224–7. This superb narrative – careful, thoughtful and humane – politely disputes Caulfield's story that the Leeson Street Bridge garrisons retreated from the roof to the warmth of the house overnight.

32. He added that the withdrawal of the ICA men from the pub at the corner of Cuffe Street also 'seemed strange'; 'their scouting, if any, seemed defective'. BMH WS 907 (Laurence Nugent).

33. Jerry Golden (BMH WS 521); Lynch counted 282 in Daly's main force, but only 6 men in the Cabra outpost.

34. BMH WS 261 (Piaras Béaslaí).

35. BMH WS 162 (Jack Shouldice).

36. BMH WS 521 (Jerry Golden).

37. BMH WS 290 (Seán McLoughlin); Balfe's testimony is quoted in the careful examination of the 'Movements of 2nd Battalion' by John Heuston in

Headquarters Battalion, Army of the Irish Republic, Easter Week, 1916 (Tallaght 1966), p. 37. Heuston, however, dismissed Balfe's statement that they reached the Mendicity by the South Quays tram, presumably unaware that it was confirmed by McLoughlin.

38. E.g. by Béaslaí himself, in 'Edward Daly's Command', *Limerick's Fighting Story 1916–21* (Tralee n.d. [1948]), p. 24.

39. BMH WS 1756 (Seumas Murphy)

40. BMH WS 280 (Robert Holland).

41. BMH WS 327 (Patrick Egan).

42. BMH WS 252 (Laurence O'Brien).

43. John F. Boyle, *The Irish Rebellion of 1916* (London 1916), p. 79.

44. BMH WS 157 (Joseph O'Connor).

45. Simon Donnelly, 'Thou Shalt Not Pass', de Valera papers, UCDA P150/504.

46. BMH WS 1687 (Harry Colley); also NLI Ms 10915.

47. Diarmuid Lynch, 'Operations, Easter Week', in Lynch, *The IRB and the 1916 Insurrection*, pp. 165–6, puts the time of this movement at 6–8 p.m.

48. Speculating that it may have been the absence of a military barracks on that side of the city that encouraged the removal of the 2nd Battalion, Hayes-McCoy pointed out, 'That may indeed be so, but the pressure which eventually reduced the GPO and crushed the rising was largely exerted from that quarter', Hayes-McCoy, 'A Military History', p. 261.

49. Max Caulfield's combination of solid research with imaginative verve is well displayed in his account of this incident; *The Easter Rebellion* (London 1963), pp. 63–5.

50. 'At Portobello Bridge', *Weekly Irish Times, Sinn Fein Rebellion Handbook* (Dublin 1917), p. 25.

51. BMH WS 445 (James Slattery).

52. BMH WS 263 (Thomas Slater).

53. *Royal Commission on the Rebellion in Ireland*, Minutes of Evidence, Cd. 8311, para. 1556–67.

7. THE BATTLE OF DUBLIN II: THE COUNTERSTROKE

1. Operations Circular No. 89, WO 35 69/1.

2. Diarmuid Lynch, *The IRB and the 1916 Insurrection* (Cork 1957), p. 160.

3. Hayes-McCoy sagely notes that this use of cavalry was 'quite in keeping with contemporary practice. If the insurgents had remained in the streets

they would doubtless have tried to ride them down. After the first few moments, however, the cavalry fought dismounted.' 'A Military History of the 1916 Rising', in K. B. Nowlan (ed.), *The Making of 1916* (Dublin 1969), p. 269.

4. Narrative of OTC actions, 26 June 1916, TCD MUN/OTC/10, Report by Major Harris, Adjutant DUOTC, to War Office, 16 May 1916, WO 32 9576.

5. OC Troops Ireland to GHQ Home Forces, 25 April; GS Irish Command to GOC 59th Division, 28 April 1916, UCDA P150/512.

6. Lady Cynthia Asquith, *Diaries 1915–1918* (London 1968), p. 163.

7. Lord Lieutenant to War Office, 24 April 1916, WO 32 9576.

8. Evidence of J. H. Campbell, Cd. 8311, para. 1627.

9. Evidence of Col. Edgeworth-Johnstone, Cd. 8311, para. 1282.

10. Birrell to Asquith, 28 April 1916, Bod, MSS Asquith 36.

11. OC Troops Ireland to GHQ Home Forces, 25 April, UCDAD P150/512; General Staff, Home Forces, Summary of Reports Received up to 1 p.m. 26th April 1916, WO 35 69/1.

12. Orders for OC. Troops disembarking from England at Queenstown [*sic*] 25/4/1916, WO 35 69/1. Since the orders were signed by 'Maj. Owen Lewis, GSO, for Brig.-General Commanding Troops in Ireland', they appear to have been issued by Lowe rather than by Friend.

13. S. Geohegan, *The Campaigns and History of the Royal Irish Regiment*, vol. 2, p. 103; Hayes-McCoy, 'A Military History', p. 281; A. N. Lee Memoir, Orpen MSS, Imperial War Museum, 66/121/1, p. 56.

14. Summary of Reports Received up to 16.00 26th April 1916, WO 35 69/1.

15. OC Troops Ireland to GHQ Home Forces, 26 April 1916, UCDA P150/512.

16. WO 32 9576.

17. Weekly Patrol Report, HM Yacht 'Helga', 30 April 1916, WO 32 9526.

18. *Weekly Irish Times, Sinn Fein Rebellion Handbook* (Dublin 1917, rep. 1998), p. 19.

19. Summary of Evidence in the Case of Captain J. C. Bowen Colthurst; statement of Lt. M. C. Morris, 11th East Surrey Regiment, WO 35 67. The Simon Commission, interestingly, rephrased these orders as 'to do his utmost to avoid conflict but keep the roadway clear'.

20. Notably in his widely circulated 'Open Letter to Thomas MacDonagh' (*Irish Citizen*, May 1915). James Stephens noted that 'there are multitudes of men in Dublin of all classes and creeds who can boast that they kicked Sheehy Skeffington, or that they struck him on the head with walking sticks and umbrellas ... he accepted blows, and indignities, and ridicule with the pathetic candour of a child who is disguised as a man.' Joseph Brennan recorded in July 1915 that David Sheehy was trying to persuade his daughter 'to take her

husband away *sub silentio*'; Sheehy 'appearing to want sympathy at having suffered under him for so many years', NLI Ms 26178.

21. Memoir by Gerald Keatinge, in possession of R. F. Foster. Keatinge himself was a student in the Trinity OTC who was trying to get in to college from Terenure when he arrived at Portobello.

22. Monk Gibbon, 'Murder in Portobello Barracks', *The Dublin Magazine* (Spring 1966), p. 15.

23. *Royal Commission on the Arrest and Subsequent Treatment of Mr Francis Sheehy Skeffington, Mr Thomas Dickson, and Mr Patrick James McIntyre*, Cd. 8376, paras. 11, 13, 7.

24. Cd. 8376, para. 16.

25. The commission of inquiry did not trouble to discover Coade's first name. It registered, however, that there was conflicting witness testimony about how he died – whether by the blow of a rifle butt, a rifle shot, or Bowen Colthurst's revolver.

26. Statement of 2/Lt W. L. P. Dobbin, 3rd Royal Irish Rifles, WO 35 67.

27. Capt. Bowen Colthurst to OC 3rd Reserve Bn Royal Irish Rifles, 26 April 1916, WO 35 67.

28. Cd. 8376, para. 42.

29. Maj.-Gen. W. Grey, 'Subject of Inquiry', WO 35 67.

30. The opinion of the Canadian journalist F. A. McKenzie, *The Irish Rebellion* (London 1916), p. 70.

31. BMH WS 310 (Seumas Grace).

32. BMH WS 309 (James Doyle).

33. NAM Brig.-Gen. E. W. S. K. Maconchy Memoir.

34. BMH WS 309 (James Doyle).

35. In his brilliantly realized account of the fight, Caulfield (*The Easter Rebellion*, London 1963, pp. 195–9) lays stress on the 'honour of the Sherwoods', though without citing direct evidence.

36. Lee Memoir, IWM 66/121/1, p. 53.

37. Ibid., p. 43.

38. BMH WS 166 (Seumas Doyle).

39. T. P. Coogan, *Eamon de Valera*, p. 69.

40. Simon Donnelly, letter to the *Irish Press*, 5 April 1962, de Valera papers, UCD P150/507.

41. Simon Donnelly, 'Thou Shalt not Pass – Ireland's Challenge to the British Forces at Mount Street Bridge, Easter 1916', IMA CD 62/3/7.

42. Sam Irwin, public letter to Simon Donnelly, 6 April 1964. Irwin noted that 'you and I are the only ones now alive who were present when he woke'. Mulcahy papers, UCDA P7/D/23.

43. Peadar O Cearnaigh, Memoir, TCD MS 3560. Few members of the

Jacob's garrison provided statements to the BMH. The only witness commissioned by the *Capuchin Annual* 'saw little military activity as I was appointed to a post within the factory'.

44. Pádraig O Ceallaigh, 'Jacob's Factory Area', *Capuchin Annual* (1966), p. 216.

45. Maire Nic Shiubhlaigh, as told to Edward Kenny, *The Splendid Years* (Dublin 1955), p. 183.

46. BMH WS 304 (James Coughlan).

47. J. M. Heuston, *Headquarters Battalion, Army of the Irish Republic, Easter Week, 1916* (Tallaght 1966), p. 44.

48. BMH WS 340 (Oscar Traynor). Harry Colley (WS 1687), who was also shot at, thought that the firing came from the GPO, but 'could never quite understand' it – he speculated that some of the men 'believed that we were a country detachment that had made its way to Dublin, and in jubilation started firing'. He remembered O'Rahilly, ever the quartermaster, fuming 'A good hundred rounds of ammunition wasted!'

49. Hayes-McCoy, 'Military History of the Rising', p. 280. Curiously, however, some observers thought that Fairview remained a 'rebel stronghold' until Friday at least. 'They still kept up a desperate fight, and for thirteen hours on one occasion, ceaseless sniping went on between them and the military.' J. F. Boyle, *The Irish Rebellion of 1916* (London 1916), pp. 72–5.

50. Heuston, *Headquarters Battalion*, p. 35.

51. Hayes-McCoy, 'A Military History of the 1916 Rising', p. 282. It is still true that 'we know very little of what was known at insurgent headquarters of the British movements; nor indeed how much Connolly and his colleagues knew of the movements of their own widely scattered forces'.

52. BMH WS 162 (John F. Shouldice).

53. P. Holohan, 'Four Courts Area', *Capuchin Annual* (1966), pp. 184–5.

54. W. Meakin, *The 5th North Staffords and the North Midland Territorials 1914–1919* (Longton, Staffs., 1920), p. 72.

55. For the military inquiry into the killings, see Ch. 10 below.

56. Possibly with some of the booty from the captured DMP station.

57. BMH WS 162 (Shouldice); Holohan, 'Four Courts Area', p. 187.

58. C.-in-C. Ireland to Secretary of State for War, 26 May 1916, WO 32 9524.

59. Brig-Gen. Hutchinson, Irish Command, to GOC 59th Division, 28 April 1916, P150/512.

60. Maj.-Gen. F. Shaw, GHQ Home Forces, to Lt.-Gen. Sir John Maxwell, 29 April; C.-in-C. Ireland, Proclamation No. 1, 28 April 1916, P150/512; Lee Memoir, p. 61.

61. WO 32 4307.

62. BMH WS 340 (Oscar Traynor).

63. W. J. Brennan-Whitmore, *Dublin Burning. The Easter Rising from Behind the Barricades* (Dublin 1996), pp. 55, 68. Of course, IV men liked to be critical of the ICA, and Brennan-Whitmore, who had written a pamphlet on street fighting, was in an odd position. One member of the Imperial Hotel garrison thought he had been 'more or less ignored all week' after failing to persuade Joseph Plunkett to follow his views on street fighting. BMH WS 360 (Seamus Daly).

64. M. Hopkinson (ed.), *Frank Henderson's Easter Rising* (Cork 1998), p. 58.

65. The *Helga* does appear to have carried a quick-firing cannon on its fo'c'sle, so Good may have been right about the 'pom-pom'.

66. Joe Good, *Enchanted by Dreams: The Journal of a Revolutionary* (Dingle 1966), pp. 36–8.

67. Liam Tannam (BMH WS 242) felt the same: the 'rather sparing' FitzGerald would later be 'heartily cursed in every jail in England where men were confined when, starving with hunger, they thought of the food they had left behind in the GPO. I myself even dreamt of it.'

68. Fergus FitzGerald, *Memoirs of Desmond FitzGerald* (London 1968), p. 144, describes how Collins 'strode in one evening with some of his men who were covered in dust, and announced that those men were to be fed if they took the last food in the place. I did not attempt to argue . . .'

69. Dick Humphreys, 'Easter Week in the GPO', NLI Ms 18829.

70. BMH WS 284 (Michael Staines).

71. Humphreys, 'Easter Week'.

72. BMH WS 284 (Michael Staines).

73. 'Thursday, 4th day of the Republic', Field Message Book, NLI Ms 4700.

74. BMH WS 497 (Eamonn Bulfin).

75. Good, *Enchanted by Dreams*, p. 56.

76. 'At the back of his mind was the knowledge that he had left a devoted wife and family to give his life in an action that not only had not the assent of his own judgment, but that had been decided upon by men who treated him as he had been treated. They had treated him as of no account and yet at their words of command he had no option but to give his life . . .' FitzGerald, *Memoirs of Desmond FitzGerald*, p. 137.

77. NLI Ms 4700.

8. THE NATIONAL RISING

1. One of the second rank of leaders, Desmond FitzGerald, who had several conversations with Pearse and Plunkett about the prospects for the rebellion,

found that they talked mainly of what might have been. He detected no confidence that outside aid would arrive. Fergus FitzGerald (ed.), *Memoirs of Desmond FitzGerald* (London 1968), pp. 139–42.

2. Humphreys, 'Easter Week in the GPO', NLI Ms 18829.

3. One of the earliest accounts, by Wells and Marlowe, dedicated a chapter to the 'rising in the provinces', and Desmond Ryan a slightly less substantial one; by contrast, Max Caulfield's history does not refer to it at all, while Foy and Barton give it a single paragraph.

4. J. Lawless, 'Fight at Ashbourne', *Capuchin Annual* (1966), p. 308.

5. BMH WS 149 (Charles Weston).

6. BMH WS 97 (Richard Hayes).

7. This group furnished Connolly's main reinforcement to the Mendicity Institute; see, e.g., BMH WS 148 (James Crenigan).

8. Maryann Valiulis, *Portrait of a Revolutionary. General Richard Mulcahy and the Founding of the Irish Free State* (Dublin 1992), pp. 13–14.

9. Lawless, 'Fight at Ashbourne', p. 309.

10. 'All through the week Ashe had moved erect and purposeful; the leader, radiating authority; the comrade pervading his whole group with a mutual confidence and understanding', UCDA, Mulcahy papers, P7/D/19.

11. BMH WS 97 (Hayes), 149 (Weston).

12. Hayes counted 17 cars; Lawless gives a figure of 'about 24', and others have suggested 15. The cars were borrowed from the 'gentry' of the surrounding areas, according to Constable Eugene Bratton, and driven by their owners' chauffeurs, BMH WS 467.

13. Ibid.

14. BMH WS 1494 (Michael McAllister).

15. There is a careful attempt to sift some of them in Terence Dooley, 'Alexander "Baby" Gray (1858–1916) and the Battle at Ashbourne, 28 April 1916,' *Ríocht na Midhe* (Records of Meath Archaeological and Historical Society), XIV (2003), pp. 194–229.

16. Lawless, 'Fight at Ashbourne', p. 312.

17. Ibid., p. 314.

18. BMH WS 177 (Jerry Golden).

19. BMH WS 467 (Eugene Bratton).

20. Seán MacEntee, *Episode at Easter* (Dublin 1966), p. 63.

21. Ibid., p. 64; see also BMH WS 494 (Peter Kieran).

22. BMH WS 212 (Seán Boylan). Hannigan's recollection, however (WS 161), is that he himself was responsible for Tara.

23. BMH WS 161 (Donal O'Hannigan).

24. MacEntee, *Episode at Easter*, pp. 80–83.

25. But one member of the column thought that only a minority left; his

estimate of its initial strength (75) was much lower than Hannigan's, and he thought that some 45 remained. BMH WS 695 (Thomas McCrave).

26. BMH WS 161 (O'Hannigan); MacEntee's recollection of the order – 'Carry out the original instructions: we strike at noon' – is closer to the orders sent by Pearse to other provincial leaders.

27. Proceedings of Court Martial on John MacEntee, 9 June 1916. *Weekly Irish Times, Sinn Fein Rebellion Handbook* (Dublin 1917), pp. 109–12.

28. BMH WS 1052 (Seán MacEntee).

29. BMH WS 143 (Gerald Byrne).

30. Boylan records that he asked Pearse in advance whether he could take his men into the city, to be told very definitely, 'Your task is communications.' Pearse pointed to the village of Mulhuddart on the map, saying, 'under no circumstances must you go beyond that line'. Boylan 'understood I was to keep communications to and from the city open', BMH WS 212 (Seán Boylan).

31. BMH WS 695 (Thomas McCrave).

32. BMH WS 269 (Peter Boylan).

33. BMH WS 124 (Joseph Connolly).

34. Denis McCullough, 'The Events in Belfast', *Capuchin Annual* (1966), p. 383.

35. He concluded tartly, but perhaps not unreasonably, 'I refrain from comment on the activities of the Belfast contingent in Tyrone, but I think these justified my contention.'

36. BMH WS 915 (Denis McCullough).

37. BMH WS 173 (Cathal McDowell).

38. BMH WS 289 (Manus O'Boyle).

39. BMH WS 178 (John Garvey); also WS 378 (Thomas Kelly).

40. BMH WS 224 (Jack Shields).

41. 'Rebellion in Tyrone, etc.'; County Inspector's Office, Omagh, 25 May 1916. In F. X. Martin (ed.), 'The McCartan Documents, 1916', *Clogher Record* (1966), pp. 55–65.

42. Tomás Ó Maoileóin (Seán Forde), in U. MacEoin (ed.), *Survivors* (Dublin 1980), pp. 79–80.

43. Mattie Neilan, 'The Rising in Galway', *Capuchin Annual* (1966), p. 324.

44. BMH WS 298 (Ailbhe O Monachain).

45. BMH WS 446 (Frank Hynes).

46. BMH WS 714 (Thomas Hynes).

47. For the same argument see also Neilan, 'The Rising in Galway', p. 325.

48. BMH WS 1330 (John D. Costello).

49. BMH WS 344 (John Broderick). He estimated that they had only 20 service rifles, however.

50. BMH WS 345 (Brian Molloy), 572 (Thomas Newell).

NOTES

51. BMH WS 298 (Ailbhe O Monachain).

52. BMH WS 446 (Frank Hynes).

53. Neilan, 'The Rising in Galway', p. 326.

54. The Society was 'the source of most of the agrarian crime and unrest in Galway.' RIC Reports, County Inspector, Galway West Riding, June–July 1916, CO 904 100.

55. BMH WS 446 (Frank Hynes).

56. BMH WS 298 (Ailbhe O Monachain).

57. Darrel Figgis, *Recollections of the Irish War* (London 1927), pp. 143–6.

58. Mannix Joyce, 'The Story of Limerick and Kerry in 1916', *Capuchin Annual* (1966), p. 339.

59. Ibid., p. 342.

60. BMH WS 164 (Charles Wall).

61. BMH WS 1042 (John Joe Neilan).

62. W.B. Wells and N. Marlowe, *A History of the Irish Rebellion of 1916* (Dublin 1916), p. 193.

63. BMH WS 1176 (Mark Kenna).

64. Peter Hart, *The IRA at War 1916–1923* (Oxford 2003), p. 120.

65. It stated that '[so-and-so] was on active Service, under Arms, on Easter Sunday night, to achieve the Freedom of Ireland as an Independent Irish Republic', BMH WS 1598.

66. Thomas Barry, Patrick Canton, Seán Murphy, James Wickham, 'Record of Cork City and County Battalion [*sic*], Easter 1916', BMH WS 1598. Michael Leahy (WS 94), who took the officer's course in January and was appointed captain, thought that the 'Committee system continued up to Easter 1916', and no other officer appointments were made in his unit.

67. BMH WS 1698 (Liam de Roiste diary).

68. BMH WS 1598.

69. Florence O'Donoghue, 'History of the Irish Volunteers', NLI Ms 31437; also Statement of Cork 1916 Committee, NLI Ms 31434.

70. Note by Major Florence O'Donoghue, 5 February 1948, BMH CD 27/2. O'Donoghue was responsible for collating the statements by Cork participants.

71. BMH WS 1598. Ríobard Langford (WS 16) recalled the note as being 'on small cream notepaper', and reading 'We start at noon today.'

72. BMH WS 90 (Cornelius Collins).

73. BMH WS 1698 (Liam de Roiste diary).

74. BMH WS 54 (Seán O'Hegarty).

75. Mary MacSwiney, 'Easter Week in Cork', UCDA P48a/407.

76. BMH WS 119 (Eithne Ni Suibhne).

77. BMH WS 1698 (Liam de Roiste diary).

78. BMH WS 144 (Michael Walsh). Almost incredibly, Walsh records that on

the Tuesday of Easter week he was able to buy two more shotguns from a gunsmiths, Atkins & Co. of Clonakilty.

79. BMH WS20 (Tom Hales). Seán O'Hegarty himself had been left without any instructions, despite sending Mary MacSwiney into Cork on Tuesday and Annie on Thursday. When approached about the Macroom attack, he said that he did not know the situation and the brigade officers did: 'he was sure they would do what was right'. BMH WS 103 (Seán O'Hegarty, Seán Lynch, Jeremiah Shea).

80. Assistant Bishop of Cork to Editor, *Cork Free Press*, 20 May 1916.

81. Court martial report and statements, WO 35 68.

82. BMH WS 590 (Thomas Treacy).

83. Tom Stallard to Josephine Clarke (née Stallard), 5 June 1951, BMH WS 699 (Josephine Clarke).

84. BMH WS 590 (Thomas Treacy).

85. BMH WS 699 (Josephine Clarke). A tantalizing damaged fragment of O'Connell's own holograph account of Easter 1916 survives with his memoir (NLI Ms 22114), but it stops on Saturday.

86. According to Tom Stallard ('who has a good memory about these things'), Head Constable Frizzell of the RIC agreed with de Loughrey 'that if Ginger would go up to the jail himself it would suit Frizzell all right, so he went up', (BMH WS 699, Josephine Clarke).

87. Seumas O Dubhighaill, 'Activities in Eniscorthy', *Capuchin Annual* (1966), p. 319.

88. P. P. Galligan papers, BMH CD105.

89. O Dubhighaill, 'Activities in Eniscorthy', pp. 319–21.

90. BMH WS 1343 (James Cullen).

91. The account of this incident by Wells and Marlowe, *Irish Rebellion*, pp. 184–5, closely matches that of the *Weekly Irish Times*.

92. O Dubhighaill, 'Activities in Eniscorthy', p. 321.

93. Col. J. A. French, Wexford, to GOC-in-C Ireland, enclosing notes from and to Capt. Robert Brennan, 30 April 1916, UCDA P150/512. A slightly amended copy of the last note is illustrated in O Dubhighaill, 'Activities in Eniscorthy', p. 322.

94. Midleton attributed the saving of the south to 'troops dispatched to Cork by Lord French while the government was still vacillating'. *Ireland – Dupe or Heroine?* (London 1932), p. 101.

95. Vice-Admiral Bayly to Secretary, Admiralty, 29 April 1916, WO 32 9526.

96. Summary of Events, Nos. 4, 6, 7, 8, 8a, 9, 10, 15, WO 32 9510.

97. OC Troops Ireland to GHQ Home Forces, 26 April 1916, UCDA P150/512.

9 · SURRENDER

1. To her brother, 18 May 1916, TCD Ms 10543. Mitchell, a writer and critic close to Yeats and Æ, had spent Easter week in 'a pretty hot spot near Portobello Barracks'.

2. W. J. Brennan-Whitmore, *Dublin Burning. The Easter Rising from Behind the Barricades* (Dublin 1996), p. 87.

3. J. J. Lee, *The Modernisation of Irish Society* (Dublin 1973), pp. 155–6.

4. Ibid., pp. 89–90.

5. James Ryan, 'In the GPO: the Medical Unit', in F. X. Martin (ed.), *The Easter Rising, 1916, and University College, Dublin* (Dublin 1966), p. 89.

6. Holograph 'Notes, 3.30 p.m. 29-4-16', and Maxwell to French, 29 April 1916, UCDA P150/512.

7. BMH WS 242 (Liam Tannam). The escorting officers (also including Michael Staines and Diarmuid Lynch) were annoyed to find themselves regarded as prisoners in the Castle, and maintained they had never surrendered. BMH WS 284 (Michael Staines).

8. BMH WS 497 (Eamonn Bulfin).

9. BMH WS 660 (Thomas Leahy).

10. BMH WS 1052 (Seán MacEntee); see p. 247 above.

11. BMH WS 340 (Oscar Traynor).

12. BMH WS 497 (Eamonn Bulfin).

13. BMH WS 1140 (Patrick Ward).

14. Or 1 p.m.; 'I am not certain which hour', Fr Aloysius, OFM, Cap., 'Personal Recollections', *Capuchin Annual* (1966), p. 284.

15. TCD Ms 3560.

16. BMH WS 995 (Eamon Price).

17. Padraig O Ceallaigh (BMH WS 376) saw 'a few Volunteers hurling their guns away in disappointed rage', but thought that for some 'there was a feeling of relief that the strain of the week was over'.

18. BMH WS 397 (Thomas Pugh).

19. Thomas Young, 'Fighting in South Dublin', *An tOglác*, 6 March 1926.

20. BMH WS 482 (Rose McManners).

21. BMH WS 203 (Edward O'Neill).

22. BMH WS 304 (James Coughlan).

23. Piaras F. MacLochlainn, *Last Words. Letters and Statements of the Leaders Executed After the Rising* (Dublin 1990), p. 117.

24. Frank Robbins, *Under the Starry Plough. Recollections of the Irish Citizen Army* (Dublin 1977), pp. 120–22.

25. BMH WS 1019 (Sir Alfred Bucknill).

26. Robbins, *Under the Starry Plough*, pp. 126–7.

27. M. Ó Dubhighaill, 'The Plan of the Rising', *Irish Independent*, 1916 Golden Jubilee Supplement (April 1966).

28. Conversation with Col. Liam Archer, Mulcahy MSS, UCDA P7/D/23.

29. Savage Armstrong to his mother, n.d. [May 1916], PRONI D/618/165.

30. Ó Dubhighaill, 'The Plan of the Rising'.

31. BMH WS 819 (Liam Archer).

32. Bill Stapleton, 'A Volunteer's Story', *Irish Independent*, 1916 Golden Jubilee Supplement (April 1966).

33. Ó Dubhighaill, 'The Plan of the Rising'.

34. Declan Kiberd, '1916: the Idea and the Action', in K. Devine (ed.), *Modern Irish Writers and the Wars* (Gerrards Cross 1999), p. 29.

35. Collins to Kevin O'Brien, 6 October 1916. Quoted in Rex Taylor, *Michael Collins* (London 1958), p. 58.

36. Printed in Appendices to Brennan-Whitemore, *Dublin Burning*, p. 131.

37. Desmond Ryan, *James Connolly* (Dublin 1924), pp. 130–1.

38. BMH WS 369 (William Whelan).

39. Sam Irwin, open letter to Simon Donnelly, 6 April 1964, Mulcahy papers, UCDA P7 D/22.

40. Joe Good, *Enchanted by Dreams: the Journals of a Revolutionary* (Dingle 1966), p. 30.

41. BMH WS 29 (Geraldine Plunkett).

42. BMH WS 293 (Aine Heron).

43. F. A. McKenzie, *The Irish Rebellion. What Happened and Why* (London 1916), pp. 84–5. His considered opinion was that 'the rebel street barricades were of very little service to them'. Many were flimsy, and the strongest were easily breached by artillery. 'Large numbers that I examined immediately after the fighting showed no signs of battle at all. Houses in all directions, however, with their riddled windows and broken walls, showed where the real fighting had been.'

44. Martin King of the ICA gave Connolly his government pass to assist in the plan of 'cutting communications to England', BMH WS 543.

45. 'Easter Week 1916. The GPO Area', Béaslaí papers, NLI Ms 33912(4).

46. R. M. Fox, *The History of the Irish Citizen Army* (Dublin 1942), pp. 172–4.

47. BMH WS 579 (Seán Byrne).

48. BMH WS 521 (Jerry Golden).

49. Maryann Valiulis, *Portrait of a Revolutionary*. (Dublin 1992), pp. 12–14.

50. Good, *Enchanted by Dreams*, p. 46.

51. Col. P. J. Hally, 'The Easter 1916 Rising in Dublin', Part I, *The Irish Sword*, 7 (29) (1966), p. 316.

52. BMH WS 1746 (Matthew Connolly).

53. 'Programme of Military Training', 13 January 1915, *Supplement to the Irish Volunteer*, UCD P48b/370.

54. BMH WS 1768 (Andrew McDonnell).

55. BMH WS 638 (Patrick Caldwell).

56. Thomas Bodkin MSS, TCD Ms 7013. There are other indirect references to the use of dumdum or 'exploding' bullets, e.g. in Henry Hanna's 'Citizen's Diary', TCD Ms 10066/92, and the autograph narrative of the St John's Ambulance volunteer, W. G. Smith, NLI Ms 24952.

57. Ó Dubhighaill, 'The Plan of the Rising'.

58. Thomas Young, 'Fighting in South Dublin', *An tOglác*, 6 March 1926. The 24 April mobilization order for A Company, 4th Battalion, preserved in NLI Ms 10972(2), specifies twelve hours' rations.

59. BMH WS 482 (Rose McManners).

60. Good, *Enchanted by Dreams*, p. 36.

61. Maire Nic Shiubhlaigh, *The Splendid Years* (Dublin 1955), p. 174.

62. TCD Ms 3560.

63. BMH WS 195 (Molly Reynolds).

64. Eilis Bean Ui Chonail, 'A Cumann na mBan Recalls Easter Week', *Capuchin Annual* (1966), p. 272.

65. BMH WS 293 (Aine Heron).

66. Nic Shiubhlaigh, *The Splendid Years*, pp. 161–8, 174–6.

67. Margaret Ward, *Unmanageable Revolutionaries: Women and Irish Nationalism* (London, 1983), pp. 110–11.

68. BMH WS 246 (Marie Perolz).

69. Brennan-Whitmore, *Dublin Burning*, p. 102.

70. BMH WS 432 (Pauline Keating).

71. McKenzie, *Irish Rebellion*, pp. 73–4; also J. V. O'Brien, *'Dear, Dirty Dublin'. A City in Distress 1899–1916* (Berkeley, CA, 1982), p. 259.

72. McKenzie, *Irish Rebellion*, pp. 75–6.

73. BMH WS 497 (Eamonn Bulfin). The planners had made some preparations for order maintenance; Bulfin noted that batons had been got ready, but in the event 'of course we could not afford men for police duty'.

74. Brennan-Whitmore, *Dublin Burning*, pp. 69–71.

75. Fergus FitzGerald (ed.), *Memoirs of Desmond FitzGerald* (London 1968), p. 137.

76. BMH WS 369 (William Whelan).

77. Seumas O'Sullivan's ten-man garrison still had six looters, 'whom we had arrested on the premises and used for fatigue work', with them when they surrendered, BMH WS 393.

78. 'A Kilmallock Lady's Experiences in Dublin during the 1916 Easter

Rising', *Journal of the Lough Gur and District Historical Society*, 6 (1990), p. 4. Anon, 'The Rebellion', 29 April 1916, NLI Ms 22725.

79. Warre B. Wells and N. Marlowe, *A History of the Irish Rebellion of 1916* (Dublin 1916), p. 161.

80. *Letters from Dublin, Easter 1916*, p. 34.

81. PP 1919 (XLII), Cmd. 30, quoted in O'Brien, *'Dear, Dirty Dublin'*, p. 260.

82. Humphreys, 'Easter week', NLI Ms 18829.

83. M. Hopkinson (ed.), *Frank Henderson's Easter Rising* (Cork 1998), p. 55.

84. NLI Ms 10915.

85. FitzGerald (ed.), *Memoirs of Desmond FitzGerald*, p. 142.

86. NLI Ms 18829.

87. 'A Kilmallock Lady's Experiences', p. 4.

88. Wells and Marlowe, *Irish Rebellion*, pp. 159–60.

89. Bonaparte-Wyse to his brother, 28 April 1916, *Irish Times*, 24 April 1965, quoted in J. Lee, *Ireland 1912–1985. Politics and Society* (Cambridge 1988), p. 32.

90. Diary of Mrs Henry, NLI Ms 7984.

91. 'Let us grieve, not over the fragment of Dublin city that is knocked down, but over at least three quarters of what has been preserved', Bernard Shaw, 'Neglected Morals of the Irish Rising', *New Statesman*, 6 May 1916.

92. J. F. Boyle, *The Irish Rebellion of 1916* (London 1916), pp. 170–80.

93. Stephens, *The Insurrection in Dublin* (Dublin 1916), pp. 37–8.

94. Ibid., p. 40.

95. Johnson's diary of Easter week, in J. A. Gaughan, *Thomas Johnson, 1872–1963* (Mount Merrion 1980), p. 50.

96. Stephens, *Insurrection in Dublin*, p. 40.

97. BMH WS 416 (Mairin Cregan).

98. Emily H. Ussher, 'The True Story of a Revolution', TCD Ms 9269. Stafford's mistake had probably been to give the Cork Volunteer commanders an undertaking that their rifles would be returned after their surrender.

10. PUNISHMENT

1. J. F. Boyle, *The Irish Rebellion of 1916* (London 1916), p. 69.

2. In Flanders 'one usually knew exactly where the enemy was', while in Dublin 'neither military nor rebels could guess where the next bullet was coming from'. Charles Duff, *Six Days to Shake an Empire* (London 1966), p. 161.

3. And where the US marines also had to re-learn urban warfare – nicknamed

FISH ('fighting in someone's house'). The net result seems to have been the destruction of much of the city.

4. Col. P. J. Hally, 'The Easter 1916 Rising in Dublin', Part I, *The Irish Sword*, 7 (29) (1966), pp. 318ff.

5. C.-in-C. Ireland to Sec. of State for War, 26 May 1916, WO 32 9524.

6. Sir George Arthur, *General Sir John Maxwell* (London 1932), p. 247.

7. These were the figures Maxwell cited in his 26 May report; military intelligence later gave them as 99 rather than 89 other ranks killed (a total of 116) and 322 wounded (a total of 368). In addition, 13 RIC and 3 DMP constables were killed, giving a total for the Crown Forces of 132; official figures lumped rebel combatants together with civilians (318 killed, 2,217 wounded) and the numbers could not be precisely established. Republican deaths in combat have been generally agreed to total 60 or 62.

8. Tom Johnstone, *Orange, Green and Khaki: The Story of the Irish Regiments in the Great War* (Dublin 1992), pp. 209–12; Keith Jeffery, *Ireland and the Great War* (Cambridge 2000), p. 51.

9. Charles Townshend, 'Martial Law: Legal and Administrative Problems of Civil Emergency in Britain and the Empire, 1800–1940', *Historical Journal*, 25 (1979).

10. Birrell to Asquith, 28 April 1916, Bod, MS Asquith 36.

11. Pencil holograph note by PPS, 10 Downing Street to Maxwell (marked 'Urgent'), 28 April 1916, WO 32 4307. The drafting discussion is recorded in the holograph minute of the Cabinet War Committee, 28 April 1916, CAB 42/12.

12. NLI Ms 22725.

13. Scheme for Further Operations to Cope with the Rebellion in the Dublin District Area, 30 April 1916, UCDA P150/512. 'This was discussed at a conference between C.-in-C. and B. Gen. Lowe & approved.'

14. Maxwell to French, 30 April 1916, UCDA P150/512.

15. Maxwell to Kitchener, 2 May 1916, loc. cit.

16. Maxwell to Robertson, 8 May 1916, loc. cit.

17. Hall to Hutchison, 5 May 1916, ibid. Three weeks later, a colleague of Hutchison on the staff of Irish Command wrote to the DPS at the War Office, 'it must be realised that although in many counties no actual rising took place, the Volunteers were merely sitting on the fence, and were ready to rise should events have taken a more favourable turn'. Byrne to Childs, 26 May 1916, WO 32 9571.

18. Instructions, No. 13989 G. O., 3 May 1916, WO 32 9568.

19. Instructions to Brig. Gen. W. H. M. Lowe, 3 May 1916, WO 32 9568. Maxwell asked for the armoured cars in his letter to French, 30 April 1916, UCDA P150/512.

20. Instructions to Brig.-Gen. W. H. M. Lowe, WO 32 9568.

21. G. I. Edmunds, *2/6th Battalion Sherwood Foresters* (privately published in Chesterfield, 1960), p. 58, for the cordon technique; Lowe to Maxwell, 27 May 1916, Bod, MS Asquith 44.

22. GOC-in-C Ireland to GHQ Home Forces, 3 July 1916, reported a total of 3,829 arms had been taken, of which 2,085 were rifles (including 448 service Lee-Enfields and 361 Mausers), 126 carbines, 1,416 shotguns, and 202 pistols. WO 32 9574.

23. OC Limerick to GOC Queenstown, PRONI I/1065/38.

24. Maxwell to Asquith, 28 June 1916, Bod, MS Asquith 37.

25. Instructions to Defensible Queenstown, General Belfast, GOC Curragh, 6 May 1916, WO 32 9568.

26. Telegram, Commandeth [C.-in-C. Ireland] to Garrison Commanders and all Officers Commanding Troops, 14 May 1916, WO 35 69.

27. RIC memo, 8 June 1916, WO 35 69/4.

28. Cabinet Memorandum by H.H.A., 'Ireland. 1 – The Actual Situation', 19 May 1916, CAB 37 148/13.

29. Byrne to Childs, 23 May 1916, WO 32 9571.

30. Dillon to Maxwell, 8 May 1916, UCDA P150/512. HC Deb., 11 May 1916, cols 938–9.

31. Brig.-Gen. Hutchison to Editor, *Freeman's Journal*, 14 May 1916; Maxwell to Bonham-Carter, 20 May 1916, UCDA P150/512.

32. Byrne to Childs, 28 April 1916 (pencil holograph), WO 32 4307.

33. Commandeth [C.-in-C. Ireland] to Cinchomfor [C.-in-C. Home Forces], 10.30 p.m., 28 April 1916, WO 32 4307.

34. Maxwell to French, 30 April 1916, UCDA P150/512.

35. Minute by Adjutant General, 4 May 1916, WO 32 4307.

36. Memorandum by Irish Law Officers, 9 May 1916, WO 32 9571.

37. 'Irish Rebels Interned in England', 15 May 1916, CAB 37/147/36. (The original draft is in HO 144/1455/2.)

38. Maxwell to Kitchener, 2 May 1916, UCDA P150/512. The difficulties probably concerned the framing of the charges, since the Defence of the Realm Act had not envisaged open rebellion.

39. There is a detailed account of the trials and executions in Brian Barton, *From Behind a Closed Door. Secret Court Martial Records of the Easter Rising* (Belfast 2002).

40. French to Maxwell, holograph, 3 May 1916, UCDA P150/512.

41. Maj.-Gen., Gen. Staff to GOC-in-C Irish Command, 3 May 1916, WO 32 4307.

42. AG to Commandeth, 12.10 a.m., 5 May 1916, WO 32 4307.

43. PM to the King, 6 May 1916, CAB 41 37 19.

44. Redmond to Asquith, 3 May 1916, NLI Ms 15165.

45. 'Press Reaction to the Rising in General', Owen Dudley Edwards and Fergus Pyle (eds), *1916: the Easter Rising* (London 1968), Appendix II, p. 255.

46. Lord Lieutenant to C.-in-C. Ireland, 8 May 1916, BL Add Ms 58372/R.

47. Leon Ó Broin, *Dublin Castle and the 1916 Rising* (London 1966), pp. 120–21.

48. Lord Lieutenant to C.-in-C. Ireland, 6 May 1916, UCDA P150/512.

49. HC Deb., 11 May 1916, cols 940–51.

50. 'Brief History of rebels on whom it has been necessary to impose the supreme penalty', Maxwell to Asquith, 11 May 1916, Bod, MS Asquith 43.

51. GOC-in-C Irish Command to War Office ('The following is for the Prime Minister'), 3.20 a.m., 11 May 1916, WO 32 4307, no. 82B.

52. 'Brief History of rebels on whom it has been necessary to inflict the supreme penalty', Bod, MS Asquith 43.

53. Maxwell to French, 4 May 1916, UCDA P150/512.

54. Notes by Eoin MacNeill, NLI Ms 11437.

55. Byrne to Childs, 23 May 1916, WO 32 9571; GOC Dublin [GOC-in-C?] to DPS, War Office, 10 p.m., 24 May 1916, WO 32 4307.

56. Maxwell to Asquith, 28 May 1916, MS Asquith 37.

57. W. E. Wylie, 'Personal recollections for his daughter, begun 26 October 1939', typescript courtesy of Miss Margaret ('Biddy') Wylie, ff. 34–5.

58. GOC Dublin to War Office, 11 May 1916, WO 32 4307. War Office to C.-in-C. Ireland, 23 May; C.-in-C. to War Office, 30 May 1916, WO 141 19.

59. C.-in-C. Ireland to WO, 5 June 1916, WO 141 20.

60. Diary of Elsie Mahaffy, 6 May 1916, TCD Ms 2074.

61. Wylie, 'Personal recollections', f. 30. Also Leon Ó Broin, *W. E. Wylie and the Irish Revolution 1916–1921* (Dublin 1989), p. 27.

62. Brian Barton, *From Behind a Closed Door*, p. 80, calls it a 'wilful and scurrilous distortion', though admitting that it is 'difficult to interpret'. He speculates (without offering any evidence for this charge) that it 'reflected deep-rooted sexual prejudice and rank misogyny'. While this (and indeed wilful distortion) is by no means impossible in a High Court judge, Wylie's memoir is generally very frank and self-deprecating. Perhaps more importantly, it is not self-evident that the court-martial record is more accurate. Had such a scene occurred, it would probably not have been recorded. Barton himself prints testimony (p. 34) that one court president, Col. Maconchy, refused to record parts of the proceedings he tried.

63. French to Maxwell, 3 May 1916, UCDA P150/512.

64. There were 10 life sentences, 1 sentence of twenty years, 33 of ten years, 3 of eight years, 1 of seven years, 18 of five years, 56 of three years, 2 of two years, 17 of one year, and 4 of six months. Irish Office, 'The Sinn Fein or Irish

Volunteers and the Rebellion', in B. MacGiolla Choille (ed.), *Intelligence Notes 1913–16* (Baile Atha Cliath 1966), pp. 221–38.

65. Redmond MSS, NLI Ms 15206.

66. Commandeth, Dublin, to Cinchomfor, London, 10 May 1916, UCDA P150/512. Copy in Asquith MS 43.

67. UCDA P102/495, quoted in Ben Novick, *Conceiving Revolution. Irish Nationalist Propaganda during the First World War* (Dublin 2001), p. 235.

68. See, e.g., Robert Barton's Scrapbook No. 3, NLI Ms 5650.

69. BMH WS 257 (Grace Plunkett).

70. Wylie claims that he continued to urge that Connolly 'should not be tried until he was well again'. Wylie did not serve as prosecutor at the court martial. 'Personal recollections', f. 33.

71. War Office minute, 15 October 1916, WO 32 4307.

72. HC Deb., 11 May 1916, cols 936–7.

73. Vane protested against his 'unemployment' to the War Office on 5 October 1916, TCD Ms 6837/23.

74. Sir Charles Mathews (DPP) to Byrne, 22 May 1916, WO 35 67.

75. Opinion by J. H. C., 31 May 1916, WO 35 67.

76. Law Officers' Opinion 'Re Bowen Colthurst', WO 35 67.

77. Byrne noted on the 23rd that the trial would begin 'on Tuesday week' – 'I do not see how in such an important case we can give him any shorter notice, especially as there are three other somewhat similar cases to be brought before the same Court.' Byrne to Childs, 23 May 1916, WO 32 9571.

78. Asquith to Maxwell, 13 May 1916, BL Add MS 58372/R.

79. Lemass to Dillon, 23 May 1916, TCD Ms 6837/23.

80. Lemass to Asquith, 13 June, 1916. Loc. cit; Lemass to Maxwell, 8, 20, 24 June 1916, WO 35 67/1.

81. *Royal Commission on the Arrest and Subsequent Treatment of Mr Francis Sheehy Skeffington, Mr Thomas Dickson, and Mr Patrick James McIntyre*, Report, 29 September 1916, Cd. 8376, para. 55.

82. Sheehy-Skeffington to Dillon, 22 October 1916, TCD Ms 6837/23.

83. 'Subject of Inquiry', n.d., WO 35 67.

84. Sheehy-Skeffington to Dillon, 4, 30 November 1916, TCD Ms 6837/23.

85. C.-in-C. Ireland to Sec. of State for War, 26 May 1916, WO 32 9524.

86. Sir George Arthur, *General Sir John Maxwell* (London 1932), p. 257. According to a trusted journalist, the solicitor representing some of the King Street families ('a temperate respectable man who honestly wants to prevent trouble') said that 'other cases will present a worse appearance than the one which has just been sat upon'. Bonham-Carter to Hutchison, 17 May 1916, UCDA P150/512.

87. French to Maxwell, 26 May 1916, loc. cit.

88. The statements taken in evidence, together with the reports to the GOC Dublin, and Maxwell's autograph comments, are in WO 141 21 and 22, with some copies in WO 35 67.

89. Report for the information of the GOC 59th Division by Col. E. W. S. K. Maconchy, President, Standing Court of Inquiry, 22 May 1916, WO 141 22.

90. Court of Inquiry proceedings, deaths of Peter Lawless, James Finnegan, Patrick Hoey and James McCarthy, WO 141 23.

91. 'Very confidential, By Sir E. Troup for information of the P.M.', WO 141 21.

92. On 27 October the Chief Secretary for Ireland asked the Judge Advocate General (who controlled the court martial records) 'to furnish copies to carry out the Prime Minister's pledge'. The JAG referred the question to the Army Council. A month later, however, he 'handed the proceedings over to the Chief Secretary and left him to determine . . . what portions of them can be published without detriment to the public interest'. Minute to AG, 20 November 1916, WO 141 27.

93. JAG, Minute of meeting with Prime Minister, 3 November 1916, WO 141 27.

94. A War Office memorandum on 9 January 1917 noted that it was not clear what 'policy' was involved, and pointed out that the Law Officers had advised that holding the courts martial in camera had been unjustified under DORA. The Judge Advocate General, however, held that martial law justified Maxwell's decision. JAG minute to Under-Secretary, 15 January 1917, WO 141 27. Also Law Officers' Opinion, 31 January 1917, loc. cit.

95. Memorandum by Col. Brade, 9 January 1917, WO 141 27.

96. Minute by Adjutant General, 10 January 1917, loc. cit.

97. Maxwell to French, 16 May 1916, UCDA P150/512.

98. He also sensibly demanded either Sir Maurice Hankey or Sir Eric Drummond as Under-Secretary, both considered irreplaceable in Whitehall. Eunan O'Halpin, *The Decline of the Union* (Dublin 1987), p. 121.

99. Roy Jenkins, *Asquith* (London 1964), p. 397.

100. 'Ireland. II. The Future', Cabinet memorandum by H. H. A., 21 May 1916, CAB 37/148/18.

101. Cesca Chenevix Trench to Francis Chenevix Trench, 29 May 1916, Trench MSS, courtesy of Anthony Fletcher.

102. *Royal Commission on the Rebellion in Ireland*, Report, 26 June 1916, Cd. 8279, paras. 4, 5 and *passim*.

103. Chalmers to Bonham-Carter, 31 May and 5 June 1916, Bod, MS Asquith 37. He did, however, applaud Samuel for his town-planning proposals ('an admirable red herring of his own netting').

104. Compensation claims, WO 141 17.

105. Report to Assistant Director, Supply and Transport, Irish Command, on Supply account of Sinn Fein prisoners 14 May–15 June 1916. WO 35 69/4; Edmunds, *2/6th Sherwood Foresters*.

106. BMH WS 242 (Liam Tannam).

107. 'Ireland. I. The Actual Situation', Cabinet memorandum by H. H. A., 19 May 1916, CAB 37/148/13.

108. Maxwell to Bonham-Carter, 20 May 1916, UCDA P150/512.

109. Bonham-Carter to Hutchison, 17 May 1916, UCDA P150/512. He added two pages of advice on the points to be made in the statement.

110. Brade to Bonham-Carter, 8 June 1916, WO 32 9523.

11. TRANSFORMATION

1. W. E. Wylie, 'Personal recollections for his daughter, begun 26 October 1939', typescript courtesy of Miss Margaret (Biddy) Wylie; Sir George Arthur, *General Sir John Maxwell* (London 1932), p. 264, referred to his 'fair-mindedness and firm grasp of the situation' – based mainly on his condemnation of the previous policy of 'drift and oscillations between "conciliation" and "coercion"'.

2. Maxwell to Lord Monteagle, quoted in ibid.

3. The numerous files (in WO 32 9525, WO 35 69, and elsewhere) prepared in response to the Prime Minister's request for details of murders committed by rebels, attest the persistence of this belief.

4. Robert H. Murray, 'The Sinn Fein Rebellion', *The Nineteenth Century and After* (June 1916), p. 1219.

5. Maxwell to Asquith, 25 May 1916, Bod, MS Asquith 43.

6. Maxwell to Bonham-Carter, 26 May 1916, loc. cit.

7. Inspector-General RIC, 'Public Attitude and Opinion in Ireland as to the Recent Outbreak', 15 May 1916, CAB 37 147/38.

8. Maxwell to Asquith, 11 June 1916, WO 32 4307.

9. Unfortunately, he said, DRR9a did not apply, and no other regulation dealt with processions or meetings. Maxwell to Asquith, 17 June 1916, Bod, MS Asquith 37.

10. Maxwell to Bonham-Carter, 7 June 1916, loc. cit.

11. 'Report on the State of Ireland since the Rebellion', 24 June 1916, p. 2, CAB 37 150/18.

12. Ibid., p. 3.

13. Memorandum by Prime Minister, 19 May 1916, HLRO, Bonar Law MSS

63/C/5, quoted in Charles Townshend, *Political Violence in Ireland* (Oxford 1983), p. 310.

14. Law Officers' opinion, attachment to Maxwell to Bonham-Carter, 20 May 1916, UCDA P150/512.

15. Maxwell to Bonham-Carter, 10 June 1916, Bod, MS Asquith 37.

16. Arthur, *Maxwell*, pp. 271–6.

17. The petition, signed 12–15 May, runs to forty pages in MS Asquith 42.

18. 'The *Irish Times* on the Easter Rising', Owen Dudley Edwards and Fergus Pyle (eds), *1916: the Easter Rising* (London 1968), Appendix I, p. 248. The later extract was quoted by Dillon in his 11 May speech in Parliament.

19. Maxwell to O'Dwyer, 6 May and 12 May 1916, O'Dwyer MSS, quoted in Jerome aan de Wiel, *The Catholic Church in Ireland 1914–1918* (Dublin 2003), pp. 104–5.

20. O'Dwyer to Maxwell, 17 May 1916, quoted in David W. Miller, *Church, State and Nation in Ireland 1898–1921* (Dublin 1973), p. 331.

21. John H. Whyte, '1916 – Revolution and Religion', in F. X. Martin (ed.), *Leaders and Men of the Easter Rising* (London 1967), p. 221.

22. J. J. Lee, *Ireland 1912–1985* (Cambridge 1989), pp. 28–9.

23. James Stephens, *The Insurrection in Dublin* (Dublin 1916), p. 76.

24. F. A. McKenzie, *The Irish Rebellion. What Happened and Why* (London 1916), pp. 105–6.

25. Warre B. Wells, *An Irish Apologia* (Dublin 1917), p. 66.

26. W. B. Wells and N. Marlowe, *A History of the Irish Rebellion of 1916* (Dublin 1916), pp. 203–4. Cf. the *Northern Whig* (1 July 1916): 'futile attempts were made at first to represent it as a sort of street brawl'.

27. Æ to Mrs Philimore, 28 July 1916, Strathcarron MSS, Bod Dep.C.714 folder 1.

28. Grace Plunkett to Asquith, 17 May 1916, Bod, MS Asquith 37.

29. Lee, *Ireland*, p. 32, proposes the 'crystallisation' idea, though he admits that the nature of the evidence prevents precise measurement of the process.

30. There is a pioneering study of press reactions in the Appendices of Edwards and Pyle (eds), *1916: the Easter Rising*, pp. 251–71. As they point out, the *Irish Times* was read by many people who detested its political line. Lee, *Ireland*, pp. 32–6, adds a further well-chosen sample of the provincial newspapers.

31. RIC Monthly Confidential Reports, July 1916, CO 904 100.

32. Cabinet Confidential Print No. 1, August 1916, Bod Dep.C.714 folder 1.

33. Maxwell to Duke, 21 September 1916, WO 35 69/6.

34. *Midland Reporter*, 14 September 1916, PRO WO 35 69/6.

35. RIC Monthly Confidential Reports, June 1916, PRO CO 904 100.

36. Confidential Print No. 3, August 1916, Bod Dep.C.714 folder 1.

37. Memoir by P. J. Matthews, NLI Ms 9873. (Matthews did think that 'a feeling of bitter hostility' changed 'overnight to one of passive admiration'.)
38. MacBride's violence to Maud Gonne during their marriage was widely known. 'It must have been some humourist who got him the post of water bailiff to the corporation', Lily added, referring to his still better-known partiality to drink. R. F. Foster, *W. B. Yeats*, vol. 2 (Oxford 2003), pp. 46–50.
39. Miller, *Church, State and Nation*, p. 341.
40. An 'intention' (as T. P. O'Connor explained to Lloyd George when he told him of this) means a wish of a religious character. O'Connor to Lloyd George, 13 June 1916, HLRO D/14/2/35.
41. HC Deb., 25 May 1916, cols. 2309–10.
42. As George Boyce says, 'if this ambiguous phrase meant anything, it was simply a promise that there would be no *automatic inclusion*' – in other words there would be further negotiations after the war. 'British Opinion, Ireland and the War, 1916–1918', *Historical Journal* 17 (3) (1974), p. 580.
43. 'Ireland 1916', memorandum by R. C., 26 June 1916, CAB 37/150.
44. According to William O'Brien's note of a meeting with Carson and Lloyd George on 30 May, the latter suggested (perhaps for Carson's benefit) that 'In six months the war will be lost', and 'clung obstinately to his view that something must be done before the American elections or Wilson would be returned and the war lost', William O'Brien, *The Irish Revolution and How it Came About* (London 1923), pp. 273–4.
45. H. J. Whigham, 5 May 1916, FO 395/6, quoted in Stephen Hartley, *The Irish Question as a Problem in British Foreign Policy, 1914–18* (London 1987), pp. 62–3.
46. William M. Leary, jr., 'Woodrow Wilson, Irish Americans, and the Election of 1916', *Journal of American History*, 54 (1) (1967), p. 59.
47. Spring Rice to Grey, 16 June 1916, in Stephen Gwynn (ed.), *The Letters and Friendships of Sir Cecil Spring Rice* (Boston 1929), vol. 2, p. 338; Roosevelt to Lee, 7 June 1916, in Elting E. Morison (ed.), *The Letters of Theodore Roosevelt* (Cambridge, MA, 1951), vol. 8, p. 1054.
48. Alan J. Ward, *Ireland and Anglo-American Relations, 1899–1921* (London 1969), p. 113. Cf. the assessments from MI1 on Irish agitation in the USA, January–July 1916, CO 616/63.
49. Conor Gearty, 'The Casement Treason Trial in its Legal Context', lecture at the Royal Irish Academy Symposium, 'Roger Casement in Irish and World History', 6 May 2000.
50. Herbert Samuel to his wife, 2 August 1916, HLRO, Samuel MSS A/157/844. The convoluted governmental discussion of the Casement case – in which Samuel's role was 'not impressive' – is carefully analysed in Bernard Wasserstein, *Herbert Samuel. A Political Life* (Oxford 1992), pp. 182–5.

51. Owen Dudley Edwards, 'American Aspects of the Rising', in Dudley Edwards and Pyle (eds), *1916: the Easter Rising*, pp. 164–9.

52. Roy Jenkins, *Asquith* (London 1964), p. 404. In fact, there were at least five discussions. Ward, *Ireland and Anglo-American Relations*, pp. 120–4.

53. George Boyce, *The Sure Confusing Drum: Ireland and the First World War* (Swansea 1993), p. 12.

54. Keith Jeffery, *Ireland and the Great War* (Cambridge 2000), pp. 57–9.

55. J. B. Lyons, *The Enigma of Tom Kettle* (Dublin 1983), p. 293. There is a lucid exploration of his ideas in Senia Paseta, 'Thomas Kettle: "An Irish Soldier in the Army of Europe"?' in A. Gregory and S. Paseta (eds), *Ireland and the Great War* (Manchester 2002), pp. 8–27.

56. *Irish Weekly Independent*, 24 June 1916, quoted in Miller, *Church, State and Nation*, pp. 337–9.

57. R. M. Henry, *The Evolution of Sinn Fein* (Dublin 1920), p. 225.

58. Mary MacSwiney to Peter MacSwiney, n.d., *Devoy's Post Bag*, II, p. 493.

59. McCartan to McGarrity, 13 May, 11 May 1916, in F. X. Martin (ed.), 'The McCartan Documents, 1916', *Clogher Record* (1966), pp. 26, 22.

60. Confidential Print No. 1, August 1916. Bod Dep.C.714 folder 1.

61. INAA and IVDF collections, RIC Reports, July 1916, CO 904 100. Michael Laffan, *The Resurrection of Ireland* (Cambridge 1999), pp. 64–8, provides a lucid account of the funds.

62. While some, like Oscar Traynor, despatched their prison experience in a couple of sentences of their Witness Statements, Bob Holland wrote over forty pages on his time in Knutsford gaol – more than on the fighting in Easter Week.

63. BMH WS 340 (Oscar Traynor), WS 242 (Liam Tannam), WS 371 (Robert Holland).

64. M. Hopkinson (ed.), *Frank Henderson's Easter Rising* (Cork 1998), p. 71.

65. Margery Forester, *Michael Collins, the Lost Leader* (London 1971), pp. 50–51.

66. HO 144 1456/661.

67. To Susan Killeen (undated, but probably written in late summer). T. P. Coogan, *Michael Collins* (London 1990), p. 50.

68. Frank Robbins, *Under the Starry Plough* (Dublin 1977), pp. 143–6.

69. BMH WS 163 (Patrick Rankin).

70. He advised Sankey that the committee should not sit as a whole, because 'if three judges were sitting together it might give the Irish section almost too judicial a character for a body which does not hear evidence according to judicial procedure'. Samuel to Sankey, 8 June 1916, Sankey papers, Bod, MS Eng. hist. c.548.

71. Aliens Advizory [*sic*] Committee minute book, Sankey papers, loc. cit.

72. HO 144 1455/62, 257.

73. HO 45 24677.

74. 'Most of the questions seemed to be directed to getting us to make a confession of being misled by our leaders and being sorry for what we had done.' (Hopkinson (ed.), *Frank Henderson's Easter Rising*, p. 74.

75. Robbins, *Under the Starry Plough*, pp. 148–9.

76. HO 144 1455/272, HO 144 1456/379.

77. Under-Secretary to Home Office, 19 July 1916, HO 144 1455/220.

78. W. J. Brennan Whitmore, *With the Irish in Frongoch* (Dublin 1917), pp. 25–30.

79. The nickname was a familiar label for 'coercive' British rulers, notably Chief Secretary W. E. Forster in the 1880s.

80. Sean O'Mahony, *Frongoch: University of Revolution* (Dublin 1987), p. 124.

81. J. J. O'Connell, 'Reorganisation 1917', NLI Ms 22114.

82. HO 144 1456/469.

83. Closing Report by Camp Commandant, HO 144 1456/615.

84. Report by E. Sebag Montefiore, 1–2 July 1916, HO 144 1455/168. Report by Sir Charles Cameron and Dr R. W. Braithwaite, December 1916, HO 144 1456/614.

85. Michael Collins to Home Secretary, 14 December 1916, HO 144 1456/598.

86. BMH WS 242 (Liam Tannam).

87. 'Official Report of the Ill-Treatment of the Irish Prisoners of War Interned at Frongoch Internment Camp', 14 November 1916, BMH CD 250/3/1.

88. Gerald Boland's reminiscences, quoted in David Fitzpatrick, *Harry Boland's Irish Revolution* (Cork 2003), pp. 58, 347.

89. BMH WS 398 (Brigid Martin).

90. HC Deb., 18 October 1916, cols. 581–93.

12. THE POLITICS OF MILITARIZATION

1. 'State of Ireland', Cabinet memorandum by W. H. Long, 21 July 1916, CAB 37 152/15.

2. Wimborne to Duke, 16 September 1916, Bod Dep.C.714 folder 1.

3. HC Deb., 18 October 1916, cols. 597–604.

4. J. F. Boyle, *The Irish Rebellion of 1916* (London 1916), pp. 258–9.

5. Note by Archbishop of Dublin, 18 July 1916, BL Add Ms 52782, f. 89.

6. Chalmers to Bonham-Carter, 7 June 1916, Bod MS Asquith 27.

7. Louis Treguiz, *L'Irlande dans la Crise Universelle* (Paris 1917), ch. 2 ('La régime provisoire: Retour aux anciennes méthodes').

8. Note of meeting between Chief Secretary and a Southern Unionist delegation, 17 November 1916, Midleton MSS, PRO 30/67/31.

9. Redmond to Asquith, 30 November 1916, Bod, MS Asquith 37.

10. RIC Monthly Confidential Reports, January 1917, CO 904 102. Duke himself gave the War Cabinet a pessimistic report of the energetic Sinn Féin rebuilding on 19 February, WC 73, CAB 23/1.

11. Seán O Luing, *I Die in a Good Cause. A Study of Thomas Ashe, Idealist and Revolutionary* (Tralee 1970), p. 121.

12. There is a vividly detailed account of the Lewes experience in David Fitzpatrick, *Harry Boland's Irish Revolution* (Cork 2003), pp. 59–88.

13. DRR cases, WO 35 95.

14. War Cabinet, 22 March 1917, CAB 32/2; *The Times*, 17 May 1917, quoted in R. B. McDowell, *The Irish Convention 1917–18* (London 1970), p. 76.

15. Sir John O'Connell, 'What Ireland Wants', *Fortnightly Review*, July 1917, p. 106.

16. 'The Military Situation in Ireland', Cabinet Memorandum by Secretary of State for War, 21 July 1917, Cabinet paper G.T. 1477, Bod Dep.C.715.

17. War Cabinet 175, 4 July 1917, Bod Dep.C.717.

18. Fitzpatrick, *Harry Boland's Irish Revolution*, p. 89.

19. Report by GOC-in-C Ireland, 25 June 1917, Bod Dep.C.715.

20. David W. Miller, *Church, State and Nation in Ireland 1898–1921* (Dublin 1973), p. 393.

21. 'Sinn Fein meetings in 1917', CO 904 23/3.

22. DMP Report, 13 July 1917, Bod Dep.C.715.

23. RIC Reports, CO 904 104.

24. BMH WS 1093 (Thomas Treacy).

25. Fitzpatrick, *Harry Boland's Irish Revolution*, pp. 98–9.

26. RIC Confidential Reports, June 1917, CO 904 103.

27. C. M. Byrne memoir, NLI Ms 21142.

28. Wimborne to Duke, 14 July 1917, Bod Dep.C.715.

29. 'The Sinn Fein Movement in Ireland', Cabinet memorandum by H. E. Duke, 10 July 1917, G.T. 1359, Bod Dep.C.717. Duke had to explain to his colleagues in this context that a hurley was not simply a sporting accessory but 'a somewhat formidable weapon'.

30. See the analysis in Ben Novick, *Conceiving Revolution. Irish Nationalist Propaganda during the First World War* (Dublin 2001), pp. 236–9.

31. C.-in-C. Irish Command to Chief Secretary for Ireland, 5 October 1917, WO 32 9515.

32. War Cabinet 249, 15 October 1917, Bod Dep.C.715.

33. C.-in-C. to CSI, 5 October 1917, WO 32 9515.

34. Margaret Ward, 'The League of Women Delegates and Sinn Féin', *History Ireland* (Autumn 1996), pp. 40–41.

35. Michael Laffan, *The Resurrection of Ireland* (Cambridge 1999), p. 119. NacNeill won 888 votes, 205 more than Cathal Brugha. Third and fourth were Richard Hayes (674) and Seán Milroy (667), followed by Markievicz (617), Count Plunkett (598) and Piaras Béaslaí (557), Michael Collins polled only 340 votes. CO 904 23.

36. Keith Jeffery, *Ireland and the Great War* (Cambridge 2000), p. 61.

37. 'Condition of Ireland', Cabinet memorandum by Chief Secretary for Ireland, 6 October 1917, G. T. 2227, Bod Dep.C.715.

38. Chief Secretary to Under-Secretary, 14 July 1917, WO 32 9515. A taste of these instructions may be had from the fourth, which reads 'Isolated acts of wearing the "rebel" uniform are not regarded in the same light as the wearing of uniform in connection with drilling or marching. The latter offence is, however, aggravated by this incident where it occurs.' For a mild military protest against the confused and 'anomalous' legal situation, see C.-in-C. Home Forces to Secretary of State for War, 14 October 1917, WO 32 9515.

39. Inspector General RIC to Under Secretary, 14 December 1916, WO 35 69/9.

40. D. G. Boyce and C. Hazlehurst, 'The Unknown Chief Secretary', *Irish Historical Studies*, 20 (79) (1977), p. 300, refuting the verdicts of Lyons and Fitzpatrick.

41. GOC Ireland to C.-in-C. Home Forces, 14 October 1917, WO 32 9515.

42. O'Connor to Duke, 22 January 1917, Bod Dep. C.714 folder 2.

43. C.-in-C. Ireland to Chief Secretary, 5 October 1917. Bod Dep.C.717.

44. War Cabinet 262, 1 November 1917, Bod Dep.C.717.

45. Memorandum by Lord Milner, 23 January, and Memorandum by H. E. Duke, 30 January 1917, HLRO, Lloyd George MSS F/14/4/18, F/37/4/8. Alan J. Ward, 'Lloyd George and the 1918 Irish Conscription Crisis', *Historical Journal*, 17 (1) (1974), pp. 108–9.

46. Ibid., pp. 110, 125.

47. War Cabinet, 28 March 1917, CAB 23/5/377.

48. 'Condition of Ireland', Cabinet memorandum by Chief Secretary for Ireland, 3 March 1918, G.T. 3798, Bod Dep.C.717.

49. Miller, *Church, State and Nation in Ireland*, pp. 404–5.

50. Inspector General RIC, Weekly Report, 'Public Feeling in Ireland', 20 April 1918, CAB 24 49/4326.

51. Ward, 'Irish Conscription Crisis', p. 128.

52. Richard Mulcahy, 'Conscription and the General Headquarters Staff', *Capuchin Annual* (1968), p. 384.

53. Fergus Campbell, 'The Social Dynamics of Nationalist Politics in the West of Ireland 1898–1918', *Past and Present*, 182 (2004), pp. 182–3.

54. RIC Reports, County Inspector, Galway East Riding, February 1918, CO 904 105.

55. Military Intelligence report, Midland and Connaught Division, March 1918, CO 904 157; Chief Secretary's Office Intelligence Notes, 1918, p. 14, CO 903 19/4.

56. Ernie O'Malley, *On Another Man's Wound* (London and Dublin 1936, 1979), p. 79.

57. Charles Townshend, *Political Violence in Ireland* (Oxford 1983), pp. 313–21.

58. Yeats to Haldane, 10 October 1918, quoted in R. F. Foster, 'Yeats at War', in *The Irish Story* (London 2001), pp. 70–71.

59. *Irish Times*, 30 December 1918, quoted in Paul Bew, 'Moderate Nationalism and the Irish Revolution, 1916–1923', *Historical Journal*, 42 (3) (1999), p. 736.

13. EPILOGUE: THE REBELLION IN HISTORY

1. Gregory to Yeats, 7 May, and Yeats to Gregory, 11 May 1916. R. F. Foster, *W. B. Yeats. A Life* (Oxford 2003), vol. 2, pp. 47–8, 51.

2. Gonne to Yeats, 8 November 1916, in ibid., p. 63. She said, justly enough, that the poem would be 'unintelligible to many', adding that 'even Iseult' (her daughter, to whom Yeats would shortly propose) had not understood it.

3. Edna Longley, 'The Rising, the Somme and Irish Memory', in M. Ní Dhonnchadha and T. Dorgan (eds), *Revising the Rising* (Derry 1991), pp. 46–7.

4. Desmond Ryan, *The Rising. The Complete Story of Easter Week* (Dublin 1949).

5. Francis MacManus, 'Imaginative Literature and the Revolution', in T. D. Williams (ed.), *The Irish Struggle 1916–1926* (London 1966), p. 23.

6. See, e.g., Charles Townshend, 'The Irish Republican Army and the Development of Guerrilla Warfare, 1916–21', *English Historical Review*, 94 (1979), pp. 318–45.

7. F. X. Martin, '1916 – Myth, Fact and Mystery', *Studia Hibernica*, 7 (1967), p. 20.

8. E.g. F. X. Martin (ed.), *Leaders and Men of the Easter Rising: Dublin 1916* (London 1967).

9. Richard English, *Armed Struggle: a History of the IRA* (London 2003), pp. 76–7.

10. Garret FitzGerald, 'The Significance of 1916', *Studies*, 55 (Spring 1966), pp. 29–37.

11. Francis Shaw, 'The Canon of Irish History – A Challenge', *Studies*, 61 (Summer 1972), p. 124.

12. Conor Cruise O'Brien, 'The Embers of Easter', in Owen Dudley Edwards and Fergus Pyle (eds), *1916: the Easter Rising* (London 1969), pp. 226–7.

13. Kevin Myers, 'The Glory that was Hijacked', *Guardian*, 30 March 1991.

14. David McKittrick, 'Rebels of 1916 Leave Mixed Legacy', *Independent*, 12 March 1991.

15. B. Bradshaw, 'Nationalism and Historical Scholarship in Modern Ireland', *Irish Historical Studies*, 26 (1988–9), pp. 329–51; D. Fennell, *The Revision of Irish Nationalism* (Dublin 1989).

16. Seamus Deane, 'Wherever Green is Read', in N Dhonnchadha and Dorgan (eds), *Revising the Rising*, pp. 91ff.

17. Ruth Dudley Edwards, *Patrick Pearse. The Triumph of Failure* (London 1977).

18. See, e.g., C. Desmond Greaves, *The Life and Times of James Connolly* (London 1972); and Austen Morgan, *James Connolly. A Political Biography* (Manchester 1988).

19. In the substantial collection of essays edited by Ciaran Brady as *Interpreting Irish History. The Debate on Historical Revisionism 1938–1994* (Dublin 1994), there are just two references to 1916.

20. David Fitzpatrick, 'Militarism in Ireland, 1900–1922', in T. Bartlett and K. Jeffery (eds), *A Military History of Ireland* (Cambridge 1996), p. 394.

21. Charles Townshend, 'The Meaning of Irish Freedom: Constitutionalism in the Free State', *Transactions of the Royal Historical Society*, 6th series, vol. 8 (1998), pp. 56–9.

22. Garret FitzGerald, *Reflections on the Irish State* (Dublin 2003), pp. 1–16.

23. Declan Kiberd, '1916: the Idea and the Action', in K. Devine (ed.), *Modern Irish Writers and the Wars* (Gerrards Cross 1999), p. 29.

24. R. V. Comerford, *Ireland* (London 2003), p. 263.

25. See, e.g., Report of Sinn Fein Concert and Lecture, Nenagh, 9 July 1917, Bod Dep.C.715, f. 21. See also Eimear Whitfield, 'Another Martyr for Old Ireland: the Balladry of Revolution', in D. Fitzpatrick (ed.), *Revolution? Ireland 1917–1923* (Dublin 1990), pp. 60–68.

26. NLI Ms 22114.

27. Fergus Campbell, 'The Social Dynamics of Nationalist Politics in the West of Ireland 1898–1918', *Past and Present*, 182 (2004), pp. 195–7.

28. Ibid., p. 201.

29. Keith Jeffery, *Ireland and the Great War* (Cambridge 2000), pp. 118–25.

Biographical Glossary

Ashe, Thomas b. 1885 in Co. Kerry; Gaelic Leaguer and pipe band enthusiast; principal of Lusk National School, Co. Dublin; Commandant of 5th Battalion, Dublin Brigade, Irish Volunteers 1916; death sentence commuted to life imprisonment; released June 1917; rearrested August 1917; led hunger strike in Mountjoy gaol; died under forcible feeding 25 September 1917.

Asquith, Herbert Henry b. 1852 in Morley, Yorkshire; barrister, Liberal MP for East Fife 1886; Home Secretary 1892–4; Chancellor of the Exchequer 1905; Prime Minister 1908–16; leader of Liberal party 1916–24; lost parliamentary seat 1924; peerage (Earl of Oxford and Asquith) 1925; d. 1928.

Blythe, Ernest (Earnan de Blaghd) b. 1889 in Co. Antrim; government clerk; junior reporter for *North Down Herald* 1909; Gaelic Leaguer and Volunteer Organizer; deported 1915; Sinn Féin MP/TD for North Monaghan 1918; minister in Dáil Cabinet, 1919–21; Minister for Finance in Free State government 1922; Vice-President (Deputy Prime Minister) 1927–32; lost parliamentary seat 1933; Senator 1933–6; retired from politics 1936; Managing Director of the Abbey Theatre 1941–67; repeatedly criticized for hiring actors for their Irish language rather than acting ability; d. 1975.

Brugha, Cathal (Charles Burgess) b. 1874 in Dublin; educated Belvedere College; co-founder of candle-making business; Gaelic Leaguer 1899; Vice-Commandant 4th Battalion, Dublin Brigade, Irish Volunteers in South Dublin Union, Easter 1916; seriously wounded and permanently crippled; Sinn Féin MP/TD 1918; presided over first meeting of Dáil Éireann 1919; Minister for Defence in Dáil Cabinet; opposed Treaty 1922; killed fighting in O'Connell Street in civil war, 7 July 1922.

Carson, Edward b. 1854 in Dublin; educated at Trinity College, Dublin; barrister 1889; Irish Solicitor General 1892; Unionist MP for Dublin University 1892–1918; prosecuting counsel in trial of Oscar Wilde 1895;

knighted 1900; Solicitor General 1900–1906; leader of Irish Unionist Party 1910; Attorney General in coalition Cabinet 1915–16; First Lord of the Admiralty 1916; MP for Belfast Duncairn 1918–21; life peer 1921; Lord of Appeal 1921–9; d. 1935.

Casement, Roger b. 1864 in Co. Dublin; went to Africa 1884; entered British consular service 1892; reported on abuse of native workers in Belgian Congo 1904; joined Gaelic League 1904; wrote nationalist articles under name 'Sean Bhean Bhocht'; consul-general at Rio de Janeiro, knighted 1911; report on conditions of workers on Putumayo River rubber plantations caused an international sensation 1912; retired 1913, joined Irish Volunteers; in Germany 1914–16 to raise Irish Brigade; returned to Ireland by submarine April 1916; tried for high treason, stripped of his knighthood, and executed 3 August 1916; the authenticity of his homosexual diaries was disputed for decades; his bones were returned to Dublin and buried at Glasnevin 1965.

Childers, Robert Erskine b. 1870 in London; grew up in Co. Wicklow; educated Haileybury and Cambridge; Clerk of the House of Commons 1895–1910; fought in Boer War with City Imperial Volunteers; wrote *In the Ranks of the CIV* 1900, *The Riddle of the Sands* 1903, *War and the Arme Blanche* 1910; became a Home Ruler 1908 and wrote *The Framework of Home Rule* 1910; ran in IV guns at Howth 1914; served in Royal Naval Air Service 1914–19, awarded DSC 1917; secretary of Irish Convention 1917; director of publicity in Dáil government 1919–21, edited *Irish Bulletin*; secretary to Irish delegation to London 1921; opposed Treaty 1922; fought on anti-treaty side in civil war; executed 1922.

Clarke, Thomas b. 1857 on Isle of Wight; in USA 1878, joined Clan na Gael; on bombing mission to England 1883, arrested and given life imprisonment; released 1898, made Freeman of Limerick city; emigrated to USA 1899; returned to Dublin 1907 to buy tobacconist's shop in Parnell Square; on Supreme Council of IRB; organized first pilgrimage to Wolfe Tone's grave at Bodenstown 1911; member of IRB military committee 1915; first signatory of 1916 proclamation of the Irish Republic; in GPO, Easter 1916; executed 3 May 1916.

Collins, Michael b. 1890 in Co. Cork; post office clerk in London; adjutant to Joseph Plunkett in GPO 1916; interned in Frongoch, released December 1916; Irish Volunteer organizer, and Sinn Féin MP 1918; Director of Organization (later Intelligence), Volunteer GHQ; President of the Supreme Council of the IRB 1919; signatory of Anglo-Irish Treaty 1921; Chairman of the Provisional Government and Commander-in-Chief of the National Army, Irish Free State, 1922; killed in ambush, Co. Cork, 22 August 1922.

Connolly, James b. 1868 in Edinburgh; served in British army at the Curragh; deserted; founded Irish Socialist Republican party 1896; founder-editor of the *Worker's Republic* from 1898; in USA 1903–10, helped found Industrial Workers of the World (the 'Wobblies'); author of *Labour in Irish History*, 1910; Ulster organizer of the ITGWU 1910, and General Secretary 1914; founder of Irish Citizen Army 1913; joined IRB military committee January 1916; Commandant-General of republican forces in Dublin area Easter 1916; executed Kimainham gaol 12 May 1916.

Cosgrave, William T. b. 1880 in Dublin; Sinn Féin member of Dublin Corporation 1909; Captain, 4th Battalion, Dublin Brigade, Irish Volunteers in South Dublin Union, 1916; death sentence commuted to life imprisonment; Sinn Féin MP for Kilkenny 1917; Minister for Local Government in Dáil cabinet 1919; President of the Executive Council (Prime Minister), Irish Free State, after death of Michael Collins in 1922; leader of Cumann na nGaedheal party 1922–33, and Fine Gael party 1934–44; d. 1965.

de Valera, Eamon b. 1882 in New York; mathematics teacher and Gaelic Leaguer; Commandant of 3rd Battalion, Dublin Brigade, Irish Volunteers 1916; death sentence commuted to life imprisonment; released June 1917; MP for East Clare July 1917; President (Priomh-Aire) of Sinn Féin and Irish Volunteers, October 1917; President of the Irish Republic 1919–21; opposed the Anglo-Irish Treaty and joined IRA 1922; left Sinn Féin party to found Fianna Fáil 1926; President of the Executive Council (Prime Minister), Irish Free State, 1933–7; Taoiseach (Prime Minister), Eire, under new constitution 1937–48, 1951–4, 1957–9; President of the Irish Republic, 1959–73; d. 1975.

Dillon, John b. 1851 in Co. Dublin; Nationalist MP 1880–83, 1885–1918 (East Mayo); Parnell's deputy in charge of 'Plan of Campaign' 1886; anti-Parnellite leader 1891–1900; deputy leader of reunited Nationalist party (UIL) 1900–18, and leader 1918 after death of John Redmond; lost East Mayo seat to Eamon de Valera, December 1918; d. 1927.

Gonne (MacBride), Maud b. 1866 in Surrey; moved to Ireland 1867; lived in France with Lucien Millevoye 1887–99; Irish nationalist activist, founder of Inghinidhe na hEireann 1900; played lead role in first performance of *Cathleen ni Houlihan*, 1902; convert to Catholicism; married John MacBride 1903, separated 1905; readopted his name after his execution 1916; interned in 'German plot' arrests 1918; Secretary of Women Prisoners Defence League 1922; autobiography *A Servant of the Queen* 1938; d. 1953.

Griffith, Arthur b. 1871 in Dublin; printer and journalist; founded the *United Irishman* and *Sinn Féin*; Vice-President of Sinn Féin party 1917; Sinn

Féin MP 1918; Acting President of Dáil government 1919–20 during de Valera's visit to USA; chief negotiator and signatory of Anglo-Irish Treaty 1921; President of Dáil and minister in Irish Free State Provisional Government 1922; d. 12 August 1922.

Hobson, John Bulmer   b. 1883 in Belfast; Quaker and Gaelic Leaguer; founding secretary of Antrim GAA 1901; founder of Fianna Eireann 1903; founder of Ulster Literary Theatre and, with Denis McCullough, the Dungannon Clubs, in 1905; Vice-President of Sinn Féin 1907–10; member of Supreme Council of the IRB and Chairman of the Leinster Executive; editor of *Irish Freedom* 1910–14; Secretary of the Irish Volunteers 1913; resigned from IRB Supreme Council after supporting Redmond's takeover of IV Executive June 1914; organized Volunteer gun-running July 1914; arrested by IRB Easter 1916; Chief of the Revenue Commissioners Stamp Department, Irish Free State, 1922; author of *A National Forests Policy* (1923) and *Ireland Yesterday and Tomorrow* (1968); d. 1969.

Johnson, Thomas   b. 1872 in Liverpool; worked for Irish fish merchant; commercial traveller 1900; Vice-President Irish TUC 1913; President 1915; co-operated with Eoin MacNeill over employers' threats to sack members of Irish Volunteers, 1915–16; organized anti-conscription strike 1918; co-drafted Democratic Programme of first Dáil Éireann; secretary of ITUC 1920–28; TD for Co. Dublin 1922–7 and Leader of Labour party; Senator 1928–36; d. 1963.

MacCurtain, Thomas   b. 1884 in Co. Cork; secretary of Blackpool branch of Gaelic League 1902; joined Sinn Féin and IRB 1907; Fianna Éireann organizer 1911; commanded Cork Brigade, Irish Volunteers 1916; imprisoned in Wakefield, Frongoch and Reading 1916–17; Sinn Féin councillor for Cork North-West in 1920 local elections; elected Lord Mayor of Cork January 1920; assassinated in his home 20 March 1920. Coroner's jury found verdict of murder against the RIC and the Prime Minister, Lloyd George.

MacDermott (MacDiarmada), Seán   b. 1884 in Co. Leitrim; emigrated to Glasgow 1900, worked as gardener and tramway conductor; moved to Belfast 1902; joined Gaelic League; appointed Dungannon Clubs organizer by Bulmer Hobson; joined IRB 1906; full-time Sinn Féin organizer 1907; manager of *Irish Freedom* 1910; crippled by polio 1912 but continued to work as organizer; Provisional Committee Irish Volunteers 1913; member of IRB military committee 1915; signatory of 1916 proclamation of the Irish Republic; in GPO Easter 1916; executed 12 May 1916.

MacDonagh, Thomas   b. 1878 in Co. Tipperary; taught in Kilkenny and Fermoy; moved to Dublin 1908 to study at UCD; first teacher on staff of St

Enda's school; also appointed to English department, UCD; play *When the Dawn is Come* produced at Abbey Theatre 1908; co-edited *Irish Review* with Joseph Plunkett; Director of Training, Irish Volunteers, 1914; joined IRB 1915; Commandant 2nd Battalion, Dublin Brigade, Irish Volunteers 1915; joined IRB military committee, 1916; signatory of proclamation of Irish Republic, 1916; commanded Jacob's Factory garrison, Easter 1916; executed 3 May 1916.

MacEntee, Seán b. 1889 in Belfast; educated St Malachy's College and Belfast Municipal College of Technology; electrical engineer and patent agent; death sentence 1916 commuted; Sinn Féin MP/TD 1918; Fianna Fáil TD 1927–69; government minister 1932–48, 1951–4, 1957–65; Tánaiste (Deputy Prime Minister) 1959–65; d. 1984.

MacNeill, Eoin b. 1867 in Co. Antrim; law clerk; co-founder of Gaelic League 1893; editor of *Gaelic Journal*, later *An Claideamh Soluis*; professor of early Irish history, UCD 1908; founder and first Chief of Staff, Irish Volunteers 1913; sentenced to penal servitude for life 1916; released 1917; MP/TD for National University 1918; Minister for Education, Irish Free State 1922; member of Boundary Commission 1924–5; forced to resign ministry and lost parliamentary seat 1927; Chairman of Irish Historical Manuscripts Commission 1927; d. 1945.

MacSwiney, Terence b. 1879 in Cork city; trained as an accountant; philosophy degree at Royal University 1907; co-founded Cork Dramatic Society with Daniel Corkery 1908; plays included *The Revolutionist*, *The Holocaust* and *The Warriors of Coole*; peripatetic teacher, Co. Cork 1911, resigned to become full-time Irish Volunteer organizer, 1915; Vice-Commandant, Cork Brigade, Irish Volunteers 1916; MP/TD for West Cork 1918; elected Lord Mayor of Cork after murder of Thomas MacCurtain; arrested and sentenced to two years' imprisonment 16 August 1920; died after seventy-four days of hunger strike 24 October 1924.

Markievicz, Constance (née Gore-Booth) b. 1868 in London; grew up at Lissadell, Co. Sligo; studied at Slade School, London 1893; married Count Casimir Dunin-Markiewicz 1900 (daughter Maeve b. 1901); co-founder of United Arts Club, Dublin 1907; joined Sinn Féin and Inghinidhe na hEireann 1908; co-founder of Na Fianna Eireann 1909, and Irish Citizen Army, 1913; in St Stephen's Green garrison Easter 1916; death sentence commuted to life imprisonment; released June 1917; converted to Catholicism; first woman MP (for Dublin) 1918; Minister for Labour in Dáil Cabinet 1919; opposed Anglo-Irish Treaty 1922; joined Fianna Fáil 1926; TD 1927; d. 1927.

Mellows, Liam   b. 1892 in Lancashire; grew up in Co. Wexford; educated Royal Hibernian Military School; clerk in Dublin 1905; joined Fianna 1909; joined IRB 1912; full-time organizer, Irish Volunteers, Co. Galway 1914–15; deported 1915; returned Easter 1916 to lead Galway Volunteers; escaped to USA after rebellion, worked on *Gaelic American*; agent for de Valera's US tour 1919–20; Director of Purchases, IRA 1921; TD for Galway 1921; member of Four Courts anti-Treaty garrison in civil war June 1922; executed 8 December 1922.

O'Brien, William   b. 1881 in Co. Cork; joined Irish Socialist Republican party 1898; close associate of Connolly and James Larkin; secretary of lockout committee during 1913 labour dispute; anti-conscription campaigner; deported and interned in Frongoch and Reading 1916; deported to Wormwood Scrubs 1920, released after hunger strike; TD for Dublin South City 1922–3, for Tipperary 1927 and 1937–8; General Secretary ITGWU; d. 1968.

O'Kelly (O Ceallaigh), Seán T.   b. 1882 in Dublin; Gaelic Leaguer, joined Celtic Literary Society; Sinn Féin 1905; Sinn Féin member of Dublin Corporation 1906–26; manager of *An Claideamh Soluis*; general secretary Gaelic League 1915; in GPO Easter 1916; MP/TD for College Green division of Dublin 1918; Speaker of Dáil Éireann 1919; envoy to international peace conference, Paris, 1919; opposed Treaty 1922; joined Fianna Fáil 1926; Minister for Local Government 1933 and Vice-President of Executive Council (Deputy Prime Minister); Minister for Finance 1941; President of Ireland 1945; d. 1966.

O'Rahilly, Michael Joseph (The O'Rahilly)   b. 1875 in Co. Kerry; local magistrate; moved to Dublin; member of national executive of Gaelic League 1912; managing director of *An Claideamh Soluis* 1913; co-founder and Director of Armaments, Irish Volunteers, 1913–16; carried MacNeill's countermanding order to western Ireland 1916; joined GPO garrison Easter 1916; killed in action, Moore Street, 28 April 1916.

Pearse, Patrick Henry   b. 1879 in Dublin; Christian Brothers' school and Royal University; barrister (took only one case, for Gaelic League); left father's stonemason's business; Gaelic Leaguer, editor of *An Claideamh Soluis* 1903–9; founder of St Enda's school 1908; joined Irish Volunteers 1913; became Director of Military Organization in Irish Volunteers, 1914; member of IRB military committee 1915; author and signatory of the 1916 proclamation of the Irish Republic; Commandant General, Commander-in-Chief of the Army of the Irish Republic, in GPO, Easter 1916; ordered surrender 30 April; executed 3 May 1916.

Plunkett, George Noble (hereditary Papal Count)   b. 1851 in Dublin; founding editor of *Hibernian*, 1882; barrister 1886; Vice-President of Royal Irish Academy, 1907–8, 1911–14; independent Sinn Féin MP for North Roscommon 1917; Minister for Foreign Affairs in Dáil Cabinet; Minister for Fine Arts 1921–2; opposed Treaty 1922, Sinn Féin abstentionist TD for Roscommon 1922–7; d. 1948.

Plunkett, Joseph Mary   b. 1887 in Dublin; educated at Belvedere College, Stonyhurst, England; graduate of UCD 1909; travelled for health reasons in Italy, Egypt and Algeria; returned to Dublin 1911, established *Irish Review* and Irish Theatre with Thomas MacDonagh and Edward Martyn; joined Irish Volunteers 1913 and IRB 1914; member of IRB military committee; travelled to Germany to meet Casement 1915; signatory of 1916 proclamation of Irish Republic; in GPO Easter 1916; married Grace Gifford in Kilmainham Gaol; executed 4 May 1916.

Redmond, John   b. 1856 in Co. Wexford; Clerk of the House of Commons 1880; Nationalist MP for New Ross 1881, North Wexford 1885, and Waterford 1891–1918; barrister 1886; leader of Parnellite section of parliamentary party 1891; reunited party under his leadership 1900; member of Land Conference 1902 leading to tenant land purchase scheme of Land Act 1903; secured introduction of Third Home Rule Bill 1911; pledged Irish support for Britain in Great War 1914; refused post in Asquith's coalition Cabinet 1915; d. March 1918.

Stack, Austin   b. 1880 in Co. Kerry; GAA enthusiast and champion hurler; founder member and commandant, Kerry Irish Volunteers 1913–16; interned 1916–17, led hunger strikes in Lewes prison; released June 1917; Sinn Féin TD for West Kerry 1918; Minister for Justice in Dáil Cabinet 1919; established Republican Courts; IRA Deputy Chief of Staff 1921; Minister for Home Affairs 1921–2; opposed Treaty 1922; abstentionist Sinn Féin TD 1923; d. 1929.

Yeats, William Butler   b. 1865 in Dublin; educated in London and Dublin; Theosophist 1887; joined Order of the Golden Dawn 1890; co-founder of National Literary Society 1892; author of *The Celtic Twilight*, 1893, *A Book of Irish Verse*, 1895 and (with Lady Gregory) *Cathleen ni Houlihan*, performed 1902 by the Irish National Theatre; co-founder of the Abbey Theatre, 1904; published four major collections of poems 1919–33 and three volumes of autobiography; member of Irish Free State Senate 1922–38; Nobel Prize for Literature 1923; founded Irish Academy of Letters 1932 with G. B. Shaw; d. 1939.

Bibliography

OFFICIAL RECORDS

Royal Commission on the Landing of Arms at Howth on 26th July 1914, Report (1914), Cd. 7631.

Royal Commission on the Rebellion in Ireland, Report (1916), Cd. 8279. Minutes of Evidence, Cd. 8311.

Royal Commission on the Arrest and Subsequent Treatment of Mr Francis Sheehy Skeffington, Mr Thomas Dickson, and Mr Patrick James McIntyre, Report (29 September 1916), Cd. 8376.

Documents Relative to the Sinn Fein Movement (1921), Cmd.1108.

Department of External Affairs, Republic of Ireland, *Cuimhneachán 1916–1966: a Record of Ireland's Commemoration of the 1916 Rising* (Dublin 1966).

CONTEMPORARY AND PARTICIPANT ACCOUNTS

'A Volunteer', 'South Dublin Union Area', *Capuchin Annual* (1966): 201–13.

Andrews, C. S., *Dublin Made Me* (Dublin 1979).

Arthur Griffith. A Study of the Founder of Sinn Fein (Dublin, no author, no date [1917]).

Béaslaí, Piaras, *Michael Collins and the Making of a New Ireland* (Dublin 1926).

——, 'Edward Daly's Command', in *Limerick's Fighting Story*, pub. by *The Kerryman* (n.d. [1948]).

Boyle, J. F., *The Irish Rebellion of 1916* (London 1916).

Brennan, James J., 'Mendicity Institution Area', *Capuchin Annual* (1966): 189–92.

Brennan, Michael, *The War in Clare 1911–1921: Personal Memoirs of the Irish War of Independence* (Dublin 1980).

Brennan, Robert, *Allegiance* (Dublin 1950).

Brennan-Whitmore, W. J., *With the Irish in Frongoch* (Dublin 1917).

——, *Dublin Burning. The Easter Rising from Behind the Barricades* (Dublin 1996).

Briollay, Sylvain (pseudonym of Roger Chauviré), *L'Irlande Insurgée* (Paris 1921).

Brooks, Sydney, 'The Irish Insurrection', *North American Review* (July 1916), pp. 57–69.

Casement, Sir Roger, *Ireland, Germany and the Freedom of the Seas. A Possible Outcome of the War of 1914?* (New York, n.d. [1914]).

Clarke, Kathleen (ed. Helen Litton), *Revolutionary Woman. Kathleen Clarke 1878–1972. An Autobiography* (Dublin 1991).

Connolly, Matt, 'City Hall Area', *Capuchin Annual* (1966): 193–200.

Cronin, Seán (ed.), *The McGarrity Papers* (Tralee 1972).

Czira, Sydney Gifford, *The Years Flew By* (Dublin 1974).

David, E. (ed.), *Inside Asquith's Cabinet. From the Diaries of Charles Hobhouse* (London 1977).

de Blaghd, Earnan, 'Organising the IRB in Donegal', *Journal of the Donegal Historical Society*, 7 (1) (1966), pp. 41–4.

Desmond, Shaw, *The Drama of Sinn Féin* (London 1923).

Devoy, John, *Recollections of an Irish Rebel* (New York 1929).

Ervine, St John, 'The Story of the Irish Rebellion', *Century Magazine* (1917).

Escouflaire, R. C., *L'Irlande ennemie . . . ?* (Paris 1918).

Figgis, Darrel, *Recollections of the Irish War* (London 1927).

FitzGerald, Fergus (ed.), *Memoirs of Desmond FitzGerald* (London 1968).

Fitzgibbon, Sean, 'The Easter Rising from the Inside', *Irish Times*, 18, 19, 20, 21 April 1949.

Fr Aloysius, OFM, Cap., 'Personal Recollections', *Capuchin Annual* (1966).

Gibbon, Monk, 'Murder in Portobello Barracks', *The Dublin Magazine*, 5 (1966): 8–32.

——, *Inglorious Soldier* (London 1968).

Good, Joe, *Enchanted by Dreams: the Journals of a Revolutionary* (Dingle 1966).

Griffin, Gerald, *The Dead March Past* (London 1937).

Hannay, J.O., 'Ireland and the War', *The Nineteenth Century and After*, 77 (August 1915): 393–402.

Henry, R. M. *The Evolution of Sinn Fein* (Dublin 1920).

Higgins, B., *The Soldier's Story of Easter Week* (Dublin 1917).

Hobhouse, Charles, *Inside Asquith's Cabinet* (London 1977).

Hobson, Bulmer, *The Creed of the Republic* (Belfast 1907).

——, *Defensive Warfare. A Handbook for Irish Nationalists* (Belfast 1909).

——, *A Short History of the Irish Volunteers* (Dublin 1918).

——, *Ireland Yesterday and Tomorrow* (Tralee 1968).

Holohan, Paddy, 'Four Courts Area', *Capuchin Annual* (1966): 179–88.

Hopkinson, M. (ed.), *Frank Henderson's Easter Rising* (Cork 1998).

Jeffery, K. (ed.), *The Sinn Féin Rebellion as They Saw it. Mary Louisa and Arthur Hamilton Norway* (Dublin 1999).

Jones, Francis P., *History of the Sinn Fein Movement and the Irish Rebellion of 1916* (New York 1917).

Joyce, Mannix, 'The Story of Limerick and Kerry in 1916', *Capuchin Annual* (1966): 327–70.

Lawless, Joseph, 'The Fight at Ashbourne', *Capuchin Annual* (1966): 307–16.

Little, P. J., 'A 1916 Document', *Capuchin Annual* (1942): 454–62.

Lynch, Arthur, *Ireland – Vital Hour* (London 1915).

Lynch, Diarmuid, *The IRB and the 1916 Insurrection* (Cork 1957).

Lyons, George, 'Occupation of the Ringsend Area', *An tOglác*, 10, 17, 24 April 1926.

McBride, Maud Gonne, *A Servant of the Queen* (London 1938).

McCullough, Denis, 'The Events in Belfast', *Capuchin Annual* (1966): 381–4.

McDonnell, Kathleen Keyes, *There is a Bridge at Bandon. A Personal Account of the Irish War of Independence* (Cork 1972).

MacEntee, Seán, *Episode at Easter* (Dublin 1966).

MacGiolla Choille, B. (ed.), *Intelligence Notes 1913–16 Preserved in the State Paper Office* (Baile Atha Cliath 1966).

McHugh, Roger (ed.), *Dublin, 1916: An Illustrated Anthology* (London 1966, New York 1967).

McKenzie, F. A., *The Irish Rebellion. What Happened and Why* (London 1916).

MacLochlainn, Piaras F., *Last Words, Letters and Statements of the Leaders Executed After the Rising* (Dublin 1990).

McLoughlin, Seán, 'Memories of the Easter Rising 1916', *Camillian Post*, 13 (1) (1948): 1–21.

Macready, Gen. Sir [Cecil Frederick] Nevil, *Annals of an Active Life* (London 1925).

Martin, F. X. (ed.), 'The McCartan Documents, 1916', *Clogher Record* (1966): 5–65.

——, 'Select Documents: Eoin MacNeill on the 1916 Rising', *Irish Historical Studies*, 12 (March 1961): 226–71.

Meakin, W., *The 5th North Staffords and the North Midland Territorials 1914–1919* (Longton 1920).

Midleton, Earl of, *Ireland – Dupe or Heroine?* (London 1932).

——, *Records and Reactions, 1856–1939* (London 1939).

Monteith, Robert, *Casement's Last Adventure* (Chicago 1932).

Mulcahy, Richard, 'Conscription and the General Headquarters Staff', *Capuchin Annual*, 35 (1968).

——, 'The Development of the Irish Volunteers: 1916–22', *An Cosantóir*, 40 (2) (1980): 35–40; (3): 67–71; (4): 99–102.

Neilan, Mattie, 'The Rising in Galway', *Capuchin Annual* (1966): 324–6.

Ni Chorra, Eilis, 'A Rebel Remembers', *Capuchin Annual* (1966): 292–300.

Nic Shiubhlaigh, Maire (as told to Edward Kenny), *The Splendid Years* (Dublin 1955).

Norway, Mrs A. H., *The Sinn Fein Rebellion as I Saw It* (London 1916).

Ó Briain, Liam, 'Saint Stephen's Green Area', *Capuchin Annual* (1966): 219–36.

O'Brien, William, *The Irish Revolution and How it Came About* (London 1923).

O'Casey, Sean, *The Story of the Irish Citizen Army* (Dublin 1919).

O Ceallaigh, Pádraig, 'Jacob's Factory Area', *Capuchin Annual* (1966): 214–18.

O Ceallaigh, Seán T., *Seán T.* (Dublin 1973).

O'Connor, Joseph, 'Boland's Mill Area', *Capuchin Annual* (1966): 237–53.

O Dubhighaill, Seumas, 'Activities in Enniscorthy', *Capuchin Annual* (1966): 317–23.

O'Duffy, Eimar, *The Wasted Island* (London 1929).

O'Hegarty, P. S., *The Victory of Sinn Fein. How it Won it, and How it Used it* (Dublin 1924).

O'Higgins, Brian, *The Soldier's Story of Easter Week, Poems of 1916, Prison Letters 1917–20 of Brian O'Higgins* (Dublin 1966).

O'Malley, Ernie, *On Another Man's Wound* (London and Dublin 1936).

O'Rahilly, Michael, *The Secret History of the Irish Volunteers* (Dublin 1915).

Pearse, Patrick H., *Collected Works of Padraic H. Pearse. Political Writings and Speeches* (Dublin 1922).

Phillips, W. Alison, *The Revolution in Ireland 1906–1923* (London 1923).

Plunkett, Geraldine, 'Joseph Plunkett's Diary of his Journey to Germany', *University Review*, 1 (12) (1968): 36–45.

Redmond-Howard, L. G., *Six Days of the Irish Republic: a Narrative and Critical Assessment of the Latest Phase of Irish Politics* (Dublin 1916).

Reynolds, John J., *A Fragment of 1916 History* (Dublin 1919).

Robbins, Frank, *Under the Starry Plough. Recollections of the Irish Citizen Army* (Dublin 1977).

Ruiséal, Liam, 'The Position in Cork', *Capuchin Annual* (1966): 371–80.

Ryan, Desmond, *James Connolly* (Dublin 1924).

——, *Remembering Sion* (London 1934).

——, *The Rising. The Complete Story of Easter Week* (Dublin 1949).

Ryan, James, 'General Post Office Area', *Capuchin Annual* (1966): 170–8.

——, 'In the GPO: The Medical Unit', in F. X. Martin (ed.), *The Easter Rising, 1916, and University College, Dublin* (Dublin 1966).

Skinnider, Margaret, *Doing My Bit for Ireland* (New York 1917).

Spindler, Karl, *The Mystery of the Casement Ship* (Berlin 1931).

Staines, M. and O'Reilly, M., 'The Defence of the GPO', *An tOglác*, 23 January 1926.

Stephens, James, *The Insurrection in Dublin* (Dublin 1916).

Stokes, Lilly, 'The Personal Experience of Miss L. Stokes, 11 Raglan Road, Dublin, during the Sinn Fein Rebellion of 1916', *Nonplus*, 4 (Winter 1960): 7–33.

Ui Chonail, Eilis Bean, 'A Cumann na mBan Recalls Easter Week', *Capuchin Annual* (1966).

Warwick-Haller, S. and A. (eds), *Letters from Dublin, Easter 1916. The Diary of Alfred Fannin* (Dublin 1995).

Weekly Irish Times, *Sinn Fein Rebellion Handbook* (Dublin 1917).

Wells, Warre B., *An Irish Apologia. Some Thoughts on Anglo-Irish Relations and the War* (Dublin 1917).

——and Marlowe, N., *A History of the Irish Rebellion of 1916* (Dublin 1916).

LATER WORKS

aan de Wiel, Jerome, *The Catholic Church in Ireland 1914–1918. War and Politics* (Dublin 2003).

Adams, R. J. Q. and Poirier, Sidney, *The Conscription Controversy in Great Britain, 1900–1918* (Basingstoke 1987).

Arthur, Sir George, *General Sir John Maxwell* (London 1932).

Asquith, Lady Cynthia, *Diaries 1915–1918* (London 1968).

Audouin-Rouzeau, Stephane and Becker, Annette, *14–18, retrouver la Guerre* (Paris 2000).

Augusteijn, Joost, *From Public Defiance to Guerrilla Warfare. The Experience of Ordinary Volunteers in the Irish War of Independence 1916–1921* (Dublin 1996).

—— (ed.), *The Irish Revolution, 1913–1923* (London 2002).

Barton, Brian, *From Behind a Closed Door. Secret Court Martial Records of the Easter Rising* (Belfast 2002).

Beckett, I. F. W., *The Amateur Military Tradition 1558–1945* (Manchester 1991).

—— (ed.), *The Army and the Curragh Incident, 1914* (London 1986).

Bew, Paul, *Ideology and the Irish Question: Ulster Unionism and Irish Nationalism, 1912–1916* (Oxford 1994).

——, 'The real importance of Sir Roger Casement', *History Ireland*, 2 (2) (1994): 42–5.

——, *John Redmond* (Dundalk 1996).

——, 'Moderate Nationalism and the Irish Revolution, 1916–1923', *Historical Journal*, 42 (3) (1999): 729–49.

Bolger, Dermot (ed.), *16 on 16* (Dublin 1989).

Bourke, Joanna, '"Irish Tommies": the Construction of a Martial Manhood 1914–1918', *Bullán*, 3 (2) (Winter 1997 / Spring 1998): 13–30.

Bourke, Marcus, 'Thomas MacDonagh's Role in the Plans for the 1916 Rising', *The Irish Sword*, 8 (32) (1968): 178–85.

Bowen, Elizabeth, *The Shelbourne. A Centre in Dublin Life for More than a Century* (London 1951).

Bowman, Tim, 'The Ulster Volunteer Force and the Formation of the 36th (Ulster) Division', *Irish Historical Studies*, 32 (2001): 498–518.

——, 'The Ulster Volunteers 1913–14: Force or Farce?', *History Ireland*, 10 (2002): 43–7.

——, *The Irish Regiments in the Great War. Discipline and Morale* (Manchester 2003).

Boyce, D. George, 'British Opinion, Ireland and the War, 1916–1918', *Historical Journal*, 17 (3) (1974).

——, *Nationalism in Ireland* (London 1982, 3rd edition, 1995).

——, *The Sure Confusing Drum: Ireland and the First World War* (Swansea 1993).

—— and Hazlehurst, Cameron, 'The Unknown Chief Secretary: H. E. Duke and Ireland, 1916–18', *Irish Historical Studies*, 20 (79) (1977): 286–311.

Boyle, Andrew, *The Riddle of Erskine Childers* (London 1977).

Callan, Patrick, 'Recruiting for the British Army in Ireland during the First World War', *The Irish Sword*, 17 (1987), pp. 42–56.

Callanan, Frank, *T. M. Healy* (Cork 1996).

Campbell, Colm, *Emergency Law in Ireland 1918–1925* (Oxford 1994).

Campbell, Fergus, 'The Social Dynamics of Nationalist Politics in the West of Ireland 1898–1918', *Past and Present*, 182 (2004): 175–209.

Cassar, George H., *Kitchener. Architect of Victory* (London 1977).

Caulfield, Max, *The Easter Rebellion* (London 1963).

Chevasse, M., *Terence MacSwiney* (Dublin 1961).

Coakley, John, 'Patrick Pearse and the "Noble Lie" of Irish Nationalism', *Studies in Conflict and Violence*, 62 (1983): 119–34.

Coldrey, Barry, *Faith and Fatherland: the Christian Brothers and the Development of Irish Nationalism, 1838–1921* (Dublin 1988).

Colls, Robert, *Identity of England* (Oxford 2002).

Comerford, R. V., *Ireland* (London 2003).

Coogan, Tim Pat, *Michael Collins* (London 1990).

——, *Eamon de Valera* (London 1993).

Crowley, Tony, *The Politics of Language in Ireland 1366–1922* (London 2000).

Curtis, L. P., jr, 'Moral and Physical Force: the Language of Violence in Irish Nationalism', *Journal of British Studies*, 27 (1) (1988): 150–89.

Daly, Dominic, *The Young Douglas Hyde* (Dublin 1974).

Dangerfield, George, *The Strange Death of Liberal England* (London 1936).

——, *The Damnable Question: a Study in Anglo-Irish Relations* (London 1977).

Davis, Richard, *Arthur Griffith and Non-violent Sinn Féin* (Dublin 1974).

Deane, Seamus, *Strange Country. Modernity and Nationhood in Irish Writing since 1790* (Oxford 1997).

Denman, Terence, 'The 10th (Irish) Division 1914–15: a Study in Military and Political Interaction', *The Irish Sword*, 17 (1987).

——, 'The Catholic Irish Soldier in the First World War: the "Racial Environment"', *Irish Historical Studies*, 27 (108) (1991): 352–65.

——, *Ireland's Unknown Soldiers. The 16th (Irish) Division in the Great War* (Dublin 1992).

De Paor, Liam, *On the Easter Proclamation and Other Declarations* (Dublin 1997).

Devine, Kathleen (ed.), *Modern Irish Writers and the Wars* (Gerrards Cross 1999).

Doerries, Reinhard, *Prelude to the Easter Rising. Sir Roger Casement in Imperial Germany* (London 2000).

Dooley, Terence, 'Alexander "Baby" Gray (1858–1916) and the Battle at Ashbourne, 28 April 1916', *Ríocht na Midhe*, 14 (2003): 194–229.

Dooley, Thomas, 'Politics, Bands and Marketing: Army Recruitment in Waterford City, 1914–15', *The Irish Sword*, 18 (72) (1991): 205–19.

——, 'Southern Ireland, Historians and the First World War', *Irish Studies Review*, 4 (Autumn 1993): 5–9.

——, *Irishmen or English Soldiers?* (Liverpool 1995).

Dudley Edwards, Owen, *Eamon de Valera* (Cardiff 1987).

——and Pyle, Fergus (eds), *1916: the Easter Rising* (London 1968).

Dudley Edwards, Ruth, *Patrick Pearse. The Triumph of Failure* (London 1977).

Duff, Charles, *Six Days to Shake an Empire* (London 1966).

Duggan, J. P., 'German Arms and the 1916 Rising', *An Cosantóir*, 30 (1970): 88–91.

Dungan, Myles, *Irish Voices from the Great War* (Dublin 1995).

——, *They Shall Grow Not Old: Irish Soldiers and the Great War* (Dublin 1997).

Elliott, Marianne, *Robert Emmet: the Making of a Legend* (London 2003).

English, Richard, *Ernie O'Malley. IRA Intellectual* (Oxford 1998).

——, *Armed Struggle: a History of the IRA* (London 2003).

Farry, Michael, *Sligo 1914–1921. A Chronicle of Conflict* (Trim, Co. Meath, 1992).

Fennell, Desmond, *The Revision of Irish Nationalism* (Dublin 1989).

Ferriter, Diarmuid, *Lovers of Liberty? Local Government in Twentieth Century Ireland* (Dublin 2001).

——, '"In such deadly earnest": The Bureau of Military History', *Dublin Review*, 5 (Winter 2001–2): 5–15.

——, *The Transformation of Ireland 1900–2000* (London 2004).

FitzGerald, Garret, 'The Significance of 1916', *Studies*, 55 (Spring 1966): 29–37.

——, *Reflections on the Irish State* (Dublin 2003).

Fitzpatrick, David, *Politics and Irish Life 1913–21. Provincial Experience of War and Revolution* (Dublin 1977).

——, 'The Overflow of the Deluge: Anglo-Irish Relationships, 1914–1922', in O. MacDonagh and W. F. Mandle (eds), *Ireland and Irish Australia* (London 1986), pp. 81–94.

——, 'The Logic of Collective Sacrifice: Ireland and the British Army, 1914–1918', *Historical Journal*, 38 (4) (1995): 1017–30.

——, 'Militarism in Ireland 1900–1922', in T. Bartlett and K. Jeffery (eds), *A Military History of Ireland* (Cambridge 1996).

——, *The Two Irelands 1912–1939* (Oxford 1998).

——, *Harry Boland's Irish Revolution* (Cork 2003).

——, (ed.), *Ireland and the First World War* (Dublin 1986).

——, (ed.), *Revolution? Ireland 1917–1923* (Dublin 1990).

Forester, Margery, *Michael Collins, the Lost Leader* (London 1971).

Foster, R. F., *Modern Ireland 1600–1972* (London 1988).

——, *Paddy and Mr Punch. Connections in Irish and English History* (London 1993).

——, *W. B. Yeats. A Life* (2 vols) (Oxford 2003).

Fox, R. M., *Rebel Irishwomen* (Dublin 1935).

——, *The History of the Irish Citizen Army* (Dublin 1943).

——, *Louie Bennett: Her Life and Times* (Dublin 1957).

Foy, Michael and Barton, Brian, *The Easter Rising* (Stroud 1999).

Garvin, Tom, 'Priests and Patriots. Irish Separatism and Fear of the Modern, 1890–1914', *Irish Historical Studies*, 25 (97) (1986): 67–81.

——, *Nationalist Revolutionaries in Ireland, 1858–1928* (Oxford 1987).

——, 'Great Hatred, Little Room: Social Background and Political sentiment among Revolutionary Activists in Ireland, 1890–1922', in D. G. Boyce (ed.), *The Revolution in Ireland, 1879–1923* (Basingstoke 1988).

Gaughan, J. A., *Austin Stack. Portrait of a Separatist* (Dublin 1977).

——, *Thomas Johnson, 1872–1963. First Leader of the Labour Party in Dáil Éireann* (Mount Merrion 1980).

Geohegan, S., *The Campaigns and History of The Royal Irish Regiment*, 2 vols (Edinburgh 1927).

Glandon, Virginia E., *Arthur Griffith and the Advanced-Nationalist Press in Ireland, 1900–1922* (New York 1985).

Goldring, Maurice, *Faith of Our Fathers. The Formation of Irish Nationalist Ideology, 1890–1920* (Dublin 1982).

——, *Pleasant the Scholar's Life: Irish Intellectuals and the Construction of the Nation State* (London 1993).

Greaves, C. D., *Liam Mellows and the Irish Revolution* (London 1971).

——, *The Life and Times of James Connolly* (London 1972).

——, *The Easter Rising in Song and Ballad* (London 1980).

——, *1916 as History: the Myth of the Blood Sacrifice* (Dublin 1991).

Gregory, Adrian and Paseta, Senia (eds), *Ireland and the Great War. 'A War to Unite Us All'?* (Manchester 2002).

Gwynn, Denis, *The Life of John Redmond* (London 1932).

Gwynn, Stephen, *John Redmond's Last Years* (London 1919).

—— (ed.), *The Letters and Friendships of Sir Cecil Spring Rice* (Boston 1929).

——, *Dublin Old and New* (London n.d.).

Hally, Col. P. J., 'The Easter 1916 Rising in Dublin: the Military Aspects', Part I, *The Irish Sword*, 7 (29) (1966): 313–26; Part II, 8 (30) (1968): 48–57.

Hart, Peter, *The IRA and its Enemies. Violence and Community in Cork, 1916–1923* (Oxford 1998).

——, *The IRA at War 1916–1923* (Oxford 2003).

Hartley, Stephen, *The Irish Question as a Problem in British Foreign Policy, 1914–18* (London 1987).

Haswell, Jock, *Citizen Armies* (London 1973).

Haydon, Anthony, *Sir Matthew Nathan: British Governor and Civil Servant* (St Lucia, Queensland 1976).

Hayes-McCoy, G. A., *Irish Battles: a Military History of Ireland* (London 1969).

——, 'A Military History of the 1916 Rising', in K. B. Nowlan (ed.), *The Making of 1916. Studies in the History of the Rising* (Dublin 1969).

——(ed.), *The Irish at War* (Cork 1964).

Hazlehurst, Cameron, *Politicians at War, July 1914 to May 1915* (London 1971).

Heuston, J., *Headquarters Battalion, Army of the Irish Republic, Easter Week, 1916* (Tallaght 1966).

Holmes, Richard, *The Little Field-Marshal. Sir John French* (London 1981).

Howie, David and Josephine, 'Irish Recruiting and the Home Rule Crisis of August–September 1914', in M. Dockrill and D. French (eds), *Strategy and Intelligence. British Policy During the First World War* (London 1996), pp. 1–22.

Hynes, Samuel, *A War Imagined: the First World War and English Culture* (London 1990).

Ireland, John de Courcy, *The Sea and the 1916 Rising* (Dublin 1966).

Jalland, Patricia, *The Liberals and Ireland. The Ulster Question in British Politics to 1914* (Brighton 1980).

Jamie, Lt. Col. J. P. W., *The 177th Brigade 1914–18* (Leicester 1931).

Janowitz, Morris, *The Military in the Political Development of New Nations: An Essay in Comparative Analysis* (Chicago 1964).

Jeffery, Keith, 'The Great War and Modern Irish Memory', in T. G. Fraser and K. Jeffery (eds), *Men, Women and War* (Dublin 1993).

——, 'Irish Culture and the Great War', *Bullán*, 1 (2) (1994): 87–96.

——, 'Irish Prose Writers of the First World War', in K. Devine (ed.), *Modern Irish Writers and the Wars* (Gerrards Cross 1999).

——, *Ireland and the Great War* (Cambridge 2000).

Jenkins, Roy, *Asquith* (London 1964).

Johnstone, Tom, *Orange, Green and Khaki. The Story of the Irish Regiments in the Great War* (Dublin 1992).

Kiberd, Declan, 'The Elephant of Revolutionary Forgetfulness', in M. Ní Dhonnchadha and T. Dorgan (eds), *Revising the Rising* (Derry 1991).

——, '1916: the Idea and the Action', in K. Devine (ed.), *Modern Irish Writers and the Wars* (Gerrards Cross 1999).

Laffan, Michael, *The Partition of Ireland, 1911–1925* (Dundalk 1983).

——, *The Resurrection of Ireland. The Sinn Féin Party 1916–1923* (Cambridge 1999).

Larsen, Stein and Snoddy, Oliver, '1916 – a Workingmen's Revolution?' *Social Studies*, 2 (1973): 377–98.

Lee, J. J., *The Modernisation of Irish Society* (Dublin 1973).

——, *Ireland 1912–1985. Politics and Society* (Cambridge 1989).

——, '*In Search of Patrick Pearse*' in M. Ní Dhonnchadha and T. Dorgan (eds), *Revising the Rising* (Derry 1991).

Leonard, Jane, 'The Reaction of Irish Officers in the British Army to the Easter Rising of 1916', in H. Cecil and P. Liddle (eds), *Facing Armageddon. The First World War Experienced* (London 1996).

Le Roux, Louis, *Patrick H. Pearse* (tr. Desmond Ryan) (Dublin, n.d. [1932]).

——, *Tom Clarke and the Irish Freedom Movement* (Dublin 1936).

Levenson, Leah, *With Wooden Sword: a Portrait of Francis Sheehy Skeffington, Militant and Pacifist* (Boston 1983).

Levitas, Ben, *The Theatre of Nation. Irish Drama and Cultural Nationalism 1890–1916* (Oxford 2002).

Liebknecht, Karl, *Militarism and Anti-militarism* (1907; English translation; Cambridge 1973).

Llobera, Josep, *The God of Modernity* (London 1994).

Longford, Earl of, and O'Neill, T.P., *Eamon de Valera* (London 1970).

Lyons, F. S. L., *Ireland since the Famine* (London 1971).

——, *Culture and Anarchy in Ireland 1890–1939* (Oxford 1979).

——, 'The Watershed, 1903–7', in W. E. Vaughan (ed.), *Ireland under the Union, II, 1870–1921* (*A New History of Ireland*, vol. 6) (Oxford 1996).

Lyons, J. B., *The Enigma of Tom Kettle* (Dublin 1983).

Macardle, Dorothy, *The Irish Republic* (London 1937).

MacCurtain, Margaret, 'Women, the Vote and Revolution', in M. MacCurtain and D. Ó Corráin (eds), *Women in Irish Society. The Historical Dimension* (Dublin 1978), pp. 46–57.

McDiarmid, Lucy, 'The Posthumous Life of Roger Casement', in A. Bradley and M. G. Valiulis (eds), *Gender and Sexuality in Modern Ireland* (Amherst, MA, 1997).

McDowell, R. B., *The Irish Convention, 1917–18* (London 1970).

MacEoin, U., *Survivors* (Dublin 1980).

McEwen, John, 'The Liberal Party and the Irish Question During the First World War', *Journal of British Studies*, 12 (2) (1972): 109–31.

McKillen, Beth, 'Irish Feminism and National Separatism, 1914–23', *Eire-Ireland*, 17 (3) (1982): 52–67; (4) (1982): 72–90.

McMahon, Deirdre, 'Roger Casement: an Account from the Archives of his Reinterment in Ireland', *Journal of the Irish Society for Archives*, 3 (new series) (1) (1996): 3–12.

Maher, Jim, *The Flying Column: West Kilkenny 1916–21* (Dublin 1987).

——, *Harry Boland. A Biography* (Cork 1998).

Malins, Edward, 'Yeats and the Easter Rising', in L. Miller (ed.), *Yeats Centenary Papers* (Dublin 1965).

Mansergh, Nicholas, *The Unresolved Question: the Anglo-Irish Settlement and its Undoing, 1912–72* (London 1991).

Martin, F. X., (ed.) *The Irish Volunteers 1913–1915. Recollections and Documents* (Dublin 1963).

——, (ed.), *The Howth Gunrunning and the Kilcoole Gunrunning, 1914* (Dublin 1964).

——, (ed.), *The Easter Rising, 1916, and University College, Dublin* (Dublin 1966).

——, '1916 – Myth, Fact and Mystery', *Studia Hibernica*, 7 (1967).

——(ed.), *Leaders and Men of the Easter Rising: Dublin 1916* (London 1967).

——, 'The 1916 Rising – A *Coup d'état* or a "Bloody Protest"?' *Studia Hibernica*, 8 (1968).

——, 'The Evolution of a Myth – the Easter Rising, Dublin 1916', in Eugene Kamenka (ed.), *Nationalism: the Nature and Evolution of an Idea* (London 1973).

——and Byrne, F. J. (eds), *The Scholar Revolutionary. Eoin MacNeill 1867–1945, and the Making of the New Ireland* (Shannon 1973).

Maume, Patrick, *The Long Gestation. Irish Nationalist Life 1891–1918* (Dublin 1999).

Maye, Brian, *Arthur Griffith* (Dublin 1997).

Miller, David W., *Church, State and Nation in Ireland 1898–1921* (Dublin 1973).

Mitchell, Arthur, *Labour in Irish Politics, 1890–1930. The Irish Labour Movement in an Age of Revolution* (Dublin 1974).

Moran, Sean Farrell, *Patrick Pearse and the Politics of Redemption* (Washington, DC, 1994).

Morgan, Austen, *James Connolly* (Manchester 1988).

Morison, Elting E. (ed.), *The Letters of Theodore Roosevelt* (Cambridge, MA, 1951).

Muenger, Elizabeth A., *The British Military Dilemma in Ireland. Occupation Politics, 1886–1914* (Lawrence, Kansas, 1991).

Mulvihill, Margaret, *Charlotte Despard: A Biography* (London 1989).

Murphy, Brian P. *Patrick Pearse and the Lost Republican Ideal* (Dublin 1991).

Newsinger, John, 'Revolution and Catholicism in Ireland, 1848–1923', *European Studies Review*, 9 (4) (1979): 457–80.

——, 'Canon and Martial Law: William O'Brien, Catholicism, and Irish Nationalism', *Eire-Ireland*, 16 (2) (1981): 59–70.

Ní Dhonnchadha, M. and Dorgan, T. (eds), *Revising the Rising* (Dublin 1991).

Norstedt, Johann A., *Thomas MacDonagh. A Critical Biography* (Charlottesville, VA, 1980).

Novick, Ben, 'Postal Censorship in Ireland, 1914–1916', *Irish Historical Studies*, 31 (123) (1999): 343–56.

——, 'The Arming of Ireland: Gun-running and the Great War', in Adrian Gregory and Senia Paseta (eds), *Ireland and the Great War* (Manchester 2002).

——, *Conceiving Revolution. Irish Nationalist Propaganda during the First World War* (Dublin 2001).

Nowlan, K. B. (ed.), *The Making of 1916. Studies in the History of the Rising* (Dublin 1969).

Oates, Lt. Col. W. C., *The Sherwood Foresters in the Great War 1914–1919* (Nottingham 1920).

O'Brien, J. V., *'Dear, Dirty Dublin'. A City in Distress 1899–1916* (Berkeley, CA, 1982).

O'Brien, R. Barry, *Munster at War* (Cork 1971).

Ó Broin, Leon, *Dublin Castle and the 1916 Rising* (London 1966).

——, *The Chief Secretary. Augustine Birrell in Ireland* (London 1969).

——, *Revolutionary Underground. The Story of the Irish Republican Brotherhood, 1858–1924* (Dublin 1976).

——, 'Revolutionary Nationalism in Ireland: the IRB 1858–1924', in T.W. Moody (ed.), *Nationality and the Pursuit of National Independence* (Belfast 1978).

——, *W. E. Wylie and the Irish Revolution 1916–1921* (Dublin 1989).

O'Connor, John, *The Story of the 1916 Proclamation* (Dublin n.d. [1986]).

O'Donoghue, Florence, 'Plans for the 1916 Rising', *University Review*, 3 (March 1963).

——, 'Guerrilla Warfare in Ireland', *An Cosantóir*, 23 (1963).

——, 'Easter Week, 1916', in G. A. Hayes-McCoy (ed.), *The Irish at War* (Cork 1964).

——, 'The Failure of the German Arms Landing at Easter 1916', *Cork Historical and Archaeological Society Journal*, 71 (1966).

O'Faolain, Sean, *Constance Markievicz, or the Average Revolutionary* (London 1934).

O'Farrell, Mick, *A Walk Through Rebel Dublin 1916* (Cork 1999).

O'Farrell, Patrick, *Ireland's English Question. Anglo-Irish Relations 1534–1970* (New York 1971).

O'Halpin, Eunan, 'H. E. Duke and the Irish Administration, 1916–18', *Irish Historical Studies*, 20 (88) (1981): 362–76.

——, 'British Intelligence in Ireland', in C. Andrew and D. Dilks (eds), *The Missing Dimension. Governments and Intelligence Communities in the Twentieth Century* (London 1984).

——, *The Decline of the Union. British Government in Ireland 1892–1920* (Dublin 1987).

O Luing, Seán, *I Die in a Good Cause. A Study of Thomas Ashe, Idealist and Revolutionary* (Tralee 1970).

O' Mahoney, Sean, *Frongoch: University of Revolution* (Dublin 1987).

O'Neill, Col. E., 'The Battle of Dublin, 1916', *An Cosantóir*, 26 (1966): 211–22.

O'Rahilly, Aodogan, *Winding the Clock: O Rahilly and the 1916 Rising* (Dublin 1991).

Orr, Philip, *The Road to the Somme. Men of the Ulster Division Tell Their Story* (Belfast 1987).

——, 'The Road to Belgrade: the Experiences of the 10th (Irish) Division in the Balkans, 1915–17', in Adrian Gregory and Senia Paseta (eds), *Ireland and the Great War* (Manchester 2002).

Parks, Edd W. and Aileen W., *Thomas MacDonagh: the Man, the Patriot, the Writer* (Athens, GA, 1967).

Paseta, Senia, *Before the Revolution. Nationalism, Social Change and Ireland's Catholic Elite, 1879–1922* (Cork 1999).

——, 'Thomas Kettle: "An Irish Soldier in the Army of Europe"?' in Adrian Gregory and Senia Paseta (eds), *Ireland and the Great War* (Manchester 2002).

Reid, B. L., *The Lives of Roger Casement* (New Haven, Conn., 1976).

Roth, Andreas, '"The German Soldier is Not Tactful": Sir Roger Casement and the Irish Brigade in Germany during the First World War', *The Irish Sword*, 19 (78) (1995).

Savage, David, 'The Attempted Home Rule Settlement of 1916', *Eire-Ireland*, 2 (3) (1967): 132–45.

Simkins, Peter, *Kitchener's Army: the Raising of the New Armies, 1914–16* (Manchester 1988).

Snoddy, Oliver, 'The Midland Volunteer Force 1913', *Journal of the Old Athlone Society* (1968).

Staunton, Martin, 'Kilrush, Co. Clare and the Royal Munster Fusiliers: the Experience of an Irish Town in the First World War', *The Irish Sword*, 14 (1986): 268–70.

Stewart, A. T. Q., *The Ulster Crisis* (London 1967).

Stubbs, J. O., 'The Unionists and Ireland 1914–1918', *Historical Journal*, 33 (4) (1990): 867–93.

Taillon, Ruth, *The Women of 1916* (Belfast 1996).

Taylor, Rex, *Michael Collins* (London 1958).

Thompson, William Irwin, *The Imagination of an Insurrection: Dublin, Easter 1916* (New York 1967).

Tierney, Michael, *Eoin MacNeill. Scholar and Man of Action, 1867–1945* (Oxford 1980).

Tóibín, Colm, 'Playboys of the GPO', *London Review of Books*, 18 April 1996.

Townshend, Charles, *The British Campaign in Ireland: the Development of Political and Military Policies 1919–1921* (Oxford 1975)

——, 'The Irish Republican Army and the Development of Guerrilla Warfare 1916–21', *English Historical Review* 94 (1979): 318–45.

——, 'Martial Law: Legal and Administrative Problems of Civil Emergency in Britain and the Empire, 1800–1940', *Historical Journal* 25 (1979).

——, *Political Violence in Ireland. Government and Resistance since 1848* (Oxford 1983).

——, 'Military Force and Civil Authority in the United Kingdom, 1914–21', *Journal of British Studies* 28 (3) (1989): 262–92.

——, 'Militarism and Modern Society', *Wilson Quarterly* (Winter 1993): 71–82.

——, 'The Suppression of the Easter Rising', *Bullán*, 1 (1) (1994): 27–47.

——, 'The Meaning of Irish Freedom; Constitutionalism in the Free State', *Transactions of the Royal Historical Society*, 6th series, vol. 8 (1998): 56–9.

——, 'Telling the Irish Revolution', in Joost Augusteijn (ed.), *The Irish Revolution, 1913–1923* (London 2002).

——, 'Religion, War and Identity in Ireland', *Journal of Modern History*, 76 (4) (2004): 882–902.

Travers, Charles J., 'Seán Mac Diarmada, 1883–1916', *Breifne* (1966): 1–46.

Tréguiz, Louis, *L'Irlande dans la Crise universelle* (Paris 1917).

Valiulis, Maryann, *Portrait of a Revolutionary. General Richard Mulcahy and the Founding of the Irish Free State* (Dublin 1992).

Van Voris, Jacqueline, *Constance de Markievicz in the Cause of Ireland* (Amherst, MA, 1967).

Vaughan, W. E. (ed.), *Ireland under the Union, II, 1870–1921 (A New History of Ireland*, vol. 6) (Oxford 1996).

Wall, Maureen, 'The Plans and the Countermand: the Country and Dublin', in K. B. Nowlan (ed.), *The Making of 1916* (Dublin 1969).

Walsh, Oonagh, *Ireland's Independence, 1880–1923* (London 2002).

Ward, Alan J., *Ireland and Anglo-American Relations 1899–1921* (London 1969).

——, 'Lloyd George and the 1918 Irish Conscription Crisis', *Historical Journal*, 17 (1) (1974): 107–29.

——, *The Easter Rising: Revolution and Irish Nationalism* (Arlington

Heights, IL, 1980).

Ward, Margaret, 'Marginality and Militancy: Cumann na mBan 1914–1936', in A. Morgan and B. Purdie (eds), *Ireland: Divided Nation, Divided Class* (London 1980).

——, *Unmanageable Revolutionaries: Women and Irish Nationalism* (London 1983).

——, *Maud Gonne. Ireland's Joan of Arc* (London 1990).

Wasserstein, Bernard, *Herbert Samuel. A Political Life* (Oxford 1992).

Williams, T. D. (ed.), *The Irish Struggle, 1916–1926* (London 1966).

Index

Achill Island 230–31
Adams, Gerry 160
Adrian, Mollie 216, 218
AE (see George Russell)
Allen, Fred 22
Aloysius, Father 249, 250
An Barr Buadh 40
Ancient Order of Hibernians (AOH)
     42, 53, 225
Andrews, C. S. (Todd) 124
Anglo-Irish Treaty 1921 344, 347
Anti-recruiting campaign 77, 143, 147
Archer, Liam 252, 253
Ardee, Co. Louth 222
Arklow, Co. Wicklow 190
Army Annual Act 34
Ashbourne, Co. Meath 215, 218
     Rath Cross ambush 218–21, 333
Ashe, Thomas (Commandant 5th
     Battalion Dublin Brigade IV)
     169, 216–21, 328
     hunger strike and death 333–4, 335
Asquith, Lady Cynthia 147–8
Asquith, Herbert Henry 29, 31, 34, 61,
     63, 72–3, 118, 188, 271–2, 275,
     279–80, 281, 286, 289, 295,
     296–7, 302, 303, 304, 310, 314,
     323, 324, 325, 326
Athenry, Co. Galway 109, 228, 229,
     242
Athlone, Co. Westmeath 38, 106, 150,
     151, 169, 186, 191
Attorney-General, Irish 36
Aud: see Libau

Balbriggan, Co, Dublin 218
Balfe, Dick 171, 172
Ballybunion, Co. Kerry 333
Ballykissane pier, Killorglin, Co, Kerry
     131, 233
Bandon, Co. Cork 47
Bank of Ireland, Dublin 185, 190, 252
Banna Strand, Co. Kerry 129–30
barricades 165–6, 170, 174, 179,
     255–6
Bayly, Admiral Sir Lewis 127, 241
Béaslai, Piaras (Vice-Commandant, 1st
     Battalion Dublin Brigade IV) xiv,
     16, 41, 53, 68, 100, 169
Beggars Bush Barracks 177–8, 196, 199
Belfast 18–19, 20, 31, 32, 34, 150, 178,
     186, 189, 225–6, 228, 233
Benedict XV, Pope 78, 123
Bethmann Hollweg, Theobald von 125
Beverley, Julian 127
Birrell, Augustine 24–5, 63, 64, 82,
     86–7, 88, 144–5, 148, 149, 150,
     188, 208, 271, 281, 296
Blackader, Brig.Gen. C. 286
Blackwood, Lord Basil 147
Blanqui, Auguste 358
Blythe, Ernest 81, 82, 148, 341–2
Boland, Harry 84, 178, 332
Boland's bakery 154, 175–6, 199, 248,
     255
Boland's mill 176
Bonar Law, Andrew 34
Bonham Carter, Maurice 299
Borris, Co. Kilkenny 239

Bowen, Elizabeth 167
Bowen-Colthurst, Captain J. C. 193–5, 290, 292
Boylan, Seán 222, 224
Brade, Colonel Sir Reginald 74, 299
Bradshaw, Brendan 352
Brennan, Michael 124
Brennan-Whitmore, W. T. 209, 243, 244, 252, 255, 262, 263, 320, 321
British army 76
  Irish Command 58, 85, 186, 190, 196, 275
  Irish enlistment in 73–7
  mobile columns 273–4
  urban warfare experience 269–70
  units:
  2nd King's Own Scottish Borderers 57
  3rd Reserve Cavalry Brigade 51, 186
  3rd Royal Irish Regiment 183–4, 202, 208
  3rd Royal Irish Rifles 184–5, 192–5, 203
  6th Reserve Cavalry Regiment 183
  2/6th South Staffordshire Regiment 206, 293
  2/7th Sherwood Foresters (Notts and Derby Regiment) 196–8, 203
  2/8th Sherwood Foresters 197
  10th (Irish) Division 75, 147
  10th Royal Dublin Fusiliers 183–4
  16th (Irish) Division 74
  25th Reserve Infantry Brigade 186
  59th (North Midland) Division 190, 195
  176th Infantry Brigade 195
  178th Infantry Brigade 190, 195–8
  Curragh Mobile Column 186
  Royal Iniskilling Fusiliers 203, 282
Broderick, John 229
Brugha, Cathal 39, 203, 238–9
Bucknill, Sir Alfred 251
Bulfin, Eamon 212, 247, 248, 263
Bureau of Military History xiv
Butt, Isaac 4, 26
Byrne, Alfie 322
Byrne, Garry 224

Byrne, Brig. Gen. Joseph
  DAG, Irish Command 183, 208, 276, 284, 285, 290
  IG RIC 326, 337
Byrne, Seán 257

Cabinet, British 188, 270–1, 277–8, 286, 312–13, 329, 337, 338
Cahill, P. J. 109, 129
Cahirciveen, Co. Kerry 129, 131
Campbell, Sir James 287, 291, 325, 338
Carney, Winifred 162, 212, 285
Carriganimma, Co. Cork 109, 140, 141, 235, 237
Carson, Sir Edward (Lord) 32, 36, 38, 42, 73, 74, 311, 329, 338
Casement, Sir Roger 42, 43, 52, 54, 67, 103–7, 124, 126, 127–8, 129, 135, 309
  Irish Brigade 116–17, 124, 125
  Kerry landing and arrest 129–30, 131, 136, 142, 149, 233
  trial and execution 312–13
'Castle Document' 125, 131–3, 135, 136
Castro, Fidel 358
Catholic Bulletin 309–10
Catholic Church, Irish 4, 78–80, 84, 123, 314, 339, 355
  Hierarchy 305, 310, 339
Caulfield, Max 199–200, 247, 349
Cavanagh, Maeve 113
Ceannt, Eamon 41, 68, 205, 250, 261
  Commandant, 3rd Battalion 93, 140, 172–3, 203
  Director of Communication, Irish Volunteers 92
  on IRB military committee 94
  trial and execution 279, 280
Cecil, Lord Robert 311
Central Committee on Recruitment in Ireland (CCORI) 147
Chalmers, Sir Robert 296, 297–8, 326
Chamberlain, Sir Neville (IG RIC) 74–5
Childers, Erskine 54–5
Christian Brothers 13
Churchill, Winston S. 28, 63, 147
City Hall, Dublin 163–4, 185

Clan na Gael 5, 104, 116

Clanwilliam House 176, 196–8, 199

Clare, county 231

Clarke, Kathleen 161, 327

Clarke, Thomas J. 18, 22, 23, 40, 53, 91, 94, 138, 141, 142, 161, 247, 248, 309, 358
  trial and execution 279

Clausewitz, Carl von 96

Clontarf, battle of 56, 99, 125, 178, 333

Cohalan, Daniel (Assistant Bishop of Cork) 238

Colbert, Cornelius (Con) 39, 173, 279, 280, 283, 309

Colivet, Michael (Commandant Limerick Brigade IV) 231, 233–4, 248

College of Surgeons, Dublin 159, 168, 259

Colley, Harry 139–40, 156, 178, 265

Collins, Cornelius (Con) 129, 235

Collins, Michael 138, 254, 321–2, 327, 328, 339, 344, 355

Colum, Mary 47

Compensation claims 297–8

Connolly, James 49, 81, 122, 134, 136, 155, 157, 158, 161, 171, 214, 246, 254, 256, 257, 261, 263, 309
  and Citizen Army 111–12
  Commandant Dublin IRA 155, 172, 204–5, 209, 224–5, 241, 243
  final communiqué 244–5
  and looting 264
  on 'military committee' 95, 98, 99
  military ideas 112–14, 166
  trial and execution 280, 282, 289

Connolly, Matthew 257–8

Connolly, Seán 162–4, 166, 185, 260

Conscription 78, 83, 87, 92, 322: see also Military Service Bill
  resistance to 338–40, 341–2, 357

Constitutional crisis of 1910-11 28–9

Cork, Assistant Bishop of 238

Cork, city 84, 234–8
  Lord Mayor 237–8

Cork, county 43, 44, 47–8, 85, 89

Cosgrave, W. T. 250, 331, 347, 348

Cotton, Alfred 98, 233

Coughlan, James 203

courts martial: see Defence of the Realm Acts

Cowan, Col. H. V. 181, 186, 208

Craig, William 42

Craughwell, Co. Galway 342

Crenigan, James 139

Cromwell, Oliver 82

Crown Alley telephone exchange, Dublin 256–7

Cumann na mBan 46–7, 56, 70, 152, 164, 175, 202, 211, 216, 229, 239, 246, 247, 250, 259, 261, 267
  GPO garrison 211
  medical service 260

Cumann na nGaedheal 10

Curragh camp 151, 186

Curragh incident 51, 58

Czira, Mrs Sidney (Gifford) 96

Daly, Edward (Ned) 248
  Commandant 1st Battalion 93, 170, 172, 204, 205–7, 257, 261
  trial and execution 279, 283

Daly, P. T. 9, 22

Daly, Seamus 56

Davis, Thomas 7, 38, 84

Davitt, Michael 2–3

Davy's public house 168, 180, 185, 192, 261

De Coeur, Bob 192

De Valera, Eamon 69, 191, 283, 324, 328, 331, 334, 335, 339, 348
  Commandant 3rd Battalion 93, 140, 154, 175–7, 178, 199–201, 248, 255, 260

Deane, Seamus 352

Defence of the Realm Acts (DORA) 82, 89, 188, 245, 276–7, 303, 325, 328, 330, 332, 333, 336
  Courts Martial under 277, 282, 287, 290–2, 306
  Defence of the Realm (Amendment) Act 1915 277

Defence of the Realm Regulation 14B 277, 285
Department of Recruiting in Ireland (DRI) 147
Detainees: *see* internment
Devlin, Joseph 42, 68, 225
Devoy, John 6, 9, 50, 53, 54, 104, 117, 122, 125, 127, 128
Dillon, John 42, 63, 87, 265, 266, 267, 269, 275–6, 280, 281–2, 289–90, 291, 292, 328
Donabate, Co. Dublin 218
Donnelly, Simon 153, 177, 199, 200
Doyle, James 198
Doyle, Paddy 154
Doyle, Seamus 241
Doyle, Sean 81
Drogheda 267, 308
Dublin
    Abbey Street 157, 209, 210, 211, 256, 266
    Amiens Street Station 178, 185, 186, 189, 204
    Bachelors Walk 57, 59, 61
    Ballybough Road 156, 185
    Beresford Place 154, 157, 171
    Bishop Street 181, 185
    Blackhall Street 152, 169
    Broadstone Station 169, 170, 205
    Cabra Road 170, 204
    Camden Street 180, 184
    Cammock River 174
    Capel Street 205, 210
    Church Street 170, 206, 207, 253
    Coulsdon Avenue 12
    Dame Street 164
    Dawson Street 42, 132, 137, 153
    Digges Street 201
    Earlsfort Terrace 153, 175
    Fairview 156, 178, 179, 244
    Grafton Street 14, 165, 265
    Grand Canal 102, 168
    Grand Canal Street 175, 177
    Great Brunswick Street 13, 42, 258
    Harcourt Street Station 165, 168
    Henry Street 158, 208–9, 210–11, 212, 213, 244, 264, 266

Jervis Street Hospital 209
Kingsbridge Station 172, 173, 186, 204
Leeson Street 154, 168–9, 253
Liffey quays 101–2, 169, 170
Marrowbone Lane 172, 173–4, 251, 259
Merrion Square 175
Moore Street 212, 244, 246, 247, 288
Mount Brown 174, 175
Mount Street 153, 175, 176, 177, 196–8, 199, 253, 255, 270
North Circular Road 171
North King Street 170, 205–6, 293
North Wall docks 186, 189, 204, 208
Northumberland Road 153, 177, 255, 270
Oakley Road, Ranelagh 154, 175
O'Connell Bridge 170, 265
Ormond Quay 170
Parnell Square 178
Portobello Bridge 168, 180, 185, 192, 193, 292
Rathmines Road 193
Redmond's Hill 153
Ringsend 175
Rotunda 247
Royal Canal 157, 169, 178, 204
Sackville Street xiv, 100, 158, 159, 165–8, 178, 190, 204, 208, 209, 211, 262, 263, 265, 266
St Stephen's Green 101, 155, 165–8, 185, 358
Sir John Rogerson's Quay 191
South Circular Road 173
Thomas Street 9
Tolka river 156
Westland Row 13, 175, 177, 185
Westmoreland Street 165, 265
Dublin, Archbishop of 132, 133
Dublin Bread Company 254
Dublin Brigade, Irish Volunteers 118, 124, 125, 152
    1st Battalion 100, 156, 158, 169–72, 248, 260

Dublin Brigade, Irish Volunteers – *cont.*
  2nd Battalion 139, 154–5, 156, 168,
    178–81, 185, 204, 217, 264
  3rd Battalion 140, 153, 175–8,
    196–9, 248, 255
  4th Battalion 140, 172–5, 202–3
  5th (Fingal) Battalion 139, 169,
    215–21
  'Headquarters Battalion' 157,
    244–5
  'Kimmage Garrison' 171, 210
Dublin Castle 9, 25, 48, 77, 80, 85,
    110, 131, 162–4, 181, 183, 184,
    186, 190, 246, 252, 272, 302,
    319: *see also* Irish Executive
Dublin Corporation 131, 263
Dublin Metropolitan Police (DMP) 25,
    26, 67, 139, 148, 187, 272, 326
  Commissioner 67, 187, 263
  Howth gunrunning 55–7
Dudley Edwards, Ruth 353
Duke, Henry E. 297, 300, 324–5, 326,
    333, 334, 335–7, 338
Dum-dum bullets 258–9, 301
Dundalk, Co. Louth 214, 222
Dungannon Clubs 19, 20, 23

East Clare by-election 331
Edgeworth-Johnstone, Lt.Col. W. 149,
    150
Egan, Patrick 175
Emmet, Robert 7, 9, 14, 23, 48, 91, 96,
    98–9, 159, 162, 163, 221, 250,
    309
Enemy Aliens Advisory Committee
    317–19
Enniscorthy, Co. Wexford 240–2
Etchingham, John 241
Evening Mail, Dublin 145

Fairyhouse races 153, 167, 181, 222
Fane, Lt.Col. Cecil (OC 2/7th Sherwood
    Foresters) 197
Fannin, Alfred 265, 267
Father Matthew Park, Dublin 42, 139,
    150, 151, 154
Fenians 1, 3, 4, 37, 92, 224, 247, 333:

  see also Irish Republican
    Brotherhood
Fenit, Co. Kerry 128–9
Fennell, Desmond 352
Fermoy, Co. Cork 238
Ffrench Mullen, Douglas 140, 203
Ffrench Mullen, Madeleine 140, 285
Fianna Eireann 20, 22, 39, 55, 83, 93,
    164
Fianna Fáil party 11, 45, 348
Figgis, Darrell 54, 55, 230–1
Fine Gael party 11, 349
First World War 60–6, 71–7, 85–9, 90,
    93–4, 113, 311–13, 329, 337, 342
  Battle of Messines 335
  Battle of the Somme 270, 313
  Church reaction to 78–80
  Suvla Bay (Gallipoli) landing 76,
    207
FitzGerald, Desmond 44–5, 82, 98,
    210, 264, 349
FitzGerald, Garret 349–50, 354–5
Fitzgibbon, Seán 41, 108–9, 136, 232
Fogarty, Michael, Bishop of Killaloe 80
food supplies 259–60
Foster, Roy 15, 352
Four Courts, Dublin 101, 169, 170,
    206, 260, 262
Freeman's Journal 276, 327
French, Field-Marshal Viscount 145,
    148, 270, 271, 272, 276, 279–80,
    283, 286, 293, 296, 338
French, Col. J. A. 241
French Revolution 4, 269
Friend, Maj.Gen. L. W. 133, 143, 145,
    148, 149, 181, 186, 189, 190,
    191, 196, 242
Frongoch camp 317, 319–22

Gaelic American 53
Gaelic Athletic Association (GAA) 7–8,
    17, 39, 83, 84
Gaelic League 8, 12–13, 17, 36, 131,
    132, 173
Galligan, Paul 240, 241
Galway 227–30, 242, 357
  agrarian conflict in 341

Gandhi, M. K. 11
Garristown, Co. Dublin 218
General Post Office, Dublin 1, 100, 101,
    155, 156, 157, 158–61, 163, 184,
    202, 204, 205, 206, 209–13, 214,
    216, 240, 244, 247, 253, 254,
    255, 259, 260, 261, 262, 264,
    266, 267, 351, 355
George V, King 299
German Imperial Government 104–6
    Navy (Kriegsmarine) 126, 128
'German Plot' arrests 338, 339–40
Gibbon, Monk 192–3, 194
Gladstone, William Ewart 29, 30, 31
Golden, Jerry 170, 216
Gonne, Maud 10, 16, 345
Good, Joe 210, 212, 255–6, 257, 259
Government of Ireland Act (1914) 61,
    64
Grace, Seamus (Jimmy) 196–7
Gray, County Inspector (RIC) 220
Great Northern Railway 178, 216
Gregory, Augusta, Lady 16, 342, 345,
    348
Grey, Sir Edward 61
Griffith, Arthur 9–12, 30, 68, 80–1, 86,
    95, 138, 242, 333, 334, 335, 347
Guerrilla tactics 83, 98, 99
Guevara, Che 358
Guinness's brewery (Parkgate, Dublin)
    172, 205, 206
Gwynn, Stephen 16, 52, 73, 77

Hacket Pain, Colonel W. 33
Haldane, Richard Burdon, Viscount 342
Hales, Tom 236–7
Hall, Captain Reginald 127
Hamilton, Gen. Sir Ian 207
Hankey, Maurice 329
Hannay, Canon 61, 75
Harrel, W. V. 55, 57, 67
Haughey, Charles 352
Hayes, Fr Michael 304
Hayes, Dr Richard (Vice-Commandant
    5th Battalion, Dublin Brigade IV)
    215, 216, 220
Healy, T. M. 5, 290

Helga, HMS 191
Henderson, Frank 124, 139, 140, 154–5,
    178, 185, 204, 209, 210, 211,
    265, 317
Henry, Mrs Elsie 266
Heron, Aine 152, 260, 262
Heuston, Seán 171–2, 204–5, 279, 280,
    283
Heygate Lambert, Col. F. A. 319–21
Hibernian Bank 256
Hobson, Bulmer xiii, 18, 19–21, 22, 30,
    39, 40, 41, 53–4, 55, 56, 66, 80,
    117, 121, 134–5, 146, 232, 333,
    343, 347, 348, 358
    arrested by IRB (21 April 1916) 136
    Defensive Warfare 20–1, 80
    on Irish Volunteer staff 92, 134
Hoche, General Lazare 106
Holland, Robert 173–4, 203–4, 259,
    316–17
Holohan, Paddy 219
'Home rule all round' (UK federalism)
    31
Home Rule, Irish 4–5, 29–32, 80, 302,
    310, 312, 329, 340: see also
    Government of Ireland Act
    (1914)
Hopkins and Hopkins, Dublin 158
House of Lords 29
Howth gunrunning 54–6
'Howth Mauser' rifles 56, 91, 201, 215
Hughes, Paddy 221
Humbert, General 107
Humphreys, Dick 211, 214, 265
Hunter, Tom 154, 155
Hyland, Mary 168

Imperial Hotel, Dublin 158, 160, 204,
    209, 211, 243, 266
Inghinidhe na hEireann 21
Inishtooskert island 126
intelligence, military (MI5) 86
intelligence, republican 163
internment without trial 275–8, 298
Irish Brigades
    in Boer War 10, 179
    in First World War 116–17, 127

Irish Citizen 46

Irish Citizen Army 41, 49–50, 93, 109, 111–13, 156–7, 162, 169, 209
  IV attitudes to 235–6
  Mallin's command 164–9, 179
  'Starry Plough' flag 160
  women's section 46, 260, 261–72

Irish civil war 344, 347, 357

Irish Convention (1917-18) 329–30, 332, 335

Irish Executive 24–5, 58, 59, 144–7, 186, 281, 296, 297
  failure to reform 324–6

Irish Free State 344, 347, 354

Irish Freedom 22, 36–7, 48

Irish Independent 137, 138, 152

Irish local authorities, established in 1898 8, 10

Irish National Aid Association Fund 316, 327

Irish National Dramatic Society 16

Irish National Foresters 39, 132

Irish National Invincibles 6

Irish National Volunteers xv, 70–1, 73, 75, 85, 131, 133

Irish Neutrality Association 10

Irish Parliamentary (Nationalist) Party 4, 9, 18, 52, 68, 78, 87, 95, 313–14, 328, 330, 335, 337, 339, 357
  destruction of 342–3

Irish Republican Army 162, 295, 344–5, 352

Irish Republican Brotherhood (IRB) 3–4, 5, 7, 18, 22, 23, 31, 39, 40, 69, 116, 123, 125, 129, 134–5, 156, 161, 232, 319, 321–2, 328
  Dublin Centres Board 39
  Leinster Executive 137
  Military committee (council) 94–5, 97, 100, 111, 116, 118, 119, 131, 134, 135, 137, 138, 139, 142, 143, 159
  Munster Executive 118
  Supreme Council 22, 91, 94, 122, 135, 328

Irish Times 191, 304, 343, 350

Irish Transport and General Workers Union (ITGWU) 41, 48–9, 157, 160

Irish Transvaal Committee 10

Irish Volunteer Dependents' Fund 315–16

Irish Volunteers xiv, 18, 23, 28, 41–8, 52, 53, 54, 56, 57, 62, 65–70, 90–1, 120, 122, 125, 128, 132, 139, 142, 143–4, 148, 153, 157, 162, 192, 214, 232, 315, 327, 332
  1914 split 68–70
  Advisory Committee 93, 94
  and agrarian agitation 1917-18 340–1
  Ballinadee company 237
  Churchill Spa company 233
  Clogough company 237
  and conscription crisis 1918 341–2
  Cork Brigade 43, 44, 48, 118, 136, 140–1, 234–8
  Dublin 45, 47, 96–7, 120: *see also* Dublin Brigade, Irish Volunteers
  Easter Day mobilisation (1916) 139–41, 143
  Ennistymon company 233
  Howth gunrunning 54–6, 114
  Limerick brigade 233–4
  Longford 70
  Louth battalion 222–5
  Mayo 70, 84
  munitions manufacture 124, 257–8
  recruitment 44, 52
  Redmondite takeover 52–3, 66–7
  reorganisation after 1916 314–15
  St Patrick's Day mobilisation (1916) 124, 148, 258
  Tralee 43, 233
  Ulster 225
  Wexford 240–1

Irish War News (25 April 1916) 161

Irish Women's Franchise League 17, 46

Irish Worker 48, 112

Irwin, Sam 201, 255

Jacob's factory, Dublin 164, 179–81, 185, 201–2, 259, 261

Jagow, Gottlieb von 105

Jameson's Distillery 173, 203
Jenkins, Roy 313
Johnson, Thomas 267
Jordan, Neil 355
Joyce, James (cellarman) 180
Joyce, James (writer) 6
Joyce, Mannix 233

Kavanagh, Seumas 153
Kearny, Peadar 179, 201–2, 249, 355
Keating, Cornelius (Con) 131
Keating, Pauline 262
Kelly, James (Alderman, Dublin) 193
Kelly, Tom (Alderman, Dublin) 131,
    132, 133
Kelly-Kenny, General 43
Kelly's store ('Kelly's fort') 158, 209–10
Kennard, Lt.Col. 181–2, 184, 185
Kent, Richard 238
Kent, Thomas 238, 279, 280
Keogh, Margaretta 262
Kickham, Charles J. 7
Kerry, county 43, 109, 128–31, 150,
    231
Kerryman, The 145
Kettle, Thomas 95, 194, 314, 358
Kilkenny 238–40
    By-election 1917 331–2
Kilmainham gaol 279, 289
King's County 75
Kingstown, Co. Dublin 176, 186, 189,
    191, 203
Kitchener of Khartoum, Field-Marshal Earl
    63–4, 73, 76, 77, 145, 148, 208,
    272, 274, 278, 290, 293, 300, 301
Knutsford gaol 316–17

Land League 3
'Land War' 2–3
Lardner, Larry (Commandant Galway
    Battalion IV) 227–8
Larkin, James 48–9
Larne gunrunning (1914) 51, 57
Lawless, Joe 215, 217, 218–19
Le Roux, Louis 94, 346
Lee, Capt. Arthur 195, 198
Lee-Wilson, Captain 248

Leek, Staffordshire 227
Lemass, Henry 291–2
Lenin, V. I. 351
Lewes gaol 170, 322, 328
Libau, SMS 126–8, 131, 149
Liberty Hall, Dublin 132, 138, 141, 150,
    157, 169, 191, 260, 318
Liebknecht, Karl 30
Limerick 125, 126, 231–2, 274
Lincoln, Abraham 340
Linenhall barracks, Dublin 205
Little, P. J. 132
Liverpool docks 79
Lloyd George, David 271, 295, 310, 312,
    313, 326, 328–9, 338, 340, 342
Logue, Michael, Cardinal 339
Long, Walter 296, 304, 311, 324, 340
looting 192, 262–5, 298
de Loughrey, Peter 239
Louth, County 221
Lowe, Brig.Gen. W. H. M. 186, 189,
    197, 198, 207, 249, 250, 272, 274
Lurgan Green, Co. Louth 223–4
Lynch, Diarmuid xiii, 94, 117, 118–19,
    139, 142, 155, 158, 160, 163,
    179, 184
Lynn, Kathleen 21, 164, 167, 260, 285
Lyons, F. S. L. 18

MacBride, John 179, 250, 279, 283,
    300, 309
McCartan, Patrick 22–3, 40, 225,
    226–7, 315
McCormick, Richard 168
McCullough, Denis 18–19, 22, 82, 94,
    119, 225, 226
MacCurtain, Thomas 136, 234, 235,
    236, 237
    assassination 344
MacDermott, Sean 40, 68, 94, 108, 110,
    119, 129, 130, 133, 135, 137,
    138, 161, 211, 214, 221, 234,
    245, 247, 280, 282, 289, 327, 358
MacDonagh, Thomas 16–17, 46, 68,
    95, 98, 125, 135, 136, 137, 143,
    155, 178, 232, 248, 249–50, 288,
    295, 300, 309, 345, 348

MacDonagh, Thomas – *cont.*
  Commandant 2nd Battalion 93,
    124, 140, 155, 179–80, 201–2,
    261
  Commandant Dublin Brigade 93,
    140
  Director of Training, Irish Volunteers
    92
  on IRB 'military committee' 95
  trial and execution 279, 288
McDonnell, Kathleen Keyes 141
McDonnell, Fr Walter 156
McDonnell, William 47
MacEntee, Seán 214, 221, 222, 223,
  247, 260, 317, 348
McGarrity, Joseph 53, 54, 66, 90, 91,
  117
McGarry, Seán 39
McGowan, Josie 174
McGuinness, Joseph 328
McKenna, Stephen 346
McKenzie, F. A. 221, 263
McManners, Rose 250–1
MacNeill, Eoin 13, 17, 37–8, 40, 41,
  42, 43, 52, 67, 80, 93–4, 104,
  117, 118, 119–21, 123, 124, 131,
  132, 133, 134, 135–7, 140, 146,
  172, 239, 343, 347, 348, 349
  arrest and trial, May 1916 283–4,
    289
  'countermanding order' (22 April
    1916) 125, 136–7, 138–9,
    141–3
  election to Sinn Féin Executive, 1917
    335
  IV Chief of Staff 43, 92, 132, 135
  Spy Wednesday orders (19 April
    1916) 132, 134
  and Volunteer split 67–8
Maconchy, Col. E. W. S. K. 197, 198,
  272, 293–4
Macready, General Sir Nevil (Adjutant
  General) 146, 271, 295–6
MacSwiney, Mary 235–6
MacSwiney, Terence 81, 84, 109, 115,
  234, 235–6
  hunger strike and death, 1920 344

Magazine Fort, Phoenix Park 155, 156,
  170
Mahaffy, Elsie 286
Mahon, Lt.Gen. Sir Bryan 75, 334, 336
Mallin, Michael 109, 111, 164, 166–8,
  169, 251, 261, 279, 280, 283
Mallow, Co. Cork 267
Malone, Michael 153, 196–7, 199
Manahan, Liam 232
Manchester Martyrs 5, 6
Mansion House, Dublin 118, 344
Markiewicz, Casimir, Count 16
Markiewicz, Constance, Countess 16,
  21–2, 37, 39, 50, 136, 138, 159,
  167, 168, 251, 261, 279, 284,
  285–6, 288, 335, 358
Marlborough Barracks 183, 184
martial law 187–8, 192–4, 242, 270–1,
  276, 278, 290, 292, 303–5, 310,
  311, 323, 325, 336
Martin, Brigid 322
Martin, Eamon 39
Martin, F. X. xiii–xv, 346
Martyn, Edward 10, 16
martyrdom, political 348–9
Maxwell, Gen. Sir John Grenfell 207–8,
  245–6, 270, 282, 283–5, 287,
  289, 290, 292, 299, 300–5, 308,
  315, 316, 323, 324, 325, 326,
  327, 335, 341
  on civil government 296
  death sentences 278–81, 287
  deportations 276–8
  Military Governor 271–2, 297, 303,
    305
  and North King Street killings 293
  policy of mass arrests 273–5
  and women prisoners 284–6
Mazzini, Giuseppe 7
Meath, County 221
Meelick, Co. Clare 124
Mellows, Liam 39, 68, 81, 82, 85, 225,
  227–30
Mendicity Institute 171–2, 184, 204–5
Messines, battle of (1917) 335
Messines Ridge Peace Tower 359
Metropole Hotel, Dublin 209, 213, 266

MI5 86, 273, 275
Middleton, Earl of 144, 146, 241, 298
militarism 30, 46, 271, 339
Military courts of inquiry, North King
    Street deaths 293–5
Military Service Bill 1918 338, 339
Milligan, Alice 19, 20
Milner, Alfred, Viscount 337
Milroy, Seán 335
Mitchel, John 12, 92
Mitchell, Susan 243
Molony, Helena 21, 22, 162, 285, 335
Monahan, Alfred (Alf) 82, 227, 228,
    229, 230
Montagu, Edwin 296
Monteith, Robert 81, 116–17, 124,
    126, 127, 129
Moore, Col. Maurice 56, 62, 71, 103
Moran, D. P. 9, 39, 41
Morrell, Lady Ottoline 61
Moylan, Seán 81
Mulcahy, Richard 217, 218, 219–20,
    257, 333, 340–1, 344, 347, 348
Mullingar, Co. Westmeath 307–8
Murphy, Seumas 172
Murphy, William Martin 28, 48–9, 160
Myers, Kevin 351, 352

Nathan, Lt.Col. Sir Matthew 87–8,
    144–6, 147, 149–51, 162, 177,
    281, 296
National Council (1903) 10
national songs 356
Nelson's Pillar, Dublin 160, 184
    blown up by IRA 1966 352
'New departure' 4
New Ireland 132
Nic Shiubhlaigh, Máire 16, 202, 261
North Dublin Union 170
North Roscommon by-election (1917)
    327
Norway, Arthur H. 88, 162
Nugent, Laurence 169

Oates, Lt.Col. W. Coape (OC 2/8th
    Sherwood Foresters) 198
Ó Briain, Liam 108–11, 168–9

O'Brien, Conor 54, 56
O'Brien, Conor Cruise 350, 351
O'Brien, Larry 175
O'Brien, William 157, 161
O'Callaghan, Donal 236
O'Casey, Seán 49–50, 258, 348
O'Connell, Daniel 3, 4, 7
O'Connell, J. J. ('Ginger') 80, 81, 82,
    83, 97, 134, 135, 157, 347, 355
    Chief of Inspection, Irish Volunteers
    92, 234
    in Frongoch camp 320
    OC Southern IV, Easter week 1916
    234, 238–40
O'Connor, Johnny ('Blimey') 257
O'Connor, Rory 132
O'Connor, T. P. 329
O'Donnell, 'Red Hugh' 1
O'Donoghue, Florence xiv, 48, 102,
    129
O'Duffy, Eimar 98, 134, 347
O'Dwyer, Edward (Bishop of Limerick)
    78–80, 305
O'Farrell, Elizabeth 246–7, 248, 249,
    251
O'Farrelly, Agnes 46
An tOglac 341–2
O'Hannigan, Donal (Dan Hannigan)
    221–5
O'Hanrahan, Michael 249, 279, 283
O'Hegarty, P. S. 88, 94, 118
O'Hegarty, Seán 236, 237
O'Higgins, Brian 346
O'Higgins, Kevin 348, 357–8
O'Kelly, Seán T. 109, 137, 161
Omagh, co. Tyrone 275
O'Malley, Ernie 341
O'Neill, Hugh 1
O'Rahilly, Michael ('The O'Rahilly')
    36–7, 38, 41, 42, 52, 53, 66, 68,
    83, 92, 131, 136, 158, 212, 260
Orange Order 33
O'Shannon, Cathal 122
O'Sullivan, Patrick 141
O'Sullivan, Sean 141, 237
Owens, Col. 184, 190

Paris Commune (1871) 269
Parliamentary Party: *see* Irish
    Parliamentary (Nationalist) Party
Parnell, Charles Stewart 4–5, 29
Parsons, Lt.Gen. Sir Lawrence 74
Pearse, Margaret 301
Pearse, Patrick H. 1, 12–16, 17–18, 30,
    37–8, 39, 46, 50, 53, 54, 66–7, 68,
    81, 90–3, 107, 112, 113, 114–15,
    118, 125, 134–5, 138, 142, 159,
    214, 222, 224, 232, 235, 240,
    241, 254, 262, 264, 300, 345,
    358
  burial in Arbour Hill prison 301
  confirmation of countermanding
    order (23 April) 138–9
  decision to surrender 243–6
  final communiqué (28 April 1916)
    141, 245
  later interpretations 353
  nationalist ideas 14–15
  orders to rise (24 April) 216, 223–4,
    228, 233, 235
  President of Irish Republic (April
    1916) 160–1
  on Robert Emmet 14, 98–9
  Rossa funeral oration 333
  trial and execution 279, 288
  'vertigo of self-sacrifice' 309
Pearse, William 279, 280, 282, 283
Perolz, Marie 162, 235, 261–2, 285
Phillips, W. Alison xiii, xv
Phoenix Park 25, 87, 187
Phoenix Park murders 6
Pim, Herbert Moore 82, 226
Plunkett, Count 16, 123, 132, 327–8
Plunkett, Countess 285
Plunkett, George (OC 'Kimmage
    Garrison') 210
Plunkett, Geraldine 99–100, 125, 288
Plunkett, Grace (Gifford) 133, 288–9,
    307
Plunkett, Sir Horace 329–30
Plunkett, Jack 56
Plunkett, Joseph 15, 16–17, 103, 108,
    115, 123, 133, 135, 136, 210,
    212–13, 214, 254, 255, 256, 309

Casement-Plunkett Strategical Plan
    106–7
  Director of Military Operations, Irish
    Volunteers 92
  editor of *Irish Review* 95–6
  military ideas 96–100
  trial and execution 279, 280, 288
Plunkett, Philomena (Mimi) 122, 128,
    288
Police, Irish: *see* DMP; RIC
  reform of 297, 326
Poole, Vincent 156
Portobello Barracks 180, 183, 192–5,
    202, 290
Post Office, Irish 88
Price, Bob 249–50
Price, Major Ivor 85, 89, 143–4, 146,
    150, 162–3, 284, 307
prisoners, republican 315–23, 328–9,
    330–1
Pro-Boers 10
Provisional Government, Irish Republic
    (1916) 138, 159, 161–2
public opinion, Irish 267–8, 301–3,
    304–10

Queen's County 75
Queenstown, Co. Cork 88, 127, 131,
    242, 268, 273

Rebellion of 1798 8–9
recruitment, British military 73–7, 147,
    148, 337–8
Redmond, John E. 9, 37, 42, 52, 53,
    62–3, 64, 65, 66, 67, 71, 72–3,
    76, 78–9, 118, 280, 287, 296,
    311, 323, 324, 325, 326–7, 328,
    329, 335
Redmond, William 335, 358
Reilly's pub ('Reilly's Fort') 170, 205,
    207
'revisionist' history 346, 347, 349,
    350–1, 352–4
Richardson, General Sir George 33, 65
Richmond Barracks, Dublin 183, 184,
    248, 249, 250, 251, 252, 279,
    316

Prime Minister's visit (16 May 1916) 275, 298
Robbins, Frank 49–50, 164, 168, 251–2, 317, 318–19
Robinson, Mary 351
Roe's Distillery 174–5
De Roiste, Liam 235, 236–7, 238
Roosevelt, Theodore 312
Rosborough, Major 192, 194, 292
Rossa, Jeremiah O'Donovan 84
funeral (August 1915) 87, 114, 115
Royal Barracks, Dublin 183, 184
Royal Commission on the 1916 rebellion (Hardinge Commission) 25, 26, 163, 183, 186, 297, 307, 326
Royal Commission on the killings in Portobello Barracks 292
Royal Dublin Society, Ballsbridge 249
Royal Hospital, Kilmainham 174, 184, 190, 208
Royal Irish Constabulary (RIC) 2, 25–6, 55, 58, 70, 129, 130, 146, 296, 301, 326, 332, 341
in Ashbourne ambush 218–21
attacks on barracks, 1916 217, 218
Black and Tans 345
Inspector General (IG) 59, 74–5, 146, 308, 339
Special Branch 146
Tyrone 179, 226–7
Russell, George ('AE') 77, 307
Ryan, Desmond 23, 67, 133, 139, 158, 231, 254, 346, 347
Ryan, James 245
Ryan, Min 289

St Enda's school 14, 16, 50, 91, 114–15, 118
Samuel, Herbert 276, 277–8, 313, 318, 322, 325
Sankey, Sir John 278, 317–19
Sarsfield, Patrick 1
Savage Armstrong, Major Raymond 338
Sayonara 146–7
'separation women' 171, 173, 174, 179, 244, 262
Separatism 12

Serbia 79
Shannon, river 106, 109, 228, 232
Shaw, Francis 350–1
Shaw, George Bernard 266, 346
Sheehan, Canon 114
Sheehy-Skeffington, Francis 46, 192, 193–4, 264, 289–92, 297, 299
Sheehy-Skeffington, Hanna 46, 161, 291, 292, 348
Shelbourne Hotel, Dublin 101, 165–7, 169, 185, 297
Ship Street Barracks, Dublin 163, 181, 184
Shortt, Edward 339
Shouldice, Jack 170
Simon, Sir John 35, 292, 296
Sinn Féin 11–12, 20–1, 64, 80–1, 131, 132, 144, 314–15, 327–35, 336, 338–9, 340–1
1918 election victory 342–3, 344
'Sinn Feiners' 64, 70, 84–5, 143–4, 194, 273, 274–5, 295, 304, 337
Skinnider, Margaret 169, 260, 262
Smith, Eugene 133
Smith, W. G. 165
Somme, battle of the (1916) 270, 313
South Africa 188, 305
Boer War 8, 10, 179
South Dublin Union 172–3, 176, 183, 184, 189, 203, 250
The Spark 81, 114
Spindler, Leutnant Karl 126–9, 131
Spring Rice, Mary 54
Stack, Austin 88, 117–18, 129–30
Stafford, General 268
Stafford gaol 316–17
Staines, Michael 45, 109, 320
Stephens, James 165–6, 266–7, 269, 308
Stokes, Lilly 165
Ni Suibhne, Eithne 236
Suvla Bay landing 76, 207
Swords, Co. Dublin 215, 216, 217

Tannam, Liam 140, 153–4
Tara 222
Thompson, William Irwin 15, 23

Tivy, Henry 145–6
Tralee, Co. Kerry 109, 117, 118, 128, 129, 130
Traynor, Oscar 139, 155, 156, 209, 247, 248, 348
Treacy, Thomas 239, 240
Trimble, William Copeland 36
Trinity College, Dublin (TCD) 101, 159, 163, 164, 190, 191, 252, 255, 286, 302, 350
  OTC 168, 185–6, 191, 285
Tubbercurry, Co. Sligo 68
Tulira Castle 230
Tynan, Katharine 76
Tyrrellspass, Co. Westmeath 227

U19 127, 128
Ulster Solemn League and Covenant 32, 33
Ulster Unionist Clubs 32
Ulster Unionist Council 33, 36
Ulster Volunteer Force 33–4, 36, 38, 54, 58, 63, 65, 227, 337
  Larne gunrunning 51–2
United Irish League (UIL) 9, 53, 64
United Irishmen 1, 12
University College, Dublin (UCD) 17, 26, 137
urban warfare 269–70
USA, public relations in 299, 310, 311–12

Vane, Sir Francis 195, 290
Victoria, Queen 12
Vinegar Hill, Co. Wexford 240

Volunteer Training Corps (VTC) 148, 177–8

Wall, Maureen 142–3
Wall, Fr Thomas 304–5
Walsh, Richard 116
War Office 146, 148, 275, 277, 295
Watkin's Brewery, Dublin 173
Weafer, Thomas 140, 156, 185, 256
Weisbach, Captain 127
Wellington Barracks 173
Wells, Warre B. 266, 306–7
Westmeath Independent 38–9
Weston, Charles 216, 217, 218–19, 220, 221
Wexford 214, 239, 240–1
Whiteboys 2
Wicklow 332
Wilson, Woodrow 329
Wimborne, Ivor Churchill Guest, 2nd baron (Lord Lieutenant) 147–51, 187, 188, 208, 270, 281, 282, 296, 297, 324, 325, 332, 337, 338
Wolfe Tone, Theobald 7, 8
Workers' Republic 81, 112, 119, 138, 145
Wylie, William E. 285, 286, 287, 288, 289, 301

Yeats, Lily 309
Yeats, William Butler 6, 13, 16, 115, 300, 309, 344, 345–6, 348, 355
  'Easter 1916' 345–6
  'Sixteen Dead Men' 348–9
Young Ireland 3, 12